Welcome to our new 2012 editic [barcode: KU-444-267] ing guide from Weight Watchers®, putting *ProPoints* values for thousands of your favourite supermarket foods at your fingertips.

Armed with 'Shop', following the Weight Watchers *ProPoints* system and staying within your *ProPoints* budget is simple and straight forward. It's the perfect resource for meal planning, grocery shopping, cooking, entertaining and tracking – giving you instant access to *ProPoints* values and highlighting **Filling & Healthy** foods.

The categories in **Shop** have been designed to mirror your supermarket layout, so it's easy for you to find the foods you are looking for. If you ever get stuck, there's an index at the back of this book.

Filling & Healthy foods are highlighted in green, like this, so they are easy to spot. They help you feel fuller for longer as you're losing weight, so try to include them in your food plan.

Enjoy using **Shop** - you are now equipped for success with *ProPoints* values for just about every food and drink you can think of.

About Shop *ProPoints* values

✳ The *ProPoints* value of every food listed in this guide is based on the amount of protein, fibre, carbohydrate and fat in the portion using the most up-to-date nutritional information available from manufacturers and supermarkets.

✳ The *ProPoints* values listed in Shop are correct at the time of going to print (July 2011). But manufacturers do sometimes change their recipes, product ranges and pack sizes throughout the year, which can affect the *ProPoints* values. If you have any doubts, you can double check using your *ProPoints* Calculator or the *ProPoints* finder® and the information on the packaging.

✳ Please note that *ProPoints* values listed are for the item on its own. So if you are adding anything to it, for example, milk to your cereal, you need to add the *ProPoints* values for that too.

WEIGHT WATCHERS on foods and beverages is the registered trademark of WW Foods, LLC and used under licence.

WEIGHT WATCHERS for services and *ProPoints* are the registered trademarks of Weight Watchers International, Inc. and are used under licence. © (2012). Weight Watchers International, Inc. All rights reserved.

The *ProPoints*® programme and these programme materials are proprietary to Weight Watchers International, Inc. and are licensed to Weight Watchers members solely for their personal use in losing and controlling their weight. Any other use, including but not limited to reproduction or distribution in any form or medium, is strictly prohibited. NOT FOR RESALE.

Weight Watchers, *ProPoints* and the *ProPoints* icon are the registered trademarks of Weight Watchers International, Inc. Patent pending.

Use the contents to find the category that the food falls into. We've designed the categories to match the usual supermarket aisles layout – so you should find it very easy to navigate. If you were looking for a 'Fresh Prepared Meal', for example, you would go to page 158.

At the front of each category there's an index of the sub-sections contained within it. Use this to find the section you want and then turn to the appropriate page. If you were looking for a 'Fresh Soup' in the 'Fresh Prepared Meal' category, for example, you would go to page 168.

At the beginning of most categories, there's a handy 'Basic Food' list – which is where you'll find generic, unbranded foods listed alphabetically. These foods – for example, an apple or a chicken breast – have the same *ProPoints* values regardless of where you buy them.

The individual brands are then listed alphabetically – under the brand name (e.g. New Convent Garden Soup Co.) or the supermarket name (e.g. Asda).

Scroll down the list until you find the food you are looking for. You'll see the *ProPoints* value for a specific portion size listed.

Index – if you can't find what you are looking for, there's an index at the back (page 272) which lists food alphabetically by type.

You may notice that some supermarkets and branded foods are not included in **Shop**. This is because they are not able to supply nutritional information on their products and without this information, we are unable to calculate the *ProPoints* values.

If you have any questions or comments, please call our Customer Service Team on **0845 345 1500**.

Weight Watchers® Cakes

a must for your shopping list

Our range of Cakes is simply delicious. Why not try our moist Slices range, luxurious Victoria Sponges or our individually wrapped Mini Rolls and Cake Bars.

1 ProPoints value *to* **3** ProPoints value

per cake

Over 10 delicious options including:
Carrot Cake Slices, Coconut Slices, Individual Victoria Sponges, Caramel Cake Bars, Belgian Chocolate Slices and Jaffa Mini Rolls

 WeightWatchers® Foods
Eat gorgeous. Feel gorgeous.

Bakery &
Patisserie

Basic Foods

Bagel, plain, 1 (80g)	6
Bread Roll, Brown, crusty, 1 (50g)	4
Bread Roll, Brown, soft, 1 (50g)	3
Bread Roll, Granary, 1 (50g)	3
Bread Roll, Sesame Seed, 1 (56g)	4
Bread Roll, White, gluten free, 1 (80g)	5
Bread Roll, White, crusty, 1 (50g)	4
Bread Roll, White, soft, 1 (50g)	4
Bread Roll, Wholemeal, 1 (50g)	3
Bread, Brown, sliced, 1 medium slice, 35g	2
Bread, Brown, gluten free,1 medium slice, 35g	3
Bread, Burger Bun, 1 (50g)	4
Bread, Calorie Controlled, 1 slice, 20g	1
Bread, Calorie Controlled, 2 slices, 40g	3
Bread, Chollah, 1 medium slice, 40g	3
Bread, Ciabatta, 1 slice, 40g	3
Bread, Currant, 1 small slice, 20g	2
Bread, Granary, sliced, 1 medium slice, 35g	2
Bread, Granary, sliced, 1 thick slice, 44g	3
Bread, Irish soda, brown, 1 slice, 40g	2
Bread, Naan, ½ medium, 70g	6
Bread, Pitta, white or wholemeal, 1 mini, 30g	2
Bread, Pitta, white or wholemeal, 1 medium, 60g	4
Bread, Pumpernickel, 1 medium slice, 26g	2
Bread, Rye, German style, 1 slice, 60g	4
Bread, Wheatgerm, 1 medium slice, 35g	2
Bread, White, farmhouse, 1 medium slice, 35g	2
Bread, White, French stick, 1 one inch slice, 15g	1
Bread, White, French stick, 1 two inch slice, 30g	2
Bread, White, gluten free,1 medium slice, 35g	3
Bread, White, gluten free, 1 thick slice, 44g	4
Bread, White, sliced, 1 medium slice, 35g	2
Bread, White, sliced, 1 thick slice, 44g	3
Bread, White, with added fibre, 1 medium slice, 35g	2
Bread, Wholemeal, sliced, 1 medium slice, 35g	2
Bread, Wholemeal, sliced, 1 thick slice, 44g	3
Chapati, made with fat, 1 (60g)	6
Chapati, made without fat, 1 (55g)	3
Chinese Pancake, 1 (10g)	1
Croissant, plain, 1 medium, 60g	6
Croutons, 1 tablespoon, 7g	1
Crumpet, 1 (60g)	2
Currant Bun, 1 (60g)	5
Danish Pastry, 1 (90g)	9
Doughnut, jam, 1 (60g)	6
Doughnut, ring, 1 (55g)	6
Eccles Cake, 1 (45g)	5
Egg Custard Tart, 1 (85g)	6
Flan Case, large, ⅛ cake, 25g	2
Flan Case, medium, ¼ cake, 19g	2
Fruit Cake, plain, 1 slice, 60g	6
Fruit Cake, Rich, 1 slice, 45g	4
Fruit Cake, Rich, Iced, 1 slice, 45g	5
Hot Cross Bun, 1 (50g)	4
Jam Tart, 1 (34g)	4
Malt Loaf, 1 small slice, 35g	3
Muffin, English, White, 1 medium, 90g	6
Pancake, Savoury or Sweet, made with whole milk, 1 (37g)	3
Scone, Fruit, 1 (55g)	5
Scone, Plain, 1 (50g)	4
Scone, Wholemeal, 1 (60g)	6
Scotch Pancake, 1 (28g)	2
Sponge Cake, plain, 1 medium slice, 50g	7
Sponge Finger, 1 (5g)	1
Taco Shell, 1 medium, 13g	2
Teacake, 1 (55g)	5
Tortilla, soft, 1 medium, 42g	3

Bread & Bread Products

Allinson

Malted Harvest Grain Batch, 1 slice, 47g	3
Malted Harvest Grain Bread, 1 slice, 47g	3
Sunflower & Pumpkin Batch, 1 slice, 47g	4
Wholemeal, 1 slice, 47g	3
Wholemeal Batch Bread, 1 small slice, 29g	2
Wholemeal Batch Bread, 1 large slice, 47g	3

Asda

Bakers Gold Tinned Open Top Wholemeal Thick, 1 slice, 44g	2
Big Loaf White Medium, 1 slice, 40g	2
Breadstick, Salted or Sesame, 1 (8g)	1
Chapattis, 1 individual, 42g	3
Cheese & Garlic Crostini, ¼ pack, 23g	3
Crumpet, 1 individual, 41g	2
Danish Soft & Light Thick Cut White Bread, Reduced Fat, 1 slice, 25g	2
Danish White, 1 slice, 25g	2
Extra Strong Garlic Petit Pains, 1 (70g)	7
Farmhouse White Bread, 1 slice, 40g	3
Flour Tortilla Wrap, large, 1 individual, 50g	4

	ProPoints value
Fruit Loaf, 1 slice, 48g	**4**
Hot Cross Bun, 1 individual, 60g	**4**
Indian Chapattis, 1 individual, 25g	**2**
Italian Garlic Ciabatta, ¼ loaf, 65g	**6**
Jalepeño Tear & Share Bread, 1 serving, 80g	**7**
Lightly Sea Salted Croutons, ¼ bag, 25g	**3**
Malted Bread, 1 slice, 35g	**2**
Medium White Bread, 1 slice, 36g	**2**
Medium Wholemeal, 1 slice, 36g	**2**
Mini Pitta Bread, White or Wholemeal, 1 individual, 30g	**2**
Muffins Traditional Style, 1 portion, 100g	**8**
Naan Breads, Plain, 1 portion, 130g	**8**
Olive Oil & Sea Salt Crostini, ¼ packet, 23g	**3**
Pan Bread Medium Brown, 1 slice, 32g	**2**
Part Baked Cheese Bread Sticks, 1 individual, 38g	**3**
Part Baked Sun-dried Tomato & Olive Ciabatta, ¼ loaf, 75g	**5**
Peshwari Naan Breads, ½ pack, 130g	**10**
Pitta Bread, White or Wholemeal, 1 individual, 55g	**4**
Plain Bread Sliced, 1 slice, 73g	**4**
Plain Mini Naan, 1 individual, 64g	**5**
Potato Farls, 1 (61g)	**3**
Ready to Bake Crusty Cobs, 1 portion, 60g	**4**
Ready to Bake Bloomers, All Flavours, 1 slice, 40g	**3**
Ready to Bake White Baguette, 1 slice, 20g	**1**
Ready to Bake White Tin Bread, 1 slice, 40g	**3**
Sandwich Baguette, 1 (100g)	**7**
Soda Farls, 1 (100g)	**6**
Soft Loaf, White or Wholemeal 1 slice, 44g	**3**
Tex Mex Bloomer, 1 slice, 27g	**2**
Thick bread, White or Wholemeal, 1 slice, 44g	**3**
Tomato & Chilli Dough Balls, 1 serving, 25g	**3**
Tortilla Wrap, 1 individual, 50g	**4**
Toasting Waffles, 1 (42g)	**5**
White Muffins, 1 (67g)	**4**
White Oven Bottom Muffin, 1 (65g)	**5**
Wholemeal Baguettes Part Baked, ½ baguette, 75g	**5**
Wholemeal Fresh for a Week, 1 slice, 35g	**2**
Wholemeal Tin Bread, 1 slice, 40g	**2**
Wholewheat Tortillas, 1 (34g)	**2**

Asda – Chosen by You

All Butter Scones, 1 (60g)	**6**
Derby Scones, 1 (59g)	**6**
Sultana Scones, 1 (63g)	**6**

Asda – Extra Special

Butter Naan Bread, ½ individual, 110g	**11**
Butter Paratha, 1 (50g)	**5**
Caramelised Onion, Cheddar & Roast Garlic Tear & Share, 1 serving, 59g	**6**
Cheese Ciabatta, 1 serving, 82g	**6**
Ciabatta, 1 serving, 68g	**5**
Crumpets, 1 individual, 65g	**3**
Extra Special Farmhouse Oatmeal Loaf, 1 slice, 44g	**3**
Feta & Roasted Vegetable Stonebaked Flatbread, ¼ loaf, 74g	**5**
Lemon Wholemeal Pitta Breads, 1 portion, 75g	**5**
Malted Loaf, 1 slice, 44g	**3**
Oatmeal Farmhouse Loaf, 1 slice, 44g	**3**
Roasted Onion & Gruyere Focaccia, 1 serving, 50g	**4**
Seeded Farmhouse Loaf, 1 slice, 44g	**2**
Slow Roasted Tomato Focaccia, ⅙ pack, 64g	**5**
Soya & Linseed White Loaf, 1 slice, 44g	**3**
Stonebaked Mini Mozzarella, Cheddar & Jalepeño Ciabatta, 1 serving, 72g	**6**
Stonebaked Cheddar, Mozzarella & Garlic Ciabatta, 2 slices, 87g	**7**
Stonebaked Garlic & Herb Bloomer, 2 slices, 59g	**5**
Stone Ground Golden Wholemeal Loaf with Blossom Honey, 1 slice, 44g	**3**
Sundried Tomato Ciabatta, ⅙ pack, 46g	**4**

Brace's Bread

Classic Sliced Malted Grain or White, 1 slice, 42g	**3**
Classic Sliced White or Wholemeal, 1 small slice, 29g	**2**
Classic Wholemeal, 1 slice, 44g	**3**
Cymru Bara Brith, 1 serving, 60g	**5**
Extra Thick Sliced White, 1 slice, 44g	**3**
Linseed & Soya Loaf, 1 slice, 40g	**3**
Malted Grain Thick Sliced, 1 slice, 38g	**2**
Medium Sliced, White, Wholemeal or Brown, 1 slice, 32g	**2**
Oat & Flax Loaf, 1 slice, 40g	**3**
Thick Brown, 1 slice, 38g	**2**
Thick Sliced White or Wholemeal, 1 slice, 38g	**2**
Wholemeal Grain & Seed Loaf, 1 slice, 40g	**3**

Dietary Specials

Brown Multigrain Sliced Loaf, 1 medium slice, 35g	**2**

Dietary Special Gluten Free Fresh White Loaf,
1 slice, 35g **3**
Multi Seeded Loaf, 1 slice, 30g **2**
White Baguettes, 1 (200g) **13**
White Sliced Loaf, 1 slice, 33g **2**

Discovery Foods

Chilli & Jalapeño Tortillas, 1 (40g) **4**
Corn Tortillas, 1 (40g) **3**
Garlic & Coriander Soft Flour Tortillas,
1 serving, 40g **3**
Mexican Soft Flour Tortillas, 1 (40g) **3**
Mexican Soft Flour Tortillas Chilli &
Jalapeño, 1 (40g) **4**
Multiseed Wrapbread, 1 (57g) **4**
Plain Flour Tortillas, 1 (40g) **3**
Taco Shell, 1 (11g) **1**
Taco Trays, 1 (9g) **1**
Tortillas, large, 1 (52g) **4**
White or White Plus Wrapbread, 1 (57g) **5**
Wholemeal Wrapbread, 1 (57g) **4**
Wrap 'n' Roll, Healthy & White Wraps, 1 (56g) **4**

Genesis

Breakfast Griddle Fruit Scones, 1 serving, 65g **5**
Fresh Brown Bread, Gluten Free, 1 slice, 35g **3**
Savoury Honey & Yogurt, Walnut & Almond,
Poppy & Sesame Seed Wheaten, 1 slice, 45g **3**
Savoury Honey & Yogurt, Almond, Poppy &
Sesame Seed Brown Soda Bread, 1 slice, 40g **2**
Sliced Oven Wheaten, 1 slice, 40g **2**
The Delicious Thick Sliced Honey & Yogurt
Brown Soda Bread, 1 slice, 40g **3**
The Delicious Thick Sliced Honey & Yogurt
Wheaten, 1 slice, 40g **3**
The Healthier Honey & Yogurt, Apricot &
Sunflower Seed Brown Soda Bread, 1 slice, 40g **3**
The Very Crafty Honey & Yogurt, Apricot &
Sunflower Seed Wheaten Sliced, 1 slice, 45g **3**
Wheaten Big Slices, 1 slice, 65g **4**
Wholemeal Sourdough with Linseed, Pumpkin
& Sunflower Seeds, 1 serving, 60g **5**

Hovis

Best of Both Invisible Crust, 1 slice, 40g **3**
Best of Both Medium Sliced White Bread,
1 slice, 40g **2**
Best of Both Thick Sliced Square Cut Bread,
1 slice, 50g **3**
Classic White, 1 medium slice, 44g **3**
Crumpets, 1 (65g) **3**
Farmhouse Best of Both, 1 slice, 44g **3**

Farmhouse White or Wholemeal Bread,
1 slice, 44g **3**
Granary Original, White or Wholemeal Bread,
1 medium slice, 40g **3**
Muffins, 1 serving, 65g **4**
Original Wheatgerm Bread, 1 slice, 40g **2**
Seed Sensations Light & Nutty Bread or
Rich & Roasted Bread, 1 slice, 44g **3**
Soft White Extra Thick Bread, 1 slice, 67g **4**
Soft White Farmhouse Bread, 1 slice, 50g **3**
Soft White Medium Bread, 1 slice, 25g **2**
Soft White Thick Bread, 1 slice, 33g **2**
Teacakes, 1 serving, 60g **4**
Wholemeal Mini Loaves, 1 (70g) **5**
Wholemeal Bread, 1 slice, 40g **2**

Juvela

Fibre Loaf, 1 slice, 33g **2**
White Sliced Loaf, 1 slice, 29g **2**

Kingsmill

50/50 White Medium, 1 slice, 40g **2**
50/50 White Thick, 1 slice, 44g **3**
50/50 with Omega 3 White medium,
1 slice, 40g **2**
Crumpets, 1 (55g) **3**
Crusts Away! 50/50 Bread or White Bread,
1 slice, 22g **1**
Gold Soft White Farmhouse, 1 slice, 47g **3**
Good as Gold Oatgrain, 1 slice, 22g **2**
Great Everyday Soft White Thick Sliced,
1 slice, 44g **3**
Great Everyday White Medium Sliced,
1 slice, 38g **2**
Great Everyday Wholemeal Medium Sliced,
1 slice, 40g **2**
Great Everyday Wholemeal Thick Sliced,
1 slice, 44g **3**
Little Big Loaf Seeds & Oats, 1 slice, 48g **3**
Little Big Loaf Tasty Wholemeal Bread,
1 medium slice, 44g **3**
Love to Toast Crumpets, 1 (55g) **3**
Love to Toast Muffins, 1 (75g) **4**
Love to Toast, Toastie Thick Bread, 1 slice, 50g **3**
Muffins, 1 (75g) **4**
Oatilicious Thick, 1 slice, 44g **3**
Plain Medium Sliced White Bread, 1 slice, 57g **4**
Seed & Oats Soft & Crunchy, 1 slice, 44g **3**
Tasty Wholemeal Medium Sliced Bread,
1 slice, 40g **2**
Tasty Wholemeal Thick Sliced Bread,
1 slice, 44g **3**

White Medium Bread, 1 slice, 40g — **3**
White Thick Bread, 1 slice, 44g — **3**

Livwell Free From

Garlic & Coriander Naan Breads, 1 (90g) — **6**
Gluten Free English Muffins, 1 (50g) — **4**
Gluten Free White Baguette, 1 serving, 125g — **9**
Gluten Free White Pitta Bread, 1 (20g) — **2**
Pitta Breads, 1 (55g) — **4**
Pizza Bases, 1 portion, 100g — **7**
Sliced Multi-Seeded Bread, 1 slice, 29g — **2**
Sliced White Bread, 1 slice, 27g — **2**

M&S

Crumpet, 1 (59g) — **3**
Gold Wholemeal Loaf, 1 slice, 47g — **3**
Italia Half Ciabatta, 1 serving, 68g — **5**
Onion Rye Bread, 1 medium slice, 66g — **4**
Soft Multigrain Loaf, 1 thick slice, 50g — **3**
Soft White Farmhouse Loaf, 1 slice, 27g — **2**
Super Soft White Loaf, 1 thick slice, 47g — **3**
White Sliced Loaf, 1 medium slice, 40g — **3**
Wholemeal Loaf, 1 medium slice, 40g — **2**

M&S – In-Store Bakery

3 Seed Baguette, 1 slice, 40g — **3**
5 Seed Golden Wholemeal Cob, 1 slice, 46g — **3**
Baguette, 1 slice, 40g — **3**
Ciabatta, 1 slice, 45g — **3**
Country Grain Loaf, 1 slice, 45g — **3**
Crusty White Bloomer, 1 slice, 50g — **4**
French Country Loaf, 1 slice, 44g — **3**
French Crusty Baguette, ¼ loaf, 65g — **4**
French Sourdough, 1 slice, 46g — **3**
French White Boule, 1 slice, 50g — **3**
Green Olive Pave, ⅛ loaf, 50g — **3**
Hot & Spicy Feta & Pepper Focaccia,
1 individual, 75g — **6**
Palmier, 1 individual, 70g — **10**
Peperonata Focaccia Slab, ⅓ loaf, 50g — **3**
Rosemary Focaccia, 1 loaf, 70g — **6**
Rustique Flute, 1 slice, 40g — **3**
Rustique Loaf, 1 slice, 50g — **3**
Sesame & Poppy Seed Roll Crown, 1 slice, 46g — **3**
Sesame Seed Golden Wholemeal Cob,
1 slice, 50g — **3**
Small French Sourdough Loaf, ¹/₁₀ loaf, 44g — **3**
Tartine Slices, 1 slice, 45g — **3**
Walnut Loaf, 1 slice, 44g — **3**
White Crusty Bloomer or Loaf, 1 slice, 45g — **3**
White Crusty Tin Bread, 1 slice, 50g — **3**
White Pave Loaf, 1 slice, 46g — **3**

Wholemeal Crusty Sandwich Loaf, 1 slice, 50g — **3**

Mission Deli

Wraps, Mediterranean Herb or Wheat & White
or Multigrain or Original, 1 (61g) — **5**
Wraps, Roasted Red Pepper, 1 (62g) — **5**

Morrisons

Barbecue Bread to Share, 1 serving, 63g — **4**
Breadsticks, Salted or Sesame, 1, (20g) — **2**
Butteries, 1 individual, 67g — **6**
Cheese Breadsticks, 1, (20g) — **2**
Cheese Ciabatte Bites to Share, 1 serving, 42g — **3**
Crumpets, 1 individual, 46g — **2**
Garlic & Coriander Naans, 1 individual, 65g — **5**
Garlic & Herb Bruschetta, ¼ packet, 23g — **3**
Pumpkin & Sunflower Seed Bruschetta,
¼ packet, 23g — **3**
Stonebaked Pizza Base, 1 pizza, 115g — **8**
Thick Sliced Malted Grain Bread, 1 slice, 40g — **3**
Three Cheese Bread to Share, 1 serving, 67g — **5**

Morrisons – Eat Smart

Thick Sliced Danish White, 1 slice, 20g — **1**

Mothers Pride

Crumpets, 1 (43g) — **2**
Original Plain White Sliced Bread,
1 slice, 61g — **4**
Scottish Plain Medium Cut, 1 slice, 50g — **3**
Scottish Plain Thick Cut, 1 slice, 62g — **4**

Nimble

Malted Wholegrain, 1 slice, 22g — **1**
White Bread, 1 slice, 20g — **1**
Wholemeal Bread, 1 slice, 20g — **1**

Patak's

Garlic & Coriander Mini Naans, 1 (60g) — **4**
Garlic & Herb Chapattis, 1 portion, 40g — **3**
Mini Pappadums, Original Assorted,
Black Peppercorn, Tikka & Plain, ⅓ bag, 25g — **3**
Original Garlic & Coriander & Plain
Naans, ½ (70g) — **5**
Original Pappadums, 1 (9g) — **1**
Original Peshwari Mini Naans, 1 (60g) — **5**
Original Plain Chapattis, 1 (20g) — **2**
Original Plain Mini Naans, 1 (60g) — **4**
Original Spicy Ready to Eat
Pappadums, 1 (10g) — **1**
Plain Ready to Eat Pappadums, 1 (8g) — **1**

Roberts Bakery

Floury White Batch Rolls, 1 (60g)	**4**
Medium Sliced Oatmeal Bread, 1 slice, 30g	**2**
Medium Sliced White or Wholemeal Bread, 1 slice, 37g	**2**
Mega-Thick Sliced White Toastie Bread, 1 slice, 66g	**4**
Seeded Farmhouse Bread, 1 slice, 37g	**3**
Thick Sliced Malted Wheatgrain, 1 slice, 46g	**3**
Thick Sliced White or Wholemeal Bread, 1 slice, 43g	**3**
White Farmhouse Bread, 1 slice, 37g	**2**

Sainsbury's

Crumpets, 1 (46g)	**2**
Extra Thick White Toastie, 1 slice, 44g	**3**
Fresh for Longer White, Medium Sliced, 1 slice, 36g	**2**
Fresh for Longer Wholemeal, Medium Sliced, 1 slice, 35g	**2**
Fresh For Longer Wholemeal, Thick Sliced, 1 slice, 44g	**3**
Irish Wheaten Loaf, 1 slice, 36g	**2**
Mini Savoury Muffins, 1 (15g)	**1**
Mini Wholemeal Pitta, 1 (30g)	**2**
Naan Bread, ½ pack, 80g	**7**
Peshwari Naan Bread, ½ pack, 90g	**7**
Pitta Bread Mini, white, 1 (31g)	**2**
Soda Farls, 1 serving, 140g	**9**
Thick Wholemeal Bread, 1 slice, 42g	**3**
Wholemeal Muffins, 1 (67g)	**4**

Sainsbury's – Be Good To Yourself

Mini Garlic & Parsley Flatbread, ½ pack, 108g	**8**
Plain Mini Naan Bread, 1 (50g)	**3**
Tortilla Wraps, 1 (50g)	**3**

Sainsbury's – Taste the Difference

Cheese & Black Pepper Muffins, 1 (70g)	**6**
Garlic & Coriander Naan Bread, ¼ pack, 70g	**6**

Sharwood's

Mini Naans Garlic & Coriander or Plain, 1 (60g)	**4**
Tandoori Naans, ½ (130g)	**10**

Soreen

The Fruity Malt Loaf, 1 slice, 27g	**2**
The Fruity Malt Loaf Snack, Ready Spread with Butter, 1 pack, 64g	**6**

Sunblest

Baker's Choice Potato Farls, 1 (100g)	**5**
Baker's Choice Sliced Soda Farls, 1 (100g)	**6**
Baker's Choice White Sliced Bread, 1 slice, 38g	**2**
Baker's Choice Wholemeal Sliced Bread, 1 slice, 36g	**2**
Muffins, 1 (57g)	**4**
Scotch Crumpets, 1 (34g)	**2**
White Medium Sliced Bread, 1 slice, 38g	**2**
White Thick Sliced Bread, 1 slice, 42g	**3**

Tesco

Baker's Soft Tasty White Bread Sliced, 1 medium slice, 40g	**3**
Baker's Soft Tasty White Bread Sliced, 1 thick slice, 44g	**3**
Baker's Soft Whole n' White Bread Medium Sliced, 1 slice, 40g	**2**
Baker's Soft Wholemeal Bread Medium Sliced, 1 slice, 40g	**2**
Café Continental Croissants, 1 individual, 80g	**8**
Café Continental Pains au Chocolat, 1 individual, 45g	**5**
Chapattis, 1 serving, 85g	**6**
Cheese & Garlic Pizza Bread, 1 serving, 98g	**11**
Cheese & Tomato Flatbread, 1 serving (¼ pack), 54g	**4**
Cheese & Tomato Tear & Share Bread, 1 serving (⅛ pack), 52g	**4**
Cheese English Muffins, 1 individual, 72g	**4**
Chilli & Coriander Naan Bread, 1 serving, 80g	**6**
Ciabatta, 1 serving, 72g	**5**
Crumpets, 1 individual, 65g	**3**
Crusty White Bloomer, 1 slice, 28g	**2**
Danish Soft White Bread, 1 slice, 18g	**1**
Danish Soft White Bread, 1 thick slice, 24g	**2**
English Muffins, White or Wholemeal, 1 individual, 72g	**4**
Garlic & Coriander Mini Naan, 1 serving, 65g	**5**
Garlic & Coriander Naan, 1 individual, 160g	**11**
Garlic & Herb Pitta Breads, 1 individual, 60g	**4**
Garlic & Parsley Flatbread, 1 serving, 50g	**4**
Garlic & Rosemary Flatbreads, 1 individual, 93g	**8**
Granary Brown Baton, 1 individual, 100g	**7**
Large White Pitta Bread, 1 individual, 85g	**5**
Large Wholemeal Pitta Bread, 1 individual, 85g	**7**
Mini Garlic Ciabattas, 1 individual, 93g	**8**
Mini White or Wholemeal Pitta, 1 individual, 30g	**2**

Oven Bottom Muffins, 1 individual, 65g	**5**
Part Baked Baguettes, 1 serving, 75g	**5**
Peshwari Naan, 1 serving, 180g	**14**
Plain Flour Tortilla Wraps, 1 individual, 64g	**5**
Plain Naan, 1 serving, 82g	**6**
Potato Farls, 1 individual, 60g	**3**
Scottish Plain Batch Bread, 1 slice, 62g	**4**
Sliced Brioche Loaf, 1 slice, 44g	**4**
Soda Farls, 1 individual, 142g	**9**
Stonebaked Loaf, 1 slice, 28g	**2**
Sun Dried Tomato & Cheese Focaccia, 1 serving, 49g	**4**
Thick Sliced White Bread, 1 slice, 44g	**3**
Tomato & Garlic Flatbreads, 1 individual, 103g	**7**
White Medium Sliced Loaf, 1 slice, 38g	**2**
White Pitta, 1 individual, 60g	**4**
White Pitta, 1 large, 90g	**6**
White Pitta, 1 mini, 30g	**2**
White Thick Sliced Danish Loaf, 1 slice, 23g	**2**
Wholemeal Bread Sliced, 1 medium slice, 36g	**2**
Wholemeal Bread Sliced, 1 thick slice, 44g	**3**
Wholemeal Oatbran Bread, 1 slice, 44g	**2**
Wholemeal Pitta Bread, 1 individual, 60g	**4**

Tesco – Finest

Cheese & Sundried Tomato Stromboli, 1 serving, 65g	**5**
Ciabatta, 1 serving, 45g	**3**
Farmhouse White Bread Sliced, 1 slice, 50g	**3**
Garlic & Coriander Naan, 1 serving, 80g	**7**
Grand Rustique, 1 serving, 100g	**7**
Kalamata Olive Bouchon, 1 roll, 80g	**6**
Mediterranean Bread, ¼ loaf, 100g	**7**
Mini Cheddar Flatbreads, 1 serving, 62g	**5**
Mini Garlic & Coriander Naan, 1 individual, 50g	**4**
Multigrain Pain Rustiques, 1 individual, 60g	**4**
Multiseed Farmhouse Batch Bread, 1 slice, 44g	**3**
Oatmeal Batch Bread, 1 slice, 44g	**3**
Part Baked Ciabatta Loaf, 1 serving, 75g	**5**
Peshwari Naan, 1 serving, 65g	**5**
Plain Naan, 1 serving, 85g	**8**
Rosemary Focaccias, 1 individual, 125g	**11**
Rustic Baguette, 1 serving, 125g	**8**
Rustic Multigrain Loaf, 1 slice, 50g	**3**
Seeded Bloomer, 1 slice, 28g	**2**

Tesco – Free From

Breakfast Muffin, 1 individual, 75g	**8**
Brown Loaf, 1 slice, 33g	**2**
Ciabatta, 1 individual, 90g	**7**
Crumpets, 1 individual, 55g	**2**
Garlic & Coriander Naan, 1 individual, 90g	**6**

Mini Breadsticks, 1 individual, 3g	**0**
Mini Brown Pitta, 1 individual, 14g	**1**
Multiseeded Sliced Loaf, 1 slice, 29g	**2**
Pitta Bread, 1 individual, 55g	**4**
Pizza Bases, 1 individual, 100g	**7**
White Loaf, 1 slice, 33g	**3**
White Sliced Loaf, 1 slice, 29g	**2**

Tesco – Healthy Living

Pitta, 1 individual, 60g	**4**
Seeded Panini, 1 individual, 85g	**6**
Seeded Wraps, 1 individual, 67g	**5**

Tesco – In-Store Bakery

Cheese & Onion Grand Rustique, 1 serving, 100g	**7**
Express White Bloomer, 1 serving, 50g	**3**
Express Wholemeal Tin, 1 serving, 50g	**3**
Mediterranean Rustique, 1 serving, 85g	**6**
Olive Bouchon, 1 serving, 80g	**6**
Panini, 1 individual, 95g	**7**
Rye & Pumpkin Rustique, 1 serving, 80g	**6**
Seeded Bloomer, 1 serving, 100g	**7**
Seeded Panini, 1 serving, 90g	**7**
Spelt & Sunflower Bloomer, ¼ loaf, 100g	**8**
Stonebaked Sourdough Bloomer, 100g	**6**
Traditional Irish Wheaten Loaf, 1 serving, 100g	**6**

Tesco – Light Choices

Garlic Baguettes, ½ baguette, 105g	**8**
Garlic Slices, 1 slice, 30g	**2**
Mini Naan, 1 individual, 65g	**4**
Plain Naan Bread, 1 serving, 70g	**5**
Tortilla Wraps, 1 individual, 64g	**5**

The Co-operative

Bloomer, Plain, 1 slice, 50g	**3**
Bread, Plain, 1 slice, 73g	**5**
Brown Loaf, 1 slice, 36g	**2**
Ciabatta, ¼ loaf, 68g	**4**
Dark Rye Caraway Cob, In-Store Bakery, ¼ loaf, 100g	**7**
Everyday Medium Sliced White Bread, 1 slice, 36g	**2**
Garlic & Coriander Naan Breads, 1 portion, 160g	**11**
Garlic Flatbread, ½ (115g)	**9**
Italian Plain Breadsticks, 1 stick, 5g	**1**
Longer Life White Bread, Medium Sliced, 1 slice, 36g	**2**
Mini Breadsticks, 1 (6g)	**1**
Muffins, Plain, 1 (60g)	**4**
Naan Breads, Healthy Living, ½ (70g)	**5**

Weight Watchers® Bread
a must for your shopping list

Ideal toasted or as part of a delicious sandwich, our tasty bread will fit into your healthy eating plan.

1 ProPoints value *to* 2 ProPoints value
per slice

6 varieties of bread:
White Danish, Brown Danish, Wholemeal Thick Sliced , Malted Danish, White Thick Sliced and Grained Thick Sliced.

ALL LOW IN SATURATED FAT. THICK AND THIN SLICED LOAVES AVAILABLE.

WeightWatchers® Foods
Eat gorgeous. Feel gorgeous.

Naan Breads, Plain, 1 (160g)	11
Naturally Healthy Wholemeal Bread, Medium Sliced, 1 slice, 36g	2
Naturally Healthy Wholemeal Pitta Breads, 1 portion, 70g	4
Oatmeal Batch Loaf, 1 slice, 44g	3
Panini, 1 (75g)	5
Pitta Breads, Plain, 1 (70g)	5
Potato Cakes, 1 (60g)	3
Scottish Square White Bread, Medium Sliced, 1 slice, 50g	3
Soda Farls, 1 (170g)	10
Sultana Scones, 1 (62g)	5
Tiger Bread, In-Store Bakery, 1 (50g)	4
Topped Ciabatta, ¼ loaf, 74g	5
White Farmhouse Batch Loaf, 1 slice, 44g	3
White Seeded Batch Loaf, ⅛ loaf, 136g	10
Wholemeal Seeded Batch Loaf, 1 slice, 44g	3

Waitrose

Baguette, large, ½ (50g)	3
Flute, 1 serving, 50g	3
French Stick, ⅛ stick, 50g	4
Garlic & Coriander Naan, large, 1 (130g)	11
Garlic & Coriander Naan, small, 1 (55g)	5
Garlic Ciabatta, ¼ pack, 88g	8
Grand Mange Blanc, 1 slice, 40g	3
Grand Mange Paysan, 1 slice, 50g	3
Grand Rustica, ½ pack, 140g	10
Multi Seeded Ficelle, 1 (25g)	2
Pain au Levain, 1 (50g)	4
Peshwari Naan, 1 (100g)	8
Plain Naan, large, 1 (145g)	11
Plain Naan, small, 1 (57g)	4
Roasted Garlic Flatbread, ¼ pack, 60g	5
Rye Bloomer with Linseed & Poppy Seeds, 1 (50g)	3
Seeded Bloomer, 1 pack, 50g	4
Stonebaked Baguette, ½ (50g)	3
Stonebaked Boule, ⅛ pack, 50g	3
Stonebaked Ficelle, 1 (25g)	2
Stonebaked Harvester Petit Pain, 1 portion, 100g	7
Stonebaked Olive Ciabatta, ⅛ pack, 50g	4
Stonebaked Pain de Campagne, 1 serving, 50g	3
Stonebaked Spelt Bread, 1 slice, 50g	3
White Muffins, 1 (60g)	4

Warburtons

Crumpets, 1 (58g)	3
Crusty Premium White Sliced Loaf, 1 slice, 30g	2
Danish Sliced White Bread, 1 slice, 26g	2

Farmhouse Soft White Sliced Bread, 1 slice, 27g	2
Farmhouse Soft White Thick Sliced Bread, 1 slice, 43g	3
Medium Sliced Wholemeal Bread, 1 slice, 24g	1
Our Thickest Slice of White Bread, 1 slice, 58g	4
Oven Bottom Muffins, 1 (65g)	5
Potato Cakes, 1 (54g)	4
Premium Brown Medium Sliced Bread, 1 slice, 24g	2
Raisin Loaf with Cinnamon, 1 slice, 33g	2
Seeded Batch, 1 slice, 30g	2
Seeded Batch Thick Sliced White Bread, 1 slice, 46g	4
Sliced Wholemeal Bread, 1 slice, 40g	2
Soft Brown or Grained Farmhouse, 1 slice, 42g	3
Stoneground Wholemeal Batch, 1 slice, 46g	3
Tasty Grains & Seeds, 1 slice, 38g	3
Tasty White Sliced Bread, 1 slice, 38g	2
Thick Sliced White Seeded Batch, 1 slice, 46g	4
Tiger Bread, Brown, Unsliced, 1 slice, 40g	2
Tiger Bread, White, Unsliced, 1 slice, 40g	3
Toastie Thick Sliced White Bread, 1 slice, 47g	3
Toasting Muffins, 1 (64g)	4
Wholemeal Sliced Bread, 1 slice, 24g	1

Weight Watchers

Fruited Malt Loaf, 1 slice, 23g	2
Mini Naan, plain 1 piece, 44g	3
Plain Wraps, 1 (42g)	3
Sliced Brown Danish Bread, 1 slice, 20g	1
Sliced Brown Danish Bread, 2 slices, 41g	2
Sliced Malted Danish Bread, 1 slice, 20g	1
Sliced Malted Danish Bread, 2 slices, 41g	3
Sliced White Danish Bread, 1 slice, 20g	1
Sliced White Danish Bread, 2 slices, 41g	3
Thick Grained Loaf, 1 slice, 29g	2
Thick Grained Loaf, 2 slices, 58g	4
Thick Sliced White Bread, 1 slice, 29g	2
Thick Sliced Wholemeal Bread, 1 slice, 29g	2
White Pitta Bread, 1 (44g)	3
Wholemeal Pitta Bread, 1 (44g)	3

Cakes

Asda

All Butter Dundee Cake, 1 slice, 76g	7
All Butter Flapjack Slices, 1 slice, 33g	4

Almond Fingers, 1 portion, 45g	5
Angel Cake, 1 slice, 34g	3
Apple & Cream Sponge, 1 slice, 51g	4
Apple & Custard Pies, 1 (64g)	7
Banana Loaf Cake, 1 slice, 20g	2
Battenburg Cake, 1 slice, 45g	5
Belgian Chocolate Flapjack Bites, 1 (30g)	4
Belgian Waffles, 1 (25g)	3
Best Wishes Cake, 1 slice, 53g	6
Blackcurrant Sponge Roll, 1 (48g)	5
Blueberry Cake Slab, 1 slice, 40g	4
Bramley Apple Crumble, ¼ serving, 150g	10
Butter Brioche Loaf, 1 portion, 50g	4
Buttermilk Pancakes, 1 portion, 32g	2
Caramel Bites Cake, 1 slice, 74g	9
Caramel Shortcake Mini Bites, 1 portion, 16g	2
Caramel Shortcake, 1 (42g)	6
Carrot Cake Slice, 1 slice, 80g	8
Celebration Chocolate Sponge Cake, 1 serving, 53g	7
Celebration Mega Party Cake, Chocolate or Vanilla, 1 portion, 47g	5
Cheese Scone, 1 (76g)	6
Cherry & Sultana Slab Cake, 1 portion, 57g	5
Cherry Cakes, 1 portion, 38g	4
Cherry Madeira Cake, 1 slice, 38g	3
Cherry Scones, 1 (76g)	6
Chocolate & Cream Sponge, 1 slice, 50g	4
Chocolate & Walnut Brownies, 1 slice, 30g	4
Chocolate & Fresh Cream Sponge, 1 (125g)	12
Chocolate Ball Donut, 1 portion, 65g	6
Chocolate Birthday Cake, 1 serving, 62g	8
Chocolate Brownie, 1 (35g)	4
Chocolate Cake Selection, 1 portion, 35g	5
Chocolate Chip Madeira Cake, 1 slice, 38g	4
Chocolate Chip Muffin, 1 (105g)	12
Chocolate Cornflake Clusters Mini Bites, 1 (14g)	2
Chocolate Covered Sponge Roll, 1 slice, 44g	5
Chocolate Iced Ring Donuts, 1 (60g)	7
Chocolate Loaf Cake, ⅕ slice, 86g	10
Chocolate Overload Cake, 1 serving, 94g	11
Chocolate Party Cake, 1 serving, 60g	7
Chocolate Present Cake, 1 serving, 71g	8
Chocolate Pudding Cake, 1 serving, 95g	10
Chocolate Sponge Roll, 1 serving, 47g	5
Chocolate Sponge Sandwich, 1 slice, 37g	4
Classico Panettone, 1 serving, 83g	9
Coconut Sponge Cake, 1 slice, 57g	7
Cornflake Cake, ¼ pack, 35g	5
Country Cake Slice, 1 slice, 26g	3
Cream & Strawberry Sponges, 1 portion, 108g	11
Double Chocolate Muffin, 1 (105g)	13
Family Madeira Cake, 1 slice, 43g	5
Flan Bases, 1 individual, 21g	2
Fondant Fancy, 1 (28g)	3
Frangipanes, 1 portion, 40g	5
Fruit Cake Slices, 1 slice, 36g	4
Fruit Flapjack Style Slices, 1 slice, 24g	3
Genoa Cake, 1 slice, 48g	5
Happy Birthday Candle Cake, 1 slice, 53g	6
Iced Coffee Cake, 1 slice, 42g	5
Iced Cranberry & Orange Tart, 1 tart, 44g	5
Iced Fairy Cakes, 1 (23g)	3
Iced Fruit Bar, ⅙ bar, 75g	7
Iced Fruit Slices, 1 serving, 50g	5
Iced Lemon Madeira, 1 slice, 42g	5
Iced Lemon Slice, 1 slice, 30g	3
Iced Rich Fruit Cake, ⅙ cake, 76g	7
Jam Filled Donuts, 1 (67g)	6
Lemon Drizzle Loaf Cake, ⅙ cake, 51g	6
Lemon Half Moon Cake, 1 portion, 50g	6
Lemon Splodgers, 1 portion, 30g	3
Lemon Sponge Cake, 1 serving, 59g	7
Lemon Sponge Roll, 1 serving, 48g	4
Marble Loaf Cake, ⅙ cake, 52g	6
Marshmallow Cake Bar, 1 portion, 27g	3
Milk Chocolate Gâteau, 1 slice, 43g	6
Mini Chocolate Classics, 1 cake, 31g	4
Mini Chocolate Éclair, 1 (13g)	2
Mini Vanilla & Choc Cones, 1 (16g)	2
Mini Victoria Cake, 1 (36g)	4
Mini Victoria Classics, 1 cake, 32g	4
Mississippi Mud Pie, 1 slice, 70g	8
Pancake, 1 (40g)	3
Parkin, 1 portion, 50g	5
Part Baked Fruit Scones, 1 (60g)	5
Party Bar Cake, 1 serving, 57g	6
Patchwork Flower Cake, 1 serving, 73g	8
Photo Chocolate Cake, 1 slice, 59g	7
Plain Pancake, 1 (62g)	4
Plain Scones, 1 (76g)	7
Plain Sponge Cakes, 1 slice, 19g	2
Really Chocolatey Cake, 1 slice, 66g	8
Rhubarb Crumble, 1 portion, 140g	9
Rich Fruit Cake, ⅒ cake, 91g	8
Rich Fruit Iced Bar, ⅛ bar, 62g	6
Round Potato Scones, 1 (45g)	3
Royal Iced Fruit Cake, 1 serving, 75g	7
Scotch Pancakes, 1 (33g)	3
Sponge Cake Fingers, 1 serving, 17g	2
Sponge Cake Selection, 1 portion, 43g	6
Sponge Flan Case, ¼ cake, 50g	5
Stollen Loaf, 1 serving, 50g	5

	ProPoints value
Stollen Slices, 1 serving, 50g	**6**
Strawberry & Cream Sponges, 1 (108g)	**11**
Strawberry Crêpes, 1 (32g)	**3**
Strawberry Jam Scones, 1 (76g)	**7**
Sugared Ring Donut, 1 (56g)	**7**
Sultana Scone, 1 (60g)	**6**
Summerberry Roll/Roulade, ⅙ cake, 53g	**4**
Tea Break Fruit Loaf, 1 slice, 36g	**3**
Tea Break Fruit Tea Cakes, 1 portion, 100g	**7**
Teatime Selection, 1 portion, 43g	**5**
Tiffin Squares, 1 portion, 40g	**6**
Toffee & Apple Loaf, 1 slice, 50g	**4**
Toffee Flavour Yum Yum, 1 (60g)	**8**
Toffee Fudge Cake (large), 1/12 cake, 100g	**11**
Toffee Fudge Cake (small), ⅛ cake, 79g	**9**
Toffee Sponge Pudding, ⅓ pack, 100g	**11**
Trifle Sponges, 1 (23g)	**2**
Very Berry Muffins, 1 (130g)	**12**
Victoria Sponge Cake, ⅙ cake, 46g	**5**
Walnut Cake, 1 slice, 41g	**4**
Yogurt Drizzled Fruit Flapjacks, 1 portion, 38g	**5**
Zesty Lemon Cake, 1 slice, 111g	**13**

Asda – Chosen by You

All Butter Flapjacks, 1 (33)g	**4**
Almond Slices, 1 slice, 26g	**3**
Blueberry Muffins, 1 (105g)	**10**
Cherry Madeira Cake, ⅛ cake, 40g	**4**
Chocolate Fairy Cakes, 1 individual, 23g	**2**
Chocolate Mini Rolls, 1 (30g)	**4**
Chocolate Roulade, 1 serving, 53g	**5**
Chocolate Swiss Roll, ⅙ roll, 32g	**4**
Coconut Mini Bites, 1 serving, 13g	**2**
Continental Belgian Waffles, 1 (25g)	**3**
Double Chocolate Gâteau, 1 portion, 60g	**5**
Fairy Cakes, 1 (23g)	**2**
Iced Fairy Cakes, 1 (23g)	**3**
Iced Madeira Cake, 1 serving, 43g	**5**
Jumbo Chocolate Swiss Roll, 1 slice, 30g	**3**
Jumbo Strawberry Swiss Roll, 1 slice, 30g	**3**
Lemon Iced Madeira Cake, ⅛ cake, 42g	**5**
Lemon Sponge Roll, 1 serving, 48g	**4**
Raspberry Swiss Roll, ⅙ roll, 31g	**3**
Strawberry & White Chocolate Muffins, 1 (115g)	**12**
Strawberry Jam Scones, 1 (77g)	**6**
Viennese Whirls, 1 individual, 32g	**5**

Asda – Extra Special

All Butter Sultana Scones, 1 portion, 70g	**6**
All Butter Sultana Sharing Scone, 1 (48g)	**4**
Apple & Sultana Cake, 1 slice, 46g	**4**
Bath Buns, 1 (65g)	**6**
Belgian Chocolate Torte, 1 serving, 62g	**7**
Caramel Shortbread, 1 square, 69g	**9**
Carrot Cake, 1 slice, 65g	**8**
Carrot Loaf Cake, 1 portion, 86g	**9**
Chocolate Caramel Shortbreads, 1 piece, 40g	**5**
Chocolate Fudge Cake, 1 slice, 78g	**10**
Coffee Cake, 1 slice, 61g	**7**
Cranberry & Orange Cake, 1 slice, 70g	**6**
Hand Finished Belgian White Chocolate & Raspberry Cake, 1 slice, 66g	**8**
Hand Finished Carrot Cake, 1 serving, 67g	**8**
Hand Finished Chocolate Fudge Cake, 1 serving, 70g	**8**
Hand Finished Coffee Cake, 1 serving, 67g	**7**
Hand Finished Lemon Cake, 1 portion, 50g	**5**
Hand Finished Occasion Cake, 1 serving, 65g	**6**
Hand Finished Victoria Sponge, 1 serving, 46g	**5**
Layered Chocolate Loaf Cake, 1 portion, 55g	**6**
Layered Madeira Cake, 1 slice, 54g	**6**
Mini Carrot Cake, 1 individual, 35g	**4**
Mini Chocolate Cakes, 1 individual, 40g	**5**
Rocky Road Squares, 1 portion, 55g	**7**
Syrup Sponge Pudding, ¼ pudding, 75g	**8**
Triple Chocolate Brownies, 1 (40g)	**4**
Triple Chocolate Cookie, 1 (68g)	**9**

Asda – Good For You

Carrot Cake Slices, 1 slice, 28g	**2**
Cherry Bakewell Slices, 1 (30g)	**3**
Cranberry & Orange Slices, 1 slice, 30g	**3**
Fruit Flapjack, 1 slice, 33g	**3**
Fruited Loaf Cake, 1 slice, 30g	**2**
Pancake, 1 serving, 60g	**4**
Toffee Slices, 1 slice, 30g	**3**

Asda – The Bakery

All Butter Flapjack Mini Bites, 1 (20g)	**2**
All Butter Fruit Flapjack Mini Bites, 1 (20g)	**2**
Belgian Bun, 1 (115g)	**10**
Black Forest Gâteau, 1 slice, 68g	**8**
Cherry Muffins, 1 (105g)	**12**
Chocolate Brownie Mini Bites, 1 portion, 15g	**2**
Chocolate Chip Mini Muffins, 1 (30g)	**3**
Chocolate Chip Muffin, 1 (75g)	**9**
Chocolate Fingers, 1 (45g)	**4**
Create Your Own Photo Cake, 1 slice, 58g	**6**
Double Chocolate Chip Muffin, 1 (70g)	**9**
Double Chocolate Mini Muffin, 1 (30g)	**4**
Gingerbread Men Mini Bites, 1 individual, 10g	**1**
Iced Finger, 1 (70g)	**7**
Mini Chocolate Topped Donuts, 1 portion, 14g	**2**
Really Chocolatey Cake, 1 slice, 100g	**11**

Red Berry Muffins, 1, (100g)	10
Shortbread Mini Bites, 1 (20g)	3
Sticky Fingers, 1 portion, 40g	4
Strawberry Fingers, 1 (25g)	2

Cadbury

Caramel Cake Bars, 1 (34g)	3
Caramel Cake Bites, 1 (14g)	2
Caramel Mini Rolls, 1 (30g)	4
Choc Chip Cake Bites, 1 piece, 16g	2
Choccy Road Mix, 1 serving, 20g	3
Chocolate Curl Cakes, 1 (32g)	4
Chocolate Flapjack, 1 bar, 75g	10
Double Choc Mini Rolls, 1 (27g)	3
Flake Cake, 1 (26g)	3
Fruit & Nut Cake Bars, 1 (40g)	5
Fruit & Nut Flapjack, 1 (75g)	10
Fudge Cake Bars, 1 (33g)	4
Highlights Chocolate Cake Bars, 1 (25g)	3
Highlights Toffee Flavour Cake Bars, 1 (25g)	3
Jaffa Mini Rolls, 1 (29g)	3
Milk Chocolate Cake Bars, 1 (35g)	4
Milk Chocolate Mini Rolls, 1 (25g)	3
Mint Crisp Bites, 1 (11g)	1
Mint Crisp Cake Bars, 1 (36g)	4
Mint Crisp Cake Bites, 1 (14g)	2
Orange Crisp Cake Bars, 1 (36g)	4
Orange Crisp Cake Bites, 1 (14g)	2
Strawberry Mini Rolls, 1 (29g)	3
Triple Choc Crisp Cake Bites, 1 (14g)	2
Triple Choc Roll, 1 (40g)	5
Vanilla Cake Bars, 1 (33g)	4

Genesis

Big Pancakes, 1 portion, 71g	5
Cherry Scones, 1 (81g)	6
Coconut Iced Fingers, 1 (64g)	6
Crafty Cinnamon & Fruit Swirl, 1 slice, 40g	4
Crafty Sourdough Healthy Fruit Loaf, 1 slice, 27g	2
Crafty The Healthier Honey & Yogurt, Wholemeal Handcrafted Scones, 1 (65g)	6
Fruit Buns, 1 (52g)	5
Fruit Scones, 1 (78g)	6
Pancakes, 1 (42g)	3
Plain Scones, 1 (74g)	6
Wheaten Scones, 1 (72g)	6

It's Nut Free

Cherry Flapjack, 1 (35g)	4
Choc Chip Flapjack, 1 large, 60g	8
Crunchy Flapjack, 1 (35g)	4
Fudge Flapjack, 1 (35g)	5

Livwell Free From

Double Chocolate Loaf Cake, 1 slice, 38g	4
Fruit Loaf, 1 slice, 36g	2
Sultana Scones, 1 serving, 124g	11
Syrup Pancakes, 1 (42g)	3

Lyons Cakes

Battenberg, 1 serving, 38g	4
Chocolate Layer Cake, 1 serving, 38g	5
Chocolate Sponge Sandwich, 1 slice, 34g	4
Coconut Sponge Sandwich, 1 slice, 38g	4
Cup Cakes - Chocolate, Orange, Lemon & Assorted, 1 (40g)	4
French Sponge Sandwich, 1 slice, 38g	4
Lemon Bar, 1 bar, 50g	6
Raspberry Bar, 1 slice, 35g	4
Raspberry Swiss Roll, 1 slice, 28g	2
St Clements, 1 slice, 43g	5
Sultana & Cherry, 1 slice, 49g	5

M&S

Chocolate Cornflake Mini Bites, 1 (9g)	1
Classic Lemon Drizzle Cake, 1 slice, 72g	8
Classic Victoria Sandwich Cake, ⅙ large, 70g	8
Extremely Chocolatey Covered Roll, ⅙ large, 46g	6
Extremely Chocolatey Mini Bites, 1 piece, 20g	3
Flapjack Mini Bites, 1 piece, 14g	2
Honeycomb Clusters, 1 piece, 14g	2
Mini Chocolate Teacakes, 3 (21g)	2
Strawberry Sponge Roll, ⅙ large, 47g	4

M&S – In-Store Bakery

Apple Turnover, 1 (102g)	10
Belgian Chocolate & Custard Doughnut, 1 (86g)	8
Belgian Chocolate Muffin, 1 (120g)	13
Blueberry Muffin, 1 (120g)	12
Carrot Cup Cake, 1 (86g)	10
Cheese Scone, 1 (80g)	10
Cherry Scone, 1 (85g)	4
Chocolate Iced Ring Doughnut, 1 (60g)	7
Devon Scone, 1 (85g)	10
Double Chocolate Muffin, 1 (127g)	15
Eccles Cakes, 1 (70g)	7
Fruit Scone, 1 (90g)	9
Glazed Ring Doughnut, 1 (57g)	6
Lemon & White Chocolate Muffin, 1 (124g)	14
Lemon Drizzle Muffin, 1 (120g)	12
Maple & Pecan Yum Yum, 1 (75g)	9
Milk Chocolate Chunk Shortbread, 1 (66g)	9

Mini Doughnut Bites, 1 (61g)	8
Mini Yum Yum, Glazed or Lemon, 1 (30g)	4
Palmier, 1 (70g)	10
Pink Iced Doughnut, 1 (60g)	7
Plain Ring Doughnut, 1 (50g)	6
Raspberry Jam Doughnut, 1 (65g)	5
Ring Doughnuts, 1 (71g)	7
Sugar Ring Doughnut, 1 (70g)	7
Very Berry Muffin, 1 (120g)	12

McVitie's

Apricot & Honey Wholegrain Cake with Sultanas, 1 slice, 40g	4
Caramel Shortcake Slices, 1 slice, 32g	4
Carrot Cake, ⅙ cake, 42g	4
Choc Chip Cake, 1 serving, 69g	7
Chocolate Brownie Slices, 1 slice, 28g	3
Chocolate Cake, 1 serving, 22g	2
Cranberry & Almond Wholegrain Cake with Sultanas, 1 slice, 40g	4
Fruit Cake, 1 slice, 32g	3
Fruit Jamaica Ginger Cake, 1 slice, 30g	3
Galaxy Cake Bars, 1 (33g)	5
Galaxy Caramel Cake Bars, 1 (30g)	4
Hobnobs Milk Chocolate Flapjacks, 1 mini, 35g	4
Hobnobs Milk Chocolate Flapjacks, 1 standard, 70g	9
Jaffa Cakes Mini Rolls, 1 (28g)	3
Jamaica Ginger Cake, 1 slice, 60g	6
Lemon Cake, 1 slice, 60g	7
Lunchers Blackcurrant or Lemon Cake Bar, 1 (31g)	3
Lunchers Strawberry, 1 (31g)	3
Mars Mini Rolls, 1 (30g)	4
MilkyWay Cake Bars, 1 (28g)	4
Oatjacks, Oat & Syrup Flapjacks, 1 (35g)	4
Orange Jamaica Ginger Cake, 1 slice, 60g	6
Penguin Cake Bars, 1 bar, 28g	4
Penguin Mini Rolls, 1 (26g)	4
Snickers Flapjacks, 1 (35g)	5
Strawberry Shortcake Slices, 1 slice, 26g	4

Morrisons

Lemon Blossom Miroir, 1 serving, 130g	13
Soda Scones, 1 individual, 25g	2
Sugared Mini Ring Doughnuts, 1 individual, 14g	2
Eat Smart Reduced Fat All Butter Croissants, 1 individual, 44g	4

Mr Kipling

Almond Slices, 1 slice, 36g	4
Angel Slices, 1 slice, 37g	4
Apple Slices, 1 slice, 27g	3
Apricot & Sultana Flapjacks, 1 (74g)	7
Battenberg, 1 slice, 38g	4
Carrot & Walnut Mini Classics, 1 (39g)	5
Cherry Slices, 1 slice, 30g	4
Chocolate Chip Cake Bars, 1 (32g)	4
Chocolate Slices, 1 slice, 33g	4
Country Slices, 1 slice, 32g	3
Cranberry & Orange Mini Classics, 1 (38g)	4
Delicious Sponge Cake Bites, All Flavours, 1 (14g)	2
Family Battenberg, 1 slice, 36g	4
Flapjack, 1 medium, 80g	10
French Fancies, 1 (28g)	3
Fruit Flapjack, 1 (75g)	9
Ginger Mini Classics, 1 (36g)	4
Lemon & Orange Fancies, 1 (27g)	3
Lemon Mini Classics, 1 (36g)	4
Lemon Slices, 1 slice, 29g	3
Manor House Cake, 1 slice, 67g	7
Milk Chocolate & Pecan Brownies, 1 (62g)	7
Millionaire's Shortcakes, 1 (70g)	10
Mini Battenbergs, 1 (35g)	4
Oatibakes, All Flavours, 1 (41g)	5
Raspberry Swiss Roll, 1 (41g)	4
Rum & Raisin Slices, 1 slice, 42g	5
Simnel Fruit Slices, 1 slice, 59g	6
St Clements Slices, 1 slice, 60g	7
The Big French Fancy, Pink or Yellow, 1/12 cake, 79g	8
Toffee Viennese Whirls, 1 (27g)	4
Victoria Mini Classics, 1 (36g)	4
Victoria Slices, 1 slice, 27g	3
Viennese Whirls, 1 (28g)	4

Mrs Crimble's

Bakewell Slices, 1 slice, 50g	6
Blackberry Shortcake Squares, 1 (50g)	5
Double Choc Brownies, 1 (48g)	6
Dutch Apple Cake, 1 slice, 48g	4
Jam Coconut Rings, large, 1 (40g)	5
Lemon & Coconut Slices, 1 slice, 50g	5
Stem Ginger Cake, 1 slice, 48g	4

OK Allergy Friendly Foods...

Almond & Apricot Cake, 1 slice, 30g	4
Ginger Cake Slices, 1 slice, 30g	3
Granola Cake Slices, 1 slice, 30g	4
Luxury Chocolate Tiffin Slices, 1 slice, 26g	3

ProPoints value

Sainsbury's

Apple & Sultana Muffin Cake, 1 (83g)	**7**
Apple Pies, 1 (46g)	**5**
Banana, Date & Walnut Slices, 1 slice, 30g	**2**
Battenberg Cake, large, 1 slice, 46g	**5**
Be Good To Yourself Banana, Date & Walnut Cake Slice, 1 slice, 24g	**2**
Belgian Buns, 1 (120g)	**11**
Bramley Apple Pie, ½ pie, 70g	**7**
Caramel Shortcake Fingers, 1 (36g)	**5**
Carrot Cake Slices, 1 slice, 30g	**3**
Champagne Chocolate Cake, 1 serving, 72g	**8**
Cherry Cakes, 1 (25g)	**3**
Chocolate Cake Bars, 1 serving, 27g	**3**
Chocolate Chip Cake Bars, 1 bar, 30g	**4**
Chocolate Flavour Swiss Roll, ½ cake, 18g	**2**
Chocolate Flavoured Mini Rolls, 1 (20g)	**2**
Chocolate Flavoured Sponge Roll, 1 serving, 50g	**4**
Chocolate Mini Rolls, 1 (29g)	**4**
Chocolate Slice, 1 slice, 28g	**3**
Chocolate Sponge Cake, 1 slice, 75g	**7**
Chocolate Swiss Roll, 1 slice, 35g	**3**
Chocolate Tray Bake, ⅕ cake, 53g	**6**
Cinnamon Buns, 1 (68g)	**6**
Cream & Jam Swiss Roll, 1 slice, 35g	**3**
Custard Doughnuts, 1 (81g)	**5**
Dairy Cream Sponge, ¼ cake, 51g	**4**
Dundee Cake, 1 slice, 82g	**7**
Farmhouse Style Fruit Cake, 1 slice, 75g	**7**
Fondant Fancies, 1 (28g)	**3**
Fresh Cream Belgian Buns, 1 (127g)	**11**
Fresh Cream Strawberry Scones, 1 (60g)	**6**
Genoa Cake, 1 slice, 80g	**8**
Happy Birthday Candle Cake, large, 1 slice, 69g	**8**
Happy Birthday Chocolate Bar Cake, 1 slice, 58g	**6**
Iced Bar Cake, 1 slice, 70g	**6**
Iced Bar Loaf, 1 slice, 72g	**7**
Iced Buns, 1 (40g)	**3**
Iced Rich Fruit Slices, 1 slice, 37g	**3**
Jumbo Chocolate Swiss Roll, 1/12 cake, 35g	**4**
Jumbo Strawberry & Vanilla Swiss Roll, 1/12 cake, 35g	**4**
Lemon Slice, 1 slice, 28g	**3**
Mini Chocolate Brownies, 1 (18g)	**2**
Mini Double Chocolate Chip Muffins, 1 (30g)	**4**
Mini Raspberry & White Chocolate Chip Muffins, 1 (30g)	**3**
Mini Rolls, 1 (22g)	**2**
Pecan, Cranberry & Raisin Muffins, 1 (63g)	**7**
Plum, Orange & Cranberry Sponge, ¼ pudding, 125g	**9**
Raisin Cakes, 1 (25g)	**3**
Raisin Fruit Slab Cake, 1 slice, 50g	**6**
Raspberry & Blackcurrant Muffin Cake, 1 slice, 80g	**8**
Rich Fruit Cake, 1 slice, 75g	**7**
Seriously Chocolate Cake, 1 slice, 80g	**10**
Sliced Fruit Loaf, 1 slice, 36g	**3**
Small Party Celebration Cake, ⅛ cake, 73g	**8**
Strawberry Sponge Roll, 1 serving, 50g	**3**
Swiss Roll with Raspberry Filling, 1 slice, 29g	**2**
Toffee Slices, 1 slice, 27g	**2**
Top Iced Cake Bar, 1 slice, 67g	**6**
Treacle Tart, 1 slice, 75g	**8**

Sainsbury's – Taste the Difference

All Butter Carrot Cake, ⅙ cake, 64g	**7**
All Butter Chocolate Fudge Cake, 1/10 cake, 64g	**7**
All Butter Victoria Sandwich, ⅙ cake, 62g	**7**
Apple & Cinnamon Hot Cross Buns, 1 (139g)	**7**
Black Cherry Panettone, 1/7 cake, 63g	**6**
Chocolate Loaf Cake, ⅙ cake, 51g	**5**
Cinnamon Star Stollen, ⅙ cake, 83g	**9**
Mini Victoria Sandwiches, 1 (78g)	**9**
Morello Cherry & Almond Streussel, ¼ cake, 112g	**10**
Rich Fruit Cake, 1 slice, 76g	**7**
Rich Fruit Slices, 1 slice, 49g	**5**
Rich Ginger Fruit Cake, ⅙ cake, 68g	**6**
Teacakes, 1 (90g)	**7**
Top Iced Rich Fruit Cake Bar, ⅙ bar, 68g	**7**
White Chocolate & Red Fruit Cake, 1 slice, 75g	**7**
Winter Fruit Crumble, ¼ pudding, 112g	**7**

Soreen

Cinnamon & Raisin Fruit Loaf, 1 slice, 25g	**2**
Lincolnshire Plum Fruit Loaf, 1 slice, 26g	**2**
Luxury Rich Fruit Loaf, 1 portion, 26g	**2**

Tesco

Almond Fingers, 1 individual, 46g	**5**
Angel Layer Cake, 1 serving, 40g	**4**
Apricot Sponge Roll, 1 serving, 47g	**5**
Banana Cake, 1 serving (⅛ cake), 42g	**4**
Belgian Bun, 1 individual, 110g	**12**
Big Chocolate Cake, 1 slice, 92g	**10**
Blackcurrant Mini Cupcakes, 1 individual, 20g	**2**
Blueberry Cheesecake Loaf Cake, 1 serving, 53g	**6**
Blueberry Muffins, 1 individual, 72g	**8**
Bramley Apple & Blackcurrant Flapjack, 1 serving, 125g	**8**
Butter Brioche Rolls, 1 individual, 35g	**3**

Butter Flapjacks, 1 individual, 33g	4
Butterfield Cakes Choc Mini Rolls, 1 individual, 27g	4
Caramelised Pear & Hazelnut Frangipanes, 1 individual, 115g	11
Carrot Cake, 1 serving (⅙ cake), 58g	7
Celebration Cake, small, 1 slice, 56g	6
Chelsea Buns, 1 individual, 85g	6
Cherry & Almond Slice, 1 individual, 60g	7
Cherry Genoa Cake, 1 serving, 44g	4
Cherry Loaf Cake, 1 serving, 59g	6
Cherry Madeira Slab Cake, 1 serving, 38g	3
Chewy Flapjack Squares, 1 individual, 14g	2
Chewy Rocky Road Clusters, 1 individual, 11g	1
Choc Cupcakes, 1 individual, 45g	6
Chocolate & Vanilla Cupcake Cones, 1 individual, 64g	9
Chocolate & Vanilla Jumbo Swiss Roll, 1 serving, 33g	3
Chocolate Brownie, 1 individual, 80g	9
Chocolate Brownie Cake, 1 individual, 90g	10
Chocolate Brownie Traybake, 1 serving, 37g	4
Chocolate Caterpillar Cake, 1 slice, 58g	7
Chocolate Celebration Cake, large, 1 serving, 68g	8
Chocolate Chip Muffins, 1 individual, 72g	8
Chocolate Drizzle Flapjack, 1 individual, 65g	8
Chocolate Flavoured Swiss Roll, 1 serving, 20g	2
Chocolate Flavoured Tiffin Squares, 1 individual, 52g	8
Chocolate Fudge Brownie Cake, 1 serving, 90g	10
Chocolate Mini Muffins, 1 individual, 27g	3
Chocolate Mini Roll, 1 individual, 30g	4
Chocolate 'n' Orange Muffins, 1 individual, 73g	7
Chocolate Parcel Cake, 1 serving, 63g	7
Chocolate Party Cake, 1 serving, 92g	10
Chocolate Party Traybake, 1 serving, 50g	6
Chocolate Slices, 1 individual, 28g	3
Chocolate Sponge Roll, 1 serving, 47g	5
Chocolate Sponge Sandwich Cake, ⅙ cake, 36g	4
Chocolate Swiss Roll, 1 serving, 33g	4
Citrus Sunshine Loaf Cake, 1 serving, 52g	6
Coconut Macaroons, 1 individual, 20g	3
Coconut Sponge Sandwich Cake, 1 serving, 42g	5
Coffee Iced Madeira Cake, 1 serving, 42g	4
Cookies & Cream Cupcakes, 1 individual, 69g	9
Cookies & Cream Muffins, 1 individual, 86g	10
Country Slices, 1 individual, 27g	3
Cream & Jam Doughnuts, 1 individual, 74g	7
Crispy Chocolate Clusters, 1 individual, 8g	1
Custard & Raspberry Doughnuts, 1 individual, 92g	6

Custard Slices, 1 individual, 108g	8
Double Chocolate Muffins, 1 individual, 72g	8
Double Chocolate Swiss Roll, 1 slice, 32g	3
Fairy Cakes, 1 individual, 23g	2
Flower Cake, 1 slice (1/16 cake), 63g	7
Fondant Fancies, 1 individual, 28g	3
Frangipanes, 1 individual, 59g	7
French Butter Crêpes, 1 individual, 30g	3
Fresh Cream Victoria Sponge, 1 individual, 70g	7
Fruit & Nut Flapjack, 1 individual, 65g	7
Fruit Slice, 1 individual, 87g	8
Fruity Mini Flooded Cupcake, 1 individual, 20g	2
Genoa Cake, 1 slice, 66g	6
Granola Traybake, 1 serving, 45g	5
Happy Birthday Cake Bar, 1 serving, 64g	7
Iced Bakewell Slices, 1 individual, 35g	4
Iced Fairy Cakes, 1 individual, 23g	3
Iced Finger Buns, 1 individual, 50g	4
Iced Fruit Cake, 1 serving, 57g	5
Iced Ginger Squares, 1 individual, 60g	5
Iced Lemon Cake, 1 serving, 49g	5
Iced Madeira Cake, 1 serving, 54g	6
Individual Carrot Cake, 1 individual, 75g	8
Individual Chocolate Fudge Cake, 1 individual, 75g	9
Individual Lemon Drizzle Cake, 1 individual, 75g	9
Large Fully Iced Rich Fruit Cake, 1 serving, 77g	7
Lemon Flavoured Cupcakes, 1 individual, 45g	6
Lemon Half Moon Cake, 1 individual, 50g	6
Lemon Iced Madeira Cake, 1 slice, 50g	5
Lemon Meringue Triple Layer Cake, 1 serving, 56g	5
Lemon Slices, 1 individual, 30g	3
Lemon Sponge Cake, 1 slice, 43g	4
Lemon Sponge Roll, 1 slice, 47g	5
Madeira Cake, 1 serving, 37g	4
Madeira Loaf Cake, 1 serving, 53g	5
Madeira Party Cake, 1 serving, 79g	9
Maple Syrup Pancakes, 1 individual, 40g	3
Marble Madeira Cake, 1 serving, 50g	6
Marvellous Chocolate Muffins, 1 individual, 100g	11
Mini Chocolate Roll Bites, 1 individual, 18g	2
Mini Sponge Flans, 1 individual, 21g	2
Mini Syrup Pancakes, 1 individual, 16g	1
Mini Yoghurt & Blueberry Clusters, 1 individual, 15g	2
Mississippi Mud Cupcakes, 1 individual, 67g	9
Pancakes, large, 1 individual, 60g	4
Raisin & Lemon Pancakes, 1 individual, 35g	2
Raspberry Sponge Sandwich, 1 serving, 38g	4
Raspberry Swiss Roll, 1/16 serving, 33g	3

Red Velvet Cupcakes, 1 individual, 67g	9
Rhubarb Crumble Cake, 1 serving, 41g	4
Rich Chocolate Mini Rolls, 1 individual, 18g	2
Rocky Road Traybake, 1 serving, 40g	5
Rocky Road Triple Layer Cake, 1 serving, 61g	7
Saltire Celebration Cake, 1 serving, 69g	8
Sliced Fruit Loaf, 1 slice, 36g	3
Snowballs, 1 individual, 86g	9
Sponge Cakes, 1 individual, 35g	4
Strawberry & Vanilla Jumbo Swiss Roll, 1 serving, 33g	3
Strawberry Cupcake Cones, 1 individual, 64g	8
Strawberry Sponge Roll, 1 slice, 47g	5
Strawberry Whoopie Pies, 1 individual, 67g	7
Sultana & Cherry Cake, 1 serving, 47g	5
Sultana Loaf Cake, 1 serving, 59g	6
Sultana Scones, 1 individual, 70g	7
Syrup Pancakes, 1 individual, 30g	2
Teacakes, 1 individual, 68g	5
Toffee & Popcorn Triple Layer Cake, 1 serving, 58g	7
Toffee Banoffee Cake, 1 serving, 88g	8
Trifle Sponges, 1 individual, 20g	2
Triple Layer Caramel Cake, 1 serving, 73g	9
Triple Layer Chocolate Cake, 1 slice, 79g	8
Vanilla Party Traybake, 1 serving, 50g	6
Victoria Sponge, 1 serving, 56g	5
Walnut Cake, 1 serving, 48g	5
White Chocolate Celebration Cake, Large, 1 serving, 68g	8
Yum Yums, 1 individual, 60g	7

Tesco – Finest

Apple & Blackberry Cake, 1 slice, 47g	5
Banoffee Cake, 1 serving, 61g	7
Belgian Chocolate Tiffin Squares, 1 individual, 40g	6
Belgian White Chocolate & Strawberry Cake, 1 serving (⅙ cake), 65g	7
Brioche Loaf, 1 serving, 50g	5
Briochettes, 1 individual, 45g	4
Butter Waffles, 1 individual, 25g	3
Carrot & Orange Cake, large, 1 serving, 61g	7
Cheese Scones, 1 individual, 70g	6
Chocolate Brownie Squares, 1 individual, 33g	4
Chocolate Indulgence Cake, large, (¹/₁₀ cake), 61g	7
Chocolate Indulgence Cake, standard, (⅙ cake), 67g	8
Coffee & Walnut Cake, 1 serving (⅙ cake), 69g	8
Cornish Butter & Sultana Scones, 1 individual, 70g	7

Cream Scones, 1 individual, 123g	12
Date & Walnut Loaf Cake, 1 serving, 52g	6
Lemon Cake, 1 slice, 50g	6
Lemon Drizzle Loaf Cake, 1 serving, 51g	5
Panettone Fruit Loaf, 1 slice, 50g	4
St. Clements Cake, 1 serving, 68g	7
Victoria Cake, 1 serving, 60g	7

Tesco – Free From

Caramel Shortcake Slice, 1 individual, 30g	4
Chocolate & Walnut Brownie, 1 individual, 28g	4
Country Cake Slice, 1 individual, 28g	3
Double Chocolate Cake Bars, 1 individual, 45g	5
Double Chocolate Muffins, 1 individual, 70g	8
Fruit Cake, 1 serving, 38g	4
Fruit Loaf, 1 slice, 36g	2
Lemon Loaf Cake, 1 serving, 38g	4
Sultana Scones, 1 individual, 120g	11
Syrup Pancakes, 1 individual, 42g	3
Victoria Sponge, 1 serving, 66g	7

Tesco – Light Choices

Carrot & Orange Cake Slices, 1 slice, 30g	2
Date & Walnut Cake Slices, 1 slice, 25g	2
Lemon Drizzle Cake Slices, 1 slice, 23g	2
Mini Victoria Cakes, 1 individual, 41g	4
Pancakes, 1 individual, 27g	2
Sultana & Honey Scones, 1 individual, 60g	5

The Co-operative

All Butter Madeira Cake, ⅕ cake, 44g	5
All Butter Viennese Whirls, 1 (30g)	4
Almond Fingers, 1 (45g)	5
Blackcurrant Sponges, 1 (105g)	7
Blueberry Muffin, In-Store Bakery, 1 (120g)	13
Bramley Apple Pies, 1 (62g)	7
Carrot & Orange Cake, 1 slice, 69g	8
Cherry & Almond Loaf Cake, 1 slice, 60g	5
Cherry Genoa Cake, 1 slice, 70g	7
Chocolate Brownie Bites, In-Store Bakery, 1 (100g)	13
Chocolate Cake, ⅙ cake, 106g	12
Chocolate Caramel Shortbread, 1 (38g)	5
Chocolate Crispy Bites, 1 (10g)	1
Chocolate Mini Rolls, 1 (29g)	4
Chocolate Sponge Sandwich, 1 slice, 40g	4
Chocolate Tiffin, 1 (41g)	5
Coconut Sponge Sandwich, 1 slice, 49g	5
Cream & Jam Doughnuts, 1 (71g)	6
Date & Walnut Loaf Cake, 1 slice, 60g	6
Double Chocolate Muffin, In-Store Bakery, 1 (120g)	13

Double Chocolate Swiss Roll, ⅐ roll, 47g	5
Dundee Cake, ⅙ cake, 61g	6
Fairtrade Butter Flapjack Squares, 1 (35g)	4
Fairtrade Chocolate Brownies, 1 (35g)	4
Fairtrade Chocolate Loaf Cake, ⅙ cake, 60g	6
Fairtrade Double Chocolate Chip Muffins, 1 (69g)	8
Fairy Cakes, 1 (27g)	3
Flapjack Bites, In-Store Bakery, 1 piece, 16g	2
Fruit Loaf, 1 slice, 36g	3
Fruited Teacakes, 1 (70g)	5
Ginger Loaf Cake, 1 slice, 60g	6
Hit the Spot Butter Flapjack, 1 (75g)	10
Hit the Spot Fairtrade Chocolate Brownie, 1 (75g)	9
Iced Fairy Cakes, 1 (22g)	2
Iced Jam & Buttercream Cake, ⅙ cake, 50g	5
Iced Lemon Layer Cake, ⅙ slice, 51g	6
Iced Rich Fruit Cake, ⅙ cake, 75g	7
Lemon Cup Cakes, 1 cake, 70g	8
Lemon Drizzle Cake, ⅙ cake, 66g	7
Pancakes, 1 (50g)	3
Party Parcels Cake, ⅙ cake, 139g	15
Raisin & Lemon Pancakes, 1 (35g)	3
Raspberry & Vanilla Swiss Roll, ⅛ roll, 34g	3
Raspberry Sponge Sandwich, 1 slice, 45g	4
Rich Fruit Cake, 1 slice, 72g	7
Toffee Cake, ⅙ cake, 63g	7
Victoria Cake, ⅙ cake, 60g	7
Walnut Layer Cake, 1 portion, 50g	6

The Fabulous Bakin' Boys

All Butter Flapjack, 1 (50g)	6
Belgian Chocolate Flapjack, 1 (50g)	7
Blueberry Muffin, 1 (87g)	9
Caramel Shortcake, 1 (75g)	10
Choc & Orange Muffin, 1 (87g)	10
Choc On Top Flapjack, 1 (75g)	10
Choco Flapjacks, 1 (28g)	4
Chocolate Chip Lunchbox Muffin, 1 (64g)	7
Chocolate Cupcakes, 1 (34g)	4
Chocolate Muffin, 1 (87g)	10
Double Chocolate Lunchbox Muffin, 1 (112g)	13
Eccles Cake Slice, 1 slice, 95g	10
Fruit Loaf Cake, 1 (80g)	9
Honey & Fruit Flapjack, 1 (75g)	9
King Cupcakes Lemon, 1 (54g)	6
King Cupcakes Triple Chocolate, 1 (54g)	7
Mighty Oat Flapjack, 1 (75g)	10
Original Cupcakes, 1 (80g)	10
Raspberry Flapjack, 1 (75g)	9
Yoghurt Flapjack Fingers, 1 (28g)	4

Thorntons

Chocolate Mini Cakes, 1 (42g)	5
Mini Caramel Shortcakes, 1 (20g)	3
Mini Chocolate Brownies, 1 (15g)	2
Mini Chocolate Orange Cakes, 1 (21g)	3
Mini Sicilian Lemon Cakes, 1 (21g)	3
Toffee Cake, 1 serving, 70g	8
Toffee Layered Patisserie Cake, 1 serving, 73g	9
Toffee Mini Cakes, 1 (44g)	6

Waitrose

Buttermilk Pancakes, 1 (35g)	2
Chocolate & Nut Tiffin Slice, 1 slice, 80g	11
Chocolate Brownie, 1 slice, 60g	7
Chocolate Sponge Sandwich, ⅛ cake, 47g	5
Dark Chocolate Melt in the Middle Pudding, ¼ pudding, 125g	12
Eve's Pudding, 1 pudding, 110g	7
Florentine, large, 1 slice, 40g	5
Iced Ring Doughnuts, 1 (65g)	7
Jam Doughnut, 1 serving, 114g	11
Lardy Cake, 1 slice, 60g	6
Pancakes, 1 (80g)	4
Vanilla Flavoured Scone, 1 serving, 125g	12
Victoria Sponge Sandwich, ⅛ cake, 45g	5

Warburtons

Fruit Loaf with Orange, 1 slice, 35g	2
Fruity Teacake, 1 (63g)	4
Hot Cross Bun Loaf, 1 slice, 35g	3
Pancakes, 1 (35g)	2
Raisin Loaf with Cinnamon, 1 slice, 36g	3

Weight Watchers

All Butter Croissant, 1 (44g)	4
Almond Cake Slice, 1 slice, 26g	3
Apple Crumble Slices, 1 slice, 21g	2
Belgian Chocolate Slices, 1 slice, 25g	2
Caramel Cake Bars, 1 bar, 21g	2
Caramel Shortcakes, 1 slice, 25g	3
Carrot Cake Slice, 1 slice, 27g	2
Chocolate Mini Rolls, 1 (20g)	2
Coconut Slice, 1 (26g)	2
Country Slice, 1 (23g)	2
Jaffa Mini Rolls, 1 (19g)	2
Lemon Cake Slice, 1 slice, 26g	2
Mini Carrot Cakes, 1 (30g)	3
Mini Chocolate Cupcakes, 1 (20g)	2
Mini Lemon Cupcakes, 1 (19g)	1
Mini Victoria Sponges, 1 (30g)	3

	ProPoints value
Pains au Chocolat, 1 (50g)	5
Wild Blueberry Muffins, 1 (60g)	5

Fresh Puddings

Asda

Bread & Butter Pudding, family size, ¼ large, 125g	6
Chocolate Fudge Sponge Pudding, 1 serving, 130g	12
Chocolate Sponge Pudding, 1 pot, 105g	11
Fruits of the Forest Sponge Pudding, 1 pot, 115g	6
Handmade Sticky Toffee Pudding, 1 pot, 105g	9
Mandarin Royale, ¼ pack, 38g	1
Profiteroles with Chocolate Sauce, ⅕ pack, 64g	6
Roly Poly Pudding, 1 pot, 114g	10
Spotted Dick Pudding, 1 pot, 115g	10
Syrup Sponge Pudding, ¼ pack, 113g	9
Toffee Apple Flapjack Dessert, 1 pot, 140g	11
Winter Fruit Crumble Dessert, 1 pot, 140g	9

Asda – Extra Special

Belgian Chocolate Gâteau, 1 serving, 98g	9
Belgian Chocolate Truffle Trifle, 1 serving, 150g	15
Fresh Cream Victoria Sponge Cake, 1 slice, 72g	7
Hand Finished Black Forest Cake, 1 serving, 68g	8
Bread & Butter Pudding, ¼ pack, 98g	7
Chocolate Sponge Pudding, ¼ serving, 100g	11
Fresh Cream Victoria Sponge Cake, 1 slice, 72g	7
Melt-in-the-Middle Chocolate Pudding, 1 portion, 151g	17
Melt-in-the-Middle Sticky Toffee Pudding, 1 individual, 150g	17

Asda – Good For You

Chocolate Muffin Dessert, ½ pack, 68g	2
Chocolate Sponge Pudding, 1 (105g)	5
Strawberry Muffin Dessert, 1 pack, 135g	4
Strawberry Sponge Pudding, 1 pot, 100g	5

Aunty's

Chocolate Sauce Steamed Pudding, 1 (120g)	9
Ginger Syrup Steamed Pudding, 1 (120g)	8
Gooey Caramel Steamed Pudding, 1 (120g)	10
Sensational Belgian Chocolate Pudding, 1 (120g)	9
Spotted Dick, Sticky Toffee or Strawberry Steamed Pudding, 1 (120g)	9

Heinz

Chocolate Sponge Pudding, 1 pot, 110g	9
Sticky Toffee Sponge Pudding, ¼ serving, 75g	6
Treacle Sponge Pudding, ¼ pot, 75g	6

Morrisons

Chocolate Sponge Pudding, 1 individual, 115g	6
Fresh Cream Mini Raspberry Trifles, 1 individual, 124g	6
Lemon Sponge Pudding, 1 individual, 115g	7
Strawberry Sponge Pudding, 1 individual, 115g	7

Sainsbury's

Blackforest Gâteau, ⅕ cake, 104g	8
Blueberry & Almond Sponge Pudding, 1 (120g)	7
Bread & Butter Pudding, ¼ pudding, 125g	7
Chocolate Melt-in-the-Middle Pudding, 1 pudding, 150g	15
Chocolate Sponge Pudding, 1 (120g)	11
Clotted Cream Rice Pudding, ¼ pudding, 125g	7
Clotted Cream Rice Pudding, 1 (160g)	9
Free From Syrup Sponge Pudding, 1 (100g)	8
Free From Chocolate Sponge Pudding, 1 (100g)	8
Ginger Sponge Pudding, 1 (120g)	11
Jaffa Cake Pudding, ¼ pudding, 100g	9
Jam Roly Poly, ¼ cake, 81g	8
Jam Roly Poly Pudding, ¼ pudding, 165g	11
Jam Roly Poly with Raspberry Jam & Custard, ¼ pudding, 49g	3
Lemon Sponge Pudding, 1 (120g)	10
Millionaire's Shortcake Dessert, 1 pot, 140g	15
Mini Black Forest Gâteau, 1 (91g)	7
Mini Lemon Syllabub & Raspberry Gâteau, 1 (93g)	6
Raspberry Jam Sponge Pudding, 1 (120g)	11
Spotted Dick, ¼ cake, 81g	7
Sticky Toffee Pudding, ¼ pudding, 110g	10
Sticky Toffee Sponge Pudding, 1 (120g)	10
Strawberry Gâteau, 1 slice, 110g	8
Syrup Sponge Pudding, ¼ pudding, 125g	12
Toffee Gâteau, 1 slice, 120g	8
Toffee Sponge Pudding, 1 serving, 130g	14
Triple Chocolate Gâteau, 1 slice, 94g	8

Sainsbury's – Taste the Difference

Belgian Chocolate Sponge Pudding, ⅓ pack, 100g	10

	ProPoints value
Belgian Chocolate Truffle Gâteau, 1 serving, 89g	10
Brioche Bread & Butter Pudding, ¼ pudding, 112g	10
Butterscotch & Pecan Sponge Pudding, ⅓ pudding, 102g	11
Chocolate & Cherry Drizzle Gâteau, ¹⁄₁₀ cake, 111g	9
Chocolate Gâteau, 1 serving, 70g	9
Chocolate Sponge Pudding, 1 (120g)	11
Chocolate Sponge Pudding, ⅓ pudding, 116g	12
Cranberry & Orange Muffin Gâteau, ¹⁄₁₀ cake, 95g	8
Melting Middle Chocolate Pudding, 1 (150g)	15
Sticky Toffee Pudding, ¼ pudding, 100g	10

Tesco

Amontillado Sherry Trifle, 1 individual, 180g	10
Apple Sponge Pudding, 1 serving, 95g	6
Bread & Butter Pudding, 1 individual, 120g	11
Chocolate Covered Profiteroles, 1 serving, 72g	8
Chocolate Sponge Pudding, 1 individual, 130g	12
Crème Caramel, 1 pot, 100g	3
Custard Slice, 1 individual, 107g	9

	ProPoints value
Double Chocolate Heaven, 1 portion, 150g	9
Fruit Cocktail Trifle, 1 serving, 150g	7
Lemon Filled Crêpes, 1 individual, 30g	3
Luxury Raspberry Roulade, 1 serving, 67g	5
Melting Middle Chocolate Sponge Pudding, 1 individual, 135g	14
Mississippi Mud Pie, 1 serving (⅙ pie), 93g	11
Raspberry Trifle, 1 serving, 150g	7
Rhubarb Crumble, 1 serving, 150g	9
Spotted Dick Pudding, 1 individual, 130g	12
Sticky Chocolate Brownie Pudding, 1 serving, 125g	12
Sticky Toffee Pudding, 1 individual, 130g	12
Sticky Toffee Pudding, ¼ pudding, 113g	11
Strawberry Jam Sponge Pudding, 1 individual, 130g	12
Syrup Sponge Pudding, 1 individual, 130g	13

Tesco – Finest

Belgian Chocolate Mousse, 1 pot, 100g	8
Belgian Chocolate Pudding, 1 portion, 107g	10
Bread & Butter Pudding, 1 serving, 148g	14
Butterscotch Mousse, 1 individual, 100g	8
Clotted Cream & Red Berry Sponge Pudding, 1 individual, 130g	10

Weight Watchers®
Sponge Desserts
a must for your shopping list

A fantastic treat or a great way to end a meal, our sponge dessert range is created for your sweet indulgence.

4 to 5 ProPoints value
per pudding

WeightWatchers® Foods
Eat gorgeous. Feel gorgeous.

Now available:
Chocolate Sponge Pudding, Lemon Sponge Pudding, Sticky Toffee Sponge Pudding and Apple, Blackcurrant & Blueberry Sponge Pudding

Clotted Cream & Toffee Sauce Sponge
Pudding, 1 individual, 125g **12**
Millionaire Dessert, 1 serving, 105g **12**
Toffee & Pecan Sponge Pudding,
1 individual, 130g **13**

The Co-operative

Bread & Butter Pudding, ¼ pack, 100g **5**
Chocolate Melt-in-the-Middle Pudding,
1 pot, 150g **16**
Chocolate Profiteroles, 1 pot, 90g **7**
Chocolate Profiteroles, ¼ large pack, 112g **8**
Fairtrade Chocolate Sponge Pudding,
½ large, 150g **16**
Fairtrade Syrup Sponge Pudding, ¼ pack, 75g **8**
Italian Tiramisu, 1 pot, 90g **6**
Raspberry Trifle, ⅕ large, 120g **5**
Raspberry Trifle, 1 pot, 150g **5**
Strawberry Trifle, 1 pot, 150g **6**
Syrup Sponge Pudding, 1 (120g) **9**

The Co-operative – Truly Irresistible

Chocolate Muffin Dessert, 1 pot, 120g **14**
Chocolate Sponge Pudding, ¼ large, 100g **10**
Clotted Cream Rice Pudding, ½ pack, 250g **13**
Sherry Trifle, 1 pot, 160g **9**
Tarte au Citron, ⅙ tart, 82g **8**
Toffee Melt in the Middle Pudding, 1 (150g) **16**

Waitrose

Bread & Butter Pudding, ¼ pack, 162g **10**
Caramel Apple Pudding, ¼ pack, 138g **12**
Chocolate Pudding, 1 (105g) **13**
Eton Mess, ⅙ pack, 71g **5**
Jam Roly Poly Pudding with Custard,
1 pot, 150g **9**
Lemon Meringue Dessert, 1 pot, 105g **9**
Lemon Yum Yum, 1 (106g) **14**
Pancakes with Lemon Sauce, ½ pack, 155g **9**
Raspberry Pavlova, ⅙ serving, 68g **5**
Raspberry Royale, 1 pot, 150g **6**
Sicilian Lemon Roulade, ⅙ pack, 65g **6**
Spotted Dick Pudding & Custard, 1 pot, 150g **8**
Stuffed Baked Apples, ½ pack, 175g **10**
Summer Berries Roulade, ⅙ pack, 65g **6**
Toffee Pecan Roulade, ⅙ pack, 60g **7**
Treacle Sponge Pudding, ¼ serving, 125g **12**

Weight Watchers

Apple, Blackberry & Blueberry
Pudding, 1 (100g) **4**

Chocolate Sponge Pudding, 1 (100g) **5**
Lemon Sponge Pudding, 1 (100g) **5**
Sticky Toffee Pudding, 1 (100g) **4**

Patisserie

Asda

All-Butter Croissants, 1 (55g) **6**
All-Butter Pains au Chocolat, 1 (75g) **9**
All-Butter Pains aux Raisins, 1 (110g) **10**
Apple & Cream Puff, 1 (150g) **16**
Apple & Cream Turnover, 1 (80g) **9**
Apple Danish Pastry (midi), 1 (43g) **4**
Bramley Apple Turnover, 1 (29g) **3**
Butter Croissants Part Baked, 1 (45g) **5**
Chocolate Éclair & Cream Doughnut, 1 (81g) **8**
Chocolate Éclair, 1 large, 54g **6**
Cinnamon Swirl, 1 (74g) **10**
Cream Doughnuts with Strawberry Jam, 1 (73g) **7**
Croissants, In-Store Bakery, 1 (55g) **7**
Custard Crown Danish (midi), 1 (43g) **4**
Custard Filled Donuts, 1 (67g) **5**
Donut Selection, 1 (76g) **7**
Double Chocolate Éclair, 1 (74g) **8**
Fresh Cream Fruited Scone, 1 (64g) **6**
Fruit Scones with Strawberry Jam &
Cream, 1 (58g) **5**
Fruited Teacakes, 1 (70g) **5**
Glazed Donuts, 1 (52g) **6**
Iced Cream Fingers, ½ pack of 2, 50g **5**
Jam Finger Donuts, 1 (76g) **8**
Maple & Pecan Plait, 1 (95g) **10**
Maple & Pecan Plait Danish Pastry, 1 (42g) **5**
Mini Chocolate Éclairs, 1 (13g) **2**
Mini Eclairs, ¼ pack, 60g **6**
Pain au Chocolat, Part Baked, 1 (56g) **6**
Pain au Raisin, 1 (91g) **9**
Petit Pain, 1 (45g) **3**
Profiterole Stack, 1 serving, 60g **7**
Raspberry Crown Danish, 1 (43g) **4**
Strawberry Jam & Fresh Cream Sponge Cake,
1 serving, 79g **6**
Strawberry Jam Scones, 1 (69g) **6**

Asda – Chosen by You

Apple Turnovers, 1 (81g) **9**
Choux Buns, Caramel or Chocolate, 1 (99g) **11**
Continental Croissants, 1 (44g) **5**

Continental Mini Croissants, 1 (35g)	**4**
Continental Mini Pains au Chocolat, 1 (29g)	**4**
Cream Horn, 1 (60g)	**7**
Cream Slices, 1 (68g)	**9**
Jam Doughnut, 1 (73g)	**7**
Mini Meringue Shells, 2 (8g)	**1**
Raspberry Turnovers, 1 (77g)	**10**
Teatime Classic Eccles Cakes, 1 (50g)	**6**
Victoria Ring, 1 portion, 50g	**4**

Asda – Extra Special

All-Butter Croissants, 1 (70g)	**9**
Chocolate Eclairs, 1 (70g)	**8**
Pain Au Chocolat, 1 (70g)	**7**
Pain Au Raisin Twists, 1 (100g)	**11**
Profiteroles, 1 portion, 110g	**10**

M&S – In-Store Bakery

All Butter Croissant, 1 individual, 90g	**10**
Apricot Danish, 1 individual, 90g	**6**
Cheese & Onion Twist, 1 individual, 85g	**9**
Chocolate Iced Ring Doughnut, 1 individual, 60g	**7**
Cinnamon Swirl, 1 individual, 80g	**10**
Cinnamon Twist, 1 individual, 75g	**12**
Lemon Swirl, 1 individual, 87g	**9**
Pain au Chocolat, 1 individual, 90g	**11**
Pain au Raisin, 1 individual, 130g	**12**
Pecan & Maple Plait, 1 individual, 87g	**11**
Pink Iced Ring Doughnut, 1 individual, 60g	**7**
Plum Danish, 1 individual, 130g	**10**
Raspberry Jam Doughnut, 1 individual, 65g	**5**
Strawberry & Raspberry Puff, 1 individual, 81g	**9**
Sugar Ring Doughnut, 1 individual, 70g	**9**

Pillsbury

Pain au Chocolat, 1 (100g)	**10**
Ready to Bake Croissants, 1 (100g)	**9**

Sainsbury's

Apple & Cinnamon Frangipane, 1 (59g)	**6**
Dutch Apple Turnover, 1 (33g)	**4**
Chocolate Profiterole Dessert, 1 pot, 100g	**10**
Fresh Cream Chocolate Choux Buns, 1 (90g)	**10**
Fresh Cream Horns, 1 (56g)	**6**
Fresh Cream Jam Doughnuts, 1 (73g)	**7**
Fresh Cream Profiterole Stack, ¼ dessert, 76g	**9**
Fresh Cream Raspberry Turnover, 1 (84g)	**9**
Pain Aux Raisin, 1 (75g)	**8**

Tesco

All Butter Croissants, 1 individual, 49g	**6**
All Butter Pains au Chocolat, 1 individual, 61g	**7**

All Butter Scones, 1 individual, 60g	**6**
Bramley Apple Turnovers, 1 individual, 88g	**8**
Café Continental Croissants, 1 individual, 80g	**8**
Café Continental Pains au Chocolat, 1 individual, 45g	**5**
Chocolate Choux Buns, 1 individual, 85g	**9**
Chocolate Eclairs, (4 pack), 1 individual, 39g	**4**
Chocolate Eclairs, (10 pack), 1 individual, 29g	**3**
Chocolate Filled Crêpes, 1 individual, 32g	**4**
Double Chocolate Eclairs, 1 individual, 69g	**8**
Fresh Cream & Strawberry Jam Slices, 1 individual, 75g	**8**
Fresh Cream Choux Buns, 1 individual, 85g	**9**
Fresh Cream Eclairs, 1 individual, 61g	**7**
Fresh Cream Horns, 1 individual, 55g	**7**
Fresh Cream Jam Doughnuts, 1 individual, 75g	**7**
Fresh Cream Meringues, 1 individual, 35g	**3**
Fresh Cream Scones, 1 individual, 75g	**8**
Mini Croissants, 1 individual, 35g	**4**
Mini Pains au Chocolat, 1 individual, 38g	**5**
Raspberry Turnovers, 1 individual, 85g	**8**

Tesco – Finest

All Butter Croissant, 1 individual, 71g	**8**
All Butter Pains au Chocolat, 1 individual, 82g	**9**
Chocolate & Caramel Eclairs, 1 individual, 93g	**10**
Profiteroles, 1 serving, 82g	**9**

The Co-operative

All Butter Croissants, 1 (44g)	**5**
Caramelised Apple Danish, 1 (130g)	**10**
Choux Bun Twin Pack, 1 (93g)	**10**
Dairy Cream Selection, 1 quantity, 100g	**9**
Fresh Cream Apple Turnovers, 1 (80g)	**7**
Fresh Cream Slices, 1 slice, 77g	**9**
Strawberry, Raspberry & Vanilla Flavour Danish, 1 (100g)	**9**

Waitrose

Almond Croissant, 1 (108g)	**14**
Blueberry Danish Crown, 1 serving, 110g	**12**
Butterscotch Pecan Yum Yum, 1 serving, 115g	**15**
Chocolate Berliner, 1 serving, 122g	**13**
Chocolate Truffle Roulade, ⅙ pack, 57g	**6**
Crêpes, ⅓ pack, 79g	**5**
Crêpes with Caramel Sauce, ½ pack, 100g	**7**
Dairy Cream Selection, 1 quantity, 100g	**9**
Fruit Flapjack, 1 bar, 78g	**9**
Lemon & Sultana Danish, 1 serving, 133g	**16**
Mandarin Royale, 1 pot, 150g	**6**
Morello Cherry & Almond Frangipane Rustic Bake, ⅙ tart, 78g	**7**

Pain au Raisin, 1 (98g)	13
Pecan Slice, 1 (55g)	7
Profiterole Dessert, 1 pack, 110g	12
Profiteroles, 4 (103g)	10
Sticky Toffee Pudding, 1 pack, 115g	11
Summer Pudding, ½ pack, 150g	6
Syrup Sponge Pudding, 1 pot, 105g	10
Winter Pudding, 1 pot, 150g	6

Rolls & Bagels

Allinson

Brown Snack Rolls, 1 (45g)	3
Giant Brown Baps, 1 (60g)	4

Asda

Barm Brack, ⅕ loaf, 67g	5
Cinnamon & Raisin Bagel, Reduced Fat, In-Store Bakery, 1 (113g)	8
Garlic & Coriander Naan Breads, 1 serving, 130g	10
Italian Garlic Ciabatta Rolls, 1 (93g)	8
Muffins, 1 (51g)	4
Multigrain Bagel, Reduced Fat, In-Store Bakery, 1 (113g)	8
Multigrain Soft Sub Roll, 1 (180g)	12
Oatmeal Ploughman's Rolls, 1 (71g)	5
Onion & Garlic Bagel, Reduced Fat, In-Store Bakery, 1 (113g)	8
Onion Bagel, Reduced Fat, 1 (85g)	6
Oven Bottomed Muffins, 1 (65g)	5
Part Baked Ciabatta Squares, 1 (60g)	4
Part Baked Cracked Wheat Rolls, 1 (60g)	4
Part Baked Multi Seed Rolls, 1 (60g)	4
Part Baked White Rolls, 1 (60g)	4
Part Baked Wholewheat Rolls, 1 (60g)	4
Pikelets, 1 (36g)	2
Plain Bagel, Reduced Fat, 1 (85g)	6
Plain Bagel, Reduced Fat, In-Store Bakery, 1 (113g)	8
Ready to Bake Granary Baps, 1 (70g)	6
Ready to Bake White Baps, 1 (70g)	6
Ready to Bake Wholemeal Baps, 1 (70g)	5
Seeded Burger Buns, 1 (58g)	4
Seeded Ploughman's Rolls, 1 (73g)	5
Sliced White Baps, 1 (64g)	4
Tea Break Fruit Loaf, 1 slice, 36g	3
White Baps, 1 (60g)	5

White Finger Roll, 1 (40g)	3
White Sliced Hot Dog Rolls, 1 (64g)	5
White Sub Roll, 1 (170g)	11
Wholemeal Bap, 1 (60g)	4
Wholemeal Ploughman's Rolls, 1 (80g)	5
Wholemeal Sub Roll, 1 (180g)	13

Asda – Chosen by You

Continental Milk Chocolate Chip Brioche Rolls, 1 (35g)	3
Continental Plain Brioche Rolls, 1 (35g)	4
Deli Style Cinnamon & Raisin Bagels, 1 (85g)	6
Deli Style Plain Bagel, 1 (85g)	6
Raisin Brioche Rolls, 1 (35g)	3

Asda – Extra Special

Ciabatta Roll, 1 (75g)	6
Grain & Raisin Bagels, 1 (90g)	7
Mixed Olive Rolls, 1 (85g)	6
Orange Blossom Honey & Sunflower Seed Bagels, 1 (90g)	7
Poppy Knot Rolls, 1 (65g)	5
Seeded Kaiser Rolls, 1 (30g)	2
Walnut Rolls, 1 (30g)	3

Brace's Bread

Soft White Big Bap, 1 (144g)	11
Soft White Finger Rolls, 1 (54g)	4
Soft Wholemeal Baps, 1 (58g)	4
White Floured Brecon Baps, 1 (58g)	4
White Soft Baps, 1 (58g)	4

Dietary Specials

Ciabatta Rolls, 1 (50g)	3
Soft White Rolls, 1 (75g)	5
Sweet Breakfast Roll, 1 (50g)	4

Genius Gluten Free

Brown Rolls, 1 roll, 320g	7

Hovis

Best of Both Sliced Rolls, 1 (62g)	4
Golden Wholemeal Rolls, 1 (65g)	4
Granary Original Deli Rolls, 1 (70g)	5
Premium White Rolls, 1 (65g)	4
Seed Sensations Rich & Roasted Deli Rolls, 1 (70g)	5
Soft White Rolls, 1 (75g)	5
Wholemeal Sliced Rolls, 1 (60g)	4

Juvela

Gluten Free Bread Rolls, 1 (85g)	7

Gluten Free Fibre Bread Rolls, 1 (85g)	**7**

Kingsmill

50/50 Soft White Rolls, 1 (63g)	**4**
Deliciously Soft White Rolls, 1 (50g)	**3**
Deliciously Soft White Rolls Part Sliced, 1 (58g)	**4**
Gold Seeds & Oats Soft & Crunchy Rolls, 1 (70g)	**5**
Great Everyday Soft White or Sliced White Rolls, 1 (58g)	**4**
Great Everyday Soft White Hot Dog Rolls, 1 (71g)	**5**
Great Everyday Tasty Wholemeal Rolls, 1 (68g)	**4**
Tasty Wholemeal Roll, 1 roll, 68g	**4**

Livwell Free From

Ciabatta Rolls, 1 (80g)	**6**
Free From Hot Cross Buns, 1 (70g)	**5**
Plain Bagels, 1 (80g)	**6**
White Rolls, 1 (60g)	**3**

M&S

Hot Cross Bun, Less than 3% Fat, 1 (65g)	**4**
Mini Submarine Rolls, 1 (30g)	**2**
Soft Oatmeal Roll, 1 (86g)	**7**
White Floured Baps, 1 (61g)	**5**

M&S – In-Store Bakery

3 Seed Roll, 1 (65g)	**4**
Bagel, 1 (100g)	**7**
Bakers Choice White Morning Rolls, 1 (65g)	**5**
Brown Roll, 1 (110g)	**6**
Eat Well Three Seed Crusty Roll, 1 (60g)	**4**
French Crusty Roll, 1 (65g)	**4**
Green & Black Olive Pave Roll, 1 (60g)	**5**
Sesame Bagel, 1 (100g)	**8**
Spiced Fruit Bread Bun, 1 (78g)	**6**
Sunflower & Honey Roll, 1 (50g)	**4**

Morrisons – In-Store Bakery

Cheese & Onion Roll, 1 (80g)	**6**
Crusty Rolls, 1 (75g)	**5**
Onion & Herb Ciabatta Rolls, 1 (85g)	**6**

New York Bakery Co.

Cinnamon & Raisin Bagel, 1 (85g)	**6**
Fruit 'n' Oats Bagel, 1 (85g)	**6**
Multi-Seeded Bagel, 1 (85g)	**6**
Onion Bagel, 1 (85g)	**6**
Original Bagel, 1 (85g)	**6**
Plain Bagel, 1 (85g)	**6**
Seeded Bran Bagel, 1 (85g)	**6**
Sesame Bagel, 1 (85g)	**6**

Sainsbury's

Butter Brioche Rolls, 1 (35g)	**3**
Giant Multiseeded Baps, 1 (86g)	**8**
Giant Wholemeal Baps, 1 (86g)	**6**
Malted Wheat Deli Rolls, large, 1 (70g)	**5**
Multiseeded Deli Sandwich Rolls, large, 1 (70g)	**5**
Plain Chocolate Chip Brioche Roll, 1 (35g)	**4**
Wholemeal Floury Batch Rolls, 1 (68g)	**4**
Wholemeal Oat Topped Deli Sandwich Rolls, large, 1 (70g)	**4**
Wholemeal Ploughman's Rolls, 1 (67g)	**4**
Wholemeal Sandwich Rolls, 1 (60g)	**4**
Wholemeal Sub Rolls, 1 (96g)	**7**

Tesco

Café Continental Brioche Rolls, 1 individual, 35g	**3**
Caramelised Onion & Poppy Seed Bagels, 1 individual, 85g	**6**
Cheese Topped Baps, 1 individual, 65g	**5**
Chocolate Chips Brioche Rolls, 1 individual, 35g	**4**
Ciabatta Rolls, 1 individual, 80g	**6**
Cinnamon & Raisin Bagels, 1 individual, 85g	**6**
Coffee Buns, 1 individual, 43g	**5**
Cracked Wheat Deli Rolls, 1 individual, 64g	**4**
Crusty Granary or White Round Rolls, 1 individual, 63g	**4**
Granary Roll, 1 individual, 90g	**6**
Honey & Oat Sub Rolls, 1 individual, 90g	**7**
Large Baps, Malted Grain, White or Wholemeal, 1 individual, 95g	**6**
Large Seeded Burger Buns, 1 individual, 95g	**7**
Maize Topped Deli Rolls, 1 individual, 65g	**4**
Mixed Seed Deli Rolls, 1 individual, 65g	**5**
Multigrain Bloomer, 100g	**6**
Multigrain Sub Rolls, 1 individual, 79g	**6**
Panini Rolls, 1 individual, 85g	**6**
Plain Bagel, 1 individual, 85g	**6**
Poppy Seed Topped Deli Rolls, 1 individual, 65g	**4**
Sesame Seeded Burger Buns, 1 individual, 55g	**4**
Sliced White Sandwich Rolls, 1 individual, 58g	**4**
Soft White Rolls, 1 individual, 72g	**5**
Submarine Roll, 1 individual, 100g	**7**
Tiger Rolls, 1 individual, 65g	**5**
Tomato & Herb Roll, 1 individual, 86g	**6**
Wheatfield Bakery Seeded Rolls, 1 individual, 76g	**5**

Wheatfield White Submarine Rolls, 1 individual, 90g	**6**
White Finger Rolls, 1 individual, 60g	**4**
White Floured Baps, 1 individual, 50g	**3**
White Hot Dog Rolls, 1 individual, 75g	**5**
White Sub Rolls, 1 individual, 90g	**7**
Wholemeal Deli Rolls, 1 individual, 65g	**4**
Wholemeal Rolls, 1 individual, 50g	**3**
Wholemeal Sub Rolls, 1 individual, 90g	**6**

Tesco – Free From

Bagels, 1 individual, 80g	**7**
Brown Rolls, 1 individual, 77g	**6**
Ciabatta Rolls, 1 individual, 80g	**6**
Multiseeded Rolls, 1 individual, 70g	**6**
Sundried Tomato Ciabatta Rolls, 1 individual, 85g	**7**
White Sub Rolls, 1 individual, 100g	**8**
White Rolls, 1 individual, 60g	**5**

The Co-operative

Burger Buns with Sesame Seeds, 1 (58g)	**4**
Long Life White Baguette, ⅓ baguette, 50g	**3**
Long Life White Petit Pain, 1 (50g)	**3**
Mixed Olive Rolls, 1 (100g)	**7**
Morning Rolls, 1 (45g)	**3**
Naturally Healthy Malted Baps, large, 1 (95g)	**6**
Naturally Healthy Wholemeal Rolls, 1 (60g)	**4**
Oat Topped Batch Rolls, 1 (70g)	**5**
Soft White Rolls, 1 (65g)	**4**
Tiger Rolls, In-Store Bakery, 1 (100g)	**7**
White Baps, large, 1 (85g)	**6**

Waitrose

Loose White Rolls, 1 (56g)	**4**
Multigrain Bagel, 1 (85g)	**7**
Pain Rustica Roll, 1 (120g)	**9**
Paysan Rustica Roll, 1 (120g)	**8**
Petit Pain, 1 (32g)	**2**
Plain Bagel, 1 (85g)	**6**
Poppy Seeded Knott, 1 portion, 100g	**7**
Rustic Wholemeal Roll, 1 (120g)	**8**
Sesame Bagel, 1 (85g)	**7**
White Crusty Rolls, 1 (85g)	**6**

Warburtons

Sandwich Rolls, large, 1 (58g)	**4**
Seeded Sandwich Rolls, 1 (77g)	**5**
Seeded Soft Rolls, 1 (77g)	**6**
Sliced White Rolls, 1 (55g)	**4**
Sliced White Rolls, large, 1 (89g)	**6**
Sliced White Sandwich Rolls, large, 1 (89g)	**6**

Sliced Wholemeal Rolls, 1 (64g)	**4**
Soft Sandwich Rolls, 1 (80g)	**6**
White Lunch Rolls, 1 (55g)	**3**
White Rolls, 1 (58g)	**4**
White Rolls, large, 1 (88g)	**6**
White Soft Rolls, 1 (80g)	**6**
Wholemeal Lunch Rolls, 1 (55g)	**3**
Wholemeal Soft Rolls, 1 (79g)	**5**

Weight Watchers

Petits Pains, 1 (50g)	**3**
Plain Bagels, 1 (67g)	**4**

Sweet Pies & Tarts

Asda

Apple & Blackberry Pie, 1 slice, 117g	**8**
Apple & Custard Tart, 1 portion, 84g	**6**
Apple Crumble, 1 pot, 140g	**10**
Apple Turnover, 1 (112g)	**10**
Autumn Fruit Cobbler, 1 serving, 91g	**4**
Bakewell Tart, ⅙ serving, 52g	**6**
Banoffee Tart, 1 portion, 76g	**8**
Bramley Apple & Blackcurrant Pie, 1 serving, 64g	**6**
Bramley Apple & Blackberry Crumble, ¼ pie, 150g	**10**
Cherry Pie, 1 serving, 117g	**9**
Chocky Rocky Road Pie, 1 serving, 135g	**10**
Chocolate Brownie Cheesecake Slices, 1 (100g)	**11**
Chocolate Cheesecake, 1 slice, 68g	**7**
Chocolate Chip & Vanilla Cheesecake, 1 slice, 57g	**6**
Egg Custard Tart, (family), ¼ serving, 80g	**5**
Gypsy Tart, 1 slice, 44g	**5**
Iced Bakewell Slice, 1 slice, 35g	**4**
Key Lime Cheesecake, 1 slice, 90g	**8**
Lemon Cheesecake Slices, 1 slice, 100g	**9**
Lemon Curd Tarts, 1 (33g)	**3**
Lemon Meringue Pie, ¼ pie, 114g	**10**
Lemon Swirled Cheesecake, 1 slice, 62g	**6**
Passion Fruit Tortes, 1 portion, 93g	**6**
Peach Melba Cheesecake, 1 slice, 90g	**8**
Pecan & Maple Pie, 1 (135g)	**9**
Raspberry Cheesecake, 1 slice, 90g	**9**
Raspberry Sponge Sandwich, 1 serving, 41g	**5**
Rhubarb & Strawberry Pie, 1 portion, 93g	**7**
Strawberry Cheesecake, 1 (100g)	**7**

Strawberry Tart, 1 portion, 102g	8
Toffee Apple Crumble, ⅓ pack, 167g	11
Toffee Apple Crumble Dessert, 1 pot, 140g	11
Toffee Cheesecake, ⅙ serving, 90g	9
Toffee Cheesecake Slices, 1 slice, 100g	10
True Love Tarts, 1 (30g)	3

Asda – Chosen by You

Apple & Custard Tarts, 1 individual, 85g	7
Apple Crumble, ¼ pack, 150g	10
Bramley Apple Crumble, 1 portion, 100g	7
Bramley Apple Pie, ¼ pie, 106g	8
Bramley Apple Pies, 1 individual, 64g	6
Egg Custard Tarts, 1 individual, 85g	6
Lemon Swirled Cheesecake, 1 portion, 125g	12
Rhubarb Crumble, 1 individual, 150g	11
Teatime Classic Bakewell Tart, ⅙ tart, 50g	6
Toffee Cheesecakes, 1 pot, 100g	8

Asda – Extra Special

Blueberry Cheesecake Slices, 1 slice, 73g	6
Bramley Apple Crumble with Mixed Seeds, 1 serving, 150g	11
Bramley Apple Pie, ⅙ pie, 117g	9
Chocolate Tortes, ½ torte, 57g	6
Double Chocolate Cheesecake Slices, 1 slice, 100g	8
Hand Finished Banoffee Pie, ⅙ pie, 94g	9
Hand Finished Raspberry Brûlèe Cheesecake, ⅙ cake, 92g	7
Key Lime Cheesecake Slices, 1 slice, 100g	9
New York Style Vanilla Cheesecake Slice, 1 slice, 100g	10
Rich Belgian Chocolate Cheesecakes, 1 individual, 100g	9
Strawberry & Cornish Clotted Cream Cheesecake, 1 serving, 75g	7
Strawberry Tarts, 1 portion, 150g	10
Summer Fruit Tarts, 1 portion, 153g	10
Tarte au Chocolat, ⅙ tart, 81g	10
Tarte au Citron Meringue, 1 serving, 95g	9
Tarte aux Poires, 1 slice, 95g	8
Tarte aux Pommes, 1 serving, 91g	7
Tarte Tatin, 1 slice, 88g	5

Asda – Good For You

Banana & Almond Slice, 1 slice, 18g	1
Lemon Slices, 1 slice, 30g	3
Strawberry Cheesecake Slices, 1 slice, 100g	6

Genesis – Crafty

Apple Crumble, ¼ pie, 158g	12

Apple Tart, ¼ tart, 150g	14

M&S – In-Store Bakery

Bakewell Tart, 1 (95g)	12
Cherry & Almond Tart, 1 (104g)	10
French Apple Tart, 1 (100g)	6
Pear & Almond Tart, 1 (117g)	12

Morrisons

Blackcurrant Cheesecake, 1 (100g)	8
Chockarocka Cream Pie, 1 serving, 113g	12
Fresh Cream Strawberry & Custard Tarts, 1 (86g)	7
Individual Apple & Cranberry Lattice Pie, 1 (155g)	8
Individual Apple Lattice Pie, 1 (160g)	8
Individual Plum Lattice Pie, 1 (142g)	14
Individual Rhubarb Lattice Pie, 1 (160g)	14
Millionaire Cheesecake, 1 serving, 88g	10
Raspberry & Strawberry Cheesecake, 1 serving, 103g	10
Summer Berry Cheesecake, 1 serving, 88g	8
Toffee Cheesecake, 1 (100g)	8

Mr Kipling

Bakewell Slices, 1 slice, 36g	4
Bakewell Tart, ⅕ pack, 70g	8
Blackberry & Custard Pies, 1 (64g)	6
Bramley Apple & Blackcurrant Pies, 1 serving, 67g	6
Bramley Apple Pies, 1 pie, 66g	6
Cherry Bakewells, 1 (47g)	6
Cherry Pies, 1 (67g)	6
Exceedingly Good Cakes Fruity Pies, 1 serving, 66g	6
Fruit Pie Selection, 1 (66g)	6
Jam Tarts, 1 (36g)	4
Lemon Bakewells, 1 (48g)	6
Treacle Tart, 1 slice, 55g	6

Sainsbury's

Almond Fingers, 1 (47g)	5
Almond Slice, 1 slice, 27g	3
Apple & Blackberry Pie, ⅙ pie, 122g	8
Apple & Blackcurrant Seeded Crumbles Pudding, 1 pudding, 140g	7
Apple Crumble, ⅛ large, 138g	8
Apple Pie, ⅙ family pack, 121g	9
Blackcurrant Cheesecakes, ¼ pudding, 75g	5
Bramley Apple Pie, 1 (64g)	6
Cherry Pie, ¼ pie, 130g	10
Custard Slices, 1 slice, 107g	9

Fresh & Fruity Strawberry Tarts, 1 tart, 125g	8
Fresh Cream Banoffee Pies, 1 pie, 112g	11
Fresh Cream Slices, 1 slice, 77g	9
Individual Lemon Cheesecake, 1 (120g)	11
Key Lime Pie, ⅙ pie, 65g	7
Lemon Cheesecake, 1 (120g)	11
Lemon Cheesecake Slices, 1 slice, 90g	8
Lemon Meringue Pie, ⅙ family pack, 72g	7
Lemon Tart, 1 slice, 75g	7
Maple & Walnut Cheesecake, 1 serving, 75g	7
New York Cheesecake, ⅙ cake, 95g	9
Pear & Blackcurrant Crumble, ¼ pudding, 125g	7
Rhubarb Crumble, 1 (136g)	10
Strawberry & Cream Tarts, 1 (127g)	10
Strawberry Cheesecakes, ¼ pudding, 75g	5
Tarte aux Fruits, ⅙ tart, 95g	7
Toffee & Apple Cheesecake, ⅙ cake, 81g	7
Toffee Bakewell, 1 tart, 42g	5
Toffee Cheesecake, ⅙ cake, 95g	9
Toffee Cheesecake Slices, 1 (105g)	10

Sainsbury's – Be Good To Yourself

Raspberry Cheesecakes, 1 (95g)	4
Toffee & Date Slices, 1 (22g)	2

Sainsbury's – Taste the Difference

Banoffee Tart, ⅙ cake, 89g	9
Blueberry & Blackcurrant Cheesecake, 1 serving, 75g	6
Bramley Apple Pie, ⅙ pie, 122g	9
Lemon & Raspberry Cheesecake, ⅙ large, 98g	8
Maple & Pecan Syrup Tart, ⅙ cake, 97g	11
Mini Banoffee Tarts, 1 (19g)	2
Mini Sicilian Lemon Cheesecakes, 1 (21g)	2
New York Vanilla Cheesecake, 1 (100g)	9
Passionfruit Orange & Mango Cheesecake, ⅙ cake, 94g	8
Raspberry & Clotted Cream Pavlova, ⅙ pudding, 70g	6
Red Berry Swirl Cheesecake, ⅙ cake, 94g	9
Scottish Raspberry & Redcurrant Roulade, ⅙ pudding, 77g	6
Sicilian Lemon Cheesecake, 1 (100g)	10
Tarte aux Apricots, ⅙ tart, 73g	8
Tarte Tatin, ⅙ tart, 100g	6

Tesco

Apple & Blackcurrant Pies, 1 individual, 60g	6
Apple & Custard Sundae Tarts, 1 individual, 87g	7
Apple & Strawberry Lattice Pie, 1 serving, 83g	7
Apple Crumble, 1 serving, 150g	10
Apple Puff Pies, 1 individual, 61g	6
Assorted Jam Tarts, 1 individual, 30g	3
Bakewell Tart, (⅙ tart), 51g	6
Banoffee Pie, 1 serving (⅙ pie), 93g	9
Bramley Apple & Blackberry Pie, 1 serving, 117g	8
Bramley Apple Crumbles, 1 individual, 135g	8
Bramley Apple Pie, 1 serving, 116g	8
Bramley Apple Pie, In-Store Bakery, 1 slice, 85g	7
Bramley Apple Tarts, 1 individual, 110g	11
Cherry Bakewell Tarts, 1 individual, 44g	5
Cherry Pie, 1 serving, 117g	9
Chocolate & Amaretto Velvet, 1 individual, 118g	14
Chocolate & Vanilla Cheesecake, 1 serving (⅙ cake), 100g	11
Chocolate Brownie Cheesecake Slices, 1 individual, 108g	12
Chocolate Whoopie Pies, 1 individual, 67g	8
Creamfields Blackcurrant Cheesecakes, 1 individual, 100g	7
Egg Custard Tarts, 1 individual, 90g	7
Key Lime Pie, 1 serving, 83g	8
Lemon Cheesecake, 1 serving, 100g	10
Lemon Curd Tarts, 1 individual, 30g	4
Lemon Meringue Pie, 1 serving, 72g	5
Morello Cherry & Almond Bakewell Tart, 1 serving, 74g	8
Morello Cherry & Plum Lattice Pie, 1 serving, 107g	7
New York Cheesecake Slices, 1 individual, 106g	10
New York Cheesecake, 1 serving, 92g	9
Pineapple Tarts, 1 serving, 65g	6
Raspberry Cheesecake, 1 serving, 100g	10
Raspberry Rapture Cheesecake Slices, 1 individual, 110g	9
Raspberry Tarts, 1 serving, 65g	7
Strawberry Cheesecake, 1 portion (⅙ cake), 98g	9
Strawberry Sundae Tarts, 1 individual, 48g	5
Strawberry Swirl Cheesecake, 1 serving, 100g	10
Strawberry Tarts, 1 individual, 128g	10
Swirly Chocolate Cheesecake, 1 individual, 125g	12
Swirly Raspberry Cheesecake, 1 individual, 125g	11
Tangy Lemon Pie, 1 serving, 120g	11

Toffee Apple Crunch, 1 serving, 115g	**10**
Toffee Iced Tarts, 1 individual, 45g	**5**
Treacle Tart, 1 individual, 63g	**7**

Tesco – Finest

Apple Pie, 1 serving, 125g	**8**
Apricot, Plum & Almond Tart Slices, 1 slice, 92g	**9**
Belgian Chocolate Cheesecake, 1 slice (⅙ cake), 113g	**14**
Belgian Chocolate Cheesecake Slices, 1 individual, 105g	**12**
Chocolate Cheesecake, 1 serving, 113g	**14**
Millionaire's Chocolate & Caramel Tarts, 1 individual, 110g	**14**
Millionaire's Cheesecake, 1 serving, 109g	**12**
New York Cheesecake Slices, 1 individual, 104g	**10**
Raspberry Brûlée Cheesecake, 1 portion (⅙ cake), 85g	**8**
Secret Berry Cheesecake, 1 pot, 129g	**9**
Strawberry & Cream Cheesecake, 1 individual, 109g	**10**
Strawberry Cheesecake Slices, 1 individual, 109g	**10**
Tarte aux Abricots, 1 serving, 83g	**8**
Tarte aux Fruits, 1 portion, 98g	**6**
Tarte au Citron, 1 serving (⅙ tart), 82g	**8**
Ultimate New York Cheesecake, 1 serving, 103g	**11**
Wild Blueberry & Almond Tart Slices, 1 individual, 90g	**9**
Wild Blueberry Cheesecake, 1 serving (⅙ cake), 111g	**10**

The Co-operative

Apple & Blackberry Pie, ¼ pie, 131g	**9**
Apple Pie, ¼ pie, 112g	**13**
Berry Cheesecake, ¼ large, 128g	**11**
Bramley Apple Pie, ¼ pie, 131g	**10**
Cherry Pie, ¼ pie, 131g	**10**
Egg Custard Tarts, 1 (85g)	**6**
Lemon Cheesecake Stackers, 1 (41g)	**6**
Lemon Swirl Cheesecake, ⅙ pie, 72g	**7**

The Co-operative – Truly Irresistible

Chocolate Cheesecake, ¼ cake, 110g	**14**

Waitrose

Apple & Mincemeat Streusel Tart, ⅙ pack, 96g	**8**
Apple Crumble, ¼ pack, 150g	**9**

Apple Frangipane Pies, 1 pie, 138g	**13**
Apple Tart, ⅙ tart, 92g	**4**
Apricot Caramel Tarte Tatins, 1 (125g)	**7**
Autumn Berry Cheesecake, 1 slice, 92g	**9**
Autumn Berry Cobbler, ¼ pack, 149g	**8**
Autumn Berry Pie, ¼ serving, 152g	**10**
Banoffee Pie, ⅙ pie, 114g	**12**
Blueberry & White Chocolate Cheesecake, ⅙ pack, 91g	**7**
Bramley Apple Charlottes, ½ pack, 100g	**5**
Bramley Apple Crumble, 1 portion, 72g	**4**
Bramley Apple Pie, ¼ large, 150g	**9**
Chocolate Cheesecake, 1 slice, 45g	**5**
Elderflower Cheesecake with a Sloe Berry Drizzle, ⅙ pack, 69g	**5**
Lemon Cheesecake, 1 slice, 45g	**5**
Lemon Curd Cheesecake, ⅙ pack, 100g	**9**
Lemon Meringue Pie, 1 (80g)	**7**
Light & Creamy Lemon Cheesecake, ¼ serving, 114g	**9**
Lime Pie, 1 slice, 100g	**10**
New York Cheesecake, 1 slice, 92g	**10**
Plum Tart, 1 slice, 95g	**5**
Raspberry Brûlée Cheesecake, ⅙ pack, 69g	**5**
Spiced Apple Crumble Tart, ⅙ pack, 89g	**7**
Strawberry & Raspberry Cheesecake, 1 pack, 100g	**9**
Tarte au Abricots, ⅛ tart, 73g	**6**
Tarte au Chocolat, ⅙ tart, 74g	**9**
Tarte au Citron, ⅛ tart, 75g	**7**
Tarte aux Pommes, ⅙ tart, 96g	**5**
Treacle Tart, ⅙ tart, 99g	**10**
Very Berry Cheesecake, 1 (100g)	**7**
Zuccotto Cheesecake, ¼ serving, 120g	**12**

Biscuits, Snacks & Confectionery

Basic Foods

Almonds, Sugared, 2 (7g)	1
Bombay Mix, 1 medium portion, 30g	4
Cheese Sandwich Biscuit, 1 (10g)	1
Coconut Ice, 1 bar, 125g	13
Cream Cracker, 1 (7g)	1
Cream Cracker, Light, 1 (7g)	1
Crispbread, Rye, 1 (10g)	1
Crispbreads, Extra Thin, 2 (10g)	1
Custard Cream, 1 (12g)	2
Digestive, 1 (13g)	2
Digestive, Chocolate, Milk or Plain, 1 (17g)	2
Digestive, Low Fat, 1 (13g)	2
Fig Roll, 1 (19g)	2
Fudge, 2 pieces, 35g	4
Garibaldi, 1 (9g)	1
Gingernut, 1 (12g)	1
Jaffa Cake, 1 (12g)	1
Malted Milk, 1 (8g)	1
Marshmallows, 2 pieces, 10g	1
Melba Toast, 6 slices, 21g	2
Oatcake, 1 (13g)	2
Popcorn, Air Popped, Plain, 1 medium portion, 25g	3
Popcorn, Microwave, 1 medium portion, 25g	4
Popcorn, Oil Popped, 1 medium portion, 25g	4
Popcorn, Sweet, 1 medium portion, 25g	3
Popping Corn, Uncooked, 1 small portion, 50g	7
Rice Cakes, 3 (21g)	2
Rich Tea, 1 (7g)	1
Rich Tea, Reduced Fat, 1 (11g)	1
Shortbread, All Butter, 1 (20g)	3
Water Biscuit, 1 (8g)	1

Biscuits

Asda

All Butter Shortbread Assortment, 1 (17g)	2
Boudoir Fingers, 1 (5g)	1
Brandy Snap Baskets, 1 serving, 20g	3
Caramel Shortcake, 1 (49g)	7
Cheese Thin Biscuit, 1 (4g)	1
Cherry Shortbread Trees, 1 (16g)	2
Choc Chip Cookies, 1 (11g)	1

Chocolate & Cream Biscuit Selection, 1 (13g)	2
Chocolate Caramel Biscuit Bar, 1 bar, 25g	4
Chocolate Chip Digestive Biscuit, 1 (14g)	2
Chocolate Digestive, Milk or Plain, 1 (17g)	2
Chocolate Flavour Biscuits, 1 (17g)	2
Chocolate Shortbread Selection, 1 (19g)	3
Chunky Chewy Toffee & Pecan Supercookies, 1 (92g)	12
Coconut Macaroons with a Chocolate Flavoured Drizzle, 1 serving, 33g	4
Coconut Macaroons, 1 (33g)	4
Custard Cream, 1 (12g)	2
Double Chocolate Chunk Cookie, 1 (45g)	6
Fruit Shortcake Biscuit, 1 (8g)	1
Hands Off My Biccy Bites!, 1 serving, 21g	3
Hands Off My Caramel Bites!, 1 serving, 20g	3
Hands Off My Coconut Bites!, 1 serving, 25g	3
Hands Off My Nutty Bites!, 1 serving, 40g	6
Hands Off My Whirly Bites!, 1 serving, 26g	3
Jaffa Cake Bar, 1 bar, 27g	3
Luxury Chocolate Biscuit Selection, 1 biscuit, 15g	2
Malted Milk Biscuits, 1 (11g)	1
Milk Chocolate Chunk Cookie, 1 (45g)	6
Milk Chocolate Take a Break, 1 bar, 21g	3
Mini Chocolate Caramel Rounds, 1 (15g)	2
Mini Chocolate Wafer Rolls, 1 (5g)	1
Mini Jaffa Cakes, 1 (5g)	1
Mini Milk Chocolate Fingers, 1 (3g)	0
Mini Raspberry Cakes, 1 (4g)	0
Morning Coffee Biscuit, 1 (5g)	1
Nice Biscuit, 1 (8g)	1
Oatmeal & Raisin Cookie, 1 (45g)	6
Orange Puffin, 1 (25g)	4
Rich Shortie, 1 (10g)	1
Scottish Shortbread, 1 individual, 17g	2
Shortbread Finger, 1 (18g)	2
Shortbread Rounds, 1 (17g)	2
Shortcake Biscuits, 1 (13g)	2
Smartie Cookie, 1 (44g)	5
Stem Ginger Biscuits, 1 (17g)	2
Strawberries & Cream Supercookies, 1 (84g)	11
Take a Break Mint Milk Chocolate Wafer, Mint or Orange, 1 (22g)	3
Toblerone Cookies, 1 serving, 60g	8
Triple Chocolate Biscuit Bar, 1 (25g)	4
Ultimate Chocolate Supercookies, 1 (92g)	12
Viennese Selection, 1 individual, 12g	2
White Chocolate Chunk Cookie, 1 (45g)	6
Winter Spiced Shortbread, 1 serving, 20g	3

Asda – Extra Special

All Butter Cinnamon Sticks, 1 (10g)	1

	ProPoints value
All Butter Shortbread Biscuit, 1 individual, 20g	3
All Butter Shortbread Rounds, 1 (20g)	3
All Butter Shortbread Selection, 1 (19g)	4
Belgian Chocolate & Hazelnut Cookies, 1 (25g)	4
Belgian Chocolate Cookies, 1 (26g)	4
Belgian Chocolate Ginger Thins Selection, 1 (10g)	1
Belgian Chocolate Lemon Cookies, 1 (25g)	4
Belgian Chocolate Shortbread, 1 (20g)	3
Belgian Chocolate Stem Ginger Cookies, 1 (25g)	3
Belgian Dark Chocolate Mint Crunch, (1) 6g	1
Belgian Milk Chocolate Almond Crunch, (1) 6g	1
Cantuccini Biscuit, 1 (9g)	1
Carrot Cake Cookies, 1 (25g)	4
Chocolate Biscuit Selection, 1 (15g)	2
Chocolate Chip Cookies, 1 (25g)	4
Chocolate, Fruit & Nut Cookies, 1 (25g)	4
Double Chocolate Chip Cookies, 1 (25g)	4
Hazelnut, Orange & Sultana Biscotti, 1 (38g)	4
Lemon Shortbread Rounds, 1 (20g)	3
Milk Chocolate Cookie, 1 (68g)	9
Milk Chocolate Viennese Swirls, 1 (17g)	2
Pecan Caramel Shortbreads, 1 square, 64g	8
Slowbaked Belgian Double Chocolate Cookies, 1 (25g)	4
Slowbaked Fruit & Oat Cookies, 1 (35g)	4
Slowbaked Stem Ginger Cookies, 1 (25g)	3
Slowbaked White Belgian Chocolate Cookies, 1 (25g)	4
Swiss After Dinner Biscuit Selection, 1 (7g)	1
Swiss Meringue Delight, 1 (8g)	1
Swiss Truffle Crème, 1 serving, 7g	1

Asda – Good For You

Chocolate Crispy Bars, 1 (22g)	3
Orange Chocolate Crispy Bars, 1 (22g)	2

Askeys

Continental Style Waffle Cones, 1 (12g)	1
Luxury Fan Wafer Biscuits, 1 (11g)	1

Blue Dragon

Fortune Cookies, 1 (6g)	1

Burton's Foods

Coconut Delight, 1 (25g)	3
Jam Teacake, 1 (12g)	1
Jammie Dodgers Berrillicious, 1 (19g)	2
Jammie Dodgers Snack Bar, 1 bar, 23g	3
Jammie Dodgers, Original, 1 (19g)	2
Mint Viscount, 1 (17g)	2

	ProPoints value
Toffypops, 1 (15g)	2
Viscount Milk Chocolate Mint Cream Biscuit, 1 (14g)	2
Wagon Wheels, Jammie, 1 (38g)	4
Wagon Wheels, Original, 1 (36g)	4

Cadbury

Choc Brownie Flavour Biscuits, 1 (18g)	2
Choc Chip Cookies, 1 (11g)	2
Chocolate Chunk Cookies, 1 (22g)	3
Chocolate Fingers, 1 finger, 5g	1
Cookies Double Choc, 1 (12g)	2
Dark Chocolate Fingers, 1 (5g)	1
Double Chocolate Fingers, 1 (5g)	1
Fingers Mini Breaks, 1 (22g)	3
Highlights Chocolate Cookie Crunch, 1 (16g)	2
Highlights Chocolate or Honeycomb Nibbles, 1 bag, 16g	2
Luxury Double Chocolate Chunk Cookies, 1 (25g)	4
Mini Fingers, 1 bag, 40g	6
Oat & Chocolate Chip, 1 (17g)	2
Toffee Crunch Fingers, 1 (5g)	1
White Chocolate Finger, 1 (6g)	1

Caxton

Pink 'n' White Jammie, 1 slice, 17g	2

Dean's

All Butter Shortbread Petticoat Tails & Fingers, 1 (12g)	2
All Butter Shortbread Rounds, 1 (13g)	2
Choc Chunk Shortbread, 1 (20g)	3
Luxury All Butter Shortbread, 1 (20g)	3
Oat Biscuits Apple & Cranberry or Coconut & Treacle, 1 (12g)	2
Oat Biscuits Original, 1 (25g)	4
Oat Biscuits Stem Ginger, 1 (25g)	3
Oat Biscuits Sultana & Heather Honey, 1 (19g)	2
Petit Fours Shortbread Rounds, 1 serving, 15g	2
Praline Pecan Shortbread, 1 (20g)	3
Shortbread Biscuit Collection - Apple Crumble or Butterscotch or Lemon & Oatflake, 1 (20g)	3
Shortbread Fingers, 1 finger, 21g	3
Shortbread Petticoat Tails, 1 (25g)	4
Toasted Coconut Shortbread, 1 (20g)	3

Doves Farm

Fairtrade Chocolate & Crispy Rice Bars, 1 bar, 35g	4
Fruity Oat Biscuits, 1 (12g)	1

Gluten Free Hazelnut or Lemon Zest
Cookies, 1 (15g) **2**
Wholewheat Digestives, 1 (13g) **2**

Duchy Original's

Butterscotch Shortbread, 1 (16g) **2**
Chocolate Butterscotch Biscuits, 1 (12g) **2**
Chocolate & Orange Biscuits, 1 (12g) **2**
Chocolate Ginger Biscuits, 1 (12g) **2**
Ginger Biscuits, 1 (16g) **2**
Highland Shortbread, 1 (16g) **2**
Lemon Biscuits, 1 (16g) **2**
Oaten Biscuits, 1 (15g) **2**
Orange Biscuits, 1 (16g) **2**

Elkes

Cow Biscuits, 1 (9g) **1**
Malted Milk, 1 (8g) **1**
Milk Chocolate Digestive Bars, 1 (19g) **3**
Milk Chocolate Malted Milk, 1 (11g) **2**

Fox's Biscuits

25% Less Fat Digestives, 1 (14g) **2**
Brandy Snaps, 1 (13g) **2**
Butter Crinkle Crunch, 1 (11g) **1**
Chocolate Chip Cookie Bar, 1 (16g) **2**
Chocolate Crinkles, 1 (15g) **2**
Chocolate Fudge Crunch Creams, 1 (14g) **2**
Chocolatey Millionaire's Shortcake, 1 (16g) **2**
Chunkie Dark Chocolate Chunk
Cookies, 1 (23g) **3**
Chunkie Extremely Chocolatey
Cookies, 1 (26g) **4**
Chunkie Milk or White Chocolate Chunk
Cookies, 1 (23g) **3**
Classic Bars, 1 (25g) **4**
Classic Cream, 1 (14g) **2**
Classics Traditional Gingers, 1 (8g) **1**
Cookie Bars, 1 (20g) **3**
Creams Golden Crunch with Real Oats, 1 (17g) **2**
Crinkles Classic, 1 (14g) **2**
Crinkles Coconut, 1 (11g) **1**
Crispy & Chunky Thick Tea, 1 (10g) **1**
Dunked Shortcake Fingers, 1 (15g) **2**
Echo Milk & White Chocolate Biscuit
Bars, 1 (25g) **4**
Echo Mint or Orange Biscuit Bars, 1 (24g) **3**
Ginger Crunch Crinkles, 1 (11g) **1**
Golden Crunch Cream, 1 (14g) **2**
Jam Creams, 1 (16g) **2**
Jam Rings, 1 (9g) **1**
Lemon Crunch, 1 (8g) **1**

Malted Milk Creams, 1 (13g) **2**
Milk Chocolate Crinkle Crunch, 1 (15g) **2**
Minis Organic Biscuits, All Flavours, 1 bag, 25g **3**
Moos Malted Milk Biscuits, 1 (9g) **1**
Moos Mini Malted Milk Biscuits, 1 pack, 25g **3**
Nice Cream, 1 (13g) **2**
Party Ring, 1 (7g) **1**
Rich Tea Cream, 1 (12g) **2**
Rocky Caramel or Chocolate or Orange
Bars, 1 (25g) **3**
Shortcake Rounds, 1 (23g) **3**
Sports Biscuit, 1 (7g) **1**
Triple Bars, 1 (25g) **3**
Viennese Chocolate or Double Chocolate
Melts, 1 (15g) **2**
Whipped Creams - Strawberry or
Lemon, 1 (26g) **4**

Fudges

Almond Flatbreads, 1 (8g) **1**
Belgian Dark Chocolate Florentines, 1 (10g) **1**
Cinnamon Flatbreads, 1 (8g) **1**
Cranberry Biscuits Half-Dipped in White
Belgian Chocolate, 1 (12g) **2**
Flapjacks, 1 (60g) **7**
Lemon Zest Biscuits, 1 (18g) **3**
Roasted Almond Biscuits, 1 (18g) **3**
Stem Ginger Biscuits, 1 (33g) **4**

Jacob's

Bourbon Creams, 1 (13g) **2**
Cheeselets, 1 serving, 25g **3**
Choc Gems, 1 bag, 25g **3**
Chocolate Rings, 1 (18g) **2**
Choice Grain, 1 (8g) **1**
Club Chocolate, 1 (23g) **3**
Club Fruit, 1 (23g) **3**
Club Milk Caramel Wafer, 1 (24g) **3**
Club Milk, Original, 1 (26g) **4**
Club Mint, 1 (22g) **3**
Coconut Creams, 1 (10g) **1**
Cookies from the Kitchen, Cranberry & White
Chocolate, 1 (25g) **3**
Cookies from the Kitchen, Hazelnut &
Chocolate Chunk, 1 (25g) **3**
Cookies from the Kitchen, Indulgent
Chocolate Chunk, 1 (25g) **3**
Digestive Creams, 1 (15g) **2**
Fig Roll, Reduced Fat, 1 (17g) **2**
Fig Rolls Bar, 1 (27g) **3**
Goldgrain, 1 (14g) **2**
Goldgrain, Reduced Fat, 1 (10g) **1**

Iced Gems, 1 small bag, 30g	3
Jaffa Cakes, 1 (15g)	1
Jam & Cream, 1 serving, 15g	2
Jam & Cream Shortcake Biscuits, 1 (15g)	2
Lemon Puff, 1 (14g)	2
Lincoln, 1 (7g)	1
Marietta, 1 (6g)	1
Mikado, 1 serving, 14g	2
Milk Chocolate Digestive, 1 (17g)	2
Milk Chocolate Goldgrain, 1 (17g)	2
Oat Crumbles, All Flavours, 1 (22g)	3
Polo, 1 (10g)	1
Polo, Milk Chocolate, 1 (17g)	2
Polo, Reduced Fat, 1 serving, 10g	1
Raspberry & Custard, 1 serving, 17g	2
Raspberry Mallow, 1 (14g)	2
Rich Tea, 1 (10g)	1
The Finest Nice, 1 serving, 11g	1
Wafers, 1 (15g)	2

Juvela

Gluten Free Digestives, 1 (9g)	1
Gluten Free Tea Biscuits, 1 (9g)	1

Kraft

Creamy White Chocolate Covered Oreo, 1 (22g)	3
Oreo Chocolate Flavoured Sandwich Biscuits, 1 (12g)	2

La Doria

Amaretti, 3 biscuits, 6g	1

M&S

All Butter Chocolate Chunk Cookie, 1 (24g)	3
All Butter Organic Scottish Shortbread Finger Biscuit, 1 finger, 18g	2
Apricot & Almond Flapjacks, 1 individual, 33g	3
Digestive Biscuit, 1 (16g)	2
Extremely Chocolatey Chocolate, Chocolate & Caramel or Chocolate & Orange Cake Bars, 1 (27g)	3
Extremely Chocolatey Ring Biscuits, 1 (23g)	3
Ginger Snaps, 1 (8g)	1
Jam Sandwich Creams, 1 (16g)	2
Mini Jaffa Cakes, 1 (5g)	1
Organic Percy Pig Biscuits, 1 (17g)	2
Viennese Sandwich, 1 (16g)	2

M&S – Eat Well

All Butter Fruity Flapjack Cookie, 1 pack, 25g	3
Blueberry & Oat Cookies, 1 pack, 20g	2
Cranberry & Orange Cookie, 1 (20g)	2
Date, Raisin & Oat Cinnamon Bars, 1 (30g)	3
Low Fat Stem Ginger Cookie, 1 pack, 22g	3
Pistachio & Almond Cookie, 1 pack, 20g	3
Rich Tea Biscuit, 1 (10g)	1
Spiced Orange & Hazelnut Cookies, 1 biscuit, 20g	3
Sultana Cookies, 1 biscuit, 17g	2

M&S – In-Store Bakery

Double Chocolate Cookie, 1 (71g)	9
Milk Chocolate Chip Cookie, 1 (73g)	10
Mini Double Chocolate Cookie, 1 mini, 17g	2
Mini Milk Chocolate Cookie, 1 mini, 17g	2
Mini White Chocolate Cookie, 1 mini, 17g	2
Oat, Fruit & Nut Cookie, 1 (68g)	8
White Chocolate Chip Cookie, 1 (73g)	5
White Chocolate Cookie, 1 (73g)	10

Maryland

Apple, Cranberry & Cinnamon Cookies, 1 (25g)	3
Choc Chip Cookie, 1 (11g)	2
Maryland Snack Bites, 1 serving, 25g	3
Minis Double Choc Cookies, 1 bag, 25g	3
Raisin, Oat, Choc Chunk & Maple Syrup Cookies, 1 (25g)	4

McVitie's

All Butter Shortbread, 1 (20g)	3
Apple Fruit Bakes, 1 bar, 35g	4
Boasters Belgian Chocolate & Hazelnuts, 1 (17g)	3
Boasters, All Flavours, 1 (17g)	2
Butter Puffs, 1 (11g)	2
Café Noir, 1 (9g)	1
Chocolate Caramel Crunch Bar, 1 (24g)	3
Chocolate Chip & Hazelnut Cookie, 1 (11g)	2
Chocolate Viennese Melt, 1 (17g)	2
Cookies White Choc Chip, 1 (30g)	4
Crispy Fruit Slices, Apple & Sultana, 1 slice, 15g	2
Digestives Caramels, 1 (17g)	2
Figfuls, 1 (15g)	1
Fruit Shortcake, 1 (8g)	1
Gold Biscuit Bar, 1 bar, 23g	3
Hobnob Creams, Chocolate or Vanilla, 1 (14g)	2
Hobnobs, 1 (17g)	2
Hobnobs Flapjack, 1 mini, 35g	4
Hobnobs Flapjack, 1 standard, 70g	9
Hobnobs Nobbly, 1 (14g)	2
Hobnobs Nobbly Biscuit Flapjacks, 1 (35g)	4
Hobnobs, Milk Chocolate, 1 (19g)	3
Honey Rice Crisp Bars, 1 (22g)	2

Jaffa Cakes, 1 (11g)	1
Jaffa Cakes Cake Bars, 1 bar, 32g	4
Jaffa Cakes, Blackberry & Apple or Cranberry & Orange or Lemon & Lime Flavour, 1 (12g)	1
Light Digestive, 1 (15g)	2
Light Hobnob, 1 (14g)	2
Light Milk Chocolate Digestive, 1 (17g)	2
Light Rich Tea, 1 (8g)	1
Milk Chocolate & Orange Digestives, 1 (17g)	2
Milk Chocolate Digestive, 1 (17g)	2
Milk Chocolate Digestive Caramel, 1 (17g)	2
Milk Chocolate Digestives Tube, 1 (17g)	2
Mini Choc Chip Orange Cookies, 1 pack, 25g	3
Mini Digestives, 1 bag, 40g	5
Mini Hobnobs, 1 bag, 25g	3
Mini Hobnobs, Milk Chocolate, 1 bag, 40g	5
Mini Jaffa Cakes, 1 (6g)	1
Mini Mallows, 1 serving, 28g	3
Mini Milk Chocolate Digestives, 1 bag, 25g	3
Original Digestive, 1 (15g)	2
Penguin, 1 (17g)	2
Penguin Bakes Chocolate, 1 (30g)	3
Penguin Big Stix Double Chocolate, 1 (13g)	2
Penguin Triple Chocolate Wafer, 1 bar, 17g	3
Penguin, Milk, 1 (22g)	3
Plain Chocolate Digestive, 1 (17g)	2
Raspberry Fruit Bakes, 1 (35g)	4
Shortbread Bites, 1 bag, 27g	4
Strawberry Jaffa Cakes, 1 (12g)	1
Strawberry Twist Fruit Bakes, 1 (23g)	2
Taxi, 1 (26g)	3
Wholemeal Crispy Fruit Slice, Raspberry & Cranberry, 1 slice, 14g	2
Yumbles Organic Choc Chip Crumblies, 1 (11g)	1
Yumbles Organic Oat Nibbles, 1 (9g)	1
Yumbles Organic Sultana & Hazelnut Crumblies, 1 (11g)	1
Yumbles Organic Wheat Nibbles, 1 (9g)	1

McVitie's – Go Ahead!

Apple & Raisin Cookies, 1 (17g)	1
Blueberry Yoghurt Breaks, 1 (43g)	5
Chocolate Chip Crispy Slices, 1 slice, 15g	2
Crispy Slices, Fruits of the Forest, 1 slice, 15g	2
Crispy Slices, Apple & Sultana, 1 slice, 43g	5
Crispy Slices, Forest Fruit, 1 slice, 15g	2
Crispy Slices, Orange & Sultana, 1 slice, 15g	2
Crispy Slices, Red Cherry, 1 slice, 14g	2
Crispy Slices, Raspberry, 1 slice, 15g	2
Fruit Bakes, Strawberry, 1 (35g)	4
Fruity Crunch Bars, Chocolate & Red Berry, 1 (21g)	2
Fruity Crunch Bars, Citrus Twist, 1 (23g)	3
Yogurt Breaks, All Flavours, 1 slice, 18g	2

Morrisons

All Butter Shortbread Fingers, 1 (18g)	2
Caramel Rice Cakes, 1 (11g)	1
Chocolate Crispy Bars, 1 bar, 22g	3
Chocolate Fingers, 1 (30g)	4
Chocolate Orange Crispy Bars, 1 (22g)	2
Custard Fingers Creams, 1 (14g)	2
Dark Chocolate Butter Biscuit, 1 (14g)	2
Dark Chocolate Praline Wafers, 1 (11g)	2
Digestive Creams, 1 (13g)	2
Divina, 1 biscuit, 23g	3
Garland Chocolate Wafer Bars, 1 (21g)	3
Ginger Fingers, 1 (8g)	1
Milk Chocolate Butter Biscuit, 1 (14g)	2
Milk Chocolate Cream Sandwich, 1 (25g)	4
Milk Chocolate Malted Milk, 1 (11g)	2
Milk Chocolate Mint Cream Sandwich, 1 (25g)	4
Milk Chocolate Oaties, 1 biscuit, 18g	2
Milk Chocolate Orange Cream Sandwich, 1 (25g)	4
Milk Chocolate Praline Wafers, 1 (11g)	2
Nice, 1 (8g)	1
Pink Wafers, 1 (8g	)1
Stem Ginger Crinkle Biscuits, 1 (11g)	1
Wholegrain Fruity or Golden Oaties, 1 biscuit, 11g	1

Nestlé

Dluc Riband, Plain & Dark, 1 (19g)	3
Breakaway, Caramac, 1 (23g)	3
Breakaway, Milk, 1 (21g)	3
Toffee Crisp Biscuit Bar, 1 (22g)	3
Yorkie Biscuit Bar, 1 (25g)	3

Rakusen's

Chocolate Digestives, 1 (22g)	3
Chocolate Oaties, 1 (22g)	3
Digestive Biscuit, 1 (17g)	2
Fruit Flapjack, 1 (19g)	3
Ginger Crunch Biscuit, 1 (18g)	2
Honey Crunch Biscuit, 1 (19g)	3

Sainsbury's

Be Good To Yourself Ginger & Chocolate Chip Cookies, 1 (17g)	2
Belgian Chocolate Millionaire's Shortbread, 1 piece, 69g	8
Double Take Wafer Biscuit, Milk or Plain Chocolate, 1 (22g)	3

Ginger Crinkle Crunch Biscuit, 1 (11g)	1
Ginger Snap, 90% Fat Free, 1 (12g)	1
Milk Chocolate Malted Biscuit, 1 (11g)	2
Pink Wafer, 1 (7g)	1

Sainsbury's – Taste the Difference

Almond Ricciarelli, 1 (23g)	3
Chocolate Biscotti, 1 (10g)	1
Italian Almond Cantuccini, 1 (9g)	1
Soft Amaretti, 1 (8g)	1

Tesco

All Butter Biscuits, 1 (8g)	1
Bourbon Creams, 1 (14g)	2
Buttery Viennese Fingers, 1 (15g)	2
Caramel Biscuit Bars, 1 (25g)	3
Caramel Milk Chocolate Covered Wafer Bars, 1 (28g)	4
Caramel Shortcake Traybake, 1 serving (⅙ pack), 49g	7
Caramel Shortcake, 1 individual, 65g	9
Caramel Wafer, 1 (30g)	4
Chocolate Chip Cookies, 1 (11g)	1
Chocolate Crunch Biscuit Bar, 1 (21g)	3
Chocolatey Fruit & Nut Cookies, 1 (25g)	4
Chocolatey Viennese Fingers, 1 (15g)	2
Chunky Chocolate Cookies, 1 (25g)	4
Coconut Rings, 1 (8g)	1
Crispy Nutty Seed Bites, 1 bite, 7g	1
Crunchy Cranberry & Raspberry Clusters, 1 individual, 15g	2
Crunchy Honeycomb Clusters, 1 individual, 12g	2
Currant & Cinnamon Cakey Cookie, 1 (25g)	3
Custard Cream Biscuits, 1 (13g)	2
Danish Butter Cookies, 1 (8g)	1
Digestive Biscuit Bars Fully Coated in Milk Chocolate, 1 (18g)	2
Double Chocolate Cakey Cookie, 1 (25g)	3
Double Chocolate Chip Cookie, 1 (11g)	1
Empire Biscuit, 1 (84g)	10
Fruit Shortcake, 1 (9g)	1
Fully Coated Milk Chocolate Sundae Biscuits, 1 (17g)	2
Jam Sandwich Creams, 1 (15g)	2
Malted Milk Biscuits Half Coated in Milk Chocolate, 1 (11g)	2
Milk Chocolate Fingers, 2 finger bar, 43g	6
Milk Chocolate Mint Cream Biscuits, 1 (14g)	2
Milk Chocolate Oaties, 1 (18g)	2

Milk Chocolate Sandwich Bars with Chocolate or Mint or Orange Cream, 1 (25g)	4
Milk Chocolate Sandwich Bars, 1 (24g)	3
Milk Chocolate Shortcake Biscuit, 1 (23g)	3
Millionaire's Shortcake, 1 individual, 16g	2
Mini All Butter Shortbread Bites, 1 (7g)	1
Mini Milk Chocolate Chip Cookies, 1 (7g)	1
Plain Chocolate Fingers, 1 (22g)	3
Plain Mint Chocolate Fingers, 1 (22g)	3
Raisin Crispy Slices, 1 (15g)	1
Reduced Fat Digestives, 25% less fat, 1 (16g)	2
Reduced Fat Rich Tea Biscuits, 1 (10g)	1
Rocky Road Clusters, 1 individual, 11g	2
Shortcake Biscuits, 1 (11g)	2
Sponge Fingers, 1 (6g)	1
Thick Milk Chocolate Jaffa Viennese Biscuits, 1 (16g)	2
Viennese Whirls, 1 (31g)	5

Tesco – Finest

Chocolate Caramel Shortbread Squares, 1 individual, 35g	5
Clotted Cream Shortbread, 1 individual, 18g	3
Petit Four Scottish Shortbread, 1 (8g)	1

Tesco – Light Choices

| Cranberry Crispy Slices, 1 slice, 15g | 1 |
| Mini Raspberry Fruit Bites, 1 bag, 25g | 2 |

The Co-operative

All Butter Scottish Shortbread Petticoat Tails, 1 piece, 12g	2
All Butter Shortbread Fingers, 1 (21g)	3
Cheese Thins, 1 (4g)	1
Choc Chip & Hazelnut Cookies, 1 (11g)	2
Choc Chip Cookies, 1 (11g)	2
Coconut Rings, 1 (8g)	1
Double Chocolate Chip Cookies, 1 (10g)	1
Everyday Chocolate Chip Cookies, 1 (11g)	2
Everyday Milk Chocolate Digestives, 1 (17g)	2
Fruit Shortcake Biscuits, 1 (8g)	1
Jam Sandwich Creams, 1 (15g)	2
Lincoln Biscuits, 1 bag, 9g	1
Milk Chocolate Malted Milk Biscuits, 1 (11g)	2
Milk Chocolate Rich Tea Biscuits, 1 (13g)	2
Oat Biscuits, 1 (15g)	2
Plain or Milk Chocolate Double Break, 1 (22g)	3
Premium All Butter Shortbread Fingers, 1 (20g)	3
Stem Ginger Cookies, 1 (17g)	2
Stem Ginger Shortbread, 1 (14g)	2

Weight Watchers®
Fruit Crumble Biscuits
a must for your shopping list

These jam topped Fruit Crumble Biscuits make a delicious treat – just one variety from our extensive range of scrumptious biscuits.

2 ProPoints value

per biscuit

Our range:
Over 17 delicious varieties of Cookies, Chocolate Biscuits, Oaty Biscuits, Wafers and Mallows

WeightWatchers® Foods
Eat gorgeous. Feel gorgeous.

Biscuits, Snacks & Confectionery   Chocolate

Trufree

All Butter Shortbread, 1 (11g)	2
Bourbon Biscuits, 1 (13g)	2
Choc Dippers, 1 pack, 52g	7
Chocolate Chip Cookies, 1 (10g)	1
Cookie Bites, 1 (8g)	1
Custard Creams, 1 (12g)	2
Digestive Biscuits, 1 (10g)	1
Ginger Snaps, 1 (11g)	1
Luxury Chocolate Biscuits, 1 (17g)	2
Milk Chocolate Nobbles, 1 (13g)	2
Mini O's, 1 (10g)	1

Tuc

Barbecue, 1 (11g)	1
Cheese Sandwich, 1 (14g)	2
Original, 1 (11g)	2
Salt & Pepper, 1 (11g)	1
Snack Pack, 1 pack, 31g	4

Tunnocks

Caramel Log, 1 (25g)	3
Caramel Wafer Biscuit, Dark Chocolate, 1 (26g)	3
Caramel Wafer Biscuits, 1 (30g)	4
Chocolate Wafer Creams Biscuits, 1 (24g)	4
Dark Chocolate Tea Cakes, 1 (24g)	3
Milk Chocolate Wafer Creams, 1 (24g)	4
Snowball, 1 piece, 20g	2
Teacakes, 1 (22g)	3

Waitrose

Butter & Sultana Cookies, 1 (13g)	2
Carrot Cake Cookie, 1 (75g)	9
Chocolate Bean Cookie, 1 (75g)	10
Chocolate Chip Cookies, 1 (19g)	2
Fig, Raisin & Walnut, 1 (20g)	2
Millionnaire's Shortbread, 1 piece, 60g	9
Oat & Sultana Cookie, 1 serving, 75g	8
Rich Tea Biscuit, Reduced Fat, 1 (10g)	1
Stem Ginger Cookies, 1 (17g)	2

Weight Watchers

Blueberry & Vanilla Oaty Biscuits, 1 (19g)	2
Caramel Mallow Wafers, 1 (17g)	1
Caramel Wafers, 1 (18g)	2
Chocolate Biscuits, 1 bar, 18g	2
Cranberry & Orange Cookies, 1 pack of 2, 19g	2
Cranberry & Sunflower Seed Oaty Biscuits, 1 (19g)	2
Double Chocolate & Orange Mini Cookies, 1 pack, 19g	2
Double Chocolate Chip Cookies, 1 pack of 2, 22g	2
Fruit Crumble Biscuits - Apple, Apricot & Peach, 1 (23g)	2
Fruit Crumble Biscuits - Apple, Blueberry & Raspberry, 1 (23g)	2
Ginger & Lemon Cookies, 1 pack of 2, 19g	2
Ginger Crunch Cookies, 1 pack of 2, 22g	2
Milk Chocolate Disgestive Biscuits, 1 (11g)	1
Mixed Seed & Honey Oaty Biscuits, 1 (19g)	2
Oat Choc Chip Cookies, 1 pack of 2, 22g	2
Oat Digestive Biscuits, 1 pack of 2, 19g	2
Oaty Chocolate Chip Mini Cookies, 1 pack, 19g	2
Raspberry & White Chocolate Cookies, 1 pack of 2, 19g	2
Sultana & Cinnamon Cookies, 1 pack of 2, 19g	2
Toffee Cookies, 1 pack of 2, 19g	2

Chocolate

Asda

Belgian Chocolate Flaked Cappuccino Truffles, 1 individual, 13g	2
Belgian Chocolate Flaked Truffles, 1 individual, 10g	2
Belgian Milk Chocolate Coins, 1 pack, 11g	2
Chocolate Puffin, 1 individual, 25g	4
Crispy Milk Chocolate, ¼ bar, 50g	7
Dark Chocolate Brandy Liqueurs, 1 serving, 10g	1
Milk Chocolate Irish County Cream Liqueurs, 1 individual, 10g	1
Milk Chocolate Bar, 1 serving, 25g	4
Milk Chocolate Crispy Bites, ⅕ bag, 30g	4
Milk Chocolate Fruit & Nut Bar, ¼ bar, 50g	7
Milk Chocolate Honeycomb, ¼ bag, 44g	6
Milk Chocolate Lollies, 1 portion, 20g	3
Milk Chocolate Peanuts, ¼ bag, 50g	7
Milk Chocolate Raisins, ¼ bag 50g	6
Milk Chocolate Turkish Delight Thins, 1 thin, 10g	1
Milk or Mint Chocolate, 1 sweet, 45g	7
Orange Chocolate, 1 bar, 45g	7
Wholenut Milk Chocolate, ¼ bar, 50g	8
Wholenut Milk Chocolate, 1 piece, 17g	3

Bendicks

Bittermint, 1 (18g)	2

Chocolate Classics, 1 pack, 50g	7
Chocolate Ginger, 1 (10g)	1
Chocolate Mint Crisps, 1 (8g)	1
Dark Chocolate, 1 bar, 25g	4
Milk Chocolate, 1 bar, 25g	4
Mingles, 1 (6g)	1
Mint Collection, ⅛ box, 28g	4
Victorian Mint, 1 (13g)	2
White Chocolate Mint, 1 (10g)	2

Cadbury

Boost, 1 treat size bar, 24g	3
Boost, 1 snack size bar, 39g	5
Boost, 1 standard bar, 55g	8
Bournville Deeply Dark Coffee, ¼ bar, 25g	4
Bournville Orange, 1 serving, 25g	3
Bournville Plain Chocolate, 1 miniature, 5g	1
Bournville Plain Chocolate, 1 standard bar, 50g	7
Bournville under 99 calories, 1 bar, 17g	3
Chomp, 1 bar, 26g	3
Cream Egg, 1 (39g)	5
Crunchie, 1 treat size bar, 17g	2
Crunchie, 1 snack size bar, 28g	3
Crunchie, 1 standard bar, 40g	5
Crunchie Nuggets, 1/4 pack, 50g	6
Curly Wurly, 1 treat size bar, 14g	2
Curly Wurly, 1 bar, 26g	3
Dairy Milk Caramel Nibbles, 1 serving 39g	5
Double Decker, 1 bar, 50g	6
Double Decker, 1 large bar, 65g	8
Flake, 1 treat size bar, 15g	2
Flake, 1 snack size, 18g	3
Flake, 1 standard, 34g	5
Flake Dipped, 1 bar, 44g	6
Flake, Dark, 1 standard, 32g	4
Milk Chocolate Clusters, 1 serving, 25g	3
Milk Chocolate Peanuts, 1 serving, 25g	4
Milk Chocolate Raisins, 1 serving, 25g	3
Picnic, 1 snack size bar, 30g	4
Picnic, 1 bar, 48g	6
Time Out, 2 fingers, 35g	5
Time Out, snack size, 2 fingers, 20g	3
Twirl, 2 fingers, 43g	6

Daim

Daim Bar, 1 bar, 28g	4

M&S

Caramel & Peanut Bar, 1 bar, 55g	8
Caramel Chocolate Bar, 1 bar, 55g	7
Marzipan in Dark Chocolate, 1 bar, 36g	5

Mars

Bounty, Dark, 1 bar, 57g	8
Bounty, Milk, 1 snack size, 28g	4
Bounty, Milk, 1 bar, 57g	7
Celebrations, All Varieties, 1 serving, 8g	1
Delight Bar, 1 pack of 2, 40g	6
Flyte, 1 bar, 22g	3
Galaxy Minstrels, ⅕ medium bag, 25g	3
Galaxy Minstrels, 1 small bag, 42g	6
Galaxy Caramel, 1 bar, 48g	7
Galaxy Dark Chocolate Block, ⅕ pack, 25g	4
Galaxy Milk Chocolate, 1 serving, 50g	8
Galaxy Raisin, Almond & Hazelnut or Roasted & Caramelised Hazelnuts, 1 standard bar, 46g	7
Galaxy Smooth Dark Chocolate, 5 squares, 21g	3
M&M's, Chocolate, ¼ bag, 31g	4
M&M's, Chocolate, 1 small bag, 45g	6
M&M's, Crispy, 1 small bag, 36g	5
M&M's, Peanut, 1 small bag, 45g	6
M&M's, Peanut, ¼ large bag, 50g	7
Maltesers Pouch, 1/10 pack, 18g	2
Mars Bar, 1 miniature, 8g	1
Mars Bar, 1 snack size bar, 42g	5
Mars Bar, 1 standard, 62g	8
Mars Bar, 1 large bar, 91g	11
Mars Dark Bar, 1 bar, 52g	7
Mars Planets, 1 bag, 37g	5
Milky Way, 1 funsize, 17g	2
Milky Way, 1 standard, 22g	3
Milky Way, Magic Stars, 1 bag, 31g	5
Revels, 1 small pack, 35g	5
Revels, ¼ large pack, 44g	6
Topic, 1 bar, 47g	6
Snickers, 1 snack size bar, 38g	5
Snickers, 1 standard bar, 58g	8
Snickers, 1 treat size bar, 20g	3
Twix, 1 finger, 29g	4
Twix, 1 standard bar, 58g	8
Twix Biscuit Fingers, 1 bar, 25g	3
White Maltesers, 1 bag, 37g	5

Milka

Milka & Daim, 1 serving, 25g	4
Milka Alpine Milk Chocolate Hazelnuts, 1 serving, 25g	4

Nestlé

Aero, 1 funsize, 11g	2
Aero, 1 snack size bar, 24g	4
Aero, 1 chunky bar, 43g	6
Aero, 1 medium bar, 46g	7

Aero Block, ¼ large bar, 31g	5
Aero Bubbles, Mint, ¼ large bar, 34g	5
Aero Milk Snack Size, 1 (20g)	3
Aero Minis, ⅕ pack, 45g	7
Aero Mint, ⅕ bar, 24g	4
Aero Peppermint, 1 snack size, 20g	3
Aero Peppermint, ¼ large bar, 34g	5
Animal Milk Chocolate Bar, ¼ bar, 19g	3
Animal Bar Milk Chocolate, 1 pack, 76g	11
Black Magic, 1 sweet, 10g	1
Black Magic Classic Favourites, 1 serving, 30g	4
Black Magic Dark Chocolate Thins, 4 sweets, 28g	4
Black Magic Dark Collection, 4 sweets, 40g	6
Black Magic Discovery, 1 pack, 59g	9
Black Magic Mellow Dark Chocolate, 1 box, 59g	8
Black Magic Mellow Dark Chocolate with Raisins & Almonds, ¼ bar, 25g	3
Collection Marc De Champagne Cocktail Truffles, 1 serving, 33g	5
Dairy Box, 1 sweet, 10g	2
Heaven Dark Vanilla Truffle Bar, ¼ bar, 25g	4
Heaven Hazelnut Crème Bar, ¼ bar, 25g	4
Heaven Milk or Dark Truffle Bar, ¼ pack, 25g	4
Heaven Swiss Dark or Milk Chocolate Bar, ¼ bar, 25g	4
Heavenly Truffle Collection, 1 small portion, 48g	8
Kit Kat, 2 fingers, 21g	3
Kit Kat, 4 fingers, 48g	7
Kit Kat, Cappuccino, 2 fingers, 21g	3
Kit Kat Chunky, 1 (51g)	7
Kit Kat Chunky, Minis, 1 (16g)	2
Kit Kat Chunky, Peanut Butter, 1 (50g)	7
Kit Kat, Dark, 2 fingers, 24g	3
Kit Kat, Dark, 4 fingers, 48g	7
Kit Kat, Milk Chocolate, 1 bar, 21g	3
Kit Kat, Mint, Orange or White, 2 fingers, 22g	3
Kit Kat Senses, 1 (31g)	5
Lion King, 1 bar, 80g	11
Little Rolo, 1 small bag, 40g	5
Milkybar, 1 small bar, 13g	2
Milkybar, 1 standard bar, 34g	5
Mini Smarties, 1 box, 14g	2
Mini Smarties, 1 pack, 25g	3
Munchies, ¼ pouch, 38g	5
Munchies Mini Bites, 1 piece, 17g	2
Quality Street Matchmakers Cool Mint or Zingy Orange, 4 sticks, 17g	2
Quality Street Selections Caramels, Toffee & Fudge, 1 serving, 37g	5

Quality Street Toffees, ¼ pack, 40g	5
Smarties Tubes, 1 tube, 38g	5
Toffee Crisp, 1 bar, 43g	6
Toffee Crisp Clusters, 1 bag, 44g	6
Toffee Crisp Mini Bites, 1 piece, 13g	2
Toffee Crisp, Snack Size, 1 bar, 30g	4
Walnut Whip Vanilla, 1 (34g)	5
Yorkie Boulders, Biscuit & Raisin, 1 (25g)	3

Paynes – Poppets

Brazils Milk Chocolate, 1 serving, 30g	5
Juicy Raisins, 1 serving, 100g	11
Mint Creams, 1 serving, 100g	12
Toffee, 1 box, 50g	7

Sainsbury's

Belgian Chocolate Fudge, 1 serving, 25g	3
Belgian Dark Chocolate, 1 bar, 40g	6
Belgian Milk Chocolate Flaked Truffles Gift Box, 1 piece, 12g	2
Chocolate Lebkuchen Hearts, 1 serving, 10g	1
Milk Chocolate Brazils, 1 sweet, 8g	1
Milk Chocolate Peanuts, ¼ packet, 62g	10
Milk Chocolate Raisins, ¼ packet, 57g	6
White Chocolate Buttons, 1 serving, 40g	6

Terry's

All Gold Dark Chocolates, 1 serving, 30g	4
All Gold Milk Chocolate, 1 serving, 30g	4
Chocolate Orange Bar, 1 bar, 40g	6
Chocolate Orange Bar, 1 large bar, 85g	12
Chocolate Orange Cosmic Toffee Crunch, 1 serving, 26g	4
Chocolate Orange Milk, 1 piece, 7g	1
Chocolate Orange Smashingly Tangy, 1 serving, 26g	4
Milk Waifa Bar, 1 bar, 35g	5
Plain Waifa Bar, 1 bar, 35g	5
Twilight, 4 pieces, 28g	4

Tesco

Choc Clusters, 1 serving, 25g	3
Chocolate Coated Peanuts, 1 serving, 25g	3
Chocolate Coated Raisins, 1 serving, 25g	3
Milk Chocolate Covered Peanuts, 1 serving, 25g	4
Milk Chocolate Covered Raisins, 1 serving, 25g	3

The Co-operative

Dairy Fudge, ¼ bag, 57g	7
English Toffee, 1 piece, 8g	1
Fairtrade Chocolate & Orange Bar, 1 (40g)	6

	ProPoints value
Fairtrade Chocolate Caramel Bar, 1 (40g)	5
Fairtrade Crispy Milk Chocolate, ⅓ bar, 50g	7
Fairtrade Crispy White Chocolate, ½ bar, 50g	7
Fairtrade Fruit & Nut Milk Chocolate, ⅓ bar, 50g	7
Fairtrade Milk & Dark Chocolate Hearts, 1 pack, 65g	9
Fairtrade Milk Chocolate Speckled Eggs, 1 pack, 95g	13
Milk Chocolate Brazils, ⅙ pack, 42g	6
Milk Chocolate Buttons, ½ bag, 35g	5
Milk Chocolate Turkish Delight Thins, 1 sweet, 10g	1
Orange Milk Chocolate Segments, ¼ pack, 45g	6

Thorntons

70% Dark Collection, ⅛ pack, 28g	4
Alpini Bar, 1 (35g)	5
Choc Chip Choccie, 1 (10g)	1
Classic Collection, 1 sweet, 13g	2
Dark Chocolate Gingers, ¼ pack, 60g	9
Dark Chocolate with Mint, ¼ pack, 22g	3
Dark Collection, ¼ pack, 61g	9
Heart, 1 piece, 14g	2
Milk Chocolate Bar, 1 (48g)	7
Milk Chocolate Collection, 1 serving, 13g	2
Mint Collection, ⅒ pack, 25g	4
Moments, 1 (8g)	1
Organic Truffle Collection, 1 sweet, 12g	2
Original Toffi Chocs, ¼ pack, 41g	6
Soft Caramels, 1 piece, 14g	2
Special Toffee Assorted, 1 serving, 25g	4
Turkish Delight Bars, 1 (45g)	5
Viennese Bar, 1 (38g)	6

Toblerone

Toblerone, 1 portion, 24g	3
Toblerone, 1 snack size bar, 35g	5
Toblerone, ½ standard bar, 50g	7
Toblerone, 1 slim bar, 50g	7
Toblerone, Dark or White, ½ standard bar, 50g	7
Toblerone, Fruit & Nut, ¼ standard bar, 25g	3
Toblerone Tobelle, 1 serving, 24g	3

Waitrose

After Dinner Mints, 1 (10g)	1
Belgian Chocolate Amaretto Cherry Dragees, ¼ box, 25g	3
Belgian Chocolate Apricot Dragees, ⅕ box, 25g	3
Belgian Chocolate Brazil Nut Dragees, ⅙ box, 25g	4

Never resist an indulgent treat...

Rich Toffee Bars

This classic mix of toffee, dark chocolate and nougat are combined to give an indulgent treat at anytime, and for a ***ProPoints*** value of only 2 per bar they're perfect for those 'treat yourself' moments.

Available now... in your meetings or through at home

WeightWatchers

Order today by calling: 08456 788 999

Weight Watchers and ***ProPoints*** are the registered trademarks of Weight Watchers International, Inc. The ***ProPoints*** Weight Loss System and formula are proprietary to Weight Watchers International, Inc. Patent pending. © (2011) Weight Watchers International, Inc. All rights reserved.

Belgian Chocolate Coffee Dragees, ⅕ box, 25g	3
Belgian Chocolate Collection, ¼ box, 66g	9
Belgian Marc de Champagne Truffle, ⅕ servings, 6g	1
Belgian Milk Chocolate Éclair, ¼ bag, 48g	5
Belgian Milk Chocolate Truffles, ⅛ pack, 6g	1
Belgian Milk Chocolate Whole Nut, ¼ bar, 50g	8
Dark & Milk Chocolate Mint Selection, 1 portion, 30g	4
Dark Chocolate Truffles with Marc DeChampagne, 1 (11g)	2
Fruit & Nut Belgian Milk Chocolate, ¼ bar, 50g	7
Gianduja Chocolate Hazelnut Dragees, ⅕ box, 25g	4
Peppermint Creams, ¹⁄₁₀ pack, 17g	2

Weight Watchers

| Rich Toffee Bar, 1 bar, 28g | 2 |

Crackers & Crispbreads

Asda

Chilli & Oregano Bruschetta Pieces, 2 pieces, 5g	1
Cream Cracker, 1 (8g)	1
Dutch Crispbake, 1 (8g)	1
Breadstick, 1 (6g)	1
French Toast, 1 (8g)	1
French Toast, 1 pack, 21g	2
Melba Toast, 2 slices, 7g	1
Mini Parmesan & Garlic Spirals, 1 serving, 28g	4
Rosemary & Sage Bruschetta Bites, 3 (8g)	1
Water Biscuit, 1 (6g)	1

Asda – Extra Special

Cracker Mix, 4 individual, 20g	2
Garlic Cracker, 1 (17g)	3
Spring Onion & Chive Crackers, 1 (17g)	2

Carr's

Melts Rosemary with Thyme, ⅙ pack, 25g	3
Melts Sesame with Chive, ⅙ pack, 25g	3
Original Melts, 1 (4g)	1
Table Water Biscuits, 1 (8g)	1

Finn Crisp

| 5 Wholegrains Crispbread, 2 (25g) | 2 |
| 5 Wholegrains Thins, 2 (15g) | 1 |

Multigrain Thins, 1 (7g)	1
Original Rye Rounds, 1 slice, 13g	1
Original Thins, 2 slices, 13g	1

Fortt's Original

| Bath Oliver Biscuits, 1 (12g) | 1 |

Fudges

Cheddar & Black Pepper Flatbreads, 1 serving, 25g	3
Cheddar Wafers, ⅕ pack, 20g	3
Cheese Topped Straws, 1 (10g)	1
Cheese Topped Straws with Rosemary, 1 (10g)	1
Marmite Biscuits, ¼ pack, 38g	4
Oat & Seeded Half Flatbreads & Half Cheddar & Black Pepper Flatbreads, ¼ pack, 45g	5
Oat Crackers, ⅙ pack, 25g	3
Poppy & Sesame Seed Biscuits, ⅓ pack, 50g	7
Pumpkin & Sesame Flatbreads, ⅓ pack, 50g	6
Spelt Seeded Flatbreads, ¼ pack, 33g	5
Stilton Wafers, 1 (12g)	2
Walnut Wafers, 1 (12g)	2

Jacob's

Cheddars Biscuits, 1 (4g)	1
Cheese Flavour Crackers, 1 serving, 25g	3
Cheese Sandwich, 1 (33g)	4
Cornish Wafer, 1 (8g)	1
Crackers with Wholewheat, Seeds & Herbs, 1 (13g)	1
Cream Cracker, 1 (8g)	1
Cream Crackers, Reduced Fat, 1 (8g)	1
Essentials Crackers, Rye & Oats, 2 (12g)	1
Garlic & Herb Bakes, 1 (6g)	1
High Bake Water Biscuits, 1 (5g)	1
Mediterranean Selection Crackers, Garlic & Herb, Pesto or Sundried Tomato Flavours, 1 pack, 24g	3
Mediterraneo Italian Crackers Olive Oil & Oregano, 1 (12g)	1
Mediterraneo Italian Crackers Premium Brand Olive Oil & Oregano or Salted, 1 (6g)	1
Mediterraneo Original Crackers, 1 (6g)	1
Oat Crackers, 1 (10g)	1
Ritz Original Cracker, 1 serving, 25g	3
Salt & Cracked Black Pepper Bakes, 1 (6g)	1
Savours Salt & Cracked Black Pepper Bakes, 1 (6g)	1
Savours Sweet Chilli Thins, 1 (4g)	1
Sesame Seed & Roasted Onion Thins, 1 (4g)	1
Snack Pack, Cream Crackers, All Flavours, 1 pack of 2, 30g	4

Biscuits, Snacks & Confectionery — Crackers & Crispbreads

Bursting with goodness

The delights of Nordic cuisine.
Brought to you by Finn Crisp.

Enjoy the true Nordic
taste experience
with Finn Crisp thins:
crispy, delicious, and
packed with healthy
wholegrains and fibre.

Nordic toppings: Nordic Herring Salad, Nordic Egg & Chive Spread, and Smoked Salmon
with Cream Cheese.   For more topping recipe ideas see www.finncrisp.com/nordicrecipes

	ProPoints value
Thai Bites, Mild Chilli, 1 small bag, 25g	2
Thai Bites, Mild Thai Flavour Rice Crackers, ¼ bag, 25g	3
Thai Bites, Oriental Spice, 1 small bag, 25g	3
Thai Bites, Seaweed, 1 small bag, 25g	3
Tuc Cheese Sandwich, 1 piece, 14g	2
Tuc Original Snack Cracker, 1 (5g)	1

Kallo

Mini Cheddar Crackers, ½ bag, 30g	4
Organic Thick Slice Rice Cakes Lightly Salted, Multigrain or Sesame, 1 slice, 8g	1
Organic Thick Slice Rice Cakes No Added Salt, 1 slice, 8g	1
Organic Wholemeal Rye Crispbread, 1 (23g)	2
Oven Baked Flatbreads, Cheese, Rosemary or Seeded, 1 (42g)	4
Savoury Rice Cake, 3 pieces, 26g	2
Snack Size Rice Cakes Flavoured with Yeast Extract, 1 bag, 50g	5
Snack Size Rice Cakes Slightly Salted with Cracked Pepper, 4 pieces, 9g	1
Thin Slice Rice Cakes No Added Salt, 1 (9g)	1

La Doria

Doriano Italian Crackers, 1 serving, 30g	4

Morrisons

Breadstick Assortment, All Flavours, 1 serving, 20g	2
Caramel Rice Cakes, 1 (11g)	1
Cheese Crispies, 1 serving, 4g	1
Cheese Twists, 1 pack from multi-pack, 28g	4
Eat Smart Crispbakes, 1 serving, 8g	1
Eat Smart Melba Toast, 1 (6g)	1
Free From Mini Chocolate or Yogurt Coated Rice Cakes, 1 pack, 40g	5
Melba Toast Flavoured with Cracked Black Pepper, 1 serving, 20g	2
Salt & Vinegar Rice Cakes, 1 (9g)	1
Slightly Salted Rice Cakes, 1 (8g)	1
Tomato & Basil Melba Toast, 1 serving, 20g	2
Wholegrain Melba Toast, 1 serving, 20g	2

Nairn's

Mini Oatcakes, 1 (4g)	1
Oat Bakes, Cheese, 1 bag, 30g	4
Oat Bakes, Mediterranean Tomato & Herb, 1 bag, 30g	4
Oatcakes, Fine Milled, 1 (8g)	1
Oatcakes, Herb, 1 (10g)	1
Oatcakes, Rough or Rough Oatmeal, 1 (11g)	1

	ProPoints value
Organic Oatcakes, Herb & Pumpkin Seed, 1 (10g)	1
Traditional Scottish Oatcakes, 1 (10g)	1

Pågen

Krisprolls Cranberries & Blueberries, 1 (13g)	1
Krisprolls Golden Wheat, 1 (10g)	1
Krisprolls Swedish Toasts Wholegrain, 1 (12g)	1

Paterson Arran

Cheese & Mild Chilli Oat Bites, 1 bag, 30g	4
Cracked Black Pepper Oatcakes, 1 (12g)	1
Olive Oil Oatcakes, 1 (12g)	1
Rough Oatcake, 1 (13g)	2
Scottish Oatcake, 1 (12g)	1

Rakusen's

99% Crackers Just 1% Fat, 1 (15g)	2
99% Crackers Just 1% Fat Herb & Onion, 1 (15g)	2
Biscuits for Cheese Selection Box, Cheese Snackers, 1 (10g)	1
Biscuits for Cheese Selection Box, Oat & Wheat Crackers, 1 (15g)	1
Biscuits for Cheese Selection Box, Plain Crackers, 1 (15g)	2
Cheese Snackers, 1 (40g)	4
Tea Matzos, 1 (15g)	2
Traditional Matzos, 1 (22g)	2
Wheaten Matzos, 1 (15g)	1

Ryvita

Dark Rye Crispbread, 1 (10g)	1
Flatbread Multi-Seed, 1 (10g)	1
Fruit Crunch Crispbread, 1 slice, 16g	2
Garlic & Rosemary Rye Crispbread, 1 (12g)	1
Hemp Seeds & Spelt Rye Crispbread, 1 (13g)	1
Multi-Grain Crispbread, 1 (11g)	1
Original Rye Crispbread, 1 (10g)	1
Original Wheat, 1 (5g)	1
Original Wheat Crackerbread, 1 (5g)	1
Pumpkin Seeds & Oats Crispbread, 1 (12g)	1
Ryvita Fruit Crunch, 1 (16g)	2
Sesame Rye Crispbread, 1 (10g)	1
Sunflower Seeds & Oats Crispbread, 1 (12g)	1
Thins Flatbread Cracked Black Pepper, 1 (10g)	1
Tomato & Basil Flavour Wholegrain Rye Crispbread, 1 (14g)	1
Wholegrain Crackerbread, 1 (6g)	1

Tesco

3 Seed Mini Breadsticks, 12 individual, 24g	3

LOW in fat,
LOW in salt...
that's CRACKERS!

Dairy free ✔ Lactose free ✔ Nut free ✔ Low in sugar ✔
Low in salt ✔ Low in fat ✔ Great source of fibre ✔

healthy eating for healthy living

Visit **www.rakusens.co.uk** for stockists

	ProPoints value
Bacon & Cheese Straws, 1 individual, 12g	1
Cheese & Onion Bites, 1 serving, 25g	4
Cheese & Chive Snacks, 1 serving, 25g	4
Cheese Thins, 1 individual, 4g	1
Cheese Twists, 1 individual, 8g	1
Chive & Onion Twists, 1 individual, 8g	1
French Toasts, 1 individual, 9g	1
Harvest Vegetable Crackers, 1 serving, 20g	2
Honey Oats Crackers, 1 individual, 20g	2
Japanese Rice Crackers, 1 serving, 25g	3
Mild Chilli Flavour Wholegrain Rice Cakes, 1 cracker, 10g	1
Mini Black Olive & Basil Twists, 12 individual, 24g	3
Oatland Rye Crisp Bread, 1 serving, 22g	2
Poppy & Sesame Thins, 4 individual, 16g	2
Reduced Fat Cream Crackers, 1 individual, 8g	1
Rough Oatcakes, 1 cracker, 10g	1
Salt & Vinegar Flavour Wholegrain Rice Cakes, 1 individual, 9g	1
Sweet Chilli Cassava Crackers, 1 serving, 20g	2

Tesco – Light Choices

Dutch Crispbakes, 1 individual, 8g	1
Dutch Melba Toast, 1 serving (1/10 pack), 20g	2
Savoury Jumbo Rice Cakes, 1 cracker, 8g	1

Weight Watchers

Wheat & Oat Crackers, 1 pack, 20g	2

Crisps & Snacks

Asda

Bombay Mix, 1/2 bag, 50g	7
Breadstick, 1 piece, 6g	1
Cheese & Onion Crisps, 1 bag, 25g	4
Cheese Balls, 1 serving (1/3 pack), 50g	8
Cheese Twists, 1 biscuit, 8g	1
Cheesy Curls, 1 bag, 17g	2
Cheesy Wiggles, 1 serving, 30g	4
Chinese Prawn Cracker, 1 pack, 25g	4
Garlic Bites, 1 serving (1/3 pack), 50g	8
Japanese Style Rice Cracker Mix, 1 bag, 25g	3
Loops Ready Salted, 1 serving, 30g	4
Mini Chive & Onion Twists, 1 serving, 9g	1
Nacho Cheese Tortilla Chips, 1/4 bag, 50g	7
Oven Baked Cheese & Onion Flavour, 1 bag, 25g	3

Oven Baked Ready Salted Flavour, 1 bag, 25g	3
Prawn Cocktail Flavour Crisps, 1 bag, 25g	4
Prawn Crackers, 1/2 bag, 35g	5
Ready Salted Crisps, 1 bag, 25g	4
Ready Salted Potato Loops, 1 bag, 25g	3
Salt & Vinegar Crunchy Sticks, 1/4 bag, 25g	3
Salt & Vinegar Flavour Crisps, 1 bag, 25g	4
Salt Your Own Potato Crisps, 1 bag, 25g	4
Snacking Wasabi Mix, 1 serving, 46g	6
Spicy Wasabi Mix, 1/6 pack, 38g	5
Thai Style Vegetable Crackers, 1 pack, 25g	4
Tortilla Chips, 1/4 bag, 50g	7
Tortilla Chips, Ready Salted, 1/4 bag, 50g	1
Wholegrain Bites Rosemary & Onion, 1 bag, 25g	3
Wholegrain Bites Sour Cream & Black Pepper, 1 bag, 25g	3

Asda – Extra Special

Belgian Milk Chocolate & Pecan Popcorn Clusters, 1/4 pack, 38g	5
Belgian White Chocolate & Strawberry Popcorn Clusters, 1 portion, 40g	5
Cracked Black Pepper Ciabatta Croutons, 1/3 bag, 28g	3
Davidstow Cheddar & Red Onion Crisps, 1/6 packet, 25g	3
Mediterranean Sea Salt Crisps, 1/6 packet, 25g	4
Pigs in Blankets Flavour Hand-Cooked Potato Crisps, 1 serving, 40g	6
Roast Turkey & Onion Gravy Flavour Hand-Cooked Potato Crisps, 1 serving, 40g	6
Scottish Heather Honey BBQ Flavour Crisps, 1 serving, 40g	6
Sea Salt & West Country Cider Vinegar Crisps, 1 serving, 40g	6
Sea Salt & Cracked Black Pepper Flavour Crisps, 1 serving, 50g	7
Sun-Dried Tomato & Chipotle Chilli Crisps, 1/6 packet, 25g	3
Sweet Parsnip Hand-Cooked Crisps, 1 serving, 40g	4
Vegetable Hand-Cooked Crisps, 1 serving, 25g	4
Wensleydale & Fruit Chutney Crisps, 1/6 packet, 25g	3

Blue Dragon

Prawn Crackers, 1 pack, 60g	9

Butterkist

Butter Flavour Microwave Popcorn, 1 serving, 25g	3

Fusion Popcorn, Chocolate Fudge Clusters, ¼ bag, 50g	6
Fusion Popcorn, Pecan & Almond Clusters, ¼ bag, 50g	7
Honey Nut Popcorn, 1 serving, 25g	3
Light Toffee Flavour Popcorn, ½ bag, 25g	2
Organic Natural Cane Sugar Popcorn, 1 serving, 25g	3
Organic Sea Salt Popcorn, 1 serving, 25g	4
Salted Microwave Popcorn, 1 serving, 25g	3
Sweet Cinema Style Popcorn, ¼ large bag, 50g	5
Sweet Flavour Microwave Popcorn, 1 serving, 25g	3
Toffee Popcorn, 1 small bag, 30g	3
Toffee Popcorn, 1 bag, 35g	4

Discovery Foods

Mexican Discovery Tortilla Chips Salted, 1 serving, 44g	6
Mexican Nacho Cheese Tortilla Rolls, ¼ pack, 31g	5
Tortilla Chips, 1 serving, 30g	4
Tortilla Chips, ¼ bag, 44g	6

Doritos

Big Eat Tangy Cheese, 1 pack, 55g	8
Chilli Heatwave, 1 small bag, 33g	5
Chilli Heatwave, ⅓ large bag, 50g	7
Collisions Chicken Sizzler/Zesty Salsa, 1 serving, 35g	5
Collisions T-Bone Steak/Grilled Pepper, 1 serving, 35g	5
Cool Original, ⅕ large bag, 35g	5
Cool Original, 1 bag, 40g	6
Cool Sour Cream & Chives Dip, ⅙ pack, 50g	4
Hint of Lime, ¼ pack, 56g	8
Latinos Chargrilled BBQ or Sour Cream & Sweet Pepper, 1 bag, 40g	5
Latinos, Mexican Grill, ⅕ bag, 35g	5
Lightly Salted, ⅓ pack, 43g	6
Tandoori Sizzler, 1 packet, 40g	6
Tangy Cheese, 1 standard bag, 40g	6

Golden Wonder

Cheese & Onion Crisps, 1 from multipack, 23g	3
Cheese & Onion Crisps, 1 bag, 34g	5
Golden Lights, All Flavours, 1 bag, 21g	3
Nik Naks, All Flavours, 1 bag, 34g	5
Pickled Onion Crisps, 1 from multipack, 25g	4
Pickled Onion Crisps, 1 bag, 34g	5
Prawn Cocktail Crisps, 1 from multipack, 25g	4
Prawn Cocktail Crisps, 1 bag, 34g	5

Ready Salted Crisps, 1 from multipack, 23g	3
Ready Salted Crisps, 1 bag, 34g	5
Ringos, All Flavours, 1 bag, 18g	2
Roast Chicken Crisps, 1 from multipack, 25g	4
Roast Chicken Crisps, 1 bag, 34g	5
Salt & Vinegar Crisps, 1 from multipack, 23g	3
Salt & Vinegar Crisps, 1 bag, 34g	5
Sausage & Tomato Crisps, 1 pack, 35g	5
Spring Onion Crisps, 1 from multipack, 25g	4
Spring Onion Crisps, 1 bag, 34g	5
Tomato Ketchup Crisps, 1 from multipack, 23g	3
Tomato Ketchup Crisps, 1 bag, 34g	5
Wheat Crunchies, All Flavours, 1 bag, 35g	5
XL Cheese Flavour Potato Crisps, 1 pack, 34g	5

Jacob's

Baby Tuc, Barbecue Flavour, 1 small bag, 30g	4
Crack 'O' Bites Mini Crispy Crackers, All Flavours, 1 serving, 25g	3
Original Baby Tuc, 1 pack, 30g	4
Rib 'N' Saucy, 1 portion, 25g	4
Thai Bites Fusions, All Flavours, 1 pack, 30g	3
Thai Bites Mild Thai Flavour with Sweet Chilli Dip, 1 serving, 25g	2
Thai Bites, Sweet Herb, 1 small bag, 25g	3
Twiglets, Original or Tangy, 1 bag, 30g	3

Kettle Foods

Camembert & Plum, 1 serving, 28g	4
Crème Fraîche, Garlic & Herbs, ¼ large bag, 38g	5
Crispy Bakes Crème Fraîche Lemon & Coriander, 1 bag, 24g	3
Crispy Bakes Mild Cheese with Sweet Onion, 1 bag, 24g	2
Crispy Bakes Salt & Malt Vinegar, 1 serving, 25g	3
Crispy Bakes, Tomato with Basil & Green Peppercorns, 1 bag, 24g	2
Honey Barbecue, 1 serving, 25g	3
Japanese Teriyaki, ¼ large bag, 38g	5
Lightly Salted, ¼ large bag, 38g	5
Mango Chilli, 1 pack, 25g	3
Mature Cheddar & Burgundy, ¼ large bag, 38g	5
Mature Cheddar & Red Onion, 1 bag, 40g	5
Mature Cheddar with Adnams Broadside Beer, 1 serving, 25g	3
Mexican Limes with a Hint of Chilli, 1 serving, 25g	3
Organics Lightly Salted, 1 bag, 40g	6
Peak Potato Crisps, Sea Salt with a Hint of Olive Oil, 1 bag, 25g	2

Red Thai Curry Medium Heat, 1 serving, 25g	3
Roast Chicken with Rosemary & Thyme, 1 serving, 40g	5
Salsa with Mesquite, ¼ large bag, 38g	5
Sea Salt & Balsamic Vinegar, ¼ large bag, 38g	5
Sea Salt with Crushed Black Peppercorns, ¼ large bag, 38g	5
Sea Salt with Crushed Black Peppercorns, 1 bag, 50g	7
Soulmate Cheeses with Onion, 1 pack, 40g	6
Sour Cream & Chive, 1 serving, 25g	3
Sour Cream & Chive, 1 bag, 40g	5
Sweet Chilli, 1 serving, 25g	4
Sweet Chilli, 1 bag, 40g	5
Undressed, 1 serving, 25g	3
Vegetable Chips Select Vegetables Parsnip, Sweet Potato & Beetroot, 1 serving, 25g	3
Vegetable Chips, Golden Parsnip, 1 serving, 25g	3
Vegetable Chips, Sweet Potato, 1 serving, 25g	4

KP Foods

Baked & Seasoned Large Peanuts Sea Salt & Black Pepper Flavour, 1 serving, 25g	4
Baked & Seasoned Large Peanuts Thai Sweet Chilli Flavour, 1 serving, 25g	4
Beef Flavour Crisps, 1 bag, 25g	4
Beef Flavour Mini Chips, 1 bag, 33g	5
Cheese & Onion Flavour Crisps, 1 bag, 25g	4
Cheese & Onion Flavour Potato Snacks, 1 bag, 28g	4
Disco's, Pickled Onion, 1 bag, 28g	4
Disco's, Salt & Vinegar Flavour, 1 bag, 28g	4
Frisps, Ready Salted, 1 bag, 28g	4
Frisps, Salt & Vinegar Flavour, 1 bag, 28g	4
Frosted Maple Syrup Flavour Nut Selection with Plain Chocolate Chunks, 1 serving, 35g	5
Jumbo Salted Peanuts, 1 serving, 50g	8
Meanies Pickled Onion, ¼ pack, 25g	3
Mexican Chilli Flavour, 1 small bag, 32g	5
Mexican Chilli Flavour, 1 bag, 50g	7
Prawn Cocktail Crunchies, 1 bag, 14g	2
Prawn Cocktail Flavour, 1 serving, 25g	4
Rancheros Bacon Flavour Potato, 1 serving, 25g	3
Ready Salted Crisps, 1 bag, 25g	4
Ridged Tortillas Hot Chilli Flavour, 1 serving, 25g	3
Ridged Tortillas Nacho Cheese Flavour, 1 serving, 25g	3
Roysters Bubbled Potato Chips, T-Bone Steak Flavour, 1 bag, 25g	4
Salt & Vinegar Flavour Crisps, 1 bag, 25g	4
Salt & Vinegar Flavour Mini Chips, 1 bag, 33g	5

Salt & Vinegar Flavour Potato Snacks, 1 bag, 28g	4
Salted Ridge Cut Potato Chips, 1 small bag, 32g	5
Salted Ridge Cut Potato Chips, 1 bag, 50g	7
Skips, Prawn Cocktail Flavour, 1 from multipack, 17g	2
Spicy Chilli Flavour Peanuts, 1 serving, 50g	8
Wheat Crunchies Crispy Bacon, 1 bag, 31g	4
Wheat Crunchies, Worcester Sauce, 1 bag, 35g	5

KP Foods – Hula Hoops

Barbecue Beef Flavour, 1 from multipack, 25g	4
Barbecue Beef Flavour, 1 bag, 27g	4
Cheese & Onion Flavour, 1 bag, 34g	5
Minis Original, 1 serving, 35g	5
Multigrain, Cheese & Onion Flavour, 1 from multipack, 23g	3
Multigrain, Cheese & Onion Flavour, 1 bag, 30g	4
Original, 1 bag, 34g	5
Original Stars & Hoops, 1 serving, 25g	4
Ridged, Salt & Vinegar Flavour, 1 from multipack, 25g	4
Ridged, Salt & Vinegar Flavour, 1 bag, 34g	5
Ridged, Steak & Onion Flavour, 1 bag, 25g	4
Ridged, Totally Cheesy Flavour, 1 bag, 30g	4
Salt & Vinegar Flavour, 1 bag, 34g	5
Shake 2 Salt, 1 bag, 25g	4
XL Nacho Cheese, 1 small bag, 37g	5

M&S

Cheese Tasters, 1 bag, 30g	4
Crunchy Combo Mix, Sour Cream & Jalapeños Flavour, ¼ large bag, 38g	5
Full On Flavour Crisps, All Flavours, 1 serving, 30g	4
Handcooked Crisps, All Flavours, ⅓ large bag, 30g	4
Nacho Cheese Baked Tortillas, 1 bag, 22g	3
Nacho Cheese Flavour Tortilla Chips, ⅓ large bag, 58g	8
Prawn Crackers, ½ large bag, 25g	4
Prawn Crackers, 1 bag, 15g	2
Ready Salted Crisps, 1 bag, 40g	6
Salt & Vinegar Chiplets, 1 bag, 35g	4

M&S – Eat Well

Lightly Salted Pretzel Sticks, ⅓ large pack, 30g	3
Red Pepper & Szechwan Cracker, ½ pack, 30g	3
Salt & Pepper Pretzels, 1 bag, 25g	2
Salt & Vinegar Crinkle Crisps, Reduced Fat, 1 bag, 40g	5

Thai Green Curry Crackers, ½ pack, 30g	**3**
Barbecue Wholegrain Snacks, 1 packet, 25g	**3**
Cheddar Cheese Popcorn, 1 bag, 25g	**4**
Sour Cream & Chive Pretzels, 1 bag, 25g	**3**
Honey BBQ Wholegrain Snacks, ½ bag, 30g	**4**
Salt & Crushed Black Pepper Pretzels, 1 bag, 25g	**2**
Crinkle Crisps Sour Cream & Chive, 1 bag, 40g	**5**
Honey Roast Ham Crisps, ½ bag, 50g	**6**
Lightly Salted Crinkles, Reduced Fat, 1 bag, 30g	**4**
Apple & Cinnamon Mini Popcorn Cakes, 1 packet, 22g	**2**
Lightly Salted Wholegrain Snacks, ½ bag, 30g	**4**
Salted Mini Pretzels, 1 packet, 25g	**3**
Giant Lightly Salted Pretzels, ¼ large pack, 50g	**5**

M&S – Count on Us

Salt & Vinegar Fries, 1 bag, 25g	**2**
Sea Salt & Malt Vinegar Baked Potato Crisps, 1 pack, 25g	**2**
Marmite Crisps, 1 bag, 25g	**4**
Marmite Oven Baked Cashews, ½ pack, 45g	**7**

McCoy's

Cheddar & Onion Flavour, 1 small bag, 32g	**5**
Cheddar & Onion Flavour, 1 bag, 50g	**7**
Flame Grilled Steak Flavour, 1 small bag, 32g	**5**
Flame Grilled Steak Flavour, 1 bag, 50g	**7**
Mature Cheddar & Onion Chutney Flavour, ⅓ large bag, 50g	**7**
Nacho Cheese & Sour Cream Flavour, 1 bag, 40g	**5**
Ridge Cut Salt & Malt Vinegar Flavour, 1 serving, 25g	**4**
Ridge Cut Salt & Malt Vinegar Flavour, 1 pack, 50g	**7**
Ridged Specials Tortillas Cool Ranch, 1 serving, 25g	**3**
Ridged Specials Tortillas Nacho Cheese & Sour Cream, 1 serving, 25g	**3**
Ridged Tortillas BBQ Chicken Flavour, 1 serving, 25g	**3**
Ridged Tortillas Cool Ranch Flavour, 1 serving, 25g	**3**
Sea Salt & Cider Vinegar Flavour, ⅓ large bag, 50g	**7**
Sizzling King Prawn, 1 bag, 50g	**7**
Sizzling King Prawn Flavour Ridge Cut Potato Crisps, 1 pack, 32g	**5**
Smoked Ham & Pickle Flavour Potato Chips, 1 pack, 40g	**6**

Specials, Oriental Ribs, 1 bag, 50g	**7**
Specials, Peppered Rib Eye Steak Crisps, ¼ bag, 40g	**6**
Specials, Tortillas Hickory Smoked Ribs, 1 serving, 25g	**3**
Spice Chinese Sizzling Beef Crisps, 1 bag, 35g	**5**
Spice Chinese Sizzling Beef Crisps, 1 large bag, 50g	**7**
Spice Thai Sweet Chicken, 1 bag, 35g	**5**
Spiced Chilli Flavour Crisps, 1 bag, 50g	**7**
Steak & Ale Flavour Crisps, 1 bag, 50g	**7**
T-Bone Steak with Onions Flavour, ⅓ large bag, 50g	**7**
Thai Sweet Chicken Flavour, 1 bag, 50g	**7**

McVitie's

Baked Mini Cheddars Crinklys Sweet Chilli Flavour, 1 serving, 25g	**3**
Baked Mini Cheddars Original, 1 serving, 25g	**4**
Crinklins, Lightly Salted, ⅙ tube, 26g	**3**
Go Ahead, Lightly Salted Crinkly Crisps, 1 from multipack, 25g	**3**
Go Ahead Sea Salt & Cracked Black Pepper Crinkly Crisps, 1 serving, 25g	**3**
Go Ahead Thai Sweet Chilli & Lime Crinkly Crisps, 1 serving, 25g	**3**
Mini Cheddars Crinkly's, Salt & Vinegar Flavour, 1 from multipack, 25g	**3**
Mini Cheddars Crinkly's, Salt & Vinegar Flavour, 1 bag, 50g	**7**
Mini Cheddars, Branston Pickle Flavour, 1 small bag, 25g	**4**
Mini Cheddars, Branston Pickle Flavour, 1 bag, 50g	**7**
Mini Cheddars, Original, 1 small bag, 25g	**4**

Morrisons

Cheese & Chilli Flavour Snack Mix, 1 from multi-pack, 25g	**4**
Cheese & Onion Crisps, 1 from multi-pack, 25g	**4**
Onion & Chive Twists, 1 pack	**4**
Prawn Cocktail Flavour Crisps, 1 from multi-pack, 25g	**4**
Ready Salted Crisps, 1 pack from multi-pack, 25g	**4**
Salt & Vinegar Potato Chips, 1 pack, 25g	**4**
Salt & Vinegar Crisps, 1 pack from multi-pack, 25g	**4**
Salted Snack Mix, 1 pack, 25g	**3**
Sweet Chilli Flavour Crisps, 1 pack from multi-pack, 25g	**4**

Morrisons – Eat Smart

Pickled Onion Flavour Potato Rings, 1 pack, 10g	1
Smokey Bacon Flavour Potato Waffles, 1 pack, 12g	1
Salt & Vinegar Flavour Potato Sticks, 1 pack, 15g	1

Mr Porky

Pork Crunch Light 'n' Crispy, 1 bag, 30g	4
Pork Scratchings, 1 bag, 30g	5
Prime Cut Scratchings, 1 pack, 35g	6

Patak's

Chilli & Lime Flavour Pappadums, ⅓ pack, 26g	3
Garlic & Coriander Pappadums, 1 serving, 10g	1
Mint Raita Flavour Pappadums, ½ bag, 40g	5
Onion Bhaji Flavour Pappadums, ½ bag, 40g	5

Penn State

Giant Pretzels, 1 bag, 25g	3
Original Salted Pretzels, 1 bag, 30g	3
Original Sea Salt & Cracked Black Pepper Poppy Seed Pretzel Stars, 1 serving, 25g	3
Original Sea Salted Pretzels, 1 pack, 30g	3
Pretzels Stars, 1 serving, 25g	3
Pretzels Sweet & Spicy Salsa Flavour, 1 serving, 25g	3
Pretzels Twists Roasted Red Pepper & Lime Flavour, 1 serving, 25g	3
Sweet & Spicy Salsa Flavour Pretzels, 1 bag, 30g	3

Pringles

Char-Grilled BBQ Beef Flavour, 1 serving, 30g	4
Cheesy Cheese, 1 serving, 25g	4
DeLight Original, 1 serving, 25g	3
DeLight, Sour Cream & Onion, 1 serving, 25g	3
Dippers, All Flavours, ¼ tube, 42g	6
Gourmet Crumbling Mature Cheese & Spring Onion Flavour, 1 serving, 25g	4
Gourmet Sea Salt & Balsamic Vinegar Flavour, 1 serving, 25g	4
Gourmet Spicy Thai Sweet Chilli & Lemongrass Flavour, 1 serving, 25g	3
Light Aromas Mediterranean Style Salsa with a touch of Oregano Oil, 1 serving, 30g	4
Light Sour Cream & Onion, 1 serving, 25g	3
Light, Original, 1 serving, 25g	3
Mini Pringles, All Flavours, 1 pack, 23g	3
Pocket Pack Original or Sour Cream & Onion, 1 pack, 35g	5

Rice Infusions Bite Size, Cheese & Onion, 1 bag, 35g	5
Rice Infusions Bite Size, Sweet BBQ Spare Rib Flavour, 1 bag, 35g	5
Rice Infusions, All Flavours, 1 serving, 25g	3
Select Italian Cheese with a Hint of Garlic, 1 serving, 25g	3
Select Sea Salt & Balsamic Vinegar, 1 serving, 25g	5
Select Sour Cream & Onion, 1 serving, 25g	3
Select Spicy Szechuan Barbecue, 1 serving, 25g	3
Select Sundried Tomato with Basil, 1 pack, 25g	3
Smokey Bacon, 1 serving, 25g	4
Smokey Bacon, 1 small pack, 43g	6
Texas BBQ Sauce, 1 serving, 25g	4
Xtreme Exploding Cheese & Chilli, 1 serving, 25g	4
Xtreme Exploding Cheese & Chilli, 1 pack, 40g	6
Xtreme Fiery Wasabi, 1 serving, 25g	4
Xtreme Flamin' Chilli Sauce, 1 serving, 25g	4
Xtreme Flamin' Chilli Sauce, 1 pack, 40g	6
Xtreme Take Away Smokin' Ribs, 1 serving, 25g	4
Zesty Lime 'n' Chilli, 1 serving, 25g	4

Quaker – Snack-a-Jacks

Barbecue, 1 (10g)	1
Barbecue, 1 bag, 26g	3
Caramel, 1 (13g)	1
Caramel, 1 bag, 25g	3
Cheese, 1 bag, 26g	3
Cheeky Chutney, 1 bag, 18g	2
Chocolate Chip, 1 (15g)	2
Hot Tomato, 1 bag, 26g	3
Jumbo Caramel, 1 serving, 13g	1
Jumbo Cheese, 1 serving, 10g	1
Jumbo Salt & Vinegar, 1 serving, 11g	1
Mini Bites, All Flavours, 1 bag, 28g	3
Oven Baked Mini Bagels, 1 bag, 35g	4
Oven Baked Mini Breadsticks, Cheese & Onion, 1 bag, 35g	4
Popcorn, Butter Toffee, 1 bag, 35g	4
Popcorn, Chocolate, 1 bag, 35g	3
Popcorn, Lightly Salted, 1 bag, 13g	1
Popcorn, Salt & Vinegar, 1 bag, 35g	4
Prawn Cocktail, 1 bag, 26g	3
Salt & Vinegar, 1 bag, 22g	2
Smokey Bacon, 1 bag, 26g	3
Sour Cream & Chive, 1 bag, 22g	2
Sweet Chilli, 1 bag, 22g	2
Sweet Chilli Crunchy Curls, 1 bag, 18g	2

Ryvita

Limbos, All Flavours, 1 bag, 20g	**2**
Minis, All Flavours, 1 bag, 30g	**3**

Sainsbury's

Bacon Crispies, 1 bag, 50g	**7**
Basic Snack Selection, 1 portion, 50g	**6**
British Potato Crisp Bakes Cheese & Onion, 1 pack, 25g	**4**
British Potato Crisp Bakes Ready Salted, 1 pack, 25g	**4**
British Potato Crisps Prawn Cocktail, 1 pack, 25g	**4**
British Potato Crisps Salt & Vinegar, 1 pack, 25g	**4**
British Potato Crisps Salt Your Own, 1 pack, 25g	**4**
Cheese Balls, ½ bag, 50g	**8**
Cheese Puffs, 1 pack, 18g	**3**
Cheese Savouries, ¼ bag, 50g	**7**
Fairtrade Fruit & Nut Mix, 1 serving, 30g	**4**
French Onion Flavour Crouton Snacks, ½ pack, 50g	**8**
Mini Poppadoms, 1 serving, 50g	**7**
Onion Rings, 1 serving, 25g	**3**
Popcorn, Butter Toffee, ½ bag, 50g	**6**
Popcorn, Sea Salt, ¼ bag, 25g	**3**
Popcorn, Sea Salt, ½ bag, 50g	**6**
Prawn Cocktail Shells, ¼ bag, 20g	**3**
Prawn Crackers, ¼ bag, 30g	**5**
Pumpkin Seeds, ½ pack, 50g	**8**
Salt & Black Pepper Flavour Crunchy Snack Mix, 1 serving, 38g	**5**
Salt & Vinegar Crunchy Sticks, ¼ bag, 25g	**3**
Sour Cream & Chive Flavour Crunchy Snack Mix, 1 serving, 37g	**5**
Sour Cream Chive Flavour Rice Cakes, 1 bag, 30g	**3**

Sainsbury's – Be Good To Yourself

Cheddar & Onion Light & Chunchy Snacks, 1 bag, 21g	**3**
Paprika Flavour Soya & Potato Snacks, 1 bag, 25g	**3**
Salt & Black Pepper Light & Chunchy Snacks, 1 bag, 21g	**3**
Spiced Lime & Coriander Flavour Soya & Potato Snack, 1 bag, 25g	**3**

Seabrook

Beefy Flavour Potato Crisps Crinkle Cut, 1 bag, 32g	**5**
Canadian Ham Flavour Potato Crisps Crinkle Cut, 1 bag, 32g	**5**
Chicken & Stuffing Flavour Potato Crisps Crinkle Cut, 1 bag, 32g	**5**
Cream Cheese & Chives Potato Crisps Crinkle Cut, 1 bag, 32g	**5**
Hot & Spicy Potato Crisps Chilli Jalapeño & Habanero, ⅓ bag, 37g	**6**
Hot & Spicy Potato Crisps Mustard Hot English, ⅓ bag, 37g	**6**
Hot & Spicy Potato Crisps Oriental Peking Ribs, ⅓ large bag, 37g	**6**
Hot & Spicy Potato Crisps Wasabi Japanese Horseradish, ⅓ bag, 37g	**5**
Potato Crisps, Cheese & Onion, 1 bag, 32g	**5**
Potato Crisps, Sea Salt, 1 bag, 32g	**5**
Potato Crisps, Sea Salt, ⅓ large bag, 50g	**8**
Prawn Cocktail Flavour Potato Crisps Crinkle Cut, 1 bag, 32g	**5**
Sea Salt & Black Pepper Flavour Straight Cut Potato Crisps, 1 serving, 25g	**4**
Sea Salt & Vinegar Potato Crisps Crinkle Cut, 1 bag, 32g	**5**
Sea Salted Potato Crisps Crinkle Cut, 1 bag, 32g	**5**
Spring Onion Flavour Potato Crisps Crinkle Cut, 1 bag, 32g	**5**
Tomato Ketchup Flavour Potato Crisps Crinkle Cut, 1 bag, 32g	**5**
Unsalted Potato Crisps Crinkle Cut, 1 bag, 32g	**5**

Tesco

Bacon Rashers, 1 serving, 25g	**4**
Bombay Mix, 1 serving, 25g	**3**
Cheese Balls, 1 serving, 25g	**4**
Cheese Puffs, 1 serving, 25g	**4**
Cheese Savouries, 1 serving, 25g	**4**
Crunchy Sticks Salt & Vinegar Flavour, 1 serving, 25g	**3**
Devonshire Cheddar & Norfolk Ale Chutney Crisps, 1 serving, 25g	**4**
Giant Salted Pretzels, 1 serving, 25g	**3**
Honey Roast Ham Flavour Crisps, 1 serving, 25g	**4**
Japanese Peanut Cracker Mix, 1 serving, 25g	**3**
Lightly Salted Crisps, 1 serving, 25g	**4**
Lightly Salted Tortilla Chips, 1 serving, 25g	**3**
Mini Poppadoms, 1 serving, 25g	**3**

Nacho Tortilla Chips, 1 serving, 25g	**3**
Onion Rings, 1 serving (⅙ pack), 25g	**3**
Potato Chips or Rings, 1 serving, 25g	**4**
Prawn Cocktail Snacks, 1 serving (¼ pack), 20g	**3**
Prawn Crackers, 1 serving (¼ pack), 20g	**3**
Ready Salted Snack Mix, 1 serving, 25g	**4**
Roasted & Salted Soya Beans, 1 serving, 25g	**3**
Salt & Vinegar Twirls, 1 serving, 25g	**3**
Salted Pretzels or Sticks, 1 serving, 25g	**3**
Sour Cream & Chive Snack Mix, 1 serving, 25g	**4**
Sundried Tomato, Garlic & Basil Flavour Crisps, 1 serving, 25g	**4**
Sweet Chilli Flavour Crisps, 1 serving, 25g	**4**
Tortillas Lightly Salted, 1 serving, 50g	**7**
Tortillas Mexican Chilli, 1 serving, 50g	**7**
Turkey, Stuffing & Onion Gravy Flavour Potato Crisps, 1 serving, 25g	**4**
Value Tortilla Chips, 1 serving, 25g	**3**

Tesco – Finest

Mature Cheddar & Caramelised Onion Crisps, 1 serving, 25g	**3**
Oak Smoked BBQ Flavour Crisps, 1 serving, 25g	**3**
Sea Salt & West Country Cider Vinegar Crisps, 1 serving, 25g	**3**
Sightly Salted Handcooked Crisps, 1 serving, 25g	**3**

The Co-operative

Assorted Potato Crisps, 1 bag, 25g	**4**
Black Olive & Basil Twists, 1 (8g)	**1**
Bombay Mix, ¼ pack, 62g	**9**
Cheese Twists, 1 (8g)	**1**
Crunchy Sticks, ½ bag, 50g	**7**
Gruyere Cheese & Poppy Seed Twists, ⅕ pack, 25g	**4**
Mediterranean Tomato & Smoked Paprika Flavour Crisps, ¼ bag, 38g	**5**
Milk Chocolate Peanuts, ½ bag, 57g	**9**
Milk Chocolate Raisins, ¼ bag, 57g	**6**
Nacho Cheese Tortillas, ⅙ large bag, 42g	**5**
Onion Rings, 1 bag, 100g	**13**
Salt & Vinegar Twirls, ½ bag, 40g	**5**
Streaky Crispies, ½ pack, 50g	**7**
Tortilla Chips, Chilli or Cool, ⅓ bag, 66g	**9**

Tyrrell's

Beetroot Vegetable Crisps with Sea Salt, 1 bag, 50g	**7**
Beetroot, Parsnip & Carrot Vegetable Crisps with a pinch of Sea Salt, 1 bag, 50g	**7**
English Summer Barbecue, 1 bag, 50g	**7**

Honey Roast Ham & Cranberry, 1 bag, 50g	**7**
Lightly Sea Salted, 1 bag, 50g	**6**
Ludlow Sausage & Mustard, 1 bag, 50g	**7**
Mature Cheddar & Chives, 1 bag, 50g	**7**
Mature Cheddar & Pickled Onion Furrows, 1 bag, 50g	**7**
Naked, 1 bag, 50g	**7**
Parsnip Vegetable Crisps with Black Pepper & Sea Salt, 1 bag, 50g	**8**
Sea Salt & Cider Vinegar, 1 bag, 50g	**7**
Sea Salt & Cracked Black Pepper, 1 bag, 50g	**7**
Sea Salt & Vinegar Furrows, 1 bag, 50g	**7**
Sea Salted Furrows, 1 bag, 50g	**7**
Sunday Best Roast Chicken, 1 bag, 50g	**7**
Sweet Chilli & Red Pepper, 1 bag, 50g	**7**
Worcester Sauce & Sundried Tomato, 1 bag, 50g	**7**

Walkers

Baked, All Flavours, 1 from multi-pack, 25g	**3**
BBQ Rib, 1 from multi-pack, 25g	**4**
BBQ Rib, 1 standard bag, 34g	**5**
Cheddar Cheese & Bacon, 1 from multi-pack, 25g	**4**
Cheese & Onion, 1 from multi-pack, 25g	**4**
Cheese & Onion, 1 standard bag, 34g	**5**
Chipsticks, Salt 'N' Vinegar Flavour, 1 bag 23g	**3**
Chipsticks, Salt 'N' Vinegar Flavour, 1 bag 37g	**5**
Crinkles, All Flavours, 1 from multi-pack, 28g	**4**
Crinkles, All Flavours, 1 standard bag, 32g	**5**
Extra Crunchy, All Flavours, 1 standard bag 30g	**4**
Frazzles, Crispy Bacon Flavour Corn Snacks, 1 bag, 17g	**2**
Frazzles, Crispy Bacon Flavour Corn Snacks, 1 bag, 23g	**3**
Frazzles, Crispy Bacon Flavour Corn Snacks, 1 bag, 43g	**6**
French Fries, Cheese & Onion, 1 bag 19g	**2**
French Fries, Cheese & Onion, 1 bag 22g	**3**
French Fries, Ready Salted, 1 bag 19g	**2**
French Fries, Ready Salted, 1 bag 22g	**3**
French Fries, Salt & Vinegar, 1 bag 19g	**2**
French Fries, Salt & Vinegar, 1 bag 22g	**3**
French Fries, Worcester, 1 bag 22g	**3**
Lights, All Flavours, 1 from multi-pack, 24g	**3**
Marmite, 1 from multi-pack, 25g	**4**
Marmite, 1 standard bag, 34g	**5**
Max, Chargrilled Steak, 1 standard bag, 50g	**7**
Max, Cheese & Onion, 1 standard bag, 50g	**7**
Max, Cheeseburger, 1 standard bag, 47g	**7**
Max, Paprika, 1 standard bag, 50g	**7**

Biscuits, Snacks & Confectionery **Crisps & Snacks**

Weight Watchers® Crinkle Crisps

a must for your shopping list

Reduced in fat* and low in **ProPoints**® values – when it comes to the crunch, our crisps are deliciously convenient!

2 ProPoints value ®

per pack

Now available in even more delicious flavours:
Ready Salted, Cheese & Onion, Roast Chicken, Salt & Vinegar and Sweet Chilli

NO ARTIFICIAL FLAVOURINGS, COLOURS, MSG OR PRESERVATIVES.

((WeightWatchers® Foods
Eat gorgeous. Feel gorgeous.

*Weight Watchers Crinkle Crisps contain at least 30% less fat than standard crinkle crisps.

Pickled Onion, 1 from multi-pack, 25g	4
Pickled Onion, 1 standard bag, 34g	5
Prawn Cocktail, 1 from multi-pack, 25g	4
Prawn Cocktail, 1 standard bag, 34g	5
Quavers, Cheese, 1 bag 16g	2
Quavers, Cheese, 1 bag 34g	5
Quavers, Cheese, 1 bag, 65g	10
Ready Salted, 1 from multi-pack, 25g	4
Ready Salted, 1 standard bag, 34g	5
Roast Chicken, 1 from multi-pack, 25g	4
Roast Chicken, 1 standard bag, 34g	5
Salt & Vinegar, 1 from multi-pack, 25g	4
Salt & Vinegar, 1 standard bag, 34g	5
Smoky Bacon, 1 from multi-pack, 25g	4
Smoky Bacon, 1 standard bag, 34g	5
Sour Cream & Chive, 1 from multi-pack, 25g	4
Squares, All Flavours, 1 bag 22g	3
Squares, All Flavours, 1 bag 25g	3
Squares, All Flavours, 1 bag 27g	3
Steak & Onion, 1 from multi-pack, 25g	4
Steak & Onion, 1 standard bag, 34g	5
Sunbites, Cheddar Cheese & Caramelised Onion, 1 bag, 25g	3
Sunbites, Light Sea Salted, 1 bag, 25g	3
Sunbites, Oven Roasted Onion & Rosemary, 1 bag 25g	3
Sunbites, Sour Cream & Cracked Pepper, 1 bag, 25g	3
Sunbites, Sour Cream & Cracked Pepper, 1 bag, 28g	4
Sunbites, Sun Ripened Sweet Chilli, 1 bag, 25g	3
Sunbites, Sun Ripened Sweet Chilli, 1 bag, 28g	4
Tomato Ketchup, 1 from multi-pack, 25g	4
Tomato Ketchup, 1 standard bag, 34g	5
Worcester Sauce, 1 from multi-pack, 25g	4
Worcester Sauce, 1 standard bag, 34g	5

Walkers – Sensations

Balsamic Vinegar & Caramelised Onion Flavour Crisps, 1 serving, 30g	4
Buffalo Mozzarella & Herbs, 1 serving, 35g	5
Buffalo Mozzarella & Herbs Flavour Crisps, ⅓ large bag, 53g	7
Chargrilled Steak & Peppercorn Sauce Flavour Crisps, 1 bag, 40g	6
Corn Chips Sweet Chilli & Coriander, ⅓ large bag, 35g	5
Corn Chips Sweet Chilli & Coriander, 1 bag, 35g	5
Olive Oil, Lightly Salted Crisps, 1 bag, 40g	6
Oriental Red Curry Flavour Crisps, 1 standard bag, 40g	5

Peking Duck & Hoisin Sauce Flavour Crisps, 1 pack, 40g	5
Peking Spare Ribs Flavour Oriental Crackers, ⅓ medium bag, 37g	5
Poppadoms Lime & Coriander Chutney Flavour Poppadom Style Snacks, ½ bag, 41g	5
Roasted Onion & Balsamic Vinegar Flavour Crisps, 1 bag, 40g	5
Sautéed Mushroom in White Wine Flavour Crisps, 1 serving, 30g	4
Sea Salt & Cracked Black Pepper Flavour Crisps, ⅓ large bag, 35g	5
Sea Salt & Cracked Black Pepper Flavour Crisps, 1 small bag, 40g	5
Southern Style Barbecue Flavour Crisps, 1 serving, 40g	5
Spicy Chargrilled Chilli Oriental Crackers, 1 serving, 25g	3
Szechuan Spice Crisps, 1 small bag, 40g	5
Roasted Chicken & Thyme Flavour Crisps, 1 serving, 30g	4
Thai Sweet Chilli Flavour Crisps, ⅓ bag, 35g	5
Thai Sweet Chilli Flavour Crisps, 1 small bag, 40g	5
Vintage Cheddar & Red Onion Chutney Flavour Crisps, ⅓ bag, 53g	7

Weight Watchers

BBQ Savoury Snacks, 1 bag, 22g	2
Chargrilled Smokey Bacon Flavour Corn Bites, 1 serving, 20g	2
Cheese & Onion Crinkle Crisps, 1 pack, 16g	2
Cheese Bites, 1 bag, 18g	2
Cheese Curls, 1 pack, 20g	2
Cheese Flavour Puffs, 1 single, 18g	2
Hot Chilli Tortillas, 1 bag, 18g	2
Mini Hoops, Ready Salted, 1 bag, 20g	2
Mini Hoops, Salt & Vinegar Flavour, 1 bag, 20g	2
Nacho Cheese Tortillas, 1 bag, 18g	2
Ready Salted Crinkle Crisps, 1 pack, 16g	2
Roast Chicken Flavour Crinkle Crisps, 1 pack, 16g	2
Salt & Black Pepper Tortillas, 1 bag, 18g	2
Sweet Chilli Flavour Crinkle Crisps, 1 pack, 16g	2

Mints & Gum

Asda

Classic Flavour Mint Imperials, 5 (6g)	1
Mint Puffin, 1 (26g)	4
Mint Selection, 2 sweets, 26g	3

Bassett's

Everton Mints, 1 sweet, 6g	1
Mint Favourites (Murray Mints, Murray Buttermints, Everton, Mint Toffees), ¼ packet, 50g	6
Mint Imperials, ¼ packet, 50g	5
Murray Mints, 1 sweet, 7g	1

Trebor

Extra Strong Mint, 1 serving, 8g	1
Peppermint, 1 serving, 8g	1

Wrigley's

Airwaves Black Mint Sugar Sugarfree Pieces, 1 pack, 20g	1
Airwaves Cherry Menthol Flavour Sugarfree Gum, 1 pack, 42g	1
Airwaves Green Mint Sugarfree Gum, 1 pack, 22g	1
Airwaves Menthol & Eucalyptus Sugarfree Gum Pieces, 1 pack, 20g	1
Cobalt, 1 pack, 31g	2
Electro, 1 pack, 31g	2
Extra Cool Breeze Sugarfree Gum, 1 pack, 22g	1
Extra Ice Sugarfree Gum, 1 pack, 14g	1
Extra Mints Peppermint Sugarfree Mints, 1 pack, 30g	2
Orbit Complete Lemon & Lime Flavour Sugarfree Gum Mega Pack, 1 pack, 20g	1
Orbit Complete Peppermint Whitening Sugarfree, 1 pack, 20g	1
Orbit Complete Spearmint Sugarfree, 1 pack, 22g	1
Orbit Complete Strawberry Flavour Sugarfree Gum, 1 pack, 20g	1
Orbit Complete Strong Mint Sugarfree, 1 pack, 20g	1
Pulse, 1 pack, 31g	2

Sweets

Asda

Cheeky Monkeys, 1 serving, 8g	1
Coconut Mushrooms, 1 (8g)	1
Liquorice Allsorts, 2 sweets, 10g	1
Liquorice Twists, 1 sweet, 10g	1
Mini Chicks & Bunnies, 2 pieces, 5g	1
Toasted Coconut Teacakes, 1 piece, 7g	1
Turkish Delight Chocolate Biscuit Bar, 1 bar, 25g	3
Turkish Delight Chocolate Biscuit Bar, ¼ large bar, 38g	5
Turkish Delights, ⅛ pack, 19g	2
White Mice, 1 piece, 5g	1
Yogurt Coated Raisins, 1 serving, 15g	2

Asda – Extra Special

Cashew Brittle, ¼ pack, 50g	7
Cashew Nut Brittle, 1 portion, 25g	4

Bassett's

Jelly Babies, ¼ large bag, 54g	5
Jelly Babies Milky, ¼ packet, 50g	5
Jelly Babies Party, ¼ packet, 45g	4
Lemon Bon Bons, 2 (10g)	1
Liquorice Allsorts, ¼ bag, 55g	6
Sherbet Lemons, ¼ packet, 50g	5
Strawberry Bon Bons, ¼ packet, 50g	5

Lofthouse's Fisherman's Friend

Original Extra Strong Lozenge, 1 (1g)	0

Nestlé

Juicy Jellies, ¼ bag, 49g	4
Rowntree's Pick & Mix Tube, ¼ pack, 40g	4

Storck

Werther's Original Butter Candies, 1 (5g)	1
Werther's Original Chocolate Caramels, 5 (30g)	5

Less than 10 calories per sweet
Werther's® Original
SUGAR FREE
Butter Candies
Enjoy the smooth and rich taste of the nation's favourite butter candy in a delicious long-lasting SUGAR FREE version.
Also available in a convenient Flip Top Box!

Werther's Original Caramelts, ¼ pack, 28g	5
Werther's Original Chewy Toffee, 1 (6g)	1
Werther's Original Chocolate, Dark, 5 (30g)	5
Werther's Original Chocolate, Milk, 5 (30g)	5
Werther's Original Sugar Free Butter Candies, 1 box, 42g	3

Tesco

American Hard Gums, 1 sweet, 6g	1
Cola Cubes, 1 sweet, 5g	1
Dairy Toffee, 1 individual, 8g	1
Fizzy Multi Coloured & Flavoured Belts, 2 (10g)	1
Fruit Pastilles, 2 (10g)	1
Jelly Babies, 1 serving, 18g	2
Jelly Beans, 1 serving (¼ pack), 63g	6
Marshmallows, 4 sweets, 28g	3
Pear Drops, 6 sweets, 23g	2
Rhubarb & Custards, 1 sweet, 9g	1
Sparkling Fruit Drops, 1 sweet, 6g	1
Strawberry Bon Bons, 1 sweet, 5g	1
Strawberry Laces, 6 individual, 24g	2
Sweet Shop Lemon Sherberts, 1 sweet, 8g	1
Wine Gums, 2 (11g)	1

The Co-operative

American Hard Gums, ½ bag, 125g	13
Blackcurrant & Liquorice, ⅕ bag, 45g	5
Fizzy Cola Bottles, 1 pack, 100g	9
Fizzy Strawberry Laces, ⅕ packet, 15g	2
Flying Saucers, 1 pack, 22g	2
Fruit Pastilles, ¼ bag, 62g	6
Jelly Babies, ⅕ bag, 50g	5
Jelly Beans, ¼ bag, 25g	3
Jelly Mix, ¼ bag, 25g	2
Midget Gems, ¼ bag, 62g	6
Strawberry Laces, ⅕ bag, 15g	2
Treacle Toffee, ¼ bag, 57g	7
Wine Gums, ⅕ pack, 50g	5

Trebor

Assorted Toffees, ¼ packet, 50g	5
Fundays Toffee Bonbons, 2 sweets, 10g	1
Toffee & Fudge Favourites, ¼ packet, 54g	6

Waitrose

Assorted Toffees, 1 serving, 20g	3
Butter Mintoes, ¼ bag, 62g	7
Clear Fruits, ¼ bag, 62g	7
Dairy Fudge, ¼ bag, 55g	6
Dairy Toffee, ¼ bag, 50g	6
Fizzy Strawberry Laces, ⅕ packet, 20g	2
Liquorice Allsorts, ¼ bag, 62g	6
Mint Assortment, ¼ bag, 50g	6
Sherbet Fruits, 1 serving, 20g	3

Weight Watchers

Fruities Duo Pack, Blackberry Flavour, 1 box, 32g	1
Fruities Duo Pack, Liquorice Flavour, 1 box, 32g	1
Fruities Duo Pack, Orange & Lemon Flavour, 1 box, 32g	1
Fruities Duo Pack, Strawberry Hearts, 1 box, 32g	1
Smooth Mints, 1 pack, 42g	2

Cereals &
Cereal Bars

Basic Foods

Bran Flakes, 1 medium bowl, 30g	**3**
Cornflakes, 1 medium bowl, 30g	**3**
Frosted Flakes, 1 medium bowl, 30g	**3**
Fruit & Fibre, 1 medium bowl, 30g	**3**
Muesli, 1 medium bowl, 50g	**5**
Oat Bran, 1 quantity, 50g	**5**
Oats or Oatmeal, 1 serving, 30g	**3**
Puffed Wheat, 1 medium bowl, 20g	**2**
Wholegrain Wheat Cereal, 1 medium bowl, 45g	**4**

Breakfast Cereals

Asda

5 Fruit Breakfast Topper, 1 serving, 50g	**4**
50% Fruit Oat, Wheat & Bran Flakes, 1 serving, 40g	**4**
Bite Size Wholegrain Wheats, 1 serving, 40g	**4**
Breakfast Mix, 1 serving, 50g	**4**
Choc Squares with a Nutty Chocolate Filling, 1 bowl, 44g	**5**
Choco Flakes or Hoops, 1 medium bowl, 30g	**3**
Choco Snaps, 1 medium bowl, 30g	**3**
Choco Squares, 1 bowl, 30g	**4**
Cranberry Wheats, 1 bowl, 50g	**5**
Golden Balls or Puffs, 1 bowl, 30g	**3**
Hawaiian Crunch, 1 serving, 45g	**5**
High Bran, 1 medium bowl, 30g	**3**
Honey Hoops, 1 bowl, 30g	**3**
Honey Nut Corn Flakes, 1 medium bowl, 30g	**3**
Malted Oaties, 1 bowl, 45g	**5**
Malted Wheaties, 1 serving, 40g	**4**
Mini Banana Wheat Bisks, 1 serving, 40g	**4**
Multigrain Hoops, 1 bowl, 30g	**3**
Passion Fruit Crisp, 1 medium bowl, 50g	**6**
Raisin & Almond Crisp, 1 serving, 45g	**5**
Raisin Honey & Almond Crunch, 1 bowl, 50g	**5**
Rice Snaps, 1 bowl, 30g	**3**
Starting Right, 1 bowl, 30g	**3**
Sultana Bran, 1 bowl, 30g	**3**
Vitality, All Flavours, 1 serving, 30g	**3**
Wheat Bisks, 1 serving, 50g	**5**
Wholegrain Wheats, 1 serving, 45g	**4**

Dorset Cereals

Breakfast Projects No.1 Original, 1 medium bowl, 30g	**3**
Breakfast Projects No.2 Apple, 1 medium bowl, 30g	**3**
Naturally Light Flakes, All Flavours, 1 bowl, 40g	**4**
Super Cranberry, Cherry & Almond, 1 medium bowl, 30g	**3**
Super High Fibre, 1 bowl, 50g	**6**
Tasty Fruit & Fibre, All Flavours, 1 bowl, 40g	**4**
Tasty Low Fat Flakes, 1 serving, 30g	**3**

Jordans

3 in 1, All Flavours, 1 large bowl, 50g	**5**
Country Crisp & Flakes Mixed Berries, 1 bowl, 50g	**6**
Country Crisp Chocolate, 1 bowl, 60g	**8**
Country Crisp Flame Raisins, 1 bowl, 62g	**7**
Country Crisp Chunky Nut, 1 bowl, 60g	**8**
Country Crisp Honey Nut, 1 bowl, 50g	**6**
Country Crisp Real Raspberries, 1 bowl, 50g	**6**
Country Crisp Real Strawberries, 1 bowl, 50g	**6**
Crunchy Oats Fruit & Nut, 1 serving, 50g	**6**
Crunchy Oats Raisins & Almond, 1 bowl, 50g	**6**
The Superfoods Breakfast Flakes, 1 bowl, 40g	**4**

Kellogg's

All Bran, 1 medium bowl, 40g	**3**
All-Bran Bran Flakes, Chocolate, 1 medium bowl, 30g	**2**
Bran Flakes, 1 medium bowl, 30g	**3**
Bran Flakes Sultana Bran, 1 medium bowl, 40g	**4**
Chocolate Hazelnut Krave, 1 medium bowl, 30g	**4**
Chocolate Wheats, 1 medium bowl, 40g	**4**
Coco Pops, 1 medium bowl, 30g	**3**
Corn Flakes, 1 medium bowl, 30g	**3**
Country Store, 1 medium bowl, 30g	**3**
Crunchy Nut, 1 medium bowl, 30g	**3**
Crunchy Nut Bites Nuts & Caramel, 1 large bowl, 40g	**5**
Crunchy Nut Clusters, Honey & Nut, 1 medium bowl, 45g	**5**
Crunchy Nut Clusters, Milk Chocolate Curls, 1 medium bowl, 45g	**6**
Crunchy Nut Clusters, Summer Berries, 1 medium bowl, 30g	**4**
Crunchy Nut Corn Flakes, 1 medium bowl, 30g	**3**
Crunchy Nut Nutty, 1 bowl, 40g	**5**
Crunchy Oatbakes, 1 bowl, 40g	**4**
Frosted Wheats, 1 medium bowl, 40g	**4**

Frosties, 1 individual pack, 40g	**4**
Frosties, Reduced Sugar, 1 medium bowl, 30g	**3**
Fruit 'n Fibre, 1 medium bowl, 30g	**3**
Honey Cornflakes, 1 medium bowl, 30g	**3**
Honey Loops, 1 medium bowl, 30g	**3**
Just Right, 1 medium bowl, 40g	**4**
Multigrain Start, 1 medium bowl, 40g	**4**
Nature's Pleasure Almond, Pecan & Cashew, 1 medium bowl, 30g	**3**
Nature's Pleasure Apple & Blackcurrant, 1 bowl, 40g	**5**
Nature's Pleasure Raspberry & Cherry, 1 bowl, 40g	**5**
Optivita Berry Oat Crisp, 1 bowl, 40g	**4**
Optivita Nut Clusters & Almonds, 1 bowl, 40g	**4**
Optivita Raisin Oat Crisp, 1 bowl, 40g	**4**
Raisin Wheats, 1 medium bowl, 40g	**4**
Rice Krispies, Multi-Grain or Original, 1 medium bowl, 30g	**3**
Ricicles, 1 medium bowl, 30g	**3**
Special K, 1 medium bowl, 30g	**3**
Special K Bliss Creamy Berry Crunch, 1 medium bowl, 30g	**3**
Special K Bliss, Strawberry & Chocolate, 1 medium bowl, 30g	**3**
Special K Medley, 1 medium bowl, 30g	**3**
Special K Oats & Honey, 1 medium bowl, 30g	**3**
Special K Sustain, 1 medium bowl, 40g	**4**
Special K Yogurty, 1 medium bowl, 30g	**3**
Special K Purple Berries, 1 medium bowl, 40g	**4**
Special K Berries, 1 medium bowl, 40g	**4**

McVitie's

Grape Nuts, 1 serving, 45g	**4**

Morrisons

Neat Wheat Biscuits, 1 bowl, 45g	**4**
Right Balance, 1 bowl, 40g	**4**
Eat Smart Trim Flakes, All Flavours, 1 bowl, 30g	**3**

Nestlé

Almond Oats & More, 1 medium bowl, 30g	**3**
Cheerios, or Cherrios Oat, 1 medium bowl, 30g	**3**
Clusters, 1 medium bowl, 30g	**3**
Coco Shreddies, 1 medium bowl, 45g	**4**
Curiously Cinnamon, 1 medium bowl, 30g	**3**
Fitnesse Honey & Nut, 1 medium bowl, 30g	**3**
Frosted Shreddies, 1 medium bowl, 45g	**4**
Golden Nuggets, 1 medium bowl, 30g	**3**
Honey Nut Cheerios, 1 medium bowl, 30g	**3**
Honey Oats & More, 1 medium bowl, 30g	**3**

Honey Shreddies, 1 medium bowl, 45g	**4**
Multigrain Fitnesse, 1 medium bowl, 30g	**3**
Nesquik Chocolate Cereal, 1 medium bowl, 30g	**3**
Oats & More Raisins, 1 medium bowl, 30g	**3**
Shredded Wheat, 1 medium bowl, 45g	**4**
Shredded Wheat Fruitful, 1 medium bowl, 40g	**4**
Shreddies, 1 medium bowl, 45g	**4**

Sainsbury's

Balance, 1 serving, 30g	**3**
Malties, 1 medium bowl, 30g	**3**
Maple & Pecan Crisp Cereal, 1 medium bowl, 40g	**5**
Wholewheat Bisk Cereal, 2 biscuits, 36g	**3**

Tesco

Apricot Wheats, 1 serving, 50g	**5**
Wheats, Blueberry or Cranberry, 1 serving, 50g	**5**
Crunchy Oats with Tropical Fruit, 1 serving, 50g	**6**
Fruit Crunch, 1 serving, 50g	**6**
Healthy Living Bran Flakes, 1 medium bowl, 30g	**3**
Honey Nut Corn Flakes, 1 serving, 30g	**3**
Light Choices Wheat Biscuits, 1 serving, 38g	**3**
Maple & Pecan Crisp Cereal, 1 serving, 50g	**6**
Pomegranate & Raspberry Wheats, 1 serving, 50g	**5**
Special Flakes with Red Fruit, 1 serving, 40g	**5**
Strawberry Crisp Cereal, 1 serving, 50g	**6**

The Co-operative

Choco Hoops or Snaps, 1 medium bowl, 30g	**3**
Crunchy Oat Cereal, 1 medium bowl, 60g	**7**
Crunchy Rice & Wheat Flakes, 1 medium bowl, 30g	**3**
Frosted Flakes, 1 medium bowl, 30g	**3**
Golden Nut Cornflakes, 1 medium bowl, 30g	**3**
Honey Hoops, 1 medium bowl, 30g	**3**
Malt Crunchie Cereal, 1 medium bowl, 30g	**3**
Maple & Pecan Crisp, 1 medium bowl, 30g	**4**
Perfect Choice, 1 medium bowl, 30g	**3**
Strawberry Crisp, 1 medium bowl, 30g	**3**
Whole Wheat Biscuits, 1 (24g)	**2**

Waitrose

Apricot & Orange Oat Crunchy, 1 bowl, 60g	**7**
Banana, Papaya & Honey Oat Crunchy, 1 bowl, 60g	**7**
Berry & Cranberry Crisp, 1 bowl, 60g	**7**
Berry & Cranberry Oat Crunchy, 1 bowl, 60g	**7**

Choco Rice Pops, 1 bowl, 40g	4
High Fibre Bran, 1 medium bowl, 40g	3
Honey Nut Cornflakes, 1 medium bowl, 30g	3
Malted Wheats, 1 medium bowl, 30g	3
Maple & Pecan Crisp, 1 bowl, 50g	6
Multigrain Hoops, 1 medium bowl, 30g	3
Special Choice, 1 medium bowl, 30g	3
Special Choice with Raspberries, Strawberries & Cherries, 1 medium bowl, 30g	3
Sultana Bran, 1 medium bowl, 30g	3
Triple Chocolate & Caramelised Nut Crisp, 1 serving, 50g	6
Wholegrain Apricot Wheats, 1 bowl, 50g	5
Wholegrain Cranberry Wheats, 1 bowl, 50g	5
Wholewheat Biscuits, 1 serving, 36g	3

Weetabix

Crunchy Bran, 1 medium bowl, 40g	3
Minis, Honey & Nut Crisp, 1 medium bowl, 36g	4
Oatibix, 1 serving, 48g	5
Oatibix Bites or Bitesize Original, 1 serving, 36g	4
Oatibix Bites Cranberry, 1 serving, 36g	4
Oatibix Bitesize with Chocolate & Raisin, 1 serving, 36g	4
Oatibix Bitesize with Sultana & Apple, 1 serving, 36g	4
Oatibix Flakes, 1 serving, 30g	3
Oatibix Flakes with Raisin, Cranberry & Blackcurrant, 1 serving, 40g	4
Oatiflakes Crispy Oat Flakes, 1 medium bowl, 40g	4
Weetabix, 2 (38g)	3
Weetabix Bitesize, 1 bowl, 40g	4
Weetabix Minis, All Flavours, 1 serving, 36g	4
Weetaflakes, 1 medium bowl, 30g	3
Weetaflakes with Raisin Cranberry & Apple, 1 bowl, 40g	4

Cereal Bars

Alpen

Apple & Blackberry with Yogurt Cereal Bar, 1 (29g)	3
Fruit & Nut Cereal Bar, 1 (28g)	3
Fruit & Nut with Milk Chocolate Cereal Bar, 1 (29g)	3
Groove Bar Nutty Chocolate, 1 (32g)	4

Groove Bar Sassy Strawberry or Lively Lemon, 1 (32g)	3
Groove Nutty Chocolate Bars, 1 (32g)	4
Groove Raspberry & Chocolate Bars, 1 (32g)	3
Light, All Flavours, 1 (21g)	2
Oat Flakes Pecan & Cherry, 1 (29g)	1
Raspberry & Chocolate Groove Bar with Tasty Chocolate Topping, 1 (32g)	3
Raspberry & Yogurt Bar, 1 (29g)	3
Strawberry & Yogurt Bar, 1 (29g)	3

Asda

1 of 5 a Day Cranberry & Apple Cereal Bars, 1 (35g)	3
Apricot, Sultana & Cinnamon Bars, 1 (35g)	4
Chocolate & Raisin Bars, 1 (27g)	3
Extra Special Nut & Apricot Bars with Belgian Chocolate, 1 (45g)	6
Fruit & Fibre Bars, 1 (29g)	3
Real Apple Fruit Bars, 1 (20g)	2
Real Strawberry Fruit Bars, 1 (20g)	2
Really Fruity Cereal Bars, All Flavours, 1 (40g)	4
Seed & Nut Bars, 1 (35g)	4
Vitality Cereal Bar, All Flavours, 1 (22g)	2

Asda – Chosen by You

Fruit & Grain Blueberry or Strawberry Bars, 1 (37g)	3
Fruit & Grain Mixed Fruit Bar, 1 (34g)	3
Fruit & Grain Apple & Cinnamon Bar, 1 (37g)	4

Asda – Good for You

Apple & Raspberry Cereal Bar, 1 (22g)	2
Banana & Toffee Cereal Bar, 1 (22g)	2
Chewy Bar, Apple & Cinnamon, 1 (25g)	2
Pomegranate Cereal Bar, 1 (22g)	2

Cadbury

Brunch Bar, Cranberry & Orange or Raisin, 1 (35g)	4
Brunch Bar, Hazelnut, 1 (35g)	5
Brunch Munch Oat & Apricot, 1 (25g)	3
Brunch Munch Oat & Honey, 1 (25g)	3

Dorset Cereals

Berries & Cherries, 1 bar, 35g	3
Delicious Cranberry & Almond Chunky Slices, 1 (50g)	5
Delicious Date & Pecan Chunky Slices, 1 (50g)	7
Delicious Pistachio & Pumpkin Seed Chunky Slices, 1 (50g)	6
Honey Granola Bars, 1 bar, 40g	5

Jordans

Absolute Nut Luxury Bars, 1 (45g)	7
All Fruit Bar, Apple & Passion Fruit, 1 (30g)	3
All Fruit Bar, Apple & Strawberry, 1 (30g)	3
Almond Marzipan Bars, 1 (45g)	6
Breakfast, Juicy Cranberries & Raspberries Multigrain Bar, 1 (40g)	4
Breakfast, Juicy Fruits & Sliced Almonds Multigrain Bar, 1 (40g)	4
Breakfast, Maple Syrup & Tasty Pecans Multigrain Bar, 1 (40g)	4
Cranberry & Almond Luxury Bars, 1 (50g)	6
Fruit & Nut Break Breakfast Bar, 1 (36g)	3
Frusli Berry Burst Bar, 1 (33g)	3
Frusli Cranberry & Apple Bar, 1 (30g)	3
Frusli Cereal Bars, All Flavours, 1 (30g)	3
Frusli Fruity Bars, All Flavours, 1 (30g)	3
Frusli Wild Berries Bar, 1 (30g)	3
Original Crunchy Maple & Pecan, 1 (33g)	3
Totally Oaty Oat Baked Bar, 1 (50g)	6

Kellogg's

Cherry Oat Baked Bar, 1 (50g)	6
Chocolate Oat Baked Bar, 1 (50g)	6
Coco Pops Cereal & Milk Bar, 1 (20g)	2
Coco Pops Coco Rocks Cereal Bars, 1 (20g)	2
Crunchy Nut Bar, 1 (25g)	4
Crunchy Nut Caramely Peanut Crisp Bars, 1 (35g)	5
Crunchy Nut Chocolate Bar, 1 (25g)	3
Crunchy Nut Chocolate Peanut Crisp Bar, 1 (35g)	5
Crunchy Nut Nuts About Nuts Bar, 1 (40g)	6
Crunchy Nut Nuts About Nuts 'n' Fruit Bars, 1 (40g)	5
Frosties Cereal & Milk Bar, 1 (25g)	3
Frosties Chocolate Cereal & Milk Bar, 1 (25g)	3
Fruit 'n Fibre Baked Bar, 1 (40g)	4
Fruit 'n Fibre Bar, 1 (25g)	3
Nutri-Grain Chewy, All Flavours, 1 (25g)	3
Nutri-Grain Elevenses, Carrot Cake Bakes, 1 (40g)	4
Nutri-Grain Elevenses, Chocolate Chip Bakes, 1 (45g)	5
Nutri-Grain Elevenses, Ginger or Raisin, 1 (45g)	5
Nutri-Grain Oat Baked Bar, Chocolate, 1 (50g)	6
Nutri-Grain Oat Baked Bar, Totally Oaty Bakes, 1 (50g)	6
Nutri-Grain Soft Baked Bars, All Flavours, 1 (37g)	4

Nutri-Grain, Cherry or Orange or Strawberry, 1 (37g)	4
Optivita, Berry Oat or Raisin Oat Bar, 1 (28g)	3
Pop Tarts, Chocotastic or Strawberry Sensation, 1 pack, 50g	5
Rice Krispies Cereal & Milk Bar, 1 (20g)	2
Rice Krispies Squares, Chocolate or Chocolate Caramel, 1 (30g)	4
Rice Krispies Squares, Chocolate Caramel, 1 snack size, 22g	3
Rice Krispies Squares Chewy Marshmallow, 1 (28g)	3
Rice Krispies Squares Crazy Choc Bars, 1 (28g)	3
Special K Apple & Pear Bar, 1 (22g)	2
Special K Bliss Bar, Mint Chocolate or Orange & Chocolate or Raspberry & Chocolate, 1 (22g)	2
Special K Chocolate Chip Bar, 1 (21g)	2
Special K Fruits of the Forest Bar, 1 (22g)	2
Special K Mini Breaks Zesty Lemon or Chocolate, 1 bar, 24g	3
Special K Mini Breaks, Original, 1 bar, 20g	2
Special K Original Bar, 1 (22g)	2
Special K Peach & Apricot Bar, 1 (22g)	2

Mars

Tracker Chocolate Chip, 1 (26g)	3
Tracker Raisin Bars, 1 (26g)	3
Tracker Roasted Nut, 1 (26g)	3

McVitie's

Apple & Sultana Cereal Bars, 1 (30g)	3
Cereal Bars with Almond, Raisin & Cranberry, 1 (30g)	3
Go Ahead Muesli Fingers Apple & Sultana, 1 finger, 13g	1
Go Ahead Hazelnut & Pistachio Cereal Bar, 1 (30g)	3
Muesli Finger, Cranberry & Sultana, 1 pack of 2, 25g	2

Morrisons

Apple & Cinnamon Fruit & Grain Bars, 1 (37g)	4
Bran, Apple, Pomegranate Bars, 1 (25g)	2
Bran & Apple Bars, 1 (25g)	2
Raspberry Fruit & Grain Bars, 1 (37g)	4

Morrisons – Eat Smart

Chewy Cereal Bars - Banoffee, Chocolate
Brownie, Lemon Curd, Strawberry Cheesecake,
Blueberry & Cream Flavoured, 1 (20g)　**2**

Nature Valley

Crunchy Granola Bar, Apple Crunch, 2 (42g)　**5**
Crunchy Granola Bar, Banana Nut, 2 (42g)　**6**
Crunchy Granola Bar, Canadian Maple
Syrup, 2 (42g)　**5**
Crunchy Granola Bar, Oats 'n' Honey, 2 (42g)　**5**
Crunchy Granola Bar, Roasted Almond, 2 (42g)　**5**
Ginger Nut Crunch, 2 (42g)　**5**

Nestlé

Cheerios Bar, 1 (22g)　**3**
Cookie Crisp Bar, 1 (22g)　**2**
Fitnesse Choc & Orange Bar, 1 (24g)　**2**
Honey Nut Cheerios Bar, 1 (22g)　**2**
Nesquik Cereal Bar, 1 (25g)　**3**
Oats & More Chocolate Chunks or Strawberry
or Juicy Cherries Cereal Bars, 1 (30g)　**3**
Shreddies Bar, 1 (25g)　**3**

Quaker

Cranberry & Berry Oat Bars, 1 (38g)　**4**
Harvest Cheweee, Choc Chip, 1 (22g)　**3**
Oat Bar, Original with Golden Syrup
Flavour, 1 (38g)　**4**

Ryvita

Goodness Bar Luxury Fruit & Nut, 1 (35g)　**3**
Goodness Bar, Mixed Berry, Strawberry or
Cranberry & Apple, 1 (23g)　**2**
Goodness Luxury Bar Cranberry, Date &
Almond, 1 (35g)　**3**

Sainsbury's

Be Good To Yourself Multigrain Balance Maple
Cereal Bars, 1 (27g)　**2**
Fruit & Nut Cereal Bars with Chocolate
Drizzle, 1 (27g)　**3**

Tesco

Chewy & Crisp Cereal Bars with Chocolate
Chips, 1 individual, 27g　**3**
Chocolate Orange Cereal Bars, 1 (25g)　**3**
Cranberry Cereal Bars, 1 (27g)　**3**
Fairtrade Apricot & Banana Chocolate Cereal
Bar, 1 (51g)　**5**

Fairtrade Mango & Apricot Chocolate Cereal
Bars, 1 (31g)　**3**
Finest Chunky Blueberry & Almond Chocolate
Cereal Bar, 1 (46g)　**5**
Finest Chunky Cranberry & Pumpkin Seed
Bar, 1 (28g)　**3**
Finest Fruit Nut & Seed Bars, 1 (40g)　**4**
Frosted Rice Cereal Bar with Marshmallow
Puffs, 1 (20g)　**3**
Fruit & Fibre Cereal Bars, 1 (27g)　**3**
Hazelnut Munch Bars, 1 (30g)　**4**
Honey Nut Cornflake Cereal Bar, 1 (27g)　**3**
Oat Bars with Cranberry & Blueberry, 1 (38g)　**4**
Oat Bars with Golden Syrup, 1 (38g)　**4**
Raisin Munch Bars, 1 (30g)　**3**
Reduced Fat Crispy Orange Flavour
Bars, 1 (22g)　**3**
Special Flake Cereal Bars All Flavours, 1 (23g)　**2**

Tesco – Light Choices

Cranberry & Blackcurrant Cereal Bar, 1 (25g)　**2**
Forest Fruit & Raisin Fruit Bar, 1 (27g)　**3**
Maple Cereal Bar, 1 (25g)　**3**
Raisin & Apple Fruit Bar, 1 (27g)　**3**

The Village Bakery Melmerby

Apricot, Date & Sultana Bars, 1 (25g)　**2**
Brazil, Cashew & Sunflower Seed Bars,
1 (37g)　**5**
Fruit, Nut & Seed Bars, 1 (25g)　**3**
Gluten Free Apricot & Orange Low Fat
Fingers, 1 finger, 25g　**2**
Organic Four Bars Nuts, 1 (42g)　**5**

Weetabix

Oaty Bars, Milk Chocolate, 1 (23g)　**2**
Oaty Bars, Strawberry, 1 (23g)　**2**
Oaty Bars, White Chocolate, 1 (23g)　**2**
Weetos, 1 (20g)　**2**

Weight Watchers

Roasted Peanut Bar, 1 (25g)　**2**

Porridge & Muesli

Asda

Blackcurrant, Apricot & Pumpkin Seed Muesli, 1 bowl, 50g	**5**
Swiss Style Muesli, 1 serving, 45g	**4**
Swiss Style Muesli, No Added Sugar, 1 serving, 45g	**4**
Swiss Style Muesli with Juicy Raisins, Hazelnuts & Almonds, 1 serving, 64g	**6**

Asda – Extra Special

Blackcurrant, Apricot & Pumpkin Seed Muesli, 1 serving, 50g	**5**
Sicilian Lemon & Ginger Crunch, 1 serving, 45g	**5**

Jordans

Fruit & Nut Muesli, 1 bowl, 50g	**5**
Quick & Creamy Porridge, 1 bowl, 65g	**7**
Super Berry Granola, 1 bowl, 50g	**6**

Morrisons

Swiss Style Muesli No Added Sugar, 1 bowl, 50g	**5**
Swiss Style Muesli, 1 bowl, 50g	**5**

Mornflake

Heart's Content Oatbran, 1 bowl, 30g	**3**
Heart's Content Organic Oats, 1 bowl, 40g	**4**
Heart's Content Original Oatbran, 1 bowl, 30g	**3**
Heart's Content Superfast Oats, 1 bowl, 45g	**4**
Hearts Content Organic Oats 2 Go, 1 bowl, 40g	**4**
Old Fashioned Jumbo Oats, 1 bowl, 45g	**4**

Quaker

Granola, Crunchy Clusters of Oats with Juicy Raisins, 1 bowl, 50g	**6**
Oat Crisp Cereal, 1 bowl, 30g	**3**
Oat So Simple, Golden Syrup or Apple & Blueberry, 1 serving, 36g	**4**
Oat So Simple, Original, 1 bowl, 27g	**3**
Oat So Simple, Sultanas, Raisins, Cranberry & Apple, 1 serving, 38g	**4**
Oat So Simple, Sweet Cinnamon or Honey & Almond or Raspberry or Mango & Passionfruit, 1 serving, 33g	**3**

Ready Brek

Chocolate Fine Porridge Oats, 1 serving (prepared), 30g	**3**
Honey Fine Porridge Oats, 1 serving (prepared), 30g	**3**
Original Fine Porridge Oats Sachets, 1 sachet (prepared), 30g	**3**

Sainsbury's

Be Good To Yourself Easy Porridge Oats with Oatbran, 1 bowl, 44g	**4**
Luxury 12 Fruit & Nut Muesli, 1 bowl, 50g	**5**

Tesco

Instant Hot Oat Cereal, 1 serving, 30g	**3**
Micro Oats Original, 1 sachet, 27g	**3**
No Added Sugar or Salt Swiss Style Muesli, 1 serving, 50g	**5**
Swiss Style Muesli, 1 serving, 50g	**5**
Wholewheat Muesli, 1 serving, 50g	**5**

Waitrose

Fruit & Fibre Muesli, 1 serving, 60g	**6**
Fruit & Seed Muesli, 1 serving, 50g	**5**
Fruit Muesli, 1 serving, 50g	**5**
High Fibre Muesli, 1 serving, 50g	**4**
Instant Hot Oat Original Flavour, 1 tablespoon, 15g	**1**
Maple Triple Nut Muesli, 1 bowl, 50g	**5**
Orchard Fruits & Berries Muesli, 1 bowl, 50g	**4**
Swiss Style Muesli, 1 bowl, 50g	**5**
Swiss Style Muesli, No Added Sugar or Salt, 1 bowl, 50g	**5**

Weetabix

Alpen, No Added Sugar, 1 bowl, 40g	**4**
Alpen High Fruit, 1 bowl, 45g	**4**
Alpen High Fibre, 1 bowl, 30g	**3**
Alpen Luxury Cinnamon Granola, 1 bowl, 50g	**6**
Alpen Luxury Granola, 1 bowl, 50g	**6**
Alpen Luxury High Fruit, 1 bowl, 50g	**2**
Alpen Original, 1 medium bowl, 40g	**4**
Alpen No Added Sugar The Swiss Recipe, 1 bowl, 45g	**4**
Alpen The Original Swiss Recipe, 1 bowl, 45g	**4**
Luxury Gluten Free Muesli, 1 bowl, 50g	**5**
Muesli Spiced with Cinnamon & Honey, 1 bowl, 50g	**5**

Cooking & Serving
Sauces & Marinades

Chinese & Oriental

Amoy

Hoisin & Shitake Mushroom Cooking Sauce, ¼ jar, 112g	4
Szechuan Tomato & Sweet Peppers Cooking Sauce, ¼ jar, 109g	2
Thai Creamy Coconut, Tomato & Red Pepper Cooking Sauce, ¼ jar, 108g	3

Amoy – Straight to Wok

Aromatic Black Bean Stir Fry Sauce, 1 serving, 60g	1
Chow Mein Stir Fry Sauce, 1 serving, 60g	2
Creamy Thai Green Curry Stir Fry Sauce, 1 serving, 60g	2
Pad Thai Stir Fry Sauce, 1 serving, 60g	2
Rich Hoisin Stir Fry Sauce, 1 serving, 64g	2
Roasted Peanut Satay Stir Fry Sauce, 1 serving, 64g	3
Succulent Szechuan Tomato Stir Fry Sauce, 1 serving, 64g	1
Sweet Soy & Spring Onion Stir Fry Sauce, 1 serving, 64g	3
Sweet Thai Chilli Stir Fry Sauce, 1 serving, 64g	2
Tangy Sweet & Sour Stir Fry Sauce, 1 serving, 64g	2
Teriyaki & Toasted Sesame Seeds Stir Fry Sauce, 1 serving, 60g	3

Asda

Black Bean & Chilli Stir Fry Sauce, ½ jar, 98g	4
Black Bean Cooking Sauce, ⅕ jar, 118g	3
Black Bean Stir Fry Sauce, ½ pouch, 63g	1
Cantonese Style Sauce, ¼ jar, 148g	4
Fresh Tastes Black Bean Stir Fry, ¼ jar, 50g	1
Green Thai Curry Cooking Sauce, ½ jar, 158g	7
Green Thai Stir Fry Sauce, ½ pouch, 63g	3
Hoisin Marinade, ¼ jar, 71g	2
Hoisin Stir Fry Sauce, ½ jar, 98g	4
Marinade in a Bag Mango & Chilli, ½ bag, 75g	2
Marinade in a Bag Red Thai, ½ bag, 75g	2
Marinade in a Bag Sweet & Sour, ½ bag, 75g	5
Sweet Chilli Stir Fry Sauce, 1 serving, 80ml	3

Asda – Good For You

Coriander & Lime Marinade, ¼ pack, 84g	1

Sweet & Sour Stir Fry Sauce, ½ pouch, 90ml	3

Blue Dragon

Black Bean Stir Fry Sauce, ½ large jar, 100ml	5
Black Bean with Roasted Garlic & Chilli Stir Fry Sauce, ½ pouch, 60g	2
Canton Black Bean Stir Fry Sauce, ½ pouch, 60g	2
Chinese B.B.Q., ¼ jar, 86g	2
Chinese Dynasty Bang Bang Stir Fry Sauce, ½ jar, 100g	5
Chinese Dynasty Capital Stir Fry Sauce, ½ jar, 100g	3
Chinese Dynasty Kung Po Stir Fry Sauce, ½ jar, 100g	3
Chow Mein Stir Fry Sauce, ½ pouch, 60g	2
Golden Plum, Ginger & Chilli Stir Fry Sauce, 1 serving, 60g	2
Hoisin & Garlic Stir Fry Sauce, ½ pouch, 60g	2
Hoisin & Sesame Stir Fry Sauce, 1 serving, 50ml	3
Hoisin Stir Fry Sauce, ½ pouch, 60g	3
Honey & Cashew Stir Fry Sauce, 1 serving, 50g	2
Hot Thai Sweet Chilli Dipping Sauce, 1 serving, 50ml	3
Malaysian Satay, ¼ pack, 86g	3
Oyster & Spring Onion Stir Fry Sauce, ½ pouch, 60g	2
Pad Thai Paste, 1 serving, 15g	1
Peking Lemon Stir Fry Sauce, ½ pouch, 60g	3
Royal Thai Green Curry Cooking Sauce, ½ pouch, 100g	4
Royal Thai Red Curry Cooking Sauce, ½ pouch, 100g	4
Satay Stir Fry Sauce, 1 serving, 50g	3
Soy, Honey & Garlic Stir Fry Sauce, ½ pouch, 100g	4
Spare Rib Sauce, 1 serving, 15ml	1
Spicy Szechuan Tomato Stir Fry Sauce, 1 serving, 60g	2
Sticky Plum Stir Fry Sauce, ½ pouch, 60g	2
Sweet & Sour Sauce, 1 serving, 50g	3
Sweet & Sour Stir Fry Sauce, ½ pouch, 60g	2
Sweet Chilli & Garlic Stir Fry Sauce, ½ portion, 60g	3
Sweet Chilli Stir Fry Sauce, 1 serving, 60g	3
Sweet Soy & Roasted Red Chilli Stir Fry Sauce, ½ pouch, 60g	1
Sweet Soy with Garlic & Ginger Stir Fry Sauce, 1 serving, 60g	1
Szechuan Tomato Stir Fry Sauce, ½ pouch, 60g	2

Tangy Lemon with Ginger & Cracked Pepper
Stir Fry, ½ pouch, 60g ... **2**
Teriyaki Marinade, 1 serving, 15ml ... **1**
Teriyaki Stir Fry Sauce, ½ pouch, 60g ... **2**
Thai Basil & Lemongrass Stir Fry Sauce,
1 serving, 60g ... **1**
Thai Green Curry Stir Fry Sauce, ½ pouch, 60g ... **1**
Thai Red Curry Cooking Sauce, ½ portion, 100g ... **4**
Thai Red Curry Stir Fry Sauce, ½ pouch, 60g ... **2**
Thai Sweet Sauce, 1 serving, 50g ... **3**

Knorr

Chinatown Hoisin & Plum Sauce, ¼ jar, 131g ... **3**
Chinatown Spicy Szechuan Sauce, ¼ jar, 129g ... **3**
Chinese Five Spice, ⅓ jar, 26g ... **4**

Knorr – Chicken Tonight

Oriental Sweet & Sour Sauce, ¼ jar, 131g ... **3**
Stir Fry Cherry Tomato, Red Chilli & Vodka,
½ jar, 85g ... **2**
Stir Fry Sticky Soy, Balsamic Vinegar &
Peppers, ¼ jar, 125g ... **5**
Stir Fry Thai Style Lime, Coconut & Red Chilli,
½ jar, 85g ... **3**
Stir Fry Thai Style Lime, Red Chilli & Coconut,
¼ jar, 125g ... **5**
Stir Fry Wild Mushrooms, Garlic & Shallots,
½ jar, 85g ... **3**

Knorr – Sizzle & Stir

Stir It Up Chinese Five Special Sauce, ¼ jar, 20g ... **3**
Sweet & Sour, ⅓ jar, 152g ... **6**
Sweet & Sour Sauce, ¼ jar, 115g ... **5**
Thai Green Curry, ¼ jar, 114g ... **7**

Loyd Grossman

Green Thai Curry Sauce, ¼ jar, 88g ... **3**
Malaysian Rendang Sauce, ¼ jar, 88g ... **4**
Red, Green or Yellow Thai Curry Sauce,
¼ jar, 88g ... **3**

Sainsbury's

Black Bean Stir Fry Sauce, ½ sachet, 75ml ... **2**
Chinese Stir Fry Sauce, Fresh, ½ sachet, 75ml ... **2**

Sainsbury's – Be Good To Yourself

Plum & Ginger Cooking Sauce, 1 serving, 125g ... **2**
Sweet Chilli Stir Fry Sauce, ½ sachet, 75ml ... **2**
Szechuan Tomato Cooking Sauce,
1 serving, 126g ... **3**

Schwartz

Low Fat Dark Soy, Sesame & Ginger Sauce,
½ pouch, 150g ... **4**
Tangy Lime & Coriander Sauce, ¼ pack, 75g ... **5**
Thai Chicken Green Curry Recipe Mix,
1 sachet, 41g ... **4**

Sharwood's

Beijing Chilli Bean, ¼ pack, 106g ... **2**
Black Bean Stir Fry Sauce, ½ jar, 98g ... **2**
Cantonese Curry Cook in Sauce, ¼ jar, 106g ... **2**
Cantonese Sweet & Sour Cook-in Sauce,
¼ jar, 106g ... **3**
Chinese BBQ & Sesame Sauce, ½ jar, 60g ... **3**
Cooking Sauce Black Bean & Red Pepper Mild,
¼ jar, 106g ... **2**
Cooking Sauce Hoisin & Plum Mild,
¼ jar, 106g ... **3**
Hoisin Spare Rib Sauce, ½ jar, 150g ... **6**
Hong Kong Sweet & Sour, ½ jar, 150g ... **3**
Indonesian Satay Cooking Sauce,
1 serving, 190g ... **9**
Indonesian Satay Oriental Curry Sauce
Medium, ¼ jar, 104g ... **5**
Kung Po, ⅓ jar, 140g ... **7**
Lemon & Sesame Stir Fry Sauce, ½ jar, 98g ... **3**
Malaysian Rendang Cooking Sauce,
½ jar, 190g ... **6**
Marinade Hoisin Sauce, ¼ jar, 75g ... **4**
Oyster & Mushroom Chinese Cooking Sauce,
¼ jar, 106g ... **2**
Pineapple & Coconut Cooking Sauce,
¼ jar, 105g ... **3**
Singapore Laksa Oriental Curry Sauce Mild,
¼ pack, 104g ... **5**
Sri Lankan Colombo Curry Sauce, ½ jar, 190g ... **6**
Sri Lankan Devil Curry, ½ jar, 190g ... **3**
Sweet & Sour Cooking Sauce, ¼ jar, 106g ... **3**
Szechuan Sweet Chilli Cook-In Sauce,
1 portion, 140g ... **3**
Teriyaki with Black Pepper, ½ jar, 98g ... **3**
Thai Green Curry Cooking Sauce, ¼ jar, 104g ... **3**
Thai Green Curry Paste, 1 serving, 25g ... **1**
Thai Green Curry Sauce, ⅓ jar, 138g ... **4**
Thai Mussaman Curry, ⅓ jar, 140g ... **4**
Thai Red Curry Cooking Sauce, ¼ jar, 104g ... **3**
Thai Red Curry Paste, 1 serving, 50g ... **2**
Thai Sweet Chilli & Herb Coating Sauce,
½ pouch, 60g ... **2**
Thai Yellow Curry Sauce, ⅓ jar, 140g ... **3**
Yellow Bean Sauce, ½ jar, 75g ... **2**

Tesco

Black Bean & Roasted Garlic Stir Fry Sauce, 1 serving, 90g	**3**
Black Bean Cooking Sauce, 1 serving, 108g	**2**
Black Bean Stir Fry Sauce, ⅓ pouch, 66g	**2**
Creamy Coconut, Lemongrass & Lime Stir Fry Sauce, 1 serving, 90g	**3**
Green Thai Cooking Sauce, ⅓ jar, 106g	**3**
Green Thai Curry Paste, 1 serving, 15g	**0**
Red Thai Cooking Sauce, ⅓ jar, 106g	**3**
Red Thai Curry Paste, 1 serving, 15g	**0**
Sticky Plum & Hoi Sin Stir Fry Sauce, 1 serving, 90g	**5**
Stir Fry Black Bean Sauce Pouch, 1 serving, 67g	**2**
Stir Fry Chow Mein Sauce Pouch, 1 serving, 67g	**1**
Stir Fry Hoisin Sauce Pouch, 1 serving, (⅓ pack), 67g	**2**
Sweet & Sour Cooking Sauce, 1 serving, 110g	**3**
Sweet & Sour Cooking Sauce, ¼ jar, 138g	**4**
Sweet & Sour Stir Fry Sauce, ⅓ pouch, 66g	**3**
Sweet Chilli & Ginger Stir Fry Sauce, 1 serving, 90g	**3**
Thai Yellow Curry Paste, 1 serving, 15g	**0**
Value Sweet & Sour Sauce, 1 can, 405g	**9**

Tesco – Finest

Coconut, Chilli & Lemongrass Stir Fry Sauce, 1 serving, 90g	**4**
Green Thai Curry Paste, 1 serving, 30g	**1**
Green Thai Curry Sauce, ½ jar, 168g	**7**
Oriental Hot Chilli Sauce, ½ jar, 182g	**6**
Red Thai Curry Paste, 1 serving, 30g	**1**
Red Thai Curry Sauce, ½ jar, 175g	**5**
Tamarind, Fresh Lime & Chilli Stir Fry Sauce, 1 serving, 90g	**6**

The Co-operative

Black Bean Cook In Sauce, ½ jar, 220g	**5**
Mango & Lime Sweet & Sour Stir Fry Sauce, 1 pack, 100g	**4**
Sichuan Cook in Sauce, ½ jar, 220g	**3**
Sichuan Rice Wine & Five Spice Stir Fry Sauce, 1 pack, 100g	**2**
Sweet & Sour Cook in Sauce, ½ jar, 225g	**5**
Sweet & Sour Stir Fry, ½ pack, 150g	**7**

Uncle Ben's

Black Bean Ready to Use Culinary Sauce, 1 pack, 100g	**2**
Black Bean with Green Peppers, ¼ jar, 125g	**2**

Cantonese Cooking Sauce, ¼ jar, 125g	**3**
Hoisin with Spring Onions Cooking Sauce, ¼ jar, 125g	**4**
Oriental Sauce for Lemon Chicken with Ginger, ¼ jar, 125g	**3**
Sweet & Sour Cooking Sauce, ¼ jar, 125g	**4**
Sweet & Sour Cooking Sauce, Light, ¼ jar, 125g	**2**
Sweet & Sour Extra Spicy Sauce, ¼ jar, 125g	**3**
Sweet & Sour Sauce with Extra Pineapple, ¼ jar, 125g	**3**
Szechuan Chilli Cooking Sauce, ¼ jar, 125g	**3**
Stir Fry Aromatic Sweet & Sour, ½ jar, 75g	**3**
Stir Fry Cantonese Soy & Sesame, ½ jar, 75g	**2**
Stir Fry Oriental Soy & Black Bean, ½ jar, 75g	**1**
Stir Fry Oriental Sweet & Spicy Chilli, ½ jar, 75g	**2**
Stir Fry Thai Red Chilli with Coconut & Cream, ½ jar, 75g	**2**
Sweet Thai Chilli Cooking Sauce, Mild, ¼ jar, 125g	**6**
Thai Coconut Curry Sauce, Mild, ¼ jar, 100g	**3**

Weight Watchers

Sweet & Sour Sauce, ½ jar, 175g	**2**

Indian

Asda

Balti Cooking Sauce, Medium, ½ jar, 160g	**3**
Balti Curry Paste, ¼ jar, 25g	**2**
Chickpea & Spinach Sauce, ¼ pack, 125g	**3**
Chip Shop Style Curry Sauce Mix, 1 tablespoon, 15g	**2**
Curry Cooking Sauce, ⅙ jar, 132g	**3**
Tikka Curry Paste, ¼ jar, 25g	**2**

Asda – Good For You

Bhuna Cooking Sauce, ¼ jar, 142g	**2**
Korma Cooking Sauce, ¼ jar, 142g	**3**
Tikka Masala Cooking Sauce, ¼ jar, 142g	**3**

Homepride

Curry Cook-in-Sauce, ¼ jar, 125g	**2**
Curry Mildly Spiced, ¼ can, 125g	**2**
Korma Cook-in-Sauce, ¼ jar, 125g	**5**
Tikka Masala Cook-in-Sauce, ¼ can, 125g	**5**

Knorr

Creamy Curry Sauce, ¼ jar, 125g	**6**
Hot Curry Sauce, 1 pack, 83g	**1**
Medium Curry Sauce, 1 pack, 47g	**1**

Knorr – Sizzle & Stir

Balti Sauce, ⅓ jar, 152g	**5**
Korma Sauce, ⅓ jar, 152g	**11**
Stir it Up Tikka Sauce, ¼ jar, 20g	**4**
Tikka Bhuna Sauce, ⅓ jar, 152g	**5**
Tikka Massala Sauce, ⅓ jar, 150g	**9**

Loyd Grossman

Balti Sauce, 1 portion, 100g	**4**
Dopiaza Curry Sauce, ¼ jar, 106g	**3**
Korma, ¼ large jar, 150g	**6**
Madras Curry Sauce, ¼ ¼ jar, 106g	**5**
Red Lentil Dhansak Curry Sauce, ¼ jar, 106g	**3**
Rogan Josh Sauce, 1 portion, 100g	**4**
Sweet Tomato Bhuna Curry Sauce, ¼ jar, 106g	**4**
Tikka Masala, ½ jar, 175g	**7**

Morrisons

Tikka Sauce, ¼ jar, 125g	**6**
Korma Sauce, ¼ jar, 125g	**6**
Free From Tikka Masala Cooking Sauce, ¼ jar, 125g	**4**

Patak's

Balti Cooking Sauce, ¼ jar, 125g	**3**
Balti Curry Paste, 1 serving, 30g	**2**
Biryani Curry Paste, 1 serving, 30g	**2**
Bombay Mango & Shallot Masala, ¼ jar, 106g	**3**
Coat & Cook, Lime & Coriander, ¼ sachet, 20g	**2**
Coat & Cook, Spicy Mango, ¼ sachet, 20g	**1**
Coat & Cook, Tikka, ¼ sachet, 20g	**1**
Dopiaza Cooking Sauce, ¼ jar, 125g	**3**
Garam Masala Curry Paste, 1 serving, 30g	**3**
Goan Spice Masala, ¼ jar, 106g	**4**
Hot & Spicy Tikka Masala, ¼ jar, 135g	**4**
Jalfrezi Cooking Sauce, ¼ jar, 125g	**3**
Jalfrezi Curry Paste, 1 serving, 30g	**3**
Karai Cooking Sauce, ¼ jar, 125g	**3**
Kashmiri Masala Curry Paste, 1 serving, 30g	**3**
Kashmiri Rogan Josh, ⅓ jar, 140g	**4**
Keralan Cashew & Chilli Masala, 1 serving, 140g	**5**
Korma Cooking Sauce, ¼ jar, 125g	**6**
Korma Curry Paste, 1 serving, 30g	**1**
Madras Cooking Sauce, ¼ jar, 125g	**3**
Madras Curry Paste, 1 serving, 30g	**2**
Madras Medium Hot, ⅓ jar, 94g	**3**

Mild Curry Paste, 1 serving, 30g	**2**
Pasanda Cooking Sauce, ¼ jar, 125g	**4**
Punjabi Saag Masala, ¼ jar, 106g	**3**
Rogan Josh Curry Paste, 1 serving, 30g	**2**
Rogan Josh Medium Hot Sauce, ¼ jar, 125g	**2**
Tandoori Curry Paste, 1 serving, 30g	**1**
Tikka Curry Paste, 1 serving, 30g	**1**
Tikka Masala Curry Paste, 1 serving, 30g	**2**
Tikka Masala Medium Sauce, ¼ jar, 125g	**3**
Vindaloo Curry Paste, 1 serving, 30g	**2**
Vindaloo Cooking Sauce, Hot, ¼ jar, 125g	**3**

Sainsbury's – Be Good To Yourself

Balti Cooking Sauce, ⅓ jar, 139g	**3**
Dopiaza Cooking Sauce, 1 serving, 126g	**2**
Korma Cooking Sauce, ¼ jar, 125g	**3**
Madras Cooking Sauce, 1 serving, 125g	**2**
Rogan Josh Cooking Sauce, 1 serving, 126g	**2**
Tikka Masala Cooking Sauce, ¼ jar, 125g	**3**

Sharwood's

Balanced Living Hot Madras, ¼ jar, 105g	**2**
Balti Cooking Sauce, 1 portion, 100g	**3**
Balti Paste, Medium, 1 serving, 20g	**3**
Bhuna Cooking Sauce, ⅓ jar, 139g	**3**
Biryani Coconut & Curry Leaf Spice & Sauce Mild, 1 serving, 144g	**2**
Biryani Mint & Coriander Spice & Sauce Medium, 1 serving, 144g	**2**
Biryani Tomato & Cumin Spice & Sauce Medium, 1 serving, 144g	**2**
Bundh Oven Sauce Achari, ⅓ jar, 140g	**5**
Bundh Oven Sauce Kashmiri, ⅓ jar, 140g	**4**
Bundh Oven Sauce Pasanda, ⅓ jar, 140g	**6**
Bundh Oven Sauce Tandoori, ⅓ jar, 140g	**5**
Dhansak Sauce, ¼ jar, 105g	**3**
Dopiaza Sauce, ⅓ jar, 139g	**3**
Jalfrezi Cooking Sauce, ⅓ jar, 139g	**4**
Kashmiri Korma, ½ jar, 150g	**6**
Korma Cooking Sauce, ⅓ jar, 139g	**6**
Korma Curry Paste, 1 serving, 20g	**2**
Lighter Balti Medium Cooking Sauce, ⅓ jar, 140g	**2**
Lighter Korma Sauce, ½ jar, 210g	**5**
Lighter Tikka Masala Cooking Sauce, ⅓ jar, 139g	**3**
Madras Cooking Sauce, ⅓ jar, 139g	**4**
Madras Curry Paste, 1 serving, 30g	**4**
Makhani Indian Cooking Sauce, Mild Medium, ¼ jar, 105g	**3**

Mughlai Tikka, ½ jar, 150g	5
Nepalese Hariyo Masala, ½ jar, 190g	5
Nepalese Lasoon Masala, ½ jar, 190g	4
Rogan Josh Cooking Sauce, ⅓ jar, 139g	4
Rogan Josh Curry Paste, 1 serving, 20g	2
Saag Masala Cooking Sauce, Medium, ¼ jar, 105g	3
Spicy Mango Coating Sauce, ½ pouch, 60g	1
Spicy Tikka Masala Cooking Sauce, ⅓ jar, 139g	4
Tandoori Coating Sauce, ½ pouch, 60g	1
Tikka Masala Cooking Sauce, ⅓ jar, 139g	5
Tikka Masala Paste, Medium, 1 serving, 20g	2

Tesco

Balti Cooking Sauce, ⅓ jar, 166g	3
Dopiaza Cooking Sauce, ⅓ jar, 166g	2
Jalfrezi Cooking Sauce, ⅓ jar, 166g	4
Korma Cooking Sauce, ⅓ jar, 166g	6
Madras Cooking Sauce, ⅓ jar, 166g	4
Rogan Josh Cooking Sauce, ⅓ jar, 166g	3
Tikka Masala Cooking Sauce, ⅓ jar, 166g	6

Tesco – Finest

Jalfrezi Sauce, ½ jar, 175g	4
Laksa Curry Sauce, ½ jar, 175g	5
Royal Korma Sauce, ½ jar, 175g	7
Tikka Masala Sauce, ½ jar, 175g	5

The Co-operative

Balti Cook In Sauce, ½ jar, 225g	6
Jalfrezi Cook in Sauce, ½ jar, 225g	4
Korma Cook in Sauce, ½ jar, 225g	10
Korma Cook in Sauce, Reduced Fat, ½ jar, 225g	6
Madras Cook in Sauce, ½ jar, 225g	7
Rogan Josh Cook in Sauce, ½ jar, 225g	4
Tikka Masala Cook in Sauce, ½ jar, 225g	8
Tikka Masala Cook in Sauce, Reduced Fat, ½ jar, 225g	4

Uncle Ben's

Balti Sauce, ¼ jar, 125g	3
Indian Korma Cooking Sauce, ¼ jar, 122g	5
Indian Medium Curry Sauce, ¼ jar, 125g	3
Indian Mild Curry Sauce, ¼ jar, 125g	2
Indian Tikka Masala Sauce, ¼ jar, 125g	3
Jalfrezi Sauce, ¼ jar, 125g	3
Madras Sauce, 1 serving, 125g	3
Rogan Josh, 1 serving, 100g	3

Waitrose

Goan Cooking Sauce, ¼ jar, 88g	6

Kashmiri Cooking Sauce, ¼ jar, 88g	5
Korma Cooking Sauce, ¼ jar, 88g	5
Pasanda Cooking Sauce, ¼ jar, 88g	6
Patia Cooking Sauce, ¼ jar, 88g	4
Tikka Sauce, ¼ jar, 88g	4

Weight Watchers

Korma Sauce with Flaked Almonds, ½ jar, 175g	3
Tikka Masala Sauce with Coriander, ½ jar, 175g	3

Italian & Pasta

Asda

Bolognese Sauce Mix, ¼ pack, 11g	1
Cheese & Bacon Pasta Bake, ¼ jar, 120g	5
Chow Mein Stir Fry Sauce, ½ jar, 98g	3
Creamy Mushroom Pasta Bake, ¼ pack, 119g	3
Creamy Tomato Pasta Bake Sauce, ¼ jar, 125g	5
Italian Beef Bolognese, ¼ portion, 125g	2
Italian Carbonara Sauce, ½ pot, 125g	7
Italian Cheese & Bacon Sauce, ¼ pot, 125g	3
Italian Creamy Tomato Sauce, ¼ pot, 125g	2
Italian Four Cheese Sauce, ½ pot, 175g	7
Italian Spicy Tomato & Pepper Sauce, ¼ pot, 125g	1
Italian White Sauce, ¼ pot, 125g	2
Red Pepper & Italian Cheese Stir Through Pasta Sauce, ½ jar, 95g	2
Tomato & Olive Stir Through Pasta Sauce, ½ jar, 95g	3

Asda – Chosen by You

Arrabbiata Sauce, Fresh, ½ pot, 175g	2
Carbonara Pasta Sauce, ½ pot, 155g	6
Four Cheese Sauce, ½ pot, 175g	6

Asda – Extra Special

Vine Ripened Tomato & Chilli Pasta Sauce, 1 serving, 113g	5
Vine Ripened Tomato & Mascarpone Pasta Sauce, 1 serving, 113g	4
Vine Ripened Tomato & Pancetta Pasta Sauce, 1 serving, 113g	5

Asda – Good For You

Carbonara Sauce, ½ pot, 175g	3
Creamy Mushroom Pasta Sauce, ¼ jar, 124g	2
Smokey Tomato & Pepper Sauce, ½ pot, 175g	2

Tomato & Mascarpone Pasta Sauce,
½ jar, 160g **2**

Bertolli

Basil Pasta Sauce Pouch, ¼ pouch, 112g **1**
Chilli & Sweet Pepper Pasta Sauce, ¼ jar, 125g **2**
Creamy Pasta Sauce Pouch, ¼ pouch, 112g **2**
Garlic Pasta Sauce Pouch, ¼ pouch, 112g **2**
Green Pesto Sauce, 2 tablespoons, 30g **5**
Grilled Vegetable Pasta Sauce, ¼ jar, 125g **2**
Mushroom & Roasted Garlic Pasta Sauce,
¼ jar, 125g **2**
Mushroom & Roasted Garlic Sauce,
3 tablespoons, 45g **1**
Original Pasta Sauce Pouch, ¼ pouch, 112g **1**
Red Pesto Sauce, 2 tablespoons, 30g **7**
Rustico Mediterranean Vegetable Sauce,
¼ jar, 80g **2**
Rustico Olives & Capers, ¼ jar, 80g **2**
Rustico Sweet Chilli & Red Onion, ¼ jar, 80g **2**
Spicy Pasta Sauce Pouch, ¼ pouch, 112g **1**
Sun-Dried Tomato & Oregano Pasta Sauce,
¼ jar, 125g **2**
Sweet Red & Yellow Pepper Sauce, ½ jar, 160g **4**
Tomato & Basil Sauce, ¼ jar, 125g **1**

Colman's

Creamy Cheese & Bacon Pasta Sauce Mix,
¼ sachet, 12g **1**
Creamy Pepper & Mushroom Sauce Mix,
¼ sachet, 6g **1**
Easy Lasagne Recipe Mix, 1 pack, 46g **4**
Spaghetti Bolognese Recipe Mix, ¼ sachet, 11g **1**
Spaghetti Bolognese with Mushrooms Sauce
Mix, ¼ sachet, 11g **1**
Tomato, Ham & Cheese Pasta Bake Recipe
Mix, 1 pack, 49g **4**
Tuna & Pasta Bake Mix, ¼ sachet, 11g **1**

Crosse & Blackwell

Cheesy Bacon Pasta Bake, ¼ jar, 125g **3**
Tomato & Herb Bolognese Sauce, ¼ jar, 125g **3**
Tomato & Herb Pasta Bake, ¼ jar, 125g **3**
Tomato & Mushroom Bolognese Sauce,
¼ jar, 125g **3**

Dolmio

Arrabbiata Sauce, ¼ jar, 125g **3**
Bolognese Sauce Extra Chunky Sweet Pepper,
¼ jar, 125g **2**
Bolognese Sauce Extra Chunky Winter
Vegetables, ¼ jar, 125g **2**

Bolognese Sauce, Extra Mushroom,
⅙ large jar, 124g **2**
Bolognese Sauce, Extra Onion & Garlic,
¼ jar, 125g **2**
Bolognese Sauce, Extra Spicy, ¼ jar, 125g **2**
Creamy Carbonara Pasta Bake, ¼ jar, 120g **4**
Creamy Tomato Pasta Bake, ¼ jar, 125g **4**
Original Light Sauce for Bolognese, ¼ jar, 125g **1**
Red Sauce for Lasagne, ⅙ large jar, 118g **2**
Red Sauce for Lasagne, ¼ jar, 125g **2**
Roasted Mediterranean Vegetable Pasta
Bake, ¼ jar, 125g **2**
Taste of Calabria Spicy Pepperoni & Tomato
Pasta Sauce, ½ jar, 175g **5**
Taste of Rome Creamy Tomato & Ricotta Pasta
Sauce, ½ jar, 175g **5**
Taste of Sicily Tomato, Basil & Garlic Pasta
Sauce, ¼ jar, 88g **2**
Taste of Sorrento Cherry Tomato & Parmesan
Pasta Sauce, ½ jar, 175g **5**
Taste of Summer Stir-in Cherry Tomato &
Pesto, ½ jar, 75g **2**
Taste of Summer Stir-in Spicy Tomato &
Sweet Onion, ½ jar, 75g **2**
Taste of Tuscany Tomato & Chianti Pasta
Sauce, ½ jar, 175g **3**
Tomato & Cheese Pasta Bake, ¼ jar, 125g **2**
White Sauce for Lasagne, ⅙ large jar, 118g **3**

Dolmio – Express

Creamy Carbonara Pasta Sauce, 1 pouch, 150g **7**
Creamy Mushroom Pasta Sauce,
1 pouch, 170g **5**
Minced Beef Bolognese Sauce, 1 pouch, 170g **4**
Minced Beef Bolognese with Extra Mushroom,
1 pouch, 170g **4**
Minced Beef Bolognese with Extra Onion &
Garlic, 1 pouch, 170g **4**
Spicy Italian Chilli Pasta Sauce, 1 pouch, 170g **2**
Sun-Ripened Tomato & Basil Pasta Sauce,
1 pouch, 170g **2**

Homepride

Pasta Bake, Cheese & Bacon, ¼ jar, 125g **2**
Pasta Bake, Creamy Carbonara, ¼ jar, 125g **4**
Pasta Bake, Creamy Tomato & Bacon,
¼ jar, 125g **3**
Pasta Bake, Creamy Tomato & Herb,
¼ jar, 125g **4**
Pasta Bake, Four Cheese, ¼ jar, 125g **3**
Pasta Bake, Mediterranean Vegetable with
Crunch Topping, ¼ jar, 134g **3**

Pasta Bake, Spicy Tomato & Pepperoni,
¼ jar, 125g **3**
Pasta Bake, Tomato & Mild Chilli, ¼ jar, 134g **2**
Pasta Bake, Tomato & Red Pepper, ¼ jar, 134g **3**
Pasta Bake, Tuna, ¼ jar, 125g **3**
Pasta Stir, Tomato & Bacon, ¼ jar, 88g **2**
Pasta Stir, Tomato & Basil, ½ jar, 175g **3**

Loyd Grossman

Bolognese Pasta Sauce, ⅓ jar, 140g **3**
Bolognese with Garden Vegetables,¼ jar, 165g **5**
Bolognese with Mushrooms, ¼ large jar, 165g **2**
Bolognese with Pancetta, ¼ large jar, 165g **4**
Bolognese with Roasted Garlic, ¼ large jar, 165g **2**
Carbonara with Smoked Pancetta Pasta
Sauce, ¼ jar, 85g **3**
For One Carbonara Pasta Sauce, 1 serving 150g **5**
For One Puttanesca Pasta Sauce,
1 serving 150g **3**
For One Tomato & Basil Pasta Sauce,
1 serving 150g **3**
For One Tomato & Chilli Pasta Sauce,
1 serving 150g **3**
For One Tomato & Smoky Bacon Pasta Sauce,
1 serving 150g **4**
Primavera Pasta Sauce, ¼ jar, 88g **2**
Puttanesca Pasta Sauce, ¼ jar, 88g **2**
Sardinian Style Tomato & Salami Sauce,
¼ jar, 88g **2**
Sicilian Style Sun-Dried Tomato & Almond,
¼ jar, 88g **2**
Sicilian Style Sun-Dried Tomato, Garlic & Basil
Sauce, ¼ jar, 88g **2**
Sicilian Style Tomato & Chilli Sauce, ¼ jar, 88g **2**
Smoky Bacon Pasta Sauce, ¼ jar, 88g **2**
Stir-In Carbonara, ¼ jar, 45g **2**
Stir-In Sun-Dried Tomato with Olive & Lemon,
¼ jar, 45g **1**
Stir-In Tomato & Basil, ¼ jar, 45g **2**
Stir-In Tomato & Pancetta, ¼ jar, 45g **1**
Stir-In Tomato & Sun-Dried Vegetables,
¼ jar, 45g **1**
Sweet Pepper Pasta Sauce, ¼ jar, 88g **2**
Tomato & Basil Pasta Sauce, ¼ jar, 88g **2**
Tomato & Chargrilled Vegetables Pasta Sauce,
¼ jar, 88g **2**
Tomato & Chilli Pasta Sauce, ¼ jar, 88g **2**
Tomato & Mascarpone with Vodka Pasta
Sauce, ¼ jar, 88g **3**
Tomato & Red Wine Pasta Sauce, ¼ jar, 88g **2**
Tomato & Roasted Garlic Pasta Sauce,
¼ jar, 88g **2**

Tomato & Sweet Red Pepper Pasta Sauce,
¼ jar, 88g **2**
Tomato & Wild Mushroom Sauce, ⅓ jar, 116g **3**

Morrisons

Bolognese Sauce, ½ pot, 175g **4**
Tomato & Smoked Bacon Pasta Sauce,
½ pot, 175g **2**
White Lasagne Sauce, ¼ jar, 109g **3**

Morrisons – Eat Smart

Pasta Sauce, ¼ jar, 125g **1**
Roasted Vegetable Pasta Sauce, ½ pot, 175g **2**
Tomato & Mascarpone Sauce, ½ pot, 175g **4**

Newman's Own

Hot & Spicy Pasta Sauce, ¼ jar, 110g **2**
Roasted Garlic & Peppers Pasta Sauce,
¼ jar, 110g **2**
Tomatoes, Peppers & Spice Pasta Sauce,
¼ jar, 110g **2**

Ragu

Basil & Oregano Sauce, ¼ jar, 125g **1**
Bolognese Sauce, ¼ jar, 125g **1**
Light White Lasagne Sauce, ¼ jar, 122g **2**
Onion & Roasted Garlic Sauce, ¼ jar, 125g **1**
Original Bolognese Sauce, ¼ jar, 125g **1**
Red Lasagne Sauce, ¼ jar, 125g **2**
Red Wine & Herb Sauce, ¼ jar, 125g **1**
Red Wine & Herbs for Bolognese, ¼ jar, 125g **1**
Traditional or Spicy Bolognese Sauce,
¼ jar, 125g **2**
Traditional Pasta Sauce, ¼ jar, 128g **2**
White Lasagne Sauce, ¼ jar, 120g **5**

Sacla

Chargrilled Aubergine Pesto, ¼ jar, 48g **5**
Classic Basil Pesto, 1 serving, 20g **3**
Coriander Pesto, ¼ jar, 48g **6**
Creamy Vine-Ripened Tomato Pesto,
1 serving, 20g **2**
Olive & Tomato, ½ jar, 95g **5**
Roasted Red Pepper Pesto, ¼ jar, 48g **3**
Salsa Rossa, ½ jar, 95g **9**
Salsa Verde, ½ jar, 95g **9**
Spicy Pepper & Tomato, ½ jar, 95g **4**
Sun-Dried Tomato & Garlic, ½ jar, 95g **4**
Sun-Dried Tomato Pesto, ¼ jar, 48g **4**
Sun-Dried Tomato Pesto, ¼ large jar, 72g **6**
Vine Ripened Tomato & Chilli Pepper, ½ jar, 95g **8**
Vine Ripened Tomato & Mascarpone, ½ jar, 95g **5**

Sacla – Sauce For Pasta

Whole Cherry Tomato & Basil, ½ jar, 145g	6
Whole Cherry Tomato & Chilli, ½ jar, 145g	6
Whole Cherry Tomato & Parmesan Sauce, ½ jar, 145g	5
Whole Cherry Tomato & Roasted Vegetables, ½ jar, 145g	4

Sacla – Stir Through Pasta Sauce

Italian Tomato & Chilli Intense Paste, ¼ jar, 48g	5
Italian Red Onion & Gorgonzola, ¼ jar, 48g	3
Oven Roasted Tomato & Rocket, 1 serving, 20g	1

Sainsbury's

Beef Bolognese Sauce, ¼ pot, 125g	3
Carbonara Sauce, ¼ large pot, 150g	5
Carbonara Sauce, ½ small pot, 175g	6
Chunky Vegetable Pasta Sauce, ¼ jar, 125g	2
Green Pesto, 1 serving, 30g	3
Light Tomato & Herb Pasta Sauce, ¼ jar, 125g	1
Mushroom Pasta Sauce, ¼ jar, 125g	2
Red Pesto, ¼ jar, 48g	6
Spicy Pepper Pasta Sauce, ¼ jar, 125g	2
Sugocasa with Herbs, ¼ jar, 175g	2

Sainsbury's – Be Good To Yourself

Carbonara Sauce, ⅓ jar, 132g	3
Green Pesto, ¼ jar, 48g	2
Pesto, 1 serving, 30g	2

Schwartz

Bacon & Mushroom Tagliatelle Recipe Mix, ¼ sachet, 8g, unprepared	1
Chargrilled Chicken Pasta Recipe Mix, ¼ sachet, 8g, unprepared	1
Chicken & Leek Bake Recipe Mix, ¼ sachet, 8g, unprepared	1
Spaghetti Bolognese Recipe Mix, ¼ sachet, 8g, unprepared	1
Spaghetti Carbonara Recipe Mix, ¼ sachet, 8g, unprepared	1
Tuna & Mushroom Pasta Melt, ¼ sachet, 8g, unprepared	1

Tesco

Carbonara Sauce, ½ tub, 175g	5
Chunky Vegetable Pasta Sauce, ¼ jar, 125g	5
Creamy Tomato & Herb Pasta Bake Sauce, 1 serving, 125g	4
Light Choices Pasta Sauce, ¼ jar, 125g	1
Mushroom Pasta Sauce, ¼ jar, 125g	2
Onion & Garlic Pasta Sauce, 1 serving, 125g	2
Original Pasta Sauce, 1 serving, 125g	2
Spicy Pepper Pasta Sauce, 1 serving, 125g	2
Spicy Tomato & Pepperoni Pasta Bake, 1 serving, 125g	3
Tomato & Chargrilled Vegetable Pasta Sauce, 1 serving, 85g	2
Tomato & Olive Pasta Sauce, 1 serving, 125g	2
Tomato & Pancetta Pasta Sauce, 1 serving, 85g	3
Trattoria Verdi Mushroom Pasta Sauce, 1 serving, 125g	1
Trattoria Verdi Tomato & Herb Sauce, 1 serving, 125g	1
Tuna & Sweetcorn Pasta Bake, 1 serving, 125g	2
White Lasagne Pasta Sauce, 1 serving, 107g	3

Tesco – Finest

Pesto Rosso, 1 serving, (¼ pack), 48g	5
Puttanesca Pasta Sauce, ¼ jar, 85g	3
Sun-Dried Tomato, Garlic & Basil Pasta Sauce, ¼ jar, 85g	3
Tomato & Chargrilled Vegetable Pasta Sauce, ¼ jar, 85g	2
Tomato & Mascarpone Pasta Sauce, 1 serving, 85g	4
Tomato & Mushroom Pasta Sauce, 1 serving, 85g	2
Tomato & Mushroom Pasta Sauce, ¼ jar, 85g	2
Tomato & Pancetta Pasta Sauce, ¼ jar, 85g	3
Whole Cherry Tomato & Chilli Pasta Sauce, ¼ jar, 85g	2

The Co-operative

Chunky Vegetable Pasta Sauce, ¼ jar, 128g	2
Italian Pesto Sauce, ¼ jar, 48g	4
Healthy Living Tomato & Herb Pasta Sauce, ¼ jar, 125g	1
Mushroom Pasta Sauce, ¼ jar, 129g	2
Pasta Sauce Carbonara, ½ jar, 168g	7
Sun-Dried Tomato & Basil Pasta Sauce, ⅓ jar, 112g	3
Tomato & Garlic Pasta Sauce, ¼ jar, 125g	2
Tomato & Herb Pasta Sauce, ¼ jar, 126g	2
Tomato & Mascarpone Pasta Sauce, ⅓ jar, 112g	4
Tomato & Olive Pasta Sauce, ⅓ jar, 112g	3

Weight Watchers®
Cooking Sauces

a must for your shopping list

A tasty lunch or dinner is hassle-free with our range of sauces. Simply cook with meat, vegetables, pasta or rice for a tasty, quick and delicious meal.

1 ProPoints value *to* **3** ProPoints value

per half jar

12 delicious sauces including:
Bolognese & Red Wine, White Lasagne, Red Lasagne, Mozzarella & Rocket, Korma, Tikka Masala, Sweet & Sour and Chilli Con Carne

WeightWatchers Foods
Eat gorgeous. Feel gorgeous.

Waitrose

Arrabbiata Pasta Sauce, ½ jar, 175g	3
Beef & Red Wine Ragu Sauce, 1 pack, 300g	8
Bolognese Sauce, ½ tub, 175g	4
Carbonara Sauce, ½ tub, 175g	8
Chianti & Olive Sauce, 1 jar, 300g	7
Mediterranean Vegetable Sauce, ½ jar, 175g	3
Napoletana, 1 jar, 320g	6
Mushroom & Madeira Sauce, ½½ pot, 150g	6
Puttanesca Pasta Sauce, ½ jar, 175g	5
Roasted Pepper & Goat's Cheese Sauce, ½ pot, 150g	2
Tomato & Basil Sauce, ¼ jar, 125g	2
Tomato & Chilli Sauce, ½ jar, 175g	3

Weight Watchers

Parmesan & Pesto Pasta Sauce, ½ jar, 175g	2
Roasted Garlic Pasta Sauce, ½ jar, 175g	2

Mexican, Tex Mex & Caribbean

Asda

BBQ Marinade, 1 tablespoon, 15g	1
Jerk Seasoning, 2 teaspoons, 10g	1
Piri Piri Marinade, 2 tablespoons, 30g	1

Colman's

Casserole Sauce Mix, Hot Chilli con Carne, ¼ packet, 10g	1
Chilli con Carne Mix, ¼ packet, 12g	1

Discovery Foods

Buffalo Wings Sauce, ¼ jar, 74g	2
Cajun Season & Sauce, ⅓ jar, 127g	2
Chili con Carne Seasoning Mix, ⅛ sachet, 4g	0
Chilli Season & Sauce, ⅓ jar, 127g	3
Creole Season & Sauce, ⅓ jar, 127g	2
Enchilada Season & Sauce, ¼ jar, 88g	1
Hot Fajita Seasoning Paste, 1 serving, 25g	1
Medium Fajita Seasoning Mix, ⅛ sachet, 4g	0
Medium Fajita Season & Sauce, ⅓ jar, 127g	2
Mild Fajita Season & Sauce, ¼ jar, 96g	2
Mild Fajita Seasoning Paste, 1 serving, 25g	1
Nacho Cheese Sauce, 1 serving, 75g	3
Red Jalapeños, ⅛ jar, 25g	1
Salsa – Hot, 1 serving, 37.5g	1
Salsa – Medium, 1 serving, 37.5g	1
Smooth Salsa – Mild, 1 serving, 37.5g	1

Soured Cream Topping, 1 serving, 35g	2
Stick Ribs Sauce, ¼ jar, 81g	4

Homepride

Chilli Cook-in-Sauce, ¼ can, 125g	2
Chilli Rich & Warming Cook-in-Sauce, ¼ jar, 125g	2
Smoky Barbecue Cook-in-Sauce, ¼ jar, 125g	4

Knorr

Californian Style Lemon Pepper, Jamaican Jerk or Mexican Fajita, ⅓ jar, 24g	4
Texan Barbecue, ⅓ jar, 26g	5

Knorr – Sizzle & Stir

Chilli con Carne, Medium, ¼ jar, 114g	4
Sizzle & Stir Chilli con Carne Medium Sauce, ¼ jar, 114g	4
Stir It Up Barbeque Sauce, ½ jar, 40g	7
Stir It Up Jamaican Jerk Sauce, ¼ jar, 20g	4
Stir It Up Mexican Fajita Sauce, ½ jar, 40g	7

Levi Roots

Caribbean Curry Sauce Mild, ¼ jar, 88g	3
Coconut Rundown Sauce, ¼ jar, 88g	2
Jamaican Brown Stew Sauce, ¼ jar, 88g	3
Reggae Reggae Cooking Sauce, ¼ jar, 88g	3
Reggae Reggae Sauce Jerk/BBQ, ¼ jar, 78g	3
Twangy Escoveitch Sauce, ¼ jar, 88g	3

Old El Paso

Hot Taco Salsa, Smooth, 1 serving, 50g	1
Spice Mix for Chilli, ¼ sachet, 10g	1
Spice Mix for Fajitas, Roasted Tomato & Peppers, ¼ sachet, 9g	1
Spice Mix for Original Beef Tacos, 1 portion, 3g	0
Spice Mix for Original Smoky BBQ Fajitas, 1 serving, 4g	0

Schwartz

Americano Spicy Meatballs Recipe Mix, 1 sachet, 25g	2
Cajun Chicken Recipe Mix, 1 sachet, 38g	3
Cajun Rice with Beef Mix, 1 sachet, 35g	2
Cajun Wedges Coating, 1 sachet, 38g	2
Chicken Fajitas Recipe Mix, 1 sachet, 35g	3
Chilli con Carne Recipe Mix, 1 sachet, 41g	3
Heat & Pour Barbecue Sauce, 1 sachet, 170g	3
Hot Chilli con Carne Recipe Mix, ¼ sachet, 10g	1
Jamaican Jerk Chicken Recipe Mix, 1 sachet, 27g	3

Tex-Mex Chilli con Carne Recipe Mix,
1 sachet, 35g **4**

Tesco

Chilli con Carne Mix, ¼ sachet, 10g **1**
Mexican Chilli Cooking Sauce, Hot or Mild,
¼ jar, 140g **2**
Sticky Barbecue Marinade, 1 serving, 72g **2**

Uncle Ben's

Medium Chilli Sauce, ¼ jar, 125g **2**
Mexican Cajun, Medium, ¼ jar, 125g **2**
Mexican Chunky Salsa, 1 jar, 100g **1**
Mexican Sauce for Chilli con Carne, Hot,
Medium or Mild, ¼ jar, 125g **2**
Mexican Texan Barbecue with Red Peppers
Mild, ¼ jar, 125g **5**

Weight Watchers

Chilli con Carne Sauce with Jalapeños,
½ jar, 175g **2**

Traditional & Other Recipes

Asda

5 Minute Moroccan Style Marinade,
½ pack, 50ml **2**
Bourguignon Casserole Sauce Mix, ¼ pack, 11g **1**
Bourguignon Cooking Sauce, ¼ jar, 138g **2**
Bread Simmer Sauce Mix, 1 serving, 171g **4**
Chasseur Cooking Sauce, ¼ jar, 140g **2**
Cheese Sauce Mix, ⅓ packet, 66g **10**
Chicken Casserole Sauce Mix, 1 serving, 40g **3**
Chicken Chasseur Casserole Mix,
¼ sachet, 19g **2**
Fresh Creamy Peppercorn Sauce, ½ tub, 150g **7**
Fresh Lemon & Dill Sauce, ½ pot, 150g **7**
Peppercorn Sauce, ½ pouch, 125g **4**
Red Wine & Rosemary Gravy, ⅙ pot, 77g **1**
Simply Cheese Sauce, Fresh, ¼ pot, 125g **3**

Asda – Extra Special

Fish Pie Sauce, ¼ jar, 85g **2**
Hollandaise Sauce, ¼ pot, 50g **5**
Spanish Style Roasted Pepper & Smoked
Paprika Cooking Sauce, ¼ pack, 88g **1**

Bisto

Cheese Sauce, (1 packet, 6g), prepared, 50ml **1**
Classic Chicken & Tomato Cooking Sauce,
¼ jar, 125g **1**
Country Vegetable Chicken Cooking Sauce,
¼ jar, 125g **1**
Cumberland Sausage & Onion Casserole
Sauce, ¼ jar, 125g **1**
Irish Stew Cooking Sauce, ¼ jar, 125g **1**
Lancashire Hotpot Cooking Sauce, ¼ jar, 125g **1**
Parsley Sauce, (1 packet, 6g), prepared, 50ml **1**
Rich Beef & Ale Cooking Sauce, ¼ jar, 125g **1**
White Sauce, (1 packet, 6g), prepared, 50ml **1**

Colman's

Beef & Ale Flavour Casserole Sauce,
¼ pack, 11g, prepared **1**
Beef & Red Wine Sauce, ¼ pack, 11g, prepared **1**
Beef Bourguignon Mix, ¼ sachet, 10g, prepared **1**
Beef Stroganoff Mix, ¼ sachet, 10g, prepared **1**
Bread Sauce Mix, ¼ sachet, 11g, prepared **2**
Casserole Sauce Mix, Mexican Fajita,
¼ sachet, 10g **1**
Casserole Sauce Mix, Red Wine & Garlic,
¼ sachet, 10g **1**
Casserole Sauce Mix, Chicken Chasseur,
¼ sachet, 11g **1**
Casserole Sauce Mix, Creamy Chicken Curry,
¼ sachet, 13g **1**
Casserole Sauce Mix, Honey Chicken,
¼ sachet, 13g **1**
Casserole Sauce Mix, Macaroni Cheese,
¼ sachet, 10g **1**
Casserole Sauce Mix, Southern Fried Nuggets,
¼ sachet, 11g **1**
Casserole Sauce Mix, Tomato Bake,
¼ sachet, 10g **1**
Cheddar Cheese Sauce Mix, 1 serving, 85ml **2**
Chicken & Potato Roast Recipe Mix,
1 pack, 25g **1**
Chicken Mozzarella Pasta Bake Mix,
¼ sachet, 12g **1**
Chicken Supreme Sauce Mix, ¼ sachet, 10g **1**
Cottage Pie Recipe, ¼ sachet, 11g **1**
Easy Chicken & Mushroom Pie Recipe Mix,
¼ sachet, 11g **1**
Easy Steak & Ale Pie Recipe Mix, ¼ sachet, 11g **1**
Four Cheese Sauce Mix, 1 serving, 85ml **2**
Hollandaise Sauce Mix, 1 serving, 85ml **3**
Honey Chicken Stir Fry Recipe Mix,
¼ sachet, 13g **1**

Hunter's BBQ Chicken Recipe Mix, ¼ sachet, 11g	1
Lamb Hotpot Sauce Mix, ¼ sachet, 10g	1
Liver & Bacon Casserole Mix, ¼ sachet, 10g	1
Onion Sauce Mix, 1 serving, 80ml	2
Parsley Sauce Mix, 1 serving, 80ml	1
Pepper Sauce Mix, 1 serving, 80ml	2
Pork Casserole Sauce, 1 portion, 78g	7
Red Wine & Garlic Casserole Sauce Mix, ¼ sachet, 10g	1
Sauce for Swedish Style Meatballs, ¼ sachet, 10g	1
Sausage Casserole Sauce Mix, ¼ sachet, 10g	1
Savoury White Sauce Mix, 1 serving, 80ml	2
Shepherd's Pie Mix, ¼ sachet, 12g	1
Spaghetti Bolognese Sauce Mix, ¼ sachet, 10g	1
Special Cheddar Cheese Pour Over Sauce Mix, 1 serving, 80ml	2
Special Hollandaise Pour Over Sauce, Ready to Use, ¼ carton, 50ml	3
Special Luxury Mushroom Sauce Mix, ¼ sachet, 10g	1
Special Luxury Peppercorn Pour Over Sauce, ½ sachet, 11g	1
Special Parsley & Lemon Pour Over Sauce, Ready to Use, ¼ carton, 50ml	2
Special Cracked Peppercorn & Cream Sauce, 1 serving, 100ml	4
Turkey Casserole Mix, ¼ sachet, 12g	1

Crosse & Blackwell

Bonne Cuisine Béchamel Sauce Mix, ¼ sachet, 75ml	1
Bonne Cuisine Hollandaise Sauce Mix, ¼ sachet, 75ml	3
Bonne Cuisine White Wine Gravy Mix, ¼ sachet, 75ml	1

Homepride

Barbecue, ¼ can, 125g	3
Beef Bourguignon, ¼ jar, 125g	1
Beef in Ale, ¼ jar, 125g	2
Chasseur, ¼ jar, 125g	1
Chicken Provencal, ¼ jar, 125g	1
Chicken Supreme, ¼ jar, 125g	4
Classic Red Wine, ¼ jar, 125g	1
Classic White Wine & Cream, ¼ jar, 125g	3
Creamy Stroganoff, ¼ jar, 125g	3
Fred's Favourites Fish Pie, ¼ jar, 125g	3
Hot Pot, ¼ jar, 125g	1
Lamb & Rosemary Warming Casserole, ¼ jar, 125g	1

Potato Bake Cheese & Onion, ¼ jar, 125g	4
Potato Bake Creamy Cheese & Ham, ¼ jar, 125g	4
Potato Bake Creamy Leek, ¼ jar, 125g	3
Potato Bake Garlic & Herb, ¼ jar, 125g	4
Roast Chicken Hearty Casserole, ¼ jar, 125g	1
Sausage Casserole, ¼ jar, 125g	1
Shepherd's Pie, ¼ jar, 125g	1
Somerset Pork Light & Fruity Casserole, ¼ jar, 125g	2

Knorr

Cheese Sauce, dried, 1 pack, 33g	1
Mushroom Sauce, 1 serving, 75ml	2
Onion Sauce, 1 serving, 75ml	2
Sausages Tonight, Red Wine & Onion, ¼ jar, 125g	1
Sausages Tonight, Hearty Cumberland Sauce, ¼ jar, 125g	1
Sausages Tonight, Ranch Barbeque, ¼ jar, 130g	3
Select Sauces Hollandaise Cream Sauce, 1 serving, 63ml	5
Select Sauces Hot Pepper Cream Sauce, 1 serving, 63ml	1
Stir It Up Lemon Pepper Sauce, ¼ jar, 20g	4
Wild Mushroom Sauce, 1 serving, 63ml	1

Knorr – Chicken Tonight

Cherry Tomato, Red Chilli & Vodka Stir Fry Sauce, ¼ jar, 125g	3
Classic Chasseur Sauce, ¼ jar, 125g	2
Country French Sauce, ¼ jar, 125g	3
Creamy Mushroom Sauce, ¼ jar, 125g	3
Creamy Peppercorn Sauce, ¼ jar, 125g	3
Honey & Mustard Sauce, ¼ jar, 131g	4
Low Fat Country French Sauce, ¼ jar, 125g	2
Low Fat Creamy Mushroom, ¼ jar, 125g	2
Low Fat Honey & Mustard, ¼ jar, 131g	3
Spanish Chicken Sauce, ¼ jar, 125g	1

Loyd Grossman

Burgundy Red Wine Pour Over Sauce, ¼ pouch, 55g	1
Pour Over Chicken, Wholegrain Mustard Sauce, ½ pouch, 110g	3
Pour Over Steak, Green & Black Peppercorn Sauce, ½ pouch, 110g	2
Seasonal Tomato & Balsamic Vinegar, ¼ jar, 88g	2
Seasonal Tomato & Red Wine Sauce, ¼ jar, 88g	2

Nando's

Extra Hot Peri-Peri Sauce, 2 tablespoons, 30ml	1
Garlic Peri-Peri Sauce, 2 tablespoons, 30ml	1
Hot Peri-Peri Marinade, 1 serving, 40g	1
Hot Peri-Peri Sauce, 2 tablespoons, 30ml	4
Lime & Coriander Peri-Peri Marinade, 1 serving, 40g	1
Medium Garlic Peri-Peri Sauce, 1 serving, 30ml	1
Medium Peri-Peri BBQ Sauce, 1 serving, 30ml	1
Medium Wild Herb Peri-Peri Sauce, 1 serving, 30ml	1
Portuguese BBQ Peri-Peri Marinade, 1 serving, 40g	1
Smoky BBQ Peri-Peri Marinade, 1 serving, 40g	5
Sun-Dried Tomato & Basil Peri-Peri Marinade, 1 serving, 40g	1
Sweet & Sticky Peri-Peri Marinade, 1 serving, 40g	1

Sainsbury's

Cheese Sauce, ¼ pot, 125g	2
Hollandaise Sauce, ½ pack, 75g	10
White Sauce with Cheese, ½ jar, 200g	7
White Wine & Herb Fish Pie Sauce, ¼ pack, 125g	3

Sainsbury's – Inspired to... Cook

Create Casserole Cooking Sauce, 1 serving, 127g	1
Create Hollandaise Sauce, 1 serving, 75g	4
Create Marie Rose Sauce, 1 serving, 37g	2
Create Mexican Cooking Sauce, 1 serving, 123g	2
Create Peppercorn Sauce, 1 serving, 74g	2
Create Spicy Tomato, Coriander & Lime Sauce, 1 serving, 74g	1
Create Tomato & Herb Cooking Sauce, 1 serving, 124g	1
Create White Wine & Herb Cooking Sauce, 1 serving, 125g	3

Schwartz

3 Cheese Sauce Mix, ¼ sachet, 10g	1
Creamy Lemon & Parsley Sauce, ¼ pack, 75g	5
Creamy Mild Peppercorn Sauce Mix, ¼ sachet, 6g	1
Creamy Parsley Sauce Mix, ¼ sachet, 7g	1
Creamy Pepper Sauce Mix, ¼ sachet, 6g	1
Creamy Watercress & Stilton Sauce, ¼ pack, 75g	3

Creamy White Wine Sauce with Herbs, 1 pack, 26g	3
Flavourful Spicy Meatballs Recipe Mix with Herbs & Spices, 1 sachet, 25g	2
French White Wine & Tarragon Sauce, ¼ pack, 75g	4
Heat & Pour Creamy Pepper Sauce, 1 pack, 170g	3
Heat & Pour Honey & Mustard Sauce, 1 pack, 170g	5
Heat & Pour Mushroom Sauce, 1 pack, 170g	6
Lamb Casserole Recipe Mix, 1 sachet, 35g	3
Low Fat Chunky Tomato, Olive & Rosemary Sauce, ½ pouch, 150g	2
Low Fat Zesty Orange & Dill Sauce, ½ pouch, 150g	2
Luxury Bread Sauce, ½ sachet, 25g	2
Moroccan Lamb Casserole Recipe Mix, ¼ sachet, 9g	1
Parsley & Chive Sauce Mix, ¼ sachet, 10g	1
Sausage Casserole Recipe Mix, ¼ sachet, 9g	1
Tuna Napolitana Recipe Mix, ¼ sachet, 8g	1

Tesco

Chicken Casserole Mix, ¼ sachet, 10g	1
Fresh White Sauce, 1 serving, 150g	4
Moroccan Tagine Sauce, 1 serving, 116g	2
Sundried Tomato & Cinnamon Sauce, 1 serving, 116g	1
Tuna Pasta Bake Mix, ¼ sachet, 11g	1

Waitrose

Bread Sauce, ¼ pack, 75g	2
Four Cheese Sauce, ½ jar, 175g	7

Weight Watchers

Creamy Mushroom Sauce, ½ jar, 175g	2
Sausage Casserole Sauce with Tomatoes, Red Wine & Haricot Beans, ½ jar, 175g	2

Dairy Products

Basic Foods

Butter, 1 teaspoon, 5g	1
Butter, 1 restaurant portion, 10g	2
Butter, Half Fat, 1 teaspoon, 5g	1
Butter, Half Fat, 1 restaurant portion, 10g	1
Buttermilk, ½ pint, 284ml	3
Cheese Slice, 1 slice, 20g	2
Cheese Slice, Low Fat, 1 slice, 20g	1
Cheese Triangle, 1 piece, 14g	1
Cheese Triangle, Low Fat, 1 piece, 14g	1
Cheese, Austrian Smoked, 1 medium portion, 40g	3
Cheese, Brie, 1 medium portion, 40g	4
Cheese, Caerphilly, 1 medium portion, 40g	4
Cheese, Camembert, 1 medium portion, 40g	3
Cheese, Cheddar, 1 medium portion, 40g	5
Cheese, Cheddar, Half Fat, 1 medium portion, 40g	3
Cheese, Cheshire, 1 medium portion, 40g	4
Cheese, Chevre Blanc, 1 medium portion, 40g	3
Cheese, Cottage Cheese, Plain, 1 small tub, 110g	3
Cheese, Cottage Cheese, Plain, Reduced Fat, 1 small tub, 110g	2
Cheese, Cream, 1 medium portion, 40g	5
Cheese, Dolcelatte, 1 medium portion, 40g	4
Cheese, Double Gloucester, 1 medium portion, 40g	4
Cheese, Edam, 1 medium portion, 40g	4
Cheese, Emmental, 1 medium portion, 40g	4
Cheese, Feta, 1 medium portion, 40g	3
Cheese, Goat's, 1 medium portion, 40g	3
Cheese, Goat's, Soft, Medium Fat, ½ small tub, 50g	4
Cheese, Gouda, 1 medium portion, 40g	4
Cheese, Gruyère, 1 medium portion, 40g	4
Cheese, Halloumi, 1 medium portion, 40g	4
Cheese, Halloumi Light, 1 medium portion, 40g	3
Cheese, Lancashire, 1 medium portion, 40g	4
Cheese, Lymeswold, 1 medium portion, 40g	5
Cheese, Mascarpone, 1 medium portion, 40g	5
Cheese, Mozzarella, 1 medium portion, 40g	3
Cheese, Mozzarella Light, 1 medium portion, 40g	2
Cheese, Paneer, Full Fat, 1 portion, 50g	5
Cheese, Parmesan, 1 tablespoon, 15g	2
Cheese, Port Salut, 1 medium portion, 40g	4
Cheese, Red Leicester, 1 medium portion, 40g	4
Cheese, Red Leicester, Half Fat, 1 medium portion, 40g	2
Cheese, Ricotta, 1 medium portion, 40g	2
Cheese, Roquefort, 1 medium portion, 40g	4
Cheese, Soft, Low Fat (less than 5% fat), 1 serving, 50g	1
Cheese, Soft, Medium Fat, 1 tablespoon, 30g	1
Cheese, Stilton, 1 medium portion, 40g	4
Cheese, Wensleydale, 1 medium portion, 40g	4
Chocolate Mousse, Low Fat, 1 small pot, 65g	2
Coffee Whitener, 1 heaped teaspoon, 5g	1
Cream, Canned Spray, 1 tablespoon, 10g	1
Cream, Clotted, 1 tablespoon, 15ml	3
Cream, Double, 1 tablespoon, 15ml	2
Cream, Half Fat, 1 tablespoon, 15ml	1
Cream, Single, 1 tablespoon, 15ml	1
Cream, Sour, 1 tablespoon, 15ml	1
Cream, UHT Single, 1 tablespoon, 15ml	1
Cream, Whipping, 1 tablespoon, 15ml	2
Crème Caramel, 1 pot, 100g	3
Crème Fraîche, 1 tablespoon, 30g	3
Crème Fraîche, Half Fat, 1 tablespoon, 30g	1
Custard, Low Fat, Ready to Serve, 1 small pot, 150g	3
Custard, Ready to Serve, 1 small pot, 150g	4
Duck Fat, 1 serving, 10g	3
Fromage Frais, Fruit, 1 tablespoon, 45g	2
Fromage Frais, Fruit, 1 portion, 125g	4
Fromage Frais, Low Fat, Fruit, 1 tablespoon, 45g	1
Fromage Frais, Low Fat, Fruit, 1 portion, 125g	3
Fromage Frais, Plain, 1 tablespoon, 45g	1
Fromage Frais, Plain, 1 portion, 125g	4
Fromage Frais, Very Low Fat, Fruit, 1 tablespoon, 45g	1
Fromage Frais, Very Low Fat, Fruit, 1 portion, 125g	2
Fromage Frais, Very Low Fat, Plain, 1 tablespoon, 45g	1
Fromage Frais, Very Low Fat, Plain, 1 portion, 125g	2
Ghee, Butter, 1 teaspoon, 5g	1
Ghee, Vegetable, 1 teaspoon, 5g	1
Lard, 1 teaspoon, 7g	2
Margarine, Hard, Animal & Vegetable Fats, 1 teaspoon, 5g	1
Margarine, Hard, Vegetable Fats, 1 teaspoon, 5g	1
Margarine, Polyunsaturated, 1 teaspoon, 5g	1
Margarine, Polyunsaturated, 1 tablespoon, 15g	2

Margarine, Soft, 1 teaspoon, 5g	**1**
Milk, Buffalo, 1 serving, 100ml	**3**
Milk, Condensed, Skimmed, Sweetened, 1 tablespoon, 15ml	**1**
Milk, Condensed, Whole, Sweetened, 1 tablespoon, 15ml	**1**
Milk, Dried, Skimmed, 2 heaped teaspoons, 10g	**1**
Milk, Evaporated, 1 tablespoon, 15ml	**1**
Milk, Evaporated, Light, 2 tablespoons, 30ml	**1**
Milk, Goat's, ¼ pint, 142ml	**2**
Milk, Semi Skimmed, ¼ pint, 142ml	**2**
Milk, Semi Skimmed, ½ pint, 284ml	**4**
Milk, Semi Skimmed, 1 pint, 568ml	**7**
Milk, Skimmed, ¼ pint, 142ml	**1**
Milk, Skimmed, ½ pint, 284ml	**3**
Milk, Skimmed, 1 pint, 568ml	**5**
Milk, Soya, Sweetened, ¼ pint, 142ml	**2**
Milk, Soya, Unsweetened, ¼ pint, 142ml	**1**
Milk, Soya, Unsweetened, ½ pint, 284ml	**2**
Milk, UHT Skimmed, ¼ pint, 142ml	**1**
Milk, Whole, ¼ pint, 142ml	**3**
Milk, Whole, ½ pint, 268ml	**5**
Milk, Whole, 1 pint, 568ml	**10**
Quark, 1 heaped tablespoon, 55g	**1**
Rice Pudding, ½ large can, 215g	**5**
Spread, Low Fat, 2 teaspoons, 10g	**1**
Spread, Soya, 1 teaspoon, 5g	**1**
Spread, Very Low Fat, 2 teaspoons, 10g	**1**
Yogurt, Greek Style, Plain, 1 small pot, 150g	**5**
Yogurt, Greek, 0% Fat, 1 small pot, 150g	**2**
Yogurt, Greek, Plain, 1 small pot, 150g	**5**
Yogurt, Low Fat, Fruit, 1 pot, 150g	**3**
Yogurt, Low Fat, Plain, 1 tablespoon, 40g	**1**
Yogurt, Low Fat, Plain, 1 small pot, 150g	**2**
Yogurt, Soya, 1 tablespoon, 40g	**1**
Yogurt, Virtually Fat Free, Fruit, 1 small pot, 150g	**2**
Yogurt, Virtually Fat Free, Plain, 1 small pot, 150g	**2**

Butter, Margarine & Spreads

Anchor

Anchor Lighter Spreadable, 1 teaspoon, 5g	**1**
Anchor Spreadable, 1 teaspoon, 5g	**1**

Asda

Best for Baking, 2 teaspoons, 10g	**2**
Cholesterol Lowering Low Fat Spread, 2 teaspoons, 10g	**1**
Olive Light Spread, 1 serving, 10g	**1**
Olive Spread, 1 teaspoon, 5g	**1**
Soft Spread, 2 teaspoons, 10g	**2**
Spreadable Light, 2 teaspoons, 10g	**2**
Spreadable, 2 teaspoons, 10g	**2**
Sunflower Light Spread, 2 teaspoons, 10g	**1**
Sunflower Spread, 1 level teaspoon, 5g	**1**
You'd Butter Believe It, 1 teaspoon, 5g	**1**

Benecol

Buttery Taste Spread, 2 teaspoons, 10g	**2**
Light Spread, 2 teaspoons, 10g	**1**
Olive Oil Reduced Fat Spread, 2 teaspoons, 10g	**1**
Olive Spread, 2 teaspoons, 10g	**1**

Bertolli

Bertolli Light Spread, 2 teaspoons, 10g	**1**
Bertolli with Olive Oil, 2 teaspoons, 10g	**2**

Flora

Buttery Taste, 1 serving, 15g	**3**
Extra Light, 2 teaspoons, 10g	**1**
Lighter than Light, 2 teaspoons, 10g	**1**
Light, 2 teaspoons, 10g	**1**
Omega 3 Plus Spread, 1 teaspoon, 5g	**1**
Original, 1 teaspoon, 5g	**1**
Pro-Activ Olive Spread, 2 teaspoons, 10g	**1**
Pro-Activ Extra Light Spread, 2 teaspoons, 10g	**1**
Pro-Activ Light Spread, 2 teaspoons, 10g	**1**
Pro Active Olive Spread, 1 serving, 15g	**1**
Pro-Activ Cholesterol Lowering Light, 1 tablespoon, 15g	**1**

I Can't Believe It's Not Butter

I Can't Believe It's Not Butter, 1 teaspoon, 5g	**1**
I Can't Believe It's Not Butter, Light, 2 teaspoons, 10g	**1**

Lurpak

Lighter Spreadable Slightly Salted, 2 teaspoons, 10g	**2**
Lurpak Salted, 2 teaspoons, 10g	**2**
Lurpak Butter with Crushed Garlic, 1 teaspoon, 5g	**1**
Lurpak Spreadable, 1 teaspoon, 5g	**1**

Spreadable Slightly Salted, 1 teaspoon, 5g **1**

St Ivel

Extra Light, 1 tablespoon, 15g **1**
Extra Light + Omega 3, 1 tablespoon, 15g **1**
Utterly Butterly, 1 teaspoon, 5g **1**
Utterly Butterly Omega 3, 1 teaspoon, 5g **1**

Tesco

Butter Me Up Light, 1 serving, 10g **1**
Butter Me Up, 1 serving, 10g **2**
Butterpak Light Spreadable, 1 serving, 10g **1**
Butterpak Spreadable, 1 serving, 10g **2**
Finest Olive Spread, 1 serving, 10g **2**
Olive Spread Lighter, 1 serving, 10g **1**
Olive Spread, 1 serving, 10g **2**
Soft Spread, 1 serving, 10g **2**
Sunflower Light Spread, 1 serving, 10g **1**

The Co-operative

Buttery, 1 serving, 10g **2**
Creamery Butter, 1 serving, 10g **2**
Olive Reduced Fat Spread, 2 teaspoons, 10g **2**
Soft Spread, 1 teaspoon, 5g **1**
Spreadable Slightly Salted, 2 teaspoons, 10g **2**
Sunflower Spread, 2 teaspoons, 10g **2**
Sunflower Spread Light, 2 teaspoons, 10g **1**

Waitrose

Olive Spread, 2 teaspoons, 10g **2**
Sunflower Spread, 2 teaspoons, 10g **2**

Cheese & Cheese Snacks

Arla

Apetina, 1 tablespoon, 15g **1**
Apetina Light Feta, 1 quantity, 100g **4**
Apetina Spreadable, 1 tablespoon, 15g **1**
Lactofree Soft White Cheese, 1 serving, 30g **2**
Salmon Whipped Soft Cheese, 1 serving, 30g **2**

Asda

Bavarian Smoked Cheese Slices with Ham,
1 slice, 19g **2**
Blackcurrant & Apple Wensleydale,
1 serving, 50g **5**
Bleu d'Auvergne, 1 serving, 25g **2**

Cheddar with Mango, Sweetfire Red Chilli &
Lime, 1 portion, 30g **3**
Cheese Food Slices with Jalapeño Peppers,
1 serving, 20g **2**
Cheese Food Slices with Onion & Chives,
1 slice, 20g **2**
Cheese Spread Triangles, 1 portion, 23g **1**
Cranberry Roulé, 1 serving, 25g **2**
Creamy Cheese Spread, 1 serving, 25g **2**
Creamy Cheese Spread Light, 1 serving, 25g **1**
Creamy Cheese Triangles, 1 serving, 20g **1**
Creamy Cheese Triangles Light, 1 serving, 20g **1**
Creamy White Stilton, 1 serving, 30g **3**
Four Cheese Mix, 1 serving, 25g **2**
French Garlic Roule, 1 serving, 40g **3**
French Lighter Roule, 1 serving, 25g **1**
Fromage Frais, Natural Virtually Fat Free,
3 tablespoons, 45g **1**
Lighter Mild Cheese, 1 serving, 25g **2**
Lighter Mild Coloured Cheese, 1 serving, 25g **2**
Lighter Red Cheese, 1 serving, 25g **2**
Lighter Soft Cheese with Garlic & Herbs,
1 serving, 50g **1**
Lighter Soft Cheese with Onion & Chives,
1 serving, 50g **1**
Lighter Soft Cheese, 1 serving, 50g **1**
Manchego, 1 serving, 50g **7**
Mediterranean Style Cheese Melters,
1 serving, 30g **3**
Mini Mozzarella Balls, 2 balls, 25g **1**
Real Yorkshire Wensleydale with Cranberries,
1 serving, 40g **4**
Red Leicester with Herbs, Garlic & Full Fat
Soft Cheese, 1 serving, 30g **3**
Sandhams Garlic Lancashire Cheese,
1 serving, 30g **3**
Soft & Creamy Cheese with Pineapple,
1 serving, 30g **2**
Soft & Creamy Cheese, 1 serving, 33g **2**
Soft Goat's Cheese with Herbs, 1 serving, 15g **1**
Soft Goat's Cheese, 1 serving, 25g **2**
Somerset White with Pomegranate &
Redcurrants, 1 serving, 30g **3**
Vintage Cheddar with Peppadew Peppers &
Peri Peri, 1 serving, 30g **3**
Wensleydale & Cranberry, 1 serving, 30g **3**
Wensleydale with Cranberries, 1 serving, 30g **3**
White Stilton with Apricots, 1 serving, 30g **3**
Y Fenni, 1 serving, 25g **2**

Asda – Extra Special

Cairati Taleggio D.O.P., 1 portion, 40g **3**

	ProPoints value
Cantroel Bleu D'Auvergne, 1 serving, 25g	2
Extra Creamy Blue Stilton, 1 portion, 40g	4
Farmhouse Creamy or Crumbly Lancashire Cheese, 1 portion, 30g	3
La Tournette Reblochon, 1 serving, 25g	2
Old Dutch Master, 1 serving, 50g	6
Ossau Iraty, 1 serving, 25g	3

Asda – Good For You

Cheese Food Slices, 1 slice, 20g	1
Cheese Spread Portions, 1 portion, 22g	1
Cottage Cheese, All Varieties, ¼ tub, 75g	2
Light Italian Mozzarella, 1 serving, 25g	1
Mature Cheese Slice, 1 slice, 20g	1
Mozzarella Pearls, 1 serving, 30g	1
Soft & Creamy Cheese with Garlic & Herb, 1 serving, 25g	1

Boursin

Garlic & Herbs, 1 serving, 30g	3
Light, 1 serving, 30g	1
Minis, 1 serving, 30g	3
Pepper, 1 serving, 30g	3
Portions, 1 (16g)	2

Cathedral City

Cathedral City Sliced, 1 portion, 40g	5
Extra Mature White Cheddar, 1 portion, 20g	2
Mature Lighter, 1 portion, 60g	5
Mature Yet Mellow Cheddar, 1 portion, 50g	6
Mature Yet Mellow Lighter, 1 slice, 20g	2
Mild Cheddar, 1 portion, 50g	6
Mild Yet Distinctive Cheddar, 1 portion, 30g	3
Red Mature, 1 portion, 50g	6
Vintage 20 Cheese, 1 portion, 30g	3

Jarlsberg

Jarlsberg Grated, 1 portion, 25g	2
Jarlsberg Wedge, 1 portion, 25g	2

Kraft

Basil Mini Tub, Light, 1 portion, 35g	1
Cracker Barrel Spreadable, 1 tablespoon, 30g	3
Full Fat Soft Cheese, 1 portion, 30g	2
Herb Garden, Basil, Chives or Garlic & Herb, Light, 1 portion, 30g	1
Light Splendips, Chive Crackers & Tomato Chutney, 1 portion, 82g	4
Medium Fat Soft Cheese, Light, 1 portion, 30g	1
Original Slices, 1 serving, 25g	2
Philadelphia Extra Light, 1 tablespoon, 30g	1
Philadelphia Light, Garlic & Herbs, 1 pack, 40g	2

Philadelphia Light, Medium Fat Soft Cheese, 1 tablespoon, 30g	1
Philadelphia Light, with Chives, 1 tablespoon, 30g	1
Philadelphia Original Full Fat Soft Cheese, ¼ pack, 75g	6

Kraft – Dairylea

Bites, 1 portion, 18g	2
Cheddar, Grated, 1 portion, 30g	3
Cheese Spread, 1 portion, 25g	2
Cheese Spread Triangle, 1 portion, 15g	1
Cheese Spread Triangle, 1 large piece, 23g	2
Double Dunkers, Nacho, 1 serving, 42g	3
Dunkers Salt 'n' Vinegar Twists, 1 pack, 38g	2
Dunkers, Baked Crisps, 1 portion, 44g	3
Dunkers, Jumbo Tubes, 1 portion, 47g	3
Dunkers, Ritz Crackers, 1 (46g)	3
Dunkers, Twists, 1 portion, 42g	2
Light Cheese Spread, 1 portion, 25g	1
Light Cheese Triangle, 1 portion, 20g	1
Light Thick Cheese Slices, 1 portion, 25g	1
Thick Cheese Slices, 1 serving, 25g	2
Dairylea Tri Bites, 1 portion, 20g	2
Strip Cheese, 1 (21g)	2

Mini Babybel

Light, 1 (20g)	1
Original, 1 (20g)	2

Primula

Cheese Spread, All Varieties, 2 tablespoons, 30g	2
Deli Soft Cheese, All Varieties, 1 serving, 40g	3
Smoked Salmon & Soft Cheese, 1 portion, 40g	3
Smokey Cheese, 1 portion, 40g	2
Wensleydale & Cranberry, 1 portion, 30g	3
White Stilton & Apricot, 1 portion, 30g	3

Sainsbury's

Breaded Goat's Cheese, 1 serving, 20g	1
Cheddar with Black Pepper, 1 serving, 30g	4
Double Gloucester with Chive & Onion, 1 serving, 30g	3
Real Yorkshire Wensleydale with Cranberries, 1 serving, 30g	3
White Stilton with Apricots, 1 portion, 40g	4

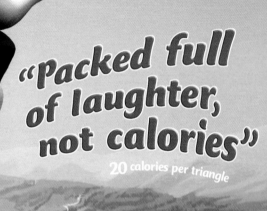

"packed full
of laughter,
not calories"

20 calories per triangle

Sainsbury's – Be Good To Yourself

British Cottage Cheese with Onion & Chive, ½ pot, 125g	2
British Cottage Cheese with Pineapple, ½ pot, 125g	3
British Natural Cottage Cheese, ½ pot, 125g	2

Tesco

Breaded Camembert, 1 individual, 75g	6
Breaded Mozzarella Sticks, 1 individual, 20g	1
Cheddar Slices with Cracked Pepper, 1 slice, 28g	3
Cheddar Slices with Wholegrain Mustard, 1 slice, 28g	3
Extra Light Soft Cheese with Garlic & Herbs, 1 portion, 30g	1
Full Fat Soft Cheese, 1 serving, 30g	2
Greek Feta Cubes in Herbs, 1 serving, 30g	3
Greek Salad Cheese Lighter, 1 serving, 30g	2
Half Fat Creamy Cheese Spread, 1 serving, 30g	1
Mascarpone Lighter, 1 serving, 30g	2
Mozzarella with Semi-Dried Tomatoes, 1 serving, 100g	8
Somerset Brie Lighter, 1 serving, 30g	2

Tesco – Healthy Living

3% Fat salad cheese, 1 portion, 30g	1
Mature Cheese Slices, Half Fat, 1 slice, 25g	2
Mozzarella, Reduced Fat, 1 serving, 30g	1

Tesco – Light Choices

Cheese Singles, 1 individual, 20g	1
Cheese Triangle, 1 individual, 18g	1
Cottage Cheese with Onion & Chives, 1 serving, 60g	1
Cottage Cheese with Pineapple & Passionfruit, 1 serving, 60g	1
Cottage Cheese with Red Pepper & Pesto, 1 serving, 60g	1

The Co-operative

Breaded Camembert with Cranberry Dip, 1 serving, 40g	3
Breaded Cheese Bite Selection, ¼ pack, 60g	4
Breaded Mozzarella Sticks with Tangy Tomato Dip, 1 stick, 10g	1
Cheese Singles, 1 slice, 17g	1
Garlic & Herb Edam, 1 portion, 40g	4
Garlic & Herb Roule, 1 portion, 40g	3

Goat's Cheese, 1 portion, 40g	3
Goat's Cheese with Black Pepper, 1 portion, 40g	4
Healthy Living Natural Low Fat Fromage Frais, ½ pot, 100g	1
Light Soft Cheese, ⅙ pack, 32g	2
Light Soft Cheese with Garlic & Herb, ⅙ pack, 32g	2
Reduced Fat Extra Light Soft Cheese, All Varieties, ⅙ pack, 32g	1
Reduced Fat Extra Light Soft Cheese with Onion & Chives, ⅙ pack, 32g	1
Reduced Fat Mature Cheese Slices, 1 slice, 23g	2
Reduced Fat Natural Cottage Cheese, ½ pot, 150g	3
Reduced Fat Onion & Chive Cottage Cheese, ½ pot, 125g	2
Reduced Fat Pineapple Cottage Cheese, ½ pot, 125g	3
Ripe & Ready French Brie, 1 portion, 40g	3
Wafer Thin Mild Cheddar Cheese Slices, 1 portion, 40g	4
White Stilton with Apricots, 1 portion, 40g	4
White Stilton with Mango & Ginger, 1 portion, 40g	4

The Laughing Cow

Cheez Dippers, 1 serving, 35g	3
Deli-Light Blue Cheese, 1 serving, 17.5g	1
Deli-Light Tomato & Basil, 1 serving, 17.5g	1
Extra Light 2% Fat, 1 serving, 17.5g	1
Light, 1 serving, 17.5g	1
Original, 1 serving, 17.5g	1

Waitrose

French Natural Fromage Frais, 1 serving, 45g	1

Weight Watchers

Low Fat Cheese Spread Triangle, Plain, 1 portion, 22g	1
Mature Cheese Block, 1 portion, 20g	1
Reduced Fat Grated Cheese Mature, 1 portion, 20g	1
Reduced Fat Sliced Mature Cheese, 1 slice, 20g	1
Soft Cheese with Roasted Onion & Chive, 1 serving, 50g	1
Soft Cheese, Plain, 1 serving, 50g	1

Wyke Farms

Superlight Somerset Mature Half Fat Cheddar, 1 portion, 40g	3

Weight Watchers® Cheese
a must for your shopping list

Yes, you can still have cheese! With all the taste, but fewer *ProPoints*® values.

per 20g portion

Weight Watchers Cheese is available in:
Block, Grated and Sliced options

SUITABLE FOR VEGETARIANS

WeightWatchers® Foods
Eat gorgeous. Feel gorgeous.

Chilled Dairy Desserts

	ProPoints value

Ambrosia

Banana Flavour Rice Pudding, 1 small pot, 150g	4
Chocolate Flavour Custard, ¼ carton, 125g	4
Creamed Rice Pudding, 1 small pot, 150g	4
Creamed Rice Pudding, ½ can, 212g	6
Creamed Rice Pudding, Low Fat, 1 small pot, 150g	4
Creamed Rice Pudding, Low Fat, ½ can, 212g	5
Low Fat Custard, 1 from multipack, 135g	3
Low Fat Custard, 1 small pot, 150g	3
Low Fat Devon Creamed Rice, 1 small pot, 150g	4
Low Fat Devon Custard, Ready to Eat, 1 pot, 135g	3
Low Fat Devon Custard, Ready to Eat, 1 serving, 160g	4
Low Fat Rice Pudding, 1 from multipack, 135g	3
Low Fat Rice Pudding, 1 small pot, 150g	4
Simply Devonly Creamy Custard, 1 small pot, 150g	4

Asda

Blackcurrant Fool, 1 pot, 114g	5
Brandy Sauce with Courvoisier VS Cognac, 1/10 tub, 50g	2
Cheesecake, Raspberry Brûlée, 1 slice, 80g	6
Chocky Rocky Road Dessert, 1 individual, 135g	10
Chocolate & Sticky Toffee Sundae, ½ dessert, 108g	11
Chocolate Chaos, 1 dessert, 130g	11
Chocolate Sundae, 1 pot, 120g	10
Chocolate Trifle, ⅓ pot, 114g	6
Crème Caramel, 1 pot, 100g	3
Fruit Cocktail Trifle, ¼ large, 150g	6
Fruit Cocktail Trifle, individual, 1 pot, 125g	5
Knickerbocker Glory, ½ pack, 105g	7
Lemon Fool, Low Fat, 1 pot, 114g	6
Raspberry Panacotta, ¼ pack, 163g	13
Raspberry Trifle, ⅛ family pack, 125g	5
Rice Pudding, 1 pot, 150g	7
Sherry Trifle, ¼ large, 150g	6
Sticky Toffee Sundae, ½ dessert, 108g	8
Strawberry & Raspberry Heaven, ⅕ large, 102g	7
Strawberry Chaos, 1 dessert, 130g	11
Strawberry Cream Tea Sundae, ½ dessert, 108g	8
Strawberry Fool, Low Fat, 1 pot, 114g	6
Strawberry Swirl Sundae, 1 pot, 136g	11
Strawberry Trifle, 1 individual, 150g	5
Toffee Chaos, 1 pot, 130g	11
Triple Chocolate Sundae, ½ dessert, 108g	8
Winterfruit Trifle, ¼ large, 150g	6

Asda – Chosen by You

British Fresh Custard, 1 serving (¼ pack), 125g	4
Chocolate Mousse, 1 pot, 60g	3
Family Dessert Tiramisu, 1 serving (¼ pack), 125g	8
Lemon Mousse, 1 pot, 60g	3
Lemon Swirled Cheesecake, 1 portion, 125g	12
Raspberry Royale, 1 portion, 150g	6
Strawberry Sundae, 1 pot, 130g	10
Strawberry Trifle, ⅛ individual, 75g	3
Tiramisu, 1 individual, 123g	9
Toffee Mousse, 1 pot, 60g	3
Toffee Sundae, 1 pot, 140g	11
Treat Yourself Profiterole Desserts, 1 pot, 100g	7

Asda – Extra Special

Belgian Chocolate Crème Brûlée, 1 portion, 96g	7
Belgian Milk Chocolate Mousse, 1 pot, 120g	6
Chocolate Mousse, 1 pot, 120g	6
Creamy Custard, ¼ pot, 125g	7
Creamy Raspberry Panna Cotta, 1 serving, 165g	11
Crème Brûlée, 1 portion, 96g	9
Eton Mess Dessert, 1 serving, 163g	10
Jamacian Rum Sauce, 1 serving, 51g	3
Raspberry Panna Cotta, 1 portion, 166g	11
Rich Belgian Chocolate Sauce, 1 tablespoon, 15g	2
Strawberry & Clotted Cream Trifle, 1 individual, 125g	6

Asda – Good For You

Chocolate Mousse, 1 pot, 61g	2
Raspberry Swirl Sundae, 1 pot, 120g	5
Raspberry Trifle, 1 pot, 125g	4
Strawberry Mousse, 1 pot, 63g	2

Bird's

Custard, Ready to Pour, 1 serving, 125g	4
Custard, Ready to Serve, 1 serving, 160g	4

Dr Oetker – Onken

Chocolate & Hazelnut Mousse, 1 pot, 125g	4
Chocolate Mousse with a Hint of Orange, 1 pot, 100g	5

Creamy Chocolate & Hazelnut Mousse, 1 pot, 115g	**4**
Creamy Orange Mango & Lime Mousse, 1 pot, 150g	**6**
Creamy Peach Mousse, 1 pot, 115g	**4**
Creamy Strawberry Mousse, 1 pot, 115g	**4**
Fruity Apple & Blackberry Mousse, 1 pot, 115g	**3**
Fruity Lemon Mousse, 1 pot, 115g	**3**
Fruity Lite Mousse, All Flavours, 1 pot, 150g	**4**
Lemon Mousse, 1 pot, 150g	**4**
Paula Chocolate Dessert with Vanilla Splodges, 1 pot, 125g	**4**
Paula Vanilla Dessert with Chocolate Splodges, 1 pot, 125g	**4**
Peach Mousse, 1 pot, 150g	**5**
Strawberry Mousse, 1 pot, 150g	**5**
Velvety Smooth Chocolate Mousse, 1 pot, 100g	**5**

M&S – Count on Us

Chocolate Mousse, 1 pot, 70g	**2**
Chocolate Muffin Dessert, 1 pot, 110g	**4**
Chocolate Sponge Puddings, 1 (95g)	**5**
Raspberry Mousse, 1 pot, 70g	**2**
Rice Puddings, 1 (170g)	**4**
Strawberry Trifle, 1 pot, 140g	**4**

Müller Rice

Mini Müller Rice, 1 snack size, 95g	**3**
Müller Rice, Original or Raspberry or Smooth Toffee, 1 pot, 190g	**5**
Müller Rice, Apple or Vanilla Custard or Strawberry, 1 pot, 190g	**6**

Sainsbury's

Banoffee Dessert, 1 pot, 140g	**11**
Be Good To Yourself Strawberry Trifles, 1 pot, 125g	**4**
Chocolate Brownie Dessert, ¼ cake, 125g	**12**
Chocolate Chip Cookie Sundae, ½ pot, 130g	**11**
Chocolate Crème Brûlée, 1 (100g)	**8**
Chocolate Shortcake Dessert, 1 (140g)	**15**
Chocolate Sundae, 1 (145g)	**12**
Chocolate Trifle, 1 (150g)	**9**
Cookies & Cream Sundae, 1 pot, 135g	**11**
Fresh Cream Meringue, 1 (35g)	**4**
Fruit Cocktail Trifles, 1 (125g)	**5**
Mandarin Royale Dessert, 1 (150g)	**6**
Raspberry Royale, 1 (150g)	**5**
Raspberry Trifle, ¼ pudding, 150g	**7**
Rocky Road Dessert, 1 pot, 135g	**10**
Strawberry Cheesecake Dessert, ½ pot, 75g	**6**
Strawberry Sundae, 1 portion, 140g	**11**

Strawberry Trifle, ¼ pudding, 150g	**7**
Summer Fruit Trifle, ¼ pudding, 150g	**8**
Tiramisu Desserts, 1 (100g)	**7**
Toffee Pavlova, ⅙ dessert, 47g	**5**

Sainsbury's – Taste the Difference

Champagne Summer Fruit Pudding, ¼ pudding, 112g	**4**
Morello Cherry & Amaretto Trifle, 1 (150g)	**11**
Panna Cotta with Raspberry Compote, ½ pudding, 185g	**16**
Pots Au Chocolate, 1 (49g)	**5**
Sherry Trifle, ⅙ pudding, 110g	**8**
Tiramisu, 1 (108g)	**10**

Tesco

Caramel Pannacotta, 1 serving, 120g	**8**
Chocolate Mousse, 1 individual, 63g	**3**
Chocolate Trifle, 1 individual, 150g	**8**
Clotted Cream Rice Pudding, 1 serving, 125g	**7**
Creamfields Strawberry Trifles, 1 individual, 125g	**5**
French Crème Brûlée, 1 individual, 100g	**9**
Fresh Cream Chocolate Muffin, 1 serving, 67g	**7**
Fresh Cream Chocolate Profiterole Stack Dessert, 1 portion, 72g	**8**
Fresh Cream Slices, 1 individual, 75g	**8**
Freshly Whipped Cream Meringues, 1 individual, 25g	**3**
Fruit Cocktail Trifles, 1 individual, 150g	**5**
Gooseberry Fruit Fool, 1 individual, 114g	**6**
Lemon Fruit Fool, 1 individual, 114g	**6**
Lemon Mousse, 1 individual, 63g	**3**
Lemoncello Dessert, 1 individual, 90g	**6**
Light Choices Ready to Serve Custard, 1 serving, 142g	**3**
Low Fat Rice Pudding, Single Pot, 1 pot, 135g	**4**
Luxury Chocolate Roulade, 1 slice, 66g	**6**
Profiteroles, 1 serving, 80g	**6**
Raspberry Ripple Sundae, 1 individual, 125g	**10**
Raspberry Sherry Trifle, 1 serving, 150g	**7**
Raspberry Trifles, 1 individual, 150g	**5**
Ready To Eat Low Fat Custard, 1 pot, 150g	**4**
Ready to Eat Rice Pudding, Single Pot, 1 pot, 135g	**4**
Ready to Serve Custard , 1 serving, 142g	**4**
Strawberry Fruit Fool, 1 individual, 114g	**5**
Strawberry Mousse, 1 individual, 63g	**3**
Strawberry Sundaes, 1 individual, 51g	**5**
Strawberry Trifle, 1 serving, 150g	**6**
Swirly Chocolate Sundae, 1 individual, 136g	**9**

Swirly Toffee Sundae, 1 individual, 136g	**11**
Tiramisu, Family, 1 serving, 100g	**7**
Tiramisu Pots, 1 serving, 100g	**7**
Triple Chocolate Trifle, 1 serving, 150g	**9**
Value Syrup Sponge Pudding, 1 serving, 100g	**8**
White Chocolate Mousse, 1 serving, 63g	**3**

Tesco – Finest

Chocolate Brownie Sundae, 1 individual, 215g	**18**
Cornish Custard, 1 serving, 125g	**8**
Lemon Ice Cream Meringue Roulade with Blueberry Sauce, 1 portion, 70g	**7**
Meal Deal Profiteroles, 1 serving, 91g	**10**
Pot au Chocolate, 1 serving, 100g	**12**
Profiterole Dessert, 1 serving, 94g	**9**
Senga Strawberry Mousse, 1 individual, 100g	**5**
Sicilian Lemon Mousse, 1 individual, 100g	**6**
Tiramisu, 1 individual, 99g	**9**
Toffee Sundae, 1 individual, 215g	**16**

The Co-operative

Chocolate Mousse, 1 pot, 62g	**3**
Crème Brûlée, 1 (100g)	**9**
Crème Caramel, 1 pot, 100g	**3**

Pot au Chocolat, Truly Irresistible, 1 pot, 55g	**6**
Reduced Fat Chocolate Muffin Dessert, 1 pot, 100g	**4**
Rhubarb Fool, 1 pot, 114g	**5**
Rice Pudding, ⅓ can, 206g	**5**
Sherry Trifle, ⅙ pot, 125g	**5**
Sherry Trifle, Truly Irresistible, 1 portion, 110g	**6**
Strawberry Trifle, from Triple Pack, 1 pot, 150g	**5**

Waitrose

A Burst of Raspberry Panna Cotta, 1 pack, 130g	**8**
Blackcurrant Fruit Fool, 1 pot, 120g	**5**
Caramel Panna Cotta, 1 pot, 120g	**9**
Chocolate Mousse, 1 pot, 120g	**9**
Coffee Panna Cotta, 1 pot, 120g	**9**
Cornish Clotted Cream Rice Pudding, ¼ pack, 162g	**9**
Crème Brûlée, 1 (96g)	**9**
Fresh Chocolate Custard, ¼ pot, 125g	**7**
Fresh Custard, ¼ pot, 125g	**4**
Fruit Trifle, 1 pack, 150g	**7**
Gooseberry Fruit Fool, 1 pot, 120g	**6**
Lemon Sundae, 1 pack, 140g	**13**

Weight Watchers® Cheesecakes
a must for your shopping list

Our smooth creamy cheesecakes with a crunchy, oaty base and gorgeous, indulgent fillings are a great way to treat yourself.

per cheesecake

Now available:
Chocolate, Lemon and Raspberry Cheesecakes

 WeightWatchers® Foods
Eat gorgeous. Feel gorgeous.

Low Fat Fresh Vanilla Custard, Black & White, ¼ tub, 125g	3
Raspberry Trifle, 1 pot, 125g	6
Scottish Raspberry & Amontillado Sherry Trifle, 1 pot, 150g	8
Strawberry Trifle, 1 pot, 125g	6
Toffee Mousse, 1 pack, 120g	10
Toffee Sundae, 1 pack, 100g	8
Vanilla Custard, ½ pack, 250g	15
Very Berry Trifle, 1 pot, 150g	7

Weight Watchers

Belgian Chocolate & Vanilla Mousse, 1 pot, 80g	3
Caramel Creamed Rice, 1 pot, 130g	3
Chocolate Cheesecake, 1 (100g)	5
Lemon Cheesecake, 1 (100g)	5
Low Fat Custard, 1 serving, 100g	2
Raspberry Cheesecake, 1 (100g)	5
Rich Chocolate Dessert, 1 pot, 70g	2
Strawberry & Vanilla Mousse, 1 pot, 80g	2
Vanilla Creamed Rice, 1 pot, 130g	3

Dairy Alternatives

Alpro

Dairy Free Dessert Vanilla Flavour, ¼ pot, 125g	3
Dark Chocolate Flavoured Dessert, 1 pot, 125g	3
Organic Plain Yogurt, ¼ pot, 125g	2
Raspberry & Vanilla Flavour, 1 serving, 125g	3
Soya Chocolate Flavoured, 1 serving, 250ml	5
Soya Dairy Free Alternative to Single Cream, 1 serving, 50ml	2
Soya Dairy Free Custard, Vanilla Flavour, 1 serving, 175g	4
Soya Light, 1 serving, 250ml	1
Soya Light, Unsweetened, 1 serving, 250ml	1
Soya Milk, Unsweetened, 1 serving, 250ml	2
Soya Organic Dairy Free Alternative to Milk, 1 serving, 250ml	3
Soya Organic, Vanilla Flavoured, 1 serving, 250ml	4
Soya Original, 1 serving, 250ml	3
Soya Smooth Chocolate Flavoured Dessert, 1 pot, 125g	3
Soya Soft Caramel Flavoured Dessert, 1 pot, 125g	3
Soya Yogurt Raspberry & Vanilla, 1 pot, 125g	3

Soya Yogurt Strawberry & Forest Fruits, 1 pot, 125g	3

Benecol

Dairy Free Strawberry & Berries Fruit & Soya Drink, 1 bottle, 68g	1
Dairy Free Tropical Fruit & Soya Drink, 1 bottle, 66g	1
Fruit & Dairy Smoothie, 1 bottle, 150ml	2

Oatly

Healthy Oat Dairy Free Alternative to Cream, 1 serving, 50ml	2
Healthy Oat Drink, Chocolate, 1 serving, 250ml	4
Healthy Oat Drink, Enriched, 1 serving, 250ml	3
Healthy Oat Drink, Organic, 1 serving, 250ml	3

Provamel

Organic Rice Drink, Vanilla, 1 medium glass, 250ml	3
Soya Soleil, Sweetened, 1 medium glass, 250ml	2
Soya Soleil, Unsweetened, 1 medium glass, 250ml	2

Rice Dream

Chocolate, 1 portion, 200ml	3
Dairy Free Milk, Hazelnut & Almond, ½ pint, 284ml	6
Dairy Free Milk, Vanilla, ½ pint, 284ml	4
Rice Dream + Calcium Rice Drink, ½ pint, 284ml	4

So Good

Chocolate Soya Milk, 1 serving, 250ml	5
Light Soya Milk Unsweetened, 1 serving, 250ml	2
So Good Fat Free, Reduced Calorie Soya Milk, 1 serving, 250ml	2
Soya Original, 1 serving, 250ml	3

Milk & Cream

Anchor

Brandy Flavoured Cream, 1 serving, 12g	1
Chocolate Flavoured Cream, 1 serving, 13g	1
Extra Thick Real Cream UHT, 1 serving, 12g	1
Light Real Cream UHT, 1 serving, 12g	1
Original Real Cream UHT, 1 serving, 12g	1

Weight Watchers®
Reduced Fat Pouring Cream
a must for your shopping list

Contains 50% less fat than single cream – now you **can** add some indulgence to your cooking every day!

3
ProPoints value

per 100ml serving

Now also available:
Low Fat Crème Fraîche and Reduced Fat Thick Cream

SUITABLE FOR COOKING AND SPOONING

WeightWatchers Foods
Eat gorgeous. Feel gorgeous.

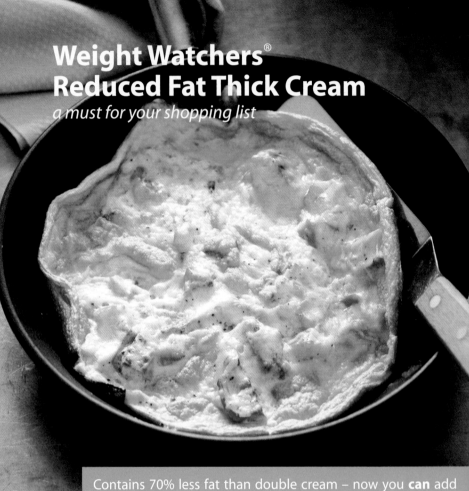

Weight Watchers®
Reduced Fat Thick Cream
a must for your shopping list

Contains 70% less fat than double cream – now you **can** add some indulgence to your cooking every day!

1
ProPoints value

per 30g serving

Now also available:
Low Fat Crème Fraîche and Reduced Fat Pouring Cream

SUITABLE FOR COOKING AND SPOONING

WeightWatchers Foods
Eat gorgeous. Feel gorgeous.

Weight Watchers®
Low Fat Crème Fraîche
a must for your shopping list

Contains less than 3% fat – now you **can** add some indulgence to your cooking every day!

1
ProPoints
value

*per 30g
serving*

Now also available:
*Reduced Fat Thick Cream and
Reduced Fat Pouring Cream*

SUITABLE FOR COOKING
AND SPOONING

WeightWatchers Foods
Eat gorgeous. Feel gorgeous.

Asda

Clotted Cream, 1 tablespoon, 15ml	3
Crème Fraîche, 1 tablespoon, 30g	2
Flavoured Milk, Banana or Chocolate, 1 glass, 250ml	5
Lemon Whipping Cream, 2 tablespoons, 30g	3
Reduced Fat Squirty Cream, 1 pack, 250g	4
Squirty Topping, 1 serving, 13g	1
Strawberry Flavoured Milk, 1 medium glass, 250ml	4
Strawberry Whipping Cream, 2 tablespoons, 30g	3
Vanilla Flavoured Milk, 1 bottle, 330ml	6

Elmlea

Aerosol Alternative to Whipped Cream, 1 tablespoon, 12g	1
Double Cream Substitute, 1 tablespoon, 15ml	1
Light Double Cream Alternative, 1 tablespoon, 15ml	1
Light Single Cream Alternative, 2 tablespoons, 30ml	1
Single Cream Substitute, 1 tablespoon, 15ml	1
Whipping Cream Substitute, 1 tablespoon, 15ml	1

Marvel

Marvel Dried Milk, 2 teaspoons, 10g	1
Original Dried Skimmed Milk, 1 serving, 57g	5

Nestlé

Carnation Condensed Milk, 1 tablespoon, 15g	1
Carnation Condensed Milk, 1 serving, 50g	4
Carnation Evaporated Milk, 1 tablespoon, 15g	1
Carnation Extra Thick Cream, Sterilised, 1 serving, 50g	3
Carnation Light Condensed Milk, 1 serving, 50g	4
Carnation Light Evaporated Milk, 2 tablespoons, 30g	1

Waitrose

Crème Fraîche, 1 portion, 20ml	2
Half Fat Select Farm Extra Thick Cream, 1 tablespoon, 15ml	1
Reduced Fat Select Farm Pouring Cream, 1 tablespoon, 15ml	1
Select Farm Extra Thick Double Cream, 1 tablespoon, 15ml	2
Select Farm Extra Thick Single Cream, 1 tablespoon, 15ml	1
Soured Cream, 1 tablespoon, 15ml	1

Weight Watchers

Low Fat Crème Fraîche, 1 serving, 30g	1
Reduced Fat Pouring Cream, 1 serving, 100ml	3
Reduced Fat Thick Cream, 1 serving, 30g	1

Yogurts & Yogurt/Milk Drinks

Asda

Active Health Drink, 1 bottle, 100g	2
Banana Flavour Milkshake Mix, 1 serving, 20g	2
Black Cherry Biopot Yogurt, 1 portion, 125g	4
Black Cherry Fruit Tumbles, ¼ pot, 44g	1
Black Cherry or Hazelnut Low Fat Yogurt, 1 pot, 150g	4
Blueberry Probiotic Yogurt Drink, 1 bottle, 100ml	2
Cherry or Mandarin Low Fat Yogurt, 1 pot, 125g	2
Cherry Squeezy Yogurt, 1 pouch, 150g	3
Chocolate Milkshake Mix, 1 serving, 20g	2
Cholesterol Lowering Blackcurrant Yogurt, 1 pot, 125g	2
Cholesterol Lowering Low Fat Blackcurrant Yogurt, 1 pot, 118g	3
Cholesterol Lowering Original Yogurt Drink, 1 bottle, 125g	3
Cholesterol Lowering Strawberry Yogurt Drink, 1 bottle, 125g	3
Crunch Split Pot Banana & Chocolate Cornflake, 1 pack, 150g	5
Crunch Split Pot Toffee & Cereal Hoops, 1 pot, 150g	5
Crunch Split Pot Vanilla & Chocolate Crunch, 1 pot, 150g	5
Fruity Probiotic Low Fat Yogurt, 1 pot, 125g	2
Greek Style Low Fat Yogurt, Strawberry or Summer Fruit Compote, 1 pot, 140g	3
Hazelnut Probiotic Low Fat Yogurt, 1 pot, 150g	3
Inner Defence Raspberry & Cranberry Probiotic Yogurt Drinks, 1 bottle, 100g	2
Light Smooth Raspberry & Cranberry Yogurt, 1 pot, 200g	3
Light Strawberry Yogurt, 1 pot, 200g	3
Low Fat Berry Probiotic Yogurt, 1 pot, 125g	2
Low Fat Blueberry Flavour Yogurt Drink with Green Tea Extract, 1 bottle, 125g	2

Mandarin Squeezy Yogurt, 1 pouch, 150g	**3**
Mango & Passion Fruit Biopot Yogurt, 1 serving, 125g	**4**
Natural Balance Peach Probiotic Yogurt, 1 pot, 125g	**3**
Natural Balance Strawberry Probiotic Yogurt, 1 pot, 125g	**3**
Natural Low Fat Yogurt with Raspberry Clusters, 1 pot, 140g	**5**
Peach & Apricot Fruit Tumbles, ¼ pot, 44g	**1**
Peach & Nectarine Yogurt, 1 pot, 150g	**3**
Peach & Passionfruit Low Fat Yogurt, ⅓ pot (large), 150g	**4**
Peach, Pineapple & Mandarin Low Fat Yogurt, 1 pot, 125g	**2**
Pineapple or Raspberry Low Fat Yogurt, 1 pot, 125g	**2**
Pro+Pre-Biotic Low Fat Blueberry Yogurts with added Fibre, 1 pot, 125g	**2**
Pro+Pre-Biotic Low Fat Strawberry Yogurts with added Fibre, 1 pot, 125g	**3**
Pro+Pre-Biotic Mixed Fruit Low Fat Yogurts with added Fibre, 1 pot, 125g	**2**
Pro+Pre-Biotic Pink Grapefruit Low Fat Yogurt with added Fibre, 1 pot, 125g	**2**
Pro+Pre-Biotic Raspberry & Cranberry Yogurt Drink, 1 bottle, 100g	**2**
Pro+Pre-Biotic Raspberry & Cranberry Yogurt with added Fibre, 1 pot, 125g	**3**
Pro+Pre-Biotic Strawberry Yogurt Drink, 1 bottle, 100g	**2**
Pro+Pre-Biotic with Omega 3 Mixed Fruit Yogurt Drinks, 1 bottle, 100g	**1**
Probiotic Yogurts with a Blueberry Compôte, 1 pot, 125g	**3**
Probiotic Yogurts with a Prune Compote, 1 pot, 125g	**3**
Raspberry & Redcurrant Low Fat Yogurt, ⅓ pot (large), 150g	**3**
Raspberry Squeezy Yogurt, 1 pouch, 150g	**3**
Spiced Apple Fruit Layer Custard Style Pots, 1 pot, 100g	**3**
Strawberry & Banana Smooth & Creamy Low Fat Yogurt, 1 pot, 150g	**3**
Strawberry & Vanilla Smooth & Creamy Low Fat Yogurt, 1 pot, 150g	**3**
Strawberry Flavour Low Fat Yogurt Drink, 1 bottle, 125g	**3**
Strawberry Flavour Milkshake Mix, 1 serving, 20g	**2**
Strawberry Fruit Tumbles, ¼ pot, 44g	**1**
Strawberry Low Fat Yogurt, 1 pot, 125g	**3**

Strawberry, Raspberry & Cherry Low Fat Yogurt, 1 pot, 125g	**3**
Strawberry Squeezy Yogurt, 1 pouch, 150g	**3**
Strawberry Wholegrain Biopot Yogurt, 1 serving, 125g	**4**
Strawberry Yogurt with Seeds & Grain, ⅓ pot, 150g	**5**
Thick & Creamy Autumn Harvest Yogurt, Apple & Blackberry, 1 pot, 125g	**4**
Thick & Creamy Autumn Harvest Yogurt, Plum, 1 pot, 125g	**4**
Toffee Flavoured Probiotic Low Fat Yogurt, 1 pot, 150g	**3**
Toffee Low Fat Yogurt, 1 pot, 125g	**2**
Totally Apricot Low Fat Yogurt, 1 pot, 150g	**4**
Totally Raspberry Low Fat Yogurt, 1 pot, 150g	**3**
Virtually Fat Free Strawberry Probiotic Yogurt, ¼ pot (medium), 38g	**1**

Asda – Chosen by You

Greek Style Yogurt with Honey, 1 pot, 200g	**9**
Inner Defence Strawberry Probiotic Yogurt Drinks, 1 bottle, 100g	**2**
Inner Defence Tropical Fruit Probiotic Yogurt Drinks, 1 bottle, 100g	**2**

Asda – Extra Special

Belgian Chocolate Milkshake, 1 serving, 375ml	**11**
Canadian Blueberry West Country Yogurt, 1 pot, 150g	**6**
Champagne Rhubarb West Country Yogurt, 1 pot, 150g	**6**
Extra Creamy Hazelnut Praline West Country Yogurt, 1 pot, 150g	**7**
Extra Creamy Lemon Curd West Country Yogurt, 1 pot, 150g	**7**
Heritage Raspberry West Country Yogurt, 1 pot, 150g	**5**
Mango & Passionfruit West Country Yogurt, 1 pot, 150g	**6**
Morello Cherry West Country Yogurt, 1 pot, 150g	**6**
Raspberry West Country Yogurt, 1 pot, 150g	**5**
Sri Lankan Pineapple West Country Yogurt, 1 pot, 150g	**6**
Strawberry & Cream West Country Yogurt, 1 pot, 150g	**6**
Timperley Rhubarb & Vanilla West Country Yogurt, 1 pot, 150g	**6**
Valencia Orange West Country Yogurt, 1 pot, 150g	**6**

White Peach West Country Yogurt, 1 pot, 150g **6**

Asda – Good For You

Granola Split Pot Yogurt, 1 pot, 170g **4**
Greek Style Yogurt, with Blackcurrants,
1 pot, 140g **3**
Natural Yogurt, ¼ pot, 125g **2**

Benecol

Benecol Strawberry, 1 pot, 125g **3**
Bio Live Yogurt Low Fat Plain, 1 pot, 125g **2**
Light Yogurt Drink, 1 bottle, 67g **1**
Peach & Apricot Yogurt Drink, 1 bottle, 68g **1**
Pineapple Yogurt Drink, 1 bottle, 68g **1**
Strawberry Low Fat Bio Yogurt, 1 pot, 125g **3**
Strawberry Yogurt Drink, 1 bottle, 68ml **1**
Yogurt Drink, 1 bottle, 70g **2**

Campina – Yazoo

Banana Flavour Milkshake, 1 bottle, 475ml **8**
Chocolate Flavour Milkshake, 1 bottle, 475ml **9**
Milk Shaken Up with Banana, 1 serving, 200ml **3**
Milk Shaken Up with Chocolate,
1 bottle, 472ml **9**
Milk Shaken Up with Strawberry,
1 serving, 200ml **3**
Strawberry Flavour Milkshake, 1 bottle, 475ml **8**

Danone – Actimel

0.1% Fat, All Flavours, 1 bottle, 100g **1**
Actimel, 1 bottle, 100g **2**
Blueberry or Cherry or Multifruit or Orange or
Raspberry or Strawberry & Banana or
Strawberry, 1 bottle, 100g **2**
Peach & Mango or Pineapple, 1 bottle, 100g **1**

Danone – Activia

Bio Fruit Yogurt Mixed Fruit, 1 pot, 125g **4**
Bio Low Fat Natural Yogurt, 1 pot, 125g **2**
Fat Free, Fruit, All Flavours, 1 pot, 125g **2**
Fibre Muesli Apple, 1 pot, 125g **4**
Fibre, Cereals, All Flavours, 1 pot, 125g **3**
Fig, 1 pot, 125g **3**
Fruit Layer, All Flavours, 1 pot, 125g **3**
Intensely Creamy, All Flavours, 1 pot, 120g **3**
Natural Bio Yogurt, 1 pot, 125g **2**
Rhubarb, 1 pot, 125g **3**
Strawberry, 1 pot, 125g **3**

Danone – Shape

Feel Fuller for Longer Fat Free Yogurt,
Raspberry or Strawberry Flavour, 1 pot, 120g **2**

Greek Style Yogurt, Orange or Lemon,
1 pot, 125g **4**

Flora – pro.activ

Pro.Activ Low Fat Yogurt, Strawberry,
1 pot, 125g **2**
Pro.Activ Cholesterol Lowering Yogurt Drink
Original, 1 bottle, 100g **1**
Pro.Activ Cholesterol Lowering Yogurt Drink
Strawberry, 1 bottle, 100g **1**

Frijj

Chocolate Fudge Brownie Flavour Milkshake,
½ bottle, 250ml **6**
Chocolate Fudge Brownie Flavour Milkshake,
1 bottle, 500ml **12**
Thick & Smooth Banana Milkshake,
1 bottle, 500ml **9**
Thick & Smooth Chocolate Fudge Brownie
Flavour Milkshake, 1 bottle, 500ml **12**
Thick & Smooth Chocolate or Chocolate Mint
Milkshake, 1 bottle, 500ml **10**
Thick & Smooth Cookie Dough Flavour
Milkshake, 1 bottle, 500ml **11**
Thick & Smooth Strawberry Milkshake,
1 bottle, 500ml **9**

M&S – Count on Us

Apple & Cinnamon Yogurt, 1 pot, 145g **2**
Chocolate & Orange Yogurt, 1 pot, 150g **2**
Peach & Apricot Yogurt, 1 pot, 145g **1**
Raspberry or Strawberry Yogurt, 1 pot, 145g **2**
Thick & Fruity Exotic Fruit Yogurt, 1 pot, 145g **2**
Thick & Fruity Papaya & Banana Yogurt,
1 pot, 145g **2**
Vanilla Yogurt, 1 pot, 150g **2**

M&S – Eat Well

Extremely Fruity Black Cherry Low Fat Yogurt,
1 pot, 170g **5**
Extremely Fruity Blueberry Low Fat Yogurt,
1 pot, 170g **4**
Extremely Fruity Peach & Apricot Creamy Low
Fat Yogurt, 1 pot, 170g **5**
Extremely Fruity Raspberry Low Fat Yogurt,
1 pot, 170g **4**
Extremely Fruity Rhubarb Low Fat Yogurt,
1 pot, 170g **4**
Extremely Fruity Strawberry Low Fat Yogurt,
1 pot, 170g **5**

Mars

Bounty Drink, 1 bottle, 250ml	**6**
Galaxy Chocolate Drink, 1 carton, 180ml	**4**
Galaxy Chocolate Drink, 1 bottle, 388ml	**9**
Thick Shake, 1 bottle, 440ml	**11**

Müller

Amore, Fruit, All Flavours, 1 pot, 150g	**6**
Amore Vanilla with Dark Chocolate Flakes or Walnut & Greek Honey, 1 pot, 150g	**7**
Corner Healthy Balance, Redberry Crunch or Strawberry, 1 pot, 150g	**5**
Crunch Corner All Flavours, 1 pot, 150g	**6**
Fruit Corner Blackberry & Raspberry, 1 pot, 175g	**5**
Fruit Corner Blueberry or Peach & Apricot, 1 pot, 175g	**5**
Fruit Corner, Raspberry & White Chocolate, 1 pot, 175g	**6**
Fruit Corner, Red Cherry or Strawberry, 1 pot, 175g	**5**
Mini Müller Corners, All Flavours, 1 pot, 85g	**3**
Müllerlight Raspberry & Cranberry, 1 pot, 190g	**2**
Müllerlight Vanilla Sprinkled with Dark Chocolate, 1 pot, 165g	**2**
Müllerlight Vanilla, Chocolate Sprinkles & Black Cherry Underlayer Fat Free Yogurt, 1 pot, 165g	**2**
Müllerlight, Apricot, 1 pot, 190g	**2**
Müllerlight, Banana & Custard, 1 pot, 190g	**3**
Müllerlight, Cherry, 1 pot, 190g	**2**
Müllerlight, Mandarin, 1 pot, 190g	**3**
Müllerlight, Peach & Pineapple, 1 pot, 190g	**2**
Müllerlight, Rhubarb or Strawberry, 1 pot, 190g	**2**
Müllerlight, Strawberry Layered Yogurt, 1 pot, 175g	**2**
Müllerlight, Toffee or Vanilla, 1 pot, 1900g	**2**

Müller – Vitality

Low Fat Pre & Probiotic Yogurt Drink, All Flavours, 1 bottle, 100g	**2**
Prebiotic Fibre + Probiotic Low Fat Yogurt, Strawberry, 1 pot, 125g	**3**
Yogurt, All Flavours, 1 pot, 125g	**3**

Nestlé

Nesquik Fresh, Chocolate or Strawberry Flavour, 1 serving, 250ml	**5**
Nesquik Go!!, 1 serving, 80g	**2**
Ski Black Cherry, 1 pot, 125g	**3**
Ski Family Pack Smooth Variety, 1 pot, 120g	**3**

Ski Smooth, All Flavours, 1 pot, 125g	**3**

Provamel – Alpro

Dairy Free Chocolate Flavour Shake, 1 bottle, 250ml	**5**
Dairy Free Strawberry Flavour Shake, 1 bottle, 250ml	**4**

Rachel's Organic Range

Bio-Live Low Fat Strawberry Yogurt, 1 pot, 125g	**3**
Bio-Live Raspberry Yogurt, 1 pot, 125g	**3**
Bio-Live Strawberry Yogurt, 1 pot, 90g	**2**
Bio-Live Wholemilk Cherry Yogurt, 1 pot, 150g	**4**
Divine Desserts Milk Chocolate Yogurt, 1 pot, 120g	**6**
Divine Desserts Orange Yogurt, 1 pot, 120g	**5**
Divine Rice Apple Sultana & Mixed Spice, 1 pot, 150g	**6**
Forbidden Fruits, Strawberry, 1 pot, 150g	**5**
Forbidden Fruits, Peach or Raspberry, 1 pot, 125g	**4**
Greek Style Orange & Lemon Bio-Live Yogurt, 1 serving, 125g	**5**
Luscious Low Fat Bio-Live Yogurt with Vanilla, 1 pot, 150g	**3**
Luscious Low Fat Cherry Yogurt, ¼ pot, 112g	**2**
Luscious Low Fat Peach Bio-Live Yogurt, 1 serving, 125g	**3**
Luscious Low Fat Raspberry, 1 pot, 150g	**3**
Luscious Low Fat Strawberry, 1 pot, 142g	**3**
Luxury Greek Style Bio-Live Yogurt with Coconut, ¼ pot, 112g	**5**
Luxury Greek Style Bio-Live Yogurt with Honey, 1 pot, 150g	**6**
Spiced Pear & Plum Bio-Live Yogurt, ¼ large pot, 112g	**3**
Taste Explorers Strawberry Drinking Yogurt, 1 serving, 100g	**2**
Tropical Fruits & Coconut Bio-Live Yogurt, 1 serving, 125g	**4**
Wholemilk Peach Yogurt, 1 serving, 125g	**3**

Tesco

Cherry Granola Yogurt, 1 pack, 190g	**6**
Cholesterol Reducing Strawberry Yogurt Drink, 1 pot, 100g	**2**
Low Fat Apricot Yogurt, 1 pot, 150g	**3**
Low Fat Black Cherry or Hazelnut or Strawberry, or Toffee or Vanilla Yogurt, 1 pot, 150g	**4**
Melon & Berries with Yogurt & Granola, 1 serving, 225g	**5**

Natural Defences Yogurt Drink, All Flavours,
1 pot, 100g **2**

Natural Light Greek Style Yogurt,
1 serving, 100g **2**

Raspberry or Strawberry Granola Yogurt,
1 pack, 190g **6**

Strawberry Yogurt Drink with LA-5, 1 pot, 100g **2**

Tropical Fruit with Yogurt & Granola,
1 serving, 235g **5**

Tesco – Finest

Black Cherry Yogurt with Chocolate Chunks,
1 pot, 135g **7**

Champagne Rhubarb Yogurt, 1 pot, 150g **6**

Devonshire Style Fudge Yogurt, 1 pot, 135g **7**

Hazelnut Yogurt, 1 pot, 150g **7**

Lemon Curd Yogurt with Meringue Pieces,
1 pot, 130g **7**

Lemon Curd Yogurt, 1 pot, 150g **7**

Madagascan Vanilla Yogurt, 1 pot, 150g **6**

Mango & Passion Fruit Yogurt, 1 pot, 150g **5**

Mediterranean White Peach Yogurt,
1 pot, 150g **5**

Scottish Raspberry Yogurt, 1 pot, 150g **5**

Strawberries & Cream Yogurt, 1 pot, 150g **5**

Strawberry Yogurt with Chocolate Chunks,
1 pot, 135g **6**

Swiss Black Cherry Yogurt, 1 pot, 150g **5**

Valencia Orange Yogurt, 1 pot, 150g **5**

Vanilla Yogurt with Chocolate Chunks,
1 pot, 135g **8**

Victoria Plum Yogurt, 1 pot, 150g **5**

Wild Canadian Blueberry Yogurt, 1 pot, 150g **6**

The Co-operative

Custard Style Apple & Blackberry Yogurt,
1 pot, 150g **6**

Custard Style Gooseberry or Rhubarb Yogurt,
1 pot, 150g **7**

Low Fat Black Cherry Yogurt, 1 pot, 125g **3**

Low Fat Hazelnut Yogurt, 1 pot, 125g **4**

Low Fat Peach or Raspberry or Strawberry or
Toffee Yogurt, 1 pot, 125g **3**

Strawberry Milk, ¼ pint, 142ml **3**

The Co-operative – Truly Irresistible

Blueberry or Vanilla Yogurt, 1 pot, 150g **6**

Champagne Rhubarb or Heritage Raspberry or
Strawberries & Cream Yogurt, 1 pot, 150g **5**

Lemon Curd Yogurt, 1 pot, 150g **8**

Total

0% Fat Free, Greek Yogurt, 1 pot, 170g **2**

0% Fat Free, Greek Yogurt with Blueberry,
1 pot, 170g **3**

0% Fat Free, Greek Yogurt with Honey,
1 pot, 150g **4**

0% Fat Free, Greek Yogurt with Strawberry,
1 pot, 150g **3**

0% Fat Free, Greek Yogurt with Tropical Fruit,
1 pot, 150g **3**

2% Fat, Greek Yogurt, 1 pot, 170g **3**

10% Fat, Greek Yogurt, 1 pot, 170g **6**

Waitrose

Apricot Fruit Fool, 1 pot, 120g **6**

Belgian Chocolate or Colombian Coffee
Flavoured Milk, 1 small glass, 100ml **3**

Madagascan Vanilla Flavoured Milk,
1 small glass, 100ml **2**

Rhubarb Fruit Fool, 1 pot, 120g **5**

Weight Watchers

Apricot Yogurt, Limited Edition, 1 pot, 120g **1**

Citrus Fruit Yogurt, Orange & Nectarine,
1 pot, 120g **1**

Citrus Fruit Yogurt, Pink Grapefruit, 1 pot, 120g **1**

Dessert Recipe Yogurt, Apricot Tart,
1 pot, 120g **1**

Dessert Recipe Yogurt, Lemon Tart, 1 pot, 120g **1**

Dessert Recipe Yogurt, Raspberry Tart,
1 pot, 120g **1**

Dessert Recipe Yogurt, Red Fruit Cheesecake,
1 portion, 120g **2**

Dessert Recipe Yogurt, Toffee Apple,
1 pot, 120g **1**

Layered Fromage Frais, Apricot, 1 pot, 100g **1**

Layered Fromage Frais, Blackberry,
1 pot, 100g **1**

Layered Fromage Frais, Cherry, 1 pot, 100g **1**

Layered Fromage Frais, Forest Fruits,
1 pot, 100g **1**

Layered Fromage Frais, Peach, 1 pot, 100g **1**

Layered Fromage Frais, Raspberry, 1 pot, 100g **1**

Layered Fromage Frais, Strawberry,
1 pot, 100g **1**

Nectarine Yogurt, Limited Edition, 1 pot, 120g **1**

Summer Fruit Yogurt, Black Cherry, 1 pot, 120g **1**

Weight Watchers® Yogurts, Desserts & Fromage Frais

a must for your shopping list

Ideal for dessert, as a tasty snack or as part of a yummy breakfast, all our Yogurts and Chilled Dairy Desserts are low in fat.

per pot

Over 25 delicious varieties of
Yogurt, Fromage Frais, Creamed Rice, Chocolate Dessert and Mousse.

WeightWatchers® Foods
Eat gorgeous. Feel gorgeous.

Summer Fruit Yogurt, Peach, 1 pot, 120g	**1**
Summer Fruit Yogurt, Raspberry, 1 pot, 120g	**1**
Summer Fruit Yogurt, Strawberry, 1 pot, 120g	**1**
Toffee Yogurt, 1 pot, 120g	**1**
Vanilla Yogurt, 1 pot, 120g	**1**

Yakult

Yakult, 1 bottle, 65ml	**1**
Yakult Light, 1 bottle, 65ml	**1**

Yeo Valley Organic

Apple & Berry Fruit Compote, ¼ pot, 113g	**2**
Bio Live Yogurt, All Flavours, 1 pot, 125g	**3**
Fat Free Bio Live Yogurt, All Flavours, 1 serving, 125g	**2**
Greek Style Yogurt with Honey, 1 pot, 100g	**4**
Low Fat Bio Live Yogurt, All Flavours, 1 pot, 125g	**3**
Natural Greek Style Yogurt, 1 pot, 100g	**4**
Probiotic Yogurt, All Flavours, 1 serving, 125g	**3**
Prune Layer Probiotic Yogurt, 1 large pot, 225g	**6**
Raspberry Layer Probiotic Yogurt, 1 pot, 125g	**3**
Smooth & Creamy Yogurt, All Flavours, ¼ large pot, 112g	**3**
Wholemilk Yogurt, All Flavours, ¼ large pot, 125g	**3**

Yoplait

Bramley Apple, 1 pot, 125g	**3**
Chocolate Yogurt, 1 pot, 125g	**4**
Forest Fruits Yogurt, 1 serving, 125g	**3**
Fruit Yogurt Raspberry, 1 pot, 125g	**3**
Hazelnut Yogurt, 1 pot, 125g	**4**
Melon & Orange Yogurt, 1 pot, 125g	**3**
Mixed Seeds Probiotic Yogurt, Peach, ¼ large pot, 125g	**4**
Peach & Strawberry Yogurt, 1 pot, 125g	**3**
Perle de Lait Classic, 1 pot, 125g	**4**
Perle de Lait Coconut, 1 pot, 125g	**5**
Perle de Lait Lemon, 1 pot, 125g	**5**
Strawberry Yogurt, 1 pot, 125g	**3**
Yop Chocolate Drink, ¼ bottle, 125g	**3**
Yop Raspberry Drinkable Yogurt, ½ bottle, 200g	**4**
Yop Strawberry Drinkable Yogurt, ½ bottle, 200g	**4**

Drinks

Basic Drinks

Advocaat, 1 pub measure, 25ml	2
Amaretto Liqueur, 1 pub measure, 25ml	2
Apple Juice, 1 small glass, 100ml	1
Barley Wine (Strong Ale), 1 bottle, 180ml	4
Beer, Bitter, Average, ½ pint, 284ml	3
Beer, Bitter, Average, 1 small can, 330ml	3
Beer, Bitter, Average, 1 pint, 568ml	6
Beer, Bitter, Bottled, 1 bottle, 330ml	4
Beer, Bitter, Bottled, 1 large bottle, 500ml	6
Beer, Bitter, Premium, ½ pint, 284ml	3
Bitter Lemon, 1 small glass, 100ml	1
Brandy, 2 teaspoons, 10ml	1
Brandy, 1 pub measure, 25ml	2
Carrot Juice, 1 small glass, 100ml	1
Champagne, 1 small glass, 125ml	3
Champagne, 1 medium glass, 175ml	5
Cherry Brandy, 1 pub measure, 25ml	2
Cider, Dry, ½ pint, 284ml	4
Cider, Dry, 1 bottle, 500ml	6
Cider, Dry, 1 pint, 568ml	7
Cider, Low Alcohol, ½ pint, 284ml	2
Cider, Low Alcohol, 1 pint, 568ml	3
Cider, Sweet, ½ pint, 284ml	4
Cider, Sweet, 1 pint, 568ml	8
Cider, Vintage, ½ pint, 284ml	10
Cider, Vintage, 1 pint, 568ml	20
Cocoa Powder, 1 heaped teaspoon, 6g	1
Coffee & Chicory Essence, 2 teaspoons, 10ml	1
Cola, 1 can, 330ml	4
Cola, Diet, 1 can, 330ml	0
Cranberry Juice, 1 small glass, 100ml	2
Cream Liqueurs, 1 pub measure, 25ml	3
Cream Soda, 1 can, 330ml	5
Drinking Chocolate, 1 tablespoon, 20g	2
Fruit Juice Drink, Carbonated, 1 small glass, 100ml	1
Fruit Juice Drink, Carbonated, 1 medium glass, 250ml	3
Fruit Juice Drink, Squash & Cordials, 1 measure, 50ml	1
Fruit Juice Drink, Squash & Cordials, Low Calorie, 1 measure, 50ml	0
Fruit Squash, 1 measure, 50ml	1
Fruit Squash, Sugar Free, 1 medium glass, 250ml	0
Gin, 40% volume, 1 pub measure, 25ml	2
Ginger Beer, 1 can, 330ml	5

Grape Juice, 1 small glass, 100ml	1
Grapefruit Juice, 1 medium glass, 250ml	2
Grenadine Syrup, undiluted, 1 tablespoon, 15g	1
Guinness, 1 pint, 568ml	6
Lager, ½ pint, 284ml	3
Lager, 1 can, 330ml	3
Lager, 1 can, 440ml	5
Lager, 1 pint, 568ml	6
Lager, Alcohol Free, ½ pint, 284ml	1
Lager, Alcohol Free, 1 pint, 568ml	1
Lager, Low Alcohol, 1 bottle, 330ml	1
Lemon Tea, Instant, 1 portion, 6g	1
Lemonade, 1 can, 330ml	2
Lemonade, Diet, 1 can, 330ml	0
Lime Juice Cordial, 1 measure, 50ml	2
Liqueurs, High Strength, 1 measure, 25ml	3
Liqueurs, Medium Strength, 1 measure, 25ml	2
Milk Shake Powder, 1 portion, 15g	2
Orange Juice Concentrate, Unsweetened, 1 serving, 50ml (undiluted)	3
Orange Juice, Unsweetened, 1 small glass, 100ml	1
Peppermint Cordial, 1 measure, 50ml	0
Pernod, 1 pub measure, 25ml	3
Pineapple Juice, 1 small glass, 100ml	1
Port, 1 pub measure, 50ml	3
Rum, 40% volume, 1 pub measure, 25ml	2
Schnapps Fruit Flavour, 1 pub measure, 25ml	3
Sherry, Dry, 1 pub measure, 50ml	2
Sherry, Medium, 1 pub measure, 50ml	2
Sherry, Sweet, 1 pub measure, 50ml	2
Soda Water, 1 medium glass, 250ml	0
Tequila, 1 pub measure, 25ml	2
Tomato Juice, 1 medium glass, 250ml	1
Tonic Water, 1 medium glass, 250ml	2
Tonic Water, Low Calorie, 1 medium glass, 250ml	0
Vermouth, Dry, 1 pub measure, 50ml	2
Vermouth, Sweet, 1 pub measure, 50ml	3
Vodka, 1 pub measure, 25ml	2
Whisky/Bourbon, 1 pub measure, 25ml	2
Wine, Lower Alcohol, 1 small glass, 125ml	2
Wine, Lower Alcohol, 1 medium glass, 175ml	3
Wine, Lower Alcohol, 1 large glass, 250ml	4
Wine, Red, 1 small glass, 125ml	3
Wine, Red, 1 medium glass, 175ml	4
Wine, Rosé, 1 small glass, 125ml	3
Wine, Rosé, 1 medium glass, 175ml	4
Wine, White, Dry, 1 small glass, 125ml	3
Wine, White, Dry, 1 medium glass, 175ml	4
Wine, White, Medium, 1 small glass, 125ml	3
Wine, White, Medium, 1 medium glass, 175ml	5
Wine, White, Sparkling, 1 small glass, 125ml	3

Wine, White, Sparkling, 1 medium glass, 175ml	4
Wine, White, Sweet, 1 small glass, 125ml	4
Wine, White, Sweet, 1 medium glass, 175ml	6

Beer, Cider & Alcopops

Asda

French Lager 2.8%, 1 can, 250ml	2
French Lager 5%, 1 can, 250ml	3

Bacardi

Breezer Lemon, 1 bottle, 275ml	5
Breezer Mango, Orange, Pineapple, Raspberry or Watermelon, 1 bottle, 275ml	3

Bulmers

Light Irish Cider, 1 serving, 250ml	3
Light Irish Cider, 1 bottle, 750ml	8

Carling

99 Calorie Bottle, 1 (330ml)	3
C2, 2% ABV Lager, 1 bottle, 300ml	3
C2, 2% ABV Lager, 1 pint, 568ml	5

Coors

Light, ½ pint, 284ml	3
Light, 1 bottle, 275ml	3

Heineken

Premium Lager Beer, 1 bottle, 330ml	5
Premium Lager Beer, 1 can, 440ml	6

Jacques

Fruit Des Bois Cider, 1 pint, 568ml	10
Fruit Des Bois Cider, 1 bottle, 750ml	14
Orchard Fruits Cider, 1 pint, 568ml	10
Orchard Fruits Cider, 1 bottle, 750ml	13

Magners

Light Irish Cider, 1 bottle, 330ml	3

Marston's

Resolution, Low Carb Beer, 1 bottle, 275ml	3

Morrisons

Shandy 1 serving, 250ml	2

Sainsbury's

German Lager Low Alcohol, 1 can, 330ml	3

Shandy Bass

Shandy, 1 serving, 250ml	2
Shandy, 1 can, 330ml	2

Smirnoff

Smirnoff Ice, 1 bottle, 275ml	5
Smirnoff Ice, 1 bottle, 700ml	13

The Co-operative

Strong Brown Ale, 1 bottle, 500ml	8

VK Lo

VK Lo, Pineapple & Grapefruit, 1 bottle, 275ml	1

Coffee, Tea, Cocoa & Instant Hot Drinks

Asda

Café Instant Cappuccino, 1 sachet, 19g	2
Café Instant Decaff Cappuccino, 1 sachet, 19g	2
Café Instant Latte, 1 sachet, 19g	2
Café Skinny Cappuccino, 1 serving, 18g	1
Drinking Chocolate, 4 teaspoons, 28g	1
Instant Malt Drink, 1 serving, 32g	3
Sleep Easy, ¼ pack, 50g	5

Cadbury

Bournville Cocoa, 1 tablespoon, 15g	1
Bournvita Malted Chocolate Drink, 2 teaspoons, 12g	1
Chocolate Break, 4 teaspoons, 28g	3
Dairy Milk Hot Choc Chunks, 1 chunk, 25g	3
Highlights Milk Chocolate Drink, 1 sachet, 11g	1

Douwe Egberts

Instant Café Latte, 1 serving, 12g	2
Instant Cappuccino, 1 serving, 12g	1
Instant Cappuccino, Less Sweet Taste, 1 serving, 12g	1
Skinny Instant Cappuccino, 1 serving, 12g	1
Skinny Instant Latte, 1 serving, 12g	1

Weight Watchers® Hot Chocolate
a must for your shopping list

Made with real chocolate – all our deliciously smooth hot chocolates are low in fat and **ProPoints**® values. The ideal me-time treat!

1 ProPoints value
per drink

Our delicious range includes:
Chocolate, Chocolate Caramel and Chocolate Mint in jars, re-sealable pouches and handy single serve sachets

SUITABLE FOR VEGETARIANS
NATURAL FLAVOURS ONLY

WeightWatchers Foods
Eat gorgeous. Feel gorgeous.

Horlicks

Extra Light Cosy Caramel or Dreamy Vanilla or Heavenly Amaretto or Malt or Malt Chocolate, 1 sachet, 11g	**1**
Light Malt, 1 serving, 32g	**3**
Light Malt Caramel Dream, 1 serving, 32g	**3**
Light Malt Refill, 1 serving, 10g	**1**
Original, 1 serving, 25g	**2**
Instant Malted Chocolate Drink, 1 sachet, 32g	**3**

Kenco

Caffé Latte, 1 serving, 20g	**2**
Cappuccino, 1 serving, 20g	**2**
Cappuccino Unsweetened Taste, 1 serving, 20ml	**2**
Cappuccino Unsweetened Taste Suchard Topping, 1 serving, 18g	**2**
Kenco 2 in 1 Smooth White Coffee, 1 pack, 8g	**1**
Smooth White Coffee with Sugar, 1 pack, 20g	**2**

Lipton

Ice Green Tea with Orange, 1 bottle, 250ml	**2**
Ice Tea, Lemon, 1 bottle, 500ml	**3**
Ice Tea, Mango, 1 bottle, 500ml	**4**
Ice Tea, Peach, 1 bottle, 500ml	**3**

Mars

Galaxy Hot Chocolate Bliss, 1 sachet, 15g	**2**
Galaxy Instant Hot Chocolate Drink, 1 sachet, 28g	**3**
Malteser Instant Hot Chocolate, 1 sachet, 15g	**2**

Maxwell House

Café Latte, 1 sachet, 14g	**2**
Café Latte Big Mugsticks, 1 serving, 15g	**2**
Cappuccino, 1 sachet, 14g	**2**
Cappuccino Original Big Mugsticks, 1 serving, 18g	**2**
Cappuccino Unsweetened Taste Big Mugsticks, 1 serving, 17g	**2**
Unsweetened Cappuccino with Chocolate Sprinkles, 1 sachet, 15g	**2**

Nescafé

Cappuccino Decaff, 1 sachet, 16g	**2**
Cappuccino Decaff, Unsweetened, 1 sachet, 16g	**2**
Caramel Latte, 1 sachet, 17g	**2**
Collection Espresso Delicate Crema, ½ pack, 50g	**1**

Dolce Gusto Cappuccino, 1 serving, 240ml	**2**
Dolce Gusto Chococino, 1 serving, 210ml	**4**
Dolce Gusto Mocha, 1 serving, 210ml	**3**
Irish Cream Latte, 1 sachet, 23g	**3**
Latte, 1 sachet, 10g	**1**
Latte Macchiato, 1 serving, 210ml	**2**
Mocha, 1 serving, 210ml	**3**
Skinny Cappuccino, 1 serving, 240ml	**1**
Skinny Latte Macchiato, 1 serving, 220ml	**2**
Vanilla Latte Macchiato, 1 sachet, 24g	**2**

Nestlé

Aero Hot Chocolate, 1 serving, 24g	**3**
Aero Instant Bubbly Hot Chocolate Drink Orange, 1 serving, 24g	**3**
Coffee-Mate, 1 teaspoon, 6g	**1**
Nestea Iced Tea & Lemon, 1 serving, 250ml	**2**
Nestea Iced Tea & Red Fruits, 1 serving, 250ml	**2**

Options

Belgian Chocolate Sachet Range, 1 sachet, 11g	**1**
Indulgent Range, All Flavours, 1 sachet, 16g	**2**

Ovaltine

Instant Hot Chocolate Double Choc, 1 measure, 11g	**1**
Night Time White Malt, 1 serving, 25g	**3**
Ovaltine Max for Milk Milkshake Powder Mix, All Flavours, 1 serving, 47g	**5**

Sainsbury's

Cappuccino, 1 serving, 50g	**5**
Fairtrade Drinking Chocolate, 1 serving, 9g	**1**
Fairtrade Hot Chocolate, 1 serving, 28g	**3**
Fairtrade Hot Chocolate Light, 1 serving, 11g	**1**
Fairtrade Instant Hot Chocolate, 3 teaspoons, 30g	**3**
Malted Drink, 3 teaspoons, 21g	**2**
Malted Drink Light, 1 serving, 25g	**2**

The Skinny Cow

Hot Chocolate, 1 serving, 10g	**1**

Weight Watchers

Hot Chocolate Drink, 1 sachet, 15g	**1**
Hot Chocolate with Caramel, 1 sachet, 15g	**1**
Hot Chocolate with Mint, 1 sachet, 15g	**1**

Fruit Juices

Asda

100% Premium Pure Clementine Juice, Not from Concentrate, 1 medium glass, 200ml	**3**
100% Pure Pressed Apple Juice, 1 medium glass, 200ml	**2**
100% Pure Pressed Grape, Apple & Cherry Juice, Not from Concentrate, 1 medium glass, 200ml	**3**
100% Pure Pressed Orange, Mango & Passionfruit Juice, 1 medium glass, 200ml	**3**
100% Pure Pressed Orchard Fruits Juice, Not from Concentrate, 1 medium glass, 200ml	**3**
100% Pure Pressed Pineapple Juice, 1 medium glass, 200ml	**3**
100% Pure Pressed Red Grape, Cranberry & Blackcurrant Juice, 1 medium glass, 200ml	**3**
100% Pure Pressed Tropical Juice, 1 medium glass, 200ml	**3**
100% Pure Pressed White Grape & Peach Juice, 1 medium glass, 200ml	**3**
100% Pure Pressed White Grape, Raspberry & Blackcurrant Juice, 1 medium glass, 200ml	**3**
100% Pure Squeezed Clementine Juice, 1 medium glass, 200ml	**3**
100% Pure Squeezed Pink Grapefruit Juice with Juicy Bits, 1 medium glass, 200ml	**2**
45% Fruit High Juice Blackcurrant, 1 serving, 250ml	**4**
50% Fruit High Juice Apple & Cranberry, 1 serving, 250ml	**3**
50% Fruit High Juice Florida Orange, 1 serving, 250ml	**3**
50% Fruit High Juice Orange & Mango, 1 serving, 250ml	**2**
50% Fruit High Juice Pineapple & Mexican Lime, 1 serving, 250ml	**3**
50% Fruit High Juice Summer Fruits, 1 serving, 250ml	**3**
50% Fruit High Juice White Grape & Peach, 1 serving, 250ml	**3**
Blueberry, Blackcurrant & Acai Smoothie, 1 medium glass, 200ml	**3**
Forest Fruits Juice Drink, 1 medium glass, 200ml	**2**
Mixed Berry Smoothie, 1 medium glass, 200ml	**3**

Orange & Mango Smoothie, 1 medium glass, 200ml	**3**
Orange & Carrot Juice Drink with added Vitamins, 1 medium glass, 200ml	**2**
Orange, Mango, Banana & Passionfruit Smoothie, 1 medium glass, 200ml	**3**
Pineapple Juice from Concentrate, 1 medium glass, 200ml	**2**
Pressed Apple & Mango Juice, 1 medium glass, 200ml	**3**
Pure Breakfast Juice, 1 serving, 250ml	**3**
Pure Orange & Pineapple Juice From Concentrate, 1 bottle, 200ml	**2**
Smoothie Orange Mango & Passion Fruit, 1 medium glass, 200ml	**3**
Smoothie Peach, Banana & Passion Fruit, 1 medium glass, 200ml	**3**
Smoothie Strawberry & Banana, 1 medium glass, 200ml	**3**
Strawberry & Banana Smoothie, 1 medium glass, 200ml	**3**
Tropical Smoothie, 1 medium glass, 200ml	**3**

Asda – Chosen by You

100% Pure Pressed Apple Juice, 1 medium glass, 200ml	**3**
100% pure Orange & Mango Juice from Concentrate, 1 medium glass, 200ml	**2**
100% Pure Pressed White Grape, Raspberry & Blackcurrant Juice, 1 medium glass, 200ml	**3**
100% Pure Squeezed Orange Juice with Juicy Bits, 1 serving, 250ml	**3**
Grape, Apple & Raspberry Juice Drink, 1 medium glass, 200ml	**2**
100% Pure Pineapple Juice from Concentrate, 1 serving, 250ml	**3**
100% Fruit Orange, Mango & Passion Fruit Smoothie, 1 serving, 250ml	**4**
100% Pure Squeezed Clementine Juice, 1 serving, 200ml	**3**
100% Pure Squeezed Orange Juice Smooth, 1 serving, 200ml	**2**
Forest Fruits Juice Drink, 1 serving, 200ml	**2**
100% Pure Breakfast Juice from Concentrate, 1 serving, 200ml	**2**
Apple & Blackberry Juice Drink, 1 serving, 200ml	**2**
Mixed Berry Smoothie, 1 serving, 250ml	**4**
Cranberry Juice Drink, 1 medium glass, 200ml	**3**
100% Fruit Strawberry & Banana Smoothie, 1 serving, 250ml	**4**

100% Pure Apple Juice from Concentrate,
1 serving, 250ml   **3**

Asda – Extra Special

100% Pure Squeezed Orange Juice Smooth,
1 medium glass, 200ml   **2**
Apple & Blackberry Smoothie,
1 small glass, 100ml   **2**
Cranberry & Raspberry Smoothie,
1 medium glass, 250ml   **4**
Freshly Squeezed Orange Juice with Bits,
1 medium glass, 250ml   **3**
Freshly Squeezed Orange Juice, Smooth,
1 medium glass, 250ml   **3**
Pineapple, Banana & Coconut Smoothie,
1 medium glass, 250ml   **6**
Pure Orange Juice with Bits, UHT,
1 serving, 200ml   **2**
Vanilla Bean, Honey & Yogurt Smoothie,
1 bottle, 250ml   **6**

Britvic

20 Winter Berry Juice Drink, 1 serving, 275ml   **3**
55 Sparkling Orange Juice Drink,
1 small bottle, 125ml   **1**
55 Sparkling Orange Juice Drink, 1 bottle, 275ml   **3**
Cranberry Juice Drink, 1 bottle, 125ml   **2**
J20 Apple & Blueberry, 1 bottle, 275ml   **3**
J20 Apple & Raspberry, 1 bottle, 275ml   **4**
J20 Orange & Pomegranate, 1 bottle, 275ml   **3**
J20 Apple & Mango, 1 bottle, 275ml   **3**
J20 Apple & Melon, 1 bottle, 275ml   **3**
J20 Orange & Passionfruit, 1 bottle, 275ml   **3**
OJ Squeezed, 1 bottle, 275ml   **3**
Orange Juice, 1 small bottle, 113ml   **1**
Pineapple Juice, 1 small bottle, 125ml   **2**
Tomato Juice, 1 small bottle, 113ml   **1**

Campbell's

V8 100% Fruit & Carrot Juice Tropical,
1 medium glass, 200ml   **2**
**V8 100% Fruit & Carrot Juice, Pomegranate &
Cranberry**, 1 serving, 150ml   **2**
**V8 100% Fruit & Vegetable Juice, Apple &
Melon**, 1 serving, 150ml   **1**
V8 100% Fruit & Vegetable Juice, Citrus,
1 serving, 150ml   **1**
**V8 100% Fruit & Vegetable Juice, Orange &
Mango**, 1 serving, 150ml   **2**
V8 100% Fruit & Vegetable Juice, Tropical,
1 serving, 150ml   **1**
V8 100% Vegetable Juice, 1 serving, 150ml   **1**

Capri Sun

100% Apple Juice, 1 pouch, 200ml   **2**
100% Orange Juice, 1 pouch, 200ml   **2**
100% Summer Fruits Juice, 1 pouch, 200ml   **3**
Apple Juice Drink, 1 pouch, 200ml   **2**
Tropical Juice Drink, 1 pouch, 200ml   **2**

Copella

Apple & Blackcurrant, 1 medium glass, 250ml   **4**
Apple & Mango Juice, 1 medium glass, 250ml   **3**
Apple & Pear Juice, 1 medium glass, 250ml   **3**

Del Monte

100% Pure Orange Juice with Juicy Bits,
1 carton, 200ml   **2**
Mango & Papaya Juice, 1 serving, 200ml   **3**
Pomegranate & Pear Juice, 1 serving, 200ml   **2**
Premium Tomato Juice, 1 serving, 200ml   **1**

Innocent

**Break Time Thickie, Yoghurt, Wholegrains,
Figs & Pears**, 1 bottle, 250ml   **7**
Cranberries, Blueberries & Cherries Smoothie,
1 serving, 250ml   **4**
Pineapples, Blueberries & Ginger Smoothie,
1 serving, 250ml   **4**
Pure Fruit Smoothie Kiwis, Apples & Limes,
1 serving, 250ml   **4**

Ocean Spray

Cranberry & Raspberry Juice Drink,
1 medium glass, 250ml   **3**
Cranberry Classic Light Juice Drink,
1 medium glass, 250ml   **0**
Cranberry Juice Drink, 1 medium glass, 250ml   **3**

Pomegreat

Pomegranate & Acai Berry Super Juice Drink,
1 medium glass, 250ml   **3**
Pomegranate & Raspberry Super Juice Drink,
1 medium glass, 250ml   **3**
Pomegranate Juice Drink,
1 medium glass, 250ml   **3**

Princes

100% Pure Grapefruit Juice from Concentrate,
1 medium glass, 200ml   **2**
Apple & Alphonso Mango Juice Drink,
1 medium glass, 200ml   **3**
Apple & Elderflower Juice Drink,
1 medium glass, 200ml   **2**

Apple, Raspberry & Pomegranate Juice Drink,
1 medium glass, 200ml **3**

No Added Sugar Blackcurrant,
1 medium glass, 250ml **1**

No Added Sugar Orange High Juice,
1 medium glass, 250ml **2**

Pear & Blackcurrant Juice Drink,
1 medium glass, 200ml **3**

Real Cranberry Juice Drink,
1 medium glass, 250ml **3**

Sainsbury's

100% Pressed Apple & Mango Juice,
1 medium glass, 250ml **3**

100% Pressed English Apple Juice,
1 medium glass, 250ml **3**

Apple & Raspberry Juice Drink, 1 bottle, 330ml **4**
Berries & Cherries Smoothie, 1 serving, 200ml **3**
Cranberry Juice Drink, 1 medium glass, 250ml **3**
Mango Juice Drink, 1 medium glass, 250ml **4**
Orange & Mango Smoothie, 1 serving, 200ml **3**
Strawberry & Banana Smoothie, 1 serving, 200g **3**

Sainsbury's – Be Good To Yourself

Cloudy Apple Juice Drink,
1 medium glass, 250ml **1**

Cranberry & Raspberry Juice Drink,
1 serving, 200ml **0**

Pomegranate Juice Drink,
1 medium glass, 250ml **1**

White Grape & Peach Juice Drink,
1 medium glass, 250ml **1**

Sunmagic

100% Pure Tropical Fruit Juice,
1 medium glass, 250ml **3**

Cranberry Juice Drink, 1 medium glass, 250ml **4**

Pure Fruit Smoothie Apple Strawberry &
Raspberry, 1 bottle, 330ml **5**

Pure Fruit Smoothie Orange Mango & Passion
Fruit, 1 bottle, 330ml **5**

Sunpride

Mango Juice Drink, 1 serving, 200ml **2**
Orange Nectar, 1 serving, 250ml **3**
Pineapple & Coconut Flavour Juice Drink,
1 serving, 200ml **3**
Tropical Juice Drink, 1 serving, 200ml **1**

The Berry Company

Acai Berry, 1 serving, 250ml **4**
Blueberry, 1 serving, 250ml **3**
Goji Berry, 1 serving, 250ml **3**
Raspberry, 1 serving, 250ml **3**
Superberry 100, All Flavours, 1 serving, 250ml **4**
Superberry Purple, 1 serving, 250ml **3**
Superberry Red, 1 serving, 250ml **3**

The Co-operative

Cloudy Apple Juice, 1 serving, 150ml **2**
No Added Sugar Orange Drink, 1 carton, 250ml **0**
No Added Sugar Orange Juice Drink with
Sweeteners, 1 carton, 250ml **0**
No Added Sugar Tropical Juice Drink with
Sweeteners, 1 carton, 250ml **0**

Tropicana

Alphonso Mango, Pineapple & A Hint of Lime
Juice, 1 medium glass, 250ml **4**
Essentials Calcium 100% Pure Squeezed
Orange Juice, 1 medium glass, 250ml **3**
Extra Juicy Bits, 1 serving, 200ml **2**
Mango Peach & Papaya, 1 medium glass, 250ml **3**
Orange & Lime Juice, 1 serving, 200ml **2**
Orange & Mango, 1 medium glass, 250ml **3**
Orange & Passionfruit Juice, 1 serving, 200ml **2**
Orange & Watermelon Juice, 1 serving, 200ml **2**
Passionfruit, Pear & Apple,
1 medium glass, 250ml **3**
Pineapple & Guava, 1 medium glass, 100ml **1**
Pineapple & Passionfruit, 1 medium glass, 250ml **3**
Raspberry, Wild Rosehip & Elderberry Juice,
1 medium glass, 250ml **4**
Red Citrus, 1 small glass, 100ml **1**
Sanguinello Sicilian Blood Orange,
1 medium glass, 250ml **3**
Smoothie, Blackberry & Blueberry,
1 medium glass, 250ml **3**
Smoothie, Mango, Passion Fruit & Pineapple,
1 medium glass, 250ml **3**
Smoothie, Raspberry & Pomegranate,
1 medium glass, 250ml **3**
Smoothie, Strawberry & Banana,
1 medium glass, 250ml **4**
Valencia Orange & Crushed Raspberry,
1 medium glass, 250ml **3**

Waitrose

Alphonso Mango & Passionfruit Smoothie,
1 medium glass, 250ml **4**

Cloudy Apple Juice, 1 small glass, 100ml	1
Pineapple, Banana & Coconut Smoothie, 1 medium glass, 250ml	5
Pressed Apple, Raspberry & Guava Juice, 1 medium glass, 250ml	3
Pure Squeezed Orange, Mango & Passionfruit Juice, 1 medium glass, 250ml	3
Strawberry Blackcurrant & Blueberry Smoothie, 1 medium glass, 250ml	4
Strawberry, Raspberry & Banana Smoothie, 1 medium glass, 250ml	4
Tropical Fruit Drink, 1 carton, 250ml	3

Welch's

Pure Grape Juice Drink, Light, 1 medium glass, 250ml	3

Soft Drinks & Squashes

Amè

Elderberry & Lemon, 1 medium glass, 250ml	2
Grape & Apricot, 1 medium glass, 250ml	2
Grape & Orange, 1 medium glass, 250ml	2
Raspberry & Blackcurrant, 1 medium glass, 250ml	2

Appletiser

Appletiser, 1 small bottle, 275ml	3
Appletiser, 1 can, 330ml	4

Asda

Apple & Berries 100% Sparkling Fruit Juice, 1 carton, 200ml	2
Apple & Blackcurrant Squash, 1 medium glass, 250ml	0
Apple Juice & Spring Water, 1 serving, 250ml	2
Apple, Blackcurrant & Acerola Smoothie, 1 medium glass, 200ml	3
Bitter Lemon, 1 medium glass, 250ml	1
Blackcurrant Juice Drink, 1 small glass, 100ml	1
Blackcurrantade, Sugar Free, 1 medium glass, 250ml	0
Blueberry, Pomegranate Juice Drink, 1 medium glass, 200ml	2
Citrus Fruit Splash, 1 bottle, 500ml	1
Dandelion & Burdock, Sugar Free, 1 medium glass, 250ml	0
Ginger Ale, 1 medium glass, 250ml	1

Ginger Beer, 1 can, 330ml	3
Grape, Apple & Raspberry Juice Drink, 1 medium glass, 200ml	2
Iron Brew, 1 medium glass, 100ml	1
Lemonade, 1 serving, 250ml	1
No Added Sugar Juice Drink Pomegranate & Blueberry, 1 serving, 250ml	1
No Added Sugar Pomegranate & Blueberry Juice Drink, 1 medium glass, 250ml	1
No Added Sugar Pomegranate & Cranberry Juice Drink, 1 medium glass, 250ml	1
North American Cranberry & Apple Hi Juice, 1 serving, 250ml	2
Orange & Mandarin 100% Sparkling Fruit Juice, 1 bottle, 250ml	3
Orange & Mango Juice, 1 medium glass, 200ml	2
Pear & Grape 100% Sparkling Fruit Juice, 1 bottle, 200ml	2
Pineapple & Mexican Lime High Juice, 1 medium glass, 250ml	3
Sparkling Apple, 1 medium glass, 250ml	2
Sparkling Orange, 1 medium glass, 250ml	2
Sparkling Tropical, 1 medium glass, 250ml	2
Summer Fruit Splash, 1 bottle, 500ml	1
Summer Fruits High Juice, 1 medium glass, 250ml	3

Asda – Extra Special

Dandelion & Burdock, 1 medium glass, 250ml	3
Extra Juicy Lemonade, 1 serving, 250ml	3
Hot Jamaican Ginger Ale, 1 serving, 250ml	2
Indian Tonic Water with Tahitian Lime, 1 serving, 250ml	2
Jamaican Ginger Beer with Lime, 1 serving, 250ml	3
Orange & Ecuadorian Passionfruit Juice Drink, 1 bottle, 275ml	4
Sicilian Bitter Lemon, 1 serving, 250ml	3
Sparkling Muscat Non Alcoholic Juice Drink, 1 bottle, 250ml	4
Sparkling Pink Muscat Non Alcoholic Juice Drink, 1 bottle, 250ml	4

Barr

Cherryade, 1 serving, 330ml	2
Dandelion & Burdock, 1 can, 330ml	4
Ginger Beer, 1 serving, 330ml	5
Orangeade, 1 serving, 330ml	3
Originals Cream Soda with a Twist of Raspberry, 1 serving, 330ml	4
Shandy, 1 serving, 330ml	2
Traditional Lemonade, 1 can, 330ml	4

Soft Drinks & Squashes Drinks

Bottle Green Drinks Company

Blossom Cottage Ginger Beer Cordial,
1 serving, diluted, 250ml **2**

Blossom Cottage Lemon & Lime Leaf Cordial,
1 serving, diluted, 250ml **2**

Classic Variety Cordial Blackberry & Russet
Apple, 1 serving, diluted, 250ml **2**

Classic Variety Cordial Cox's Apple & Plum,
1 serving, diluted, 250ml **2**

Classic Variety Cordial Williams Pear &
Elderflower, 1 serving, diluted, 250ml **2**

Cordial Orange & Mango, 1 serving, 250ml **2**

Party Apple & Elderflower Sparkling Drink,
1 serving, 200ml **2**

Red Grape Sparkling Juice Drink,
1 serving, 200ml **2**

Sparkling Elderflower, 1 serving, 200ml **2**

Sparkling Williams Pear & Elderflower,
1 serving, 200ml **2**

White Grape Sparkling Juice Drink,
1 serving, 200ml **2**

Britvic

55 Apple, Raspberry & Cranberry Juice Drink,
1 bottle, 275ml **3**

7Up, 1 medium glass, 250ml **3**

Bitter Lemon, 1 medium glass, 250ml **2**

Pepsi, 1 can, 330ml **4**

Pepsi Raw, 1 can, 150ml **2**

Pepsi Regular, 1 medium glass, 250ml **3**

R Whites Premium Lemonade, 1 can, 330ml **1**

Tango Cherry or Citrus, 1 can, 330ml **1**

Coca Cola Company

Cherry, 1 can, 330ml **4**

Coca Cola Original, 1 can, 330ml **4**

Coca Cola Original, 1 bottle, 500ml **6**

Dr Pepper, 1 can, 330ml **4**

Fanta Fruit Twist, 1 can, 330ml **5**

Fanta Orange, 1 serving, 150ml **1**

Fanta Still, Orange Tropical,
1 medium glass, 250ml **2**

Fanta World Pineapple Flavour, 1 can, 330ml **4**

Lilt, 1 can, 330ml **2**

Lilt Pineapple & Grapefruit, 1 can, 330ml **2**

Oasis Citrus Punch, 1 bottle, 375ml **2**

Oasis Mixed Berry Fruit Drink, 1 serving, 250ml **1**

Oasis Summer Fruits, 1 bottle, 375ml **2**

Sprite, 1 can, 330ml **4**

Feel Good Drinks

Cranberry & Lime Sparkling Juice Drink,
1 medium glass, 250ml **2**

Gently Sparkling White Grape & Peach Juice
Drink, 1 bottle, 750ml **8**

Lemon Sparkling Juice Drink, 1 bottle, 250ml **3**

Orange & Passion Fruit Sparkling Juice Drink,
1 bottle, 250ml **2**

Innocent – This Water

Passion Fruit, Peaches & Spring Water with
Natural Antioxidants, 1 bottle, 420ml **4**

Pomegranates, Lychees & Blackcurrants,
1 medium glass, 250ml **2**

This Water Cranberries, Raspberries & Spring
Water, 1 bottle, 420ml **3**

Irn Bru

Irn Bru, 1 can, 330ml **4**

Irn Bru, 1 medium glass, 250ml **3**

Ocean Spray

Cranberry & Pomegranate for Water,
1 serving, undiluted, 50ml **3**

Cranberry & Raspberry for Water,
1 serving, undiluted, 50ml **2**

Cranberry Classic for Water,
1 serving, undiluted, 50ml **2**

Cranberry Classic Light for Water Reduced
Sugar, 1 serving, undiluted, 50ml **1**

Old Jamaica

Ginger Beer, 1 can, 330ml **6**

Light Ginger Beer, 1 can, 330ml **0**

Princes

Jucee Apple & Blackcurrant Squash,
1 medium glass, 200ml **0**

Jucee Fruit Squash Orange, Lemon &
Pineapple, 1 medium glass, 200ml **1**

Jucee Orange, Lemon & Pineapple Squash,
1 medium glass, 100ml **0**

Jucee Summer Fruits Squash,
1 medium glass, 200ml **0**

Ribena

Blackcurrant, 1 can, 330ml **4**

Blackcurrant, 1 serving, 250ml **3**

Blackcurrant Spark, 1 can, 330ml **5**

Really Light Blackcurrant, 1 carton, 200ml **0**

Robinsons

Apple & Blackcurrant, No Added Sugar,
1 measure, 50ml — **0**

Be Natural, All Flavours, 1 measure, 50ml — **3**

Fruit & Barley No Added Sugar Orange,
1 measure, 50ml — **0**

Fruit & Barley, Peach, 1 measure, 50ml — **0**

Fruit Shoot 100% Juice, All Flavours,
1 bottle, 250ml — **3**

Fruit Shoot H2OC, 1 bottle, 300ml — **0**

Fruit Shoot Juice Drink Summer Fruits,
1 bottle, 300ml — **0**

Fruit Shoot Low Sugar Apple Juice Drink,
1 bottle, 300ml — **0**

Fruit Shoot Low Sugar, All Flavours,
1 bottle, 200ml — **0**

Fruit Shoot, Blackcurrant & Apple,
1 bottle, 200ml — **0**

Original Whole Orange Squash,
1 measure, 50ml — **1**

Summer Fruits, No Added Sugar,
1 measure, 50ml — **0**

Robinsons – Fruit & Barley

Apple & Blackcurrant Smooth Juice,
1 medium glass, 250ml — **3**

Classic Lemon Barley Water, 1 measure, 50ml — **1**

Fruit & Barley, Apple & Blackcurrant,
1 measure, 50ml — **1**

High Juice, Apple, Cherry & Raspberry,
Concentrate, 1 measure, 50ml — **2**

High Juice, Apple, Concentrate,
1 measure, 50ml — **3**

High Juice, Apple, Strawberry & Lychee,
Concentrate, 1 measure, 50ml — **2**

High Juice, Grape & Melon, Concentrate,
1 measure, 50ml — **3**

High Juice, Orange, Concentrate,
1 measure, 50ml — **2**

High Juice, Peach, Concentrate,
1 measure, 50ml — **2**

High Juice, Pink Grapefruit, Concentrate,
1 measure, 50ml — **2**

Original Orange & Pineapple Squash,
1 measure, 50ml — **1**

Original Summer Fruits Squash,
1 measure, 50ml — **1**

Sainsbury's

Cloudy Lemonade, 1 medium glass, 250ml — **4**

Cranberry & Raspberry Juice Drink,
1 medium glass, 250ml — **3**

Fiery Ginger Beer, 1 medium glass, 250ml — **0**

Fruit Cocktail Juice Drink, 1 serving, 50ml — **1**

Fruit Crush Sparkling Lemon & Lime,
1 medium glass, 250ml — **0**

Fruit Crush Sparkling Orange,
1 medium glass, 250ml — **0**

Fruit Crush Sparkling Orange Twist,
1 medium glass, 250ml — **0**

Fruit Crush Sparkling Pineapple & Grapefruit,
1 medium glass, 250ml — **0**

Lemon & Lime, 1 medium glass, 250ml — **3**

Limeade, 1 medium glass, 250ml — **0**

No Added Sugar Fizzy Strawberry,
1 bottle, 250ml — **0**

Orangeade, 1 medium glass, 250ml — **0**

Orange Squash, 1 serving, 250ml — **3**

Pineapple & Coconut Cooler,
1 medium glass, 250ml — **5**

Pomegranate & Blueberry Juice Drink,
1 medium glass, 250ml — **3**

Red Grape & Cranberry Cooler,
1 medium glass, 250ml — **3**

Sparkling Orange Fruit Crush,
1 medium glass, 250ml — **0**

Schweppes

Canada Dry Ginger Ale, 1 can, 330ml — **3**

Classic Cloudy Lemonade, 1 can, 330ml — **3**

Cordial Lime, 1 serving, 200ml — **0**

Cordial Orange, 1 serving, 200ml — **1**

Ginger Ale, 1 serving, 200ml — **2**

Indian Tonic Water, 1 medium glass, 250ml — **1**

Indian Tonic Water with a Hint of Pomegranate,
1 medium glass, 250ml — **1**

Indian Tonic with Lemon, 1 medium glass, 250ml — **2**

Lemonade, 1 serving, 150ml — **1**

**Lightly Sparkling Apple Pear & Cinnamon or
Pomegranate & Blueberry**, 1 small glass, 100ml — **1**

Original Bitter Lemon, 1 medium glass, 250ml — **2**

Original Lemonade, 1 can, 330ml — **2**

Peppermint Cordial, 1 measure, 50ml — **0**

Russchian, 1 medium glass, 250ml — **2**

Straightcut Lemon, 1 medium glass, 250ml — **3**

Straightcut Pomegranate & Blueberry,
1 serving, 200ml — **2**

Summer Punch Lemonade, 1 serving, 200ml — **1**

White Lemonade, 1 serving, 200ml — **2**

Shloer

Red Grape, 1 small glass, 125ml — **1**

Red Grape, 1 can, 250ml	3
Sparkling Juice Drink Apple, 1 serving, 250ml	3
Sparkling Rosé Grape Juice Drink, 1 serving, 250ml	3
White Grape, 1 small glass, 125ml	1
White Grape & Elderflower, 1 small glass, 125ml	1
White Grape Raspberry & Cranberry, 1 small glass, 125ml	1
White Grape, Mango & Passionfruit, 1 bottle, 275ml	3

Snapple

Cranberry Raspberry Juice Drink, 1 bottle, 500ml	6
Guava Mania, 1 bottle, 500ml	6
Snapple Apple Juice Drink, 1 bottle, 500ml	7

Sunny D

Caribbean Tropical Juice Drink, 1 serving, 200ml	2
Florida Style Orange Juice Drink, 1 serving, 200ml	2

The Co-operative

Apple & Blackcurrant Squash, 1 measure, 50ml	0
Apple, Strawberry & Redcurrant Squash, 1 measure, 50ml	0
Blackcurrant Cordial, 1 measure, 50ml	0
Cloudy Lemonade, 1 medium glass, 250ml	0
Ginger Ale, 1 medium glass, 250ml	1
Grape Apple & Raspberry Juicy Water, 1 medium glass, 250ml	2
High Juice Apple Squash, 1 measure, 50ml	3
High Juice Blackcurrant, 1 measure, 50ml	3
High Juice Orange Squash, 1 measure, 50ml	2
High Juice Pineapple & Grapefruit, 1 measure, 50ml	3
High Juice Summer Fruits Squash, 1 measure, 50ml	3
High Juice Tropical Fruit Squash, 1 measure, 50ml	2
Lemon & Lime Flavour Sparkling Spring Water Drink, ¼ bottle, 250ml	0
Lime Cordial, 1 measure, 50ml	0
Mandarin & Cranberry Flavour Still Spring Water Drink, ⅙ bottle, 240ml	0
Mango & Orange Juicy Water, 1 medium glass, 250ml	3
Mixed Fruit Flavour Squash, 1 measure, 50ml	0
Orange & Cranberry Flavour Sparkling Spring Water Drink, ¼ bottle, 250ml	0
Orange, Lemon & Pineapple Squash, 1 measure, 50ml	0

Peach Flavour Sparkling Spring Water Drink, ¼ bottle, 250ml	0
Soda Water, 1 medium glass, 250ml	0
Sparkling Blackcurrant Flavour Juice Drink, ⅓ bottle, 248ml	2
Sparkling Cranberry Juice Drink with Spring Water, 1 can, 330ml	4
Sparkling Lemonade Shandy, 1 serving, 250ml	0
Tonic Water with a Twist of Lemon, 1 medium glass, 250ml	1
Tropical Juicy Water, 1 bottle, 250ml	2
Whole Lemon Squash, 1 measure, 50ml	0
Whole Orange Squash, 1 measure, 50ml	0

Vimto

Vimto Fizzy, 1 serving, 250ml	3

Volvic

Revive Berry Blast Flavour with Ginseng & Guarana, 1 bottle, 500ml	0
Touch of Fruit Original Still Strawberry Flavour, 1 small bottle, 500ml	3
Touch of Fruit Sugar Free Still Lemon & Lime Flavour, 1 bottle, 500ml	0

Waitrose

Apple & Blackcurrant Squash, 1 medium glass, 250ml	1
Apple, Red Grape & Pomegranate Sparkling Juice Drink, 1 medium glass, 250ml	2
Apple, Red Grape & Rhubarb Sparkling Juice Drink, 1 medium glass, 250ml	3
Cloudy Lemonade, 1 medium glass, 250ml	3
Lemonade with Real Lemon Juice, 1 can, 330ml	4
Lemonade with Spanish Lemon, 1 carton, 250ml	3
Sicilian Bitter Lemons, 1 carton, 250ml	4
Sparkling Lemonade, 1 medium glass, 250ml	1
Still Lemonade, 1 medium glass, 250ml	3
Traditional Cream Soda, 1 small glass, 100ml	1
Tropical Crush, 1 medium glass, 250ml	3
White Grape, Apple & Elderflower Sparkling Juice Drink, 1 medium glass, 250ml	2
White Grape, Apple & Raspberry Sparkling Juice Drink, 1 medium glass, 250ml	2

Spirits, Sherry, Port & Vermouth

Bailey's

Bailey's The Original Irish Cream, 1 serving, 25ml	2
Bailey's with a Hint of Crème Caramel, 1 serving, 25ml	2
Bailey's with a Hint of Mint Chocolate, 1 serving, 25ml	2

Tesco

Bianco Vermouth, 1 measure, 25ml	1
Extra Dry Vermouth, 1 measure, 25ml	1
Rosso Vermouth, 1 measure, 25ml	1

Sports & Energy Drinks

Asda

Blue Bolt, 1 can, 250ml	3
Blue Charge, 1 medium glass, 250ml	3
Glucose Energy Drink, 1 medium glass, 250ml	4
Isotonic Sports Drink, All Flavours, 1 bottle, 500ml	4
Orange Glucose Energy Drink, 1 serving, 250ml	5

Britvic

Energise Sport, 1 bottle, 500ml	3

Firefly

Chill Out Blackcurrant & Currant + Cinnamon & Bitter Orange Flower, 1 can, 330ml	3
Detox Lemon, Lime & Ginger, 1 can, 330ml	3

Lucozade

Body Fuel, Orange, Raspberry or Tropical, 1 bottle, 500ml	3
Hydrate Carbohydrate & Sodium Drink Mix, Orange, 1 serving, 24g	0
Lucozade Sport Hydro Actice, Citrus or Summer Fruits, 1 bottle, 500ml	1
Mixed Citrus Body Fuel, 1 bottle, 500ml	3
Sport Body Fuel Orange, 1 bottle, 330ml	2

Powerade

Berry & Tropical Fruits, Cherry, Mango or Orange, 1 bottle, 500ml	3

Red Bull

Red Bull Energy Drink, 1 can, 250ml	3
Red Bull, Sugar Free, 1 can, 250ml	0

Rowan Glen

Cranberry in Tune Probiotic Health Drink, 1 serving, 100g	2
Orange in Tune Probiotic Health Drink, 1 small glass, 100ml	2

Wine & Champagne

Banrock Station

Light Chardonnay & Sauvignon Blanc, 1 serving, 125ml	2
Light Shiraz Rosé, 1 serving, 125ml	2

Blossom Hill

Pinot Grigio, 1 serving, 125ml	3
Signature Blend California Red, 1 serving, 125ml	3
Signature Blend California White, Aromatic & Fruity, 1 serving, 125ml	3

Echo Falls

Spritz with White Zinfandel Rosé, 1 bottle, 250ml	3
Spritz with Chardonnay, 1 bottle, 250ml	3
Lambrini Light, 1 bottle, 275ml	6

Le Piat d'Or

Piat d'Or Chardonnay, 1 serving, 125ml	3
Piat d'Or Grenache Rosé, 1 serving, 125ml	3
Piat d'Or Merlot, 1 serving, 125ml	3

Weight Watchers

Fruity White Wine, 1 small glass, 125ml	2
Grenache Rosé, 1 small glass, 125ml	3
Purely Pink Wine, 1 small glass, 125ml	2
Refreshing Rosé, 1 small glass, 125ml	2
Riesling, 1 small glass, 125ml	2
Smooth Red, 1 small glass, 125ml	3

Weight Watchers®
Wines

2 ProPoints value *to* 3 ProPoints value

per 125ml glass

Our delicious range is unique in that each wine is lower in **ProPoints**® values than many other wines on shelf.

Our range of 5 full flavoured, easy drinking wines:
*Fruity White, Purely Pink and Refreshing Rosé each have a **ProPoints**® value of 2 per 125ml glass, Grenache Rosé and Smooth Red each have a **ProPoints** value of 3 per 125ml glass. Maximum 9% abv.*

 WeightWatchers® Foods
Eat gorgeous. Feel gorgeous.

Customers must be 18 years or over to purchase alcohol. www.drinkaware.co.uk

Fish, Meat & Poultry

Basic Foods

Bacon Medallions, 2 rashers, 40g	**1**
Bacon, Back, raw, 1 medium rasher, 25g	**1**
Bacon, Streaky, raw, 1 medium rasher, 20g	**2**
Beef, Braising Steak, braised, 1 quantity, 100g	**6**
Beef, Braising Steak, Lean, cooked, 1 quantity, 100g	**5**
Beef, Braising Steak, Lean, raw, 1 quantity, 100g	**3**
Beef, Brisket, 1 medium portion, 90g	**5**
Beef, Corned, 1 medium slice, 45g	**2**
Beef, Fillet Steak, Lean, grilled, 1 steak, 105g	**5**
Beef, Fillet Steak, Lean, raw, 1 medium steak, 105g	**4**
Beef, Fillet Steak, raw, 1 steak, 100g	**4**
Beef, Fillet Steak, raw, 1 medium steak, 200g	**8**
Beef, Fore-Rib/Rib-Roast, roasted, 1 medium slice, 35g	**3**
Beef, Mince, Extra Lean, raw, 1 portion, 125g	**6**
Beef, Mince, Extra Lean, cooked, 1 medium portion, 140g	**6**
Beef, Mince, raw, 1 medium portion, 125g	**7**
Beef, Silverside, cooked, 1 thin slice, 28g	**1**
Beef, Silverside, Lean, raw, 1 quantity, 100g	**3**
Beef, Sirloin Steak, Lean, raw, 1 medium steak, 225g	**7**
Beef, Stewing Steak, Lean, raw, 1 medium portion, 100g	**3**
Beef, Topside, raw, 1 quantity, 100g	**5**
Beef Burger, fried, 1 standard, 36g	**3**
Beef Burger, fried, 1 quarter pounder, 90g	**8**
Beef Burger, grilled, 1 standard, 36g	**3**
Beef Burger, grilled, 1 quarter pounder, 90g	**8**
Beef Burger, raw, 1 (56g)	**4**
Beef Burger, raw, 1 large, 114g	**9**
Biltong, 1 portion, 100g	**6**
Black Pudding, Dry Fried, 1 medium slice, 30g	**2**
Bratwurst, 1 (75g)	**5**
Brawn, 1 quantity, 100g	**4**
Chicken Roll, 2 medium slices, 24g	**1**
Chicken, Breast, Skinless, raw, 1 medium, 165g	**4**
Chicken, Breast, with Skin, cooked, 1 medium, 130g	**6**
Chicken, Breast, Skinless, grilled, 1 (120g)	**4**
Chicken, Drumstick, Skinless, cooked, 1 piece, 44g	**2**
Chicken, Drumstick, Skinless, raw, 1 medium, 47g	**1**

Chicken, Drumstick, with Skin, cooked, 1 (62g)	**3**
Chicken, Leg Quarter, Skinless, Boneless, raw, 1 medium, 135g	**7**
Chicken, Leg Quarter, with Skin, roasted, 1 (190g)	**12**
Chicken, Leg, Skinless, raw, 1 medium, 110g	**3**
Chicken, Mince, raw, 1 medium portion, 140g	**4**
Chicken, roast, meat only, 1 medium slice, 30g	**1**
Chicken, roasted with Skin, 1 medium slice, 30g	**2**
Chicken, roast, rotisserie, ¼ (300g)	**13**
Chicken, Skin, roasted or grilled, 1 small portion, 10g	**1**
Chicken, Thigh, Skinless & Boneless, raw, 1 (85g)	**4**
Chicken, Thigh, with Skin, cooked, 1 (85g)	**5**
Chicken, Wafer Thin, 1 medium portion, 30g	**1**
Chicken, Wing, with Skin, cooked, 1 (25g)	**1**
Chorizo Sausage, 1 portion, 30g	**2**
Cockles, cooked, 1 portion, 50g	**1**
Cod Roe, Battered, 1 medium portion, 160g	**8**
Cod, baked, 1 medium fillet, 120g	**3**
Cod, raw, 1 medium fillet, 90g	**2**
Cod, Smoked, raw, 1 medium fillet, 120g	**2**
Cod, Smoked, raw, 1 large fillet, 175g	**3**
Crab, boiled, 1 medium, 110g	**4**
Crab, raw, 1 quantity, 100g	**2**
Crabsticks, 3 sticks, 51g	**1**
Crayfish, raw, 1 medium portion, 85g	**1**
Dover Sole, whole, raw, 1 (250g)	**5**
Duck, Breast, Skinless, raw, 1 medium, 150g	**5**
Duck, Breast, with Skin, raw, 1 (160g)	**9**
Duck, Breast, with Skin, roasted, 1 serving, 170g	**10**
Duck, Leg, with Skin, raw, 1 (90g)	**6**
Duck, Skinless, mixed meat, roasted, 1 portion, 25g	**1**
Eel, 1 medium portion, 100g	**4**
Frankfurter, regular, 1 (47g)	**4**
Frogs Legs, raw, 1 serving, 75g	**1**
Gammon Steak, raw, 1 medium, 170g	**6**
Gammon/Ham Joint, raw, 1 slice, 23g	**1**
Goat, raw, 1 quantity, 100g	**2**
Goose, roasted, 1 medium slice, 25g	**2**
Grouper, raw, 1 fillet, 259g	**5**
Guinea Fowl, raw, 1 (275g)	**10**
Haddock, raw, 1 medium fillet, 120g	**2**
Haddock, smoked & steamed, 1 medium fillet, 120g	**3**
Haddock, steamed, 1 small fillet, 50g	**1**
Haddock, steamed, 1 medium fillet, 120g	**2**
Haddock, steamed, 1 large fillet, 170g	**4**
Haggis, boiled, 1 portion, 100g	**9**

	ProPoints value
Hake, grilled, 1 serving, 100g	3
Hake, raw, 1 steak, 100g	2
Halibut, grilled, 1 medium steak, 150g	4
Halibut, raw, 1 fillet, 120g	3
Ham, Parma, 2 thin slices, 34g	2
Ham, Premium, 1 medium slice, 35g	1
Ham, Prepacked, 3 thin slices, 33g	1
Ham, Wafer Thin, 1 medium portion, 30g	1
Haslet, Pork, 1 slice, 14g	1
Herring, raw, 1 medium fillet, 120g	6
Hoki, grilled, 1 fillet, 190g	6
Hoki, raw, 1 medium fillet, 120g	2
Jellied Eels, 1 medium portion, 100g	3
John Dory, raw, 1 medium fillet, 120g	3
Kangaroo Steak, raw, 1 steak, 125g	3
Kidney, Lamb, raw, 1 (25g)	1
Kidney, Pig, cooked, 1 medium, 74g	3
Kidney, Pig, raw, 1 (140g)	4
King Prawns, cooked, 1 quantity, 100g	3
King Prawns, raw, 8 (64g)	1
Kipper, grilled, 1 medium, 130g	9
Kipper, raw, 1 medium, 150g	9
Lamb, Boneless Leg Steak, Lean, raw, 1 medium, 100g	5
Lamb, Breast, Lean, roasted, 1 medium slice, 35g	3
Lamb, Breast, roasted, 1 slice, 30g	3
Lamb, Chump Chop, Boneless, raw, 1 medium, 130g	8
Lamb, Heart, raw, 1 medium, 200g	6
Lamb, Leg, Lean, raw (23% bone), 1 quantity, 100g	4
Lamb, Leg, Lean, roasted, 1 medium slice, 30g	2
Lamb, Leg, raw, 1 joint, 270g	13
Lamb, Leg, roasted, 1 slice, 30g	2
Lamb, Loin Chop, raw, 1 medium, 60g	5
Lamb, Mince, Lean (less than 16% Fat), 1 medium portion, 140g	8
Lamb, Mince, raw, 1 medium portion, 140g	9
Lamb, Neck Cutlet, Boneless, raw, 1 (86g)	7
Lamb, Neck Fillet, raw, 1 quantity, 100g	7
Lamb, Rack, Weighed with Bone, raw, 1 quantity, 100g	6
Lamb, Shank, Weighed with Bone, Meat Only, raw, 1 quantity, 100g	5
Lamb, Shoulder, Lean, raw, 1 quantity, 100g	6
Lamb, Shoulder, Lean, roasted, 1 quantity, 100g	5
Lamb, Sweetbread, raw, 1 portion, 25g	1
Lemon Sole, grilled, 1 medium fillet, 170g	4
Lemon Sole, raw, 1 fillet, 170g	3
Liver Sausage, 1 medium slice, 17g	1
Liver, Calf, raw, 1 medium slice, 50g	1
Liver, Chicken, raw, 1 quantity, 100g	2

	ProPoints value
Liver, Lamb, raw, 1 quantity, 100g	3
Liver, Ox, raw, 1 quantity, 100g	4
Liver, Pig, raw, 1 quantity, 100g	3
Lobster with Shell, boiled, ½ (300g)	3
Lobster, boiled, 1 portion, 85g	2
Lobster, raw, 1 quantity, 100g	2
Luncheon Meat, 1 medium slice, 14g	1
Mackerel, raw, 1 medium fillet, 150g	9
Mackerel, Smoked, 1 medium fillet, 150g	14
Monkfish, grilled, 1 medium portion, 70g	2
Monkfish, raw, 1 medium portion, 70g	1
Mullet, Grey, grilled, 1 fillet, 100g	4
Mullet, Grey, raw, 1 medium fillet, 120g	3
Mullet, Red, grilled, 1 fillet, 100g	3
Mullet, Red, raw, 1 medium fillet, 120g	3
Mussels, Without Shells, boiled, 1 medium portion, 40g	1
Mussels, Without Shells, boiled, 1 quantity, 100g	3
Mussels, Weighed with Shells, boiled, 4 (96g)	1
Mussels, Weighed with Shells, boiled, 1 quantity, 1000g	7
Octopus, raw, 1 portion, 85g	2
Orange Roughy, raw, 1 medium fillet, 120g	4
Ostrich, Mince, raw, 1 quantity, 100g	4
Ostrich, Tenderloin, raw, 1 medium, 107g	3
Oxtail, raw, 1 piece, 44g	2
Oysters, Flesh Only, raw, 12 (120g)	2
Oysters, Weighed with Shells, raw, 12 (504g)	1
Pancetta, 1 slice, 7g	1
Partridge, cooked, 1 serving, 260g	14
Pastrami, 2 medium slices, 24g	1
Pheasant, Meat Only, roasted, ¼ medium, 108g	6
Pigeon, cooked, 1 medium, 115g	5
Pigeon, Meat Only, raw, 1 serving, 100g	4
Pike, raw, 1/2 fillets, 198g	4
Plaice, cooked, 1 medium fillet, 106g	2
Plaice, raw, 1 fillet, 130g	3
Pollock, raw, 1 fillet, 105g	2
Polony, 1 medium slice, 30g	2
Pork Crackling, 1 portion, 30g	4
Pork Escalope, raw, 1 medium, 130g	5
Pork Joint, Shoulder, Boneless, raw, 1 quantity, 100g	3
Pork Joint, Shoulder, Boneless, raw, 1/10 joint, 210g	6
Pork, Belly Slices, raw, 1 slice, 96g	7
Pork, Chitterlings, raw, 1 portion, 100g	5
Pork, Fillet, Lean, grilled, 1 quantity, 100g	4
Pork, Fillet, Lean, raw, 1 quantity, 100g	4
Pork, Leg Joint, Lean, roasted, 1 medium slice, 35g	2

Lean on
Turkey

'Turkey is a great meat, it's got great flavour, great texture and one of the beauties of turkey is the versatility of it and hence the dishes that you can make with it "

Turkey Ambassador Marco Pierre White

...to achieve your target!

From turkey steaks and risottos, to salads and pasta dishes, the versatility of turkey means there is plenty for you to try. Whether you want a quick fix weekday favourite or hearty family meal to tempt your tastebuds, your mealtimes needn't leave you uninspired!

Turkey breast meat is...
- ✓ high in protein
- ✓ low in saturated fat
- ✓ a good source of natural vitamins and minerals

Brought to you by

Bernard Matthews farms

The **Lean on Turkey** campaign is supported by a fantastic website packed full of culinary inspiration, including low fat meal ideas masterclasses with Marco and nutritional advice.

Lean on Turkey .co.uk

Be inspired at **www.leanonturkey.co.uk**

Pork, Leg Joint, raw, 1 medium, 235g	**17**
Pork, Leg Joint, roasted, 1 slice, 35g	**2**
Pork, Leg, Bone In, raw, ⅛ joint, 125g	**6**
Pork, Leg, Boneless, raw, ⅛ joint, 125g	**7**
Pork, Loin Steak, Lean, grilled, 1 steak, 120g	**5**
Pork, Loin Steak, Lean, raw, 1 medium, 150g	**7**
Pork, Mince, raw, 1 medium portion, 140g	**6**
Pork, Spare Ribs, Meat Only, cooked, 1 portion, 140g	**11**
Pork, Spare Ribs, Weighed with Bone, cooked, 1 portion, 220g	**8**
Pork, Spare Ribs, Meat Only, raw, 1 quantity, 100g	**5**
Pork, Spare Ribs, Weighed with Bone, raw, 1 medium portion, 80g	**2**
Pork, Tenderloin, raw, 1 medium portion, 150g	**5**
Prawns, All Types, raw or cooked, 1 serving, 100g	**2**
Quail, raw, 1 portion, 92g	**3**
Rabbit, raw, 1 portion, 128g	**4**
Rock Salmon (Huss, Dog Fish), raw, 1 medium portion, 175g	**7**
Roe, Herring, Soft, fried, 1 medium portion, 85g	**6**
Roe, Herring, Soft, raw, 1 medium portion, 85g	**2**
Roll Mop Herring, 1 serving, 90g	**4**
Salami, 1 small slice, 5g	**1**
Salmon, raw, 1 medium fillet, 130g	**6**
Salmon, Smoked, 1 medium portion, 60g	**2**
Sardines, raw, 1 portion, 100g	**4**
Sausage, Pork, raw, 1 thin, 20g	**2**
Sausage, Pork, raw, 1 large, 40g	**3**
Sausage, Vienna, 1 slice, 16g	**1**
Sausage, Beef, grilled, 1 (50g)	**4**
Sausage, Beef, raw, 1 thin, 20g	**2**
Sausage, Beef, raw, 1 large, 40g	**3**
Sausage, Pork, Reduced Fat, 1 thin, 20g	**1**
Sausage, Pork, Reduced Fat, 1 standard, 40g	**2**
Saveloy, 1 (65g)	**5**
Scallops, steamed, 9 small, 54g	**2**
Scallops, raw, 1 quantity, 100g	**2**
Sea Bass, cooked, 1 fillet, 130g	**3**
Sea Bass, raw, 1 medium fillet, 120g	**3**
Sea Bream, raw, 1 medium fillet, 120g	**3**
Seafood Selection, 1 medium portion, 100g	**2**
Shark, raw, 1 medium steak, 100g	**2**
Shrimps, cooked, 1 quantity, 100g	**2**
Shrimps, raw, 1 medium portion, 60g	**1**
Skate, grilled, 1 medium wing, 290g	**5**
Skate, raw, 1 medium wing, 290g	**4**
Snail, raw, 6 (90g)	**2**
Sprats, cooked, 3 (24g)	**1**
Sprats, cooked, 1 medium portion, 220g	**10**
Squid, raw, 1 medium portion, 60g	**1**

Swordfish, grilled, 1 medium steak, 140g	**5**
Tilapia, raw, 1 medium fillet, 120g	**2**
Trout, Fillet, raw, 1 medium fillet, 115g	**4**
Trout, Rainbow, grilled, 1 fillet, 155g	**5**
Trout, Rainbow, raw, 1 (230g)	**7**
Trout, Smoked, 1 serving, 60g	**2**
Tuna, raw, 1 medium steak, 140g	**5**
Turbot, grilled, 1 fillet, 204g	**6**
Turbot, raw, 1 serving, 100g	**2**
Turkey, Breast, Fillet, grilled, 1 serving, 100g	**4**
Turkey, Breast, Skinless & Boneless, raw, 1 (125g)	**3**
Turkey, Mince, raw, 1 medium portion, 140g	**5**
Turkey, Rasher, raw, 1 rasher, 25g	**1**
Turkey, roasted, 1 medium slice, 25g	**1**
Turkey, Steak, raw, 1 medium, 150g	**4**
Turkey, Thigh, Diced, raw, 1 medium portion, 100g	**3**
Turkey, Wafer Thin, 1 medium portion, 30g	**1**
Turkey, Whole, Weighed with Bone, raw, 1 portion, 100g	**3**
Turkey, with Skin, roasted, 1 medium slice, 30g	**1**
Veal Escalope, raw, 1 medium, 130g	**3**
Venison, Haunch Meat Only, raw, 1 serving, 100g	**2**
Whelks, cooked, 1 portion, 30g	**1**
Whitebait, fried, 1 quantity, 100g	**15**
Whiting, cooked (steamed), 1 fillet, 92g	**2**
Whiting, raw, 1 quantity, 100g	**2**
Wild Boar, raw, 1 medium portion, 100g	**3**
Wild Boar, roasted, 1 slice, 40g	**1**
Winkles, cooked, 1 small portion, 50g	**1**

Bacon, Sausages & Burgers

Asda

100% Prime Beef Burger, 1 individual, 47g	**3**
American Style Beef Burger, 1 individual, 42g	**2**
Beef & Onion Quarter Pounders, 1 serving, 84g	**5**
Beef Meatballs, 1 serving, 23g	**1**
Beef Quarter Pounders, 1 individual, 114g	**8**
Cumberland Sausage, 1 individual, 53g	**3**
Krakowska, ½ pack, 40g	**2**
Lorne Sausage, 1 slice, 60g	**4**
Mini Hot Dogs, 1 pack, 100g	**8**
Peppered Beef Grillsteaks, 1 steak, 170g	**11**
Pork & Tomato Sausage, 1 individual, 48g	**3**
Pork Salami Snack, ¹⁄₁₀ pack, 10g	**1**
Pork Sausages, 1 individual, 57g	**4**

Bacon, Sausages & Burgers · **Fish, Meat & Poultry**

123

Ready to Eat Cooked Cocktail Sausage,
1 individual, 10g **1**
Reduced Fat Chipolatas Pork, 1 individual, 53g **2**
Smoked Pork Sausage, 1 individual, 50g **5**

Asda – Extra Special

100% Aberdeen Angus Beef Burgers,
1 individual, 170g **10**
5oz Scottish Beef Burgers, 1 (142g) **9**
Aberdeen Angus Beef Sausage, 1 serving, 67g **4**
Beef & Mull of Kintyre Cheddar Burgers,
1 individual, 107g **7**
Beef & Sun Dried Tomato Burgers,
1 individual, 114g **8**
Beef Burgers with Wholegrain Mustard &
Tarragon, 1 serving, 114g **7**
British Pork & Herb Chipolatas, 1 individual, 40g **3**
British Pork Feta, Roasted Tomato & Basil
Sausages, 1 individual, 100g **5**
Classic Sausage & Bacon Rolls, 1 roll, 15g **1**
Cranberry & Apple Chipolatas, 1 pack, 20g **1**
Cumberland Chipolatas, 1 individual, 20g **1**
Cumberland Ring Sausage, 1 ring, 203g **15**
Extra Special Beef & Sun-Dried Tomato
Burgers, 1 (114g) **8**
Extra Special Spicy Roquito Pepper & Soft
Cheese Pork Sausages, 1 sausage, 67g **4**
Extra Special Sweet Cherrywood Smoked
Pork Sausages, 1 sausage, 67g **4**
Feta, Roasted Tomato & Basil Sausages,
1 serving, 73g **3**
Fillet Steak Burgers, 1 individual, 95g **5**
Hot & Spicy Beef Burgers, 1 individual, 110g **7**
Jumbo Cumberland Sausages, 1 individual, 95g **7**
Jumbo Pork Sausages, 1 individual, 95g **6**
Lightly Spiced Cumberland Pork Sausage,
1 individual, 67g **4**
Pork & Herb Chipolatas, 1 individual, 24g **2**
Pork Chipolatas British Pork, 1 serving, 40g **3**
Pork, Parma Ham, Garlic & Red Wine Sausages,
1 serving, 68g **5**
Premium Pork Cocktail Sausages Wrapped in
Whisky Barrel Smoked Bacon, 1 individual, 20g **2**
Salaminis, ½ serving, 90g **11**
Thai Spiced Sausages, 1 serving, 69g **4**
Venison Burgers, 1 (114g) **4**

Feasters

Bacon Quarter Pounder 100% Beef Burger
with Bacon & Cheese, 1 (215g) **15**
Hot Dog Premium Smoked, 1 (140g) **9**

Herta

Frankfurters Chicken, 1 (35g) **2**
Frankfurters Minis, 1 (27g) **2**

Mattessons

Garlic Smoked Pork Sausage, ¼ large, 57g **5**
Hot & Spicy Smoked Pork Sausage,
1 serving, 50g **3**
Lightly Smoked Turkey Rashers,
1 serving, 50g **1**
Original Smoked Pork Sausage, ¼ pack, 57g **5**
Original Turkey Rashers, 1 serving, 50g **1**
Reduced Fat Smoked Pork Sausage,
¼ pack, 57g **4**

Morrisons

Beef Burger with Cheese Melt, ½ pack, 186g **15**
Beef Burgers with Cheese & Jalepeño,
½ pack, 186g **14**
British Beef Burgers with Chilli, 1 (113g) **7**
British Beef Burgers with Onion, 1 (57g) **4**
French Saucisson Sec, 1 serving, 50g **6**
Prime British Beef Burgers, 1 (57g) **4**
Prime British Beef Quarter Pounders, 1 (113g) **8**
Quarter Pounder Beef Burger with
Cheese, 1 (113g) **8**

Morrisons – Eat Smart

Pork Sausages, 1 (57g) **3**

Porkinson

Pork Sausages, 1 (66g) **4**
Pork Sausages with a Hint of Lemon &
Nutmeg, 1 (66g) **4**

Porky Whites

Pork Sausage Originals, 1 (76g) **5**
Surrey Pork Sausage, 1 (75g) **5**

Richmond

Fresh Sausages Thick, 1 (57g) **5**
Irish Recipe Cocktail Sausage, 1 (15g) **1**
Irish Recipe Sausages, 1 thin, 28g **2**
Irish Recipe Sausages, 1 large, 45g **4**
Irish Recipe Skinless Sausage, 1 (27g) **2**

Sainsbury's

Bacon & Cheese Bites, 1 (18g) **2**
Beef Burgers with Onion & Seasoning, 1 (57g) **4**
British Pork & Chestnut Stuffing,
1 serving, 100g **5**

Fish, Meat & Poultry   Bacon, Sausages & Burgers

British Pork Cocktail Sausages, 5 (50g)	**4**
British Pork, Cranberry & Apple Stuffing, 1 serving, 100g	**5**
British Pork Quarter Pound Sweet Chilli Burger, 1 (92g)	**5**
British Sweetcure Gammon with Smoked Bacon & Bayleaf, 1 serving, 100g	**4**
Butcher's Choice Cumberland Cocktail Sausages, 1 (18g)	**1**
Butcher's Choice Pork Cocktail Sausage, 1 (14g)	**1**
Cocktail Sausages, 5 (50g)	**4**
Extra Lean Cumberland Sausage, Less than 3% Fat, 1 (57g)	**2**
Liver Sausage Slices, 1 slice, 12g	**1**
Mini Beef Burgers, 1 (67g)	**6**
Pork Breakfast Sausage, 1 serving, 21g	**1**
Pork Cocktail Sausage, 1 (10g)	**1**
Pork Cocktail Sausage Bites, 1 (7g)	**1**
Pork Sausage Slices, 1 slice, 14g	**1**
Quarter Pounder Beef Burger, 1 (114g)	**8**
Sausage & Bacon Wraps, 1 (15g)	**1**
Smoky Bacon Cocktail Sausage, 1 (20g)	**1**
Thick Cut Smoked Rashers Back Bacon, 1 rasher, 50g	**4**
Thick Cut Unsmoked Rashers Back Bacon, 1 rasher, 50g	**4**
Unsmoked Bacon Joint, 1 serving, 100g	**7**
Unsmoked Bacon Steaks, 1 (105g)	**8**

Sainsbury's – Taste the Difference

British Pork & Fresh Bramley Apple Stuffing Ball, 1 ball, 30g	**2**
British Pork & Mushroom Stuffing Parcels, 1 (20g)	**1**
British Pork Burgers with Bramley Apples & Fresh Sage, 1 (142g)	**8**
British Pork, Cranberry & Bramley Apple Chipolatas, 1 (31g)	**2**
British Ultimate Outdoor Reared Pork Sausagemeat, ¼ pack, 70g	**4**
Dry-Cured Unsmoked British Bacon Steaks, 1 steak, 44g	**3**
Pancetta & Parmesan Sausage, 1 (58g)	**6**
Pork & Chestnut Stuffing Parcels Wrapped in Dry-Cured Bacon, 1 serving, 52g	**5**
Pork & Sun-Dried Tomato Sausage, 1 (50g)	**3**
Pork Cocktail Sausage & Dry-Cured Smoked Streaky Bacon Rolls, 1 (16g)	**1**
Pork, Roasted Red Pepper & Sweetflamed Chilli Sausage, 1 serving, 100g	**8**
Scotch Beef Burgers, 1 (142g)	**10**

Scotch Beef Burgers with Fresh Garden Herbs, 1 (142g)	**9**
Scotch Beef Burgers with Smoked Jalapeño Chilli, 1 (142g)	**9**
Scottish Half Pounder Scotch Beef Burger, 1 (227g)	**15**
Scottish Wild Venison & Red Wine Sausage, 1 (57g)	**3**
Sweet Prunes in Dry-Cured Bacon with Pork Cocktail Sausages, 1 pack, 170g	**14**
Ultimate Scotch Beef Burgers, 1 (142g)	**9**

Tesco

Butcher's Choice Cumberland, Lincolnshire or Pork Sausages, 1 individual, 57g	**4**
Chicken Burger Quarter Pounder, 1 serving, 101g	**3**

Tesco – Finest

British Pork & Caramelised Red Onion Sausage, 1 individual, 67g	**5**
Cumberland Chipolata Sausages, 1 individual, 31g	**2**
Cumberland Pork Sausages, 1 individual, 76g	**6**
Cumberland Sausage, 1 individual, 76g	**6**
Hickory Smoked Pork Sausages, 1 individual, 67g	**4**
Lincolnshire Chipolata, 1 individual, 31g	**2**
Lincolnshire Sausages, 1 individual, 76g	**5**
Pork & Apple Sausages, 1 individual, 76g	**6**
Pork & Apricot Sausages, 1 individual, 67g	**5**
Pork & Italian Cherry Tomato Sausage, 1 individual, 67g	**4**
Pork & Leek Sausage, 1 individual, 76g	**5**
Pork & Sweet Chilli Sausages, 1 individual, 76g	**5**
Pork Chipolata Sausages, 1 individual, 31g	**2**
Pork Cocktail Sausages, 1 individual, 16g	**1**
Pork Toulouse Style Sausages, 1 individual, 67g	**5**
Pork, Herb & Lemon Sausages, 1 individual, 67g	**4**
Pork, Mustard & Honey Sausages, 2 (14g)	**1**
Scottish Beef Sausages, 1 individual, 76g	**5**
Traditional Pork Chipolata Sausages, 1 individual, 31g	**2**
Traditional Pork Sausages, 1 individual, 76g	**5**
Venison Sausage, 1 individual, 50g	**2**
Venison, Pork & Red Wine Sausages, 1 individual, 58g	**4**

The Co-operative

Aberdeen Angus Beef Burgers, 1 (114g)	**7**
Butcher's Choice British Pork & Leek Sausages, 1 (50g)	**3**

Butcher's Choice Cumberland or Lincolnshire or Pork Sausages, 1 (50g) **3**

Butcher's Choice Pork Chipolata Sausages, 1 (19g) **2**

Butcher's Choice Thick Pork Sausages, 1 (43g) **3**

Butcher's Choice Thin Pork Sausages, 1 (38g) **3**

Jumbo Pork Sausages, 1 (100g) **7**

Ready to Eat Pork Cocktail Sausages, 1 (10g) **1**

Reduced Fat Bacon Medallions, 1 (10g) **1**

Reduced Fat Pork Sausages, 1 (50g) **2**

Thick Pork & Beef Sausages, 1 (57g) **4**

Thick Pork Sausages, 1 (56g) **4**

Thin Pork Sausages, 1 (38g) **3**

The Co-operative – Truly Irresistible

Aberdeen Angus Beef & Vintage Cheddar Burgers, 1 (114g) **7**

Aberdeen Angus Beef Burgers, 1 (114g) **6**

Aberdeen Angus Beef Sausages with Black Pepper, 1 pack, 66g **5**

Honey & Mustard Sausages, 1 (67g) **5**

Lightly Smoked Maple Cured Back Bacon, 1 pack, 250g **9**

Pork & Bramley Apple Sausages, 1 (67g) **4**

Pork & Sweet Chilli Sausages, 1 (100g) **7**

Pork Chipolatas, 1 (34g) **2**

Pork Sausages, 1 (66g) **5**

Suffolk Recipe Freedom Foods Pork Sausages, 1 (67g) **4**

Waitrose

100% Aberdeen Angus Beef Quarter Pounders, ¼ pack, 114g **8**

Aberdeen Angus Half Pounder Beef Burgers, 1 (227g) **15**

Beechwood Smoked Frankfurters, 1 (35g) **3**

British Beef Burgers, 1 (114g) **7**

Cooked Cocktail Sausages, 1 (10g) **1**

Smoked Streaky Bacon Sweet Cured with Black Treacle, 1 rasher, 21g **1**

Smoked Sweetcured Back Bacon with Black Treacle, 1 rasher, 25g **2**

Smoked Thick Cut British Bacon, 1 rasher, 41g **2**

Sweetcure English Loin, 1 serving, 100g **6**

Wall's

Brilliant Bacon Unsmoked Rashers, 1 pack of 2, 47g **3**

Classic Rashers Bacon Rashers Smoked, 1 pack of 2, 47g **3**

Cumberland Sausages, 1 (114g) **10**

Micro Sausages, 1 (46g) **4**

Micro Sausages Classic Pork Sausages, 1 serving, 92g **7**

Micro Sausages Hot & Spicy Sausages, 1 serving, 92g **7**

Succulent Pork Sausages, 1 (114g) **10**

The Finest Cuts Classic Pork Sausages, 1 (99g) **7**

The Finest Cuts Cumberland Sausages, 1 (98g) **7**

The Finest Cuts Lincolnshire Sausages, 1 (98g)) **6**

The Finest Cuts Skinless Pork Sausages, 1 (48g) **4**

Thick Lincolnshire Sausages Seasoned with a Hint of Sage & Onion, 1 (114g) **11**

Thick Pork Sausage, 1 (57g) **5**

Thick Pork Sausage, Lean Recipe, 1 (57g) **3**

Thin Pork Sausage, 1 (28g) **2**

Weight Watchers

Cumberland Sausages, 1 (39g) **1**

Extra Trimmed Oak Smoked Back Bacon, 1 rasher, 25g **1**

Extra Trimmed Unsmoked Back Bacon, 1 rasher, 21g **1**

Premium Pork Sausages, 1 (39g) **1**

Cooked Deli Meat & Pâté

Asda

Ardennes & Brussels Pâté Layered with Sundried Tomatoes, ½ pack, 85g **6**

Ardennes Pâté, 1 serving, 50g **3**

Bavarian Ham, 1 serving, 30g **1**

Brussels & Garlic Pâté, 1 serving, 50g **3**

Chicken & Garlic Pâté, 1 serving, 50g **4**

Chicken & Smoked Bacon Pâté, 1 serving, 40g **3**

Chicken Pâté, ½ pack, 85g **5**

Chicken, Smoked Bacon & Red Wine Pâté, ¼ pack, 38g **3**

Coarse Country Style Pâté, 1 serving, 30g **2**

Corned Beef, 1 slice, 50g **3**

Country Style Pâté, ¼ pack, 38g **3**

Duck & Orange Pâté, 1 serving, 43g **4**

Farmhouse Pâté with Mushrooms, 1 serving, 43g **3**

Fish, Meat & Poultry — Cooked Deli Meat & Pâté

French Garlic Sausage, 1 serving, 50g — **3**
Italian Mortadella, 1 slice, 10g — **1**
Maple Drycure Ham, 1 slice, 37g — **1**
Mustard Dry Cure Ham, 1 slice, 33g — **1**
Pork & Apricot Pâté, ¼ pack, 38g — **2**
Pork Lunch Tongue, 1 slice, 30g — **1**
Rustico, 1 serving, 50g — **1**
Sage & Onion Chicken, 1 serving, 100g — **5**
Wafer Thin Chargrilled Style Chicken,
⅓ pack, 50g — **1**
Wiejska, ⅓ pack, 36g — **1**
Yorkshire Ham, 1 serving, 100g — **4**

Asda – Deli

Cooked Ham on the Bone, 1 slice, 20g — **1**
Black Country Ham, 1 slice, 50g — **2**
Breaded Wiltshire Cured Ham, 1 slice, 25g — **1**
Brussels Pâté, 1 serving, 50g — **5**
Carver Ham, 1 slice, 20g — **1**
Chopped Pork, 1 serving, 50g — **3**
Pastrami, 1 serving, 20g — **1**
Pork & Egg Gala Slice, 1 slice, 100g — **9**
Sliced Cured Pork Shoulder with Breadcrumbs,
1 slice, 50g — **1**

Asda – Extra Special

Bramley Apple Wiltshire Cure Ham,
1 pack, 100g — **3**
Butter Roast Turkey Breast, 1 pack, 145g — **5**
Duck & Apple Pâté, ¼ pack, 43g — **3**
Duck Liver Pâté with Chardonnay & Apple Jelly,
1 serving, 30g — **3**
Duck Pâté with Rioja, ⅓ pack, 50g — **4**
Farmhouse Pâté with Jonagold Apples,
⅓ pack, 50g — **4**
Wild Alaskan Hot Smoked Salmon Pâté,
1 pack, 115g — **7**
Wild Mushroom & Garlic Pâté, 1 serving, 30g — **2**
Wiltshire Cured Blossom Honey Roast Ham,
1 serving, 50g — **2**
Yellowfin Tuna Pâté, 1 serving, 20g — **1**

Asda – Good For You

Brussels Pâté, 1 serving, 50g — **3**
Mini Brussels & Mushroom Pâté, 1 serving, 40g — **2**

Asda – Ready to Eat

Chinese Style Chicken Drumsticks,
1 serving, 211g — **9**
Chinese Style Chicken Pieces, ½ pack, 135g — **6**
Chinese Style Chicken Wings,
1 serving, 103g — **5**

Chinese Style Cooked & Sliced Chicken,
⅓ pack, 78g — **2**
Chinese Style Mini Chicken Fillets, ½ pack, 100g — **3**
Chinese Style Sliced Chicken Breast,
½ pack, 52g — **2**
Duck & Orange Pâté with Orange Liqueur,
1 serving, 10g — **1**
Flamegrilled Cooked Mini Chicken Breast
Fillets, ½ pack, 100g — **3**
Hot & Spicy Chicken Wings, 1 serving, 128g — **7**
Jalfrezi Cooked & Sliced Chicken Breast,
⅓ pack, 78g — **2**
Mexican Style Cooked & Sliced Chicken,
⅓ pack, 78g — **3**
Mexican Style Cooked Mini Chicken Breast
Fillets, 1 fillet, 145g — **5**
Sticky Chilli BBQ Cooked Chicken Drumsticks,
¼ pack, 96g — **4**
Sweet Chilli Cooked & Sliced Chicken Breast,
1 serving, 140g — **4**
Tandoori Style Cooked Chicken Breast Pieces,
½ pack, 108g — **4**
Tandoori Style Cooked Mini Chicken Breast
Fillets, 1 fillet, 145g — **4**
Tikka Cooked & Sliced Chicken Breast,
½ pack, 70g — **2**
Tikka Style Mini Chicken Breast Fillets,
1 serving, 200g — **6**
5 Snack Salami, 1 stick, 25g — **3**

Bernard Matthews

Chicken Breast, 1 slice, 20g — **1**
Honey Roast Turkey Breast, 1 slice, 20g — **1**
Roast Turkey Breast Chunks, 1 (50g) — **1**
Sage & Onion Turkey Breast, 1 slice, 20g — **1**
Tikka Turkey Breast Chunks, 1 (50g) — **1**
Turkey Breast, 1 slice, 20g — **1**
Turkey Ham Sandwich Slices, 2 slices, 26g — **1**
Turkey Sandwich Slices, 2 slices, 22g — **1**
Wafer Thin American Fried Chicken, 1 slice, 20g — **1**
Wafer Thin Honey Roast Turkey Ham,
1 slice, 20g — **1**
Wafer Thin Turkey, 1 slice, 20g — **1**
Wafer Thin Turkey Ham, 1 slice, 20g — **1**

Mattessons – Fridge Raiders

Chicken Bites Chinese Spare Rib Flavour
Chicken, 1 (65g) — **3**
Chicken Bites, Roast Flavour, 1 (65g) — **3**
Chicken Bites Sweet Chilli Flavour, 1 (65g) — **3**
Chicken Bites, Tikka Flavour, 1 (65g) — **3**

Cooked Deli Meat & Pâté Fish, Meat & Poultry

127

Morrisons

Pork & Mustard Grillsteak, 1 individual, 75g	**7**
Pork Ribs with a Chinese Style Glaze, ¼ pack, 250g	**13**
Shredded Beef Brisket, 1 serving, 100g	**4**
Shredded Pork, 1 serving, 100g	**6**
Sliced Pork & Stuffing, 1 serving, 20g	**1**
Stuffed Belly Pork, 1 serving, 30g	**2**

Peperami

Barbecue Flavour, 1 (25g)	**3**
Barbecue Flavour Lunchbox Mini, 1 (10g)	**1**
Firestick, 1 (25g)	**3**
Hot Bunch, 1 (25g)	**3**
Spicy or Original, 1 mini, 10g	**1**
Spicy or Original, 1 standard, 25g	**3**
Spicy, 1 large, 40g	**6**
Wideboy Spicy Meat Snack, 1 (40g)	**6**

Sainsbury's

Ardennes Pâté, 1 serving, 43g	**3**
Ardennes Pâté with Apricots, 1 serving, 30g	**2**
British Breaded Ham, 2 slices, 35g	**1**
British Mustard Ham Slices, 2 slices, 35g	**1**
British Pork, Sage & Onion Stuffing Balls, 1 serving, 25g	**2**
Brunswick Ham, 1 slice, 20g	**1**
Brussels Pâté, 1 serving, 43g	**5**
Brussels Pâté with Cranberries, 1 serving, 10g	**1**
Chicken & Campagne Layered Pâté, 1 serving, 10g	**1**
Chicken Liver Pâté, 1 serving, 28g	**3**
Chicken Liver Pâté with Wiltshire Bacon, 1 serving, 10g	**1**
Chinese Style Chicken Breast Slices, ½ pack, 65g	**2**
Cubetti di Pancetta with Herbs, ¼ pack, 40g	**4**
Duck & Orange Pâté, ⅓ pack, 56g	**6**
Fine Liver Pâté, ¼ pack, 28g	**2**
German Salami Selection Slices - Black Pepper Coated, 3 slices, 10g	**1**
German Salami Selection Slices - Green Peppercorn Infused, 3 slices, 10g	**1**
German Salami Selection Slices - Mustard Seed Salami, 3 slices, 10g	**1**
German Sausage Selection Pack - Bierwurst, 5 slices, 15g	**1**
German Sausage Selection Pack - Extrawurst Sausage, 5 slices, 16g	**1**
German Sausage Selection Pack - Schinkenwurst, 5 slices, 16g	**1**

Layered Pâté, 1 serving, 30g	**2**
Layered Pâté with Port, 1 serving, 10g	**1**
Liver Sausage Slices, 1 slice, 12g	**1**
Mackerel Pâté, 1 serving, 30g	**3**
Medium Coarse Ardennes Pâté, 1 serving, 30g	**2**
Mushroom Pâté, ½ pack, 58g	**2**
Pâté de Campagne, 1 serving, 30g	**2**
Pork Lunch Tongue Slices, 1 slice, 25g	**1**
Premium Corned Beef Slices, 1 slice, 42g	**2**
Smooth Brussels Pâté, 1 serving, 10g	**1**
Southern Fried Chicken Fillets, ¼ pack, 112g	**6**
Spanish Meat Selection, Serrano Ham, 2 slices, 30g	**2**
Tuna Pâté, ½ pack, 58g	**6**

Sainsbury's – Be Good To Yourself

Ardennes Pâté, 1 serving, 30g	**1**
British Breaded Ham, 1 slice, 20g	**1**
Brussels Pâté, 1 serving, 30g	**2**
Chicken Liver Pâté, 1 serving, 50g	**3**
Roast Chicken & Stuffing, 1 slice, 25g	**1**
Spreadable Brussels Pâté, 1 serving, 30g	**2**
Thick Cut Cooked Ham, 1 slice, 25g	**1**
Tikka Sliced Chicken Breast, Cooked, ⅓ pack, 68g	**2**
Turkey Pastrami Slices, 2 slices, 67g	**2**

Sainsbury's – Taste the Difference

Antipasto from Parma Region, Coppa, 2 slices, 12g	**1**
Antipasto from Parma Region, Felino Salami, 2 slices, 27g	**3**
Antipasto from Parma Region, Parma Ham, 2 slices, 27g	**2**
Breaded Ham Slices, Dry Cured, 1 slice, 27g	**1**
Breaded Wiltshire Ham, 1 slice, 35g	**1**
Breaded Yorkshire Ham, 1 slice, 35g	**2**
British Breaded Ham, 1 slice, 27g	**1**
British Finely Sliced Salt Beef, 4 slices, 35g	**1**
British Free Range Hand Carved Oak Smoked Chicken Breast, 1 slice, 30g	**1**
British Outdoor Reared Hand Carved Maple Cured Ham, 1 slice, 30g	**1**
British Outdoor Reared Hand Carved Peppered Ham, 1 slice, 30g	**1**
British Salt Beef Slices, 4 slices, 35g	**1**
British Thick Cut Breaded Ham, 1 slice, 42g	**2**
British Wiltshire Breaded Ham, 1 slice, 35g	**1**

Chicken Breast with Pork, Sage & Onion Stuffing, 1 slice, 38g	1
Chicken Live Pâté with Chadonnay & Wild Mushrooms, 1 serving, 30g	3
Chicken Liver Pâté with Wild Mushrooms, ¼ pack, 42g	5
Duck Liver Pâté with Truffles & Champagne, 1 serving, 25g	3
Honey & Wholegrain Mustard British Ham Slices, 1 slice, 26g	1
Iberico Bellota Selection, Chorizo, 2 slices, 12g	2
Iberico Bellota Selection, Lomo, 2 slices, 13g	1
Iberico Bellota Selection, Paleta, 2 slices, 12g	1
Isle of Sky Smoked Salmon Pâté, ½ pack, 58g	4
Slowcooked Suffolk Cured Ham Hocks, ½ pack, 350g	11
Suffolk Black Ham, 1 slice, 41g	1
Venison Pâté, 1 serving, 30g	2
Yorkshire Mustard Ham Slices, 1 slice, 35g	1
Yorkshire Peppered Ham Slices, 1 slice, 35g	1

Spam

Chopped Ham & Pork, 1 serving, 50g	4
Lite Chopped Ham & Pork, 1 serving, 50g	3

Tesco

Ardennes Pâté, 1 serving, 40g	3
Ardennes Pâté with Bacon, 1 serving, 40g	3
Bacon & Egg Bites (20 pack), 1 individual, 12g	1
Barbecue Chicken Wings, 1 serving, 105g	6
BBQ Drumsticks, 1 serving, 160g	6
Bresaola della Valtellina PGI, 1 serving, 20g	1
Brussels Pâté 175g, 1 serving, 40g	4
Brussels Pâté with Garlic, 1 serving, 40g	4
Chicken Garlic & Herb Mini Fillets, 1 serving, 140g	9
Chicken Hot & Spicy Mini Breast Fillets, 1 serving, 137g	7
Chicken Liver Pâté, 1 serving, 40g	4
Chicken Roll, 1 slice, 13g	1
Chicken Tikka Slices, 1 individual, 165g	12
Culatello, 1 serving, 18g	1
Deli Corned Beef, 1 slice, 31g	2
Duck & Orange Pâté, 1 serving, 40g	4
Farmhouse Pâté with Mushrooms, 1 serving, 40g	4
Garlic Sausage, 1 slice, 13g	1
German Black Pepper Coated Salami, 1 serving, 30g	3
Grab & Go Sliced Chorizo, 1 serving, 30g	3
Ham & Cheese Slices, 1 individual, 165g	13
Herb Crumbed Wiltshire Cured Ham, 1 slice, 35g	1

Liver & Bacon Spreading Pâté, 1 serving, 25g	2
Liver Sausage, 1 slice, 13g	1
Mini Crumbed Ham, 1 slice, 28g	1
Pâté de Campagne, 1 serving, 40g	3
Pizza Diced Ham, 1 serving, 50g	1
Pork & Sweet Onion Pâté, 1 serving, 40g	4
Pork Lunch Tongue, 1 slice, 26g	1
Pork Luncheon Meat, 1 slice, 14g	1
Reduced Fat Brussels Pâté, 1 serving, 40g	2
Salamini Piccanti, 1 serving, 18g	2
Sandwich Pâté Slices, 1 serving, 40g	3
Smoked Flavoured Pancetta, 1 serving, 38g	4
Smoked Mackerel Pâté, 1 serving, 40g	3
Tuna Pâté, 1 serving, 40g	3
Wholegrain Mustard Wiltshire Cured Ham, 1 slice, 30g	1

Tesco – No Added Water

Corned Beef, 1 slice, 38g	2
Crumbed Ham, 1 slice, 25g	1
Honey Roast Ham, 1 slice, 26g	1
Mustard Ham, 1 slice, 26g	1
Peppered Beef, 1 slice, 25g	1
Roast Pork, 1 slice, 26g	1
Roast Turkey, 1 slice, 25g	1
Smoked Ham, 1 slice, 26g	1
Thick Sliced Crumbed Ham, 1 slice, 21g	1
Thick Sliced Honey Roast Ham, 1 slice, 21g	1
Wafer Thin Cooked Ham, 1 slice, 18g	1
Wafer Thin Crumbed Ham, 2 slices, 33g	1
Wafer Thin Honey Roast Ham, 1 slice, 18g	1
Wafer Thin Roast Chicken, 2 slices, 18g	1
Water Wafer Thin Smoked Ham, 1 slice, 18g	1

Tesco – Finest

Ardennes Pâté, 1 serving, 40g	4
Beechwood Smoked Ham, 2 slices, 20g	1
Brussels Pâté, 1 serving, 40g	4
Chicken & Stuffing, 1 slice, 30g	1
Chicken Liver Parfait, 1 serving, 40g	3
Culatello, 1 slice, 10g	1
Duck Pâté with Port, 1 serving, 40g	3
Mortadella Bologna PGI, 1 serving, 33g	3
Saucisson Sec, 1 serving, 30g	3
Scottish Venison Pâté, 1 serving, 40g	2
Smoked Pancetta, 1 serving (¼ pack), 28g	3
Smoked Salmon Pâté, 1 serving, 40g	2

The Co-operative

Antipasto Pack, ½ pack, 60g	5
Ardennes Pâté with Plum & Brandy, ¼ pack, 44g	4

Weight Watchers®
Wafer Thin Cooked Ham

a must for your shopping list

Our delicious Wafer Thin Cooked Ham makes a great snack, straight from the fridge. It's ideal for popping in your lunchbox with some salad and fabulous in sandwiches or on crispbreads.

1 ProPoints value

per 60g serving

Also available:
Cooked Ham, Thick Cut Ham, Thick Cut Breaded Ham, Roast Chicken Slices, Wafer Thin Cooked Chicken and Thick Cut Chicken

WeightWatchers® Foods
Eat gorgeous. Feel gorgeous.

Beef Pastrami, ½ pack, 40g	**1**
Brussels Pâté with Forest Mushroom, ⅓ pack, 56g	**4**
Chicken, Red Wine & Bacon Pâté, ¼ pack, 44g	**3**
Chunky Flame Grilled Chicken, ½ pack, 70g	**2**
Chunky Sweet Chilli & Lime Chicken, ½ pack, 70g	**2**
Chunky Tikka Chicken, ½ pack, 70g	**3**
Coarse Cut Pâté, ¼ pack, 44g	**4**
Coarse Cut Pâté with Black Mushrooms, ¼ pack, 42g	**4**
Duck Pâté with Orange & Cream, ¼ pack, 42g	**3**
Everyday Corned Beef, ¼ pack, 62g	**3**
Flame Grilled Chicken Mini Fillets, ½ pack, 100g	**3**
German Peppered Salami, ½ pack, 50g	**4**
Hot & Spicy Wings, 1 serving, 100g	**7**
Mild Cured Honey Roast Ham, 1 slice, 25g	**1**
Mustard Ham, 1 slice, 25g	**1**
Peppered Ham, 1 slice, 25g	**1**
Pork Lunch Tongue, 1 slice, 20g	**1**
Premium Dry Cured Cumberland Marinated Silverside Ham, 1 slice, 33g	**2**
Premium Dry Cured Breaded Ham, 1 slice, 33g	**1**
Reduced Fat Brussels Pâté, ¼ tub, 44g	**2**
Roast Skin-on Chicken Thighs Browned with Sugar & Dextrose, ½ pack, 200g	**12**

Waitrose

Applewood Smoked Gammon Ham,1 slice, 40g	**1**
Black Forest Ham, 1 serving, 70g	**5**
British Honey & Ginger Roast Ham, 1 slice, 34g	**1**
British Honey & Muscovado Sugar Roast Ham, 1 slice, 40g	**1**
British Oak Smoked Ham, 1 slice, 17g	**1**
British Oak Smoked Ham, Reduced Fat & Salt, 1 slice, 20g	**1**
British Ox Tongue, 1 serving, 113g	**6**
Cured Breaded Gammon Ham, 1 slice, 35g	**1**
Dry Cured Heather Honey Roast Hampshire Gammon Ham, 1 slice, 20g	**1**
Dry Cured Oak Smoked Hampshire Gammon Ham, 1 slice, 20g	**1**
German Brunswick Smoked Ham, 1 slice, 20g	**1**
German Pepper Salami, 1 slice, 8g	**1**
Molasses Roast Hampshire Gammon Ham, 1 slice, 20g	**1**
Napoli Piccante Salami, 1 slice, 10g	**1**
Napoli Salami, 1 slice, 6g	**1**
Roast Chicken Honey & Mustard Mini Fillets, 1 fillet, 33g	**1**
Roast Chicken Mexican Fajita Pieces, 1 serving, 130g	**4**

Roast Chicken Sea Salt & Black Pepper Chicken, 1 piece, 65g	**2**
Roast Chicken Spanish Smoked Paprika Drumsticks, ¼ pack, 156g	**7**
Roast Ham, Reduced Fat & Salt, 1 slice, 20g	**1**
Roast Stuffed Chicken Thighs, 1 (60g)	**3**
Salame Brianza, 1 portion, 10g	**1**
Saucisson Saint Andre, 1 serving, 70g	**7**
Saucisson a L'Ail, 1 serving, 50g	**3**
Saucisson a la Pistache, 1 serving, 50g	**5**
Saucisson de Jambon, 1 serving, 20g	**2**
Saucisson Sec with Herbes De Provence, 1 serving, 70g	**7**
Sliced Strong Garlic Sausage, 2 slices, 10g	**1**

Weight Watchers

Cooked Ham, 3 slices, 30g	**1**
Roast Chicken, 3 slices, 50g	**1**
Thick Cut Breaded Ham, 2 slices, 50g	**1**
Thick Cut Chicken, 2 slices, 50g	**1**
Thick Cut Ham, 2 slices, 50g	**1**
Wafer Thin Chicken, 1 serving, 60g	**1**
Wafer Thin Ham, 1 serving, 60g	**1**

Fresh, Prepared & Breaded Fish

Asda

Boned Kippers, 1 piece, 129g	**8**
Breaded Chunky Cod Fillets, 1 fillet, 125g	**5**
Breaded Cod Goujons, 1 (43g)	**3**
Breaded Hot & Spicy Tiger Prawns, 1 serving, 71g	**5**
Breaded Plaice Fillets, 1 portion, 116g	**7**
Breaded Plaice Goujons, 1 (52g)	**4**
Breaded Wholetail Scampi, 1 portion, 75g	**5**
Chilli & Coriander King Prawns, 1 portion, 85g	**2**
Chunky Breaded Haddock Fillets in Light Crunchy Breadcrumbs, 1 (126g)	**6**
Cod & Mango Kebabs, 1 serving, 82g	**2**
Cod Fishcake, 1 (66g)	**4**
Dressed Layer Crab, ½ pot, 100g	**5**
Filo Prawns, 1 portion, 10g	**1**
Fish Bake, ½ pack, 225g	**9**
Haddock Fishcakes, ½ pack, 150g	**8**
Haddock Ruskoline, ½ pack, 142g	**8**
Lemon & Black Pepper Scottish Salmon Flakes, 1 pack, 120g	**6**
Lemon & Pepper Salmon Roasties, 1 pack, 120g	**8**

Mini Wild Alaskan Salmon Fishcakes, ¼ pack, 50g	**3**
Monkfish Tails, 1 quantity, 100g	**1**
Natural River Cobbler Fillet, 1 fillet, 150g	**4**
Prawn Cocktail, ½ pack, 70g	**7**
Prawn Kebabs, 1 (70g)	**2**
Ruskoline Coated Mackerel Fillets, ½ pack, 100g	**10**
Salmon Fillets topped with a Pesto Crust, ½ pack, 145g	**12**
Salmon with a Lemon & Herb Butter, ½ pack, 125g	**9**
Sardines with Lemon & Rosemary, ½ pack, 175g	**11**
Scallop & Bacon Brochettes, 1 (31g)	**2**
Scottish Mussels in Garlic Butter Sauce, 1 serving, 134g	**4**
Scottish Salmon Fillets with a Honey & Ginger Glaze, ½ pack of 2, 155g	**8**
Seabass with Thai Butter, ½ serving, 143g	**8**
Seafood Casserole with Cod, Mussels & Prawns, ½ pack, 400g	**6**
Tail On King Prawns with a Sweet Chilli Dip, 1 serving, 120g	**3**
Thai Fish Cakes, 1 (17g)	**1**
Thai King Prawns in a Fragrant Marinade of Lemon Grass, ½ pack, 118g	**7**
Tikka Salmon Kebabs, 1 serving, 100g	**2**
Trout Kebabs in a Sweet Chilli Sauce, 1 (58g)	**2**
Tuna Fishcake, 1 (75g)	**5**
Tuna Steaks in a Smokey Chilli & Lime Marinade, 1 serving, 90g	**3**
Wild Alaskan Salmon Fillets in a Sweet & Tangy Lime & Coriander Flavour Marinade, 1 (97g)	**4**
Wild Alaskan Salmon Tikka Kebabs, 1 (86g)	**2**

Asda – Chosen by You

Breaded 100% Plaice Fillets, 1 fillet, 125g	**8**
Breaded Chunky 100% Cod Fillets, 1 fillet, 125g	**6**

Asda – Extra Special

Battered Chunky Cod Loins, 1 individual, 113g	**5**
Battered Chunky Haddock Loins, 1 individual, 113g	**6**
Cod, Feta & Roasted Red Pepper Fishcakes, 1 individual, 115g	**6**
Cod, Tiger Prawn & Pancetta Fishcakes, 1 individual, 103g	**5**
Mini Scottish Smoked Haddock & Vintage Cheese Fishcakes, 2 individual, 51g	**4**

Rosemary Crusted Wild Salmon Portions, 1 portion, 161g	**7**
Salmon en Croute, ½ pack, 215g	**19**
Seafood Gratin, ½ pack, 218g	**14**
Skinless & Boneless Scottish Mackerel Fillets with Olive Oil & Lemon, 1 pack, 125g	**8**
Smoked Haddock & Vintage Cheddar Fishcakes, 1 (115g)	**9**
Smoked Haddock Fishcakes, 1 individual, 58g	**3**
Smoked Salmon Escalopes with Honey-Ginger Cornish Butter, ½ pack, 142g	**7**
Trout Parcels with Cream Cheese & Pesto, 1 individual, 146g	**8**
Wild Salmon, Spinach & Dill Fishcakes, 2 (115g)	**7**

Asda – Fresh Tastes

Cod Fillets in Mornay Sauce, 1 (180g)	**6**
Haddock Fillets in Cheese Sauce, 1 (180g)	**5**
Salmon Fillets in Creamy Florentine Sauce, 1 (180g)	**6**

Asda – Good For You

Breaded Chunky Cod Fillets, 1 fillet, 125g	**3**
Cod with Sweet Red Pepper Sauce, ½ pack, 170g	**3**
Prawn Cocktail, ½ pack, 100g	**4**

Birds Eye – Simply Baked to Perfection

Chunky Basa Fillets with a Chilli & Lemongrass Butter Sauce, 1 portion, 140g	**4**
Chunky Wild Alaska Pollock Fillets with a Herb Butter Sauce, 1 portion, 140g	**4**
Chunky Wild Pink Salmon Fillets with a Lemon & Herb Butter Sauce, 1 portion, 140g	**5**
North Atlantic Haddock Fillets with a Lemon & Chive Butter Sauce, 1 portion, 140g	**5**
Succulent King Prawns with a Sweet Chilli Sauce, ½ pack, 140g	**7**

Lyons Seafoods

Crayfish Medley, 1 serving, 220g	**4**
King Prawn Cocktail, 1 serving, 130g	**4**
Ready to Eat Seafood Selection, 1 portion, 100g	**2**
Sweet Chilli King Prawn Cocktail, 1 serving, 130g	**4**

Morrisons

Breaded Prawn Skewers, 1 (13g)	**1**
Cracked Black Pepper & Red Chilli Breaded Prawn Skewer, 1 (13g)	**1**

Lime & Coriander Breaded Prawn Skewer, 1 (13g)	1
Tempura King Prawns, 1 (13g)	1

Sainsbury's

Breaded Butterfly King Prawns, 1 (16g)	1
Breaded Haddock Fillets, ½ pack, 142g	8
British Honey Flavour Hot Smoked Mackerel Fillets, 1 serving, 100g	11
British Peppered Hot Smoked Mackerel Fillets, 1 serving, 100g	9
Chunky Cod Fillet in Breadcrumbs, 1 (150g)	7
Chunky Lemon Sole Fillets, 1 (170g)	10
Chunky Plaice Fillets in Breadcrumbs, 1 (160g)	9
Cod Fillets in Crispy Breadcrumbs, 1 (142g)	8
Dressed Layered Crab, 1 pack, 200g	9
Fish Pie Mix, 1 quantity, 100g	4
Honey Roasted Salmon Fillets, ½ pack, 68g	4
Lemon Sole Goujons in Breadcrumbs, ½ pack, 100g	7
Lightly Dusted Lemon Sole Fillets, 1 (133g)	7
Line Caught Chunky Cod Fillet in Light & Crispy Signature Breadcrumb, 1 (134g)	6
Line Caught Cod Fillet in Light & Crispy Signature Breadcrumb, 1 (131g)	7
Line Caught Cod Fishcake, 1 (89g)	4
Line Caught Haddock Fishcake, 1 (88g)	4
Marinated Anchovies, ⅓ pack, 66g	3
Mussels in Garlic Butter, ½ pack, 250g	6
Prawn Cocktail, ½ tub, 100g	8
Ready Prepared Mackerel Fillet,1 serving, 100g	6
Ready to Cook Scallops with Soy & Ginger Butter, ½ pack, 68g	3
Salmon Fish Cake, ½ pack, 90g	5
Scottish Cooked Mussels in a Garlic Butter Sauce, 1 portion, 206g	5
Scottish Cooked Mussels in a White Wine Sauce, 1 portion, 210g	5
Scottish Mackerel Kebabs with a Sweet Chilli Glaze, 1 (89g)	7
Scottish Responsibly Sourced Honey Roast Salmon Flakes, ½ pack, 68g	4
Shetland Isle Layered Dressed Crab, ½ pack, 100g	5
Sweetflame Tomato & Basil Marinated King Prawns, ½ pack, 70g	1
Tempura Jumbo King Prawns, 1 (25g)	2
Tempura King Prawns, 1 (24g)	2
Thai Style Marinated Prawns, ½ pack, 70g	1

Sainsbury's – Be Good To Yourself

Hake Fillets in a Crunchy Seeded Breadcrumb, ½ pack, 106g	4
Mackerel Fillets in Lemon, Pepper & Oat Breadcrumbs, ½ pack, 100g	8
Mackerel Fishcake, ½ pack, 100g	6
Prawn Cocktail, Reduced Fat, ½ pot, 100g	4
Smoked Mackerel & Rocket Fishcakes, 1 portion, 90g	6
Tuna Fishcake with Lime & Coriander Sauce, ½ pack, 100g	6

Sainsbury's – Taste the Difference

Cod & Cheddar Fishcakes, ½ pack, 115g	6
Cod & West Country Cheddar Fishcakes, 1 (115g)	6
Gravadlax with a Mustard & Sweet Dill Sauce, 1 serving, 60g	3
Isle of Skye Responsibly Sourced Smoked Salmon Parcels, ½ pack, 57g	4
King Scallop Shells with King Prawns & Prawn Mousse, 1 serving, 120g	3
Layered Prawn & Cucumber Terrines, ½ pack, 60g	3
Poached Salmon Appetiser, 1 pack, 142g	6
Prawn Cocktail, ½ pot, 100g	9
Responsibly Sourced Gravadlax, 1 serving, 60g	4
Salmon & Mozzarella Fishcakes, ½ pack, 115g	3
Sea Bass with Roasted Fennel & Orange Butter, ½ pack, 115g	6
Shetland Isles Dressed Crab, 1 pack, 150g	7
Trout with Wild Flower Honey, Orange & Thyme Butter, ½ pack, 263g	9
Wholetail Breaded Scampi, ½ pack, 82g	5
Wild Alaskan Salmon with Rosemary & Rock Salt Butter, ½ pack, 140g	7
Wild Nova Scotia Lobster, 1 pack, 175g	8
Yellowfin Tuna Steaks with Sun-Dried Tomato & Balsamic Butter, ½ pack, 124g	5

Tesco

Battered Cod, 1 serving, 200g	10
Breaded Scampi, 1 serving, 125g	7
Garlic & Herb Prawn Skewers, 1 serving, 45g	1
Hot Smoked Salmon Fillets with Sweet Chilli, 1 serving, 93g	5
Piri-Piri Smoked Mackerel Fillets, 1 serving, 80g	6

Roasted Salmon Fillets with Cracked Black Pepper, 1 serving, 93g **5**

Roasted Salmon Fillets with Dark Treacle, 1 serving, 93g **5**

Smoked Haddock & Cheese Sauce Fishcakes, 1 (210g) **11**

Tesco – Finest

Smoked Salmon & Dill Terrrine, 1 serving, 55g **3**

Smoked Salmon & Vegetable Roulades, 1 serving, 50g **2**

Smoked Salmon Blinis, 1 individual, 18g **1**

Smoked Salmon Canapes, 1 serving, 40g **2**

Thai Fishcakes With a Sweet Chilli Dip, 1 serving (½ pack), 175g **9**

The Co-operative

Breaded Haddock Fillets, 1 (150g) **8**

Hoki with Parsley Sauce, 1 serving, 210g **5**

Pollock Fishcakes, 1 (60g) **4**

Salmon with Watercress Sauce, 1 serving, 170g **7**

Scottish Salmon Fishcakes, 1 (60g) **3**

Simply Salmon Fillets with Lemon & Herb Butter, ½ pack, 120g **10**

Waitrose

Battered Cod Fillets, ¼ pack, 150g **8**

Battered Haddock Fillets, ¼ pack, 150g **8**

Breaded Fish Bites, ½ pack, 150g **8**

Chunky Breaded Haddock Fillets, ½ pack, 138g **6**

Chunky Breaded Haddock Fingers, 1 (55g) **3**

Chunky Breaded Lemon Sole Fillets, 1 (120g) **7**

Chunky Breaded Plaice Fillets, 1 (125g) **8**

Cod & Parsley Fish Cakes, ½ pack, 85g **4**

Haddock Fillets in a Seeded Crust, ½ pack, 130g **7**

Haddock Mornay, 1 pack, 190g **5**

Salmon & Dill Fish Cakes, 1 (115g) **6**

Scottish Salmon Fillets, 1 (120g) **6**

Tuna & Red Pepper Fish Cakes, 1 (85g) **4**

Young's

Bantry Bay Mussels in Creamy Garlic Sauce, ½ pack, 225g **5**

Basa Fillets Lightly Dusted with Sea Salt & Cracked Black Pepper, 1 (160g) **7**

Battered Calamari, ½ pack, 150g **8**

Breaded Basa Fillets, 1 (125g) **7**

Breaded Fish Fillets, ½ pack, 150g **9**

Fish & Chips, 1 portion, 300g **13**

Isle Of Lewis Premium Whole Scampi, 1 quantity, 100g **6**

Lemon & Pepper Salmon Fillets, ¼ pack, 125g **8**

Mussels in Creamy Garlic Sauce, ½ pack, 225g **4**

Premium Wholetail Scampi Kievs, ¼ pack, 63g **4**

Salmon Fillets with Garlic & Herb, 1 (125g) **7**

Fresh & Prepared Meat

Asda

American Texan Style Pork Ribs, 1 (60g) **4**

Applewood Smoked Gammon Joint, 1 portion, 160g **8**

BBQ Ribs, ½ pack, 180g **12**

Beef & Pork Meatballs in a Tomato & Basil Sauce, 1 serving, 115g **6**

Beef Braising Steak with Gravy, 1 serving, 180g **5**

Beef in Ale, ½ pack, 250g **5**

Beef Joint with a Pepper Coating, ¼ pack, 125g **5**

Chinese Style Pork Shoulder Steaks, 1 portion, 100g **5**

Corned Beef Slices, 1 slice, 30g **2**

Cranberry & Mint Stuffed Lamb Shoulder, 1 serving, 167g **12**

Cured Pork Shoulder, ¼ pack, 125g **3**

Gammon Joint with Three Cheese & Mustard Crust, ⅓ joint, 162g **5**

Halal Lamb Chops, 1 portion, 100g **9**

Hot & Spicy Thin Sliced Beef Steaks, 1 steak, 80g **4**

Hot & Spicy Buffalo Wings, ¼ pack, 150g **8**

Lamb Meatballs, 1 (85g) **6**

Lamb Ribs in a Chinese Style Marinade, 1 serving, 100g **11**

Lamb Ribs in a Mint Flavour Marinade, 1 serving, 100g **13**

Lamb Shoulder Chops in a BBQ Marinade, 1 serving, 100g **9**

Meatloaf with Onion Gravy, 1 serving, 175g **8**

Mini BBQ Pork Ribs, 1 (50g) **3**

Minted Lamb Leg Chops, 1 (100g) **5**

Minted Lamb Loin Chops, 1 (100g) **7**

Minted Lamb Riblets, ⅓ pack, 99g **10**

Minted Lamb Shanks, 1 quantity, 100g **5**

Pork Belly Crackling Joint, 1 serving, 120g **14**

Pork In Cider, ½ pack, 250g **8**

Pork Joint with Gravy, 1 serving, 180g **6**

Pork Loin Steaks with Garlic Butter, 1 pack, 100g **6**

Pork Meatballs, 1 serving, 40g **2**

Pork Steaks in a Texan Style BBQ Sauce, 1 serving, 166g	**8**
Salmon Cut Beef Steaks, 1 steak, 113g	**7**
Salt & Pepper Beef Meatball Kebabs, 1 (50g)	**3**
Shish Kebab, 1 (26g)	**2**

Asda – Chosen by You

Ready To Roast Pork Loin Joint with Apple & Sage Stuffing, 1 serving (cooked), 188g	**10**

Asda – Extra Special

14 Day Matured Cherrywood Smoked Silverside Gammon Joint, 1 serving, 110g	**4**
14 Day Matured Unsmoked Silverside Gammon Joint, 1 serving, 110g	**4**
British 14 Day Matured Rack of Lamb with Garlic & Herb Crust, 1 portion, 100g	**6**
Butterflied Beef, ½ serving, 243g	**9**
Chilli & Garlic Marinated Rump Steaks, 1 pack, 240g	**8**
Double Rack of British Lamb, 1 quantity, 100g	**8**
Garlic & Herb Marinated Lamb Steaks, 1 pack, 240g	**12**
Hickory Smoked Ribs with Bourbon, ½ pack, 200g	**11**
Lamb Shanks in Garlic & Rosemary Gravy, 1 serving, 280g	**12**
Lamb Shanks in Mint Gravy, 1 serving, 277g	**13**
Slow-Cooked Lamb with Pomegranate & Chickpoas, ½ pack, 250g	**8**
Sous Vide Pork Shanks in Mustard Sauce, ½ pack, 250g	**11**
Venison Haunch Joint, ½ pack, 150g	**4**

Asda – Fresh Tastes

Beef Medallions in a Creamy Peppercorn Sauce, 1 serving, 165g	**11**
Lamb Chops in a Sweet Mint & Balsamic Sauce, ½ pack, 160g	**10**
Mixed Grill, 1 serving, 360g	**15**
Peppered Beef Steaks with Garlic Butter, 1 serving, 30g	**1**
Pork Loin Steaks in a Chunky Apple Sauce, ½ pack, 170g	**11**

Highland Game

Diced Venison, ¼ pack, 75g	**2**
Medallions of Venison, 1 (70g)	**2**
Venison Steaks, 1 (130g)	**3**

Morrisons

British Beef Grillsteaks, 1 (86g)	**6**

Beef Wellington, ½ pack, 205g	**14**
Beef Rump Steaks with Peppercorn Sauce, ½ pack, 185g	**8**
Cooked Half Rack Pork Rib in Barbecue Sauce, 1 pack, 225g	**9**
Lamb Grillsteaks, 1 (85g)	**7**
Lamb Kebabs, 1 (28g)	**2**
Lamb Rack with a Herb Crust, ½ pack, 185g	**8**
Pork & Mustard Grillsteak, 1 individual, 75g	**7**
Pork Ribs with a Chinese Style Glaze, ¼ pack, 250g	**13**
Pork Steaks, 1 serving, 125g	**8**

Sainsbury's

American Style Pork Rib Selection Pack, 1 portion, 25g	**2**
Applewood Smoke Flavour Pork Rib Racks with Cider Drizzle, 1 portion, 22g	**2**
BBQ Boneless Pork Ribs with Bourbon Drizzle, 1 portion, 22g	**2**
Beef Meatballs, 3 balls, 87g	**6**
British Roast Pork Slices, 1 slice, 25g	**1**
British Beef Kebabs with Sweet Chilli Seasoning, 1 (68g)	**4**
British Beef Lean Diced Steak & Kidney, ½ pack, 250g	**7**
British Boneless Barbecue Ribs with a Bourbon Drizzle, 1 slice, 62g	**6**
British Pork Drumsticks with a Hot & Spicy Herb Rub, 1 portion, 81g	**3**
British Pork Kebabs with Peppers & a Barbecue Drizzle, 1 (40g)	**2**
British Pork Kebabs with Sweet Chinese Seasoning, 1 (72g)	**4**
British Pork Loin Steak with a Sweet Chilli Marinade, 1 (109g)	**8**
British Pork Loin Steaks with a Fire Roasted Pineapple & Coriander Relish, 1 (83g)	**5**
British Pork Meaty Ribs with a Hot & Spicy Marinade, 1 (57g)	**4**
British Pork Mini Ribs with Barbecue & Chinese Marinade, 1 (39g)	**3**
British Pork Rack of Ribs with a Barbecue Applewood Marinade, 1 portion, 61g	**3**
British Pork Ribs with American Style Barbecue Marinade, 1 portion, 112g	**9**
British Pork Sage & Onion Stuffed Joint, 1 portion, 100g	**6**
British Pork Shoulder Steaks with a Chinese Marinade, 1 (61g)	**4**
Lamb Kofta Kebab, 1 (58g)	**4**

Item	ProPoints
Lamb Rump Steak Topped with a Mint & Red Chilli Marinade, 1 steak, 104g	8
Minted Lamb Shish Kebab, 1 (85g)	5
Pork & Lamb Kofta, 1 (20g)	1

Sainsbury's – Inspired to... Cook

Item	ProPoints
Gammon with Pineapple, ½ pack, 170g	6
Pork Loin Steaks with a Spiced Tomato & Apricot Sauce, ½ pack, 165g	8
Pork Fillet Medallions with Red Wine & Bramley Apple Sauce, ½ pack, 180g	6
Pork Steaks with Prosciutto & Sicilian Lemon Butter, 1 serving, 146g	10

Sainsbury's – Inspired to... Roast

Item	ProPoints
Lamb Leg Joint, 1 serving, 200g	9
Pork Crackling Joint, 1 serving, 146g	11
Scottish Beef with Onion Gravy, ⅓ joint, 183g	7

Sainsbury's – Taste the Difference

Item	ProPoints
British Beef Meatballs, ½ pack, 210g	12
British Pork, Roasted Onion & Fresh Sage Stuffing, 1 serving, 67g	4
Outdoor Reared Pork Joint with Bramley Apple Stuffing, 1 serving, 100g	6
Pheasant Breast Fillets, 1 (78g)	4
West Country Veal Mince, 1 pack, 227g	8
Whole Partridge, ½ pack, 125g	7
Whole Pheasant, 1 serving, 120g	7
Wood Pigeon Breast Fillet, 1 pack, 160g	7

Scan

Item	ProPoints
Swedish Kitchen Premium Meatballs Pork & Beef, ¼ pack, 88g	5
Swedish Meatballs, 1 portion, 87g	6

Tesco

Item	ProPoints
Bacon Lattice Chicken Joint with Stuffing, 1 serving, 130g	6
BBQ Balti Burger Quarter Pounders, 1 individual, 114g	8
Beef & Pork Meatballs, 1 serving, 64g	5
Beef Brisket Joint with a Mediterranean Style Stuffing, 1 serving, 145g	5
Beef Grill Steaks, 1 serving, 80g	4
Beef Joint with Horseradish & Mustard, 1 serving, 144g	7

Item	ProPoints
Beef Quarter Pounders, 1 burger (raw), 114g	7
Bone in Lamb Leg Joint With a Rosemary & Mint Crust, 1 serving, 115g	6
Carvery Leg of Lamb with Garlic & Rosemary, 1 serving, 120g	5
Chinese Style Pork Ribs, 1 serving, 75g	6
Chunky Bacon Pieces, 1 serving, 100g	3
Counter Peppered Beef Steak, 1 serving, 100g	3
Gammon Joint topped with an Orange Style Marmalade, 1 serving, 115g	7
Gammon Joint with a Sweet Glaze, 1 serving, 120g	5
Ken Hom's Spare Ribs, 1 serving, 200g	9
Lamb Breast Rib With Mint Glaze, 1 serving, 90g	10
Make a Meal with Char Sui Pork, 1 serving, 90g	3
Make a Meal with Chilli Beef, 1 serving, 85g	3
Make a Meal with Peppered Beef Steak, 1 serving, 85g	2
Make a Meal with Wholegrain Mustard Gammon, 1 serving, 100g	3
Minted Lamb Steaks, 1 serving, 60g	4
Moroccan Style Lamb Chops, 1 serving, 54g	5
Pork Loin Joint with Crackling & Pork, Sage & Onion Stuffing, 1 serving, 130g	9
Pork Shanks with a Creamy Mustard & Honey Sauce, 1 serving, 180g	7
Rosemary & Mint Lamb Meatball Kebabs, 1 serving, 85g	5
Rosemary & Mint Lamb Steaks, 1 serving, 65g	4
Simply Add Beef Chilli, 1 serving, 300g	10
Sweetcure Roast Pork Loin, 1 slice, 16g	1

Tesco – Finest

Item	ProPoints
Steak Au Poivre, 1 serving (½ pack), 225g	9
Venison Grillsteak, 1 individual, 170g	5

The Co-operative

Item	ProPoints
Aberdeen Angus Grills, 1 (142g)	8
Beef Meatballs, ½ pack, 170g	11
Chinese Pork Loin Steaks, ½ pack, 125g	6
Chinese Pork Ribs, ¼ pack, 138g	6
Easy Cook Beef Steaks, 1 steak, 200g	9
Easy to Cook Beef Steaks with Mushroom & Mozzarella Topping, ½ pack, 150g	5
Garlic & Rosemary Lamb Chops, ½ pack, 175g	9
Lamb Chump Steak, ½ pack, 80g	5
Lamb Mince 20% Fat, 1 serving, 100g	7
Lamb Shoulder Chops with a Mint Glaze, 1 (150g)	11
Peppered Beef Slices, 1 slice, 50g	2
Pork & Pepper Kebabs, 1 pack, 74g	2

Simply British Beef Steaks with Pepper Sauce, ½ pack, 150g	4
Tennessee Pork Ribs, 1 serving, 100g	5

The Co-operative – Hot Food Rotisserie

BBQ Rack of Ribs, 1 pack, 100g	6
Brisket of Beef, 1 serving, 100g	3
Chinese Style Rack of Ribs, 1 quantity, 100g	6
Minted Lamb Joint, 1 quantity, 100g	5
Pork Belly Mini Joint, 1 serving, 100g	4

The Co-operative – Truly Irresistible

Butter Basted Turkey Breast, 1 quantity	3
Butterflied Leg of Lamb, 1 serving, 100g	4
Finely Sliced Aberdeen Angus Silverside Beef, 1 serving, 100g	6
Rack of Lamb, 1 serving, 100g	8
Sweetcure Freedom Food British Gammon Joint with an Orange Glaze, 1 serving, 100g	3

Waitrose

Aberdeen Angus Beef Meatballs, 1 (36g)	3
British Beef Meatballs, 1 (15g)	1
Smoked Bacon Chops Sweet Cured with Maple Syrup, 1 (50g)	3
Steak & Kidney, ½ pack, 225g	9

Fresh, Prepared & Breaded Poultry

Asda

Barbecue Chicken Thighs, 1 piece, 150g	10
Basted Chicken, 1 serving, 100g	5
Battered Chicken Breast Steaks, 1 individual, 93g	4
Breaded Chicken Bites, ¼ portion, 50g	4
Breaded Chicken Steaks, 1 steak, 123g	6
Butter Basted Turkey Breast Joint with Sage & Onion, ⅓ joint, 149g	6
Butter Basted Turkey Breast Joint, 1 portion, 100g	4
Cheddar & Ham Chicken Kievs, 1 serving, 133g	7
Cheese & Garlic Chicken Kievs, 1 serving, 136g	8
Chicken & Mushrooms in White Wine, ½ pack, 250g	8

Chicken Breast Joint with Sage & Onion Stuffing, 1 serving, 172g	7
Chicken in Tomato, ½ pack, 250g	4
Chinese Style British Chicken Drumsticks, 1 serving, 100g	4
Chinese Style Chicken Wings, 1 pack, 24g	1
Dipping Chicken, ⅓ pack, 122g	8
Four Cheese Chicken Escalopes, 1 portion, 164g	10
Garlic Basted British Whole Chicken, 1 serving, 100g	5
Lemon & Black Pepper Chicken Steaks, 1 steak, 118g	7
Lemon Basted British Whole Chicken, 1 serving, 100g	4
Mexican Style Cooked Mini Chicken Breast Fillets, 1 serving, 200g	7
Pork, Sage & Onion Stuffed Whole Chicken without Giblets, 1 serving, 100g	5
Roast Chicken Drumsticks, 1 serving, 100g	4
Roast Chicken Kebabs with Peppers, 1 pack, 160g	3
Roast Chicken Kebabs, 1 pack, 160g	4
Southern Fried Chicken Bites, ½ pack, 100g	7
Southern Fried Chicken Steaks, 1 portion, 121g	6
Southern Fried Chicken Thighs & Drumsticks, 1 serving, 125g	9
Southern Fried Whole Chicken Mini Fillets, ½ pack, 175g	11
St. Clement's Basted Chicken, 1 serving, 100g	4
Three Bird Roast, 1 serving, 175g	7
Tikka Mini Chicken Fillets, ½ pack, 105g	4
Turkey Breast & Thigh Joint with Pork, Sage & Onion Stuffing, 1 serving, 163g	7
Turkey Breast Joint with Cranberry & Orange Stuffing, 1 serving, 153g	6
Turkey Breast Joint with Cranberry & Orange Stuffing, 1 serving, 153g	6
Turkey Breast Joint with Pork, Sage & Onion Stuffing, 1 portion, 100g	4
Turkey Crown with Pork, Sage & Onion Stuffing, 1 portion, 100g	4
Whole Breaded Mini Chicken Breast Fillets, 1 serving, 153g	9
Whole Chicken Breast Breaded Fillet, ½ pack, 175g	10

Asda – Extra Special

British Lamb Leg Joint with Shallot & Garlic Butter, 1 portion, 100g	5
Butter Roast Chicken Breast, 1 pack, 125g	4

Butter-Roasted British Chicken Breast with
Stuffing, 1 portion, 100g   **3**
Whole Chicken Fillet Garlic Kievs, ½ pack, 145g   **9**
Yakitori Chicken Skewers,
1 skewer (cooked), 18g   **1**

Asda – Fresh Tastes

Chicken Breasts in a Honey & Mustard
Marinade, 1 serving, 138g   **5**
Chicken Breasts in a Mushroom & White Wine
Sauce, 1 serving, 166g   **6**
Chicken Breasts in a Pesto Crumb,
1 serving, 134g   **6**
Chicken Breasts in a Rich Red Wine Sauce,
1 serving, 150g   **5**
Chicken Breasts in a Smoky Barbecue Sauce,
½ pack, 185g   **8**
Chicken Breasts in a Spicy Piri Piri Sauce,
½ pack, 190g   **5**
Chicken Breasts in a Sweet & Sour Sauce,
1 serving, 166g   **5**
Chicken Breasts in a Tomato & Olive Sauce
with Chorizo, ½ pack, 190g   **6**
Chicken Breasts with Green Thai Curry Sauce,
½ pack, 210g   **7**
Chicken Breasts with Leeks & Cheese Crumb,
½ pack, 115g   **5**
Chicken Caesar Melts with a Three Cheese
Topping & Smoked Streaky Bacon,
1 serving, 138g   **6**
Chicken Enchiladas, 1 serving, 173g   **9**
Chicken Supreme with Carrots, Mushrooms &
Peas in a White Wine Sauce, 1 serving, 155g   **5**
Chicken Thighs in a Lemon & Garlic Marinade,
1 serving, 208g   **10**
Chicken Thighs in a Tomato & Chilli Marinade,
1 serving, 186g   **9**
Mediterranean Style Chicken Breasts in
a Rich Tomato Sauce with Feta Cheese,
1 serving, 180g   **5**
Mexican Style Chicken Breast with Onion Rings
& a Cheese Chilli Topping, 1 serving, 148g   **7**
Mexican Style Chicken Breasts, 1 serving, 132g   **6**
Whole Breaded Chicken Breast Fillets,
1 serving, 118g   **5**

Asda – Go Cook

Chicken Breasts in a Memphis Style Barbecue
Sauce, ½ pack, 175g   **8**
Chicken Fajitas, 1 serving, 293g   **12**
Chicken Mini Roasts Breast Fillets,
1 serving, 220g   **8**

Chicken Thighs with Peppers, Onions & Peas
in a Spanish Style Marinade, 1 serving, 274g   **11**

Bernard Matthews

BBQ Turkey Drumstick, 1 serving, 220g   **9**
Butter Basted Turkey Breast Joint with Herbs,
1 serving, 125g   **6**
Chicken Escalope, 1 (130g)   **9**
Creamy Pepper Turkey Escalope, 1 (136g)   **9**
Crispy Chicken, 1 (116g)   **8**
Golden Norfolk Turkey Breast Joint,
1 serving, 125g   **5**
Ham & Cheese Chicken Escalope, 1 (136g)   **9**
Hot & Spicy Turkey Escalope, 1 (121g)   **9**
Lemon & Pepper Turkey Escalope, 1 (120g)   **10**
Southern Fried Crispy Chicken, 1 (116g)   **8**
Southern Fried Turkey Escalope, 1 (121g)   **9**
Southern Fried Turkey Steaks, 1 (117g)   **9**
Turkey Escalope, 1 (123g)   **10**
Turkey Goujons, 1 (28g)   **2**
Turkey Steaks, 1 (117g)   **10**

Big Al's

Chicken Dippers, ½ pack, 135g   **7**
BBQ Chicken Grills, 1 (200g)   **11**
Breaded Chicken Burgers, 1 (280g)   **15**
Chunky Chicken Bites, 1 serving, 220g   **13**
Chunky Chicken Fillets, 1 (220g)   **9**
Hot 'n' Spicy Chicken Fillets, 1 (220g)   **11**
Hot 'n' Spicy Chicken Strips, 1 serving, 220g   **12**
Poppin' Chicken, 1 serving, 220g   **17**
Roasted Chicken Fillets, 1 (250g)   **10**
Roasted Mini Fillets, 1 pack, 200g   **5**
Southern Fried Chicken Fillets, ½ pack, 105g   **6**
Spicy Chicken Grills, 1 (200g)   **11**
Sweet Chilli Mini Fillets, 1 serving, 220g   **6**

Morrisons

Chicken Burgers, 1 (50g)   **4**
Chicken Quarter Pounders, 1 (104g)   **7**
Crunchy Crumb Chicken Fillets, 1 (94g)   **6**

M&S

Breaded Chicken Breast Fillets, ¼ pack, 125g   **6**
Breaded Chicken Goujons, ½ pack, 112g   **6**
Chicken Kiev, 1 (160g)   **11**
Roast Chicken Portion, 1 portion, 210g   **9**

Sainsbury's

Battered Chicken Breast Chunks,
1 serving, 68g   **3**
Battered Chicken Nuggets, ¼ pack, 75g   **4**

BBQ & Honey Roast Chicken Portions, ¼ pack, 175g	**10**
BBQ Style Chicken Breast Slice, 1 portion, 64g	**2**
Breaded BBQ Chicken Mini Fillets, ½ pack, 175g	**10**
Chicken Breast Fillets with a Sun-Dried Tomato & Basil Marinade, 1 (115g)	**4**
Chicken Drumsticks with a Barbecue Marinade, 1 portion, 66g	**3**
Chicken Drumsticks with a Chinese Marinade, 1 portion, 64g	**3**
Chicken Jumbo Thighs, 1 portion, 143g	**8**
Chicken Large Drumsticks, 1 portion, 92g	**4**
Chicken Mini Fillet Kebabs with a Tikka Marinade, 1 serving, 25g	**2**
Chicken Mini Fillets with a Sunbaked Tomato & Basil Marinade, 1 serving, 38g	**1**
Chicken Thighs with a Thai Marinade, 1 serving, 76g	**5**
Chicken Thighs with a Tikka Marinade, 1 portion, 120g	**5**
Chicken Wings with a Barbeque Marinade, 1 (45g)	**3**
Chicken Wings with a Hot & Spicy Marinade, 1 (112g)	**7**
Skin on Chicken Breast Fillets, 1 (130g)	**6**
Chicken Breasts with a Mushroom & Spinach Melt, 1 serving, 182g	**7**
Chicken Dippers, 1 portion, 66g	**4**
Chicken Goujons, Breaded, ⅓ pack, 89g	**7**
Chicken Kiev Cordon Bleu (Gruyere Cheese & Ham), ½ pack, 161g	**9**
Chicken Kiev Hot & Spicy, ½ pack, 112g	**5**
Chicken Kiev with Garlic & Parsley, Boneless, ½ pack, 130g	**10**
Chicken Nuggets, 1 portion, 73g	**5**
Chicken Pieces with Brown Cap Mushrooms, Smoked Bacon & Red Onion, 1 serving, 173g	**10**
Chicken Steaks with Lemon & Pepper, 1 (86g)	**6**
Chicken Tikka Breast Pieces, ⅓ pack, 71g	**2**
Chilli & Lime Corn Fed Chicken Breast Fillet Kebabs with Soy Sauce Drizzle, 1 portion, 105g	**4**
Chinese Style Chicken Breast Slice, ⅓ pack, 63g	**2**
Chinese Style Chicken Wing, 1 portion, 84g	**5**
Dragon's Fire Chicken Thigh, 1 portion, 119g	**8**
Garlic Butter Filled Chicken Kiev, 1 portion, 125g	**9**
Hot & Spicy Chicken Breast Fillets, ½ pack, 112g	**6**
Hot 'n' Spicy Chicken Thigh, 1 portion, 108g	**7**
Hot 'n' Spicy Chicken Wing, 1 serving, 79g	**5**

Mexican Style Chicken Breast Slice, ⅓ pack, 63g	**2**
Mini Chicken & Olive Skewers, 1 (30g)	**1**
Moroccan Chicken Breast Fillet Kebabs, 1 portion, 34g	**1**
Nuggets Battered Chicken Breast Chunks, 1 portion, 67g	**4**
Oven Ready BBQ Basted Whole Chicken, 1 portion, 113g	**5**
Oven Ready Garlic Basted Whole Chicken, 1 portion, 114g	**5**
Oven Ready Whole Chicken with an Apple & Parsnip Stuffing, 1 portion, 184g	**9**
Oven Ready Whole Chicken with Pork, Sage & Onion Stuffing, 1 serving, 100g	**4**
Peking Whole Crispy Aromatic Duck, 1 serving, 125g	**8**
Roast Chicken Breasts, ¼ pack, 120g	**5**
Roast Chicken Drumsticks, 1 80g	**3**
Salt & Cracked Black Pepper Spatchcock Chicken, 1 serving, 122g	**4**
Smoked Bacon & Mushroom Chicken Kiev, 1 portion, 120g	**7**
Southern Fried Chicken Breast Fillet, 1 (112g)	**6**
Southern Fried Chicken Goujons, 3 (70g)	**5**
Southern Fried Chicken Mini Fillets, 1 serving, 170g	**10**
Southern Fried Chicken Nuggets, 6 pieces, 72g	**4**
Southern Fried Coated Chicken Strip, 1 portion, 109g	**6**
Southern Fried Style Chicken Breast Pop'ems, ½ pack, 112g	**7**
Southern Fried Style Chicken Drumsticks & Thighs, 1 portion, 91g	**5**
Spicy Herb Chicken Breast Fillet Kebabs with Lemon & Thyme Drizzle, 1 serving, 89g	**4**
Sweet & Smoky Chicken Breast Mini Fillet, 1 portion, 144g	**8**
Sweet Chilli Chicken Breast Slices, ½ pack, 65g	**2**
Sweet Chilli Chicken Fillets, ⅓ pack, 66g	**2**
Tikka Chicken Breast, ½ pack, 65g	**2**
Tikka Chicken Breast Kebabs, 1 (20g)	**1**
Tikka Chicken Breast Mini Fillet Kebabs, 1 portion, 33g	**2**
Tomato & Mozzarella Chicken Kiev, 1 portion, 124g	**7**

Sainsbury's – Inspired to... Cook

Chicken & White Wine Sauce, ½ pack, 185g	**5**
Chicken Breast Joint Stuffed with Sage & Onion, ⅓ pack, 165g	**7**

Chicken Breast Topped with Cheddar Cheese & Bacon, 1 serving, 139g **6**

Chicken Breasts Topped with Cheese & Ham, ½ pack, 170g **7**

Chicken en Croute, ½ pack, 195g **13**

Chicken in Red Wine Sauce, ½ pack, 175g **5**

Chicken Topped with Cheese & Smoked Flavoured Ham, 1 serving, 135g **5**

Chicken Topped with Sausagemeat & Bacon, ½ pack, 180g **10**

Chicken with Sunbaked Tomato, ½ pack, 165g **6**

Sun-Dried Tomato & Black Olive Chicken, ½ pack, 160g **7**

Sainsbury's – Taste the Difference

Butter Basted Turkey Breast Slices, 1 slice, 32g **1**

Chicken Breast Fillet Kebabs with Chorizo & Red Pepper Chutney, 1 serving, 117g **5**

Free Range Bronze Turkey Breast Joint with Roast Chestnut Stuffing, 1 serving, 150g **5**

Free Range Gressingham Goose, 1 serving, 150g **12**

Gressingham Duck Breast Mini Fillets, 1 serving, 90g **3**

Gressingham Duck Fillets with Zesty Orange Sauce, 1 serving, 150g **9**

Gressingham Duck with Pork, Apricot & Orange Stuffing, 1 serving, 150g **11**

Guinea Fowl with Pork & Caramelised Red Onion Stuffing, 1 serving, 150g **9**

Roast Garlic & Parsley Chicken Kiev, ½ pack, 150g **10**

Tesco

Bacon & Cheese Chicken Escalopes, 1 individual, 153g **11**

Bacon & Cheese Chicken Fillets, 1 individual, 173g **8**

Bacon & Cheese Chicken Kievs, 1 individual, 130g **8**

Bacon & Cheese Chicken Topped Goujons, 1 serving, 126g **10**

BBQ Sweet Chilli Chicken Skewers, 1 individual, 20g **1**

Breaded Chicken Breast Chicken Fillets, 1 individual, 150g **7**

Breaded Chicken Goujons, 1 serving, 86g **6**

Breaded Chicken Mini Fillets, 1 serving, 145g **9**

Breaded Chicken Pops, 1 serving, 50g **4**

Breaded Chicken Steaks, 1 individual, 126g **8**

Cajun Chicken, 1 serving, 55g **1**

Chicken Breaded Escalopes, 1 individual, 128g **10**

Chicken Breast Joint & Stuffing, 1 serving, 125g **6**

Chicken Breasts Topped with Cheese & Wrapped in Bacon, 1 serving, 150g **5**

Chicken Breasts with BBQ Hunters Style Sauce, 1 serving, 160g **6**

Chicken Breasts with Cheese, Ham & Mushroom, 1 serving, 175g **5**

Chicken Breasts with Mediterranean Vegetables, 1 serving, 145g **4**

Chicken Breasts with Piri Piri Marinade, 1 serving, 150g **5**

Chicken Butter Basted Joint, 1 serving, 125g **5**

Chicken Creamy Mushroom Fillets, 1 individual, 173g **8**

Chicken Tikka Kebabs, 1 serving, 80g **2**

Chicken, Tomato & Mozzarella Kievs, 1 individual, 130g **8**

Chilli Chicken, 1 serving, 100g **3**

Chunky Barbecue Chicken, 1 serving, 100g **3**

Chunky Flame Grilled Chicken, 1 serving, 100g **3**

Chunky Hot & Spicy Chicken, 1 serving, 100g **3**

Chunky Tikka Chicken, 1 serving, 100g **3**

Creamy Garlic Chicken Kievs, 1 individual, 130g **8**

Creamy Peppercorn Chicken Escalopes, 1 individual, 153g **10**

Creamy Peppercorn Chicken Kievs, 1 individual, 130g **8**

Crumb Coated Chicken Breasts with Garlic Mushrooms, 1 serving, 140g **5**

Extra Tasty Chicken Breast Fillets Skin On, 1 serving, 140g **5**

Garlic & Herb Spatchcock Chicken, 1 serving, 140g **8**

Garlic Chicken Kievs, 1 individual, 130g **10**

Hickory Style BBQ Chicken Fillets, 1 serving, 80g **3**

Hoisin Mini Fillets, 1 serving, 100g **3**

Hot & Spicy Chicken Breast Fillets, 1 individual, 173g **7**

Hot & Spicy Chicken Wings, 1 serving, 105g **5**

Mexican Fajita Chicken, 1 serving, 100g **3**

Mini Flame Grilled Chicken Fillets, 1 serving, 100g **2**

Piri Piri Mini Chicken Fillets, 1 serving, 100g **3**

Popcorn Chicken, 1 serving, 46g **3**

Red Thai Chicken Kebabs, 1 serving, 100g **3**

Red Thai Style Mini Fillets, 1 serving, 100g **3**

Reduced Fat Garlic Chicken Kievs, 1 individual, 130g **8**

Roast BBQ Chicken Wings, 1 serving (⅓ pack), 126g	**7**
Roast Chicken Tikka Mini Fillets, 1 serving, 100g	**3**
Southern Fried Chicken Breaded Goujons, 1 serving, 83g	**5**
Southern Fried Chicken Breast Fillets, 1 individual, 165g	**7**
Southern Fried Chicken Drumsticks, 1 serving, 238g	**13**
Southern Fried Chicken Pops, 1 serving, 52g	**4**
Southern Fried Chicken Steaks, 1 individual, 126g	**8**
Southern Fried Chicken Straws, 1 individual, 12g	**1**
Southern Fried Chicken Wings, 1 serving, 159g	**10**
Southern Fried Mini Fillets, 3 mini fillets, 137g	**8**
Spicy Chicken Parcels, 1 individual, 18g	**2**
Sticky Barbecue Chicken Wings, 1 serving, 56g	**3**
Sweet Chilli Chicken Sticks, 1 serving, 58g	**5**
Three Bird Roast, 1 serving, 120g	**5**
Tikka Mini Chicken Breast Fillets, 1 serving 100g	**3**

Tesco – Finest

Butter Roast Turkey, 1 slice, 30g	**1**
Chicken Kiev, 1 individual, 208g	**12**
Roast Chicken with Sage, Onion & Thyme Stuffing, 1 slice, 30g	**1**

The Co-operative

Chicken Breast Joint with Wild Mushroom & Bacon Stuffing, ¼ joint, 150g	**5**
Freedom Food Easy Carve Stuffed Whole Duck, ⅛ pack, 125g	**11**
Garlic & Herb Chicken Thighs, 1 (115g)	**7**
Hoisin Chicken Drumsticks, ¼ pack, 188g	**6**
Hot & Spicy Chicken Wings, 1 serving, 100g	**5**
Kansas BBQ Chicken Drumsticks, ¼ pack, 156g	**7**
Ready to Cook British Chicken Parcels with a Red Pepper Filling, ½ pack, 158g	**6**
Ready to Cook British Chicken Parcels with a Three Cheese Filling, ½ pack, 163g	**6**
Roast Half Chicken, 1 serving, 100g	**5**
Sea Salt & Black Pepper Chicken Portions, 1 portion, 175g	**11**
Southern Fried Chicken Portions, ¼ pack, 175g	**11**
Tomato & Basil Part Boned Chicken Breasts, 1 pack, 250g	**7**

The Co-operative – Hot Food Rotisserie

Chinese Style Chicken Drumstick, 1 quantity, 100g	**4**
Cooked Chicken Fillets, 1 serving, 100g	**4**
Cooked Chicken Quarters, 1 serving, 100g	**4**
Peppered Southern Fried Chicken Fillets, 1 serving, 100g	**5**

Waitrose

BBQ Maple Mesquite Style Rotisserie Chicken Whole, 1 portion, 200g	**7**
Chicken Cordon Bleu, 1 pack, 160g	**9**
Cooked Chicken Flamegrilled Pieces, 1 serving, 130g	**4**
Crispy Crumb Chicken, ½ pack, 112g	**6**
Crispy Crumb Chicken Goujons, ½ pack, 125g	**7**
Garlic Rotisserie Chicken Whole, 1 portion, 200g	**7**
Hand Carved Turkey Breast with Stuffing, 1 serving, 100g	**3**
Honey & Mustard Rotisserie Chicken Whole, 1 portion, 200g	**8**
Roast Chicken Chinese Style Wings, 1 serving, 100g	**6**
Roast Chicken Drumsticks, 1 pack, 105g	**5**
Roast Chicken Hot & Spicy Wings, 1 (50g)	**3**
Roast Chicken Leg Quarters, 1 (150g)	**8**
Roast Chicken Lemon & Herb Mini Fillets, 1 fillet, 25g	**1**
Roast Chicken Pesto Mini Fillets, 1 fillet, 25g	**1**
Roast Chicken Sticky Chilli Chicken Wings, 1 (62g)	**3**
Roast Chicken Sticky Maple BBQ Chicken Wings, 1 (62g)	**3**
Roast Chicken Sweet Chilli Mini Fillets, 1 (33g)	**1**
Roast Chicken Tandoori Mini Fillets, 1 fillet, 33g	**1**
Roast Chicken Thighs, 1 (55g)	**4**
Roast Chicken Tikka Pieces, 1 piece, 65g	**2**
Rosemary & Thyme Rotisserie Chicken Whole, 1 portion, 200g	**10**
Southern Fried Chicken Breast Mini Fillets, 1 quantity, 100g	**5**

Smoked & Marinated Fish

Asda

Honey Roast Scottish Salmon Flakes, 1 portion, 135g	7
Hot Smoked Salmon Flakes, ½ pack, 55g	2
Lemon & Pepper Salmon Roasties, ½ pack, 60g	3
Peppered Mackerel Fillets, 1 portion, 100g	8
Smoked Scottish Mackerel Strips, 1 portion, 100g	8
Smoked Scottish Salmon Crescent, ½ pack, 125g	6
Smoked Scottish Salmon Parcels, 1 individual, 50g	2
Smoked Scottish Salmon Pâté, 1 serving, 50g	2
Sweet Cured Mackerel Strips, ¼ pack, 50g	5

Asda – Extra Special

Applewood & Beech Smoked Scottish Salmon, 1 serving, 50g	3
Golden Roast Scottish Smoked Salmon Slices, ⅓ pack, 50g	2
Hot Smoked Mackerel Strips with Chilli & Garlic, ½ pack, 100g	10
Peppered Hot Smoked Salmon Fillet, ½ pack, 100g	5
Smoked Scottish Salmon Terrine Slice, 1 slice, 15g	1
Smoked Scottish Salmon with Lemon Oil & Cracked Black Pepper, ½ pack, 50g	2

Sainsbury's

Hot Smoked Mackerel Fillet, ½ pack, 125g	12
Hot Smoked Mackerel Fillets with Honey Flavoured Glaze, ½ pack, 110g	12
Marinade Herring, 1 pack, 126g	7
Scottish Peppered Hot Smoked Salmon, ½ pack, 114g	8
Scottish Responsibly Sourced Hot Smoked Salmon Roasties, 1 pack, 120g	7
Scottish Responsibly Sourced Smoked Salmon Mousse Crescent, ½ pack, 72g	4
Scottish Responsibly Sourced Smoked Salmon Sandwich Pack, 1 slice, 16g	1
Smoked Salmon & Asparagus Mini Roulades, 1 serving, 80g	4
Scottish Smoked Salmon Mousse Crescent, ¼ pack, 36g	2
Smoked Mackerel Peppered Fillet, ½ pack, 125g	12

Sainsbury's – Taste the Difference

Arbroath Hot Smoked Trout Fillets, ½ pack, 62g	2
Birch & Juniper Smoked Salmon, 1 serving, 100g	4
Hot Smoked Salmon with a Creamy Prawn & Salmon Filling, ½ pack, 60g	3
Hot Smoked Scottish Stuffed Salmon Slices, ½ pack, 60g	3
Line Caught Smoked Haddock & Spinach Fishcakes, 1 (107g)	6
Marinade Herring with Fresh Lemon, ½ pack, 74g	5
Responsibly Sourced Birch & Juniper Smoked Salmon, ½ pack, 60g	3
Smoked Salmon Blinis, 1 (15g)	1
Smoked Salmon Parcels, ½ pack, 58g	4
Smoked Salmon Shot, ½ pack, 90g	6

Young's

Inverness Smokehouse Scottish Smoked Salmon Slices, 1 serving, 100g	4
Mussels Marinated in Vinegar, ½ pack, 125g	1
Smoked Haddock Fillets, 1 fillet, 112g	2

Food on the Go

ProPoints value

Basic Foods

Coleslaw, 1 tablespoon, 40g	3
Coleslaw, Reduced Calorie, 1 tablespoon, 40g	1
Cucumber Raita, 2 tablespoons, 30g	0
Cucumber Raita, 3 tablespoons, 45g	1
Guacamole, 1 tablespoon, 30g	1
Houmous, 1 tablespoon, 30g	3
Houmous, Reduced Fat, 1 tablespoon, 30g	2
Potato Salad, 1 tablespoon, 45g	2
Salsa, Fresh, 1 tablespoon, 30g	0
Taramasalata, 1 tablespoon, 30g	4
Tzatziki, 1 tablespoon, 30g	1

Dips & Fillers

Asda

30% Less Fat Sour Cream & Chive Dip, 1 serving, 50g	2
BBQ Chicken Filler, 1 serving, 30g	1
Caramelised Onion Houmous, ⅕ tub, 50g	3
Cheddar Cheese & Chive Dip, ⅕ pot, 40g	3
Cheddar Cheese & Cracked Black Pepper Dip, 1 serving, 42g	5
Chicken & Stuffing Filler, 1 serving, 25g	2
Chicken Fajita Filler, 1 serving, 30g	1
Chilli Cheese Dip, 1 tablespoon, 15g	2
Chinese Sweet & Sour Dip, 1 tablespoon, 15g	1
Chinese Sweet Chilli Dip, 1 tablespoon, 15g	1
Cracked Black Pepper Houmous, 1 tablespoon, 15g	1
Creamy Red Pepper Dip, 1 serving, 42g	5
Egg & Salad Cream Filler, ⅕ pot, 50g	2
Indian Pakora Dip, 1 pack, 70g	1
Mango Dip, 2 tablespoons, 30g	1
Mexican Style Cheese Filler, 1 serving, 50g	5
Nut Free Satay Dip, 1 tablespoon, 15g	1
Pecorino, Basil & Pine Nut Dip, ¼ pot, 50g	7
Red Salmon Filler, ½ pack, 125g	10
Reduced Fat Cheese & Onion Filler, 1 serving, 30g	1
Reduced Fat Chicken Mayonnaise Filler, 1 serving, 30g	1
Reduced Fat Chicken Tikka Filler, 1 serving, 25g	1
Reduced Fat Rocket Houmous, 1 serving, 50g	3
Reduced Fat Soured Cream & Chive Dip, 1 serving, 50g	2
Reduced Fat Tuna & Sweetcorn Filler, ½ pack, 125g	4
Sour Cream Dip, 1 tablespoon, 30g	2
Soured Cream & Chive Dip, 1 serving, 42g	2
Sweet Chilli Dipping Sauce, 1 serving, 30g	2
Thai Dip, 2 tablespoons, 30g	3
Thousand Island Dip, 1 serving, 42g	3

Asda – Chosen by You

30% Less Fat Houmous, 1 serving, 50g	3
30% Less Fat Lemon & Coriander Houmous, 1 serving, 37g	2
50% Less Fat Egg Mayonnaise, 1 tablespoon, 15g	1
Chargrilled Red Pepper Houmous, 1 serving, 50g	4
Cheese & Onion Deli Filler, ⅕ pot, 50g	5
Chicken & Bacon Deli Filler, ⅕ pot, 50g	3
Chicken & Sweetcorn Deli Filler, 1 serving, 30g	1
Chicken Caesar Deli Filler, ⅕ pot, 50g	3
Chicken Tikka Deli Filler, ⅛ pot, 50g	3
Chilli Cheese Dip, 1 serving, 40g	3
Corned Beef & Onion Deli Filler, ⅕ pot, 50g	3
Coronation Chicken Deli Filler, ⅕ pot, 50g	3
Egg & Bacon Deli Filler, ⅕ pot, 50g	3
Egg & Smoked Bacon Deli Filler, ¼ pot, 50g	3
Egg Mayonnaise Deli Filler, ⅕ pot, 50g	3
Greek Salad Deli Filler, ⅕ pot, 50g	3
Guacamole, 1 serving (¼ pack), 43g	2
Honey & Mustard Chicken Deli Filler, ⅕ pot, 50g	2
Moroccan Spiced Houmous, 1 serving, 50g	4
Onion & Garlic Dip, 1 serving (¼ pack), 50g	3
Prawn Mayonnaise Deli Filler, ⅕ pot, 50g	3
Seafood Cocktail Deli Filler, ⅕ pot, 50g	4
Sour Cream & Chive Dip, ¼ pot, 50g	3
Tuna & Sweetcorn Deli Filler, 1 pack, 60g	3

Asda – Extra Special

Sweet Mango & Habanero Chilli Salsa, 1 serving, 30g	1
Vintage Cheddar & Caramelised Onion Dip, 1 serving, 50g	4

Asda – Good For You

Cheese & Chive Dip, 1 serving, 50g	2
Chicken Tikka Deli Filler, ½ pot, 125g	4
Egg Mayonnaise Deli Filler, ⅕ pot, 50g	2
Tuna & Sweetcorn Deli Filler, ⅕ pot, 50g	1

Crosse & Blackwell

Mango & Chilli Dip, 1 tablespoon, 15g	1
Red Pepper & Redcurrant Dip, 1 tablespoon, 15g	1
Roasted Tomato & Sweet Chilli Dip, 2 tablespoons, 30g	1
Spicy Apricot & Onion Dip, 1 tablespoon, 15g	1

Discovery Foods

Guacamole, 1 serving, 36g	1

Heinz

Chicken Sandwich Filler, 1 serving, 52g	3
Mild Chicken Tikka Sandwich Filler, 1 serving, 52g	3
Tuna & Sweetcorn Sandwich Filler, 1 serving, 52g	3

John West

Smoked Salmon & Soft Cheese Deli Filler, ½ pack, 90g	8
Tuna Mayonnaise Deli Filler, ½ pack, 100g	8

Morrisons – Eat Smart

Cheese & Chive, 1 serving, 50g	3
Houmous, ½ large pot, 85g	6
Lemon & Coriander Houmous, ½ large pot, 85g	5
Onion & Garlic, 1 serving, 50g	2
Roasted Red Pepper Houmous, ½ large pot, 85g	5
Soured Cream & Chive, 1 serving, 50g	2
Thousand Island, 1 serving, 50g	2
Tuna & Sweetcorn, 1 serving, 50g	2

Primula

Nacho Cheese Dip, 1 tablespoon, 15g	1
Roasted Garlic Dip, ¼ tub, 42g	3
Sour Cream & Chive Dip, 1 tablespoon, 15g	1
Spicy Salsa or Spring Onion Dip, 4 tablespoons, 60g	1

Sainsbury's

Cajun Chicken Deli Filler, ⅕ pot, 50g	2
Cannelini Bean & Lime Dip, ¼ pot, 50g	3
Caramelised Onion Houmous, ¼ pot, 50g	4
Cheddar Cheese & Chive Dip, ¼ pot, 58g	6
Cheese & Onion Deli Filler, ⅓ pot, 56g	5
Chicken & Sweetcorn Deli Filler, ⅕ pot, 60g	3
Chicken Tikka Deli Filler, ¼ pot, 62g	3
Chicken, Bacon & Sweetcorn Deli Filler, ¼ pot, 62g	3
Chunky Salsa Dip, ¼ pot, 58g	1
Coronation Chicken Sandwich Filler, ¼ pot, 62g	4

Egg & Bacon Deli Filler, ¼ pot, 62g	4
Egg Mayonnaise Deli Filler, ¼ pot, 42g	3
Free Range Egg Mayonnaise Deli Filler, ¼ pot, 62g	3
Garlic & Herb Dip, 1 tablespoon, 30g	3
Guacamole, 1 tablespoon, 30g	2
Indian Stacker - Coriander Raita, 1 pot, 60g	1
Indian Stacker - Mango & Lime Riata, 1 pot, 60g	1
Indian Stacker - Tomato & Onion Relish, 1 pot, 60g	1
Jalapeño Houmous, ¼ pot, 50g	4
Lemon & Coriander Houmous, ¼ pot, 50g	4
Mexican Style Dip, 1 tablespoon, 30g	3
Mixed Olive & Tomato Houmous, ¼ pot, 50g	4
Moroccan Style Houmous, ¼ pot, 50g	3
Nacho Cheese Dip, 1 serving, 25g	2
Onion & Garlic Dip, 1 tablespoon, 30g	3
Pea, Yogurt & Mint Dip, 1 tablespoon, 30g	2
Pecorino & Basil Dip, ¼ pot, 50g	4
Pesto Style Houmous, ¼ pot, 50g	4
Prawn Mayonnaise Deli Filler, ¼ pot, 62g	3
Roasted Vegetable Houmous, ¼ pot, 50g	4
Seafood Cocktail Deli Filler, ¼ pot, 75g	5
Smoked Salmon Taramasalata, 1 tablespoon, 30g	4
Sour Cream & Chive Dip, 1 tablespoon, 30g	3
Taramasalata, 1 tablespoon, 30g	4
Thousand Island Dip, 1 tablespoon, 30g	3
Tuna & Red Onion Deli Filler, ¼ pot, 42g	2
Tuna & Sweetcorn Deli Filler, ¼ pot, 42g	2
Yogurt & Cucumber Dip, 1 tablespoon, 30g	2

Sainsbury's – Be Good To Yourself

Coronation Chicken Sandwich Filler, ¼ pot, 62g	2
Coronation Tuna Sandwich Filler, ½ pot, 40g	1
Egg Mayo Deli Filler, ¼ pot, 62g	2
Lemon & Coriander Houmous, ¼ pot, 50g	2
Reduced Fat Guacamole, ¼ pot, 42g	1
Roasted Red Pepper Houmous, ¼ pot, 50g	2
Sour Cream & Chive Dip, 1 serving, 46g	2
Tuna & Sweetcorn Sandwich Filler, ¼ pot, 62g	2

Tesco

Barbecue Chicken Sandwich Filler, 1 serving, 50g	3
Caramelised Onion Houmous, 1 serving, 50g	3
Cheese & Chive Dip, 1 serving, 50g	5
Cheese & Ham or Cheese & Onion or Cheese & Pickle Sandwich Filler, 1 serving, 50g	5

	ProPoints value
Chicken & Bacon Sandwich Filler, 1 serving, 50g	3
Chicken & Stuffing Sandwich Filler, 1 serving, 50g	3
Chicken & Sweetcorn Sandwich Filler, 1 serving, 50g	3
Chicken Tikka Sandwich Filler, 1 serving, 50g	2
Chunky Houmous Dip, 1 serving, 50g	4
Chunky Seafood Cocktail Sandwich Filler, 1 serving, 50g	4
Coronation Chicken Sandwich Filler, 1 serving, 50g	4
Egg & Bacon Sandwich Filler, 1 serving, 50g	3
Egg Mayonnaise Sandwich Filler, 1 serving, 50g	3
Flavoured Houmous Selection Dips, 1 pot, 70g	5
Focaccia Sticks with Reduced Fat Houmous, 1 serving, 75g	6
Frijomole Dip, 1 serving, 50g	3
Guacamole Dip, 1 serving, 50g	3
Healthy Living Soured Cream & Chive Dip, 1 serving, 50g	4
Jalapeño & Red Pepper Houmous Dip, 1 serving, 50g	5
Lemon & Coriander Houmous, ¼ pot	4
Lemon & Herb Chicken Sandwich Filler, 1 serving, 50g	3
Light Choices Prawn Cocktail, 1 pot, 140g	6
Mild Mexican Salsa, 1 serving, 30g	5
Mini Tex Mex Dips, 1 serving, 50g	2
Moroccan Chickpea Pâté, 1 serving, 40g	3
Moroccan Style Houmous Dip, 1 serving, 50g	3
Nacho Cheese Dip, 1 serving, 50g	5
Oaktree Estate Houmous, 1 serving, 50g	3
Oaktree Estate Lemon & Herb Houmous, 1 serving, 50g	3
Olive & Sundried Tomato Houmous, 1 serving, 50g	3
Onion & Garlic Dip, 1 serving, 50g	5
Piri Piri Sandwich Filler, 1 serving, 50g	4
Prawn Mayonnaise Sandwich Filler, 1 serving, 50g	3
Red Pepper Pesto Houmous, 1 serving, 50g	4
Reduced Fat Caramelised Onion Houmous, 1 serving, 50g	3
Reduced Fat Cheese & Onion Sandwich Filler, 1 serving, 50g	3
Reduced Fat Classic Dip, 1 serving, 65g	3
Reduced Fat Guacamole Dip, 1 serving, 50g	2
Reduced Fat Houmous Dip, 1 serving, 50g	3
Reduced Fat Onion & Garlic Dip, 1 serving, 50g	3
Reduced Fat Red Pepper Houmous, 1 serving, 50g	4
Reduced Fat Soured Cream & Chive Dip, 1 serving, 50g	3
Sea Salt & Black Pepper Houmous, 1 serving, 50g	4
Smoked Salmon Taramasalata, 1 serving, 50g	7
Soured Cream & Chive Dip, 1 serving, 50g	4
Sweet Chilli Houmous, 1 serving, 50g	3
Taramasalata, 1 serving, 50g	7
Tex Mex Multipack Dips, 1 serving (⅛ pack), 54g	3
Tuna & Sweetcorn Sandwich Filler, 1 serving, 50g	3
Tuna Crunch Sandwich Filler, 1 serving, 50g	4
Tzatziki, 1 serving, 50g	2
West Country Cheddar Dip, 1 serving, 50g	5

The Co-operative

Cheese & Chive Dip, ¼ tub, 50g	7
Cheese & Onion Deli Filler, ¼ tub, 50g	6
Chicken & Bacon Deli Filler, ¼ tub, 50g	3
Corned Beef & Onion Deli Filler, ¼ tub, 50g	4
Coronation Chicken Deli Filler, ¼ tub, 50g	4
Egg Mayonnaise Deli Filler, ¼ tub, 50g	3
Guacamole Dip, ¼ tub, 50g	3
Onion & Garlic Dip, ¼ tub, 50g	6
Pesto Topped Houmous, ¼ tub, 50g	5
Prawn Marie Rose Deli Filler, ¼ tub, 50g	3
Reduced Fat Onion & Garlic Dip, 1 level tablespoon, 15g	1
Reduced Fat Tuna & Sweetcorn Deli Filler, ¼ tub, 50g	2
Roasted Red Pepper Houmous, ¼ tub, 50g	4
Sour Cream & Chive Dip, ¼ tub, 50g	4
Tuna & Sweetcorn Deli Filler, 1 serving, 100g	7

Sandwiches, Salads & Sushi

Asda

All Day Breakfast Sandwich, 1 (228g)	13
Baby Potato Salad, ⅕ pack, 50g	3
BLT Sandwich, 1 (172g)	13
Butternut Squash & Carrot Salad, ½ pack, 110g	6
Celery, Fruit & Nut Salad, ¼ pack, 75g	5
Cheese & Onion Sandwich, 1 (154g)	12
Cheese & Spring Onion, 1 pack, 158g	16
Cheese & Bacon Roll, 1 individual, 16g	1
Cheese Pasta Salad, ¼ tub, 150g	11

Cheese Ploughman's Sandwich, 1 (191g)	**10**
Chicken & Bacon Caesar Pasta Salad, ½ tub, 140g	**10**
Chicken & Stuffing Sandwich, 1 (219g)	**13**
Chicken & Sweetcorn Sandwich, 1 (181g)	**10**
Chicken Salad Sandwich, 1 (221g)	**10**
Chicken Tikka & Onion Bhaji Wrap, 1 (213g)	**12**
Classic Chicken Tip & Mix Salad, ½ pack, 125g	**4**
Coronation Coleslaw, ½ pack, 140g	**7**
Egg & Cress Sandwich, 1 (164g)	**8**
Egg Mayonnaise Sandwich, 1 (149g)	**9**
Egg Salad Sandwich, 1 (208g)	**9**
Egg Salad, Deep Fill, 1 pack, 213g	**10**
Ham & Mushroom Pasta Salad, ½ pack, 125g	**8**
Ham Sandwich, 1 (131g)	**7**
Ham, Cheese & Pickle Sandwich, 1 (192g)	**12**
Italian Style Pasta Salad, 1 serving, 125g	**4**
Mixed Bean & Tuna Pasta, 1 serving, 50g	**2**
Mushroom Rice Salad, ½ pack, 125g	**5**
Nacho Chicken Wrap, 1 (195g)	**10**
New York Deli Sandwich, 1 (203g)	**8**
Peking Duck Wrap, 1 (195g)	**11**
Prawn Mayonnaise Sandwich, 1 (221g)	**12**
Red Leicester Salad Sandwich, 1 (200g)	**10**
Roast Vegetable Rice Salad, ½ pack, 125g	**4**
Roasted Butternut Squash Topped Couscous, ½ pack, 125g	**7**
Salmon & Cucumber Sandwich, 1 (153g)	**8**
Sour Cream & Chive Carrot Snack Pack, 1 pack, 115g	**6**
Sun-Dried Tomato Couscous, ½ pack, 125g	**5**
Three Bean & Vegetable Couscous, 1 pack, 250g	**9**
Tomato & Basil Chicken Topped Pasta Salad, ½ pack, 110g	**6**
Tuna Pasta Salad, ½ pack, 140g	**5**

Asda – Chosen by You

30% Less Fat Creamy Coleslaw, ¼ tub, 150g	**6**
Basil Pesto Pasta Salad, 1 serving, 50g	**4**
Beetroot Salad, 1 serving, 50g	**1**
Chicken & Sweetcorn Pasta Salad, 1 serving, 50g	**3**
Creamy Coleslaw, ¼ tub, 150g	**6**
Creamy Potato Salad, ¼ tub, 113g	**5**
Garlic & Herb Coleslaw, ¼ pack, 75g	**3**
Moroccan Style Chicken Cous Cous, 1 serving, 50g	**2**
Piri Piri Chicken Pasta Salad, 1 serving, 50g	**3**
Prawn Coleslaw, 1 serving, 50g	**2**
Spicy Sausage Pasta Salad, 1 serving, 50g	**2**
Three Cheese Pasta Salad, 1 serving, 50g	**4**

Tomato & Roasted Vegetable Pasta, ¼ pot, 150g	**5**
Tuna & Sweetcorn Pasta Salad, 1 serving, 50g	**3**

Asda – Extra Special

3 Cheese Coleslaw, 1 serving, 50g	**4**
American Deli Style Coleslaw, ¼ pot, 75g	**5**
Chicken Caesar Pasta Salad, 1 serving, 50g	**2**
Fruited Couscous, 1 serving, 50g	**3**
Greek Style Couscous, 1 serving, 50g	**3**
Moroccan Inspired Couscous, 1 serving, 50g	**3**
Oriental Style Edamame Bean Salad, 1 serving, 50g	**3**
Pesto & Spinach Pasta, ⅓ pot, 66g	**4**
Potato Salad, ⅓ pot, 100g	**4**
Prawn Cocktail, 1 serving, 100g	**8**
Prima Verra, ⅓ pack, 66g	**2**
Roasted Tomato & Mozzarella Pasta Salad, ½ pack, 110g	**4**

Asda – Good For You

Chicken Pasta Salad, ½ pack, 125g	**4**
Chilli Prawn Noodle, 1 pack, 290g	**8**
Creamy Potato Salad, 1 serving, 50g	**2**
Lightly Dressed Crunchy Coleslaw, ½ pack, 125g	**2**
Lightly Dressed Pasta Salad, ½ pack, 118g	**3**
Mediterranean Style Salad Kit, ½ pack, 88g	**2**
Pasta & Sundried Tomato Salad, ¼ pack, 75g	**2**
Pitta & Homous Snack Pack, 1 pack, 105g	**7**
Spicy Vegetable Cous Cous, ½ pack, 125g	**4**
Thai King Prawn Pasta Salad, 1 pack, 180g	**3**
Tomato & Basil Chicken Pasta Salad, ½ pack, 120g	**4**
Tomato, Rocket & Mozzarella Pasta Salad, ½ pack, 142g	**5**
Tuna Pasta Salad, ½ pack, 125g	**5**

M&S

Bacon, Lettuce & Tomato Sandwich, 1 (196g)	**16**
Beef & Rocket Baguette, 1 baguette	**13**
Brie & Rocket Baguette, 1 baguette	**16**
Cheddar Cheese & Celery, 1 pack, 200g	**15**
Cheddar Cheese Ploughman's, 1 sandwich, 208g	**14**
Cheese & Coleslaw, 1 sandwich, 200g	**16**
Couscous & Roasted Vegetables Salad, 1 pack, 200g	**9**
Egg & Bacon Baguette, 1 baguette	**16**
Ham & Cheese Baguette, 1 baguette	**14**
Hoisin Duck Wrap, 1 (236g)	**12**
Mexican 3 Bean Wrap, 1 (240g)	**12**
Mexican Chicken Wrap, 1 (247g)	**15**

Mini Chicken Salad, 1 baguette	7
Mini Egg & Tomato, 1 baguette	8
Mini Smoked Salmon & Cream Cheese, 1 baguette	8
Organic Herby Roast Chicken Sandwich, 1 (183g)	14
Prawn & Mayonnaise Sandwich, 1 (168g)	11
Prawn & Salmon Nigiri, 1 pack, 151g	6
Super Wholefood Salad with a Lemon & Herb Dressing, 1 pack, 330g	9
Sushi Snack Pack, 1 pack, 105g	4
Wrap Selection (Chicken Caesar, Chicken Fajita, Beef Enchilada), 1 (298g)	19

M&S – Count on Us

Chicken Tikka Sandwich, 1 (186g)	7
Greek Salad Wrap, 1 (180g)	6
Lemon Chicken & Mangetout Salad, 1 pack, 100g	4
Roast Chicken Sandwich, No Mayo, 1 (160g)	7

M&S – Eat Well

British Roast Chicken & Sweetcorn Sandwich, 1 (194g)	9
Chicken & Salad Sandwich, 1 (218g)	11
Free Range Egg & Watercress Sandwich, 1 (179g)	9
Poached Salmon Sandwich, 1 (171g)	9
Prawn Mayonnaise Sandwich, 1 (162g)	8
Rare Roast British Beef & Horseradish Mayonnaise Sandwich, 1 (205g)	11
Tuna & Sweetcorn Sandwich, 1 (195g)	10
Tuna & Three Bean Salad, 1 pack, 350g	9

M&S – Fuller for Longer

Chicken & Bacon Sandwich on Malted Bread, 1 (207g)	11
Ham, Taw Valley Cheese & Mustard Sandwich on Malted Brown, 1 (177g)	8
Deep Filled Roast Chicken & Chorizo Flatbread, 1 (173g)	7
Deep Filled Roast Chicken & Pesto Flatbread, 1 (207g)	8
Deep Filled Tandoori Chicken & Lentil Daal Flatbread, 1 (182g)	8

Morrisons

Cheese & Tomato Pasta Salad, 1 serving, 50g	2
Chicken Triple Sandwich, 1 (273g)	16
Coronation Rice Salad, 1 serving, 50g	2
Couscous with Cranberries & Apricots, 1 serving, 50g	2

Mexican Style Tuna Salad, 1 packet, 250g	11
Tomato & Basil Couscous, 1 serving, 50g	3
Tuna Triple, 1 sandwich, 247g	13

Morrisons – Eat Smart

Cheese Pasta Salad, 1 serving, 83g	5
Chicken Fajita Wrap, 1 (174g)	7
Egg & Cress, 1 sandwich, 162g	8
Prawn Mayonnaise, 1 sandwich, 162g	7
Reduced Fat Cheese & Onion, 1 sandwich, 146g	9
Tomato & Sweet Chilli Couscous, 1 serving, 75g	2
Tuna & Sweetcorn, 1 sandwich, 151g	7

Sainsbury's

3 Bean Salad, ¼ pot, 68g	2
Brunch Triple, 1 pack, 264g	16
Chargrilled Artichokes, ⅓ pot, 59g	2
Cheese & Tomato Pasta Salad, 1 pack, 301g	16
Cheese Coleslaw, ¼ pot, 75g	5
Cheese Ploughman's Baguette, 1 (225g)	15
Chicken & Bacon Salad Sandwich, 1 (195g)	11
Chicken & Stuffing Sandwich, 1 (174g)	10
Chicken Fajita Wrap, 1 (260g)	12
Coronation Wild Rice Salad, ¼ pot, 75g	4
Deep Fill BLT, 1 pack, 205g	12
Deli Style Coleslaw, ¼ pot, 75g	4
Deli Style Coleslaw & Tomato, ¼ pack, 125g	7
Egg & Cress Sandwich, 1 (145g)	9
Florida Salad, ¼ pot, 75g	3
Free Range Egg & Watercress, 1 pack, 204g	11
King Prawn & Avocado Cocktail, 1 pack, 200g	8
Lunch Triple, 1 sandwich, 277g	12
Meatball Baguette, 1 (237g)	15
Pesto Pasta Salad, ⅓ pot, 66g	4
Potato Salad, ¼ pot, 75g	3
Prawn Mayonnaise Sandwich, 1 (150g)	9
Roasted Vegetable Couscous, ¼ pot, 75g	3
Hot Smoked Salmon & Beetroot Cocktail, 1 pack, 200g	13
Smoked Ham & Mustard Sandwich, 1 (154g)	3
Steak & Onion Baguette, 1 (200g)	12

Sainsbury's – Be Good To Yourself

Beetroot Salad, ¼ pot, 62g	1
Coleslaw & Beetroot Twin Pack, Coleslaw, ¼ pot, 62g	2
Coleslaw & Beetroot Twin Pack, Beetroot, ¼ pot, 62g	1
Egg & Cress Sandwich, 1 (144g)	7

Potato Salad, ¼ pot, 75g	3
Roast Chicken Salad Sandwich, 1 (180g)	7
Tuna & Cucumber Sandwich, 1 (195g)	8

Sainsbury's – Taste the Difference

Balsamic Roasted Vegetable Couscous, ⅓ pack, 73g	2
Cheese & Sunbaked Tomato Pasta Salad, 1 serving, 200g	12
Cheese Coleslaw, ¼ tub, 75g	6
Coleslaw & Potato Salad, Coleslaw, ⅓ pack, 83g	7
Coleslaw & Potato Salad, Potato Salad, ⅓ pack, 83g	5
Couscous & Feta Salad, ¼ pack, 72g	4
Edamame & Butterbean Salad, ⅓ pack, 61g	2
Farro & Wild Rice Salad, ⅓ pack, 79g	4
Mediterranean Tomatoes, ¼ pack, 60g	3
Moroccan Style Couscous, ⅓ pot, 75g	3
Torchietti Pesto with Rocket Pasta, ⅓ pack, 66g	5
Tortellini & Sweet Flamed Pepper Salad, ⅓ pot, 73g	3
Waldorf Salad, ¼ pot, 69g	5

Tesco

All Day Breakfast, 1 sandwich, 189g	12
American Coleslaw, 1 serving, 50g	2
Apple & Grapes with Cheddar Bites, 1 serving, 115g	4
Bacon Lettuce Tomato Malted Brown Bread Sandwich, 1 (217g)	14
Bean & Red Pepper Couscous, 1 serving, 30g	2
Beetroot Salad, 1 serving, 50g	1
Big & Tasty Ham Cheese & Mustard Sandwich, 1 (226g)	15
Big & Tasty Spicy Chicken Sandwich, 1 (253g)	11
Caesar Salad, 1 serving, 117g	5
Cajun Chicken Sandwich, 1 (209g)	12
Cajun Chicken Wrap, 1 (180g)	12
Celery, Fruit & Nut Salad, 1 serving, 50g	5
Chargrilled Chicken & Bacon Pasta, 1 pack, 200g	11
Chargrilled Chicken Pasta Snack Salad, 1 pack, 275g	11
Chargrilled Mushroom Pasta, 1 serving, 50g	3
Chargrilled Vegetables & Couscous Salad, 1 individual, 225g	9
Cheese & Onion Brown Bread Sandwich, 1 (172g)	14
Cheese & Pickle Sandwich, 1 (139g)	10

Cheese & Tomato Salad, 1 individual, 300g	15
Cheese Bowl Mini Salad, 1 individual, 180g	9
Cheese Coleslaw Sandwich, 1 (168g)	13
Cheese Coleslaw, 1 serving, 50g	3
Cheese Layer Salad, 1 individual, 190g	11
Cheese Layered Salad, 1 individual, 380g	16
Cheese Triple Sandwich, 1 (251g)	19
Chicken & Bacon Club Sandwich, 1 (257g)	15
Chicken & Bacon Layer Salad Bowl, 1 individual, 360g	15
Chicken & Bacon Mini Salad, 1 individual, 180g	8
Chicken & Bacon Pasta, 1 serving, 55g	3
Chicken & Bacon Salad Bowl, 1 individual, 180g	6
Chicken & Bacon Sandwich, 1 (164g)	13
Chicken & Bacon Sub Roll, 1 pack, 203g	15
Chicken & Bacon Wrap, 1 (179g)	15
Chicken & Chorizo Sandwich, 1 (180g)	11
Chicken & Spicy Couscous, 1 tablespoon, 30g	2
Chicken & Sweetcorn Sandwich, 1 (161g)	10
Chicken & Vegetable Sushi, 1 pack, 148g	6
Chicken Caesar Wrap, 1 (188g)	13
Chicken Fajita Wrap, 1 (205g)	11
Chicken Masala Wrap, 1 (225g)	12
Chicken Salad Sandwich, 1 (217g)	10
Chicken Triple Sandwich, 1 (253g)	15
Chicken, Bacon & Lettuce Sandwich, 1 (208g)	13
Chicken, Tomato & Basil Couscous, 1 tablespoon, 30g	1
Chicken, Tomato & Basil Pasta Snack, 1 individual, 350g	17
Chilli Beef Pasta Salad, 1 individual, 280g	10
Chirashi, ½ pack, 179g	10
Chunky Cheese Roll, 1 (100g)	7
Classic Ranch Style Salad, 1 serving, 100g	2
Creamy Coleslaw, 1 serving, 50g	3
Creamy Potato Salad, 1 serving, 50g	2
Deep Fill BLT Sandwich, 1 (218g)	14
Deep Fill Chicken & Bacon Sandwich, 1 (221g)	13
Deep Fill Ham, Cheese & Pickle Sandwich, 1 (224g)	13
Deep Fill Smoked Ham & Cheddar Sandwich, 1 (199g)	15
Egg & Cress Sandwich, 1 (170g)	11
Egg & Tomato Sandwich, 1 (168g)	8
Egg & Bacon Sandwich, 1 (220g)	13
Flame Roasted Red Peppers with Feta, 1 serving, 45g	1
Florida Salad, 1 serving, 50g	2
Free Range Egg Florentine Sandwich, 1 (198g)	11
Garlic Mushrooms, 1 serving, 100g	6
Garlic Stuffed Olives, 1 serving, 45g	2
Greek Halkidiki Olives, 1 serving, 60g	4

Ham & Cheddar Croissant, 1 (128g)	11
Ham & Cheddar Sub, 1 (196g)	14
Ham & Cheese Sandwich, 1 (157g)	10
Ham & Cheese Sub Roll, No Mayo, 1 (182g)	14
Ham & Egg Sandwich, 1 (192g)	9
Ham & Mustard Roll, 1 (140g)	10
Ham Cheese & Pickle Brown Bread Sandwich, 1 (206g)	12
Ham Salad Sandwich, 1 (190g)	8
Ham Triple Sandwich, 1 (225g)	14
Hoisin Duck Wrap, 1 (184g)	9
Honey & Mustard Chicken Pasta, 1 individual, 200g	12
Hot Smoked Salmon Pasta, 1 individual, 270g	12
Indian Chicken Balti Wrap, 1 (219g)	10
Indian Chicken Korma Wrap, 1 (223g)	14
Indian Chicken Tikka Masala Wrap, 1 (225g)	12
Indian Onion Bhaji Wrap, 1 (231g)	16
Italian Pasta Salad, 1 serving, 55g	2
Jalapeño Chicken Sandwich, 1 (200g)	11
Jalapeño Pasta, 1 serving, 50g	2
Just Ham Sandwich, 1 (116g)	6
Mexican Style Rice Salad, 1 serving, 100g	3
Mini Salmon Sushi, 1 pack, 106g	5
Moroccan Chicken Couscous, 1 individual, 275g	11
Pesto Chicken Pasta, 1 individual, 300g	16
Pesto Chicken Sandwich, 1 (213g)	11
Pesto Pasta Salad, 1 serving, 100g	6
Ploughman's Sandwich, 1 (204g)	12
Prawn & Egg Sandwich, 1 (190g)	10
Prawn Bowl Mini Salad, 1 individual, 180g	7
Prawn Layered Pasta Salad Bowl, 1 individual, 190g	7
Prawn Mayo & Avocado Wrap Sushi, 1 pack, 109g	5
Prawn Mayonnaise Oatmeal Bread Sandwich, 1 (148g)	10
Prawn Mayonnaise Triple Sandwich, 1 (222g)	14
Prawn Pasta, 1 serving, 55g	3
Prawn, Tuna & Vegetable Sushi, 1 pack, 150g	6
Red Cheddar & Tomato Sandwich, 1 (178g)	13
Red Leicester Salad Sandwich, 1 (201g)	15
Red Salmon Salad Sandwich, 1 (165g)	8
Roast Chicken & Stuffing Roll, 1 (175g)	14
Roast Chicken & Stuffing Sandwich, 1 (200g)	13
Roast Chicken Sandwich, 1 (167g)	10
Roast Chicken, Bacon & Stuffing Sandwich, 1 (208g)	15
Roasted Vegetables & Houmous with Pitta, 1 serving, 200g	15
Salmon & Cucumber (Wrap) Sushi, 1 pack, 105g	5

Salmon & Cucumber Sandwich, 1 (150g)	8
Salmon & Rocket Sandwich, 1 (175g)	12
Salmon & Vegetable Sushi, 1 pack, 142g	6
Sausage & Egg Sandwich, 1 (174g)	10
Sausage Pasta, 1 pack, 275g	14
Sausage, Bacon & Egg Triple Sandwich, 1 (288g)	19
Seafood Cocktail Sandwich, 1 (170g)	10
Smoked Ham & Cheddar Sandwich, 1 (170g)	12
Smoked Ham & Mustard Sandwich, 1 (161g)	11
Southern Fried Chicken Sandwich, 1 (185g)	11
Southern Fried Chicken Wrap, 1 (196g)	12
Southern Fried Layer Bowl, 1 pack, 180g	7
Spicy Couscous, 1 serving, 30g	2
Spicy King Prawn Pasta Salad, 1 pack, 235g	6
Sushi Feast, 1 pack, 170g	8
Sushi Variety, 1 pack, 229g	10
Sushi Selection, 1 pack, 140g	7
Sushi Taster, 1 pack, 148g	6
Sweet Chilli Chicken Wrap, 1 (192g)	13
Sweet Chilli Pasta, 1 serving, 50g	2
Three Bean Salad, 1 serving, 35g	1
Tomato & Basil Pasta, 1 serving, 100g	4
Tomato & Chicken Pasta Salad, 1 pack, 300g	15
Tuna & Cucumber Sandwich, 1 (170g)	10
Tuna & Sweetcorn Pasta Snack, 1 pack, 350g	18
Tuna Crunch Pasta, 1 pack, 280g	16
Tuna Layered Salad Bowl, 1 serving, 175g	8
Tuna Sweetcorn Malt Bread Sandwich, 1 (171g)	9
Vegetarian Sushi Taster, 1 pack, 151g	7
West Country Cheddar, Soft Cheese & Chives Sandwich, 1 (183g)	14

Tesco – Finest

All Day Breakfast Sandwich, 1 (293g)	17
British Maple Cure Bacon & Brie Sandwich, 1 (187g)	16
British Roast Beef Sandwich, 1 (209g)	11
British Roast Chicken & Ham Hock Sandwich, 1 (200g)	11
Caesar Salad, 1 serving, 115g	4
Chargrilled Vegetable Couscous, 1 serving, 35g	2
Cheese Coleslaw, 1 serving, 55g	4
Chicken & Bacon Club Sandwich, 1 (274g)	16
Chicken & Mascarpone Sandwich, 1 (208g)	12
Coleslaw, 1 serving, 50g	4
Couscous & Lentil Salad, 1 serving, 50g	2
Crayfish & Rocket Sandwich, 1 (180g)	10
Deli Potato Salad, 1 serving, 50g	3
Edamame & Pea Salad, ½ pack, 105g	4
Fireroast Tomato & Red Pepper Pasta Salad, 1 pack, 200g	9

Fruity Coleslaw, 1 serving, 50g	**3**
Goat's Cheese & Caramelised Red Onion Sandwich, 1 (200g)	**11**
Ham Hock & Vintage Cheddar Sandwich, 1 (192g)	**16**
Italian Salami & Mozzarella Sandwich, 1 (208g)	**15**
King Prawn & Avocado Sandwich, 1 (187g)	**10**
Mexican Chicken Flatbread, 1 (156g)	**7**
Moroccan Chicken Flatbread, 1 (136g)	**8**
Mozzarella Tomato & Basil Sandwich, 1 (222g)	**13**
Potato Salad, 1 serving, 50g	**3**
Salt Beef Sandwich, 1 (185g)	**9**
Scottish Honey Roast Salmon Sandwich, 1 (226g)	**12**
Scottish Smoked Salmon & Cream Cheese Sandwich, 1 (192g)	**15**
Sunblush Tomato Pasta, 1 serving, 50g	**3**
Tabbouleh & Feta, 1 pot, 225g	**8**
Thai Green Chicken Sandwich, 1 (197g)	**13**
Tortellini Salad, 1 serving, 50g	**2**
Waldorf Salad, 1 serving, 55g	**4**
Wensleydale & Chutney Sandwich, 1 (197g)	**13**

Tesco – Light Choices

Chicken & Bacon Sandwich, 1 (185g)	**8**
Chicken & Couscous Wrap, 1 (197g)	**9**
Chicken Salad Sandwich, 1 (191g)	**7**
Chicken Salad, Ham Salad, Prawn Mayonnaise, 1 (231g)	**9**
Chicken Salsa & Chicken Caesar Wrap Duo, 1 pack, 207g	**8**
Crayfish & Rocket Wrap, 1 (172g)	**7**
Egg & Cress Sandwich, 1(162g)	**8**
Egg Mayonnaise Sandwich, 1 pack, 162g	**7**
Ham Salad Sandwich, 1 (193g)	**8**
Ham, Cheese & Pickle Sandwich, 1 (175g)	**8**
Spicy Vegetable Chapatti Wrap, 1 (194g)	**8**
Tomato & Basil Chicken Salad, 1 pack, 192g	**6**

The Co-operative

Aberdeen Angus Beef with Vine Ripened Tomato & Rocket Sandwich, 1 (202g)	**10**
Aromatic Duck Wrap, 1 (187g)	**10**
Babyleaf Salad with Blackberry & Mint Dressing & Seed Sprinkles, ½ pack, 75g	**2**
BLT, Prawn Mayonnaise, Chicken Salad Triple Pack Sandwich, 1 (268g)	**13**
Breakfast Sub Roll, 1 (204g)	**15**
Broad Bean & Spinach Falafel Wrap, 1 (208g)	**12**
Caesar Salad, ¼ pack, 60g	**3**

Celery, Nut & Sultana Salad, 1 heaped tablespoon, 50g	**2**
Cheese & Onion Sandwich, 1 (155g)	**12**
Cheese & Tomato Sandwich, 1 (158g)	**12**
Cheese Coleslaw, 1 heaped tablespoon, 50g	**4**
Cheese Sandwich, 1 (139g)	**11**
Chicken & Bacon Caesar Wrap, 1 (201g)	**14**
Chicken & Bacon Sub Roll, 1 (166g)	**11**
Chicken Fajita Wrap, 1 (210g)	**11**
Chicken Salad Sandwich, 1 (180g)	**8**
Chicken Sandwich Triple Pack, 1 (271g)	**14**
Classic BLT Sandwich, 1 (165g)	**9**
Coleslaw, 1 heaped tablespoon, 50g	**2**
Coronation Rice, 1 heaped tablespoon, 50g	**3**
Creamy Coleslaw, 1 heaped tablespoon, 50g	**3**
Deep Fill All Day Breakfast Sandwich, 1 (204g)	**12**
Deep Fill BLT Sandwich, 1 (200g)	**12**
Deep Fill Cheese Ploughman's Sandwich, 1 (223g)	**13**
Deep Fill Chicken Salad Sandwich, 1 (188g)	**8**
Deep Fill Chicken, Stuffing & Red Onion Sandwich, 1 (193g)	**11**
Deep Fill Egg & Bacon Sandwich, 1 (200g)	**15**
Deep Fill Ham, Cheese & Pickle Sandwich, 1 (176g)	**11**
Deep Fill Tuna & Sweetcorn Sandwich, 1 (194g)	**11**
Deep Fill Chicken, Bacon & Tomato Sandwich, 1 (203g)	**13**
Florida Salad, 1 heaped tablespoon, 50g	**2**
Free Range Egg & Cress Sandwich, 1 (150g)	**10**
Ham & Cheese Sandwich, 1 (158g)	**11**
Ham Salad Sandwich, 1 (181g)	**8**
Honey & Mustard Chicken Pasta Snack Salad, 1 pack, 200g	**11**
Italian Pasta Salad, 1 heaped tablespoon, 50g	**2**
Italian Style Chicken Pasta Snack Salad, 1 pack, 200g	**7**
Mexican Bean Pasta Snack Salad, 1 pack, 200g	**11**
Pasta & Bacon Salad, 1 heaped tablespoon, 50g	**4**
Potato Salad, 1 heaped tablespoon, 50g	**3**
Prawn Cocktail, ⅓ pack, 66g	**6**
Prawn Layered Salad, 1 pack, 300g	**14**
Prawn Mayonnaise Sandwich, 1 (152g)	**8**
Premium Pasta & Mushroom Salad, 1 heaped tablespoon, 50g	**3**
Premium Pasta Salad with Chargrilled Chicken, 1 heaped tablespoon, 50g	**3**
Reduced Fat Coleslaw, 1 heaped tablespoon, 50g	**1**
Reduced Fat Potato Salad, 1 heaped tablespoon, 50g	**2**

Salmon & Cucumber Sandwich, 1 (174g)   **8**
Tuna & Sweetcorn Sandwich, 1 (165g)   **8**

The Co-operative – Healthy Living

Chicken & Bacon Sandwich, 1 (150g)   **6**
Chicken Pasta Salad, 1 pot, 260g   **7**
Chicken Pasta Salad with Honey & Mustard, 1 pack, 250g   **9**
Chicken Pasta Salad with Tomato & Rocket, 1 pack, 250g   **8**
Chicken Salad Sandwich, 1 (198g)   **7**
Chicken Tikka Wrap, 1 (171g)   **7**
Pasta & Tuna Snack Salad, 1 pack, 200g   **4**
Prawn Mayonnaise Sandwich, 1 (165g)   **7**
Tuna & Cucumber Sandwich, 1 (192g)   **7**
Tuna Layer Salad, 1 pack, 300g   **8**

The Co-operative – Truly Irresistible

Chicken & Sweetcure Bacon Sandwich, 1 (194g)   **15**
Coleslaw, 1 heaped tablespoon, 50g   **3**
Denhay Mature Cheddar Cheese & Plum Chutney Sandwich, 1 (222g)   **13**
Greek Salad, 1 pack, 270g   **6**
Mixed Olives with Soft Cheese, 1 pack, 165g   **11**
Potato Salad, ⅕ pot, 50g   **3**
Smoked Salmon, Cucumber & Watercress Sandwich, 1 (194g)   **10**

Waitrose

Atlantic Prawns with Creamy Mayonnaise Sandwich, 1 (169g)   **11**
British Ham with English Mustard Sandwich, 1 (151g)   **9**
Chicken Caesar Salad Wrap with Smoky Sweetcure Bacon & Parmigiano Reggiano, 1 (213g)   **14**
Egg Mayo & Bacon Sandwich, 1 (240g)   **15**
Egg Mayo with Cress Sandwich, 1 (177g)   **11**
Irish Mature Cheddar with Crunchy Red Onion & Mayonnaise Sandwich, 1 (165g)   **10**
Irish Mature Cheddar with Vine Ripened Tomatoes Sandwich, 1 (181g)   **11**
Poached Salmon Pasta Salad, 1 bowl, 225g   **11**
Roast Chicken & Bacon with Dijon Mustard Mayonnaise Sandwich, 1 (175g)   **10**
Roast Chicken with Mixed Leaves, Vine Tomatoes, Cucumber & Mayonnaise Sandwich, 1 (205g)   **12**

Sweet Chilli Chicken, Coconut & Lime Wrap, 1 (200g)   **12**
Tuna Mayo & Crunchy Sweetcorn Sandwich, 1 (211g)   **13**
Tuna Niçoise Salad, 1 bowl, 360g   **10**
Wild Alaskan Salmon with Chunky Cucumber Sandwich, 1 (137g)   **7**

Weight Watchers

BLT Sandwich, 1 (153g)   **6**
Chicken Caesar Wrap, 1 (172g)   **8**
Chicken Fajita Wrap, 1 (191g)   **8**
Egg Mayonnaise & Cress Sandwich, 1 (150g)   **7**
Mexican Chicken Pasta Salad, 1 pack, 249g   **8**
Roast Chicken & Stuffing Sandwich, 1 (158g)   **7**
Southern Style Chicken Wrap, 1 (164g)   **9**
Sweet Chilli Chicken Wrap, 1 (164g)   **8**
Triple Pack: Prawn, Egg & Chicken Sandwich, 1 (234g)   **10**
Tuna & Sweetcorn Pasta Salad, 1 pack, 250g   **7**

Weight Watchers®
Sandwiches, Wraps & Salads
a must for your shopping list

Great for a working lunch, as well as picnics and buffets, our Sandwiches, Wraps & Salads are convenient and tasty.

6 ProPoints value *to* **10** ProPoints value

per pack

Our range includes:
BLT, Egg Mayonnaise, Chicken Fajita Wrap, Chicken Caesar Wrap and more

WeightWatchers® Foods
Eat gorgeous. Feel gorgeous.

Fresh Fruit & Vegetables

Basic Foods

	ProPoints value
Alfalfa Seeds Sprouted, 1 portion, 100g	0
Apple, 1 medium, 150g	0
Apple, Cooking, 1 medium, 210g	0
Apricots, 3 (120g)	0
Artichoke Hearts, edible portion, cooked, 1 (50g)	0
Artichoke, Globe, 1 portion, 100g	0
Artichoke, Jerusalem, boiled in unsalted water, 1 portion, 100g	0
Asparagus, 5 spears, 125g	0
Aubergine, ½ medium, 130g	0
Avocado Pear, ½ medium, 78g	4
Babycorn, 1 portion, 80g	0
Banana, 1 medium, 100g	0
Beans, Broad, 1 heaped tablespoon, 35g	1
Beans, French, 1 portion, 100g	0
Beans, Green, 1 portion, 100g	0
Beans, Runner, 1 medium portion, 90g	0
Beansprouts, 1 portion, 100g	0
Beetroot, 1 slice, 10g	0
Blackberries, 1 medium portion, 100g	0
Blackcurrants, 1 medium portion, 100g	0
Blueberries, 1 medium portion, 100g	0
Breadfruit, ¼ medium, 96g	0
Broccoli, Green, 1 medium portion, 85g	0
Brussels Sprouts, 1 serving, 80g	0
Butternut Squash, 1 portion, 100g	0
Cabbage, 1 medium portion, 95g	0
Carambola, Star Fruit, 1 medium, 127g	0
Carrots, canned, drained, 1 serving, 80g	0
Carrots, old, 1 medium, 80g	0
Carrots, young, 1 serving, 80g	0
Cassava, ¼ medium, 102g	4
Cauliflower, 1 floret, 10g	0
Celeriac, 1 portion, 480g	0
Celery, 1 serving, 80g	0
Cherries, 1 medium portion, 100g	0
Chicory, 1 portion, 100g	0
Chilli, Green or Red, 1 teaspoon, 5g	0
Chinese Leaves (Amaranth Leaves), 1 quantity, 100g	0
Chips, Home Made, Thick Cut, Fried, 1 small portion, 100g	5
Chips, Home Made, Thick Cut, Fried, 1 medium portion, 150g	8
Chips, Home Made, Thick Cut, Fried, 1 large portion, 200g	11
Clementines, 2 medium, 140g	0
Corn on the Cob, 1 medium, 125g	2
Courgette, 1 medium, 100g	0
Cranberries, 1 medium portion, 100g	0
Cucumber, 1 medium portion, 60g	0
Custard Apple, 1 medium, 100g	0
Damson (without stone), 6 medium, 90g	0
Date, raw without stone, 1 (25g)	0
Dragonfruit, 1 (330g)	0
Durian, ½ medium, 300g	0
Elderberries, 1 portion, 100g	0
Fennel, 1 medium portion, 100g	0
Fig, fresh, 2 (110g)	0
Fruit Salad, fresh, no added sugar, 1 small portion, 100g	0
Garlic, 1 small, 5g	0
Gooseberries, 1 medium portion, 100g	0
Gooseberries, stewed with sugar, 1 medium portion, 100g	2
Gourd, (karela), 1 portion, 100g	0
Grapefruit, ½ medium, 170g	0
Grapes, Black or White, 1 small bunch, 100g	0
Greengage, without stone, 1 (50g)	0
Guava, 1 medium, 90g	0
Jicama (Mexican Turnip), raw, 1 small, 365g	0
Kale, 1 medium portion, 50g	0
Kiwi Fruit, 1 medium, 60g	0
Kumquats, 8 (64g)	0
Laverbread, 1 serving, 150g	3
Leek, 1 medium, 80g	0
Lemon, 1 teaspoon, 5g	0
Lemon, 1 zest of 1, 10g	0
Lettuce, 4 small leaves, 20g	0
Lime, 1 teaspoon, 5ml	0
Loganberries, 1 medium portion, 100g	0
Lychees, 6 (90g)	0
Mandarin, peeled, 3 (180g)	0
Mange-tout, 1 quantity, 100g	0
Mango, 1 medium slice, 45g	0
Marrow, 1 large, 260g	0
Melon, Cantaloupe, 1 medium slice, 150g	0
Melon, Galia, ½ medium, 250g	0
Melon, Honeydew, 1 medium slice, 200g	0
Mushrooms, 1 small portion, 30g	0
Mustard & Cress, 1 tablespoon, 5g	0
Nashi Pear, 1 medium, 130g	0
Nectarine, 1 medium, 140g	0
Okra, 1 portion, 10g	0
Onion, All Types, 1 large, 240g	0
Orange, 1 medium, 160g	0
Orange Juice, Freshly Squeezed from Fruit, 1 serving, 250ml	2

Pak Choi, 1 portion, 50g	0
Papaya, Paw-Paw, 1 medium, 300g	0
Parsnip, 1 medium, 90g	2
Passion Fruit, 6 medium, 90g	0
Peach, 1 medium, 110g	0
Pear, 1 medium, 160g	0
Peas, canned, drained, 1 serving, 80g	2
Peas, Sugar Snap, 1 medium portion, 60g	0
Pepper, All Types, 1 medium, 160g	0
Physalis, Cape Gooseberry, 9 (90g)	0
Pineapple, 1 quantity, 250g	0
Plantain, cooked, 1 medium, 180g	6
Plums, (without stone), 3 small, 90g	0
Plums, stewed with sugar, 1 medium portion, 100g	2
Pomegranate, 1 medium, 154g	0
Pomelo, flesh only, 1 medium portion, 100g	0
Potato Cake, 1 (60g)	4
Potato Croquette, 1 medium, 14g	1
Potato, boiled, 1 medium portion, 100g	2
Potato, Jacket, (weighed when cooked), 1 medium, 225g	8
Potato, Mashed (plain), 1 scoop, 60g	1
Potato, Mashed with Margarine, 1 scoop, 60g	2
Potatoes, New, 1 medium portion, 100g	2
Potatoes, New, 1 large portion, 200g	4
Potatoes, Old, 1 medium portion, 100g	2
Potatoes, Old, roasted in blended oil, 1 serving, 100g	4
Potatoes, Old, roasted in corn oil, 1 serving, 100g	4
Prickly Pear, peeled, 1 medium, 86g	0
Pumpkin, 1 medium portion, 60g	0
Quince, 1 medium, 108g	0
Radish, 1 medium, 8g	0
Raspberries, 1 portion, 100g	0
Redcurrants, 1 portion, 100g	0
Rhubarb, 1 medium portion, 250g	0
Rhubarb, stewed with sugar, 1 medium portion, 150g	2
Rocket, 1 portion, 25g	0
Satsumas, 2 medium, 140g	0
Shallots, 4 medium, 60g	0
Sharon Fruit (Persimmon), 1 medium, 110g	0
Spinach, 1 portion, 100g	0
Spring Onions, 1 medium, 10g	0
Strawberries, 1 medium portion, 150g	0
Swede, 1 portion, 100g	0
Sweet Potato, 1 medium, 150g	4
Sweetcorn, Baby, 1 can, drained, 230g	0
Sweetcorn, canned, drained, 2 tablespoons, 60g	2
Tamarillo, 1 medium, 120g	0

Tangerines, 2 medium, 140g	0
Tomato, 1 small, 65g	0
Turnip, 1 large portion, 120g	0
Watercress, ¼ bunch, 20g	0
Watermelon, 1 medium slice, 250g	0
Yam, 1 medium, 100g	3

Fruit

Asda

Berry Fruit Salad, 1 pack, 250g	0
Ripe & Juicy Summer Fruits, ½ pack, 250g	0

Sainsbury's

Deglet Nour Dates, 1 serving, 50g	4

Waitrose

Tropical Fruits with Passion Fruit Coulis, ¼ pack, 112g	2

Salads & Prepared Vegetables

Asda

Battered Onion Rings, 3 rings, 45g	4
Crispy Potato Slices, 1 serving, 116g	11
Honey Glazed Root Vegetables, 1 serving, 200g	4
Neeps & Tatties, ½ pack, 250g	3
New Potatoes with Herbs & Butter, ½ pack, 180g	4
Slow Braised Spiced Red Cabbage, 1 serving, 150g	7
Water Chestnut & Bamboo Shoot Stir Fry, 1 serving, 87g	1

Asda – Fresh Tastes

Baby Potato & Free Range Egg Side Salad, ½ pack, 152g	3
Butternut Squash & Sweet Potato Slices, ¼ pack, 138g	2
Colcannon with Cabbage, Onion & Butter, ¼ pack, 100g	3
Mini Jackets with Garlic & Thyme Butter, 1 serving, 230g	7
New Potatoes & Herbs & Butter, 1 serving, 181g	4

Root Mash, 1 serving, 200g — **4**
Sweetcorn Wheels with Butter, 1 serving, 87g — **2**

Asda – Good For You

Mini Jacket Potatoes with Garlic Butter,
1 pack, 225g — **5**

Sainsbury's

Baby Potatoes with Butter & Herbs,
¼ pack, 148g — **6**
British Baby Potatoes Lightly Seasoned,
½ pack, 192g — **4**
British Baby Potatoes with Mint Butter &
Herbs, ¼ pack, 148g — **3**
British Diced Potato with Onion, Garlic &
Herbs, ½ pack, 200g — **8**
British Mashed Potato, ½ pack, 200g — **4**
British Roast Potatoes, ½ pack, 200g — **8**
Buttery Mashed Potato, ¼ family pack, 200g — **6**
Cabbage & Bramley Apple, ½ pack, 150g — **4**
Mashed Potato, ½ pack, 200g — **4**
Mixed Pepper Stir Fry, ½ pack, 150g — **0**

Tesco

Brussels Sprouts with Thyme Butter,
1 serving, 90g — **3**
Casserole Vegetables, 1 serving, 100g — **1**
Classic Layered Vegetables, 1 serving, 150g — **3**
Edamame Bean & Butternut Stir Fry,
½ pack, 210g — **3**
Finest Tender Vegetables with Caesar Butter,
1 serving, 120g — **2**
Garden Layered Vegetables, 1 serving, 150g — **3**
Healthy Living Potato Salad, 1 tub, 250g — **6**
Hot & Spicy Stir Fry, ½ pack, 115g — **1**
Prepared Butternut Squash & Sweet Potato,
1 serving, 100g — **1**
Ready to Roast Root Vegetables,
1 serving, 100g — **1**

The Co-operative

Aromatic Salad with a Thai Style Dressing,
½ bag, 65g — **2**
Classic Salad with Green Herb Dressing,
½ pack, 90g — **2**
Diced Butternut Squash & Sweet Potato,
½ pack, 150g — **3**
Exotic Stir Fry, ½ pack, 138g — **1**
Power Stir Fry, ½ pack, 125g — **2**
Simply Baby Potatoes with Seasoned Butter,
½ pack, 180g — **5**

Vegetables

Asda

Crispy Potato Slices, 1 serving, 116g — **11**
Extra Special Slow Roasted SunBlush
Tomatoes, 1 tub, 240g — **9**
Extra Special Slow Braised Spiced Red
Cabbage, 1 serving, 150g — **7**
Mixed Pepper Stir Fry, 1 serving, 151g — **2**
Mixed Vegetable Stir Fry, 1 serving, 192g — **3**
Sliced Black Olives Spanish Olives in Brine,
1 pack, 180g — **8**

Asda – Chosen by You

Garlic Mushrooms, 1 pack, 180g — **4**
Garlic & Chilli Chargrilled Artichokes,
1 tub, 150g — **9**
Beetroot Salad, 1 pot, 230g — **3**
30% Less Fat Creamy Potato Salad,
½ tub, 150g — **4**
Garlic & Herb Coleslaw, ¼ pack, 75g — **3**

Sainsbury's

British Casserole Vegetables, 1 serving, 82g — **1**
British Roast Root Vegetables Lightly
Seasoned, ¼ pack, 100g — **2**
Honey & Mustard Parsnips, ¼ pack, 100g — **2**
Mediterranean Vegetables, ¼ pack, 100g — **2**

Tesco

New Potatoes With Herbs & Butter,
1 serving, 125g — **3**
Potato Wedges with an Oil and Parsley
Dressing, 1 serving, 138g — **2**

The Co-operative

Cooked Baby Beetroot in a Cayenne Pepper
Marinade, ¼ pack, 38g — **1**
Crunchy Salad Mix, ½ pack, 100g — **1**
Mini Jacket Potatoes with Butter, ½ pack, 160g — **4**
Simply - Maris Piper Mashed Potato,
½ pack, 200g — **4**
Stuffed Peppers, ½ pack, 150g — **3**

Fresh Prepared Meals

PING!

Fresh Chilled Bread

Asda

Garlic Baguettes, ¼ baguette, 43g	4
Cheese & Onion Panini Rolls, 1 roll, 85g	7
Cheese & Ham Ciabatta, ¼ loaf, 76g	6
Cheese, Onion & Chive Baguettes, ¼ baguette, 43g	4
Cheesy Garlic Bread, 1 serving, 70g	6
Garlic Bread Slices, 1 individual, 26g	3
Garlic Pizza Bread, ½ pack, 118g	10
Italian Cheese & Chive Baguettes, ¼ pizza, 105g	9
Mixed Peppers & Cheese Flatbread, 1 individual, 52g	4
Reduced Fat Garlic & Herb Baguettes (50% Less Fat), ½ baguette, 105g	7
Reduced Fat Garlic Slices, 1 slice, 30g	2
Stonebaked Garlic Bread, ¼ pack, 48g	4
Sun-Dried Tomato & Cheese Flatbread, 1 individual, 55g	5

Asda – Chosen by You

Cheese & Bacon Tear & Share, 1 serving, (¼ pack), 66g	6

Asda – Extra Special

Garlic & Herb Bloomer, 1 slice, 30g	3
Sundried Tomato, Olive & Oregano Pitta Bread, 1 pack, 75g	5

Asda – Good For You

Garlic & Herb Petit Pains, 1 roll, 60g	4
Onion & Cheese Flatbread, 1 pack, 110g	7

Asda – Italian

Roasted Garlic & Parmesan Ladder Bread, 1 serving, 66g	5
Garlic & Cheese Tear & Share Focaccia, 1 individual, 36g	3
Cheese & Chive Baguette, 1 individual, 42g	4
Garlic & Cheese Slices, 1 individual, 32g	3

Chicago Town

Take Away Sides Cheese & Garlic Dough Balls, 1 pack, 145g	13

Morrisons

Mini Garlic Baguette, ½ baguette, 53g	4
Reduced Fat Cheese & Garlic Pizza Bread, ¼ pizza, 69g	5

Morrisons – Eat Smart

Garlic Baguettes, 1 serving, 47g	4
Garlic Slices, 1 slice, 30g	2

M&S

Garlic Bread, 2 slices, 45g	4
Garlic Naan, ½ pack of 2, 150g	10
Stromboli (Italian stuffed bread), ⅙ pack, 49g	5

Pizza Express

Garlic Bread, ½ pack, 114g	9
Garlic Bread with Caramelised Garlic, 1 serving, 115g	10
Garlic Bread with Mozzarella, 1 serving, 130g	11

Sainsbury's

Cheese & Garlic Pizza Bread, ¼ portion, 69g	6
Garlic Dough Balls, 2 balls, 60g	6
Garlic & Herb Butter Dough Balls, 1 serving, 30g	3
Garlic & Herb Tear & Share Bread, ⅙ pack, 45g	4
Garlic Slices, 1 slice, 26g	3
Multi-Seed Garlic Baguette, ½ pack, 84g	9
Red Pepper & Chilli Flatbread, ⅓ pack, 63g	5
Tomato & Basil Tear & Share Bread, 1 portion, 45g	4
Tomato & Garlic Flatbread, ⅓ pack, 73g	5
Whole & White Garlic Slices, 1 slice, 28g	2

Sainsbury's – Be Good To Yourself

Mini Garlic & Parsley Pizza Breads, 1 pizza, 95g	7

Sainsbury's – Taste the Difference

Canapé Blinis, 3 (11g)	1
Garlic Baguette, 1 portion, 95g	9
Garlic Ciabatta, ¼ pack, 75g	7
Garlic & Parmesan Mini Flatbreads, 1 piece, 130g	11
Party Cocktail Blinis, 1 (10g)	1
Pesto & Gruyère Cheese Tear & Share Bread, ⅓ pack, 82g	8
Wheat Beer Bread, ¼ pack, 80g	6

Tesco – Finest

Garlic Ciabatta, 1 portion, ¼ pack, 66g	**7**
Roasted Balsamic Garlic Ciabattas, 1 individual, 138g	**13**

The Co-operative

Garlic Baguette, ½ baguette, 95g	**8**
Garlic Butter Slices, 1 slice, 23g	**2**

Waitrose

Bite Size Garlic Doughballs, ¼ pack, 49g	**4**
Cheese & Chive Baguette, large, ¼ pack, 65g	**6**
Cheese, Onion & Roasted Garlic Tear & Share, ½ pack, 142g	**12**
Garlic Slices, 1 slice, 22g	**2**
Garlic & Mozzarella Pizza Bread, ½ pack, 132g	**13**
Pesto & Provolone Pizza Bread, ½ pack, 118g	**13**
Red Pesto & Parmesan Tear & Share, ½ pack, 150g	**12**
San Marzano Tomato & Roast Garlic Pizza Bread, ½ pack, 135g	**10**
Three Seed Garlic Baguette, ½ pack, 88g	**9**

Weight Watchers

Garlic & Coriander Chilled Naan Bread, 1 piece, 60g	**3**
Garlic & Herb Ciabatta, 1 pack, 94g	**6**
Garlic & Herb Dough Balls, 4 balls, 52g	**4**

Fresh Meal Accompaniments

Asda

Bombay Potato, ½ pack, 150g	**4**
Carrot & Swede Mash, ½ pack, 225g	**7**
Cauliflower Cheese & Potatoes, 1 pack, 300g	**9**
Cheddar Mash, ½ pack, 200g	**5**
Cheese Pasta Salad, ¼ tub, 150g	**11**
Chicken & Bacon Caesar Pasta Salad, ½ tub, 140g	**10**
Chicken Pakoras, 1 (26g)	**2**
Chicken & Mango Spring Rolls, 1 (25g)	**2**
Chicken Spring Rolls, ¼ pack, 60g	**4**
Chicken Tikka Samosa, 1 (50g)	**3**
Chinese Snack Selection, ¼ pack, 83g	**6**
Colcannon, ½ pack, 225g	**7**
Gobi Aloo Saag, ½ pack, 150g	**4**
Lamb Samosa, 1 (60g)	**4**
Mash, ½ pack, 225g	**5**

Mashed Potato with Cabbage & Spring Onion, ½ pack, 200g	**5**
Mature Cheddar Cauliflower Cheese, ½ pack, 225g	**7**
Mini Chicken Satay Sticks, 1 (10g)	**1**
Mini Chicken Spring Rolls, 1 (60g)	**4**
Mini Chicken Tikka Samosa, 1 (23g)	**2**
Mini Chicken Tikka Satay, 1 (10g)	**1**
Mini Onion Bhaji, 1 (35g)	**2**
Mini Onion Pakora, 1 (30g)	**2**
Mini Vegetable Samosas, ¼ pack, 23g	**2**
Mini Vegetable Spring Rolls, 1 (25g)	**2**
Onion & Red Pepper Pakora, 1 pack, 80g	**6**
Onion Bhaji, 1 (80g)	**6**
Pilau Rice from Curry Pot, ½ serving, 250g	**12**
Pilau Rice, ⅓ pack, 66g	**3**
Potato Gratin, ¼ pack, 113g	**4**
Prawn Toasts, 1 (25g)	**2**
Prawn Wonton, 1 (18g)	**1**
Singapore Style Noodles from Curry Pot, 1 serving, 250g	**5**
Special Chow Mein, ½ pack, 200g	**6**
Special Fried Rice, ½ pack, 200g	**9**
Sprouts with Roast Onion & Bacon, ½ pack, 150g	**4**
Tricolour Basmati Rice from Curry Pot, ½ serving, 250g	**11**
Tricolour Rice, ½ pack, 125g	**6**
Vegetable Samosa, 1 (59g)	**3**

Asda – Chosen by You

30% Less Fat Creamy Coleslaw, ¼ pack, 150g	**6**
Creamy Coleslaw, ¼ tub, 150g	**7**
Duck Spring Rolls, 3 individual, 54g	**4**
Vegetable Spring Rolls, 1 individual, 60g	**3**

Asda – Extra Special

Broccoli & Petit Pois, 1 pack, 300g	**6**
Broccoli & Petit Pois with Hollandaise Sauce, ½ pack, 150g	**3**
Cauliflower Cheese, ½ pack, 200g	**5**
Creamy Mash, ½ pack, 215g	**7**
Davidstow Cheddar Mash, ½ pack, 225g	**7**
Honey Roasted Parsnips, ½ pack, 200g	**10**
Orange & Honey Chantenay Carrots & Parsnips, ¼ pack, 150g	**2**
Paella Rice, 1 portion 60g	**3**
Prawn Money Bags, 1 individual, 15g	**1**

Asda – Good For You

Bombay Potato, less than 10% fat, ½ pack, 200g	**6**

	ProPoints value
Mashed Potato, 1 serving, 150g	3
Moroccan Style Cous Cous Break, 1 portion, 60g	2
Potato Dauphinoise, ½ pack, 215g	4
Special Chow Mein, ½ pack, 200g	5

M&S

Carrot & Swede Crush, ½ pack, 150g	3
Cauliflower Cheese, ½ pack, 225g	6
Crispy Prawns with Dipping Sauce, ½ pack, 120g	7
Frites, ½ pack, 100g	5
Poppadum, 1 (8g)	1
Potato Croquettes, ½ pack, 125g	6
Swede & Carrot Mash, ½ pack, 225g	6
Ultimate Mash, ½ pack, 225g	11

M&S – Count on Us

Cauliflower Cheese, ½ pack, 200g	4
Potato Mash with Cabbage & Spring Onion, ½ pack, 225g	4
Potato Mash with Carrot & Swede, ½ pack, 225g	5

Mash Direct

Champ, ½ pack, 200g	5
Cheese & Onion Mash, ½ pack, 200g	7
Colcannon, ½ pack, 200g	5
Mashed Potato, ½ pack, 200g	5
Mashed Turnip, ½ pack, 200g	2

Morrisons

Bubble & Squeak Parcels, 1 serving, 40g	2
Onion Bhaji Dippers, 1 (15g)	1
Plain Pappadums, 1 (10g)	1
Sage & Onion Baked Yorkshire Puddings, 1 (19g)	1
Sage & Onion Spreadable Stuffing, 1 serving, 50g	1
Spiced Pappadums, 1 (10g)	1
Vegetable Spring Rolls, 1 (20g)	1
Beef Kofta Kebab, 1 (28g)	2
Bombay Potato Fritters, 1 (12g)	1
Bubble & Squeak Parcels, 1 serving, 40g	2
Chicken Tikka Samosa, 1 (30g)	2
King Prawns in a Coconut Breadcrumb, 1 (10g)	1
King Prawns in a Crisp Breadcrumb, 1 (10g)	1
King Prawns in a Crisp Tempura Batter, 1 (10g)	1
King Prawns in Filo Pastry, 1 (10g)	1
Onion Bhaji, 1 (12g)	1
Sag Aloo Bites, 1 (12g)	1
Chicken Wontons, 1 (15g)	1
Prawn Toasts, 1 (13g)	1
Vegetable Spring Rolls, 1 (16g)	1

Sainsbury's

	ProPoints value
Aloo Saag, ½ pack, 150g	6
Bombay Potato, ½ pack, 150g	4
Broccoli Cheese, ½ pack, 200g	4
British Carrot & Swede Potato Mash, ½ pack, 200g	4
British Mini Jacket Potatoes with Roasted Garlic Butter, 1 pack, 355g	10
Butter Roast Potatoes, ⅓ pack, 165g	7
Buttery Mashed Potato, ¼ large pack, 200g	6
Buttery Mashed Potato with Black Pepper, ½ pack, 225g	7
Carrot & Swede Mash, 1 small pack, 200g	6
Carrot & Swede Mash, 1 pack, 450g	13
Cauliflower Cheese, ½ pack, 200g	4
Cheese & Bacon Potato Skin, ½ pack, 210g	13
Chicken & Chilli Spring Rolls, 1 (50g)	3
Cheese & Onion Crispbakes, 1 serving, 82g	6
Chicken Tikka Samosa, 1 (50g)	3
Chicken Yakitori, 1 (22g)	1
Colcannon Potato Mash, ½ pack, 225g	7
Creamed Cabbage, ½ pack, 150g	3
Creamed Spinach, ½ pack, 150g	3
Crispy Breaded Mushrooms, ½ pack, 155g	12
Crispy Seaweed, ½ pack, 35g	6
Duck, Hoi Sin & Spring Onion Wontons, 1 (14g)	1
Duck Spring Rolls, 1 (25g)	2
Garlic Roast Potatoes, ½ pack, 225g	11
Indian Poppadoms, 1 serving, 20g	3
Mini Aloo Tikkas, 1 (25g)	1
Mini Onion Bhajias, 1 (22g)	1
Mini Spinach Pakoras, 1 (22g)	2
Mini Vegetable Samosas, 1 (25g)	2
Mushroom Pilau Rice, 1 pack, 250g	11
Onion Bhajia, 1 (35g)	3
Oriental Vegetable Stir Fry, 1 serving, 80g	2
Peshwari Rice, 1 pack, 200g	10
Pilau Rice, 1 pack, 250g	8
Potato Croquette, 1 (42g)	2
Potato Gratin, ½ pack, 200g	6
Potato Slices, 1 serving, 100g	7
Prawn Spring Roll, 1 (28g)	2
Prawn Toasts, 1 (65g)	7
Prawn Wontons, 1 (45g)	3
Roast Parsnips, ¼ pack, 125g	7
Roast Potatoes, ¼ pack, 112g	4
Roast Potatoes with Bacon, ½ pack, 200g	7
Rumbledethumps, ½ pack, 213g	5
Saag Paneer, ½ pack, 150g	7
Spicy Potato Wedges & Dip, ½ pack, 225g	13
Thai Coconut Rice, 1 pack, 200g	10

Vegetable Rice, ½ pack, 200g	**7**
Vegetable Samosa, ¼ pack, 58g	**4**
Vegetable Selection, ½ pack, 175g	**3**
Vegetable Spring Rolls, 1 serving, 61g	**4**

Sainsbury's – Be Good To Yourself

Carrot & Swede Mash, 1 pack, 200g	**3**

Sainsbury's – Taste the Difference

Bombay Potato, ½ pack, 112g	**2**
Braised Red Cabbage, ½ pack, 150g	**4**
Cauliflower Cheese, ½ pack, 200g	**8**
Cheddar Mash with Canadian Reserve Cheddar Cheese, ½ pack, 225g	**7**
Cheddar Mashed Potato, ½ pack, 225g	**4**
Chunky Chips, ½ pack, 200g	**7**
Coriander Pilau Rice, 1 pack, 250g	**10**
Gruyère & Rosemary Croquettes, ½ pack, 125g	**8**
Jersey Butter Mash, ½ pack, 225g	**10**
Maris Piper Potato Wedges, ½ pack, 180g	**5**
Roasted Baby Potatoes with Garlic & Rosemary, ½ pack, 200g	**5**
Roasted Potatoes with Goose Fat, ½ pack, 225g	**6**

Sharwood's

Bombay Potatoes Mild, ½ pack, 150g	**4**
Flame Baked Peshwari Mini Naans, 1 (40g)	**3**
Peshwari Mini Naans, 1 (40g)	**3**
Saag Aloo Mild, ½ pack, 150g	**4**
Tarka Dahl Mild, ½ pack, 150g	**4**
Vegetable Curry Medium, ½ pack, 150g	**3**

Tesco

Broccoli Cheese, 1 serving, 175g	**7**
Bubble & Squeak, 1 serving, 163g	**4**
Carrot & Swede Mash, 1 serving, 250g	**5**
Cheddar Mash, 1 serving, 250g	**8**
Cheesy Roasted Potatoes, 1 serving, 200g	**9**
Chicken Spring Rolls, 1 individual, 68g	**4**
Colcannon, 1 serving, 250g	**6**
Cooked Basmati Rice, 1 serving, 270g	**11**
Creamy Spring Greens with Savoy Cabbage, 1 serving, 125g	**3**
Crispy Potato Slices, ½ pack, 180g	**7**
Exquisa Potatoes with Jersey Butter, 1 serving, 125g	**3**
Fresh Mash, 1 serving, 250g	**6**
Fresh Potatoes with Tomato, Paprika & a Hint of Chilli, 1 serving, 125g	**3**

Garlic Roast Potatoes, 1 serving, 250g	**11**
Honey Roasted Parsnips, 1 serving, 125g	**6**
Leek Gratin, 1 serving, 175g	**6**
Maris Piper Mashed Potato, 1 serving, 213g	**5**
Onion Bhajis, 1 individual, 47g	**3**
Petit Pois with Leeks & Pancetta, 1 serving, 125g	**4**
Pilau Rice, 1 serving, 250g	**10**
Potato Dauphinoise, 1 serving, 225g	**10**
Potato Gratin, 1 serving, 225g	**9**
Rice Noodles, 1 serving (⅓ pack), 125g	**7**
Root Vegetable Mash, 1 serving, 250g	**6**
Root Vegetables For Mashing, 1 serving, 100g	**1**
Saag Aloo, 1 serving, 150g	**5**
Sweet Potato Wedges with an Oil & Parsley Dressing, 1 serving, 170g	**5**
Vegetable Samosas, 1 (64g)	**4**
Vegetable Spring Rolls, 1 (19g)	**1**

Tesco – Finest

Basmati Rice, ½ pack, 150g	**6**
Boulangere Potatoes, ½ pack, 225g	**6**
Cauliflower Cheese, 1 serving, 175g	**6**
Cheddar Mash, 1 serving, 125g	**6**
Chunky Chips, 1 serving, 225g	**8**
Creamed Spinach, 1 serving, 125g	**5**
Creamy Garlic Mushrooms, 1 serving, 150g	**7**
Creamy Mash, 1 serving, 250g	**10**
Green Beans with Caramelised Onions & Almonds, 1 serving, 100g	**2**
Honey Roasted Root Vegetables, 1 serving, 200g	**7**
Horseradish Mash, 1 serving, 250g	**6**
Mediterranean Vegetables, 1 serving, 150g	**4**
Oven Baked Potatoes with Smoked Bacon, 1 serving, 200g	**6**
Parsnip & Parmesan Mash, 1 serving, 250g	**7**
Parsnip Dauphinoise, 1 serving, 200g	**6**
Prawn Toasts, 1 serving, 27g	**2**
Rosemary Roasted Potatoes, 1 serving, 225g	**9**
Saag Paneer, 1 serving, 150g	**8**

Tesco – Light Choices

Cauliflower Cheese, 1 serving, 175g	**3**
Fresh Carrot & Swede Mash, 1 serving, 200g	**3**
Fresh Mash, 1 serving, 225g	**5**

Tesco – Ken Hom

Duck Spring Rolls, 1 (41g)	**3**
Egg Fried Rice, 1 pack, 250g	**10**
Sesame Noodles, 1 pack, 250g	**11**
Special Fried Rice, 1 pack, 300g	**11**

The Co-operative

Mini Duck Spring Rolls with Hoisin Dip, 1 (29g)	**2**
Summer Eating Potato Wedges with Lemon Zest & Rosemary, ½ pack, 200g	**4**
Vegetable Samosas, 1 (50g)	**3**

Waitrose

Bombay Potatoes, ½ pack, 150g	**4**
Chicken & Coconut Samosas, ¼ pack, 188g	**12**
Colcannon, ½ pack, 225g	**5**
Egg Fried Rice, 1 portion, 200g	**10**
Garlic & Coriander Couscous, 1 pack, 110g	**10**
Grilled Mushrooms with Garlic & Chilli, 1 serving, 25g	**1**
Lamb Samosa, 1 (50g)	**4**
Beef Dripping Yorkshire Pudding To Share, Large, 1 portion, 34g	**3**
Large Duck & Hoisin Spring Rolls, ¼ pack, 117g	**8**
Mini Yorkshire Puddings, 1 (12g)	**1**
Nine Jewel Rice, 1 portion, 200g	**8**
Onion Bhaji, 1 (45g)	**3**
Potato & Spinach Pakoras, 1 (43g)	**3**
Spinach & Carrot Pilau, ½ pack, 175g	**6**
Vegetable Samosas, 1 (54g)	**3**
Yorkshire Puddings, 1 (30g)	**2**

Weight Watchers

Creamy Carrot & Swede Mash, 1 pack, 250g	**5**

Fresh Pasta & Pasta Sauces

Asda

Beef Ravioli, ½ pack, 150g	**9**
Chicken & Mushroom Tortellini, ½ pack, 150g	**7**
Ham & Cheese Tortellini, ½ pack, 150g	**9**
Meat Ravioli, ½ pack, 150g	**10**
Mushroom & Ricotta Tortellini, ½ pack, 150g	**8**
Ricotta & Basil Tortelloni, ½ pack, 150g	**9**
Spinach & Ricotta Cannelloni, 1 pack, 400g	**13**
Tomato & Mozzarella Ravioli, ½ pack, 150g	**10**
Tomato & Mozzarella Tortellini, ½ pack, 150g	**8**

Asda – Chosen by You

Four Cheese Tortelloni, ½ pack, 150g	**9**
Garlic & Herb Tortelloni, ½ pack, 150g	**7**
Ham & Cheese Tortellino, ½ pack, 150g	**7**
Spicy Sausage Tortelloni, ½ pack, 150g	**8**

Asda – Extra Special

Beef & Amarone Ravioli, ½ pack, 150g	**9**
Gorgonzola & Walnut Ravioli, ½ pack, 150g	**12**
Hand-Filled Beef Cannelloni, ½ pack, 150g	**14**
Mortadella & Prosciutto Ravioli, ½ pack, 150g	**10**
Mushroom & Marsala Pasta Sauce, ½ tub, 175g	**6**
Porcini Mushroom Girasole, ½ pack, 150g	**8**

Asda – Good For You

Carbonara Sauce, ½ pot, 150g	**3**
Four Cheese Sauce, ½ pot, 175g	**4**
Fresh Beef Ravioli, ½ pack, 200g	**4**
Fresh Grilled Vegetable Tortelloni, ½ pack, 150g	**7**

Sainsbury's

Napoletana Sauce, ½ pot, 175g	**2**
Spinach & Ricotta Tortelloni, 1 pack, 400g	**15**
Spinach & Ricotta Tortellini, 95% Fat Free, 1 pack, 250g	**14**
Tomato & Mozzarella Tortelloni, 1 serving, 150g	**8**

Sainsbury's – Italian

Amatriciana Sauce, 1 serving, 108g	**1**
Arrabiata Sauce, ¼ large pot, 150g	**1**
Arrabiata Tortelloni, ½ pack, 150g	**8**
Cheese & Ham Pasta Bake Sauce, 1 serving, 124g	**3**
Creamy Petit Pois, Green Bean & Asparagus Sauce, 1 serving, 175g	**5**
Crème Fraîche & Black Pepper Sauce, 1 serving, 176g	**5**
Emmental & Mushroom Ravioli, ½ pack, 150g	**8**
Fig & Goat's Cheese Tortelloni, ½ pack, 150g	**9**
Five Cheese Tortelloni, ½ pack, 150g	**8**
Garlic & Herb Tortelloni, ½ pack, 150g	**9**
Mediterranean Vegetable Sauce, 1 serving, 173g	**2**
Spicy Tomato Pasta Bake Sauce, 1 serving, 126g	**1**
Spicy Tomato Sauce, 1 serving, 176g	**2**
Spinach & Ricotta Sauce, 1 serving, 175g	**5**
Spinach & Ricotta Tortelloni, 1 serving, 175g	**10**
Three Cheese Sauce, 1 serving, 175g	**6**
Tomato & Basil Sauce, 1 serving, 174g	**2**
Tomato & Herb Pasta Bake Sauce, 1 serving, 125g	**2**
Tomato & Mascarpone Sauce, 1 serving, 175g	**4**
Tomato & Smoked Bacon Sauce, 1 serving, 174g	**2**

Tesco

Arrabbiata Sauce, 1 serving, 175g **2**
Beef & Red Wine Ravioli, 1 serving, 150g **8**
Beef Bolgnese Fresh Pasta Sauce,
1 serving, 175g **5**
Chargrilled Vegetable Sauce, 1 serving, 175g **2**
Cheese & Smoked Ham Cappelletti,
1 serving, 150g **7**
Cheese & Smoked Ham Tortelloni,
1 serving, 150g **8**
Cheese Fresh Pasta Sauce, 1 serving, 175g **6**
Cheese, Tomato & Basil Tortelloni,
1 serving, 150g **9**
Chicken & Bacon Tortelloni, 1 serving, 150g **9**
Chilli & Tomato Sauce, 1 serving, 65g **6**
Four Cheese Tortelloni, 1 serving, 150g **8**
Grana Padano & Rocket Ravioli, 1 serving, 150g **9**
Green Pesto, Fresh, 1 serving, 50g **7**
Italian Cheese, Tomato & Basil Tortellini,
½ pack, 150g **9**
Italian Sausage & Ham Tortelloni,
1 serving, 150g **8**
Napoletana Sauce, 1 serving, 175g **2**
Pesto Tortelloni, 1 serving, 150g **8**
Smoked Ham, Bacon & Tomato Tortelloni,
1 serving, 150g **8**
Spinach & Ricotta Tortelloni, 1 serving, 150g **8**
Sweet Pepper & Tomato, 1 serving, 65g **6**
Tomato & Mascarpone Sauce, 1 serving, 175g **5**
Tomato & Olive, 1 serving, 65g **5**
Tomato Pasta Sauce, 1 serving, 150g **2**
Trattoria Verdi Italian Sausage Tortelloni,
1 serving, 200g **16**
Trattoria Verdi Spinach & Ricotta Tortelloni,
1 serving, 200g **15**
Wild Mushroom Tortelloni, 1 serving, 150g **9**

Tesco – Finest

Asparagus Ravioli, 1 serving, 150g **9**
Basil Pesto, 1 serving, 65g **8**
Beef & Chianti Ravioli, 1 serving, 125g **7**
Beef Cannelloni, ½ pack, 180g **17**
Beef Cannelloni Al Forno, 1 pack, 400g **17**
Cherry Tomato Sauce, ½ pot, 175g **5**
Chicken Mozzarella & Smoked Pancetta
Ravioli, 1 serving, 150g **10**
Four Cheese Fresh Pasta Sauce, 1 pot, 350g **14**
Italian Wild Mushroom Pappardelle,
1 pack, 400g **16**
Porcini Mushroom Ravioli, 1 serving, 125g **8**
Pumpkin Ravioli, 1 serving, 125g **7**

Salami Napoli & Red Pepper Saccottini,
1 serving, 125g **7**
Spinach & Ricotta Cannelloni, 1 serving, 180g **11**
Spinach & Ricotta Girasoli, ½ serving, 150g **9**
Sundried Tomato & Mozzarella Ravioli,
1 serving, 125g **8**
Tomato & Mascarpone Sauce, ½ pot, 175g **5**
Tomato & Sausage Ragu Sauce,
1 serving, 175g **5**
Venison Ravioli, 1 serving, 125g **7**
Wild Mushroom Fresh Pasta Sauce,
1 pot, 350g **12**

Tesco – Italian

Carbonara Fresh Pasta Sauce, ½ pot, 175g **6**
Fresh Cheese & Tomato Filled Tortelloni,
½ pack, 150g **8**
Italian Gnocchi, ¼ pack, 125g **5**

Tesco – Light Choices

Spinach & Ricotta Pasta, 1 pack, 350g **12**
Spinach & Ricotta Tortelloni, ½ pack, 150g **10**

The Co-operative

Bolognese Pasta Sauce, ½ pot, 150g **3**
Carbonara Pasta Sauce, ½ pot, 150g **6**
Cheese & Sun-Dried Tomato Ravioli,
½ pack, 150g **12**
Fire Roasted Tomato Pasta Sauce, ½ pot, 150g **4**
Garlic & Herb Free Range Egg Tagliatelle,
Fresh, ¼ pack, 125g **9**
Ricotta Cheese & Spinach Free Range Egg
Tortelloni, ½ pack, 150g **10**

Waitrose

Chicken, Lemon & Basil Raviolo, ½ pack, 125g **8**
Fresh Beef & Red Wine Stuffed Cannelloni,
½ pack, 170g **11**
Fresh Beef, Pancetta & Red Wine Ravioli,
½ pack, 125g **9**
Fresh Cheese & Porcini Mushroom Cappelletti,
½ pack, 125g **10**
Fresh Cheese & Smoked Ham Tortelloni,
1 serving, 125g **9**
Fresh Cheese, Tomato & Basil Ravioli,
½ pack, 125g **7**
Fresh Pancetta & Spinach Stuffed Ravioli,
½ pack, 125g **9**
Fresh Prosciutto & Cheese Cappelletti,
½ pack, 125g **10**
Fresh Pumpkin & Pine Nut Stuffed Fiorelli,
½ pack, 125g **7**

Fresh Pasta & Pasta Sauces — Fresh Prepared Meals

Fresh Red Pepper & Chilli Tagliatelle, ½ pack, 125g	9
Fresh Roasted Vegetable Stuffed Cannelloni, ½ pack, 170g	8
Fresh Sausage & Fennel Stuffed Fiorelli, ½ pack, 125g	7
Fresh Ricotta & Spinach Stuffed Cannelloni, ½ pack, 170g	8
Fresh Ricotta & Spinach Stuffed Ravioli, ½ pack, 125g	6
Fresh Roasted Vegetable Stuffed Ravioli, ½ pack, 125g	5
Pancetta & Parmesan Sauce, ½ pot, 150g	8
Roasted Mushroom & Parmesan Raviolo, ½ pack, 125g	7
Spinach & Ricotta Ravioli, ½ pack, 125g	7
Spinach & Ricotta Tortelloni, ½ pack, 125g	7
Tomato & Bacon Sauce, ½ pot, 175g	3

Fresh Pizza

Asda

Bacon Double Cheese Burger Pizza, 1 individual, 187g	12
Cheese & Tomato, 1 individual, 87g	6
Cheese & Tomato, 1 small, 90g	6
Deep Cheese Feast, 1 serving, 230g	17
Deep Dish, Cheese & Tomato, ½ pizza, 150g	11
Deep Dish, Pepperoni, ½ pizza, 150g	11
Deep Ham & Pineapple, ½ pizza, 243g	14
Deep Pan Hot & Spicy Chicken, ½ pizza, 238g	14
Deep Pan Meat Feast, ½ pizza, 233g	15
Deep Pan Pepperoni Feast, ½ pizza, 218g	18
Garlic Chicken, ½ pizza, 215g	12
Hawaiian, ½ pizza, 201g	12
Large Margherita Stonebaked, ¼ pizza, 101g	7
Mexican Style Chicken Quiche, 1 serving, 200g	13
Mini Stonebaked Margherita, 1 pizza, 23g	1
Stuffed Crust Barbecue Chicken, ½ pizza, 255g	17
Stuffed Crust Cheese Feast, ½ pizza, 235g	16
Stuffed Crust Ham & Pineapple, ½ pizza, 248g	16
Stuffed Crust Meat Feast, ½ pizza, 238g	16
Stuffed Crust Pepperoni, ½ pizza, 232g	17
Stuffed Crust Spicy Barbecue Chicken, 1 serving, 248g	15
Sweet BBQ Chicken, ½ pizza, 204g	12
Sweet Chilli Chicken, ½ pizza, 211g	11
Thin & Crispy Cheese & Tomato, ½ pizza, 173g	11

Thin & Crispy Meat Feast, ½ pizza, 158g	11
Thin & Crispy Pepperoni, ½ pizza, 138g	11
Thin Ham & Pineapple, ½ pizza, 169g	10
Thin Sausage & Onion, ½ pizza, 163g	10
Vegetable, ½ pizza, 230g	11

Asda – Extra Special

Four Cheese Stonebaked, ½ pizza, 210g	15
Roasted Pepper, Mature Cheddar, & Thyme Focaccia, 1 individual, 61g	5
Slow Roasted Tomato & Mature Cheddar Focaccia, 1 individual, 63g	5
Stonebaked Italian Ham, Mushroom & Mascarpone, ½ pizza, 231g	15
Stonebaked Pepperoni & Roasted Pepper, ½ pizza, 235g	15
Stonebaked Roasted Vegetable & Pesto, ½ pizza, 248g	14
Stonebaked Slow Roasted Cherry Tomato & Buffalo Mozzarella, ½ pizza, 213g	15
Wood-Fired Buffalo Mozzarella & Cherry Tomato, ½ pizza, 200g	14
Wood-Fired Ham & Wild Porcini Mushroom Snack, 1 individual, 120g	7
Wood-Fired Italian Four Cheese, ½ pizza, 200g	14
Wood-Fired Italian Style Meats, ½ pizza, 200g	14

Morrisons

Mini Cheese & Pepperoni, 1 pizza, 111g	8
Mini Cheese & Ham, 1 pizza, 111g	7
Deep Pizza Crust, 10", ½ pizza, 150g	12
Mini Cheese & Tomato, 1 pizza, 106g	7
Deep Pizza Crust, 14", ¼ pizza, 145g	11
Mini Cheese & Hot Dog, 1 pizza, 111g	8

M&S

Ham, Pepperoni & Milano Salami Thin Crust, ½ pizza, 165g	9
Stonebaked Cheese & Tomato, ½ pizza, 182g	13

M&S – Count on Us

Mushroom & Ham, 1 (245g)	10

Pizza Express

American, 1 pack, 256g	15
Diavolo, ½ small, 150g	8
Funghi Piemontese, ½ pizza, 190g	11
La Reine, ½ pizza, 142g	8
Margherita, 1 pack, 270g	15
Salami Toscana, ½ pizza, 210g	14
Sienese Spinach & Mascarpone, ½ pizza, 142g	8
Romana Etna, ½ pizza, 130g	9

Sloppy Giuseppe, ½ large, 322g — 16

Sainsbury's

Cheese & Ham, 1 pizza, 96g — 6
Cheese & Tomato, 7", 1 pizza, 129g — 9
Deep & Loaded Cheese Feast, ½ pizza, 197g — 13
Deep & Loaded Chilli Beef, ½ pizza, 244g — 15
Deep & Loaded Ham & Pineapple, ½ pizza, 258g — 15
Deep & Loaded Pepperoni, ½ pizza, 230g — 17
Pizza Bases Thin & Crispy, 1 (165g) — 13
Stuffed Crust Cheese Feast, ½ pizza, 232g — 16
Stuffed Crust Double Pepperoni, ½ pizza, 257g — 19
Thin & Crispy Barbecue Chicken, ½ pizza, 170g — 11
Thin & Crispy Cajun Chicken, ½ pizza, 160g — 9
Thin & Crispy Cheese & Tomato, ½ pizza, 138g — 12
Thin & Crispy Ham & Pineapple, ½ pizza, 180g — 11
Thin & Crispy Meat Feast, ½ pizza, 178g — 14
Thin & Crispy Pepperoni, ½ pizza, 152g — 13
Thin & Crispy Vegetable Feast, ½ pizza, 164g — 9
Thin & Crispy Vegetable Supreme, ½ pizza, 172g — 10

Sainsbury's – Be Good To Yourself

Cajun Chicken, 1 pizza, 200g — 11
Smoked Paprika Chicken, 1 pizza, 187g — 10
Spinach & Ricotta, 1 pizza, 220g — 12

Sainsbury's – Italian

Chicken & Bacon, 1 portion, 178g — 16
Deep Pan Pizza Base, 1 (220g) — 19
Ham & Pineapple, 1 portion, 189g — 13
Hot & Spicy, 1 portion, 192g — 13
Margherita, 1 portion, 181g — 13
Mediterranean Vegetable, 1 portion, 207g — 12
Pepperoni, 1 portion, 168g — 13
Quattro Formaggi, 1 portion, 162g — 12
Spicy Meat Feast, 1 portion, 158g — 12
Spinach & Ricotta, 1 portion, 197g — 13

Sainsbury's – Taste the Difference

Chicken & Chorizo, ½ pizza, 258g — 17
Four Cheese, ½ pizza, 240g — 17
Goat's Cheese & Spinach Flamme, ⅓ pack, 76g — 6
Mozzarella & SunBlush Tomato, ½ pizza, 270g — 19
Smoked Bacon Flamme, ⅓ pack, 76g — 6
Spicy Etruscan Pepperoni & Roquito Pepper, ½ pizza, 250g — 18
Sunbaked Tomato & Mozzarella Flatbread, ½ pack, 143g — 11

Yorkshire Ham, Mushroom & Mascarpone, ½ pizza, 260g — 17

Tesco

12" Stonebaked Pepperoni, 1 serving, 133g — 10
Cheese & Tomato, 1 serving, 170g — 13
Chicken, Bacon & Fontal Calzone, 1 serving, 166g — 11
Family Cheese & Tomato, 1 serving, 128g — 11
Family Pepperoni, 1 serving, 123g — 11
Full-on-Flavour Ham & Pineapple Deep Crust, 1 serving, 230g — 18
Full-on-Flavour Spicy Meat Feast Deep Crust, 1 serving, 223g — 17
Full-on-Flavour BBQ Chicken Deep Crust, 1 serving, 225g — 16
Full-on-Flavour Cheese Feast Deep Crust, 1 serving, 228g — 19
Full-on-Flavour Cheese Feast Deep Crust, 1 serving, 350g — 27
Full-on-Flavour Cheese Feast Thin Stonebaked, 1 serving, 135g — 10
Full-on-Flavour Cheese Feast Thin Stonebaked, 1 serving, 184g — 14
Full-on-Flavour Chilli Beef Deep Crust, 1 serving, 225g — 18
Full-on-Flavour Ham & Mushroom Thin Stonebaked, 1 serving, 145g — 9
Full-on-Flavour Ham & Pineapple Thin Stonebaked, 1 serving, 147g — 9
Full-on-Flavour Just Pepperoni Deep Crust, 1 serving, 220g — 19
Full-on-Flavour Meat Feast Deep Crust, 1 serving, 349g — 27
Full-on-Flavour Meat Feast Thin Stonebaked, 1 serving, 149g — 12
Full-on-Flavour Mighty Vegetable Thin Stonebaked, 1 serving, 156g — 9
Full-on-Flavour Pepperoni Thin Stonebaked, 1 serving, 133g — 11
Full-on-Flavour Pepperoni Thin Stonebaked, 1 serving, 191g — 16
Italian Stonebaked Margherita, 1 serving, 149g — 11
Mini Cheese & Tomato, 1 serving, 95g — 7
Mini Garlic & Cheese, 1 serving, 79g — 7
Mini Ham & Cheese, 1 serving, 95g — 7
Mini Pepperoni, 1 serving, 95g — 7
Pepperoni, 1 serving, 173g — 15
Romana Chicken & Pancetta, 1 serving, 132g — 10
Romana Ham, Mushroom & Mascarpone, 1 serving, 144g — 10

Weight Watchers® Chilled Pizza

a must for your shopping list

Delicious pizzas ready in just 10 minutes. Perfect for those days when only a pizza will do.

6 ProPoints value *to* **12** ProPoints value

per pizza

Also available:
Pizza Oval Chicken Arrabbiata, Pizza Oval Chilli Beef, Feta & Onion Stonebaked Pizza, BBQ Chicken Stonebaked Pizza, Thin & Crispy Sweet Chilli Vegetable Pizza and Thin & Crispy Hot & Spicy Chicken Pizza

WeightWatchers® Foods
Eat gorgeous. Feel gorgeous.

Romana Italian Meats, 1 serving, 127g	9
Romana Margherita, 1 serving, 115g	9
Romana Pepperoni, 1 serving, 116g	10
Spicy Meat Feast, 1 serving, 132g	12
Spicy Meatball Calzone, 1 serving, 173g	10
Stonebaked Meat Feast, 1 serving, 181g	14
Stonebaked BBQ Chicken, 1 pizza, 400g	22
Stonebaked Ham & Pineapple, 1 serving, 169g	11
Stonebaked Margherita, 1 serving, 122g	9
Stonebaked Pepperoni, 1 serving, 169g	14
Stonebaked Spinach & Ricotta, 1 serving, 189g	12
Stuffed Crust Cheese Feast, 1 serving, 215g	16

Tesco – Finest

Chicken & Chorizo, 1 serving, 160g	11
Chilli Chicken, 1 serving, 163g	10
Four Seasons, 1 serving, 195g	14
Ham, Mushroom & Mascarpone, 1 serving, 228g	16
Margherita, 1 serving, 153g	11
Mozzarella, Tomato & Basil, 1 serving, 237g	15
Salami Piccante, 1 serving, 213g	16
Salami, Spinach & Ricotta, 1 serving, 210g	16

The Great Texas Pizza Co.

American Style Deep Pan Cheese, ½ pizza, 180g	13
American Style Deep Pan Ham & Pineapple, ½ pizza, 190g	13
American Style Deep Pan Pepperoni, ½ pizza, 180g	14
American Style Thin & Crispy Cheese, ½ pizza, 120g	10

Waitrose

American Style Chilli Beef, ⅓ pizza, 172g	11
Buffalo Mozzarella with Basil Pesto Dressing, ½ pizza, 192g	13
Caramelised Onion, Feta & Rosemary with Balsamic Dressing, ½ pizza, 242g	16
Chargrilled Vegetable Antipasti with Basil Oil, ½ pizza, 210g	10
Deep & Crispy Cheese & Tomato, ½ pizza, 180g	11
Deep & Crispy Ham & Pineapple, ½ pizza, 180g	12
Deep & Crispy Hot & Spicy Pepperoni, ½ pizza, 175g	14
Formaggio Piccolo, 1 pizza, 160g	9
Four Seasons with Olive & Anchovy Dressing, ⅓ pizza, 135g	9
Ham & Pineapple, ½ pizza, 222g	13
Hickory Steak, ⅓ pizza, 178g	11

Italian Salami, Ricotta & Olive, ½ pizza, 212g	14
Margherita Piccolo, 1 pizza, 150g	9
Mozzarella & Sausage, ⅓ pizza, 190g	13
Napoli Salami Piccolo, 1 pizza, 155g	11
Stone Baked Funghi, ½ pizza, 188g	9
Stone Baked Quattro Favoriti, ½ pizza, 220g	12
Stone Baked Quattro Stagioni, ½ pizza, 245g	12
Stone Baked Salami & Prosciutto Cotto, ½ pizza, 180g	11
Thin & Crispy Cheese & Tomato, ½ pizza, 152g	10
Thin & Crispy Ham & Pineapple, ½ pizza, 135g	8
Thin & Crispy Pepperoni, ½ pizza, 130g	10

Waitrose – Pizzeria

Bacon & Mushroom, ½ pizza, 215g	14
Cheese & Tomato, ½ pizza, 218g	14
Fire Roasted Peppers & Red Onion, ½ pizza, 218g	12
Four Cheese, ⅓ pizza, 125g	9
Goat's Cheese, Peppers & Caramelised Onion, ½ pizza, 205g	12
Mushroom & Mascarpone, ½ pizza, 220g	14
Pepperoni, ½ pizza, 218g	15
Spicy Pepperoni, ½ pizza, 230g	16

Weight Watchers

BBQ Chicken Stonebaked, 1 (220g)	11
Caramelised Onion & Feta Stonebaked, 1 (217g)	11
Chicken Arrabbiata Oval, 1 (130g)	6
Chilli Beef Oval, 1 (120g)	6
Hot & Spicy Chicken, 1 (225g)	12
Sweet Chilli Vegetable, 1 (265g)	11

Fresh Soup

Asda

Bacon & Lentil, ½ pot, 300g	4
Chilli Bean, 1 serving, 160g	2
Extra Special Creamy Chantenay Carrot & Parsnip, ½ pot, 300g	4
Leek & Potato, ½ pot, 300g	2
Minestrone, ½ pot, 300g	4
Slow Roasted Tomato & Basil, ½ pot, 300g	4
Spiced Moroccan Style, ½ pot, 300g	5

Asda – Chosen by You

Chicken Curry, ½ pot, 300g	6

Pea & Ham, ½ pot, 300g   **4**

Duchy Originals

Beetroot with Dill, ½ carton, 300g	**5**
Carrot with Orange, ½ carton, 300g	**3**
Celeriac, Bacon & Leek, ½ carton, 300g	**4**
Chicken & Leek with Lemon & Parsley, ½ carton, 300g	**6**
Parsnip with Ginger, ½ carton, 300g	**3**
Roasted Vegetable with Rosemary, ½ carton, 300g	**4**
Spinach with Nutmeg & Sage, ½ carton, 300g	**7**
Tomato with Rosemary, ½ carton, 300g	**4**

Morrisons

Broccoli & Stilton, ½ carton, 300g	**5**
Creamy Vegetable, ½ carton, 300g	**3**
Minestrone, ½ carton, 300g	**2**
Moroccan Chicken, 1 carton, 400g	**8**
Organic Lentil, ½ carton, 300g	**5**
Ten Vegetable Broth, ½ carton, 300g	**3**
Tuscan Style Chicken & Vegetable Broth, 1 carton, 400g	**5**

New Covent Garden Food Co.

Apple Vichyssoise, Sweet, 1 serving, 300g	**4**
Asparagus, ½ carton, 300g	**4**
Beef & Vegetable, ½ carton, 300g	**5**
Beetroot & Redcurrant, Sweet, 1 serving, 300g	**2**
Broccoli & Stilton, ½ carton, 300g	**5**
Carrot & Coriander, ½ carton, 300g	**4**
Chicken, ½ carton, 300g	**8**
Chicken Mulligatawny, ½ carton, 300g	**6**
Chicken, Vegetable & Pearl Barley, 1 serving, 300g	**5**
Chilli Bean, ½ carton, 300g	**5**
Cock-a-Leekie, ½ carton, 300g	**5**
Creamy Parsnip, ½ carton, 300g	**5**
Leek & Potato, ½ carton, 300g	**4**
Lentil & Smoked Bacon, ½ carton, 300g	**6**
Mediterranean Vegetable & Herb, ½ carton, 300g	**3**
Minestrone, ½ carton, 300g	**3**
Moroccan Spiced Chickpea, ½ carton, 300g	**5**
Pea & Ham, ½ carton, 300g	**5**
Pea & Mint, ½ carton, 300g	**5**
Plum Tomato & Basil, ½ carton, 300g	**4**
Plum Tomato & Mascarpone, ½ carton, 300g	**4**
Root Vegetable & Rosemary, ½ carton, 300g	**3**
Salmon & Watercress, ½ carton, 300g	**5**
Smoked Haddock Chowder, ½ carton, 300g	**5**

Spicy Butternut Squash & Sweet Potato, ½ carton, 300g	**5**
Spinach & Nutmeg, ½ carton, 300g	**4**
Sweet Potato & Corn Chowder, ½ carton, 300g	**5**
Thai Chicken, ½ carton, 300g	**6**
Three Bean & Red Lentil, ½ carton, 300g	**5**
Tomato & Chunky Vegetable, ½ carton, 300g	**4**
Toulouse Sausage & Puy Lentil, ½ carton, 300g	**5**
Wild Mushroom, ½ carton, 300g	**3**
Winter Vegetable, ½ carton, 300g	**4**

Sainsbury's

Broccoli & Stilton, 1 serving, 300g	**5**
Butternut Squash, 1 serving, 300g	**3**
Chunky Carrot & Sweetcorn, 1 serving, 300g	**2**
Cream of Chicken, 1 serving, 300g	**5**
Lentil & Bacon, 1 serving, 300g	**5**
Minestrone, 1 serving, 300g	**4**
Thai Green Chicken, 1 serving, 300g	**6**
Three Bean, 1 serving, 300g	**4**
Tomato & Basil, ½ carton, 300g	**3**

Sainsbury's – Taste the Difference

Butternut Squash, Cumin & Chilli, 1 serving, 300g	**4**
Pamplona Picante Chorizo & 3 Bean, 1 serving, 300g	**5**
Roasted Sweet Potato & Paprika, 1 serving, 298g	**4**
Vine Ripened Tomato & Puy Lentil, 1 serving, 300g	**4**

Tesco

Broccoli & Stilton, 1 serving, 300g	**6**
Carrot & Coriander, 1 serving, 300g	**4**
Chicken & Vegetable, 1 carton, 400g	**5**
Chicken & Sweetcorn, 1 serving, 300g	**5**
Chicken & Vegetable, 1 serving, 300g	**3**
Cream of Mushroom, 1 serving, 300g	**3**
Cream of Tomato, 1 serving, 300g	**5**
Creamy Vegetable, 1 serving, 300g	**4**
Garden Pea & Wiltshire Cured Ham, 1 serving, 300g	**5**
Leek & Potato, 1 serving, 300g	**5**
Lentil & Smoked Bacon, 1 serving, 300g	**5**
Mexican Chilli Bean, 1 serving, 300g	**4**
Tomato & Basil, 1 serving (as purchased), 300g	**3**
Vegetable Mulligatawny, 1 serving, 300g	**5**

Tesco – Finest

Celeriac & Truffle Oil, 1 serving, 300g	**8**

Chicken Mulligatawny, 1 serving, 300g	**7**
French Onion, 1 serving, 300g	**3**
Moroccan Chicken, 1 serving, 300g	**5**
Oxtail, 1 serving, 300g	**3**
Provencale, 1 serving, 300g	**4**
Puy Lentil & Vine Ripened Tomato, 1 serving, 300g	**5**
San Marzano Tomato & Mascarpone, 1 serving, 300g	**6**
Sri Lankan Chicken, 1 serving, 300g	**7**
Thai Chicken, 1 serving, 300g	**7**
Wild Mushroom, 1 serving, 300g	**7**

Waitrose

Broccoli & Stilton, ½ pot, 300g	**4**
Butternut Squash & Ginger, ½ pot, 300g	**6**
Carrot & Fresh Coriander, ½ pot, 300g	**4**
Celeriac & Potato, ½ pot, 300g	**4**
Chickpea & Smoked Bacon, ½ pot, 300g	**4**
Chunky Vegetable, ½ pot, 300g	**3**
Cream of Tomato, ½ pot, 300g	**3**
French Onion, ½ pot, 300g	**3**
Green Thai Chicken, ½ pot, 300g	**6**
Italian Bean, ½ pot, 300g	**5**
Keralan Spiced Chicken, ½ pot, 300g	**6**
Leek & Potato, ½ pot, 300g	**3**
Lentil & Tomato, ½ pot, 300g	**3**
Minestrone, ½ pot, 300g	**3**
Moroccan Chicken, ½ pot, 300g	**4**
Pea & Ham, ½ pot, 300g	**3**
Tomato & Fresh Basil, ½ pot, 300g	**4**
Spinach, Crème Fraîche & Nutmeg, ½ pot, 300g	**7**
Smoked Haddock, ½ pot, 300g	**6**
Spiced Parsnip, ½ pot, 300g	**5**
Vegetable & Lentil, ½ pot, 300g	**4**

Ready Meals

Asda

American Potato Wedges, ¼ pack, 138g	**7**
Baked Bean & Cheese Filled Jacket Potato, 1 pack, 300g	**8**
BBQ Chicken Pasta Bake, ½ pack, 360g	**12**
Beef Burritos, ¼ pack, 108g	**4**
Beef Chilli Filled Jacket Potato, 1 pack, 300g	**6**
Beef Dripping Potatoes Ready to Roast, ¼ pack, 113g	**6**

Beef in Black Bean Sauce with Egg Fried Rice, 1 pack, 450g	**21**
Beef Madras from Curry Pot, 1 serving, 400g	**15**
Beef Meatloaf with Tomato Sauce, 1 serving, 150g	**8**
Beef Stew with Dumplings, 1 pack, 450g	**15**
Bombay Potato from Curry Pot, 1 pack, 400g	**11**
Butternut Squash Risotto, 1 pack, 380g	**13**
Caesar Chicken Fettuccine Superbowl, 1 pack, 450g	**12**
Cajun Chicken Pasta, 1 pack, 400g	**12**
Cajun Chicken Pieces with a Smoky Barbecue Sauce, ¼ pack, 150g	**8**
Chargrilled Chicken & Tomato Tagliatelle, 1 pack, 400g	**11**
Cheese & Bacon Potato Skins, ½ pack, 188g	**11**
Cheese & Onion Potato Skins, ½ pack, 188g	**11**
Cheese & Bacon Loaded Skins, ½ pack, 125g	**8**
Cheese & Chive Chicken Escalopes, 1 serving, 160g	**10**
Cheese Chicken Escalopes, ½ pack, 170g	**10**
Cheesy Broccoli Bake, 1 serving, 400g	**11**
Cheesy Mash with Butter, ½ pack, 200g	**6**
Chicken & Bacon Pasta Bake, ¼ family pack, 375g	**16**
Chicken & Bacon Pasta Bake, 1 pack, 400g	**17**
Chicken & Broccoli Cumberland Pie, 1 pack, 500g	**16**
Chicken & Cashew Chinese Meal for One, 1 pack, 460g	**14**
Chicken & Cashew Nut with Egg Fried Rice, 1 pack, 450g	**13**
Chicken & Mushroom Pie with Mash, 1 pack, 500g	**15**
Chicken & Mushroom with Egg Fried Rice, 1 pack, 550g	**23**
Chicken & Vegetable Pie, 1 pack, 400g	**8**
Chicken Balti, 1 pack, 400g	**14**
Chicken Bhuna & Pilau Rice, 1 pack, 550g	**21**
Chicken Bhuna from Curry Pot, 1 pack, 400g	**13**
Chicken Biryani, 1 pack, 450g	**16**
Chicken Breasts in a Smoky Barbecue Sauce, ½ pack, 93g	**4**
Chicken Burritos, 1 pack, 450g	**16**
Chicken Caesar Fettucine, 1 pack, 450g	**15**
Chicken Casserole with Dumplings, 1 pack, 300g	**10**
Chicken Chow Mein, ½ pack, 200g	**4**
Chicken Dopiaza from Curry Pot, 1 pack, 400g	**13**
Chicken Enchiladas, ½ pack, 225g	**11**
Chicken Fajita, 1 pack, 440g	**20**
Chicken Hotpot, 1 pack, 400g	**9**

Chicken Hotpot, 1 pack, 500g	**12**
Chicken in Black Bean Sauce, ½ pack, 125g	**3**
Chicken Jalfrezi & Pilau Rice, 1 pack, 550g	**19**
Chicken Joint in a White Wine Sauce, ½ pack, 270g	**9**
Chicken Kashmiri, 1 pack, 450g	**15**
Chicken Korma & Pilau Rice, ½ pack (large), 450g	**18**
Chicken Korma & Pilau Rice, 1 pack, 550g	**22**
Chicken Korma, 1 pack, 350g	**17**
Chicken Madras & Pilau Rice, 1 pack, 550g	**17**
Chicken Madras, 1 pack, 350g	**13**
Chicken Nachos, ½ pack, 150g	**11**
Chicken Rogan Josh from Curry Pot, 1 serving, 400g	**10**
Chicken Tandoori & Pilau Rice, 1 pack, 450g	**18**
Chicken Tikka Masala & Pilau Rice, ½ pack (large), 450g	**16**
Chicken Tikka Masala, 1 pack, 350g	**10**
Chicken Tikka, ½ pack, 350g	**11**
Chicken Vindaloo from Curry Pot, 1 serving, 440g	**15**
Chicken with Tomato & Mascarpone, 1 pack, 400g	**14**
Chilli & Wedges, 1 pack, 400g	**12**
Chilli Beef Chimichangas, 1 serving, 60g	**4**
Chilli Beef Enchiladas, ½ pack, 225g	**10**
Chilli Beef Nachos, ½ pack, 150g	**11**
Chilli Beef Pasta Bake, ¼ family pack, 375g	**14**
Chilli Beef Pasta Bake, ½ pack (large), 360g	**13**
Chilli Beef Tortilla Superbowl, ½ pack, 225g	**13**
Chilli Chicken, 1 pack, 350g	**20**
Chinese Battered Chicken Balls with Sweet & Sour Dip, 1 pack, 220g	**11**
Chinese Battered Chicken Balls with Sweet Chilli Dip, 1 pack, 210g	**11**
Chinese Chicken & Black Pepper, 1 pack, 450g	**8**
Chinese Chicken & Mushroom with Egg Fried Rice, 1 pack, 450g	**14**
Chinese Chicken Curry & Egg Fried Rice, 1 serving, 225g	**9**
Chinese Chicken Curry from Curry Pot, 1 serving, 400g	**14**
Chinese Chow Mein, 1 pack, 450g	**16**
Chinese Crispy Duck & Pancake Kit, 1 serving, 65g	**4**
Chinese Style Chicken Curry & Egg Fried Rice, 1 pack, 550g	**28**
Chinese Style Chicken Curry, ½ pack, 170g	**6**
Chorizo & Potato Quesadillas, 1 serving, 65g	**4**
Chorizo & Sweetcorn Fritter, 1 serving, 30g	**2**
Corned Beef Hash, 1 pack,450g	**14**
Creamy Chicken & Bacon Bake, 1 pack, 400g	**14**
Creamy Chicken Korma, 1 pack, 340g	**16**
Creamy Fish Pie, ½ pack, 225g	**8**
Cumberland Sausage & Gravy, ⅓ pack, 400g	**12**
Duck & Mushroom from Curry Pot, 1 pack, 366g	**10**
Faggots & Mash, 1 pack, 450g	**13**
Fresh Spinach & Ricotta Ravioli, ½ pack, 150g	**9**
Garlic & Herb Roast Potatoes, ½ pack, 200g	**8**
Garlic Mushroom Spaghetti, 1 pack, 400g	**14**
Ham & Cheddar Cheese Filled Jacket Potato, 1 pack, 300g	**8**
Ham & Mushroom Tagliatelle, 1 pack, 400g	**15**
Hot Chicken Tikka Masala & Pilau Rice, 1 pack, 450g	**17**
Hot Meatball Sub, 1 pack, 195g	**13**
Hot Sweet & Sour King Prawns, 1 pack, 375g	**15**
Irish Stew, 1 pack, 400g	**6**
Jambalaya, 1 pack, 450g	**14**
Kung Po Chicken from Curry Pot, 1 pack, 367g	**12**
Kung Po Chicken, ½ pack, 170g	**5**
Lamb Balti, 1 pack, 500g	**20**
Lamb Rogan Josh & Pilau Rice, 1 pack, 550g	**22**
Lancashire Hotpot, 1 pack, 400g	**13**
Lemon Chicken, 1 pack, 350g	**16**
Liver & Bacon with Mash, 1 pack, 450g	**12**
Macaroni Cheese, 1 pack, 400g	**17**
Meal For One, Cottage Pie, 1 pack, 500g	**15**
Meal for One, Cumberland Pie, 1 pack, 500g	**18**
Meal for One, Liver & Bacon with Mash, 1 pack, 400g	**13**
Meal for One, Minced Beef Hotpot, 1 pack, 400g	**12**
Meal for Two, Liver & Onions, ½ pack, 225g	**5**
Meal for Two, Meat Feast Pasta Bake, ½ pack, 400g	**15**
Meatballs & Mash, 1 serving, 100g	**3**
Mediterranean Vegetable Ratatouille, ½ pack, 175g	**2**
Mexican Chilli con Carne, 1 pack, 450g	**15**
Mexican Meatballs, 1 pack, 450g	**15**
Minced Beef & Vegetable Casserole, 1 pack, 400g	**10**
Minced Beef & Vegetable Pie, 1 pack, 400g	**8**
Minced Beef & Vegetable Casserole with Dumplings, 1 pack, 300g	**9**
Minced Lamb Hotpot, 1 pack, 300g	**6**
Mini Classics Baked Bean & Cheese Jacket Potato, 1 pack, 300g	**8**
Mini Classics Lamb Hotpot, 1 pack, 300g	**6**
Mini Classics Moussaka, 1 pack, 300g	**10**
Mozzarella & Tomato Pasta Bake, 1 pack, 400g	**15**

Oriental Ribs, ½ pack, 78g	**7**
Pepperoni Pasta Bake, 1 pack, 400g	**9**
Potato & Pea Curry, 1 pack, 450g	**9**
Red Thai Vegetable Noodles, 1 pack, 400g	**14**
Reduced Fat Garlic Chicken Kievs, 1 individual, 130g	**10**
Sausage & Mash, 1 pack, 450g	**13**
Sausage Casserole, 1 serving, 408g	**14**
Shepherd's Pie, 1 pack, 500g	**14**
Southern Fried Chicken & Curly Fries, ½ pack, 300g	**15**
Spaghetti & Meatballs, 1 pack, 400g	**15**
Spaghetti Bolognese, 1 pack, 400g	**15**
Spaghetti Carbonara, 1 pack, 400g	**17**
Spicy Chicken Tacos, 1 pack, 340g	**19**
Spicy Tomato Chicken, 1 pack, 450g	**16**
Steak & Mushroom Pie with Mash, 1 pack, 500g	**14**
Steak & Stout with Mash, 1 pack, 450g	**25**
Steak & Kidney Casserole with Dumplings, 1 pack, 450g	**13**
Steak & Mash, 1 pack, 450g	**12**
Sweet & Sour Chicken with Egg Fried Rice, 1 pack, 550g	**24**
Sweet Chilli Beef Noodles, 1 pack, 470g	**20**
Szechuan Chicken, 1 pack, 400g	**11**
Tandoori Chicken Balti, 1 pack, 500g	**20**
Tandoori Chicken Masala & Pilau Rice, 1 pack, 450g	**16**
Tex Mex Combo, ½ pack, 200g	**15**
Thai Sticky Rice, ½ pack, 225g	**9**
Thai Style Sweet & Sour Chicken, 1 pack, 350g	**7**
Tomato & Ham Pasta, 1 pack, 400g	**11**
Tuna Pasta Bake, ¼ pack, 100g	**4**
Vegetable Bake, 1 serving, 400g	**11**
Vegetable Biryani, ½ pack, 150g	**6**
Vegetable Casserole with Cheese & Herb Dumplings, 1 pack, 400g	**13**
Vegetable Chow Mein, 1 pack, 400g	**14**
Vegetable Lasagne, 1 pack, 340g	**11**
Yorkshire Pudding with Roast Chicken, 1 pack, 360g	**12**

Asda – Chosen by You

Beef Cannelloni, 1 pack, 360g	**14**
Cheese Omelette, 1 serving, 108g	**6**
Minced Beef Casserole, 1 pack, 300g	**10**
Minced Beef Hotpot, 1 pack, 400g	**11**
Vegetarian Roasted Vegetable Lasagne, 1 pack, 450g	**14**
Vegetarian Tomato & Meatballs Al Forno, 1 pack, 450g	**13**

Asda – Extra Special

Aromatic Crispy Duck, ¼ pack, 138g	**9**
Beef in Peppercorn Sauce with Potato Wedges, ½ pack, 225g	**6**
Beef Lasagne with Garlic Bread, 1 pack, 500g	**27**
Beef Stroganoff with Rice, 1 pack, 400g	**16**
Beef Stroganoff, 1 pack, 400g	**13**
Braised Beef Shins in Yorkshire Ale Gravy, ½ serving, 210g	**6**
Braised Steak & Mash, 1 pack, 451g	**13**
British Steak in Peppercorn Sauce, 1 portion, 225g	**10**
Chicken in Mushroom & Madeira Sauce with Potato & Parsnip Gratin, ¼ pack, 113g	**3**
Chicken Korma with Saffron Rice, 1 pack, 500g	**26**
Chicken Panierine Pasta with Dolcelatte, 1 pack, 400g	**16**
Chicken with Roasted Mushrooms & Madeira Sauce, ½ pack, 200g	**6**
Chilli & Rice, 1 pack, 450g	**16**
Classic Shepherd's Pie, 1 pack, 400g	**13**
Classic Spinach & Ricotta Mezzaluna, 1 pack, 370g	**14**
Classic Steak Diane, 1 serving, 225g	**7**
Creamy Scallop Gratin, 1 pack, 230g	**12**
Cumberland Sausage with Colcannon Mash, 1 pack, 450g	**14**
Four Cheese Macaroni, 1 pack, 400g	**20**
Sun-Dried Tomato & Basil Meatballs, 1 pack, 400g	**27**
Fish Pie, 1 pack, 400g	**13**
Four Cheese Macaroni, ¼ pack, 100g	**4**
Hot-Smoked Salmon Risotto, 1 pack, 400g	**18**
Italian Style Lamb Casserole with Rosemary Roast Potatoes, 1 pack, 450g	**16**
Lamb Casserole with Rosemary Roast Potatoes, ½ pack, 225g	**6**
Lasagne Al Forno, 1 pack, 400g	**14**
Meatballs with Paprika-Spiced Potatoes, 1 pack, 450g	**17**
Mushroom Risotto, ½ pack, 200g	**8**
Oven Roasted Meatballs with Paprika Spiced Potatoes, ½ pack, 225g	**8**
Oven-Baked Lamb Moussaka, 1 pack, 400g	**14**
Oven-Roasted Potatoes with Smoked Bacon, ½ pack, 200g	**7**
Paella, 1 pack, 450g	**19**
Roast Chicken, Yorkshire Pudding & Rich Gravy, 1 pack, 450g	**14**
Slow Cooked Duck Legs in Orange Sauce, ½ pack, 300g	**9**

Slow Cooked Lamb Casserole & Potatoes, 1 pack, 450g	**11**
Slow Cooked Lamb Shanks in Garlic & Rosemary Gravy, ½ pack, 370g	**15**
Slow Cooked Lamb Shanks in Mint Gravy, ½ pack, 370g	**15**
Slow Cooked Lamb with Honey-Roast Vegetables, 1 pack 400g	**12**
Slow Cooked Lamb, 1 serving, 400g	**11**
Slow Cooked Pork Shanks in Wholegrain Mustard Sauce, ½ pack, 250g	**9**
Spaghetti & Meatballs, ½ pack, 200g	**11**
Spaghetti Bolognese, ¼ pack, 113g	**4**
Spicy Chilli Steak & Rice, 1 pack 450g	**15**
Spicy King Prawn Linguini, 1 pack, 400g	**15**
Steak Diane, ½ pack, 225g	**6**
Steak in Peppercorn Sauce, ¼ pack, 113g	**5**
Succulent King Prawns with Orzo Pasta, 1 pack, 245g	**11**
Tewkesbury Mustard Beef, ½ pack, 200g	**6**
Thai Fish Cakes, 1 pack, 300g	**13**

Asda – Fresh Tastes

Beef & Pork Meatballs in a Tomato & Basil Sauce, ⅕ pack, 108g	**5**
Beef Stew, 1 pack, 277g	**5**
Char Sui Pork, 1 pack, 400g	**11**
Cheese & Ham Whole Chicken Breast Kievs, ½ pack, 145g	**7**
Chicken & Mushroom Linguine, 1 pack, 400g	**11**
Chicken & Prawn Paella, ½ pack, 264g	**9**
Chicken & Smoked Bacon Wraps with Caesar Dressing, ½ pack, 260g	**12**
Chicken & Spinach Crêpes with a Creamy Cheese Sauce, 1 serving, 205g	**9**
Chicken Arrabbiata, 1 pack, 398g	**10**
Chicken BBQ Beef Noodles, 1 pack, 400g	**13**
Chicken Breasts in a Stroganoff Sauce, ½ pack, 185g	**6**
Chicken Breast in a Tomato & Basil Sauce, 1 serving, 143g	**4**
Chicken Breasts in a Caribbean Style Marinade, ½ pack, 190g	**8**
Chicken Breasts in a Sweet Chilli Sauce, ¼ pack, 90g	**4**
Chicken Breasts in a Tomato & Chilli Marinade, 1 portion, 165g	**6**
Chicken Breasts in an Orange Sauce, ½ pack, 185g	**8**
Chicken Breasts with Cheddar & Mozzarella wrapped in Bacon, ½ pack, 145g	**7**

Chicken Breasts with Cheese, Ham & Mushrooms, ½ pack, 195g	**8**
Chicken Breasts with Cheese, Leeks & Ham, ½ pack, 200g	**8**
Chicken Breasts with Garlic Mushrooms, ½ pack, 160g	**6**
Chicken Breasts with Mango & a Sweet Chilli & Lime Glaze, ½ pack, 190g	**8**
Chicken Breasts with Sun-Dried Tomato & Olive Butter, ½ pack, 138g	**7**
Chicken Enchiladas Topped with Spicy Salsa & Cheese, 1 serving, 173g	**9**
Chicken Encroute with Mature Cheddar & Ham, ½ pack, 220g	**16**
Chicken Kievs filled with Garlic Butter & Coated in a Parmesan & Basil Crumb, ½ pack, 200g	**12**
Chicken Mini Roast, ½ pack, 218g	**9**
Chicken Supremes, ½ pack, 150g	**5**
Chicken Thighs in a Spanish Style Marinade, 1 individual, 163g	**6**
Chicken Tikka Masala, 1 pack, 400g	**10**
Chicken, Tomato & Basil Pasta, 1 pack, 500g	**11**
Chinese Chicken Pancakes with Hoisin Sauce, ½ pack, 270g	**11**
Cod in White Wine, 1 pack, 394g	**7**
Cumberland Sausages, 1 portion, 139g	**11**
Gammon Steaks in a Creamy Cheddar Cheese Sauce, ½ pack, 180g	**9**
Gammon Steaks with Pineapple, ½ pack, 195g	**6**
Garlic & Cheese Stuffed Mushrooms, 1 individual, 114g	**5**
Garlic & Herb Whole Chicken Breast Kievs, ½ pack, 145g	**8**
Green Thai Chicken, 1 pot, 350g	**9**
Indian Chicken Dhal, 1 pack, 400g	**14**
Indian Style Whole Chicken Breast Mini Fillets, 1 serving, 124g	**7**
Italian Style Whole Chicken Breast Fillets, 1 serving, 121g	**7**
King Prawn & Pesto Pasta, 1 pack, 400g	**13**
King Prawn Biryani, 1 pack, 500g	**11**
King Prawn Linguine, 1 pack, 396g	**9**
Malaysian Prawn Curry, 1 pack, 400g	**10**
Mango, Lime & Coriander Chicken, 1 pack, 500g	**14**
Mediterranean Style Chicken Breasts, ½ pack, 164g	**4**
Mexican Chicken Wraps, ½ pack, 260g	**11**
Mexican Salsa Beef, 1 pack, 400g	**12**
Moroccan Spiced Chicken, 1 pack, 400g	**14**
Nacho Chicken Breasts with Spicy Salsa & Soured Cream, ½ pack, 205g	**8**

	ProPoints value
Red Thai Chicken Curry, ½ pack, 170g	4
Red Thai Chicken Curry, 1 pack, 400g	10
Rice Noodles with Spring Onions, 1 pack, 375g	14
Salmon Niçoise, 1 pack, 350g	9
Salmon Teriyaki, 1 pack, 388g	13
Salmon with Watercress Sauce, 1 pack, 390g	9
Seafood Paella, 1 pack, 400g	12
Singapore Chicken Noodles, 1 pack, 400g	10
Smoked Haddock Kedgeree, 1 pack, 400g	12
Southern Style Whole Chicken Breast Mini Fillets, 1 serving, 124g	7
Spaghetti & Meatballs, ¼ pack, 100g	3
Spaghetti Carbonara with Chicken & Bacon, 1 portion, 422g	17
Spicy Italian Chicken, 1 pack, 400g	14
Sweet & Sour Chicken, 1 pack, 498g	10
Sweet Chilli Beef, ½ pack, 200g	5
Sweet Chilli King Prawn, 1 pack, 400g	9
Sweet Chilli King Prawn Noodles, 1 pack, 400g	12
Tandoori Chicken Breasts with a Masala Sauce, ½ pack, 190g	8
Tandoori Chicken Chapatti Wraps with Mint Yogurt, 1 portion, 271g	12
Thai King Prawn Noodles, 1 pack, 400g	11

Asda – Go Cook

Chicken & Chorizo Paella with Rice, Ham, Peppers & Peas, 1 serving, 465g	18
Cod Fillets in a Mornay Sauce, 1 serving, 153g	6
Fish Haddock Fillets in a Cheese & Chive Sauce, 1 pack, 169g	6
Sweet Chilli Beef Noodles with Mixed Peppers & Onions, 1 pack, 391g	14

Asda – Good For You

Beef Cannelloni, ¼ pack, 100g	3
Beef In Red Wine, 1 pack, 396g	5
Bombay Potato, Less than 10% Fat, 1 pack, 400g	12
Braised Beef & Roasted New Potatoes, 1 pack, 450g	6
Braised Beef, ¼ pack, 100g	2
Cajun Chicken Fettuccine, 1 pack, 400g	12
Cheese & Chive Filled Jacket Potatoes, ½ pack, 200g	5
Chicken & Basil Niçoise, 1 pack, 400g	9
Chicken & Broccoli Pie, 1 pack, 400g	8
Chicken & Prawn Paella, 1 pack, 400g	11
Chicken Arrabiata, 1 pack, 450g	10
Chicken Breast with Tomato & Mascarpone, 1 pack, 400g	12
Chicken Chasseur, 1 pack, 450g	9

	ProPoints value
Chicken Enchiladas, ½ pack, 225g	7
Chicken in Black Bean Sauce, 1 pack, 450g	7
Chicken Jalfrezi, 1 pack, 350g	10
Chicken Piri Piri, 1 pack, 398g	11
Chicken Sizzler, 1 pack, 350g	7
Chicken Tikka Masala & Pilau Rice, 1 pack, 450g	11
Chilli & Wedges, 1 pack, 400g	10
Chilli Beef & Mushrooms, 1 pack, 400g	9
Chilli con Carne & Rice, 1 pack, 400g	12
Cottage Pie, 1 pack, 450g	10
Cumberland Pie, 1 pack, 450g	11
Fish Pie, 1 pack, 450g	11
Hake Florentine & Mash, 1 pack, 400g	8
Ham & Mushroom Tagliatelle, 1 pack, 400g	9
Honey & Mustard Chicken, 1 pack, 400g	9
King Prawn & Salmon Pasta Bake, 1 pack, 400g	11
King Prawn Spaghetti, 1 pack, 375g	11
Lasagne, ¼ pack, 100g	2
Liver & Bacon with Mashed Potato, 1 pack, 400g	12
Liver & Bacon, 1 pack, 400g	8
Meal for One Cajun Chicken Fettuccini, 1 pack, 400g	10
Mediterranean Style Chicken, 1 pack, 400g	11
Mushroom Stroganoff, 1 pack, 400g	9
Nutritionally Balanced Prawn Linguine, 1 pack, 400g	9
Nutritionally Balanced Salmon Teriyaki, 1 pack, 400g	9
Nutritionally Balanced Singapore Noodles, 1 pack, 400g	9
Nutritionally Balanced Sweet Chilli Prawns, 1 pack, 403g	7
Peppercorn Beef, 1 pack, 400g	12
Prawn Linguine, 1 pack, 400g	9
Red Thai Chicken, 1 pack, 400g	8
Sausage & Mash, 1 pack, 400g	11
Seafood Gratin, 1 pack, 400g	10
Shepherd's Pie, 1 pack, 400g	9
Smoked Salmon Tagliatelle, 1 pack, 400g	10
Spaghetti Bolognese, 1 pack, 400g	10
Sweet & Sour Chicken with Egg Fried Rice, 1 pack, 400g	13
Sweet Chilli Chicken Noodles, ½ pack, 25g	1
Tomato & Mozzarella al Forno, 1 pack, 450g	12
Tuna Pasta Bake, 1 pack, 400g	10

Asda – Indian

Beef Madras Indian Meal for One, 1 pack, 460g	15

Buttery Chicken Masala, 1 pack, 450g	18
Chicken Dopiaza, 1 pack, 450g	12
Chicken Jalfrezi, 1 pack, 450g	13
Chicken Tandoori Masala, 1 pack, 450g	15
Chicken Tikka Masal, 1 pack, 450g	14
Chicken Vindaloo, 1 pack, 450g	13
Lamb Rogan Josh from Curry Pot, 1 pack, 400g	12
Mango Chicken, 1 pack, 450g	10

Asda – Italian

Bacon & Mushroom Tagliatelle, ½ pack, 200g	7
Spaghetti & Meatballs, 1 pack, 400g	13
King Prawn Linguine, 1 pack, 380g	11
Lasagne, 1 pack, 400g	14
Chicken & Bacon Pasta Bake, 1 pack, 400g	17
Chargrilled Chicken & Tomato Tagliatelle, 1 pack, 400g	11
Spaghetti Carbonara, 1 pack, 400g	17
Pepperoni Pasta Bake, 1 pack, 400g	20
Ham & Mushroom Tagliatelle, 1 pack, 400g	15
Roasted Mushroom Pasta Bake, 1 pack, 400g	17

Bombay Foods

Butter Chicken, 1 pack, 350g	18
Chicken Kashmiri, 1 pack, 400g	22
Chicken Rajasthani, 1 pack, 400g	21
Goan Fish Curry, 1 pack, 350g	21
Kadhai Fish, 1 pack, 350g	17
Lamb Bhuna, 1 pack, 350g	14
Lamb Rogan Josh, 1 pack, 350g	14
Prawn Masala, 1 pack, 350g	15
Saffron Rice, 1 pack, 350g	20

Feasters

100% Beef Quarter Pounder with Cheese, 1 portion, 100g	8
Bacon Butty, 1 pack, 100g	6
BBQ Ribsteak Sandwich, 1 pack, 155g	10
Chicken Breast Sandwich, 1 pack, 140g	8
Feasters All Day Breakfast Hot & Crusty Baguette, 1 pack, 185g	12
Fish Finger Sandwich, 1 pack, 135g	9
Flame Grilled Quarter Pounder with Cheese, 1 pack, 200g	13
Flamegrilled 100% Beef Burger with Bacon & Cheese, 1 pack, 215g	14
Hot Dog, 1 pack, 140g	9
Jacket Potato with Chilli con Carne, 1 pack, 340g	7
Premium Smoked Chilli Dog, 1 pack, 140g	9
Spicy Chicken Sandwich with Jalapeño Cheese, 1 pack, 140g	9

Innocent – Veg Pots

Indian Daal Curry with Spicy Cauliflower & Fresh Spinach, ½ pot, 200g	5
Moroccan Squash Tagine with Giant Couscous & Fresh Coriander, 1 pot, 400g	9
Mexican Sweet Potato Chilli with Chargrilled Peppers & Smoky Paprika, 1 pot, 400g	10
Roasted Aubergine Moussaka, with Borlotti Beans, Tomato & Mint, 1 pot, 400g	8
Roasted Beetroot Quinoa, with Pumpkin Seeds & Fresh Spinach, 1 pot, 400g	10
Thai Coconut Curry with Soya Beans, Pak Choi & Wild Rice, 1 pot, 400g	8
Tuscan Bean Stew with Tomatoes, Kale & Fresh Parsley, 1 pot, 400g	8

M&S

Bangers & Mash, 1 pack, 430g	14
Beef Cannelloni, 1 pack, 400g	18
Beef Lasagne, 1 pack, 400g	17
Braised Steak, Meal for One, 1 pack, 450g	10
Chicken Fajitas, ½ pack, 230g	10
Chicken Tikka Masala, ½ pack, 175g	7
Chilli con Carne & Rice, 1 pack, 450g	16
Cottage Pie, 1 pack, 400g	11
Ham & Mushroom Tagliatelle, 1 pack, 400g	13
Macaroni Cheese, 1 pack, 400g	18
Roast Beef Yorkshire Pudding, 1 pack, 330g	17
Spaghetti Carbonara, 1 pack, 400g	15
Sticky Chilli Chicken, ½ pack, 225g	12
Sweet & Sour Battered Chicken, ¼ pack, 75g	4
Sweet & Sticky Mini Spare Ribs, ½ pack, 150g	8

M&S – Count on Us

Bangers & Mash, 1 pack, 430g	11
Beef Casserole with Dumplings, 1 pack, 400g	9
Beef Lasagne, 1 pack, 400g	11
Beef Stroganoff with Rice, 1 pack, 400g	10
Braised Beef in Ale, 1 pack, 400g	10
Cajun Chicken Fettucine, 1 pack, 400g	10
Cherry Tomato Risotto, 1 pack, 360g	9
Chicken & Asparagus Risotto, 1 pack, 385g	9
Chicken & Pineapple with Rice, 1 pack, 400g	11
Chicken Arrabiata, 1 pack, 400g	10
Chicken Balti & Rice, 1 pack, 400g	11
Chicken Breast Fillets in Red Wine Sauce with Mash, 1 pack, 400g	8
Chicken Breast in Tomato Sauce with Mash, 1 pack, 400g	8
Chicken Breasts in Mushroom & Red Wine Sauce, ½ pack, 200g	4

Chicken Breasts in Tomato & Basil Sauce, ½ pack, 200g	4
Chicken Casserole with Herb Dumplings, 1 pack, 400g	9
Chicken Tagliatelle, 1 pack, 400g	9
Chicken Tikka Masala with Rice, 1 pack, 400g	11
Chicken Tikka with Rice, 1 pack, 400g	11
Chicken with Cashew Nuts & Rice, 1 pack, 400g	9
Chilli con Carne, 1 pack, 400g	10
Chilli Jacket, 1 pack, 300g	7
Chilli Wedge Bowl, 1 pack, 400g	10
Cottage Pie, 1 pack, 300g	7
Fish Pie, 1 pack, 400g	8
Haddock Mornay, ½ pack, 190g	4
Hickory Steak Penne, 1 pack, 400g	8
Jalfrezi Chicken Chapatti, 1 pack, 168g	6
Lamb Casserole, 1 pack, 390g	7
Lemon & Ginger Chicken with Apricot Rice, 1 pack, 400g	11
Mushroom Risotto, 1 pack, 360g	8
Paella, 1 pack, 400g	10
Pork Fillet in Light Mustard Sauce, ½ pack, 200g	5
Ricotta & Spinach Cannelloni, 1 pack, 400g	9
Smoked Ham Tagliatelle, 1 pack, 400g	11
Spaghetti & Meatballs, 1 pack, 400g	10
Spaghetti Carbonara with Smoked Ham & a Creamy Cheese Sauce, 1 pack, 365g	10
Steak Yorkshires, ½ pack, 160g	5
Sweet & Sour Chicken with Rice, 1 pack, 400g	9
Thai Green Curry & Rice, 1 pack, 380g	10
Tuna & Pasta Bake, 1 pack, 360g	10
Vegetable Lasagne, 1 pack, 400g	9

M&S – Eat Well

Aromatic Duck & Jasmine Rice, 1 pack, 400g	16
Beef Stroganoff, 1 serving, 400g	12
Chicken & Prawn Laksa, 1 pack, 400g	11
Feta & Falafel Snackpot, 1 pot, 300g	8
Ginger Chilli King Prawn, 1 pack, 400g	12
Ham Hock & Mash, 1 pack, 400g	9
Hoisin Duck & Noodles, 1 pack, 380g	14
Loch Muir Salmon & Watercress Meal, 1 pack, 385g	10
Meal for One Cod Mornay, 1 pack, 400g	8
Roast Beef & Mash, 1 pack, 400g	9
Roast Chicken with New Potatoes, 1 pack, 400g	9
Roast Lamb & New Potatoes, 1 pack, 400g	10
Roast Lamb in Mint Gravy, 1 pack, 200g	4
Roast Pork & Mash, 1 pack, 430g	10
Seafood Linguine, 1 pack, 400g	12
Singapore Noodles, 1 pack, 400g	11
Spicy Chicken Coconut Curry, 1 pack, 400g	13

Thai Green Chicken Curry, 1 pack, 400g	11
Thai Red Chicken, 1 pack, 390g	13

M&S – Steam Cuisine

Green Thai Chicken with Jasmine Rice, 1 pack, 400g	11
Loch Muir Salmon Niçoise, 1 pack, 365g	9
Moroccan Chicken, 1 pack, 400g	9
Sweet Chilli Chicken with Noodles, 1 pack, 400g	10

McIntosh

Haggis Neeps & Tatties, 1 pack, 340g	12
Macaroni Cheese, 1 pack, 250g	10
Mince & Tatties, 1 pack, 340g	6
Scottish Stovies, 1 pack, 100g	3

Morrisons

Chilli Beef Nachos, ½ pack, 200g	11
Coq au Vin, ½ pack, 275g	9
Cottage Pie Meal, 1 pack, 450g	11
Deli Beef Lasagne, 1 serving, 440g	17
Deli Cottage Pie, 1 serving, 440g	14
Deli Lamb Moussaka, 1 serving, 420g	15
Deli Red & Green Bell Peppers filled with Cream Cheese, 1 serving, 50g	3
Deli Tandoori Chicken, 1 serving, 400g	13
Gammon Shank with Maple Sauce, ½ pack, 315g	13
Lancashire Hotpot, 1 pack, 500g	11
Mascarpone & Tomato Bake, 1 pack, 400g	17
Pork Medallions with Apple & Cider Sauce, ½ pack, 146g	6
Thai Green Chicken Curry, ½ pack, 222g	7

Morrisons – Eat Smart

Braised Beef & Mash, 1 pack, 375g	8
Chicken Arrabbiata, 1 pack, 450g	12
Chicken Breast with Red Wine Sauce & Garlic Potatoes, 1 pack, 375g	8
Chicken in Peppercorn Sauce, 1 pack, 375g	9
Chicken in Tomato & Basil Sauce, 1 pack, 375g	7
Chicken Pasta Bake, 1 pack, 400g	10
Chicken Tikka Masala with Pilau Rice, 1 pack, 400g	11
Chilli Wedge Bowl, 1 pack, 450g	7
Crispy Sweet & Sour Chicken with Rice, 1 pack, 350g	9
Fish Pie, 1 pack, 450g	10
Ham & Mushroom Tagliatelle, 1 pack, 400g	9
Lasagne, 1 pack, 400g	10
Minced Lamb Hotpot, 1 pack, 400g	9

Sausage & Mash, 1 pack, 450g — **10**
Spaghetti Bolognese, 1 pack, 400g — **10**

New Covent Garden Food Co.

Chicken & Pancetta, 1 pack, 420g — **14**
Chicken & Cherry Tomatoes, 1 pack, 450g — **13**
Fresh & Natural Asparagus Risotto,
1 pack, 500g — **12**
Meatballs & Mediterranean Vegetables,
1 pack, 450g — **12**
Moroccan Lamb & Chickpeas, 1 pack, 450g — **9**
Red Pepper & Spinach Open Ravioli,
½ pack, 200g — **4**
Risotto Sun-Dried Tomato & Mascarpone,
1 pack, 250g — **8**
Risotto Wild Mushroom & Parmesan,
1 pack, 250g — **6**
Root Vegetable & Bean Cassoulet with Cheesy
Cobblers, ½ pack, 200g — **4**
Salmon & Crayfish, 1 pack, 400g — **11**
Three Bean Tostada, ½ pack, 200g — **6**

Rustlers

BBQ Rib, 1 pack, 170g — **12**
Chicken Tikka Naan, 1 pack, 160g — **8**
Fiery Beef Burger, 1 (182g) — **13**
Flame Grilled Bacon Quarter Pounder with
Cheese, 1 pack, 205g — **15**
Flame Grilled Chicken Sandwich, 1 pack, 150g — **10**
Flame Grilled Quarter Pounder with Cheese,
1 pack, 190g — **14**
Flame Grilled The Zingy Chicken,
1 portion, 131g — **8**
Italian Chicken Fillet Sandwich, 1 pack, 100g — **5**
Sausage & Bacon Breakfast Bap, 1 pack, 166g — **12**
The Big One, 1 pack, 243g — **18**
The Flame Grilled Mighty Angus, 1 pack, 185g — **13**
The Mexican Chilli Quarter Pounder,
1 pack, 182g — **14**
The New York Chilli Dog, 1 portion, 126g — **8**
The Oriental Spicy Pork Rib, 1 pack, 162g — **12**
The Texan Chipotle Burger, 1 portion, 180g — **15**
Zingy Chicken with Peri Peri Hot Sauce,
1 pack, 131g — **8**

Sainsbury's

Aromatic Tomato Chicken Curry & Rice,
1 serving, 440g — **17**
Bacon & Mushroom Tagliatelle, 1 pack, 400g — **14**
Baked Potato with Cheddar Cheese Filling,
½ pack, 215g — **6**

BBQ Chicken Wing, ½ pack, 150g — **9**
BBQ Pork Rib, 1 (64g) — **4**
Beef in a Pot with Yorkshire Puddings,
1 pack, 450g — **14**
Beef Lasagne, 1 pack, 400g — **10**
Beef Stew with Dumplings, 1 pack, 450g — **13**
Beef Stroganoff, 1 pack, 400g — **10**
Beer Battered Cod & Chunky Maris Piper Chips,
1 pack, 450g — **22**
Braised Beef & Mashed Potato, 1 pack, 450g — **12**
British Classic Beef Stew with Dumplings,
1 serving, 370g — **17**
British Classic Chicken Hotpot,
1 serving, 451g — **10**
British Classic Filled Jacket Potato with Chilli,
1 pack, 400g — **14**
British Classic Filled Yorkshire Pudding with
Beef & Potatoes, 1 pack, 400g — **16**
British Classic Filled Yorkshire Pudding with
Sausage & Mash, 1 pack, 430g — **19**
British Lamb Shish Kebabs with Mint, 1 (72g) — **5**
British Poussin Halves with Hoisin Marinade,
½ pack, 150g — **8**
British Slow Cooking Beef Shin, Tomato &
Thyme Casserole with Carrots & Swede,
1 serving, 324g — **7**
Chicken & Coriander Pesto Pastry
Parcel, 1 (19g) — **1**
Chicken Curry with Rice, 1 pack, 345g — **12**
Chicken Fajitas, ½ pack, 250g — **10**
Chicken Hotpot, 1 pack, 355g — **8**
Chicken in a Pot, 1 pack, 450g — **10**
Chicken Lasagne, 1 pack, 450g — **15**
Chicken Tikka, 1 pack, 388g — **13**
Chicken Tikka Masala with Rice, 1 pack, 500g — **21**
Chilli Beef Nachos, ½ pack, 210g — **16**
Chilli Chicken & Prawn Laksa, 1 pack, 400g — **10**
Chilli Wedge Bake, ⅕ large pack, 405g — **17**
Cod & Chips, 1 pack, 320g — **17**
Creamy Chicken Curry & Rice, 1 pack, 450g — **19**
Crispy Chicken Bites, ½ pack, 140g — **9**
Cumberland Pie, 1 pack, 450g — **15**
España Chicken & Chorizo Bean Stew,
1 pack, 400g — **11**
España Chicken in Garlic Sauce with
Rosemary Potatoes, 1 pack, 400g — **10**
España Pork Escalopes in Madeira Sauce with
Sweet Potatoes, 1 pack, 400g — **12**
España Spicy Meatballs with Rosemary
Potatoes, 1 pack, 400g — **15**
Fish Pie, 1 pack, 400g — **13**
Fusilli Bolognese, 1 pack, 400g — **17**

Greek Style Meatball, 1 pack, 95g	**5**
Green Thai Chicken, 1 pack, 400g	**9**
Honey Roast Chicken Kebab, 1 pack, 400g	**13**
Hot Smoked Salmon with New Potatoes & Vegetables, 1 pack, 400g	**11**
Jambalaya, 1 pack, 450g	**15**
King Prawn Makhani & Rice, 1 pack, 500g	**20**
Lamb in a Pot, 1 pack, 450g	**13**
Lancashire Hot Pot, 1 pack, 450g	**14**
Lasagne, 1 pack, 400g	**13**
Liver & Bacon with Mash, 1 pack, 450g	**13**
Malaysian Beef Rendang Curry & Sticky Rice, 1 pack, 500g	**21**
Mediterranean Salmon Burgers, 1 (100g)	**5**
Minced Beef Hotpot, 1 pack, 450g	**10**
Minced Lamb Casserole with Mint Dumplings, 1 pack, 450g	**15**
Mini Fish Finger Sandwiches, 1 (28g)	**2**
Mini Mature Cheddar Cheese & Bacon Frittatas, 1 (18g)	**1**
Mini Steak & Red Wine Pie, 1 serving, 136g	**11**
Paella, 1 pack, 400g	**10**
Prawn Curry with Rice, 1 pack, 400g	**15**
Quick Mash Sweetcorn & Tuna Flavour, 1 pack, 60g	**2**
Quick Pasta Cheese Sauce & Ham Flavour, 1 bag, 63g	**2**
Quick Pasta Chicken & Mushroom Flavour, 1 bag, 61g	**2**
Quick Pasta Spaghetti Bolognese Flavour, 1 bag, 63g	**2**
Red Thai Chicken, 1 pack, 400g	**11**
Roast Beef with Mashed Potato, Carrots, Broccoli & Gravy, 1 pack, 400g	**8**
Roast Chicken Breast with New Potatoes, Carrots & Beans, 1 pack, 400g	**7**
Rumbledethumps, 1 serving, 213g	**5**
Sausage & Mash, 1 pack, 450g	**12**
Seafood Linguine, 1 pack, 394g	**13**
Shepherd's Pie, 1 pie, 450g	**11**
Southern Fried Chicken & Fries, ½ pack, 300g	**16**
Southern Fried Chicken Portion, 1 serving, 100g	**7**
Sweet & Sour Chicken with Rice, 1 pack, 450g	**16**
Tandoori King Prawn Sizzler & Rice, 1 pack, 500g	**17**
Thai Chicken Satay, 1 pack, 250g	**12**
Thai Green Chicken Curry & Sticky Rice, ½ pack, 250g	**9**
Thai King Prawn Penang Curry & Jasmine Rice, 1 pack, 500g	**20**
Thai Lamb Massaman Curry & Sticky Rice, 1 pack, 500g	**19**

Tomato & Mozzarella Bake, 1 pack, 400g	**13**
Tomato, Mozzarella & Basil Deep Filled Quiche, ⅓ pack, 132g	**8**
Tuna & Tomato Pasta Bake, 1 pack, 400g	**14**
Vegetable Curry, ½ pack, 200g	**4**
Vegetable Dansak, ½ pack, 200g	**4**

Sainsbury's – Basics

Chicken Curry & Rice Mild, 1 pack, 300g	**7**
Chicken Curry & Rice, 1 pack, 340g	**10**
Chilli con Carne & Rice, 1 pack, 340g	**10**
Cottage Pie, 1 pie, 300g	**7**
Cottage Pie, ¼ family pie, 375g	**8**
Fisherman's Pie, 1 pack, 300g	**6**
Liver & Mash, 1 portion, 297g	**6**
Macaroni Cheese, 1 pack, 300g	**11**
Meat Lasagne, ¼ family pack, 375g	**10**
Spaghetti Bolognese, 1 pack, 300g	**6**
Sweet & Sour Chicken & Rice, 1 serving, 500g	**14**
Tuna Pasta, 1 pack, 300g	**9**

Sainsbury's – Be Good To Yourself

Achaari Chicken, ½ pack, 200g	**4**
Cauliflower Cheese, 1 portion, 250g	**4**
Cheese & Ham Chicken Kiev, 1 portion, 132g	**7**
Chicken & Mushroom with Multigrain Rice, 1 pack, 328g	**10**
Chicken & Pasta Bake, 1 pack, 400g	**10**
Chicken Arrabiata, 1 pack, 400g	**12**
Chicken Casserole & Herb Dumpling, 1 pack, 400g	**7**
Chicken Jalfrezi, 1 pack, 400g	**12**
Chicken Korma, 1 pack, 400g	**11**
Chicken Korma & Pilau Rice, 1 pack, 400g	**11**
Chicken Provencal with Garlic Mash, 1 pack, 345g	**8**
Chilli con Carne, 1 pack, 400g	**11**
Chilli con Carne & Rice, 1 pack, 400g	**12**
Cottage Pie, 1 pack, 450g	**10**
Cumberland Fish Pie, 1 pack, 490g	**10**
Cumberland Pie, 1 pack, 450g	**10**
Ham & Roasted Mushroom Tagliatelle, 1 pack, 400g	**11**
Indian Spiced Chicken with Tomato & Mushroom & Basmati Rice, 1 pack, 400g	**10**
Jacket Potato with Chilli, 1 pack, 350g	**9**
King Prawn Masala, 1 pack, 400g	**12**
King Prawn Spaghetti, 1 pack, 400g	**8**
Lasagne, 1 pack, 400g	**9**
Macaroni Cheese, 1 pack, 375g	**13**

Moroccan Style Chicken with Vegetable
Cous Cous, 1 pack, 400g **11**
Mushroom Risotto, 1 pack, 400g **11**
Penne Bolognese Bake, 1 pack, 450g **13**
Risotto Rice with Cherry Tomatoes & Roasted
Red Onion, 1 pack, 400g **11**
Sausage & Mash with Red Wine & Onion
Gravy, 1 pack, 400g **9**
Spinach & Ricotta Cannelloni, 1 pack, 300g **7**
Sweet & Sour Chicken with Rice, 1 pack, 400g **11**
Thai Green Chicken Curry, 1 pack, 400g **11**
Thai Red Chicken Curry, 1 pack, 398g **11**
Three Bean Chilli with Pearl Barley, 1 pack, 400g **7**
Tomato & Basil Chicken & Roasted Baby
Potatoes, 1 pack, 450g **9**
Vegetable Curry, 1 pack, 400g **8**

Sainsbury's – British Classic

Bangers & Mash, 1 pack, 450g **18**
Beef Stew with Dumplings, 1 pack, 450g **18**
Beef in a Pot with Yorkshire Puddings,
1 pack, 450g **14**
Braised Steak & Mash, 1 pack, 431g **13**
Chicken & Asparagus with Baby Potatoes,
1 pack, 450g **13**
Chicken & Mushroom Suet Pudding with Mash,
1 serving, 350g **18**
Chicken Breast Meal, 1 serving, 377g **12**
Chicken Breast with Cheese, Smoked Bacon &
Roasted Potatoes, 1 pack, 374g **12**
Chicken Casserole with Dumplings,
1 serving, 457g **17**
Chicken with Cheese & Bacon, 1 serving, 385g **16**
Chicken, Mushroom & White Wine with Mash,
1 pack, 440g **13**
Chicken, Tomato & White Wine Casserole with
Mash, 1 pack, 450g **10**
Cottage Pie, 1 pie, 450g **11**
Cumberland Pie, 1 pack, 450g **18**
Filled Jacket Potato with Beans & Cheese,
1 pack, 400g **14**
Fish Pie, 1 pack, 400g **13**
Ham Hock & Mustard Suet Pudding with Mash,
1 serving, 353g **18**
Lancashire Hotpot, 1 pack, 450g **12**
Liver & Bacon, 1 serving, 257g **9**
Liver & Bacon with Mash, 1 pack, 450g **14**
Meatballs & Mash, 1 pack, 450g **14**
Meatballs with Gravy, 1 serving, 260g **9**
Minced Beef Cobbler with Savoury Scones,
1 pack, 450g **19**

Minced Beef Hotpot, 1 pack, 450g **14**
Minced Lamb Casserole with Minted
Dumplings, 1 pack, 411g **14**
Sausage Casserole, 1 serving, 357g **16**
Shepherd's Pie, 1 pack, 450g **12**
Steak & Kidney Casserole, 1 serving, 250g **5**
Steak & Kidney Cobbler, 1 pack, 500g **20**
Slow Cooked Beef Topside Meal, 1 pack, 400g **9**

Sainsbury's – Inspired to... Cook

Bacon Lattice Chicken Joint with an Apple,
Pork & Sage Stuffing, ⅓ pack, 134g **5**
Beef Meatballs with Tomato & Bacon Sauce,
½ pack, 230g **10**
Chicken Breast with Cream Cheese wrapped in
Prosciutto Ham, ½ pack, 160g **7**
Chicken Breasts & Leek Crumble, ½ pack, 172g **7**
Chicken Breasts Topped with Leeks & Cheddar
Cheese, ½ pack, 172g **7**
Chicken Breasts with Garlic Mushrooms,
½ pack, 162g **5**
Chicken Breasts with Sunbaked Tomato, Feta
& Olives, ½ pack, 130g **5**
Chicken en Croûte, ½ pack, 195g **13**
Chicken Topped with Sage & Onion Stuffing &
Sausage, ½ pack, 180g **10**
Cod Mornay, ½ pack, 170g **6**
Creamy Basil Chicken Wrapped in Prosciutto
Ham, 1 serving, 161g **7**
Haddock with Leek & Cheddar Sauce,
½ pack, 170g **5**
Lemon & Coriander Marinated Chicken,
½ pack, 150g **4**
Pork & Chorizo Burger, ½ pack, 170g **12**
Square Yorkshire Pudding, ⅙ pack, 32g **2**
Wild Salmon en Croûte, ½ pack, 190g **15**

Sainsbury's – Inspired to... Roast

Roast Butter Basted Chicken Joint,
⅓ pack, 148g **6**
Stuffed Chicken Breast Joint, ⅓ pack, 148g **7**

Sainsbury's – Italian

Bacon & Leek Pasta Bake, 1 pack, 400g **17**
Bacon & Mushroom Tagliatelle, 1 pack, 400g **14**
Beef Cannelloni, 1 pack, 400g **14**
Beef Lasagne, ¼ pack, 375g **14**
Carbonara Tortelloni, 1 pack, 300g **16**
Chicken & Bacon Ravioli, 1 pack, 300g **13**

Chicken Lasagne, 1 pack, 400g	13
Chicken Pasta Bake, ¼ pack, 375g	14
Chicken, Spinach & Bacon Pasta Bake, ½ pack, 400g	17
Heat & Stir Chicken & Creamy Basil, 1 pack, 370g	13
Heat & Stir Chicken with Sicilian Lemon Dressing, 1 pack, 370g	14
Heat & Stir Chicken with Tomato & Mascarpone, 1 pack, 370g	13
Heat & Stir King Prawn with Creamy Pea & Rocket, 1 pack, 370g	12
Heat & Stir Meatballs with Chargrilled Pepper & Tomato Sauce, 1 pack, 370g	16
Lasagne, ½ pack, 450g	13
Macaroni Cheese, 1 pack, 400g	16
Meat Cappelletti, ¼ large pack, 125g	7
Meat Cappelletti, 1 small pack, 150g	8
Meatball Pasta Bake, ¼ family pack, 375g	13
Mushroom Risotto, 1 pack, 400g	15
Penne Bolognese Bake, ¼ family pack, 375g	16
Pesto & Goat's Cheese Tortelloni, 1 pack, 300g	17
Potato Gnocchi, ½ pack, 250g	10
Smoked Salmon & Dill Ravioli, ½ pack, 150g	8
Spinach & Ricotta Cannelloni, 1 pack, 400g	13
Tomato & Mozzarella Bake, 1 pack, 400g	13
Tomato & Mozzarella Tortelloni, ½ pack, 150g	8
Tuna & Tomato Pasta Bake, 1 pack, 400g	14
Walnut & Gorgonzola Tortelloni, ½ pack, 150g	8
Wild Mushroom Tortelloni, ½ pack, 150g	8

Sainsbury's – Oriental

Battered Chilli King Prawns, ½ pack, 150g	8
Battered Sweet & Sour Chicken, ½ pack, 200g	8
Chicken Curry & Rice, 1 pack, 450g	13
Chicken Stir Fry with Lemon, Ginger & Egg Noodles, 1 pack, 450g	12
Duck Stir Fry with Plum & Hoi Sin Sauce & Egg Noodles, 1 pack, 400g	14
Indonesian Spiced British Chicken & Prawn Stir Fry & Egg Noodles, 1 pack, 450g	12
King Prawn Stir Fry with Blackbean Sauce & Udon Noodles, 1 pack, 450g	13
Sweet & Sour Chicken with Rice, 1 pack, 450g	16
Teriyaki Chicken Noodles, 1 pack, 400g	10
Thai Fish Cakes with Sweet Chilli Dip, ⅓ pack, 82g	3
Thai Red Chicken Curry, ½ pack, 200g	8
Thai Style Chicken Noodles, 1 pack, 400g	9
Vegetable & Cashew Nut Noodles, 1 pack, 400g	12

Sainsbury's – Taste the Difference

Aubergine & Mushroom Biryani, 1 pack, 450g	17
Aubergine Masala, ½ pack, 125g	5
Beef & Chianti Bake, 1 pack, 400g	19
Beef & Chianti Ravioli, ½ pack, 210g	10
Beef Madras with Lemon Pilau Rice, 1 pack, 500g	22
Beer Battered Cod & Chunky Maris Piper Chips, 1 pack, 393g	19
British Chicken Breast with Wild Mushroom Sauce & Herby Risotto, 1 pack, 450g	13
Cannelloni, 1 pack, 400g	16
Chargrilled King Prawn & Chicken Paella, 1 serving, 355g	15
Chicken Korma & Coriander Rice, 1 pack, 500g	21
Chicken Madras, ½ pack, 200g	6
Chicken Tikka with Raita Dip, ½ pack, 118g	4
Cottage Pie, 1 pack, 400g	15
Cumberland Pie, 1 pack, 400g	14
Daal Makhani, ½ pack, 125g	5
Five Mushroom Stroganoff with Long Grain & Wild Rice, 1 pack, 450g	9
French Style Pork Cassoulet, 1 pack, 450g	14
Handmade Prosciutto di Speck & Radicchio Panzerotto, 1 serving, 165g	8
Handmade Ricotta & Rocket Tortellaccio, 1 serving, 165g	9
Italian Meatballs, 1 serving, 220g	9
King Prawn Bhuna with Coriander Rice, 1 pack, 500g	16
King Prawn Biryani, 1 pack, 500g	21
King Prawn Masala, ½ pack, 200g	6
Lamb Burgers Moroccan Influenced Spices & Fresh Coriander, 1 (115g)	7
Lamb Cobbler with Honey Roasted Root Vegetables, 1 pack, 400g	17
Lamb Kofta Kleftico, ½ pack, 200g	9
Lasagne, 1 pack, 400g	16
Luxury Fish Pie with Smoked Haddock, 1 pack, 400g	17
Macaroni Cheese & Spinach, ½ pack, 250g	14
Mushroom & Nut Roast, ½ pack, 275g	14
New Zealand Lamb's Liver & Bacon with Jersey Butter Mash, 1 pack, 450g	17
Roasted Butternut Squash Risotto, 1 pack, 450g	18
Shepherd's Pie, 1 pack, 400g	14
Shepherd's Pie with Jersey Butter Mash, ½ large pack, 360g	13

Shepherd's Pie with Jersey Butter Mash, 1 pack, 400g	**14**
Slow Cooked New Zealand Lamb Shanks, ½ pack, 555g	**18**
Slow Cooked Beef in Ale with Dumplings, 1 pack, 400g	**12**
Slow Cooked Beef Rogan Josh, ½ pack, 200g	**7**
Slow Cooked Lancashire Hotpot, 1 pack, 450g	**11**
Slow Cooked Shin of Beef, ½ pack, 335g	**12**
Slow Cooked Steak & Kidney with Cheddar Mash, 1 pack, 400g	**12**
Slow Cooked Steak au Poivre, ½ pack, 200g	**6**
Slow Cooked Steak Diane, ½ pack, 200g	**9**
Slow Cooked Steak & Ale, 1 serving, 222g	**8**
Slow Cooked Steak & Ale with Dumplings, 1 serving, 389g	**21**
Smoked Fish Pie, 1 pack, 400g	**14**
Spaghetti Bolognese, 1 pack, 400g	**16**
Steak & Kidney with Cheddar Mash, 1 pack, 400g	**12**
Steak in Ale with Dumplings, 1 pack, 400g	**12**
Tagliatelle Carbonara, 1 pack, 400g	**17**
Tandoori Chicken, ½ pack, 200g	**9**
Thai Green Chicken Curry, 1 pack, 500g	**23**
Thai Red Chicken Curry with Toasted Shallot & Lime Rice, 1 pack, 500g	**22**
Toad in the Hole, 1 pack, 400g	**21**
Ultimate Sausage & Mash, 1 pack, 500g	**21**
Vegetable Moussaka, 1 pack, 345g	**12**

Tesco

Baked Potatoes & Cheese, 1 serving, 225g	**6**
Beef Stroganoff & Rice, 1 pack, 450g	**15**
Bolognese Bake, 1 pack, 400g	**17**
Braised Beef & Mash, 1 pack, 450g	**9**
Braised Lamb & Mash, 1 pack, 450g	**10**
Braised Steak & Mash, 1 serving, 250g	**7**
Cauliflower Cheese, 1 serving, 175g	**5**
Chana Masala, 1 serving, 150g	**6**
Cheese & Onion Crispbakes, 1 individual, 90g	**6**
Chicken & Bacon Pasta Bake, 1 pack, 400g	**17**
Chicken Bhuna & Pilau Rice, 1 pack, 550g	**18**
Chicken Biryani, 1 pack, 500g	**20**
Chicken Curry & Rice, 1 pack, 550g	**17**
Chicken Curry Noodles, 1 pack, 400g	**13**
Chicken Dopiaza, 1 pack, 350g	**11**
Chicken Enchiladas, 1 pack, 450g	**18**
Chicken Jalfrezi, 1 pack, 350g	**10**
Chicken Korma & Pilau Rice, 1 pack, 550g	**25**
Chicken Korma, 1 pack, 350g	**16**
Chicken Madras, 1 pack, 350g	**12**
Chicken Makhani, 1 pack, 350g	**15**

Chicken Tikka Masala & Pilau Rice, 1 pack, 550g	**23**
Chicken Tikka Masala, 1 pack, 350g	**15**
Chicken Vindaloo, 1 pack, 350g	**10**
Chicken with Cheese & Bacon & Crushed Potatoes, 1 pack, 450g	**15**
Chilli con Carne & Rice, 1 pack, 450g	**14**
Chow Mein Stir Fry, 1 pack, 200g	**8**
Cottage Pie, 1 pack, 450g	**11**
Crispy Aromatic Half Duck with Pancakes & Hoisin Sauce, 1 serving, 39g	**3**
Cumberland Pie, 1 serving, 450g	**13**
Curry Leaf Chicken Bhuna & Rice, 1 pack, 450g	**13**
Curry Leaf Chicken Biryani, 1 pack, 450g	**17**
Curry Leaf Chicken Jalfrezi & Rice, 1 pack, 450g	**15**
Curry Leaf Chicken Korma & Rice, 1 pack, 450g	**20**
Curry Leaf Chicken Madras & Rice, 1 pack, 450g	**16**
Curry Leaf Chicken Tikka & Rice, 1 pack, 450g	**16**
Duck Noodles, 1 pack, 385g	**18**
Fish Pie, 1 pack, 450g	**12**
French Bearnaise Chicken & Parmentier Potatoes, 1 pack, 450g	**16**
French Chicken & Mushroom Gratin, 1 pack, 450g	**14**
French Chicken Chasseur & Potatoes, 1 pack, 450g	**12**
French Prawn Provencal & Rice, 1 pack, 450g	**15**
French Steak Au Poivre & Frites, 1 pack, 400g	**14**
French Toulouse Sausages & Potatoes, 1 pack, 450g	**21**
Haddock & Mash, 1 pack, 250g	**9**
Hot Chicken Tikka Masala & Pilau Rice, 1 pack, 550g	**24**
Italian Lasagne, 1 pack, 400g	**15**
Lamb Rogan Josh & Pilau Rice, 1 pack, 550g	**21**
Lamb Rogan Josh, 1 pack, 350g	**11**
Lamb Shanks in a Red Wine & Herb Sauce Sauce, 1 serving, 425g	**18**
Lamb Shanks in Mint Gravy, 1 serving, 200g	**9**
Lasagne, 1 pack, 500g	**16**
Lentil Moussaka, 1 pack, 300g	**14**
Liver & Bacon with Mash, 1 pack, 450g	**11**
Liver & Bacon, 1 serving, 200g	**6**
Meatloaf with Onion Gravy, 1 serving, 150g	**6**
Minced Beef Hot Pot, 1 serving, 225g	**8**
Minced Lamb & Dumpling, 1 serving, 250g	**10**
Mushroom Lasagne, 1 pack, 400g	**18**
Mushroom Risotto, 1 pack, 400g	**15**
Oaktree Estate Cottage Pie, 1 pack, 400g	**8**

Oaktree Estate Sausage & Mash, 1 pack, 400g	11
Oriental Beef Noodles, 1 pack, 400g	14
Pancetta Wrapped Chicken Risotto, 1 pack, 375g	13
Peppered Beef with Potato Cakes, 1 pack, 450g	17
Prawn Masala & Pilau Rice, 1 pack, 500g	19
Roast Chicken Dinner, 1 serving, 250g	10
Roast Chicken Leg & Chips, 1 pack, 308g	13
Roasted Garlic Mushroom Pasta Bake, 1 pack, 400g	16
Root Vegetable Casserole with Herb Dumplings, 1 pack, 450g	11
Sausage & Mash, 1 pack, 450g	14
Shepherd's Pie, 1 pack, 450g	9
Simply Add Beef & Ale, 1 serving, 300g	8
Simply Add Bolognese, 1 serving, 300g	8
Simply Add Chicken Tikka Masala, 1 serving, 300g	14
Simply Add Creamy Chicken & Mushroom, 1 serving, 300g	10
Simply Add Meatballs & Tomato Sauce, 1 serving, 300g	10
Simply Add Mexican Chicken, 1 serving, 300g	7
Simply Add Mushroom Stroganoff, 1 serving, 300g	8
Smoked Pancetta & Tomato Bucatini, 1 pack, 400g	21
Southern Fried Chicken Pasta, 1 individual, 350g	20
Spaghetti Carbonara, 1 pack, 400g	17
Spicy Chicken Pasta, 1 individual, 275g	11
Spicy Tomato & Bacon Spaghetti, 1 pack, 400g	13
Spinach & Ricotta Cannelloni, 1 pack, 400g	14
Steak & Murphy's Stout with Cheddar Mash, 1 serving, 450g	12
Stuffed Mini Jacket Potatoes, 1 serving, 150g	6
Sweet & Sour Chicken with Egg Fried Rice, 1 pack, 550g	17
Sweet & Sour Chicken with Rice, 1 pack, 500g	20
Three Bean Enchiladas, 1 pack, 450g	18
Tomato & Mozzarella Pasta Bake, 1 pack, 400g	14

Tesco – Finest

Aberdeen Angus Cottage Pie, ½ pack, 400g	11
Aberdeen Angus Cottage Pie, meal for one, 1 pack, 430g	12
Aberdeen Angus Meatballs with Tomato Sauce, ½ pack, 250g	9
Asparagus & Barbers Cheddar Filo Parcels, 1 individual, 160g	12
Aubergine Curry, ½ pack, 150g	6

Baked Potatoes with Cheddar, 1 individual, 245g	10
Beef Cannelloni, 1 serving, 350g	13
Beef Cheeks with Horseradish Mash, ½ pack, 475g	15
Beef Goulash, 1 pack, 375g	12
Beef Lasagne, ½ pack, 310g	10
Beef Lasagne, to serve one, 1 pack, 400g	17
Beef Madras & Rice, 1 pack, 500g	23
Beef Stroganoff, 1 pack, 500g	21
Beef Wellington, 1 serving, 195g	12
Braised Beef with Melton Red Ale, 1 serving, 225g	6
Breaded Cod Fishcake & Gruyere Cheese Sauce, 1 individual, 210g	12
Breaded Lemon Sole Goujons with Lemon Mayonnaise, 1 serving, 115g	10
Butter Chicken & Rice, 1 pack, 475g	20
Butternut Squash Risotto, 1 pack, 400g	14
Cheese & Spinach Cannelloni Al Forno, 1 pack, 350g	17
Cheese & Spinach Cannelloni, 1 pack, 350g	16
Chianti Beef & Roasted Potatoes, 1 pack, 390g	13
Chicken & Bacon Pasta Bake, 1 pack, 400g	18
Chicken & Butternut Squash Risotto, 1 pack, 385g	13
Chicken & Pork Cassoulet, 1 pack, 340g	15
Chicken & Wild Mushroom Pasta, 1 pack, 400g	14
Chicken Biryani, 1 packet, 500g	21
Chicken Breast with Mozzarella & Pancetta, ½ pack, 225g	9
Chicken Breasts in Madeira Sauce with Mushrooms, ½ pack, 200g	7
Chicken Breasts with Mascarpone, Pancetta & Onions, ½ pack, 200g	8
Chicken Chasseur, ½ pack, 200g	5
Chicken Chorizo & Cheese Potato Bake, 1 pack, 450g	17
Chicken En Croute, 1 serving, 264g	16
Chicken Jalfrezi & Ric, 1 pack, 500g	18
Chicken Jalfrezi, 1 pack, 375g	10
Chicken Korma & Rice, 1 pack, 500g	22
Chicken Stuffed with Mushroom Risotto, ½ pack, 303g	11
Chicken Tikka & Rice, 1 pack, 500g	22
Chicken Tikka Masala, 1 pack, 375g	16
Chicken Tikka Saag & Rice, 1 pack, 500g	19
Chicken, Chorizo & King Prawn Paella, 1 pack, 400g	14
Chicken, Creme Fraiche & Pasta, 1 pack, 385g	12

Chilli Chicken Fried Rice, 1 pack, 400g	**16**
Chinese Hoisin Duck Noodles, 1 pack, 385g	**15**
Classic Battered Cod & Chips, 1 pack, 360g	**15**
Cooked Beef in a Tomato & Wine Sauce, ½ pack, 275g	**8**
Coq Au Vin, 1 serving, 325g	**13**
Crab, Rocket & Chilli Linguine, 1 pack, 350g	**19**
Creamy Fish Pie, ½ pack, 350g	**13**
Creamy Fish Pie, 1 pack, 400g	**14**
Cumberland Sausages with Butter Mashed Potato, 1 pack, 500g	**22**
Daal Makhani, 1 serving, 150g	**6**
Duck a L'Orange, ½ pack, 300g	**12**
Haddock, Chips & Pea Puree, 1 pack, 450g	**18**
Ham & Mushroom Tagliatelle, 1 pack, 450g	**16**
Ham Hock Casserole, 1 pack, 298g	**7**
Hunter's Chicken, ½ pack, 325g	**13**
Italian Spinach & Ricotta Filo Parcels, 1 individual, 150g	**11**
Japanese Chilli Chicken Yaki Soba, 1 pack, 400g	**12**
Japanese Teriyaki Beef Noodles, 1 pack, 400g	**10**
King Prawn Farfalle with Champagne Sauce, 1 pack, 400g	**16**
King Prawn Laksa, 1 pack, 400g	**9**
Lamb in a Redcurrant & Port Jus with Roasted Potato, ½ pack, 353g	**13**
Lamb in a Sloe Gin Gravy with Dauphinoise Potatoes, 1 pack, 450g	**18**
Lamb Moussaka, 1 pack, 350g	**16**
Lamb Rogan Josh & Rice, 1 pack, 500g	**20**
Lamb Rogan Josh, 1 pack, 350g	**12**
Lancashire Hotpot, 1 pack, 450g	**14**
Lasagne, ½ pack, 350g	**12**
Lasagne, 1 pack, 400g	**14**
Lemon Chicken Kiev, 1 individual, 209g	**11**
Malaysian Beef Rendang, 1 pack, 400g	**13**
Moroccan Spiced Lamb Meatballs, 1 serving, 250g	**8**
Moroccan Style Couscous, ½ pot, 133g	**5**
Mushroom Leek & Gruyere Filo Parcels, 1 individual, 160g	**12**
Pad Thai, 1 pack, 400g	**13**
Paella, 1 pack, 475g	**17**
Pea & Pesto Risotto, 1 serving, 200g	**7**
Piri Piri Chicken & Rice, 1 pack, 500g	**16**
Pork & Chorizo Meatballs with Paprika Roasted Potatoes, 1 serving, 425g	**14**
Pork & Ginger Beer with Mashed Potato, 1 pack, 450g	**16**
Pork Belly with Caramelised Apples in a Cider Jus, ½ pack, 293g	**20**

Prawn Tikka & Rice, 1 pack, 475g	**19**
Prosciutto Wrapped Chicken Breast in Cheese Sauce, ½ pack, 280g	**12**
Roast Chicken & Pancetta Bake, 1 pack, 400g	**17**
Roasted Red Pepper, Sweet Potato & Spinach Lasagne, 1 pack, 350g	**11**
Scallop & Crab Cannelloni, 1 serving, 230g	**16**
Seafood Gratin, ½ pack, 275g	**15**
Shepherd's Pie, 1 pack, 430g	**14**
Slow Cooked Beef with Roasted Potatoes, 1 pack, 400g	**13**
Slow Cooked Paprika Beef, 1 serving, 250g	**6**
Smoked Haddock Gratin with Broccoli & Leeks, 1 pack, 400g	**9**
South Indian Prawn Biryani, 1 pack, 500g	**21**
Spaghetti Bolognese, 1 pack, 450g	**19**
Spaghetti Carbonara, 1 pack, 450g	**22**
Spaghetti Carbonara, 1 pack, 450g	**16**
Steak & Ale with Vintage Cheddar Mashed Potato, 1 pack, 500g	**16**
Steak Diane, 1 serving, 225g	**10**
Steak Ragu & Pappardelle, 1 pack, 400g	**16**
Stuffed Mushrooms, 1 serving, 130g	**5**
Tagliatelle Bolognese, 1 pack, 400g	**15**
Tandoori Chicken, 1 pack, 600g	**26**
Thai Red Chicken Curry, 1 pack, 400g	**12**
Tian of Lamb, 1 pack, 300g	**13**
Vietnamese Chicken Curry, 1 pack, 400g	**13**

Tesco – Healthy Living

Cauliflower Cheese, ½ pack, 250g	**4**
Chicken Chow Mein, 1 pack, 450g	**8**
Chicken Korma & Rice, 1 pack, 450g	**13**
Chicken with Crème Fraîche, Lemon & Coriander Dressing, 1 pack, 165g	**7**
Seafood Risotto, 1 pack, 365g	**8**
Slow Cooked Pork with Smoked Chilli Beans, 1 pack, 365g	**7**

Tesco – Light Choices

Baked Potato with Cheese, ½ pack, 225g	**6**
Baked Potatoes with Cheese, 1 serving, 225g	**6**
Beef Enchiladas, 1 pack, 400g	**11**
Braised Beef & Mash, 1 pack, 400g	**8**
Cheese & Broccoli Pasta, 1 pack, 400g	**12**
Chicken & Bacon Pie, 1 pack, 400g	**10**
Chicken & Pasta Bake, 1 pack, 400g	**11**
Chicken Breasts in Creamy Mushroom & White Wine Sauce, ½ pack, 200g	**4**
Chicken in Suffolk Cider with Mustard Mash, 1 pack, 400g	**8**
Chicken Lasagne, 1 pack, 400g	**9**

Chicken Prawn Chorizo Paella, 1 pack, 350g	10
Chicken Tikka Masala & Rice, 1 pack, 400g	11
Chicken Tomato Pasta, 1 pack, 350g	11
Chicken with Baby Potatoes, 1 pack, 370g	6
Chicken with Chilli Sauce & Rice, 1 pack, 380g	13
Chilli con Carne & Rice, 1 pack, 450g	13
Chilli Prawn Tagliatelle, 1 pack, 350g	9
Cod & Prawn Cumberland Pie, 1 pack, 450g	10
Cottage Pie, 1 pack, 450g	10
Creamy Mushroom Pasta, 1 pack, 350g	11
Garlic Mushroom Pasta, 1 pack, 400g	11
Haddock, Prawn & Potato Crumble, 1 pack, 400g	9
Ham & Mushroom Tagliatelle, 1 pack, 400g	11
King Prawn & Roasted Garlic Linguine, 1 pack, 350g	8
Lamb Moussaka, 1 pack, 350g	8
Lasagne, 1 pack, 430g	11
Macaroni Cheese, 1 pack, 385g	12
Minced Beef & Potatoes, 1 pack, 350g	5
Pasta & Roasted Vegetables, 1 pack, 320g	9
Prawn Noodles, 1 pack, 350g	7
Red Thai Chicken Curry, 1 pack, 350g	8
Ricotta & Spinach Cannelloni, 1 pack, 400g	9
Salmon & Broccoli Pie, 1 pack, 400g	9
Sausage & Mash, 1 pack, 400g	9
Sausage & Tomato Pasta, 1 pack, 350g	12
Smoked Salmon Linguine, 1 pack, 350g	8
Spaghetti & Meatballs, 1 pack, 400g	10
Spaghetti Bolognese, 1 pack, 400g	11
Spaghetti Carbonara, 1 pack, 400g	12
Spicy Beef Pasta, 1 pack, 350g	11
Spinach & Ricotta Cannelloni, 1 pack, 400g	9
Tomato & Mozzarella Pasta Bake, 1 pack, 400g	10
Tomato & Cheese Pasta Bake, 1 pack, 350g	10
Tuna Pasta Bake, 1 pack, 400g	10
Vegetable Curry, 1 pack, 350g	9
Vegetable Lasagne, 1 pack, 400g	9

Tesco – Ken Hom

Chicken & Black Bean, 1 pack, 350g	12
Chicken & Cashew Nuts, 1 pack, 350g	14
Chicken & Mushrooms, 1 pack, 350g	7
Chicken Chow Mein, 1 pack, 450g	13
Chicken Noodles, 1 pack, 400g	12
Crispy Chilli Beef, 1 pack, 250g	18
Crispy Chilli Prawns, 1 pack, 300g	17
Crispy Sweet & Sour Chicken, 1 pack, 400g	18
Kung Po Chicken & Egg Fried Rice, 1 pack, 550g	20
Shredded Aromatic Duck & Pancakes, 1 serving, 35g	2

Spicy Szechuan Noodle Bowl, 1 pack, 400g	12
Sweet & Sour Chicken, 1 pack, 350g	9

Tesco – Italian

Beef Cannelloni, 1 pack, 400g	15
Chicken & Ham Pasta Bake, 1 pack, 400g	16
Chicken & Mushroom Risotto, 1 pack, 400g	12
Chicken Arrabiatta, 1 pack, 400g	13
Chicken Lasagne, 1 pack, 400g	12
Garlic Dough Ball Pasta Bake, 1 pack, 400g	19
Ham & Mushroom Tagliatelle, 1 pack, 400g	14
Pepperoni Pasta Bake, 1 pack, 400g	18
Spaghetti & Meatballs, 1 pack, 400g	13
Spaghetti Bolgnese, 1 pack, 400g	16
Tuna Pasta Bake, 1 pack, 400g	14

The Co-operative

American Style BBQ Ribs, ½ pack, 225g	14
Beef, Tomato & Red Wine Ravioli, ½ pack, 150g	11
Chicken Curry & Rice, Value, 1 pack, 500g	13
Chicken in Blackbean Sauce with Chinese Rice, 1 pack, 400g	10
Chicken in Green Thai Curry Sauce with Oriental Rice Meal For One, 1 pack, 475g	13
Chicken Tikka Masala with Pilau Rice, 1 pack, 400g	14
Chilli con Carne & Rice, 1 pack, 400g	11
Cottage Pie, 1 pack, 400g	11
Ham & Mushroom Tagliatelle, 1 pack, 400g	10
Healthy Living Cottage Pie, 1 pack, 400g	9
Indian Chicken Madras Bag for One, 1 pack, 665g	27
Lasagne, 1 pack, 400g	14
Liver & Bacon with Mashed Potato, 1 pack, 400g	11
Macaroni Cheese, 1 pack, 400g	9
Macaroni Cheese Pasta & Sauce, 1 portion, 110g	4
Mini Classics Fish Pie, 1 pack, 300g	7
Mini Classics Bolognese Bake, 1 pack, 300g	11
Mini Classics Cauliflower Cheese & Sauted Potato, 1 pack, 300g	6
Mini Classics Chicken Casserole & Dumplings, 1 pack, 300g	8
Mini Classics Minced Beef Hot Pot, 1 pack, 300g	8
Mini Classics Minced Lamb Hot Pot, 1 pack, 300g	7
Mini Classics Sausage Casserole, 1 pack, 300g	7
Mini Classics Tomato Penne Pasta, 1 pack, 300g	9

Weight Watchers®
Chilled Prepared Meals
a must for your shopping list

All of our mouth-watering Chilled Prepared Meals are delicious, low fat and convenient. Bursting with flavour and quick to prepare, they will fit perfectly into your busy lifestyle.

7 ProPoints value *to* **10** ProPoints value

per serving

Over 20 delicious meals to choose from including:
Piri Piri Chicken with Wild Rice, Roasted Vegetable Arrabiata and Chicken & Mushroom Pie

 WeightWatchers® Foods
Eat gorgeous. Feel gorgeous.

Mini Indian Vegetarian Selection, ½ pack, 168g	9
Shepherd's Pie, 1 pack, 400g	9
Simply British Beef & Ale Casserole, 1 pack, 360g	11
Simply Chicken Breasts with Garlic Mushrooms, ½ pack, 172g	7
Simply Lamb & Winter Vegetable Casserole, 1 pack, 360g	12
Spaghetti Bolognese, 1 pack, 400g	12
Spaghetti Carbonara, 1 pack, 400g	15
Spicy Potato Wedges & Dip, 1 pack, 450g	20
Spinach & Ricotta Cannelloni, 1 pack, 400g	12
Sweet & Sour Chicken with Chinese Rice, 1 pack, 400g	11

The Co-operative – Truly Irresistible

Chicken Fillets with Asparagus & Bacon in a Creamy Gorgonzola Sauce, ½ pack, 230g	8
Cottage Pie, 1 pack, 400g	12
Fish Pie, 1 pack, 400g	12
Lasagne, 1 pack, 400g	13
Lincolnshire Pork & Bacon Parcels with Bramley Apple & Mustard Relish, ½ pack, 235g	9
Salmon in a White Wine Sauce, 1 pack, 380g	19

Waitrose

Aloo Gobi Saag, 1 pack, 300g	10
Asparagus & Babycorn Masala, 1 portion, 200g	4
Beef in Black Bean Sauce, 1 portion, 200g	4
Beef Lasagne, 1 pack, 400g	12
Beef Stew with Dumplings, 1 pack, 450g	11
Cauliflower Cheese, 1 pack, 450g	19
Chicken & Mango Curry, ½ pack, 375g	16
Chicken Balti, 1 portion, 200g	7
Chicken Cordon Bleu, 1 portion, 160g	9
Chicken Jalfrezi, 1 pack, 400g	13
Chicken Korma, ½ pack, 200g	9
Chicken Madras, 1 pack, 400g	15
Chicken Saag Masala, 1 portion, 200g	7
Chicken Tikka Makhani, 1 pack, 400g	15
Chicken Tikka Masala, ½ pack, 200g	8
Chicken Tikka Masala with Pilau Rice, 1 pack, 500g	20
Chicken Vindaloo, 1 pack, 400g	12
Chilli con Carne, 1 pack, 450g	18
Cumberland Pie, 1 pack, 400g	13
Duck Parcels, 1 (22g)	2
Dum Ka Korma, 1 portion, 200g	8
Green Thai Chicken Curry, 1 portion, 200g	7
Green Thai Chicken Spring Roll, ½ pack, 450g	23
Lamb Bhuna, ½ pack, 375g	17

Lamb Jardaloo, 1 portion, 200g	7
Lamb Rogan Josh, 1 pack, 400g	15
Masala Dal, 1 portion, 200g	6
Meatball Pasta Bake, ¼ pack, 100g	3
Red Thai Chicken Curry, 1 pack, 300g	8
Salmon & Prawn Gratin, 1 pack, 400g	13
Sambhar, ½ pack, 375g	11
Spinach & Mushroom Lasagne, 1 pack, 400g	10
Szechuan Chicken Wonton, 1 pack, 210g	16
Tomato & Basil Chicken Kebabs, 1 pack, 135g	4
Vegetable Tempura, ¼ pack, 105g	8
Wild Mushroom & Chestnut Grills, 1 (88g)	4
Wild Rice, Lentil & Pumpkin Seed Gratins, 1 (140g)	7

Waitrose – Delicatezze

Adriatic Anchovies with Braised Fennel, 1 pack, 150g	7
Edamame Bean, Artichoke & Lemon Pesto Tortilla, 1 pack, 400g	14
Lemon & Ginger Chicken Kebabs, 1 pack, 150g	8
Pancetta & Gruyère Flamè, 1 pack, 300g	22
Pissaladiere, 1 pack, 150g	10
Pork & Apricot Meatballs, 1 pack, 136g	8
Sardine Stuffed Cherry Peppers, 1 pack, 160g	5

Weight Watchers

Bolognese Al Forno, 1 pack, 400g	9
Chicken & Butternut Squash Curry Pot, 1 pot, 250g	6
Chicken Balti with Pilau Rice, 1 pack, 400g	10
Chicken Tikka with Coriander Rice, 1 pack, 400g	10
Chicken, Tomato & Spinach Lasagne, 1 pack, 400g	8
Chilli Beef & Potato Wedges, 1 pack, 400g	9
Classic Beef Lasagne, 1 pack, 400g	9
Classic Cottage Pie, 1 pack, 400g	9
Ham & Mushroom Tagliatelle, 1 pack, 400g	9
Macaroni Cheese, 1 pack, 400g	9
Mediterranean Vegetable Pasta, 1 pack, 400g	7
Moroccan Vegetable Tagine Pot, 1 pot, 250g	6
Mushroom Stroganoff with Wild Rice, 1 pack, 400g	8
Red Thai Chicken Curry with Jasmine Rice, 1 pack, 400g	9
Sausages & Mash, 1 pack, 400g	9
Spicy Meatballs & Penne Pasta Pot, 1 pot, 250g	6
Spicy Veggie Curry with Pilau Rice, 1 (400g)	8
Spinach, Ricotta & Tomato Cannelloni, 1 pack, 400g	9

Weight Watchers® Pots
a must for your shopping list

Ideal for when you need a tasty meal in a hurry or a change from your usual packed lunch. The authentic flavours and ingredients will really satisfy you.

6 ProPoints value

per pot

3 delicious options to choose from:
Moroccan Vegetable Tagine, Chicken & Butternut Squash Curry, Spicy Meatballs & Penne Pasta

WeightWatchers Foods
Eat gorgeous. Feel gorgeous.

EACH POT COUNTS AS 1 OF YOUR 5 A DAY

Savoury Pies & Quiches

Fresh Prepared Meals

Sweet & Sour Chicken with Long Grain Rice, 1 pack, 400g — 9
Sweet Chilli Chicken with Thai Sticky Rice, 1 pack, 400g — 10
Tuna Pasta Bake, 1 pack, 400g — 8

Ye Olde Oak Foods

Chicken Korma, 1 pack, 575g — 26
Chicken Sweet & Sour, 1 pack, 575g — 13
Chicken Tikka Masala, 1 pack, 100g — 4
Chicken Vindaloo, 1 pack, 575g — 16
Thai Green Curry, 1 pack, 575g — 17

Young's

Mediterranean Fish Gratin, 1 pack, 350g — 11
Mornay Fish Gratin, 1 pack, 350g — 10
Salmon en Croute, ½ pack, 185g — 14

Savoury Pies & Quiches

Asda

Bacon & Leek Quiche, ⅓ tart, 110g — 8
Cheese & Onion Mini Rolls, 1 individual, 15g — 1
Cheese & Onion Pasty, 1 individual, 150g — 12
Cheese & Onion Quiche, 1 slice, 150g — 10
Cheese & Onion Rolls, 1 standard, 65g — 5
Cherry Tomato & Mozzarella Quiche, ½ pack, 300g — 17
Chicken & Mushroom Individual Pie, 1 (150g) — 12
Chicken & Mushroom Pasty, 1 (150g) — 10
Chicken & Mushroom Pie, 1 portion, 147g — 10
Chicken & Mushroom Slice, 1 slice, 165g — 11
Chicken Korma Samosa, 1 individual, 50g — 4
Chicken Puff Pastry Pie, ¼ pack, 150g — 10
Cornish Pasty (Top Crimped), 1 individual, 171g — 14
Cornish Pasty, 1 individual, 150g — 12
Cornish Plait, ⅓ pack, 133g — 10
Creamy Chicken & Mushroom Puff Pastry Pie, 1 individual, 150g — 11
Deep Fill Ham Hock & Pea Flan, ⅓ pack, 120g — 8
Ham, Cream Cheese & Chive Quiche, ¼ pack, 106g — 8
Individual Steak Pie, 1 pie, 150g — 12
Meat Feast Quiche, ¼ pack, 110g — 6
Melton Mowbray Pork Pie, 1 pack, 160g — 18
Minced Beef & Onion Pie, 1 pack, 149g — 11
Mini Cumberland Sausage Rolls, 1 portion, 15g — 1

Mini Melton Mowbray Pork Pies with Pickle, 1 (50g) — 5
Mini Onion Bhaji, 1 individual, 18g — 1
Mini Toad in the Hole, 1 individual, 20g — 1
Mini Traditional Cornish Pasty, 1 pack, 70g — 6
Party Mini Chicken Tikka Pasties, 1 (30g) — 3
Party Mini Sausage Rolls, 1 individual, 8g — 1
Pork & Egg Gala Pie, 1 pie, 110g — 10
Pork, Chicken & Ham Pie, ½ pie, 114g — 9
Puff Pastry Steak Pie, ¼ pack, 150g — 11
Reduced Fat Cheese & Onion Quiche, 1 pack, 170g — 11
Reduced Fat Quiche Lorraine, 1 pack, 170g — 11
Roast Chicken & Sweetcorn Lattice, ⅓ pack, 132g — 10
Salmon & Broccoli Lattice, ⅓ pie, 133g — 10
Sausage & Onion Quiche, 1 serving, 200g — 14
Shortcrust Chicken & Mushroom Pie, ¼ pack, 150g — 10
Shortcrust Chicken Pie, ¼ large, 150g — 10
Shortcrust Chicken Pie, 1 individual, 250g — 16
Shortcrust Lamb & Vegetable Pie, ¼ pie, 150g — 11
Shortcrust Minced Steak & Onion Pie, ¼ pie, 150g — 12
Shortcrust Minced Steak & Onion Pie, 1 individual, 250g — 21
Shortcrust Steak & Kidney Pie, ¼ pie, 150g — 11
Shortcrust Steak Pie, ¼ pie, 150g — 11
Shortcrust Steak Pie, 1 individual, 250g — 18
Snack Chicken & Mushroom Pies, 1 pie, 65g — 5
Snack Eggs, 1 individual, 20g — 2
Snack Minced Beef & Onion Pies, 1 pie, 65g — 5
Steak & Kidney Pie, ¼ pack, 203g — 14
Steak & Onion Lattice, ⅓ pie, 133g — 9
Traditional Style Cottage Pie, large, ¼ pack, 375g — 11
Vegetable & Cheese Pies in Golden Puff Pastry, 1 portion, 138g — 10
Vegetable Bhaji from Curry Pot, mini, 1 pack, 23g — 1

Asda – Chosen by You

Bistro Ultimate Steak Pie, 1 pie, 250g — 17
Chicken Tikka Slices, 1 individual, 165g — 13
Melton Mini Pork Pies, 1 pie, 50g — 6
Melton Snack Pork Pies, 1 pie, 80g — 9
Minced Steak & Onion Puff Pastry Pie, 1 individual, 200g — 15
Minced Steak & Onion Slices, 1 individual, 165g — 12
Mini Pork Sausage Rolls, 1 individual, 15g — 1
Mini Savoury Eggs, 1 individual, 12g — 1
Peppered Steak Slices, 1 individual, 165g — 12

Scotch Eggs, 1 individual, 113g	**7**
Spicy Pork Sausage Roll, 1 individual, 66g	**5**
Steak & Kidney Puff Pastry Pie, 1 individual, 200g	**13**

Asda – Deli

Bacon & Gruyère Tartlet, 1 tart, 150g	**13**
Cheese & Onion Pasty, 1 (150g)	**12**
Cornish Pasties, 1 individual, 70g	**5**
Giant Sausage Roll, 1 roll, 179g	**16**
Large Traditional Cornish Pasty, 1 (165g)	**13**
Mini Cornish Pasties, 1 (70g)	**7**
Mini Steak Pies, 1 pack, 100g	**7**
Picnic Egg, 1 snack size, 55g	**4**
Pork, Cheese & Pickle Rolls, 1 roll, 67g	**7**
Premium Sausage Roll, 1 roll, 55g	**6**
Sausage Rolls, 1 roll, 55g	**6**
Spinach & Ricotta Tartlet, 1 (150g)	**11**

Asda – Extra Special

Beechwood Smoked Bacon, Baby Leek & Roquefort Tart, 1 serving, 115g	**10**
Brie & Cranberry Filo Parcels, 1 individual, 14g	**2**
Brie & Roast Cherry Tomato Tartlets, 1 individual, 130g	**12**
Caramelised Butternut Squash & Wyke Farm Cheddar Tarlets, 1 pack, 260g	**19**
Caramelised Onion & Wyke Farm Mature Cheddar Quiche, ¼ pack, 100g	**7**
Chicken & Bacon Pie, ½ pack, 250g	**19**
Classic British Mini Chicken Pie, 1 pie, 30g	**3**
Classic British Mini Cottage Pie, 1 pie, 27g	**2**
Classic British Mini Pork Sausage Rolls, 1 individual, 35g	**4**
Classic Quiche Lorraine, ¼ tart, 100g	**7**
Davidstow Cheddar & Caramelised Onion Quiche, ¼ tart, 100g	**8**
Maple-Cured Bacon, Parmesan & Rocket Tartlets, 1 individual, 130g	**11**
Mini Beef Wellington, 1 serving, 20g	**2**
Quiche Lorraine, ¼ pack, 100g	**7**
Somerset Brie & Bacon Quiche, ¼ tart, 100g	**7**
Spinach & Goat's Cheese Tart, 1 serving, 115g	**10**
Steak & Ale Pies, 1 individual, 225g	**17**
Steak Pie, ¼ pack, 125g	**10**
Wensleydale & Roasted Tomato Quiche, ¼ tart, 100g	**8**

Asda – In-Store Bakery

Cheese & Onion Roll, 1 mini, 41g	**3**
Cheese & Onion Roll, 1 standard, 123g	**11**
Chunky Steak Pie, 1 individual, 180g	**14**

Meat & Potato Pies, 1 individual, 190g	**16**
Sausage Roll, 1 large, 113g	**10**
Sausage Roll, 1 mini, 41g	**4**
Steak & Kidney Pie, 1 pie, 174g	**13**

Ginster's

Buffet Bar, 1 (90g)	**7**
Cheddar Cheese & Onion Pasty, 1 (145g)	**13**
Cheese & Onion Slice, 1 slice, 155g	**12**
Cheese & Onion Pasty, 1 (60g)	**5**
Chicken & Mozzarella Bake, 1 (175g)	**13**
Chicken & Mushroom Pie, 1 (250g)	**18**
Chicken & Mushroom Slice, 1 slice, 180g	**12**
Chicken Lattice, 1 portion, 133g	**10**
Cornish Pasties, 1 (130g)	**10**
Deep Fill Chicken & Mushroom Slice, 1 slice, 180g	**14**
Deep Fill Ham & Cheese Slice, 1 slice, 180g	**14**
Deep Fill Peppered Steak Slice, 1 slice, 180g	**13**
Deep Fill Steak Pie, 1 (250g)	**17**
Deep Fill Steak Slices, 1 slice, 300g	**22**
Individual Pork Pie, 1 (140g)	**14**
Large Ploughman's Roll, 1 (140g)	**13**
Large Sausage Roll, 1 (150g)	**15**
Melton Mowbray Pork Pie, 1 (135g)	**15**
Mexican Style Spicy Chicken Pasty, 1 (180g)	**12**
Mini Festive Rolls, 1 (20g)	**2**
Mini Sausage Rolls, 1 (20g)	**2**
Original Cornish Pasty, 1 (227g)	**15**
Ploughman's Roll, 1 (150g)	**16**
Sausage Rolls, 1 (80g)	**8**
Scotch Egg Bar, 1 (90g)	**8**
Snack Sausage Roll, 1 (40g)	**4**
Spicy Chicken Slice, 1 slice, 180g	**12**
Steak & Onion Lattice, 1 portion, 133g	**9**
Steak & Onion Pie, 1 (180g)	**13**
Steak Pie, 1 (180g)	**12**
Steak Slice, 1 slice, 104g	**7**

Higgidy

Asparagus & Herby Summer Vegetable Quiche, ⅓ pack, 132g	**8**
Broccoli & Stilton Quiche with Crunchy Cheddar Crumb, 1 portion, 133g	**10**
Chicken Pot Pie with Ham & Leek, 1 serving, 250g	**19**
Herby Sausage Roll with Bacon & Leek, 1 serving, 150g	**13**
Little Mushroom & Slow Roast Tomato Quiche, 1 (154g)	**12**
Little Smoked Bacon & Cheddar Quiche, 1 (155g)	**13**

Savoury Pies & Quiches Fresh Prepared Meals

189

Little Spinach & Roasted Red Pepper
Quiche, 1 (155g) **11**
Smoked English Bacon & Mature Cheddar
Family Quiche, 1 serving, 150g **12**
Smoked Salmon Quiche with Fresh Basil
Pesto, ⅓ pack, 132g **10**
Spinach, Feta & Roasted Red Pepper Quiche,
⅓ pack, 132g **8**

M&S

Aberdeen Angus Minced Beef Pie,
⅓ large pie, 183g **14**
Cheese & Onion Quiche, ¼ tart, 100g **7**
Chicken Pie, 1 pie, 170g **12**
Roast Chicken Plate Pie, ¼ large pie, 138g **10**

McDougalls

Chicken & Vegetable Pie, 1 pie, 142g **10**
Steak & Mushroom Pie, 1 pie, 170g **11**

Morrisons

Cheese & Ham Slice, 1 slice 180g **15**
Cheese & Onion Rolls, 1 (15g) **1**
Cheese & Onion Slice, 1 slice, 147g **11**
Chicken & Ham Pie, ¼ pie, 250g **16**
Chicken & Mushroom Slice, 1 slice, 147g **10**
Chicken & Vegetable Pie, 1 serving, 169g **11**
Chicken Balti Pie, 1 (195g) **16**
Coronation Chicken Pie, ¼ pie, 250g **16**
Individual Pork Pie, 1 (121g) **12**
Minced Beef & Vegetable Pie, 1 serving, 164g **12**
Minced Beef & Vegetable Slice, 1 slice, 147g **11**
Mini Cheddar Cheese & Onion Pasties, 1 (21g) **2**
Mini Cheese & Onion Quiche, 1 (21g) **2**
Mini Sausage & Stuffing Lattice, 1 (20g) **2**
Mini Steak & Ale Pies, 1 (30g) **3**
Oven Fresh 8 inch Cumberland Sausage Roll,
1 serving, 131g **12**
Pork & Apple Pie, ½ pie, 250g **18**
Pork & Egg Roll, 1 (25g) **1**
Sausage & Bacon Rolls, 1 (25g) **2**
Short Crust Lidded Mince Pie, 1 (51g) **6**
Steak & Kidney Pie, 1 serving, 169g **11**
Steak Pie, 1 serving, 169g **11**
Steak Slice, 1 slice, 147g **9**
Turkey & Bacon Slice, 1 slice, 180g **15**

Morrisons – Eat Smart

Chicken & Broccoli Pie, 1 pack, 450g **10**
Crustless Cheese & Onion Quiche, 1 (160g) **8**
Crustless Quiche Lorraine, 1 (160g) **7**

Peter's

Chicken Curry, 1 pie, 235g **18**
Corned Beef Pasty, 1 (165g) **13**
Oval Steak & Kidney Pie, 1 (184g) **14**
Premier Pasty Chicken, 1 (100g) **7**
Premier Pasty Cornish, 1 (100g) **8**
Premier Pasty Pilgrims Choice Cheese & Spring
Onion Pasty, 1 (100g) **8**
Premier Pasty Pork & Cider, 1 (100g) **8**
Roast Chicken 'Perfect Crunch' Flaky Pastry,
1 pie, 235g **17**
Steak & Fullers Deliciously Deep Fill,
1 pie, 235g **18**

Pork Farms

Big Hit Recipe Strongly Seasoned Sausage
Rolls, 1 roll, 70g **8**
Bowyer's Recipe Lightly Seasoned Sausage
Rolls, 1 roll, 70g **8**
Bowyer's Recipe Mild Sweet Cured Snack Pork
Pies, 1 serving, 80g **10**
Cheese & Ham Slice, 1 slice, 175g **14**
Cheese & Onion Slice, 1 slice, 175g **13**
Chicken & Bacon Slice, 1 slice, 175g **13**
Chicken & Mushroom Slice, 1 slice, 175g **14**
Individually Wrapped Sausage Rolls,
1 serving, 50g **6**
King Size Sausage Roll, 1 roll, 142g **17**
Large Cornish Pasty, 1 (227g) **17**
Large Pork Pie, 1 serving, 56g **6**
Mild Sweet Cured Snack Pork Pie,
1 serving, 80g **10**
Original Individual Pork Pie, 1 serving, 142g **16**
Original Large Pork Pie, 1 serving, 56g **6**
Original Mini Pork Pie, 1 serving, 50g **5**
Peppered Steak Slice, 1 (175g) **14**
Pork & Egg Pie, 1 (56g) **5**
Pork & Pickle Pie, 1 pie, 100g **12**
Pork Farms Sausage Roll, 1 serving, 70g **8**
Snack Pork Pie, 1 (80g) **9**
Spicy Chicken Slice, 1 (175g) **14**
The Big Hit Kingsize Sausage Roll,
1 roll, 133g **15**
The Big Hit Sausage Roll, 1 roll, 100g **12**

Pukka-Pies

All Steak, ¼ pie, 175g **13**
Beef & Onion, 1 pie, 231g **15**
Chicken, 1 pie, 175g **12**

Sainsbury's

Aberdeen Angus Minced Beef Shortcrust Pastry Pie, 1 pie, 250g	**19**
Bacon & Cheese Quiche, ⅓ pack, 132g	**9**
Bacon & Leek Quiche, ⅓ pack, 133g	**9**
British Classic Chicken & Mushroom Pie, 1 pack, 450g	**17**
Broccoli, Tomato & Cheese Quiche, ⅓ pack, 133g	**9**
Butcher's Choice Cumberland Sausage Roll, 1 (85g)	**7**
Butcher's Choice Deep Filled Sausage Roll, 1 (85g)	**7**
Butcher's Choice Cumberland Sausage Roll, 1 (85g)	**7**
Cheese & Onion Pasty, 1 (150g)	**13**
Cheese & Onion Puff Pastry Slice, 1 slice, 165g	**14**
Cheese & Onion Quiche, ⅓ pack, 133g	**9**
Cheese & Onion Roll, 1 (66g)	**5**
Chicken & Broccoli Puff Pastry Pie, ⅓ pie, 198g	**14**
Chicken & Gravy Deep Fill Puff Pastry Pie, 1 (250g)	**16**
Chicken & Gravy Puff Pastry Pie, 1 (235g)	**16**
Chicken & Gravy Shortcrust Pastry Pie, ⅓ family pack, 198g	**14**
Chicken & Gravy Shortcrust Pastry Pie, 1 (235g)	**17**
Chicken & Mushroom Puff Pastry Pie, 1 (150g)	**12**
Chicken & Mushroom Puff Pastry Slice, 1 slice, 165g	**12**
Chicken & Smoked Bacon Puff Pastry Pie, ⅓ packet, 198g	**14**
Chicken Curry Puff Pastry Pie, 1 (150g)	**12**
Chicken, Broccoli & Mushroom Shortcrust Pastry Roll, ⅓ roll, 112g	**8**
Chilli Beef Empanadas, 1 (22g)	**2**
Cornish Pasty, 1 (150g)	**11**
Cornish Pasty, 1 large, 175g	**13**
Crusty Bake Mini Pork Pie, 1 (50g)	**5**
Crusty Bake Pork Pie, 1 (65g)	**7**
Egg & Bacon Bites, 1 (18g)	**1**
Ham Hock & Pea Shortcrust Pastry Pie, 1 (235g)	**18**
Ham Hock, Cheese & Leek Lattice Squares, 1 (35g)	**3**
Jumbo Sausage Roll, 1 (145g)	**15**
Lincolnshire Snack Sausage Roll, 1 (34g)	**4**
Mediterranean Style Vegetable Quiche, 1 (170g)	**9**
Melton Mowbray Mini Pork Pie, 1 (50g)	**5**
Melton Mowbray Pork Pie, 1 (140g)	**16**
Melton Mowbray Snack Pork Pie, 1 (75g)	**8**

Minced Beef & Onion Puff Pastry Pie, 1 (150g)	**13**
Minced Beef & Onion Puff Pastry Slice, 1 slice, 165g	**13**
Minced Beef & Onion Shortcrust Pastry Pie, ¼ pack, 150g	**12**
Minced Beef & Onion Shortcrust Pastry Pie, individual, 1 (235g)	**19**
Minced Beef & Onion Shortcrust Pastry Roll, ½ roll, 177g	**14**
Mini Cheese & Onion Roll, 1 (16g)	**1**
Mini Cornish Pasty, 1 (40g)	**3**
Mini Cornish Pasty Bites, 1 (30g)	**3**
Mini Sausage Roll Bites, 1 (10g)	**1**
Mini Sausage Rolls, 1 (15g)	**2**
Mushroom Medley Quiche, ¼ large, 100g	**6**
Pork & Stuffing Bites, 1 portion, 60g	**5**
Pork, Cheese & Pickle Bites, 1 pack, 216g	**16**
Quiche Lorraine, ⅓ tart, 132g	**9**
Quiche Lorraine, 1, (170g)	**13**
Reduced Fat Snack Sausage Roll, 1 (34g)	**3**
Salmon & Broccoli Deep Filled Quiche, ⅓ tart, 132g	**8**
Sausage & Onion Puff Pastry Plait, ⅓ plait, 120g	**13**
Sausage Bacon & Tomato Deep Filled Quiche, ⅓ tart,132g	**9**
Smoked Bacon & Cheese Puff Pastry, 1 (165g)	**13**
Smoky Bacon Sausage Roll, 1 (66g)	**7**
Snack Cheese & Onion Rolls, 1 (34g)	**3**
Spinach & Ricotta Quiche, ⅓ tart, 132g	**8**
Steak & Cornish Ale Pasty, 1 (175g)	**14**
Steak & Guinness Puff Pastry Pie, ⅓ pie, 198g	**14**
Steak & Guinness Deep Fill Puff Pastry Pie, 1 (250g)	**17**
Steak & Kidney Puff Pastry Pie, 1 (250g)	**14**
Steak & Kidney Shortcrust Pastry Pie, 1 (235g)	**16**
Steak & Mushroom Puff Pastry Slice, 1 slice, 165g	**12**
Steak & Red Wine Shortcrust Pastry Pie, 1 (250g)	**19**
Steak Pie, 1 portion, 133g	**8**
Steak Puff Pastry Pie, ⅓ portion, 198g	**14**
Steak Puff Pastry Pie, 1 (235g)	**17**
Steak Puff Pastry Pie, individual, 1 (150g)	**12**
Steak Shortcrust Pastry Pie, ⅓ pie, 200g	**15**
Wiltshire Ham & Tewkesbury Mustard Quiche, ⅓ tart, 132g	**8**

Sainsbury's –
Be Good To Yourself

Cheese & Onion Quiche, 1 tart, 170g	**8**
Cherry Tomato & Cheese Quiche, ⅓ tart, 132g	**6**

Chicken & Broccoli Pie, 1 pie, 450g	8
Chicken & Mushroom Pie, 1 pie, 450g	10
Mediterranean Vegetable Quiche, ⅓ tart, 132g	6
Mushroom Quiche, 1 slice, 170g	8
Quiche Lorraine, ⅓ tart, 132g	7
Roasted Vegetable Quiche, ⅓ tart, 132g	6
Shepherd's Pie, 1 pack, 450g	9

Sainsbury's – Taste the Difference

British Pork Sausage Rolls made with All Butter Puff Pastry, 1 (18g)	2
Cherry Tomato, Mozzarella & Pesto Quiche, ¼ tart, 119g	8
Chicken & Buttered Leek Pie, 1 (250g)	21
Goat's Cheese & Spinach Flamme, ⅓ tart, 77g	6
Hand Crimped Cheese & Onion Pasty, 1 (200g)	15
Hand Crimped Steak Pasty, 1 (200g)	13
Moroccan Spiced Vegetable & Feta Tart, ⅓ tart, 132g	9
Quiche Lorraine, ⅓ tart, 157g	11
Ricotta & Spinach Quiche, ½ tart, 85g	7
Steak & Ale Pie, ⅓ pie, 82g	6
Steak & Stilton Pie, 1 (250g)	20
Steak Pie, ⅓ pie, 198g	14
Steak Pie, 1 (250g)	18
Three Cheese & Caramelised Onion Quiche, ⅓ packet, 56g	5
Topcrust Chicken & Buttered Leek Pie, ½ pie, 300g	17
Topcrust Steak Pie, ⅓ pie, 198g	9
West Country Chicken & Wild Mushroom Pie with Jersey Butter Mash, 1 (400g)	14
West Country Chicken & Wild Mushroom Pie, 1 (400g)	14
West Country Chicken & Buttered Leek Pie, ½ pie, 300g	22

Tesco

Bacon & Brie Quiche, 1 serving, 100g	7
Bacon & Egg Snack Eggs, 1 individual, 45g	3
Bacon & Leek Quiche, 1 serving, 100g	6
Bacon, Egg & Tomato Quiche, 1 serving, 90g	5
Bacon, Sausage & Tomato Quiche, 1 serving, 100g	7
Beef, Mushrooms, Bacon & Red Wine Dorset Pie, 1 individual, 280g	21
Bite Size Cheesy Chilli Beef Pasties, 1 individual, 30g	2
Bite Size Cornish Pasties, 1 individual, 30g	3
Bite Size Mini Eggs, 1 individual, 12g	1
Bite Size Savoury Eggs, 1 individual, 12g	1

British Roast Chicken & Gravy Pie, 1 individual, 250g	18
British Roast Chicken & Ham Hock Pie, 1 individual, 250g	19
British Steak & Wild Mushroom Pie, 1 individual, 250g	17
British Steak Pie, 1 individual, 250g	18
Broccoli & Mushroom Quiche, 1 serving, 90g	5
Broccoli & Tomato Quiche, 1 serving, 100g	6
Cheese & Onion Pasty, 1 individual, 150g	12
Cheese & Onion Quiche, 100g	8
Cheese & Onion Slices, 1 individual, 165g	14
Cheese & Vegetable Lattice, ⅓ pack, 127g	9
Cheese & Bacon Crispbakes, 1 individual, 90g	6
Cheese & Bacon Quiche, 1 serving, 100g	7
Chicken & Mushroom Slices, 1 individual, 165g	14
Chicken & Sweetcorn Slices, 1 individual, 105g	8
Chicken & Mushroom Pie, 1 individual, 150g	11
Chicken Curry Pie, 1 individual, 150g	12
Cornish Pasties, 1 individual, 150g	15
Crustless Cheese & Bacon Quiche, 1 serving, 85g	5
Deep Fill Bacon, Cheese & Onion Quiche, 1 serving, 100g	7
Deep Fill Goat's Cheese & Pepper Quiche, 1 serving, 100g	7
Deep Fill Puff Steak & Ale Pie, 1 serving, 183g	12
Deep Fill Tomato, Mozzarella Quiche, 1 serving, 100g	6
Deep Fill Vintage Cheddar Quiche, 1 serving, 100g	8
Extra Large Crispy Bake Pork Pie, 1 serving, 98g	10
Extra Large Melton Mowbray Pork Pie, 1 serving, 99g	9
Family Minced Steak & Onion Pie, 1 serving, 167g	12
Family Sausage & Onion Pie, 1 serving, 167g	12
Family Shortcrust Pastry Steak Pie, 1 serving, 200g	14
Giant Pasty, 1 individual, 210g	18
Ham Hock, Apple & Cider Dorset Pie, 1 individual, 280g	21
Hand Crimped Steak Pasty, 1 individual, 200g	14
Individual Cheese & Onion Quiche, 1 individual, 175g	14
Individual Quiche Lorraine, 1 individual, 175g	12
Large Crispy Bake Pork Pie, 1 serving, 110g	11
Medium Melton Mowbray Pork Pie, 1 serving, 140g	14
Minced Beef & Onion Pie, 1 (150g)	14
Minced Steak & Onion Slices, 1 individual, 165g	13

Mini Beef Casserole & Dumpling, 1 pack, 250g	**10**
Mini Cornish Pasty, 1 individual, 70g	**7**
Mini Egg & Bacon Savoury Bites, 1 individual, 18g	**1**
Mini Melton Mowbray Pork Pies, 1 individual, 50g	**5**
Mini Pork Pies with Mustard & Honey, 1 individual, 50g	**5**
Mini Pork, Pickle & Cheese Pies, 1 individual, 50g	**5**
Mini Savoury Eggs, 1 individual, 20g	**2**
Oaktree Estate Quiche Lorraine, 1 serving, 100g	**7**
Pork & Egg Gala Pie, 1 serving, 113g	**11**
Pork & Egg Gala Slices, 1 individual, 125g	**11**
Pork & Egg Loaf, 1 slice, 21g	**1**
Pork & Caramelised Onion Pie, 1 serving, 133g	**13**
Pork & Chicken Layer Pie, 1 serving, 133g	**12**
Pork & Pâté Pie with Cranberry & Port Jelly, 1 serving, 83g	**10**
Pork & Pickle Mini Pork Pies, 1 individual, 50g	**5**
Puff Pastry Chicken & Asparagus Lattice, 1 serving, 133g	**11**
Puff Pastry Chicken & Bacon Lattice Pie, 1 serving, 138g	**10**
Puff Pastry Chicken & Broccoli Pie, 1 individual, 200g	**14**
Puff Pastry Chicken Pie, 1 individual, 200g	**13**
Puff Pastry Chilli Beef Pie, 1 individual, 200g	**17**
Puff Pastry Deep Fill Chicken & Mushroom Pie, 1 serving, 183g	**12**
Puff Pastry Deep Fill Ham Hock & Leek Pie, 1 serving, 183g	**12**
Puff Pastry Deep Fill Lamb Hot Pot Pie, 1 serving 183g	**12**
Puff Pastry Deep Fill Roast Chicken Pie, 1 serving, 183g	**12**
Puff Pastry Deep Fill Steak & Mushroom Pie, 1 serving, 183g	**12**
Puff Pastry Steak Pie, 1 individual, 200g	**14**
Quiche Lorraine, 1 serving, 100g	**7**
Roast Chicken & White Wine Dorset Pie, 1 individual, 280g	**20**
Roast Chicken Pie, 1 pack, 450g	**10**
Sausage & Bean Lattice, ⅓ pack, 127g	**12**
Scotch Egg, 1 (114g)	**7**
Shortcrust Pastry Chicken & Gravy Pie, 1 serving, 183g	**15**
Shortcrust Pastry Chicken Curry Pie, 1 individual, 235g	**18**
Shortcrust Pastry Minced Steak & Onion Pie, 1 serving, 183g	**16**

Shortcrust Pastry Steak & Kidney Pie, 1 serving, 183g	**13**
Shortcrust Pastry Steak Pie, 1 serving, 183g	**13**
Small Melton Mowbray Pork Pie, 1 (145g)	**15**
Snack Crispybake Pork Pies, 1 individual, 65g	**7**
Snack Melton Mowbray Pork Pies, 1 individual, 75g	**8**
Snack Pork & Pickle Pies, 1 individual, 75g	**7**
Snack Savoury Eggs, 1 individual, 45g	**3**
Spinach Ricotta & Sundried Tomato Filo Tartlets, 1 individual, 135g	**10**
Steak & Kidney Pie, 1 individual, 150g	**12**
Steak & Kidney Pudding, 1 individual, 190g	**12**
Steak Pies, 1 individual, 150g	**12**
Stilton, Bacon & Pear Quiche, 1 serving, 100g	**8**
Three Cheese Quiche, 1 serving, 90g	**6**
Uncured Pork, Red Leicester Cheese & Pickle Pie, 1 serving, 133g	**12**
Walkers Fluted Pork Pie, 1 serving, 110g	**11**
Walkers Pork Pie, 1 serving, 133g	**12**

Tesco – Light Choices

Chicken & Broccoli Pie, 1 pack, 450g	**10**
Chicken & Gravy Pie, 1 pack, 450g	**11**
Crustless Green Vegetable Quiche, 1 tart, 160g	**6**
Crustless Quiche Lorraine, 1 tart, 160g	**7**
Quiche Lorraine, 1 serving, 100g	**5**

Tesco – Finest

Chicken, Leek & Bacon Filo Pie, 1 pack, 225g	**15**
Gruyere Pancetta Onion Tart, 1 serving, 106g	**9**
Mini Melton Mowbray Pork Pies, 1 individual, 50g	**6**
Pumpkin & Goat's Cheese Filo Tarts, 1 individual, 160g	**9**
Roasted Vegetable Tart, 1 serving, 113g	**6**
Scotch Steak Pie 150g, 1 individual, 150g	**10**
Scotch Steak Pie 250g, 1 individual, 250g	**18**
Smoked Haddock & Prawn Filo Pies, 1 individual, 210g	**13**

The Co-operative

Cheese & Tomato Quiche, ¼ large tart, 88g	**6**
Chicken & Mushroom Pie, 1 pie, 150g	**11**
Chicken & Mushroom Slices, 1 slice, 165g	**11**
Minced Beef & Onion Slices, 1 slice, 165g	**13**
Mini Sausage Rolls, 1 roll, 15g	**1**

Vale of Mowbray

Family Pork Pie, 1 serving, 109g	**11**
Pork Pies, 1 (85g)	**10**

Waitrose

Asparagus, Broccoli & Mange Tout Tarts, 1 tart, 150g	**10**
Bacon & Gruyère Quiche, 1 tart, 170g	**12**
Bacon, Brie & Cranberry Tarte, ¼ pack, 100g	**9**
Bacon, Leek & Roquefort Tarte, ¼ pack, 100g	**9**
Balsamic Onion & Somerset Cheddar Tarte, ¼ pack, 100g	**9**
Bean & Tomato Cumberland Pie, 1 pie, 400g	**7**
Broccoli & Gruyère Quiche, ¼ tart, 100g	**7**
Buttered Leek Quiche, ¼ tart, 100g	**7**
Butternut Squash & Cherry Tomato Tarts, 1 tart, 150g	**8**
Butternut Squash Tarte, ¼ pack, 100g	**7**
Cooked Cocktail Sausages, 1 pack, 100g	**9**
Cumberland Sausage Rolls, 1 (35g)	**3**
Cumberland Sausage Scotch Eggs, 1 (114g)	**7**
Deep Filled Pork & Bramley Apple Sausage Roll, 1 (115g)	**8**
Deep Filled Pork Sausage Roll, 1 (115g)	**12**
Extra Mature Cheddar & Onion Quiche, ¼ tart, 100g	**7**
Ham & Emmental Savoury Slices, ¼ pack, 100g	**8**
Hand Crimped Cheddar & Onion Pasty, 1 (200g)	**15**
Hand Crimped Cornish Pasty, 1 (200g)	**15**
Hand Crimped Steak & Stilton Pasty, 1 (200g)	**16**
Hand Crimped Vegetable Pasty, 1 (200g)	**13**
Jumbo Sausage Roll, 1 (145g)	**14**
Melton Mowbray Mini Pork Pies, 1 (50g)	**6**
Melton Mowbray Pork Pies, 1 (75g)	**7**
Mini Chorizo Picnic Eggs, 1 (20g)	**2**
Mini Cornish Pasties, 1 (75g)	**6**
Mini Cumberland Picnic Eggs, 1 (20g)	**2**
Pork & Mustard with Crumb Topping, ½ pack, 150g	**16**
Pork Pie, 1 (140g)	**15**
Quiche Lorraine, 1 tart, 170g	**10**
Pepper Tarte, ¼ tarte, 100g	**7**
Salmon & Watercress Tartlet, 1 (130g)	**9**
Sausage Rolls, 1 (35g)	**3**
Sausage Rolls, 1 (75g)	**7**
Sautéed Mushroom Quiche, ¼ tart, 100g	**6**
Slow Roast Tomato & Brie Tartlets, ½ pack, 130g	**9**
Spinach & Ricotta Quiche, ¼ tart, 100g	**7**
Spinach Tarte, ¼ tarte, 100g	**7**
Steak & Mushroom Pie, ¼ pie, 170g	**13**
Stilton & Pear Chutney Tartlets, 1 pack, 260g	**21**
Wild Mushroom & Bacon Tartlets, 1 pack, 260g	**18**
Wiltshire Ham, Tomato & Cheddar Quiche, ¼ tart, 100g	**6**

Wall's

Classic Cornish Pasty, 1 (240g)	**18**
Classic Scotch Egg, 1 (105g)	**8**
Individual Pork & Pickle Pie, 1 pie, 130g	**13**
Individual Pork Pie, 1 (130g)	**15**
Snack Pork Pies, 1 (65g)	**7**
The Finest Cuts Classic Sausage Roll, 1 (140g)	**14**

Weight Watchers

Bacon, Leek & Cheese Quiche, 1 (165g)	**9**
Cheese & Onion Crustless Quiche, 1 (160g)	**7**
Mediterranean Vegetable Crustless Quiche, 1 (160g)	**7**
Quiche Lorraine, 1 (165g)	**9**

Frozen Foods

ProPoints value

Basic Foods

Chips, microwave, 1 small box, 100g	6
Chips, straight cut, fried in oil, 1 small portion, 100g	8
Chips, thick cut, oven baked, 1 small portion, 100g	5
Chips, thick cut, oven baked, low fat, 1 small portion, 100g	4
Choc Ice, 1 (50g)	4
Fish Finger, Cod, grilled, 1 (28g)	2
Ice Cream, flavoured, 1 scoop, 60g	4
Ice Cream, vanilla, 1 scoop, 60g	3
Ice Cream, low fat, 1 scoop, 60g	2
Lemon Sorbet, 1 scoop, 60g	1
Peas, 1 serving, 80g	2
Peas, Petits Pois, 2 heaped tablespoons, 70g	1
Scampi in Breadcrumbs, deep fried, 1 medium portion, 100g	7
Summer Fruits Mix, no added sugar, ¼ pack, 125g	0
Turkey, Escalope in Breadcrumbs, 1 medium, 145g	9

Breads

Asda

Cheesy Garlic Pizza Bread, ½ pack, 105g	11
Deep Pan Garlic Bread, 9 inch, ½ pack, 74g	6
Garlic & Cheese Pizza Bread, ¼ pack, 75g	6
Good for You Garlic Baguettes, ¼ baguette, 48g	5

Iceland

Garlic Baguettes, ⅓ baguette, 56g	6

The Co-operative

Garlic Baguettes, ¼ baguette, 40g	4
Garlic Pizza Bread, ½ pizza, 120g	10
Garlic Slices, 1 slice, 28g	2
Reduced Fat Garlic Baguettes, ½ baguette, 80g	6

ProPoints value

Desserts, Fruit & Sweet Pies

Asda

Banoffee Pie, 1 individual, 135g	10
Black Forest Gâteau, 1 serving, 75g	4
Bramley Apple & Blackberry Pie, ⅙ pie, 112g	8
Bramley Apple Crumble, ½ pudding, 200g	14
Bramley Apple Pie, ¼ pie, 106g	9
Caramel Crunch Dessert, 1 pot, 95g	8
Chocolate Brownie Dessert, ⅙ individual, 64g	5
Chocolate Sponge Pudding, ¼ family pack, 104g	9
Dessert Mandarin, ½ serving, 100g	6
Double Chocolate Gâteau, ⅒ cake, 60g	5
Family Apple Pie, ⅙ pie, 117g	9
Ice Cream Rolls, 1 individual, 42g	2
Lemon Meringue Pie, ¼ pie, 119g	9
Lemon Tart, 1 portion (⅙ tart), 58g	5
Milk Choc Moments, 1 serving, 83g	7
Mini Jam Doughnuts, 1 individual, 25g	3
New York Style Vanilla Cheesecake, 1 serving, 70g	7
Raspberry Pavlova, 1 slice, 53g	3
Rhubarb Crumble, ⅓ pack, 167g	11
Rocky Road Dessert, 1 pot, 75g	6
Spotted Dick Puddings with Custard, 1 serving, 130g	8
Sticky Toffee Pudding, ¼ family pack, 104g	9
Strawberry Cheesecake, 1 slice, 86g	6
Strawberry Gâteau, ⅒ cake, 63g	3
Syrup Sponge Pudding, ¼ family pack, 104g	10

Asda – Chosen by You

Black Forest Gâteau, 1 serving (⅒ pack), 63g	4
Bread & Butter Pudding, ¼ family pack, 104g	5
Jam Roly Poly, ⅕ pack, 60g	11
Sponge Puddings with Raspberry Jam & Custard, ½ individual, 130g	9
Sticky Toffee Puddings, 1 individual, 110g	10
Syrup Sponge Pudding, ¼ family pack, 104g	10

Asda – Extra Special

Banoffee Pie, 1 slice, 87g	9
Belgian Chocolate Meringue Stack, ⅙ cake, 83g	9
Belgian Chocolate Meringue Stack, 1 serving, 78g	8
Chocolate Profiteroles, 1 pack of 2, 100g	11
Chocolate Profiteroles, 1 funsize, 15g	2

Hand-Rolled Raspberry Roulade, 1 slice, 75g	6
Hand-Rolled Toffee & Pecan Roulade, 1 slice, 70g	7
Jam Roly Poly, ¼ family pack, 104g	7
Jam Roly Poly, ½ pack, 150g	10
Raspberry Meringue Roulade, ⅙ serving, 77g	6
Scottish Raspberry Tart, ⅛ tart, 69g	5
Special Strawberry & Clotted Cream Brûlée Cheesecake, 1 slice, 83g	8
Strawberry & Champagne Russe, 1 serving, 77g	4
Summerfruit Pannacotta, ⅙ dessert, 113g	8
Tarte au Citron, 1 serving, 75g	6
Tarte aux Framboises, ⅛ pack, 69g	4
Tiramisu Ice Cream Dessert, 1 serving, 162g	9
Wild Blueberry & Almond Tart, ⅛ tart, 63g	6

Asda – Good For You

Mandarin Cheesecake, ⅙ cake, 92g	5
Summerfruits Cheesecake, ⅙ cake, 94g	5

Aunt Bessie's

Apple Crumble, ¼ pack, 138g	8
Bramley Apple & Blackberry Pie, 1 serving, 137g	10
Fruit Scones, Ready to Bake, 1 (70g)	7
Jam Roly Poly, 1 slice, 75g	8
Morello Cherry Pie, ¼ pie, 138g	10
Spotted Dick, 1 serving, 75g	8
Summer Fruits Lattice Tart, 1 slice, 120g	9

Iceland

Apple Crumble, ¼ crumble, 125g	6
Chocolate Fudge Sensation Cake, ⅙ cake, 75g	8
Chocolate Gâteau, ⅙ gâteau, 61g	4
Chocolate Strawberries, 3 (26g)	2
Custard Slices, 1 slice, 40g	4
Jam Doughnuts, 1 (49g)	4
Strawberry Cheesecake, ⅙ cheesecake, 90g	6
Sticky Toffee Cheesecake, ⅙ cheesecake, 76g	6

Sainsbury's

Blackcurrant Cheesecake, 1 slice, 85g	6
Profiteroles with Chocolate Sauce, 1 serving, 80g	7

The Co-operative

Country Store Mixed Fruit, 1 serving, 80g	1
Blackcurrant Cheesecake, 1 serving (⅙ cake), 78g	7
Finest Toffee Pecan Meringue Roulade, 1 serving, 60g	5
Finest Banoffi Tart, 1 serving (⅙ tart), 87g	8

The Co-operative

Apple Pie, ¼ pie, 106g	8
Belgian Chocolate Eclairs, 1 (22g)	3
Blackforest Gâteau, ⅙ cake, 102g	7
Mandarin Cheesecake, ⅙ cake, 94g	7
Raspberry Pavlova, ⅙ cake, 52g	4
Rhubarb Crumble, ½ pack, 200g	14
Strawberry Splits, 1 (73ml)	2
Summer Fruits, ¼ pack, 112g	1
Toffee Pavlova, ⅙ dessert, 50g	5
Truly Irresistible Red Berry Roulade, ⅙ dessert, 78g	7

Waitrose

Apple & Blackberry Crumble, ⅓ crumble, 139g	8
Apple & Blackberry Pie, 1 slice, 71g	5
Apple Pie, ¼ pie, 175g	12
Black Cherry & Almond Frangipan, ⅙ pack, 64g	6
Black Forest Gâteau, ⅛ cake, 84g	8
Caramel & Vanilla Cheesecake, ⅙ cake, 95g	9
Caramel Surprise, 1 pot, 150g	8
Chocolate & Vanilla Cheesecake, ⅙ cake, 95g	11
Chocolate Delice, ⅙ pack, 87g	7
Chocolate Gâteau, ⅛ cake, 79g	7
Chocolate Pavlova, ¼ pack, 80g	9
Chocolate Sundae, 1 pot, 140g	12
Cinnamon Apple Pie, ¼ pie, 106g	8
Dark Chocolate & Fig Tart, ⅛ tart, 62g	6
Gooseberry Crumble, ¼ crumble, 98g	7
Lemon & Berry Cheesecake, ⅙ cake, 100g	8
Marbled Chocolate Fondant Torte, ⅙ pack, 68g	7
Milk Chocolate Cheesecake, ⅙ cake, 87g	8
Mixed Berry & Sicilian Lemon Gâteau, ⅛ cake, 80g	6
Raspberry & Hazelnut Truffle Torte, ⅙ pack, 75g	5
Sticky Toffee Pudding, 1 pudding, 90g	8
Strawberries & Cream Cheesecake, ⅛ cake, 69g	4
Tarte au Chocolat, ⅛ tart, 62g	6
Tarte au Citron Meringuée, ⅙ tart, 90g	8
Tarte aux Myrtilles, ⅛ tart, 62g	5
Tarte aux Poires, ⅛ tart, 69g	5
Tarte aux Pommes Normande, ⅙ tart, 133g	10
Tiramisu, ⅙ pack, 85g	6
White Chocolate & Amaretto Ganache, ¼ pack, 150g	17

Weight Watchers from Heinz

Banoffee Dessert, 1 (80g)	5
Caramel Crunch Desserts, 1 (89g)	5

Chocolate Mint Tortes, 1 (88g)	**5**
Chocolate Mousse Cake, 1 (75g)	**4**
Chocolate Top Dessert, 1 (75g)	**5**
Creamy Lemon Cheesecake, 1 (98g)	**5**
Creamy Strawberry Cheesecake, 1 (110g)	**5**
Double Chocolate Brownie, 1 (86g)	**4**
Double Chocolate Sponge Pudding, 1 (75g)	**5**
Lemon Meringue Desserts, 1 (85g)	**4**
Mandarin Cheesecake, 1 (102g)	**5**
Mint & Chocolate Sundae, 1 pot, 82g	**3**
Mint Choc Top Dessert, 1 (75g)	**5**
Taste temptations Belgian Éclair, 1 (30g)	**2**
Taste Temptations Chocolate Profiteroles Desserts, 1 (88g)	**5**
Taste Temptations Triple Chocolate Delight, 1 (110g)	**5**
Toffee Apple Crumble, 1 (98g)	**5**
Vanilla Raspberry Pannacotta, 1 (122g)	**5**

Fish & Seafood

Asda

Battered Cod Fillets, 1 serving, 125g	**7**
Battered Haddock Fillets, 1 serving, 125g	**7**
Breaded Cod Fillet, 1 serving, 130g	**7**
Breaded Haddock Fillet, 1 fillet, 128g	**7**
Chunky Breaded Cod Fillets, 1 fillet, 125g	**6**
Cod & Bacon Encroute, 1 serving, 160g	**12**
Cod Fillet Fish Fingers, 1 serving, 30g	**2**
Family Salmon with Dill Encroute, 1 serving, 175g	**11**
Fish Cakes, 1 individual, 50g	**3**
King Prawns in Filo Pastry, 1 serving, 100g	**5**
Mini Classics Fish Pie, 1 pack, 300g	**8**
Salmon & Prawn Encroute, 1 serving, 160g	**11**

Asda – Chosen by You

Battered Chunky 100% Haddock Fillets, 1 fillet, 125g	**6**
Breaded Chunky 100% Cod Fillets, 1 fillet, 125g	**6**
Breaded Wholetail Scampi, 1 portion (¼ pack), 70g	**4**
Omega 3 Fish Fingers, 3 fingers, 84g	**5**

Birds Eye

100% Cod Fillet Fish Fingers, 1 (30g)	**2**
100% Fillet Fish Fingers Minis, 1 (17g)	**1**
100% Haddock Fillet Fish Fingers, 1 (28g)	**2**
Cajun Chicken Fillet Burgers, 1 (92g)	**4**
Chunky Wild Pink Salmon Fillets with a Lemon & Herb Butter Sauce, 1 (140g)	**5**
Cod Cakes in Crunch Crumb, 1 (50g)	**2**
Cod Fillets in Light Golden Breadcrumbs, 1 (112g)	**5**
Cod Fillets with a Fresh Parsley Butter Sauce, 1 (140g)	**5**
Cod Steaks in a Butter Sauce, 1 portion, 170g	**5**
Cod Steaks in a Parsley Sauce, 1 portion, 170g	**4**
Crispy Batter Cod Fillet Fish Finger, 1 (30g)	**2**
Extra Large Fish Fillets in Crunchy Crumbs, 1 (160g)	**9**
Fish Bake with Mixed Vegetables, 1 portion, 191g	**5**
Fish Fillets in Crispy Batter, 1 (100g)	**6**
Fish Fillets in Crunchy Breadcrumbs, 1 (100g)	**6**
Fish Fingers in a Crispy Batter, 1 (30g)	**2**
Fish Finger Megas, 1 serving, 110g	**6**
Haddock Fillet Fish Fingers, 1 (30g)	**1**
Haddock Fillets in Light Golden Breadcrumbs, 1 (112g)	**6**
Large Cod Fillets in a Light & Crispy Batter, 1 (120g)	**7**
Large Cod Fillets in Crunchy Golden Breadcrumbs, 1 (120g)	**6**
Large Haddock Fillets in a Light & Crispy Batter, 1 (120g)	**7**
Large Haddock Fillets in Crunchy Golden Breadcrumbs, 1 (120g)	**6**
Omega 3 Fish Steaks in a Butter Sauce, 1 (150g)	**4**
Salmon Fish Fingers, 1 (80g)	**5**
Simply Cod Fillets Light & Crispy Batter, 1 (112g)	**6**
Simply Cod Fillets Light Crunch Crumb, 1 (119g)	**6**
Simply Haddock Fillets in Light & Crispy Batter, 1 (112g)	**6**
Simply Haddock Fillets Light Crunch Crumb, 1 (109g)	**6**
Simply Salmon Lightly Seasoned Garlic & Herb Fillets, 1 (112g)	**5**
Simply Wholetail Scampi, 1 piece, 123g	**7**
Value Fish Fingers, 1 (25g)	**1**

Iceland

Battered Cod Fillets, 1 (103g)	**6**
Breaded Fish Fingers, 4 fingers, 89g	**5**
Cod Fishcakes, 1 (37g)	**2**
Cooked & Peeled King Prawns, 1 pack, 375g	**5**
Filo Prawns, 1 pack, 140g	**8**

Lyons

Batter Crisp Calamari, ¼ pack, 112g	6
Prawn Pockets, ¼ pack, 138g	4
Smoked Salmon Canapés, 1 pack, 100g	6

Ross

Battered Cod Portions, 1 portion, 81g	5
Battered Fish, 1 portion, 86g	5
Battered Haddock Portions, 1 portion, 84g	5
Fish Cakes, 1 portion, 43g	2
Fish Cakes in Golden Breadcrumbs, 1 portion, 84g	4
Fish Fingers, 1 portion, 24g	1
Fish Pie, 1 pie, 318g	8

The Co-operative

Battered Fish Portions, 1 portion, 100g	5
Breaded Chilli Butterfly Prawns, 1 (12g)	1
Breaded Scampi, ½ pack, 162g	10
Fish Cakes, 1 (50g)	2
King Prawn Ring with Sweet Chilli Sauce, 1 pack, 175g	1
Lightly Dusted Haddock Fillets, 1 fillet, 130g	5
Lightly Dusted Yellow-Fin Sole Fillets, 1 fillet, 120g	5
Salmon Bites, 1 (20g)	2
Scottish Kipper Fillets with Butter, ½ pack, 85g	5
Smoked Haddock Fillets with Butter, 1 fillet, 170g	4

Waitrose

Breaded Chunky Cod Fillets, 1 pack, 198g	9
Chunky Battered Haddock Fingers, 1 finger, 75g	4
Chunky Breaded Cod Fingers, 1 finger, 67g	4
Cod Fillet Fish Fingers, 1 finger, 30g	2
Large Madagascan Crevettes, 1 pack, 300g	8
Salmon en Croute, 1 (200g)	14
Smoked Haddock Fish Cakes, 1 (115g)	5
Wild Salmon & Seafood Medley, ½ pack, 200g	5

Whitby Seafoods

Breaded Fillet Goujons, 1 serving, 133g	9
Breaded Scampi, ½ serving, 125g	9
Salmon with Lemon & Dill Fish Cakes in Crispy Breadcrumbs, 1 serving, 71g	3
Smoked Haddock & Spring Onion Fish Cakes in Crispy Breadcrumbs, 1 serving, 79g	4

Young's

Admiral's Pie, 1 pack, 340g	9

Basa Fillets in Lemon & Herb Tempura Batter, 1 (160g)	7
Chunky Battered Wild Alaskan Pollock Fillets, 1 (140g)	7
Chunky Breaded Fish Fillets Omega 3, 1 (100g)	5
Chunky Fish Fillet Nuggets, 1 portion, 70g	4
Chunky Haddock Fillets in a Butter Sauce, 1 (140g)	3
Cod Cakes, 1 (50g)	2
Cod Steaks in Butter Sauce, ¼ pack, 140g	3
Famous Fish Pie, 1 pack, 350g	10
Fish & Chips, 1 pack, 300g	12
Fish & Vegetable Pie, 1 pack, 360g	12
Fish Cakes in a Crisp Bubbly Batter, 1 (50g)	3
Fish Fingers & Chips, 1 pack, 300g	11
Fish Pie with Butter Sauce, ¼ pack, 194g	5
Fish Pie with Parsley Sauce, ¼ pack, 194g	6
Fish Steaks in Butter Sauce, 1 pack, 100g	2
Fisherman's Crumble, 1 pack, 340g	10
Fisherman's Pie, 1 pack, 340g	9
Great Grimsby Cod Fillet Fish Fingers, 1 serving, 50g	2
Haddock Fillets in a Mornay Sauce, 1 (140g)	3
Jumbo Specials Extra Large Beer Batter Fish Fillets, 1 (165g)	10
Jumbo Specials Extra Large Fish Fillets in a Crispy Bubbly Batter, 1 (105g)	6
Jumbo Specials Extra Large Haddock Fillets, 1 (190g)	11
Jumbo Specials Extra Large Sea Salt & Malt Vinegar Fish Fillets, 1 (165g)	10
Kipper Fillets with Butter, ½ pack, 100g	7
Low Fat Ocean Crumble, 1 pack, 300g	7
Mariner's Pie, 1 pack, 340g	10
Micro Fish Fingers, 1 portion, 100g	6
Naturally Delicious Fish Chunky Haddock Fillets in Signature Breadcrumbs, 1 (105g)	6
Ocean Pie, 1 pack, 300g	8
Premium Wholetail Scampi with a Hint of Lemon, ½ pack, 125g	7
Salmon & Broccoli Pie, 1 pack, 360g	13
Salmon Crumble, 1 pack, 320g	9
Salmon Pie, 1 pie, 375g	12
Seafood Dippers, 1 (14g)	1
Smoked Fish En Croute, ½ pack, 170g	14
Smoked Haddock Fish Cakes, 1 (115g)	5
The Original Ocean Pie, 1 pack, 400g	11
Vintage Cheddar Fish Bake with Ciabatta Crumb, ½ pack, 175g	5
Wild Alaskan Salmon En Croute, 1 (170g)	12

Fish & Seafood Frozen Foods

Ice Cream

Asda

Belgian Milk or White Chocolate Moments, 1 (83g)	7
Belgian Mint Chocolate Moments, 1 (87g)	7
Blackcurrant Ice Lolly, 1 individual, 81g	2
Chocolate & Nut Cones, 1 individual, 67g	5
Chocolate Ice Cream, 1 serving, 140ml	4
Chocolate Soft Scoop, 1 scoop, 60g	3
Coffee Ice Cream, 1 serving, 100ml	4
Cornish Soft Scoop, 1 scoop, 50g	3
Creamy Summerfruit Cheesecake Dairy Ice Cream, 1 serving, 91g	3
Dark Choc Ices, 1 individual, 42g	4
Double Chocolate Ice Cream, 1 scoop, 60ml	3
Milk Choc Ices, 1 individual, 41g	4
Milk Chocolate Moments, 1 pack, 100ml	9
Mint Choc Chip Cones, 1 individual, 67g	5
Mint Choc Chip Flavour Soft Scoop, 1 scoop, 45g	2
Mint Ice Cream, 1 scoop, 60ml	3
Neapolitan Soft Scoop, 1 scoop, 44g	2
Orange Ice Lolly, 1 individual, 81g	2
Raspberry Pavlova Ice Cream, 1 serving, 100ml	5
Raspberry Ripple Screwball, 1 individual, 54g	3
Raspberry Ripple Soft Scoop, 1 scoop, 46g	2
Really Creamy Raspberry Pavlova Dairy Ice Cream, 1 scoop, 57g	3
Really Creamy Triple Chocolate Dairy Ice Cream, 1 scoop, 53g	3
Rocket Lolly, 1 individual, 58ml	1
Strawberries & Cream Ice Cream, 1 serving, 176g	5
Strawberry & Vanilla Cone, 1 individual, 68g	5
Strawberry Easy Scoop, 1 serving, 100ml	4
Strawberry Ice Cream Dessert, 1 serving, 140g	4
Toffee & Vanilla Cone, 1 individual, 68g	5
Toffee Ice Cream, 1 serving, 100ml	5
Vanilla & Toffee Ice Cream Dessert, 1 serving, 139g	4
Vanilla Ice Cream, 1 scoop, 60ml	3
Vanilla Soft Scoop, 1 scoop, 44g	2
White Chocolate Moments, 1 serving, 100ml	9

Asda – Extra Special

Belgian Chocolate & Vanilla Mini Cones, 1 individual, 25g	2
Caramel Butterscotch Crunch Ice Cream, 1 serving, 76g	5
Chocolate Fudge Brownie, 1 scoop, 65g	4
Chocolate Ice Cream Swirl, 1 serving, 126g	4
Cookies & Cream Ice Cream, 1 serving, 65g	4
Ice Cream Fondue, 1 scoop, 50g	3
Madagascan Vanilla Ice Cream Chocolates, 1 serving, 20g	1
Raspberry Pannacotta Ice Cream, 1 serving, 65g	4
Rocky Road, 1 scoop, 64g	4
Rum & Raisin Ice Cream, 1 serving, 65g	4
Strawberry Cheesecake Ice Cream, 1 scoop, 65g	4
Tiramisu Ice Cream, 1 serving, 64g	3
Vanilla Clotted Cream Ice Cream, 1 serving, 69g	4

Asda – Good For You

Chocolate & Vanilla Cones, 1 (68g)	4
Vanilla Dairy Ice Cream, 1 scoop, 52g	2
Vanilla Soft Scoop, 1 scoop, 48g	1

Beechdean

Dairy Ice Cream Vanilla, 1 portion, 100g	6

Ben & Jerry's

Baked Alaska, 1 scoop, 60g	4
Cherry Garcia Frozen Yogurt, 1 scoop, 60g	3
Chocolate Fudge Brownie Frozen Yogurt, 1 scoop, 60g	3
Cookie Dough Ice Cream, 1 scoop, 60g	4
Dublin Mudslide, 1 scoop, 60g	4
Fairtrade Vanilla Toffee Crunch, 1 scoop, 60g	5
Fossil Fuel Ice Cream, 1 scoop, 60g	5
Jamaican Me Crazy Sorbet, 1 scoop, 60g	2
Mango Berry Swirl Sorbet, 1 scoop, 60g	2
Minter Wonderland Ice Cream, 1 portion, 100ml	7
Oh My! Apple Pie!, 1 portion, 100ml	7
Peace of Cake Ice Cream, 1 portion, 100ml	7
Phish Food Frozen Yogurt, 1 scoop, 60g	4
Phish Food Low Fat Frozen Yogurt, 1 scoop, 60g	4
Strawberry Cheesecake Frozen Yogurt, 1 scoop, 60g	3

Häagen-Dazs

Baileys Original Irish Cream Ice Cream, 1 portion, 100ml	6

Banoffee Ice Cream, 1 portion, 100ml	6
Belgian Chocolate Ice Cream, 1 portion, 100ml	8
Choc Choc Chip Ice Cream, 1 portion, 100ml	7
Chocolate Midnight Cookies, 1 portion, 100ml	7
Cookie Dough Chip, 1 portion, 100ml	7
Cookies & Cream Ice Cream, 1 portion, 100ml	6
Dulce de Leche Ice Cream, 1 portion, 100ml	7
Ice Cream Smoothie Mango & Apricot, ¼ tub, 125ml	5
Ice Cream Smoothie Raspberry & Summer Berries, ¼ tub, 125ml	5
Pralines & Cream Ice Cream, 1 portion, 100ml	7
Strawberry Cheesecake Ice Cream, 1 portion, 100ml	7
Summer Berries & Cream, 1 portion, 100ml	6
Tiramisu Ice Cream, 1 portion, 100ml	7

Iceland

Belgian Chocolate Majestics, 1 (120ml)	6
Choc & Nut Cones, 1 (110ml)	5

Lyons Maid

Vanilla & Chocolate Ice Cream Sandwich Bars, 1 portion, 95ml	4
Vanilla Flavour Ice Cream Block, 1 portion, 125ml	2

Mars

Bounty Ice Cream, 1 standard, 59ml	5
Bounty Milk Ice Cream, 1 large, 100ml	8
Galaxy Caramel Swirl Ice Cream, 1 stick, 100ml	8
Galaxy Ice Cream Bar, Vanilla, 1 from multipack, 54ml	5
Galaxy Triple Choc Ice Cream, 1 portion, 125ml	6
Maltesers Ice Cream, ¼ tub, 125ml	5
Maltesers Ice Cream Bar, White, 1 from multipack, 45ml	3
Maltesers Ice Cream Bar, Milk, 1 from multipack, 54ml	4
Mars Ice Cream, 1 from multipack, 59ml	5
Mars Ice Cream, ¼ tub, 125ml	6
Mars Midnight Ice Cream, 1 from multipack, 59ml	5
Snickers Ice Cream Bar, 1 single, 63ml	6
Twix Ice Cream, 1 scoop, 120ml	11

Nestlé

After 8 Dessert, 1 portion, 100ml	4
After Eight, 1 stick, 100ml	8
After Eight Ice Cream Cones, 1 (90ml)	4
Cheesecake, 1 portion, 115ml	7
Fab, 1 (58ml)	2

Fab Ice Cream Cone, 1 (100ml)	5
Lion Ice Cream Bars, 1 (60ml)	5
Milkybar Ice Cream, 1 portion, 100ml	4
Mint Crisp Lolly, 1 (75ml)	6
Munchies Ice Cream Bars, 1 (60ml)	5
Nesquik Ice Cream, 1 portion, 100ml	3
Nestlé Ice Cream Rolo, 1 portion, 100ml	4
Rowntree's Fruit Pastilles Lollies, 1 (65ml)	2
Smarties Ice Cream Cone, 1 (90ml)	5
Smarties Pop Up with Mini Smarties, 1 (90ml)	3
Strawberry & Cream Mivvi Ice Cream, 1 (90ml)	3
Toffee Crisp Ice Cream, 1 (60ml)	4
Toffee Crumble Cones, 1 (100ml)	5

Sainsbury's

Café Latte Indulgence, 1 stick, 100ml	6
Cornish Dairy Ice Cream with Clotted Cream, 1 portion, 85g	3
Cornish Ice Cream Vanilla Flavour, 1 portion, 85g	4
Dark Choc Ices, 1 (80ml)	7
Milk Choc Ices, 1 (70ml)	6
Rocket Ice Lolly, 1 (58ml)	1
Soft Scoop Chocolate Ice Cream, 1 portion, 85g	4
Soft Scoop Dairy Vanilla Ice Cream, 1 scoop, 75g	3
Soft Scoop Neapolitan Ice Cream, 1 portion, 85g	4
Soft Scoop Raspberry Ripple Ice Cream, 1 scoop, 75g	3

Sainsbury's – Taste the Difference

Devon Farmhouse Coffee Dairy Ice Cream, ¼ tub, 125ml	8
Devon Farmhouse Rum & Raisin Dairy Ice Cream, ¼ tub, 125ml	8
Devon Farmhouse Strawberry & Rhubarb Dairy Ice Cream, ¼ tub, 125ml	6
Devon Farmhouse Vanilla Dairy Ice Cream, ¼ tub, 125ml	8

Tesco

Caramella Ice Cream, 1 scoop, 60g	4
Cherrylicious Ice Cream, 1 scoop, 60g	3
Chewy Caramel Premium Ice Cream, 1 scoop, 60g	4
Chocolate & Vanilla Ice Cream Sundae, 1 individual, 70g	4
Chocolate & Nut Cones, 1 cone, 63g	5
Chocolate Fudge Cake Ice Cream, 1 scoop, 60g	3
Chocolate Ice Cream Dessert, 1 serving, 59g	3

WALL'S

Solero brings you a range of irresistible products, all 90 calories or under, ideal as guilt free treats!

Unilever

Solero

Berry Explosion

with delicious fruit pieces

without artificial
90 KCAL
colours & flavours

Solero

Exotic Explosion

Now with delicious fruit pieces

With a smooth indulgent centre and a gorgeous fruit sorbet coating full of real fruit pieces, **Solero Exotic** and **Berry Explosion** are 90 calories and 1.5g of fat per stick!

Deliciously refreshing, **Solero Fruit Ice** has juicy bits of fruit inside. With less than 0.5g of fat per product, **Pineapple is 55 calories per stick and Orange is 65 calories per stick.**

GREAT VALUE

GREAT VALUE

Solero
fruit ice
3 Pineapple
made with juicy pineapple pieces

No artificial
55 KCAL
colours & flavours

Solero
fruit ice
3 Orange
made with juicy orange pieces

No artificial
65 KCAL
colours & flavours

Chocolate Soft Scoop Ice Cream, 1 scoop, 60g	3
Chocolatino Ice Cream, 1 scoop, 60g	3
Cookies & Cream Ice Cream, 1 scoop, 60g	4
Cornish Ice Cream, 1 scoop, 60g	3
Double Chocolate Choc Ices, 1 individual, 43g	4
Freshly Squeezed Orange Juice Ice Lollies, 1 individual, 80g	2
Healthy Living Chocolate & Vanilla Sundae, 1 individual, 79g	3
Ice Cream Rolls, 1 individual, 50g	3
Jennie's Cornish Ice Cream, 1 scoop, 60g	3
Light Choices Vanilleta Ice Cream, 1 serving, 55g	2
Milk Choc Ices, 1 individual, 43g	4
Mint Choc Chip Soft Scoop Ice Cream, 1 scoop, 60g	3
Mint Cones, 1 cone, 68g	5
Mintillicious Ice Cream, 1 scoop, 60g	4
Mmmm... Milk Chocolate & Almond Ice Cream Lollies, 1 individual, 67g	6
Mmmm... Mint & Chocolate Ice Cream Lollies, 1 individual, 68g	6
Neapolitan Soft Scoop Ice Cream, 1 scoop, 60g	3
Rainbow Fruit Ice Lollies, 1 individual, 40g	1
Raspberry Pavlova Ice Cream, 1 serving, 100g	5
Raspberry Ripple Soft Scoop Ice Cream, 1 scoop, 60g	3
Rocky Road Ice Cream, 1 scoop, 60g	3
Strawberry & Vanilla Cones, 1 individual, 64g	5
Strawberry Cheesecake Ice Cream, 1 scoop, 60g	3
Toffee & Vanilla Cones, 1 individual, 68g	5
Toffee Ice Cream, 1 scoop, 60g	3
Toffee Neapolitan Soft Scoop Ice Cream, 1 scoop, 60g	3
Vanilla Flavour Ice Cream, 1 scoop, 60g	2
Vanilla Ice Cream Block, 1 serving, (1/10 pack), 45g	2
Vanilla Soft Scoop Ice Cream, 1 scoop, 60g	3

Tesco – Finest

Caribbean Rum & Raisin Ice Cream, 1 scoop, 60g	4
Colombian Coffee Ice Cream, 1 scoop, 60g	4
Devon Toffee & Fudge Ice Cream, 1 scoop, 60g	4
Lemon Sorbet, 1 scoop, 60g	2
Mango & Blackcurrant Sorbet, 1 scoop, 60g	2
Raspberry Sorbet, 1 scoop, 60g	2

The Co-operative

Assorted Fruit Splits, 1 (73ml)	3
Assorted Push Up Ice Lollies, 1 (80ml)	1

Belgian Milk Chocolate, Toffee & Honeycomb Ice Creams, 1 (90ml)	9
Belgian White Chocolate & Raspberry Shortcake Ice Cream, 1 (90ml)	9
Black Forest Ice Cream, 1 serving, 92g	5
Choc or Dark or Milk Choc Ice, 1 (70ml)	4
Chocolate Ice Cream, 1 serving, 92g	4
Chunky Mint Choc Chip Ice Creams, 1 (90ml)	9
Deliciously Dairy Vanilla Flavour Ice Cream, 1 serving, 79g	4
Double Chocolate Fudge Flavour Ice Cream, 1 serving, 92g	6
Ice Cream Sponge Roll, 1/5 serving, 45g	3
Mascarpone & Lemoncello Ice Cream, 1 serving, 92g	5
Mint Choc Chip Ice Cream, 1 serving, 90g	5
Neapolitan Ice Cream, 1 serving, 92g	4
Orange Juice Lollies, 1 (73ml)	1
Raspberry Ripple Ice Cream, 1 serving, 92ml	4
Reduced Fat Chocolate & Vanilla Cones, 1 (110ml)	6
Reduced Fat Vanilla Iced Dessert, 1 serving, 87g	3
Rocket Lollies, 1 (58ml)	1
Strawberry & Vanilla Ice Cream Cones, 1 (110ml)	5
Strawberry Cheesecake Flavour Ice Cream, 1 serving, 91g	5
Strawberry Ice Cream Cones, 1 (110ml)	8
Toffee Fudge Flavour Ice Cream, 1 serving, 92g	5
Vanilla Ice Cream, 1/5 pot, 100ml	4

The Skinny Cow

Berry Blush Smoothie Stick, 1 (100ml)	3
Cheeky Choc Brownie, 1 (100ml)	5
Completely Mintal Ice Cream, 1/5 tub, 100ml	5
Dreamy Creamy Cookie, 1 (100ml)	5
Madly Deeply Ice Cream, 1/5 tub, 100ml	4
Toffee & Honeycomb Stick, 1 (110ml)	4

Waitrose

Belgian Chocolate Ice Cream, 1 scoop, 60g	3
Chocolate Ice Cream, Organic, 1 scoop, 120ml	5
Cornish Dairy Ice Cream, 1 scoop, 60g	2
Dairy Vanilla Ice Cream, 1 scoop, 60g	2
Stem Ginger Ice Cream, 1 scoop, 60g	3
Vanilla Ice Cream, Organic, 1 scoop, 60g	2
Vanilla Soft Ice Cream, 1 scoop, 60g	1

Wall's

Calippo Mini, 1 (60ml)	1
Calippo Shots, Strawberry & Lemon, 1 portion, 80g	1

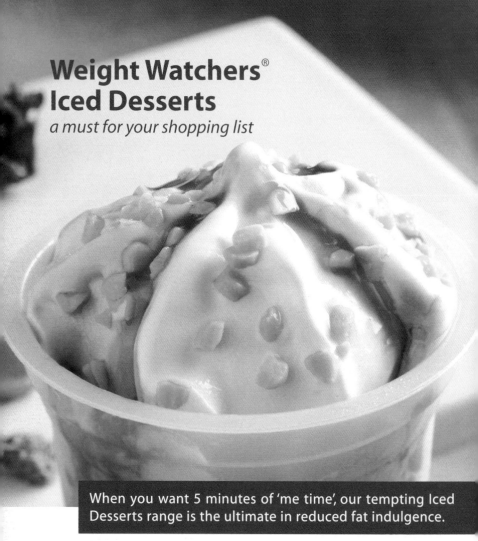

Weight Watchers®
Iced Desserts
a must for your shopping list

When you want 5 minutes of 'me time', our tempting Iced Desserts range is the ultimate in reduced fat indulgence.

2 ProPoints value *to* **4** ProPoints value

per serving

Our delicious range includes:
Three tempting Sundaes, two crunchy Cones, two magnificent Mini Pots, extravagant White & Milk Chocolate Mini Sticks, a wicked Ice Cream Wave and two delightful Whirls. Look out for more flavours during the year.

WeightWatchers® Foods
Eat gorgeous. Feel gorgeous.

Calippo, Orange, 1 (105ml)	**3**
Calippo, Strawberry Tropical, 1 (105ml)	**2**
Cornetto Love Disc, 1 (90ml)	**6**
Cornetto Mini, Chocolate or Classico, 1 (19g)	**2**
Cornetto Mint, 1 (60g)	**5**
Cornetto Strawberry, 1 (120ml)	**8**
Cream of Cornish Dairy Ice Cream, Sliceable, 1 slice, 100ml	**3**
Cream of Cornish Ice Cream, 1 scoop, 44g	**2**
Feast Mini, Chocolate Flavour, 1 mini, 60ml	**5**
Feast Original, 1 portion, 92ml	**8**
Magnum Almond, 1 (120ml)	**8**
Magnum Ecuador Dark, 1 (86g)	**7**
Magnum Mint, 1 (110ml)	**7**
Magnum Temptation Caramel & Almonds, 1 (68g)	**7**
Magnum Temptation Chocolate, 1 (68g)	**6**
Magnum, Classic or White, 1 (86g)	**7**
Magnum, Double Caramel, 1 (110ml)	**10**
Mini Magnum, Almond or White, 1 (50g)	**5**
Mini Twister, Chocolate, 1 (50ml)	**1**
Mini Twister, Strawberry, 1 (39g)	**1**
Soft Scoop Chocolate or Neopolitan, 1 scoop, 45g	**2**
Soft Scoop Light Vanilla Ice Cream, 1 portion, 100ml	**4**
Soft Scoop Mint Choc Chip, 1 scoop, 46g	**2**
Soft Scoop Raspberry Ripple, 1 scoop, 48g	**2**
Soft Scoop Vanilla Flavour Ice Cream, 1 portion, 100ml	**5**
Solero Berry Explosion, 1 (90ml)	**3**
Solero Exotic Explosion, 1 (90ml)	**3**
Solero Fruit Ice Orange, 1 (55ml)	**2**
Solero Fruit Ice Pineapple, 1 (55ml)	**2**
Twister, Pineapple, Lemon & Strawberry, 1 (80ml)	**2**
Viennetta, Mint, 1 slice, 49g	**4**
Viennetta, Original Vanilla, 1 slice, 49g	**3**

Wall's – Carte D'Or

Caramel Cinnamon Waffle, 1 portion, 56g	**3**
Chocolate Inspiration, 1 portion, 56g	**3**
Crema di Mascarpone, 1 portion, 58g	**3**
Greek Yoghurt & Honey, 1 portion, 60g	**3**
Lavazza Latte Macchiato, 1 portion, 53g	**3**
Lemon Sorbet, 1 portion, 100ml	**2**
Light, Vanilla, 1 portion, 50g	**2**
Mango Sorbet, 1 portion, 100ml	**2**
Selection Dulce de Leche, 1 portion, 55g	**3**
Strawberry & Yogurt Délice, 1 portion, 56g	**3**
Vanilla, 1 portion, 50g	**3**

Weight Watchers

Chocolate & Vanilla Cone, 1 (58g)	**4**
Chocolate Brownie Luxury Iced Dessert, 1 (60g)	**3**
Chocolate Honeycomb Swirl Minipot, 1 pot, 56g	**2**
Chocolate Whirls, 1 (100ml)	**2**
Mini Milk Chocolate Sticks, 1 stick, 31g	**2**
Mini White Chocolate Sticks, 1 stick, 31g	**3**
Strawberry & Vanilla Cone, 1 (58g)	**4**
Strawberry & Vanilla Sundae, 1 (180ml)	**4**
Strawberry Whirls, 1 (100ml)	**2**
Toffee Swirl Minipots, 1 pot, 55g	**2**
Vanilla & Chocolate Ice Cream Waves, 1 (100ml)	**3**
Vanilla Iced Dessert, 1 (30g)	**1**

Meat & Poultry

Asda

BBQ Pork Riblets, 1 individual, 75g	**4**
Beef Burgers, 1 individual, 57g	**4**
Breaded Chicken Breast Burgers, 1 individual, 57g	**3**
Cheese Quarter Pounder, ¼ pack, 114g	**7**
Chicken Breast Fillets (with Added Water), ½ pack, 250g	**7**
Chinese Style Pork Ribs, ⅓ pack, 190g	**12**
Cooked Chicken Breast Strips, ¼ pack, 94g	**3**
Garlic & Herb Chicken Thighs, ¼ pack, 138g	**8**
Lemon & Pepper Breaded Chicken Breast Steaks, 1 individual, 95g	**5**
Marinated Chicken Skewers, 1 individual, 35g	**1**
Meat Free Sausage Rolls, 1 individual, 45g	**4**
Prime Lamb Quarterpounder, 1 individual, 85g	**6**
Ready to Roast Large Turkey Breast Joint with Sage & Onion Stuffing, 1 serving, 150g	**6**
Ready to Roast Turkey Breast Joint with Sage & Onion Stuffing, 1 serving, 150g	**6**
Sausage Sizzlers, 1 individual, 140g	**9**
Southern Fried Chicken Breast Steaks, 1 steak, 116g	**5**
Southern Fried Chicken Portions, ¼ pack, 175g	**13**

Asda – Chosen by You

Battered or Breaded Chicken Breast Dippers, 1 individual, 18g	**1**
Battered Chicken Breast Steaks, 1 individual, 93g	**4**

Beef Filled Giant Yorkshire Pudding, 1 individual, 385g	**15**
Breaded Chicken Breast Steaks, 1 individual, 95g	**5**
Cottage Pie, 1 pack, 400g	**10**
Garlic Chicken Breast Kievs, 1 individual (baked), 125g	**8**
Roast Beef Dinner, 1 pack, 375g	**8**
Roast Chicken Dinner, 1 pack, 375g	**11**
Sliced Beef in Gravy, 1 serving, 200g	**4**
Sweet & Sour Chicken, 1 pack, 375g	**10**

Bernard Matthews

Cheese & Turkey Ham Mini Kievs, 1 (21g)	**1**
Chicken Escalopes, 1 (138g)	**10**
Crispy Crumb Turkey Burgers, 1 (64g)	**5**
Crispy Crumb Turkey Steaks, 1 (67g)	**4**
Free Range Golden Norfolk Turkey Breast Joint Butter Basted, 1 serving, 125g	**5**
Golden Drummers, 1 (50g)	**4**
Golden Norfolk Bronze Turkey, 1 serving, 125g	**5**
Golden Norfolk Butter Basted Turkey Breast Joint, 1 serving, 125g	**6**
Golden Norfolk Free Range Turkey, 1 serving, 125g	**4**
Golden Norfolk Turkey Ballotine with a Sticky Fruit Stuffing, 1 serving, 100g	**4**
Golden Norfolk Turkey Breast Crown, 1 serving, 125g	**5**
Golden Norfolk Turkey Roulade with Sage, Roast Onion & Apple, 1 serving, 125g	**4**
Golden Norfolk Turkey, small, 1 serving, 125g	**5**
Mini Kievs, 1 (21g)	**1**
Southern Fried Golden Drummers, 1 (50g)	**3**
Turkey Nuggets, 1 (18g)	**1**

Birds Eye

100% Beef Quarter Pounders, 1 portion, 89g	**7**
100% Chicken Fillet Burger, Cajun, 1 (92g)	**3**
Aberdeen Angus Burgers, 1 (114g)	**11**
BBQ Mini Chicken Griddlers, 1 portion, 77g	**3**
Beef Burgers with Fresh Onion, 1 portion, 57g	**4**
Beef Burgers, 1 (57g)	**5**
Beef Grillsteaks, 1 (85g)	**7**
Beef Quarter Pounders, 1 portion, 114g	**10**
Bolognese with Mini Meatballs, 1 portion, 100g	**3**
Chicken Chargrill, All Varieties, 1 (92g)	**4**
Chicken Fillet Kievs with Aromatic Garlic & Herbs, 1 portion, 150g	**8**
Chicken Fingers, 1 portion, 75g	**4**
Ciabatta Crumb Kievs, ½ pack, 150g	**7**

Ciabatta Crumb Kievs Tomato & Mozzarella, 1 portion, 150g	**7**
Ciabatta Crumb Kievs, Green Pesto & Mozzarella, 1 portion, 150g	**8**
Cracked Pepper Seasoned Chicken, 1 portion, 100g	**4**
Crispy Chicken, ½ pack of 2, 90g	**6**
Crispy Chicken Dippers, 1 portion, 88g	**6**
Hot & Spicy Chicken, 1 portion, 95g	**6**
Meatballs, ½ pack, 100g	**6**
Original Beef Burgers with Fresh Onion, 1 portion, 43g	**3**
Original Beef Quarter Pounders with Fresh Onion, 1 pack, 114g	**9**
Roasted Chicken Bites, 1 (81g)	**4**
Southern Fried Chicken, ½ pack, 100g	**6**
Southern Fried Chicken Dippers, 1 (18g)	**1**
Steakhouse Sticky Chinatown Chicken Wings, 1 portion, 140g	**8**
Thai Seasoned Chicken, 1 portion, 97g	**4**
Whole Chicken Fillet Kievs, 1 (150g)	**8**
Whole Chicken Fillets, 1 (140g)	**6**
Whole Chicken Fillets in a Light & Crispy Batter, 1 (108g)	**6**
Whole Chicken Fillets in a Light Crunch Crumb, 1 (108g)	**6**
Whole Chicken Fillets in a Delicate Lightly Seasoned Crumb, 1 portion, 150g	**7**

Iceland

Bacon & Sausage Rolls, 1 (24g)	**2**
Beef Quarter Pounders, 1 (94g)	**7**
Chicken Breast Quarter Pounders, 1 (92g)	**3**
Cocktail Sausages, 1 (10g)	**1**
Irish Recipe Pork & Beef Sausages, cooked, 2 (84g)	**6**
Minted Lamb Quarter Pounders, 1 (86g)	**6**
Thick Pork Sausages, cooked, 2 (84g)	**6**

Morrisons

Battered Chicken Dippers, 1 serving, 65g	**4**
Breaded Chicken Goujons, 1 serving, 75g	**5**
Breaded Chicken Nuggets, 1 serving, 74g	**5**
Butcher's Style Pork Sausagemeat, 1 portion, 50g	**3**
Cooked Chicken Quarters in BBQ Sauce, 1 serving, 275g	**9**
Crispy Battered Chicken Fillets, 1 (93g)	**5**
Crunchy Crumb Chicken Steaks, 1 (89g)	**6**
Garlic & Herb Chicken Fillets, 1 (98g)	**5**
Garlic & Herb Chicken Steaks, 1 (79g)	**6**
Garlic Chicken Kievs, 1 (125g)	**10**

Hot & Spicy Chicken Steaks, 1 (88g) **5**
Irish Recipe Thick Frozen Sausages, 1 (43g) **3**
Southern Fried Chicken Fillets, 1 (92g) **4**
Southern Fried Chicken Steaks, 1 (87g) **5**
Southern Fried Chicken Wings, 1 serving, 195g **14**
Thick Pork & Beef Sausages, 1 (43g) **3**
Thick Pork Sausages, 1 (43g) **3**

Mr Brain's

Pork Faggots, 2 (188g) **7**

Ross

Beef Quarter Pounders with Onion,
1 portion, 100g **8**
Beef Tender Grillsteaks, 1 portion, 100g **9**
Irish Sausages, 1 portion, 40g **3**
Tendergrill Beef Grill Steaks, 1 portion, 58g **5**

Sainsbury's

100% Beef Burger, Without Onion, 1 (57g) **4**
100% Beef Quarter Pounders with a Hint of
Seasoning, 1 (114g) **8**
Aberdeen Angus Quarter Pounders, 1 (114g) **8**
Beef Burger with Onion, 1 (57g) **4**
British Beef Peppered Grillsteak, 1 (140g) **8**
Cocktail Pork Sausages, 4 (56g) **5**

Tesco

Corned Beef Hash, 1 pack, 450g **14**
Micro Cheese Burger, 1 burger, 115g **8**

The Co-operative

Beef Burgers, 1 pack, 114g **9**
Beef Burgers with Onion, 1 (114g) **8**
Beef Quarter Pounder Burgers, 1 (114g) **9**
Breaded Chicken Goujons, ½ pack, 114g **6**
Breaded Chicken Nuggets, ¼ pack, 26g **2**
Chinese Chicken Drumsticks, ¼ pack, 188g **6**
Hickory Glazed BBQ Pork Ribs, ¼ pack, 175g **12**
Pork Cocktail Sausages, 1 (14g) **1**
Thick British Pork & Beef Sausages, 1 (56g) **3**
Thick British Pork Sausages, 1 (56g) **3**
Thin British Pork Sausages, 1 (28g) **1**

Young's

Salmon Fillet Dinner, 1 pack, 380g **8**

Pizza

Asda

Cheese & Tomato Toast a Pizza, ½ pizza, 175g **12**
Cheesy Garlic Pizza Bread, 1 pack, 210g **22**
Deep Pan Garlic Bread, 9 inch, ½ pizza, 74g **6**
Double Decker Pepperoni, ½ pizza, 194g **14**
Loaded Baguette Cheese & Tomato Pizzas,
1 baguette, 125g **7**

Chicago Town

5 Cheese Take Away Original, ¼ pizza, 142g **11**
Deep Dish Barbeque Chicken, 1 pizza, 170g **11**
Deep Dish Four Cheese, 1 pizza, 160g **12**
Deep Dish Ham & Pineapple, 1 pizza, 170g **11**
Deep Dish Meat Combo, 1 pizza, 170g **12**
Deep Dish Pepperoni, 1 pizza, 170g **13**
Deep Dish Supreme, 1 pizza, 170g **12**
Edge to Edge Deep Pan Miami Meaty,
¼ pizza, 99g **7**
Edge to Edge Deep Pan New Orleans Cheese,
¼ pizza, 94g **7**
Edge to Edge Deep Pan Texas BBQ Chicken,
¼ pizza, 100g **6**
Edge to Edge Thin & Crispy California Cheese,
¼ pizza, 73g **6**
Edge to Edge Thin & Crispy Manhattan Chicken,
¼ pizza, 80g **5**
Edge to Edge Thin & Crispy New York Deli,
¼ pizza, 83g **6**
Four Cheese, 1 pizza, 270g **21**
Gorgeous Pepperoni & Red Onion,
1 serving, 100g **8**
Ham & Pineapple, 1 (170g) **10**
Pepperoni, 1 (170g) **14**
Supreme Take Away Original, 1 portion, 151g **11**
Takeaway Footy Feast, 1 portion, 189g **14**
Takeaway Original Chicken Supreme,
¼ pizza, 154g **10**
Takeaway Original Hawaiian Heaven,
¼ pizza, 152g **10**
Takeaway Personal Pepperoni Pile-Up,
½ pizza, 140g **11**
Takeaway Sauce Stuffed Crust Chicken
Supreme, ¼ pizza, 169g **10**
Takeaway Sauce Stuffed Crust Five Cheese,
¼ pizza, 159g **12**

Takeaway Sauce Stuffed Crust Four Cheese, ¼ pizza, 158g	**11**
Takeaway Sauce Stuffed Crust Pepperoni Pile-Up, ¼ pizza, 164g	**13**
The Thin Dish BBQ Chicken, 1 portion, 119g	**7**
The Thin Dish Cheese, Tomato & Basil Pesto, 1 portion, 111g	**8**

Dietary Specials

Mozzarella & Tomato, ½ pizza, 160g	**10**
Thin & Crispy Ham & Pineapple, 1 portion, 173g	**9**
Thin & Crispy Margherita, 1 portion, 140g	**8**
Thin & Crispy Pepperoni, 1 portion, 150g	**9**

Dr Oetker – Bistro

Baguette Hawaii, 1 pizza, 125g	**7**
Baguette Jambon a la Parisienne, 1 pizza, 125g	**7**
Baguette Salami a la Lyonnaise, 1 pizza, 125g	**8**
Baguette Tomate - Fromage, 1 pizza, 125g	**8**

Dr Oetker – Ristorante

Hawaii, ½ pizza, 178g	**10**
Piccola Mozzarella, 1 pizza, 155g	**11**
Piccola Pizza Salame, 1 pizza, 140g	**10**
Pizza Bolognese, ¼ pizza, 94g	**5**
Pizza Funghi, ½ pizza, 182g	**12**
Pizza Vegetale Piccante, ½ pizza, 175g	**10**
Pollo, ½ pizza, 178g	**10**
Quattro Formaggi, ½ pizza, 170g	**12**
Rigga with Mushroom, ¼ pizza, 65g	**4**
Speciale, ½ pizza, 165g	**11**

Findus

French Bread, Cheese & Tomato, 1 pack, 140g	**8**
French Bread, Ham & Pineapple, 1 portion, 153g	**8**
French Bread, Pepperoni Supreme, 1 portion, 145g	**9**
French Bread, Pepperoni Supreme, 1 pizza, 300g	**18**

Goodfellas

Deeply Delicious Chicken Supreme, 1 serving, 160g	**9**
Deeply Delicious Ham & Pineapple, 1 serving, 200g	**13**
Deeply Delicious Loaded Cheese, ½ pizza, 200g	**14**
Deeply Delicious Massive on Meat, 1 serving, 152g	**10**
Deeply Delicious Meat Feast, 1 pizza, 213g	**14**
Deeply Delicious Meatballs, ½ pizza, 204g	**14**
Deeply Delicious Meaty Mayhem, 1 pizza, 119g	**9**

Deeply Delicious Nacho Chicken, ½ pizza, 206g	**13**
Deeply Delicious Pepperoni Perfecto, ½ pizza, 223g	**15**
Deeply Delicious Spicy Chicken Jolt, ½ pizza, 221g	**15**
Delicia Classic Chicken Provencal, ½ pizza, 160g	**11**
Delicia Classic Margherita, ½ pizza, 160g	**11**
Delicia Pepperoni Thin Classic, ½ pizza, 165g	**12**
Delicia Thin Cajun Chicken, 1 pizza, 154g	**9**
Delicia Thin Mozzarella, 1 pizza, 132g	**10**
Delicia Thin Pepperoni, ½ pizza, 155g	**12**
Four Cheese Stonebaked Solos, 1 pizza, 116g	**9**
Friday Fever BBQ Bonanza, 1 slice, 141g	**9**
Friday Fever Cheese Supreme, 1 slice, 121g	**8**
Friday Fever Meateor, 1 slice, 135g	**10**
Friday Fever Triple Pepperoni, 1 slice, 134g	**10**
La Bottega Stonebaked Ciabatta Ham & Mushroom, 1 slice, 208g	**12**
La Bottega Stonebaked Ciabatta Mozzarella & Pesto, 1 slice, 193g	**13**
La Bottega Stonebaked Ciabatta Pepperoni Classico, 1 slice, 200g	**14**
La Bottega Stonebaked Ciabatta Sweet Chilli Chicken, 1 slice, 200g	**12**
La Bottega Stonebaked Ciabatta Sweet Chilli Chicken, 1 slice, 200g	**12**
La Bottega Stonebaked Ciabatta, Mozzarella, ½ pizza, 192g	**13**
Margherita Classic Thin, 1 serving, 158g	**11**
Mini Mighty Solos 2 Stonebaked Hawaiian, 1 pizza, 130g	**8**
Pepperoni Classic Thin, 1 serving, 155g	**12**
Pepperoni Stonebaked Solos, 1 pizza, 121g	**10**
Pizzeria Cajun Spiced Chicken, ½ pizza, 168g	**10**
Pizzeria Mozzarella Pearls with Pesto, ½ pizza, 149g	**10**
Pizzeria Pepperoni & Chorizo, ½ pizza, 151g	**11**
Solos Chicken Pesto, 1 pizza, 144g	**10**
Solos Meat Speciale, 1 pizza, 140g	**10**
Solos Pepperoni, 1 pizza, 137g	**11**
The Big Takeout Triple Pepperoni, 1 serving, 134g	**10**
The Original Stonebaked Delicia Chicken & Chorizo, 1 serving, 165g	**12**
The Original Stonebaked Delicia Chicken Provencal, 1 serving, 195g	**13**
The Original Stonebaked Delicia Ham & Mushroom, 1 serving, 166g	**11**
The Original Stonebaked Delicia Ham & Pineapple, 1 serving, 173g	**11**

Frozen Foods • Pizza

The Original Stonebaked Delicia Ham, Tomato & Basil, ½ pizza, 172g **12**
The Original Stonebaked Delicia Margherita, 1 serving, 158g **11**
The Original Stonebaked Delicia Mediterranean Vegetable, 1 serving, 175g **10**

Iceland

BBQ Chicken, ½ pizza, 189g **11**
Extra Thin & Crispy Four Cheese, ½ pizza, 136g **10**
Thin & Crispy Cheese & Ham, ½ pizza, 174g **10**
Thin & Crispy Chicken Fajita, ½ pizza, 172g **10**
Thin & Crispy Double Pepperoni, ½ pizza, 180g **13**
Thin & Crispy Four Cheese, ½ pizza, 157g **11**
Thin & Crispy Ham & Pineapple, ½ pizza, 180g **10**

McCain

Anytime Four Cheese, 1 pizza, 142g **9**
Anytime Ham & Pineapple, 1 pizza, 150g **9**
Anytime Spicy Chicken, 1 pizza, 150g **9**
Maximo American Hot Pepperoni, Jalapeño & Chilli, 1 slice, 150g **9**
Maximo Cheesy Garlic, 1 slice, 150g **10**
Micro Cheese & Tomato, 1 pizza, 135g **10**
Micro Pizza, Chargrilled Chicken, 1 pizza, 121g **8**
Micro Pizza, Cheese & Tomato, 1 pizza, 128g **9**
Micro Pizza, Pepperoni, 1 pizza, 135g **10**
Pizza Fingers, Cheese & Tomato, 1 finger, 30g **2**

Morrisons

Ciabatta Mozzarella & Sundried Tomato, 1 serving, 88g **6**
Deep Pan Meat Feast, 1 serving, 178g **12**
Deep Pan Ham & Pineapple, 1 serving, 188g **13**
Deep Pan Smokey Sausage & Bacon, 1 serving, 174g **12**
Thin & Crispy Sweet Chilli Chicken, 1 serving, 195g **11**

Tesco

Pizzeria Stonebaked Four Cheese, ½ pizza, 207g **14**
Pizzeria Stonebaked Meat Feast, ½ pizza, 224g **16**

The Co-operative

Cheese & Tomato Bruschetta, 1 pizza, 38g **2**
Cheese & Tomato Stonebaked Snacks, ½ pack, 112g **7**
Deep Pan Cheese & Tomato, ½ pizza, 220g **14**
Deep Pan Meat Feast, ½ pizza, 225g **13**
Everyday Cheese & Tomato, ½ pizza, 134g **8**
Pepperoni Stonebaked Snacks, ½ pack, 116g **7**

Stonebaked BBQ Chicken, ½ pizza, 178g **9**
Stonebaked Ham & Pineapple, ¼ pizza, 89g **5**
Stonebaked Margherita, ½ pizza, 175g **10**
Stonebaked Pepperoni, ½ pizza, 170g **11**
Truly Irresistible Margherita, ½ pizza, 198g **12**
Truly Irresistible Stonebaked Margherita, ½ pizza, 232g **14**

Weight Watchers from Heinz

Chicken Italiano Pizza, 1 (185g) **8**
Ham & Mushroom Pizza, 1 (165g) **8**

Ready Meals

Asda

All Day Breakfast, 1 pack, 400g **20**
BBQ Chicken Melt, 1 serving, 400g **15**
Bean & Bacon Melt, 1 pack, 400g **13**
Beef Chilli & Potato Wedges, 1 pack, 400g **10**
Beef Curry, 1 pack, 400g **14**
Beef In Blackbean, ¼ pack, 100g **3**
Beef Roast Dinner, 1 pack, 400g **11**
Beef Stew & Dumplings, 1 pack 450g **13**
Bolognese Pasta Bake, pack, 400g **14**
Braised Steak, ¼ pack, 300g **14**
Cajun Chicken Pasta, 1 pack, 400g **12**
Char Sui Pork, 1 serving, 400g **19**
Cheesy Broccoli & Potato Bake, 1 pack, 400g **11**
Chicken & Mushroom, 1 pack, 400g **16**
Chicken & Bacon Pasta Bake, 1 pack, 400g **17**
Chicken Curry with Egg Fried Rice, 1 serving, 450g **18**
Chicken Filled Giant Yorkshire Pudding, 1 individual, 385g **17**
Chicken Hotpot, 1 pack, 400g **12**
Chicken in Mushroom & Bacon Sauce, 1 pack, 300g **10**
Chicken Korma, 1 pack, 450g **23**
Chicken Madras, 1 pack, 400g **12**
Chicken Roast Dinner, ½ pack, 200g **6**
Chicken Tikka, 1 pack, 400g **16**
Classic Beef Stew & Dumplings, 1 pack, 400g **9**
Fish Pie, 1 pack, 360g **9**
Ham Tagliatelle, 1 pack, 400g **12**
Italian Pasta & Meatballs, 1 pack, 400g **12**
Lamb Casserole, 1 portion, 600g **20**
Lamb Hot Pot, 1 pack, 400g **10**

Macaroni Cheese, 1 pack, 400g	**15**	
Minced Beef Hotpot, 1 pack, 400g	**11**	
Mini Classics Chip Shop Chicken Curry & Chips, 1 pack, 300g	**7**	
Mushroom Fried Rice, 1 pack, 225g	**8**	
Pasta & Meatballs, ½ pack, 200g	**6**	
Penne Arrabbiata, 1 pack, 400g	**13**	
Shepherd's Pie, 1 serving, 153g	**5**	
Southern Fried Chicken & Chips, 1 pack, 400g	**16**	
Spaghetti Bolognese, 1 pack, 400g	**11**	
Spaghetti Carbonara, 1 pack, 400g	**14**	
Steak & Stout Casserole, 1 pack, 400g	**7**	
Sweet & Sour Chicken with Rice, 1 pack, 400g	**12**	
Tandoori Chicken, ¼ pack, 100g	**2**	
Tomato & Black Olive Pasta, 1 pack, 400g	**15**	
Tuna & Lemon Pasta, 1 pack, 400g	**14**	
Vegetable Bake, 1 pack, 400g	**11**	
Zesty Tuna Pasta, 1 pack, 400g	**14**	

Asda – Chosen by You

Beef Curry with Rice, 1 pack, 400g	**12**
Beef Filled Giant Yorkshire Pudding, 1 individual, 385g	**15**
Beef Lasagne, 1 pack, 400g	**11**
Beef Madras, 1 serving, 188g	**7**
Chicken Chow Mein, 1 pack, 375g	**10**
Chicken Curry with Rice, 1 pack, 400g	**13**
Cottage Pie, 1 pack, 400g	**10**
Creamy Mushroom Tagliatelle, 1 pack, 400g	**11**
Prawn Curry with Rice, 1 pack, 400g	**12**
Roast Beef Dinner, 1 pack, 375g	**8**
Roast Chicken Dinner, 1 pack, 375g	**11**
Sausage Filled Giant Yorkshire Pudding, 1 individual, 385g	**18**
Sliced Beef in Gravy, 1 serving, 200g	**4**
Sweet & Sour Chicken, 1 pack, 375g	**10**

Asda – Extra Special

Beef Stroganoff, 1 pack, 400g	**15**
Chicken Béarnaise, ⅓ pack, 300g	**17**
Chicken Madeira, 1 pack, 430g	**17**
Thai Green Chicken Curry with Jasmine Rice, 1 portion, 400g	**13**
Yorkshire Puddings, 1 individual, 39g	**3**

Asda – Good For You

Beef Lasagne, 1 pack, 400g	**10**
Chicken & Asparagus Pasta, 1 pack, 400g	**10**
Chicken Balti, 1 pack, 400g	**10**
Chicken Hot Pot, 1 pack, 400g	**7**

Chicken in Black Bean Sauce, 1 pack, 450g	**7**
Chicken in Peppercorn, 1 pack, 400g	**11**
Chicken Korma, 1 pack, 400g	**11**
Chicken Madras, 1 pack, 399g	**12**
Chicken Tikka Masala, 1 pack, 400g	**11**
Chicken, Tomato & Mozzarella Risotto, 1 pack, 400g	**9**
Chilli con Carne, 1 pack, 400g	**12**
Cottage Pie, 1 pack, 400g	**10**
Fish Pie, 1 pack, 400g	**10**
Honey & Mustard Chicken Linguine, 1 pack, 400g	**11**
Hot-Smoked Salmon Linguine, 1 pack, 400g	**9**
Macaroni Cheese, 1 pack, 400g	**11**
Moroccan Style Lemon Chicken, 1 pack, 400g	**11**
Oriental Beef Noodles, 1 pack, 400g	**10**
Peppercorn Chicken, 1 pack, 400g	**11**
Roasted Vegetable Lasagne, 1 pack, 425g	**8**
Seafood Paella, 1 pack, 400g	**10**
Spicy Tomato Chicken, 1 pack, 400g	**7**
Spinach & Ricotta Cannelloni 400g, 1 pack, 400g	**7**
Tomato & Basil Chicken Pasta, 1 pack, 400g	**11**
Zesty Salmon with Baby New Potatoes, 1 pack, 400g	**7**

Aunt Bessie's

Cottage Pie, 1 pack, 400g	**11**
Homestyle Dumplings, 1 (49g)	**5**
Sage & Onion Stuffing Balls, ⅛ pack, 39g	**3**

Birds Eye

100% Chicken Breast in a Creamy Sauce with Ham, Vegetables & Pasta, 1 pack, 400g	**11**
Beef Curry with Rice, 1 pack, 395g	**12**
Beef Lasagne with a Béchamel Sauce & Cheddar Cheese Topping, ¼ pack, 100g	**3**
Beef Stew & Dumplings, 1 pack, 400g	**10**
Big Eat Beef Lasagne, 1 pack, 504g	**15**
Big Eat Chicken Balti, 1 pack, 500g	**17**
Big Eat Sausage & Mash, 1 pack, 500g	**10**
Big Eat Sweet Chilli Chicken, 1 pack, 505g	**14**
Cauliflower Cheese, ½ pack, 167g	**4**
Cheese Ravioli, 1 portion, 320g	**10**
Cheese Tortellini, 1 portion, 320g	**11**
Chicken Breast in a Sweet & Sour Sauce, 1 pack, 404g	**10**
Chicken Breast in a Tomato & Basil Sauce with Pasta, 1 pack, 404g	**9**
Chicken Curry with Rice, 1 pack, 400g	**13**
Chicken Jalfrezi with Rice, 1 pack, 350g	**10**
Chicken Korma with Rice, 1 pack, 350g	**10**

Chicken Pie, 1 pack, 160g	12
Chicken Stew & Dumplings, 1 pack, 398g	9
Chicken Supreme with Rice, 1 pack, 367g	12
Chicken Tikka Masala with Rice, 1 pack, 400g	12
Chicken Tikka Masala with Rice, 1 pack, 419g	13
Chicken, Tomato & Mozzarella Bake, 1 portion, 285g	8
Chilli con Carne, 1 pack, 285g	9
Chilli con Carne with Rice, 1 portion, 284g	8
Classic Crumb Chicken Goujons, 1 portion, 82g	7
Fish Bake with Broccoli & Cheese, 1 pack, 380g	13
Great British Menu Roast Beef Dinner, 1 portion, 344g	8
Great British Menu Roast Chicken Dinner, 1 portion, 369g	10
Great British Menu Roast Lamb Dinner, 1 portion, 342g	9
Great British Menu Roast Pork Dinner, 1 portion, 333g	8
Ham & Cheese Tortellini, 1 serving, 320g	11
Hot 'n' Spicy Chicken Burger, 1 (105g)	7
Macaroni Cheese with Fresh Pasta, 1 pack, 303g	13
Pasta, Broccoli & Green Beans in a Light Tomato & Herb Sauce, 1 portion, 171g	4
Penne Arrabiata, 1 portion, 365g	10
Prawn Curry with Rice, 1 pack, 400g	14
Roast Beef in Gravy, 1 medium pack, 227g	7
Roast Chicken in Gravy, 1 portion, 159g	3
Roast Turkey Dinner, 1 pack, 342g	11
Salmon Fillet in a Creamy Sauce with Pasta, 1 portion, 398g	9
Shepherd's Pie, 1 pack, 400g	9
Shepherd's Pie with Peas, 1 portion, 300g	6
Spaghetti Bolognese with Fresh Pasta, 1 pack, 340g	10
Traditional Beef Dinner, 1 pack, 340g	8
Traditional Chicken Dinner, 1 pack, 368g	9
Traditional Lamb Dinner, 1 pack, 340g	9
Traditional Turkey Dinner, 1 pack, 340g	8
Tuna Pasta Bake, 1 portion, 361g	9
Vegetable Fingers, 1 portion, 59g	3
Vegetable Quarter Pounders, 1 portion, 114g	8

Birds Eye – Healthy Options

Chicken Curry with Rice, 1 pack, 350g	9
Cottage Pie, 1 pack, 350g	8
Fish Pie, 1 pack, 350g	7
Minced Beef Hotpot, 1 pack, 400g	10
Spicy Chilli & Wedges, 1 pack, 350g	7

Sweet & Sour Chicken, 1 pack, 350g	10

Findus

Beef Lasagne, 1 pack, 400g	12
Cheesy Pasta Bake with Bacon & Peas, 1 pack, 360g	10
Chicken & Bacon Crispy Pancake, 1 (62g)	3
Chicken Fajita Wraps, ½ pack, 100g	4
Chilli Beef Wraps, ½ pack, 100g	5
Crispy Pepperoni & Mozzarella Cheese Bites, 1 portion, 80g	4
Crispy Sausage & Baked Bean Bites, 1 portion, 79g	4
Macaroni Cheese, 1 pack, 360g	13
Minced Beef Crispy Pancake, 1 (60g)	2
Spaghetti Bolognese, 1 portion, 411g	11
Tagliatelle Carbonara, 1 pack, 360g	11
Three Cheese Crispy Pancake, 1 (63g)	3

Findus – Jean Christophe Novelli

Curried Cream Potato Dauphinoise, 1 portion, 183g	6
Haddock Mornay, 1 portion, 300g	13
Lasagne Novelli, 1 portion, 200g	5
Lemon & Honey Roast Chicken, 1 portion, 393g	15
Mediterranean Vegetable Piperade, 1 portion, 169g	6
Prime Cod Fillet Tower, 1 portion, 293g	11
Salmon Harissa, 1 portion, 280g	12

Iceland

Caribbean Chicken with Rice, 1 meal, 600g	17
Chicken, Prawn and Chorizo Paella, 1 meal, 600g	18
Chicken Tikka Masala, 1 meal, 354g	10
Kashmiri Chicken Tikka, 1 meal, 353g	12
Kung Po Chicken, 1 meal, 354g	12
Meal for One Chicken Curry with Rice, 1 meal, 500g,	17
Meal for One Chicken Roast Dinner, 1 meal, 422g	10
Meal for One Cottage Pie, 1 meal, 500g	17
Meal for One Lasagne, 1 pack, 500g	19
Meal for One Ocean Pie, 1 pie, 405g	12
Meal for One Spaghetti Bolognese, 1 meal, 500g	12
Meal for One Toad in the Hole, 1 meal, 250g	15
Shredded Duck with Pancakes, 1 pancake roll with 33g shredded duck	2

Morrisons

2 Cheese Omelettes, ½ pack, 120g	7
All Day Breakfast, 1 pack, 400g	16
Beef Casserole & Cobblers, 1 pack, 500g	23
Beef Curry & Rice, 1 pack, 400g	12
Beef Dinner, 1 pack, 400g	11
Beef Filled Yorkshire Pudding, 1 pack, 450g	16
Beef in Ale Sauce with Mashed Potato, 1 pack, 500g	13
Beef Lasagne, 1 serving, 250g	11
Beef Stew & Dumplings, 1 pack, 450g	13
Chicken & Broccoli Pasta Bake, 1 pack, 450g	16
Chicken Balti & Rice, 1 pack, 500g	17
Chicken Casserole with Cobblers, 1 pack, 500g	17
Chicken Chow Mein, 1 pack, 500g	12
Chicken Curry & Rice, 1 pack, 400g	13
Chicken Dinner, 1 pack, 400g	12
Chicken in Black Bean Sauce, 1 pack, 500g	15
Chicken Korma & Rice, 1 pack, 500g	17
Chicken Stew filled Yorkshire Pudding, 1 pack, 450g	14
Chicken Supreme, 1 pack, 450g	15
Chicken Tagliatelle Carbonara, 1 pack, 450g	17
Chicken Tikka Masala, 1 pack, 500g	19
Chilli con Carne, 1 pack, 450g	19
Cottage Pie, 1 pack, 400g	12
Cumberland Pie, 1 pack, 500g	15
Fisherman's Pie, 1 pack, 450g	15
Gammon Dinner, 1 pack, 400g	10
Mushroom & Spinach Stroganoff, 1 pack, 450g	15
Prawn Curry & Rice, 1 pack, 400g	13
Sliced Beef in Gravy, ½ pack, 105g	2
Spaghetti & Meatballs, 1 pack, 500g	18
Spinach & Ricotta Cannelloni, 1 pack, 450g	17
Sweet & Sour Battered Chicken & Rice, 1 pack, 500g	20
Sweet & Sour Chicken with Rice, 1 pack, 400g	11
Sweet Chilli Pork Noodles, 1 pack, 500g	19
Tuna & Pasta Bake, 1 pack, 400g	10
Vegetable Balti, 1 pack, 450g	11
Vegetable Hotpot, 1 pack, 450g	7

Morrisons – Eat Smart

Beef Lasagne, 1 pack, 400g	13
Chicken & Pasta Bake, 1 pack, 400g	10
Chicken Curry, 1 pack, 400g	12
Chicken Dinner, 1 pack, 375g	10
Chicken Hotpot, 1 pack, 400g	8
Cottage Pie, 1 pack, 400g	8
Cumberland Pie, 1 pack, 400g	8

Minced Beef Hotpot, 1 pack, 400g	10
Sweet Chilli Chicken, 1 pack, 400g	9

Sainsbury's

Beer Battered Cheese & Onion Fingers, 1 finger, 22g	2
Brie, Mozzarella & Cranberry Wedges, 1 portion, 20g	2
British Classic Fish Pie, 1 pack, 450g	15
Cauliflower Cheese Grills, 1 portion, 92g	5
Cheese & Spring Onion Crispbakes, 1 portion, 107g	6
Mini Toad in the Hole, 1 (18g)	1
Mini Vegetable Fajitas, 1 (18g)	2
Red Jalapeño Peppers, 1 (24g)	2
Sausage & Mash, 1 pack, 400g	12

Sharwood's

Cantonese Chicken with Chive Rice, 1 pack, 375g	11
Cantonese Chow Mein Noodle Box, 1 pack, 350g	13
Chicken & Mushroom with Rice, 1 pack, 450g	13
Chicken Balti with Naan Bread, 1 pack, 375g	14
Chicken Balti with Pilau Rice, 1 pack, 450g	14
Chicken Chow Mein Noodle Bowl, 1 pack, 375g	11
Chicken in Oyster & Mushroom Sauce with Rice, 1 pack, 375g	11
Chicken in Tikka Masala Sauce with Pilau Rice, 1 pack, 450g	14
Chicken Korma with Pilau Rice, 1 pack, 375g	15
Chicken Rogan Josh with Pilau Rice, 1 pack, 375g	11
Chicken with Ginger & Spring Onions with Chive Rice, 1 pack, 375g	9
Hong Kong Sweet & Sour Noodle Box, 1 pack, 350g	11
Rice Bowl Lime, Honey & Red Chilli Chicken, 1 pack, 350g	14
Rice Bowl Thai Green Chicken Curry, 1 pack, 350g	15
Rice Bowl Thai Red Chicken Curry, 1 pack, 350g	13
Spicy Chinese Noodles Noodle Bowl, 1 pack, 375g	11
Spicy Oriental Chicken with Rice, 1 pack, 450g	15
Sweet & Sour Battered Chicken Rice Bowl, 1 pack, 375g	12
Sweet & Sour Chicken with Mango & Rice, 1 pack, 375g	12
Taste of China Spicy Szechuan Chicken with Rice, 1 pack, 375g	15

Frozen Foods Ready Meals

Thai Red Curry Noodle Box, 1 pack, 350g	12

Tesco

Bangers & Mash, 1 pack, 400g	11
Battered Sweet & Sour Chicken with Egg Rice, 1 pack, 400g	15
Beef Cannelloni, 1 pack, 400g	14
Beef Curry with Rice, 1 pack, 385g	13
Beef Dinner, 1 pack, 400g	11
Beef Lasagne, 1 pack, 400g	14
Beef Stew & Dumplings, 1 pack, 450g	12
Cauliflower Cheese, 1 pack, 400g	14
Cheese Omelette, 1 individual, 108g	6
Chicken Balti with Pilau Rice & Naan Bread, 1 pack, 550g	19
Chicken Chow Mein, 1 pack, 400g	9
Chicken Cottage Pie, 1 pack, 400g	9
Chicken Curry with Rice, 1 pack, 400g	13
Chicken Dinner, 1 pack, 400g	11
Chicken Tikka & Rice, 1 pack, 400g	13
Chilli con Carne with Rice, 1 pack, 400g	15
Chips & Curry Sauce, 1 pack, 400g	12
Corned Beef Hash, 1 pack, 400g	12
Cottage Pie, 1 pack, 400g	10
Fish & Chips, 1 pack, 400g	22
Fisherman's Pie, 1 pack, 360g	9
Lasagne, To Share, ½ pack, 275g	10
Macaroni Cheese, 1 pack, 400g	16
Micro Cheeseburger, 1 (115g)	9
Minced Beef Hotpot, 1 pack, 400g	12
Prawn Curry with Rice, 1 pack, 400g	15
Shepherd's Pie, 1 pack, 400g	8
Sliced Beef in Gravy, 1 pack, 210g	4
Spaghetti Bolognese, 1 pack, 400g	11
Sweet & Sour Battered Chicken with Egg Rice, 1 pack, 550g	21
Sweet & Sour Chicken with Rice, 1 pack, 400g	11
Tagliatelle Carbonara, 1 pack, 400g	11
Toad in the Hole, 1 pack, 250g	15
Tuna Pasta Bake, 1 pack, 400g	12
Turkey Dinner, 1 pack, 400g	13

The Co-operative

All Day Breakfast, 1 pack, 400g	15
Beef Curry with Rice, 1 pack, 375g	11
Beef Lasagne, 1 pack, 400g	11
Breaded Cheese Bites, ¼ pack, 58g	6
Cauliflower Cheese, 1 pack, 350g	5
Chicken Breast Satay, 2 (20g)	1
Chicken Caesar Pasta Salad, 1 pack, 200g	14
Chicken Curry with Rice, 1 pack, 400g	11
Chilli con Carne with Rice, 1 pack, 400g	9

Cooked Long Grain White Rice, 1 quantity, 100g	4
Cottage Pie, 1 pack, 400g	9
Cumberland Sausage & Mash, 1 pack, 450g	14
Garlic Butter Chicken Kievs, 1 pack, 283g	22
Minced Beef Hot Pot, 1 pack, 400g	11
Oriental Prawn Selection & Sweet Chilli Sauce, ¼ pack, 58g	3
Roast Beef Dinner, 1 pack, 400g	10
Roast Chicken Dinner, 1 pack, 400g	11
Sausage & Mash, 1 pack, 400g	12
Sausage, Beans & Mash, 1 pack, 340g	12
Sliced Beef in Gravy, 1 pack, 200g	3
Spaghetti Bolognese, 1 pack, 400g	13
Sweet & Sour Chicken with Rice, 1 pack, 400g	12
Toad In The Hole, 1 (250g)	12

Waitrose

Beef Bourguignon, 1 pack, 400g	9
Broccoli & Walnut Bakes with Tangy Tomato Sauce, ½ pack, 140g	5
Fish Pie, 1 pack, 400g	12
Meatball Pasta Bake, 1 pack, 400g	12
Mini Roast Chicken Dinner, 1 pack, 250g	7
Mini Sausage & Mash, 1 pack, 250g	10
Shepherd's Pie, 1 pack, 400g	13
Vegetable Ratatouille, 1 pack, 400g	4

Weight Watchers from Heinz

Beef & Black Bean with Rice, 1 packet, 320g	8
Beef & Red Wine Casserole, 1 pack, 330g	7
Beef & Vegetable Hotpot, 1 pack, 300g	6
Beef Hotpot, 1 pack, 320g	6
Beef Lasagne, 1 pack, 300g	7
Chicken & Mushroom Pies, 1 pie, 136g	9
Chicken & Mushroom Risotto, 1 pack, 320g	9
Chicken Casserole, 1 pack, 300g	5
Chicken Casserole & Dumplings, 1 pack, 400g	8
Chicken Curry, 1 pack, 300g	8
Chicken Hotpot, 1 pack, 320g	7
Chicken in a Creamy Mushroom Sauce, 1 pack, 330g	9
Chicken in Tomato & Basil Sauce, 1 pack, 320g	6
Chicken Tikka Masala, 1 pack, 330g	9
Chicken, Lime, Chilli & Coconut Noodles, 1 serving, 400g	3
Chilli con Carne, 1 pack, 300g	7
Cottage Pie, 1 pack, 300g	5
Creamy Chicken & Mushroom, 1 pack, 330g	9
Fisherman's Pie, 1 pack, 320g	6
Home Comforts Beef & Red Wine Casserole, 1 serving, 330g	7

Frozen Foods — Vegetables, Potato Products & Chips

Home Comforts Chicken & Dumpling Casserole, 1 serving, 330g **6**
Mushroom & Broccoli Wedge Melt, 1 pack, 300g **7**
Ocean Pie, 1 pack, 300g **5**
Oriental Beef & Black Bean with Rice, 1 pack, 320g **8**
Oriental Sweet & Sour Chicken with Rice, 1 packet, 330g **8**
Oriental Sweet Chilli Chicken with Rice, 1 packet, 330g **8**
Salmon & Broccoli Wedge Melt, 1 pack, 320g **8**
Shepherd's Pie, 1 pack, 320g **6**
Spaghetti Bolognese, 1 pack, 320g **8**
Steak & Mushroom Pie, 1 pie, 136g **9**
Sweet & Sour Chicken, 1 pack, 320g **8**
Tagliatelle Bolognese, 1 pack, 300g **8**
Tomato & Basil Chicken, 1 pack, 330g **7**

Savoury Pies & Quiches

Asda

Breaded Garlic Mushrooms, ¼ pack, 114g **7**
Cheddar Cheese & Onion Rolls, 1 individual, 13g **1**
Cheddar Cheese & Onion Slices, 1 slice, 139g **12**
Cheese & Onion Slices, 1 slice, 147g **12**
Cheese & Bacon Quiche, ⅓ tart, 133g **10**
Chicken & Mushroom Pastry Slice, 1 slice, 128g **11**
Chicken & Vegetable Pie, 1 serving, 147g **11**
Chicken Breast in Creamy Mushroom Sauce Pie in Shortcrust Pastry, ¼ pie, 170g **12**
Cornish Pasties, 1 individual, 150g **11**
Deep Filled Chicken & Mushroom Pie, 1 serving, 193g **11**
Deep Filled Roast Chicken & Rich Gravy Pie, 1 serving, 193g **10**
Deep Filled Steak & Rich Gravy Pie, 1 serving, 193g **11**
Large Sausage Rolls in Golden Puff Pastry, 1 individual, 44g **5**
Roast Chicken Breast in Rich Gravy Pie in Shortcrust Pastry, ¼ large, 170g **11**
Sausage Rolls, 1 individual, 45g **5**
Steak & Mushroom Pie, 1 pack, 142g **10**
Steak & Onion Slices, 1 individual, 147g **11**
Steak & Rich Gravy Pies, 1 serving, 147g **12**
Steak in a Rich Gravy Pie in Shortcrust Pastry, ¼ large, 170g **12**

Asda – Chosen by You

Cheese & Onion Rolls, 1 roll, 15g **2**
Vegetable & Cheese Pies, 1 pie, 156g **11**

Asda – Extra Special

Broccoli Swiss Gruyère & Mature Cheddar Tarts, 1 serving, 148g **14**
Roast Chicken Pie, ¼ large, 175g **11**
Chicken & Chestnut Mushroom Pie, 1 individual, 225g **15**

Aunt Bessie's

Extra Large Yorkshire Puddings, 1 (40g) **3**
Midweek Minis Yorkshire Puddings, 1 (8g) **1**
Original Yorkshire Puddings, 1 (18g) **1**
Toad in the Hole, Single, 1 (190g) **13**

Birds Eye

Chicken & Vegetable Pie, 1 portion, 156g **12**
Chicken Lattice Bacon & Cheddar Cheese, 1 (134g) **11**
Chicken Lattice Cheddar Cheese & Broccoli, 1 (134g) **11**
Chicken Pie, 1 portion, 154g **13**
Minced Beef & Onion Pies, 1 portion, 155g **13**
Steak & Kidney Pie, 1 portion, 157g **13**
Steak & Mushroom Pie, 1 portion, 154g **11**

Waitrose

Chicken & Red Pepper Tarte Fine, ½ pack, 175g **14**
Tomato & Mozzarella Tarte Fine, 1 (185g) **15**

Weight Watchers from Heinz

Chicken & Mushroom Pie, 1 pie, 136g **9**
Steak & Mushroom Pie, 1 pie, 135g **9**

Vegetables, Potato Products & Chips

Asda

Cauliflower Cheese, 1 pack, 400g **9**
Chargrilled Sliced Aubergines, ¼ serving, 125g **1**
Chargrilled Vegetables with a Basil & Garlic Dressing, ¼ pack, 175g **7**

Chopped Garlic, 1 portion, 150g	7
Crispy Home Style Chips, 1 serving, 125g	6
Curly Chips, 1 serving, 125g	7
Home Style Mashed Potato Microwave Cook, 1 serving, 151g	4
Mini Potato & Carrot Waffles, ⅕ pack, 91g	5
Onion Rings, 1 bag, 25g	1
Oven Chips, 1 portion (small), 100g	4
Parsnips for Roasting, 1 serving, 125g	7
Potato Wedges, 1 portion (small), 100g	5
Ready to Roast Potatoes, 1 serving, 167g	5
Southern Fried Potato Wedges, 1 serving, 104g	6
Steak Cut Oven Chips, 1 serving, 180g	9
Straight Cut Chips, 1 portion (small), 180g	9

Asda – Chosen by You

Battered Onion Rings, 3 rings, 45g	2
Chips & Curry Sauce, 1 pack, 400g	15
Crinkle Cut Frying Chips, 1 portion, 125g	7
Happy Stars, 3 individual, 60g	4
Oven Cook American Style Fries, 1 serving (baked), 125g	8
Oven Cook Crispy Potatoes, 1 serving (baked), 125g	4
Oven Cook Potato Croquettes, 1 serving, 90g	5

Asda – Extra Special

British King Edward Creamy Mash, 1 serving, 150g	6
British King Edward Roast Potatoes with Goose Fat, 1 portion, 150g	7
Chunky Oven Chips, ¹⁄₁₂ pack, 125g	5
Maris Piper Seasoned Wedges, 1 portion, 100g	3
Sweet Potato Mash, 1 serving, 151g	4
West Country Farmhouse Cheddar Mash, 1 portion, 150g	5

Asda – Good For You

Potato Wedges, 1 portion, 100g	5
Straight Cut Oven Chips, 1 portion, 181g	8

Aunt Bessie's

Cauliflower Cheese, 1 portion, 125g	2
Cheese & Potato Pie, ½ pack, 400g	10
Creamed Leeks, ¼ pack, 125g	3
Homestyle Chips, 1 portion, 100g	4
Homestyle Crispy Roast Potatoes, 1 portion, 100g	4
Honey Glazed Roast Parsnips, 1 portion, 125g	5
Jacket Wedges, 1 portion, 75g	3
Mashed Carrot & Swede, 1 portion, 125g	1
Mashed Potato, ¼ pack, 162g	5

Red Cabbage & Apple, 1 portion, 125g	2
Roast Mix Potatoes, Parsnips, Carrots & Red Onions, 1 portion, 100g	2

Birds Eye

Crispy Vegetable Fingers, 1 finger, 28g	1
Essentials Mixed Vegetables Carrots, Peas & Sweetcorn, 1 serving, 95g	1
Leeks with Cream, ½ bag, 150g	3
Original Vegetable Rice, ¼ bag, 170g	5
Oven Bake Potato Fritters, 1 (100g)	4
Pasta, Peas & Sweetcorn, 1 bag, 160g	6
Potato Waffles, 1 (57g)	3
Steam Bags Rice, Broccoli, Sweetcorn & Peas with a Hint of Herb Seasoning, 1 bag, 180g	6
Steam Bags Rice, Carrot, Asparagus & Peas with a Hint of Herb Seasoning, 1 bag, 180g	5

Iceland

American Style Curly Fries, ⅙ pack, 125g	10
Button Sprouts, 1 portion, 100g	0
Freshly Frozen Broccoli Florets, 1 portion, 100g	0
Freshly Frozen Broccoli Mix, 1 portion, 100g	0
Freshly Frozen Cauliflower Florets, 1 portion, 100g	0
Freshly Frozen Country Mixed Vegetables, 1 portion, 100g	1
Freshly Frozen Floret Mix, 1 portion, 100g	0
Freshly Frozen Garden Peas, 1 portion, 100g	2
Freshly Frozen Very Fine Whole Green Beans, 1 portion, 100g	0
Garlic Baguettes, ⅓ baguette, 55g	5
Garlic Breaded Mushrooms, 1 portion, 100g	6
Oven, Grill or Fry American Style Slim Fries, 1 portion, 100g	8
Oven, Grill or Fry Crinkle Cut Chips, 1 portion, 100g	6
Oven, Grill or Fry Steak Cut Chips, 1 portion, 100g	5
Oven, Grill or Fry Straight Cut Chips, 1 portion, 100g	5
Potato Waffles, 1 (56g)	3
Sweetcorn, 1 portion, 100g	3
Yorkshire Puddings, 1 pudding, 18g	1

McCain

Beer Battered RidgeCut Chips, 1 serving, 135g	6
Chunky Croquettes, 1 serving, 103g	5
Crinkle Micro Chips, 1 box, 100g	4
Crinkle Oven Chips, 1 serving, 100g	4
Crispy Bites, ¼ pack, 162g	6
Crispy French Fries, 1 serving, 120g	6

Vegetables, Potato Products & Chips   Frozen Foods

Crispy Slices, ¼ pack, 150g	**6**
Curly Fries, 1 serving, 136g	**6**
Diced Potatoes with Leek, Onion & Parmesan (Potato Gourmet), ½ pack, 100g	**4**
Extra Chunky Oven Chips, 1 serving, 100g	**3**
Hash Browns, 2 (100g)	**5**
Home Roasts, 1 portion, 136g	**4**
Homebakes in a Creamy Cheese Sauce, 1 serving, 178g	**6**
Homebakes in a Creamy Garlic Sauce, 1 serving, 173g	**6**
Lattices, 1 serving, 100g	**4**
Micro Chips, 1 box, 100g	**4**
Micro Chips Straight Cut, 1 serving, 100g	**4**
Oven Wedges, ¼ pack, 188g	**6**
Potato Gourmet Spicy Potato Bravas, 1 pack, 400g	**9**
Potato Gourmet, Mature Cheddar Cheese & Wholegrain Mustard Gratin, ½ pack, 200g	**8**
Potato Winners Curly Fries, 1 serving, 100g	**5**
Potato Winners Southern Fries, 1 serving, 100g	**5**
Potato Winners Winter Herb Wedges, 1 serving, 100g	**4**
Roast Potatoes Basted in Goose Fat, 1 serving, 100g	**5**
Rosti, 1 serving, 115g	**5**
Rustic Oven Chips Skins-On, 1 serving, 165g	**5**
Rustic Roasts, 1 serving, 100g	**3**
Sea Salt & Black Pepper Wedges, 1 serving, 135g	**5**
Simply Gorgeous Chunky Chips, 1 portion, 119g	**7**
Simply Gorgeous Roasting Potatoes, 1 portion, 130g	**6**
Smiles, 1 serving, 75g	**4**
Southern Fries, 1 serving, 113g	**5**
Steak Cut Fry Chips, 1 serving, 100g	**3**
Straight Oven Chips, 1 serving, 100g	**4**
Summer Wedges with a Hint of Pesto, 1 serving, 135g	**6**
Sweet Potato with Rosemary & Garlic, 1 serving, 100g	**3**
The Original Oven Chips, 1 serving, 100g	**3**

McCain – Veg Express

Baby Carrots & Green Beans in a Honey & Mustard Sauce, 1 pack, 150g	**2**
Baby Carrots, Baby Corn & Red Pepper in a 5 Spice Sauce, 1 pack, 150g	**2**
Broccoli, Pepper & Soya Beans in a Tomato & Herb Sauce, 1 pack, 150g	**2**
Yellow & Orange Carrots in a Light Soy Sauce, 1 pack, 150g	**1**

Sainsbury's

Carrots, Broccoli & Sweetcorn, 1 bag, 135g	**2**
Carrots, Cauliflower & Peas, 1 bag, 135g	**1**
Cauliflower Cheese, 1 serving, 80g	**2**
Chips, 1 serving, 165g	**7**
Chunky Vegetables, 1 serving, 80g	**1**
Crinkle Cut Chips, 1 serving, 165g	**8**
Diced Onions, 1 serving, 81g	**1**
Hash Browns, 1 serving, 120g	**7**
Mixed Special Vegetables, 1 serving, 80g	**1**
Mixed Vegetables, 1 serving, 79g	**1**
Potato Croquettes, ½ pack, 125g	**7**
Potato Waffles, 1 (46g)	**3**
Roasting Vegetables, 1 serving, 81g	**1**
Stew Pack, 1 serving, 80g	**0**
Stir Fry, 1 serving, 79g	**1**
Supersweet Mini Corn Cobs, 1 serving, 84g	**3**
Supersweet Sweetcorn, 1 serving, 80g	**2**
Sweetcorn, 1 serving, 80g	**2**
White Rice, Broccoli, Sweetcorn & Peas, 1 serving, 136g	**4**

Tesco

Beef Dripping Roast Potatoes, 1 serving, 125g	**6**
Cheesy Mashed Potato, 1 serving, 130g	**4**
Chunky Chips, 1 serving, 200g	**8**
Crinkle Cut Oven Chips, 1 serving, 125g	**5**
Crispy Lattice Potatoes, 1 serving, 125g	**8**
Crispy Potato & Bacon, 1 serving, 150g	**5**
Crispy Potatoes, 1 serving, 125g	**6**
Curly Oven Potato Chips in a Seasoned Coating, 1 serving, 125g	**7**
Curry Chips, 1 serving, 125g	**6**
Fluffy Mashed Potato, 1 serving, 130g	**4**
Goose Fat Roasting Potatoes, 1 serving, 125g	**6**
Hash Browns, 1 individual, 40g	**2**
Light Choices Straight Cut Oven Chips, 1 serving, 125g	**4**
Oven Chips, 1 serving, 125g	**4**
Potato Croquettes, 1 serving, 110g	**6**
Potato Waffles, 1 individual, 50g	**3**
Potato Wedges, 1 serving, 175g	**8**
Roast Potatoes, 1 serving, 160g	**5**
Roasted Potatoes with Goose Fat, 1 serving, 225g	**9**
Spicy Potato Wedges, 1 serving, 114g	**3**
Spicy Potato Wedges, 1 serving, 125g	**6**
Steak Cut Chips, 1 serving, 125g	**5**
Steak Cut Oven Chips, 1 serving, 125g	**6**
Straight Cut Fry Chips, 1 serving, 125g	**7**
Straight Cut Oven Chips, 1 serving, 125g	**6**

Thin & Crispy Oven Chips, 1 serving, 125g | **7**

The Co-operative

Battered Onion Rings, ⅙ pack, 77g	**4**
Breaded Garlic Mushrooms, ¼ pack, 78g	**3**
Breaded Onion Rings, ⅙ pack, 77g	**5**
Crinkle Cut 3-Way Cook Chips, ½ pack, 150g	**5**
Crinkle Cut Chips for Frying, ⅙ pack, 151g	**5**
Crinkle Cut Oven Chips, ⅙ pack, 151g	**5**
Crispy Potatoes, ⅙ pack, 125g	**5**
Healthy Living Oven Chips, 1 serving, 154g	**4**
Minted Peas, 3 heaped tablespoons, 80g	**2**
Roast Potatoes, ⅙ pack, 170g	**7**
Steak Cut 3-Way Cook Chips, ⅙ pack, 306g	**9**
Steak Cut Chips for Frying, ⅙ pack, 151g	**4**
Steak Cut Oven Chips, ⅙ pack, 170g	**5**
Straight Cut 3-Way Cook Chips, ⅙ pack, 306g	**9**

Waitrose

Courgette Fritters, 1 serving, 100g	**10**
Grilled Peppers, 1 serving, 80g	**1**
Straight Cut Frying Chips, 1 portion, 165g	**6**
Straight Cut Oven Chips, 1 portion, 165g	**6**

Weight Watchers from Heinz

Oven Chips, 1 portion, 100g	**5**
Roast Potatoes, Oven Baked, 1 serving, 100g	**4**
Spring Onion Mash, 1 serving, 100g	**2**

Home Baking

Basic Foods

Almonds, 5 (10g)	2
Apple Rings, Dried, 4 rings, 26g	3
Apricots, Dried, 3 (50g)	3
Arrowroot, 1 level tablespoon, 20g	2
Baking Powder, 1 teaspoon, 5g	0
Baking Powder, 1 tablespoon, 15g	1
Banana Chips, Dried, 1 portion, 25g	4
Beef Dripping, 1 teaspoon, 5g	1
Bicarbonate of Soda, 1 teaspoon, 5g	0
Blancmange Powder, 1 sachet, 33g	1
Bovril, 1 teaspoon, 5g	0
Bovril, 1 tablespoon, 15g	1
Brazil Nuts, 2 (6g)	1
Breadcrumbs, Dried, 1 tablespoon, 20g	2
Breadcrumbs, Fresh, 2 tablespoons, 16g	1
Buckwheat, 1 tablespoon, 10g	1
Calorie Controlled Cooking Spray, 4-18 sprays, 0.8-3.6ml	0
Calorie Controlled Cooking Spray, 19-54 sprays, 3.8-10.8ml	1
Candied Mixed Peel, 1 tablespoon, 25g	2
Capers, in Brine, 1 teaspoon, 5g	0
Caraway Seeds, 1 tablespoon, 7g	1
Cashew Nuts, 10 (10g)	2
Cashew Nuts, Roasted & Salted, 1 small bag, 25g	4
Cherries, Glacé, 1 tub, 100g	7
Chestnut Purée, 1 tablespoon, 26g	1
Chestnuts, 4 (40g)	2
Chocolate, Any Type, 2 squares, 14g	2
Cocoa Butter, 1 teaspoon, 5g	1
Coconut, Creamed, 1 sachet, 50g	10
Coconut, Desiccated, 1 tablespoon, 10g	2
Coconut, Fresh, 1 portion, 100g	10
Coconut Milk, Canned, ¼ can, 100ml	5
Corn Meal, 1 medium portion, 100g	10
Cornflour, 1 level tablespoon, 20g	2
Cream of Tartar, 1 tablespoon, 25g	2
Currants, 1 heaped tablespoon, 25g	2
Curry Paste, All Types, 1 teaspoon, 15g	1
Custard Powder, 1 tablespoon, 15g	2
Date, Dried, 1 (15g)	1
Dumplings, Suet, 1 (70g)	4
Egg, 1 medium, 45g	2
Egg White, 1 (32g)	0
Egg White, 2 (64g)	1
Egg Yolk, 1 medium, 20g	2

Egg, Duck, 1 medium, 85g	4
Egg, Goose, 1 (144g)	7
Egg, Quail, 2 medium, 18g	1
Fennel Seed, 1 teaspoon, 5g	1
Fig, Dried, 1 (22g)	1
Flour, Chapati, Brown or White, 1 level tablespoon, 20g	2
Flour, Chick Pea, 1 quantity, 100g	9
Flour, Soya, Full Fat, 1 quantity, 100g	12
Flour, Soya, Low Fat, 1 quantity, 100g	9
Flour, Wheat, Brown, 1 quantity, 100g	9
Flour, Wheat, Strong White Breadmaking, 1 quantity, 100g	10
Flour, Wheat, White, Plain or Self Raising, 1 level tablespoon, 20g	2
Flour, Wheat, Wholemeal, 1 quantity, 100g	9
Fructose, 1 teaspoon, 5g	1
Garlic Purée, 1 teaspoon, 5g	1
Gelatine, 1 sachet, 12g	1
Gelatine, Fine Leaf, 15 sheets, 25g	2
Gravy Powder/Granules, Dry, 2 teaspoons, 6g	1
Hazelnuts, 10 individual, 10g	2
Herbs, Dried, 1 teaspoon, 5g	0
Herbs, Fresh, 1 teaspoon, 5g	0
Icing, Ready to Roll, 1 portion, 100g	11
Jaggery, 1 level teaspoon, 5g	1
Jaggery, 1 heaped teaspoon, 15g	2
Jelly, Made with Water, ¼ packet, 142g	2
Jelly, Ready to Eat, 1 small pot, 125g	3
Jelly, Sugar Free, Ready to Eat, 2x125g pots	1
Linseed (Flaxseed), 1 tablespoon, 15g	2
Macadamia Nuts, 5 (10g)	2
Malt Extract, 1 teaspoon, 5g	0
Malt Extract, 1 tablespoon, 15g	1
Mango, Dried, 1 portion, 25g	2
Marzipan, 1 small portion, 50g	6
Matzo Meal, 1 heaped tablespoon, 25g	3
Meringue Nest, 1 (12g)	1
Miso, 1 tablespoon, 15g	0
Mixed Dried Fruit, 1 heaped tablespoon, 25g	2
Mixed Dried Fruit, 1 small pack, 50g	4
Molasses, Blackstrap, 1 tablespoon, 20g	1
Oil, Avocado, 1 teaspoon, 5ml	1
Oil, Coconut, 1 teaspoon, 5ml	1
Oil, Corn, 1 teaspoon, 5ml	1
Oil, Cottonseed, 1 teaspoon, 5ml	1
Oil, Grapeseed, 1 teaspoon, 5ml	1
Oil, Hazelnut, 1 teaspoon, 5ml	1
Oil, Olive, 1 teaspoon, 5ml	1
Oil, Palm, 1 teaspoon, 5ml	1
Oil, Peanut, 1 teaspoon, 5ml	1
Oil, Rapeseed, 1 teaspoon, 5ml	1

Oil, Safflower, 1 teaspoon, 5ml	1
Oil, Sesame, 1 teaspoon, 5ml	1
Oil, Soya, 1 teaspoon, 5ml	1
Oil, Sunflower, 1 teaspoon, 5ml	1
Oil, Vegetable, Any Type, 1 teaspoon, 5ml	1
Oil, Walnut, 1 teaspoon, 5ml	1
Oil, Wheatgerm, 1 teaspoon, 5ml	1
Orange Flower Water, 1 teaspoon, 5ml	0
Pastry, Filo, Raw, 1 sheet, 15g	1
Pastry, Filo, Raw, 1 large sheet, 45g	3
Pastry, Puff, Block, 1 quantity, 100g	11
Pastry, Puff, Ready Rolled Sheets, 1 sheet, 213g	22
Pastry, Shortcrust, Block, 1 quantity, 100g	13
Pastry, Shortcrust, Ready Rolled Sheets, 1 sheet, 225g	28
Peaches, Dried, 1 portion, 25g	2
Peanuts, Dry Roasted, 1 serving, 10g	2
Peanuts, Dry Roasted, 1 small bag, 50g	8
Peanuts, Plain, 1 small bag, 50g	8
Peanuts, Roasted or Salted, 1 small bag, 50g	8
Pears, Dried, 1 portion, 25g	2
Pecan Nuts, 3 (18g)	4
Pine Nut Kernels, 1 tablespoon, 15g	3
Pistachios, 15 (15g)	3
Pizza Base Mix, ¼ pack, 35g	3
Pizza Base, Thin & Crispy, 9", 1 medium, 120g	10
Poppy Seeds, 1 tablespoon, 10g	2
Prunes, Dried, 1 small pack, 50g	2
Pumpkin Seeds, 1 tablespoon, 10g	2
Raisins, 1 heaped tablespoon, 30g	2
Sesame Seeds, 1 teaspoon, 4g	1
Stock Cube, All Types, 2 cubes, 20g	1
Stuffing Mix, 1 portion, 50g	5
Sugar, Caster, 1 teaspoon, 5g	1
Sugar, Demerara, 1 teaspoon, 5g	1
Sugar, Icing, 1 teaspoon, 5g	1
Sugar, Light Brown, 1 teaspoon, 5g	1
Sugar, Muscovado, 1 teaspoon, 5g	1
Sugar, White, 1 teaspoon, 5g	1
Sultanas, 1 heaped tablespoon, 30g	2
Sunflower Seeds, 1 tablespoon, 10g	2
Sweetcorn, Creamed, 2 tablespoons, 60g	1
Syrup, Any Type, 2 level teaspoons, 16g	1
Tandoori Spice Mix, 1 teaspoon, 5g	0
Tandoori Spice Mix, 1 tablespoon, 15g	1
Thai Fish Sauce, 1 tablespoon, 15g	0
Thai Fish Sauce, 1 serving, 45g	1
Tikka Spice Mix, 1 teaspoon, 5g	0
Tikka Spice Mix, 1 tablespoon, 15g	1
Treacle, Black, 2 level teaspoons, 16g	1
Vanilla Extract, 1 teaspoon, 5ml	0

Vanilla Extract, 1 tablespoon, 15ml	1
Vinegar, All Types, 1 tablespoon, 15ml	0
Vinegar, Rice Wine, 1 tablespoon, 15ml	0
Walnut Halves, 3 (9g)	2
Yeast, 3 teaspoons, 15g	1
Yeast, Compressed, 1 quantity, 100g	1
Yorkshire Pudding, 1 (20g)	1

Bread, Cakes, Cookie & Pizza Mixes

Asda

Fruit Cake Mix, ½ pack, 59g	6
Ginger Cake Mix, 1 serving, 60g	6
Madeira Cake Mix, 1 serving, 60g	6
Ready to Bake Ginger Cookie Dough with Currants, 1 serving, 28g	4
Ready to Bake Shortbread Dough with Chocolate Beans, 1 serving, 29g	4
Shake to Bake Carrot Cake Mix with Frosting, 1 serving, 31g	3
Shake to Bake Chocolate Muffin Mix, 1 serving, 30g	3
Shake to Bake Lemon Fairy Cake Mix, 1 serving, 35g	4
Shake to Bake Pancake Mix, 1 serving, 38g	2
Yorkshire Puddings, 1 individual, 15g	1

Asda – Extra Special

Rich Chocolate Cake Mix, 1 serving, 66g	7
Spiced Carrot Cake Mix, 1 serving, 68g	7

Atora

Light Shredded Vegetable Suet, 1 portion, 25g	5
Original Atora Shredded Suet, 1 quantity, 25g	6

Aunt Bessie's

Large Light & Crispy Yorkshire Pudding Batters, ¼ pack, 62g	3
Large Light & Crispy Yorkshire Puddings, 1 (28g)	2

Betty Crocker

American Style Pancake Mix, ⅛ pack, 19g	2
Traditional Style Pancake Mix, ⅛ pack, 19g	2

Cadbury

Buttons Cake Mix, ⅙ pack, 42g	5
Chunky Chocolate Brownie Mix, ⅙ pack, 80g	8

| Super Chunk Muffin Mix, ⅙ pack, 60g | **6** |
| Triple Chocolate Cookie Mix, 1 cookie, 37g | **5** |

Dr Oetker

Apple Decorating Kit Chocolate & Caramel Flavour, ⅙ pack, 43g	**6**
Brown Bread & Roll Mix, 1 serving, 64g	**6**
Cupcake Kit, ⅛ pack, 39g	**5**
Flapjack Mix, 1 serving, 90g	**11**
Healthier Option Carrot Cake Mix, 1 serving, 71g	**7**
Healthier Option Chocolate Fudge Brownie Mix, 1 serving, 86g	**10**
Healthier Option White Bread & Roll Mix, 1 serving, 65g	**6**
Shake It! Pancake Mix, 2 servings, 170g	**4**
Tarte aux Amandes, ⅕ tart, 56g	**6**
Unsweetened Suet & Dumpling Mix, 1 serving, 69g	**8**
White Chocolate Chunk Brownie Mix, 1 serving, 37g	**5**

Goldenfry

| Yorkshire Pudding Mix, 1 portion, 100g | **9** |

McDougalls

Batter Mix, 1 portion, 38g	**2**
Crumble Mix, ¼ pack, 56g	**7**
Crumble Topping, 1 quantity, 100g	**3**
Easy Peasy Mini Muffins Recipe Kit, 1/12 pack, 21g	**2**
Granary Malted Brown Bread & Roll Mix, 1 serving, 31g	**3**
Savoury Scone Mix, 1 serving, 38g	**4**
Shortcrust Pastry Mix, 1 portion, 100g	**13**
Sponge Mix, 1 slice, 33g	**3**

Morrisons

| Apple Crumble Spice Mix, 1 bag, 40g | **4** |
| Batter Mix, 1 serving (as prepared), 91g | **5** |

Weight Watchers

Double Chocolate Cookie Mix, 1 (11g)	**1**
Double Choc Mini Muffin Mix, 1 (16g)	**1**
Mini Lemon Cup Cake Mix, 1 (17g)	**1**

Breadcrumbs

Paxo

| Golden Breadcrumbs, 1 serving, 70g | **7** |

| Natural Breadcrumbs, 1 serving, 70g | **7** |

The Co-operative

| Garlic & Coriander Croutini, ⅓ bag, 28g | **4** |
| Garlic & Herb Croutons, ½ pack, 25g | **3** |

Coating & Stuffing Mixes

Asda

American Style Reason to Season, ¼ pack, 9g	**1**
Apricot & Orange Stuffing Mix, 1 pack, 140g	**6**
Carrot Parsnip & Potato Stuffing Mix, 1 pack, 140g	**6**
Indian Style Reason to Season, ¼ pack, 9g	**1**
Nut Roast Mix, 1 serving, 150g	**14**
Parsley Lemon & Thyme Stuffing Mix, 1 pack, 140g	**5**
Parsley, Lemon & Thyme Stuffing Mix, 1 pack, 140g	**5**
Sage & Onion Stuffing Mix, 1 portion, 25g	**1**
Sage & Onion with Garlic Stuffing Mix, 1 pack, 140g	**6**
Sausage Meat Flavour Stuffing Mix, 1 pack, 140g	**7**
Tomato & Onion Cous Cous Stuffing Mix, 1 pack, 140g	**6**

Aunt Bessie's

| Pork Sausagemeat Stuffing Balls, 1 ball, 25g | **1** |

Goldenfry

| A Mix for Chip-Shop Batter, 1 portion, 100g | **8** |

Merchant Gourmet

| Chestnut Stuffing with Couscous & Herbs, ¼ pack, 50g | **2** |

Morrisons

Bake in a Bag - Biryani, 1 bag, dried, 35g	**4**
Bake in a Bag - Italian Pasta, 1 bag, dried, 35g	**3**
Bake in a Bag - Jambalaya, 1 bag, dried, 30g	**3**
Bake in a Bag - Spicy Mexican Stew, 1 bag, dried, 25g	**2**

Patak's

| Original Coat + Cook! Garlic & Coriander, Mild, ¼ pack, 20g | **2** |
| Original Coat + Cook! Tandoori, Medium, ¼ pack, 20g | **1** |

Dried Fruit, Nuts & Seeds *(side tab)*

Home Baking *(side tab)*

Sainsbury's – Taste the Difference

British Pork & Roasted Chestnut Stuffing,
1 serving, 75g **5**

British Pork, Fresh Bramley Apple & Caramelised Date Stuffing, 1 serving, 78g **5**

Schwartz

Garlic & Herb Wedges Coating, 1 sachet, 38g **1**
Nacho Cheese Wedges Coating, 1 serving, 38g **2**

Waitrose

Cranberry, Orange & Thyme Stuffing,
1 pack, 225g **19**
Redcurrant & Rosemary Stuffing, 1 pack, 225g **18**
Sage & Onion Stuffing, ½ pack, 112g **8**

Dinner Kits

Ainsley Harriott

Bengali Keema Masala with Roti Bread Mild,
½ pack, 175g **17**
Moroccan Tagine with Herbs Medium,
¼ pack, 61g **5**
Vietnamese Kho, ½ pack, 131g **15**

Discovery Foods

Complete Nachos Kit, ¼ pack, 148g **11**
Enchilada Kit, ⅛ pack, 74g **6**
Fajita Kit, ⅛ pack, 59g **5**
Taco Shells, 1 (11g) **1**
Taco Tray Kit, ¼ pack, 68g **9**

Old El Paso

Stand & Stuff Taco Dinner Kit, Taco Shells,
1 individual, 13g **1**

Tesco

Fajita Meal Kit, ⅛ pack, 59g **3**
Nachos Meal Kit, ¼ pack, 125g **8**
Tacos Meal Kit, ¼ pack, 69g **5**

Dried Fruit, Nuts & Seeds

Amoy

Reduced Fat Coconut Milk, ¼ can, 100ml **3**
Rich & Creamy Coconut Milk, 1 tablespoon, 15ml **1**
Rich & Creamy Coconut Milk, ¼ can, 100ml **5**

Asda

Berry Mix, 1 serving, 50g **4**
Blackcurrant Burst, ¹⁄₁₀ pack, 17g **2**
Caribbean Jerk Nut Mix, ⅛ pack, 25g **4**
Chilli Spiced Seeds & Almonds, 1 serving, 40g **5**
Chopped Mixed Nuts, ½ bag, 75g **12**
Coconut & North American Cranberries,
¼ pack, 31g **2**
Cut Mixed Peel, ¼ pot, 50g **4**
Dried Fruit, Nut & Seed Selection, ½ pack, 50g **6**
Dried Mango Pieces, ½ pack, 50g **4**
Dried Pineapple Pieces, ½ pack, 50g **4**
Exotic Mix, 1 serving, 50g **5**
Fruit & Nut Selection, ⅛ pack, 50g **6**
Fruit Bowl, 1 serving, 100g **1**
Golden Raisins & North American Cranberries,
¼ pack, 31g **2**
Habanero Chilli Peanuts, ⅕ bag, 40g **6**
Hazelnuts in Shell, 1 serving, 50g **9**
Indian Tikka Nut Mix with Apricots, ⅛ pack, 25g **4**
Kick Start Chocolate, Yogurt & Fruit Mix,
1 serving, 40g **4**
Kick Start Fruit, Almond & Vanilla Pumpkin
Seed Mix, 1 serving, 40g **5**
Kick Start Trail Mix, 1 serving, 75g **8**
Medjool Dates, ¼ pack, 45g **4**
Mixed Nuts & Fruit, 1 serving, 50g **7**
Mixed Nuts & Jumbo Raisins, ¼ pack, 50g **6**
Mixed Nuts in Shell, 1 serving, 50g **9**
Multigrain & Mixed Seed Sprinkle, ½ pack, 38g **9**
North American Dried Cranberries, ⅓ pack, 20g **2**
Nut Selection, ¼ pack, 88g **16**
Orchard Mix, ¼ pack, 50g **3**
Peanuts, Raisins & Chocolate Coated Peanuts,
¼ pack, 50g **6**
Ready to Eat Dried Apricots, Stoned, 1 (100g) **5**
Soft Fruits Apple Chunks, 1 pack, 75g **6**
Soft Fruits Apricots, 1 pack, 75g **5**
Soft Fruits Peach Slices, 1 pack, 75g **5**
Soft Fruits Prunes, 1 pack, 75g **4**

Tropical Fruit & Nut Mix, ⅙ pack, 51g	**6**
Tropical Mix, ¼ pack, 62g	**5**
Wholefoods Chewy Banana Slices, 1 serving, 40g	**3**
Yogurt Coated Raisins, 1 serving, 15g	**2**

Asda – Extra Special

Berry Mix, 1 pack, 190g	**15**
Californian Almonds with BBQ Smoked Seasoning, 1 serving, 25g	**4**
Jumbo Salted Cashew Nuts, 1 serving, 50g	**8**
Large Crunchy Cashew Nuts, 1 serving, 25g	**4**
Lightly Salted Nut Selection, 1 serving, 25g	**5**
Lightly Salted Vietnamese Jumbo Cashew Nuts, 1 serving, 25g	**4**
Luxury Fruit & Nut Mix, ⅕ pack, 50g	**7**
Luxury Mixed Natural Nuts, ⅕ pack, 50g	**10**
Macadamia Nuts with Spanish Orange Blossom Honey, 1 serving, 25g	**5**
Salted Mixed Nuts, 1 serving, 25g	**5**
Smoky Flavour Roasted Almonds, 1 serving, 40g	**5**
Tropical Fruit Medley, 1 portion, 190g	**16**
Vietnamese Cashews, 1 serving, 25g	**4**
World Fruit & Nut Collection, 1 serving, 25g	**4**

Asda – Wholefoods

Sunflower Seeds, 1 serving, 25g	**4**
Pistachio Nut Kernels, 1 serving, 10g	**2**
Pecan Nuts, ½ bag, 45g	**9**
Pumpkin Seeds, 1 pack, 50g	**8**
Golden Linseeds, 1 serving, 25g	**4**

Blue Dragon

Coconut Milk, ½ can, 200ml	**9**
Coconut Milk, Reduced Fat, ½ can, 200ml	**5**
Creamed Coconut, 1 serving, 13g	**3**
Organic Coconut Milk, ¼ can, 100ml	**5**

Cypressa

Roasted & Salted Pistachio Nuts, ¼ pack, 25g	**4**
Roasted & Salted Pumpkin Seeds, ¼ pack, 25g	**4**
Roasted & Salted Sunflower Seeds, ¼ pack, 25g	**4**

Dormen's – Salad Toppers

Caramelised Cashews, 1 serving, 50g	**7**
Jumbo Cashews Roasted & Salted, 1 serving, 50g	**9**
Jumbo Pistachios Roasted & Salted, 1 serving, 50g	**8**

Oven Baked Mixed Nuts Unsalted, 1 serving, 50g	**9**
Oven Baked Mixed Nuts with a Touch of Olive Oil & Salt, 1 serving, 50g	**9**

Fruit Bowl

Fruit Flakes Apple with Strawberry Flavour, 1 pack, 20g	**2**
Fruit 'O's Berry Fruits, 1 (35g)	**5**
Fruit 'O's Lemon & Lime, 1 (35g)	**5**
Fruit 'O's Strawberry, 1 (35g)	**5**
Fruit Flakes, Blackcurrant, 1 pack, 25g	**2**
Fruit Flakes, Blackcurrant with a Yogurt Coating, 1 serving, 25g	**3**
Fruit Flakes, Raisins with a Yogurt Coating, 1 serving, 30g	**4**
Fruit Flakes, Raspberry with a Yogurt Coating, 1 serving, 25g	**3**
Fruit Flakes, Strawberry with a Yogurt Coating, 1 serving, 25g	**3**
Fruit Flakes, Strawberry, 1 serving, 20g	**2**
Seed Flakes Pumpkin Seeds with a Yogurt Coating, 1 pack, 25g	**4**
Seed Flakes Sunflower Seeds with a Yogurt Coating, 1 pack, 25g	**4**

Good Seed

Slightly Salted Lightly Toasted Hemp Seed, ⅒ pack, 20g	**2**
Sweet & Crunchy Lightly Toasted Hemp Seed, 1 serving, 15g	**2**

Humdinger

Fruit Crisps Apple, 1 pack, 20g	**2**
Ready to Eat Apricots, 1 serving, 100g	**5**

Kellogg's

Fruit Winders Doubles, Strawberry & Apple, 1 sweet, 17g	**2**
Fruit Winders Doubles, Strawberry & Blackcurrant, 1 sweet, 17g	**2**
Strawberry Fruit Winders, 1 sweet, 17g	**2**

KP Foods

Baked & Seasoned Large Peanuts Lime & Coriander Flavour, 1 serving, 40g	**7**
Baked & Seasoned Mixed Nuts Chill & Lemongrass, 1 serving, 35g	**6**
Baked & Seasoned Mixed Nuts Sea Salt & Rosemary, 1 serving, 35g	**6**
Baked & Seasoned Peanuts, 1 serving, 50g	**8**
Big Nuts Peanuts, All Flavours, 1 serving, 25g	**4**

Cheese Crunchies, 1 bag, 14g	**2**
Deliciously Crunchy Sea Salt & Cracked Black Pepper Flavour Cashews, ¼ bag, 25g	**4**
Deliciously Sweet Maple Syrup Peanuts & Cashews, ¼ bag, 82g	**13**
Dry Roasted Peanuts, ½ large bag, 40g	**6**
Dry Roasted Peanuts, 1 bag, 50g	**8**
Frosted Honey Roast Nut Selection with Milk Chocolate Honeycomb, 1 serving, 35g	**5**
Frosted Maple Syrup Flavour Premium Nut Selection, 1 serving, 35g	**6**
Honey Roast Peanuts, ½ bag, 50g	**8**
Jumbo Salted Peanuts, 1 serving, 50g	**8**
McCoy's Roast Beef & Mustard Flavour Potato Chips, 1 bag, 40g	**6**
Original Salted Peanuts, 1 bag, 50g	**8**
Roasted Salted Peanuts, 1 bag, 50g	**9**
Roasted & Salted Cashews, 1 serving, 55g	**10**
Roasted & Salted Pistachios, 1 bag, 55g	**9**
Salt & Vinegar Flavour Peanuts, 1 serving, 50g	**8**
Salted Roasted Cashews, ½ bag, 50g	**9**

Loyd Grossman

Indulgent Nut Mix with Black Olive Wedges, 1 serving, 48g	**8**
Indulgent Nut Mix with Caramelised Red Onion, 1 serving, 48g	**7**
Indulgent Nut Mix with Sun-Dried Tomatoes, 1 serving, 48g	**7**

Lyme Regis Foods

Chewy Fruit Bars Tropical Fruit, 1 bar, 25g	**2**
Fruitus Chewy Apricot Bites, 1 bag, 25g	**2**
Fruitus Chewy Blackcurrant Bites, 1 bag, 25g	**2**
Fruitus Chewy Fruit Bars Pear & Apple, 1 bar, 25g	**2**
Fruitus Chewy Raspberry Bites, 1 bag, 25g	**2**

Merchant Gourmet

Whole Chestnuts, 1 serving, 25g	**1**

Morrisons

Californian Seedless Raisins, 1 serving, 50g	**4**
Cherry Fruiti-Tots, Ready to Eat, 1 pack, 25g	**2**
Dried Blueberries Ready to Eat, 1 pack, 75g	**6**
Mixed Fruit, 1 serving, 50g	**4**
Raisin & Cherry Mix, Ready to Eat, 1 pack, 35g	**3**
Ready To Eat Prunes, Ready to Eat, 1 pack, 50g	**2**
Strawberry Fruiti-Tots, Ready to Eat, 1 pack, 25g	**2**
Tropical Fruiti-Tots, Ready to Eat, 1 pack, 25g	**2**

Munchy Seeds

Pumpkin Mix, 1 serving, 25g	**4**
Vanilla Pumpkin Mix, 1 serving, 25g	**3**

Ocean Spray

Craisins, 1 tablespoon, 15g	**1**
Craisins Juicy Dried Cranberries with Mixed Berries, 1 serving, 40g	**4**
Craisins Juicy Dried Cranberries with Mixed Nuts & Seeds, 1 serving, 40g	**5**
Dried Cranberries, 1 serving, 50g	**4**

Planters

Infusions Indonesian Gado Gado Flavoured Peanuts, 1 serving, 50g	**9**
Peanuts Raisins & Chocolate Buttons, ¼ pack, 42g	**5**
Salted Peanuts & Toasted Corn Mix, ¼ pack, 42g	**7**
Salted Redskin Peanuts Mix, ¼ pack, 42g	**7**

Sainsbury's

Blueberries, Dried & Sweetened, ½ bag, 38g	**3**
Dried Pink Lady Apple, 1 serving, 20g	**2**
Fruit & Nut Mix with Yoghurt Coated Cranberries, ¼ pack, 50g	**6**
Fruit, Nut & Seed Mix, 1 serving, 40g	**5**
Glace Ginger, 1 quantity, 100g	**8**
Jumbo Salted Peanuts & Cashews, 1 serving, 50g	**9**
Mango, ¼ pack, 25g	**2**
Mixed Fruit, 1 serving, 25g	**2**
Pine Nuts, ⅓ pack, 30g	**6**
Poppy Seeds, ½ pack, 50g	**7**
Ready to Eat Exotic Sweetened Dried Fruits, ⅓ pack, 83g	**6**
Sunflower Seeds, ½ pack, 50g	**8**
Sweetened & Tenderised Coconut, 1 quantity, 100g	**16**

Sainsbury's – Taste the Difference

Canadian Maple Syrup Roasted Nut Mix, 1 serving, 50g	**8**
Chocolate Coated Nut Selection, 1 serving, 30g	**5**
Cracked Black Pepper Colossal Cashews, 1 serving, 50g	**8**
Dried Fruit & Nut Selection, 1 serving, 30g	**4**
Fruit & Nut Mix, 1 serving, 50g	**6**

Sun-Maid

California Raisins, 1 serving, 30g	**2**
California Raisins, 1 box, 42g	**4**
Organic California Raisins, 1 serving, 30g	**2**

Sunsweet

Californian Large Stoned Prunes, 1 serving, 125g	**8**
Extra Large Super Soft Ultimate Figs, 1 serving, 25g	**2**
HumZingers Variety Pack Fruit Stix Orchard Fruits, 1 pack, 15g	**1**
HumZingers Variety Pack Fruit Stix Summer Fruits, 1 pack, 15g	**1**
Ultimate Dark Apricots, 1 serving, 25g	**2**
Variety Pack Fruit Stix Orchard Fruits, 1 pack, 15g	**1**

The Co-operative

Chopped Mixed Nuts, 1 quantity, 50g	**8**
Dry Roasted Peanuts, ½ pack, 50g	**8**
Fairtrade Cashew & Raisin Snack Pack, 1 pack, 55g	**7**
Honey Roasted Peanuts & Cashews, ½ pack, 50g	**9**
Luxury Dried Mixed Fruit, 1 quantity, 100g	**8**
Macadamias & Cranberries, ¼ bag, 30g	**4**
Medjool Whole Partially Dried Dates, ¼ box, 50g	**4**
Mixed Fruit & Nuts Snack Pack, ½ bag, 35g	**4**
Mixed Nuts & Raisins, ¼ pack, 50g	**7**
Naturally Healthy Mixed Fruit & Nuts, ⅙ pack, 25g	**4**
Naturally Healthy Mixed Nut Kernels, Almonds, Hazelnuts, Brazil Nuts & Walnuts, ⅕ pack, 24g	**4**
Raw Monkey Nuts, 1/10 bag, 40g	**6**
Ready to Eat Dried Figs, ⅕ pack, 50g	**3**
Ready to Eat, Partially Dried Prunes, 1 pack, 50g	**2**
Roasted & Salted Mixed Nuts, ⅕ bag, 50g	**9**
Roasted & Salted Peanuts, 1 serving, 50g	**8**
Sea Salt & Black Pepper Cashews, ⅕ bag, 50g	**8**
Sugar Rolled Chopped Dates, ⅕ pack, 50g	**4**

Waitrose

Cranberry & Port Mincemeat, 1 quantity, 100g	**8**
Five Seed Mix, 1 portion, 25g	**4**
Glace Fruits Italian Cut Mixed Peel, 1 quantity, 100g	**8**
Honey Roasted Mixed Nuts, ¼ bag, 50g	**8**
Macadamia Nut Halves, ½ pack, 50g	**11**
Nut Mix, 1 serving, 25g	**4**
Nut, Seed & Fruit Mix, 1 serving, 50g	**7**
Soft Dried Five Fruit Medley, ¼ pack, 125g	**8**
Soft Malatya Apricots, 1 serving, 50g	**3**
Soft Prunes, ¼ pack, 125g	**5**
Soft Tropical Fruit Medley, 1 serving, 30g	**2**

Whitworths

Apricots, Fruit Snack Pack, 1 pack, 25g	**1**
Apricots, Ready to Eat, ⅕ large pack, 50g	**2**
Banana Chips, 1 serving, 25g	**4**
Banana Chips Honey Coated, 1 serving, 25g	**4**
Dates, Ready to Eat, ⅕ large pack, 50g	**4**
Dried & Sweetened Blueberries, 1 pack, 75g	**6**
Dried & Sweetened Cranberries or Sour Cherries, 1 pack, 75g	**7**
Dried Mixed Fruit, 1 serving, 25g	**2**
Exotic Fruit Medley, ⅙ large pack, 50g	**4**
Fruit & Nut Mix, 1 serving, 25g	**3**
Fruit, Seed & Nut Harvest Mix, 1 serving, 25g	**3**
Mango Slices, 1 serving, 25g	**2**

Flour & Yeasts

Carrs

Sauce Flour, 1 tablespoon, 15g	**1**

Doves Farm

Buckwheat Flour, 1 portion, 100g	**9**
Gluten & Wheat Free Brown Bread Flour, 1 quantity, 100g	**9**
Gluten & Wheat Free Plain White Flour, 1 quantity, 100g	**9**
Gluten & Wheat Free White Self-Raising Flour, 1 quantity, 100g	**9**
Gluten Free White Bread Flour, 1 quantity, 100g	**9**
Mixed Grain Barleycorn Bread Flour, 1 quantity, 100g	**9**
Stoneground Gram Flour, 1 quantity, 100g	**9**
Stoneground Rice Flour, 1 quantity, 100g	**10**
Wholegrain Kamut Bread Flour, 1 quantity, 100g	**9**

Rakusen's

	ProPoints value
Cake Matzo Meal, 1 portion, 100g	10
Fine Matzo Meal, 1 portion, 100g	10
Medium Matzo Meal, 1 portion, 100g	10

Gravies & Stock

Ainsley Harriott

	ProPoints value
Instant Gravy for Beef, 1 serving, 70ml	1
Instant Gravy for Chicken, 1 serving, 70ml	1

Asda

	ProPoints value
Beef Gravy, ¼ pouch, 75g	1
Chardonnay, Chicken & Thyme Gravy, ⅙ pot, 77g	1
Chicken Stock, ½ pack, 250g	1
Chinese Style Reason to Season, ¼ pack, 9g	1
Gravy Granules for Chicken, 1 tablespoon, 20g	3
Gravy Granules for Meat, 1 serving, 20g	3
Gravy Granules For Vegetables, 1 serving, 5g	1
Gravy Granules Vegetarian, 1 tablespoon, 20g	2
Gravy Granules with Onion, 1 serving, 5g	1
Gravy Mix for Beef, 1 pack, 25g	2
Gravy Mix for Chicken, 1 pack, 25g	2
Mediterranean Style Reason to Season, ¼ pack, 9g	1
Mexican Style Reason to Season, ¼ pack, 9g	1
Moroccan Style Reason to Season, ¼ pack, 9g	1
Onion Gravy, ¼ pouch, 88g	1
Onion with Gravy Granules, 1 serving, 20g	2
Poultry Gravy, 1 serving, 83g	1

Asda – Extra Special

	ProPoints value
Chicken Gravy, ½ pack, 125g	2
Chicken Stock, 1 pack, 125g	0
Fish Stock, 1 cube, 2g	0
Red Wine Gravy, ¼ pack, 75g	1
Roast Chicken Gravy, ⅛ pot, 68g	1

Batchelors

	ProPoints value
Gravy, 1 pack, 100g	8
Instant Gravy Mix, 1 pack, 100g	9

Bisto

	ProPoints value
Beef Heat & Pour Gravy, ¼ carton, 75g	1
Best Beef Gravy with a Hint of Caramelised Onion, 1 serving, 7g	1
Best Beef Gravy with a Hint of Red Wine & Shallot, 1 serving, 7g	1
Best Caramelised Onion Gravy, 1 serving, 6g	1
Best Chicken Gravy with a Hint of Sage & Onion, 1 serving, 7g	1
Best Gravy Granules, 4 teaspoons, 20g	2
Best Lamb Gravy with a Hint of Mint, 1 serving, 7g	1
Best Onion Gravy with a Hint of Sage & Thyme, 1 serving, 7g	1
Best Pork Gravy with a Hint of Sage, 1 serving, 8g	1
Best Rich & Roasted Beef Gravy, 1 serving, 6g	1
Best Rich & Roasted Chicken Gravy, 1 serving, 6g	1
Best Rich & Roasted Pork Gravy, 1 serving, 6g	1
Best Rich Beef Gravy, 1 serving, 7g	1
Best Roast Beef Flavour Gravy Granules, 4 teaspoons, 20g	2
Best Roast Chicken Flavour Gravy Granules, 4 teaspoons, 20g	2
Best Roast Lamb Gravy, 1 serving, 6g	1
Best Roast Onion Flavour Gravy Granules, 4 teaspoons, 20g	2
Best Roast Pork Flavour Gravy Granules, 4 teaspoons, 20g	2
Best Roast Vegetable Gravy Granules, 4 teaspoons, 20g	2
Best Roasted Winter Vegetable Gravy, 1 serving, 6g	1
Best Turkey Gravy with a Hint of Sage, 1 serving, 8g	1
Chicken Gravy Granules, 1 serving, 50g	6
Chicken Heat & Pour Gravy, ¼ carton, 75g	1
Favourite Gravy Granules, 1 serving, 6g	1
Gravy Granules for Chicken Dishes, 4 teaspoons, 20g	2
Gravy Granules for Every Meal Occasion, 4 teaspoons, 20g	2
Gravy Granules for Turkey Dishes, 4 teaspoons, 20g	2
Gravy Granules for Vegetable Dishes, 4 teaspoons, 20g	2
Gravy Granules with Onion, 4 teaspoons, 20g	2
Pour Over Gravy, All Types, 1 pack, 200g	1
Reduced Salt Favourite Gravy Granules, 1 serving, 7g	1
The Original Gravy Powder, 4 teaspoons, 20g	1
Vegetarian Gravy Granules, 4 teaspoons, 20g	2

Bovril

	ProPoints value
Beef Extract, 1 serving, 12g	0
Beef Extract, 2 servings, 24g	1
Beef Stock Cubes, 1 cube, 6g	0

Beef Stock Cubes, 2 cubes, 12g **1**

Colman's

Beef Gravy Mix, ¼ sachet, 11g **0**
Bolognese Pasta Bake Recipe Mix,
¼ sachet, 13g **1**
Chicken Gravy Mix, ¼ sachet, 10g **0**
Lamb & Mint Gravy, ¼ sachet, 10g **0**

Goldenfry

Onion Gravy Granules, 1 portion, 5g **0**
Reduced Salt Gravy Granules For Beef,
1 pack, 170g **2**
Rich & Meaty Gravy Granules, 1 portion, 5g **0**
Rich & Meaty Onion Gravy Granules,
1 serving, 70ml **1**

Kallo – Just Bouillion

Concentrated Stock, Beef, 1 serving, 10g **0**
Gravy Granules, All Types, 1 serving, 7g **1**
Premium Stock Cubes, All Types, 1 cube, 11g **0**
Specially Prepared Gravy Concentrate,
All Types, 1 serving, 10g **0**

Knorr

Beef Stock Granules, 1 serving, 2g **0**
Beef Stock Pot, 1 pot, 28g **1**
Chicken Stock Granules, 1 serving, 2g **0**
The Cube, All Types, 1 cube, 10g **0**
Vegetable Stock Granules, 1 teaspoon, 5g **0**
Vegetable Stock Pot, 1 pot, 28g **1**

OXO

Beef Gravy, 1 serving, 7g **1**
Beef Gravy with a Hint of Pink Peppercorn,
1 serving, 7g **1**
Beef Gravy with a Hint of Winter Berry &
Shallot, 1 serving, 7g **1**
Chicken Gravy with a Hint of Sage & Onion,
¼ pack, 8g **1**
Concentrated Beef Liquid Stock, 1 serving, 20ml **1**
Concentrated Chicken Liquid Stock,
1 serving, 20ml **1**
Concentrated Lamb Liquid Stock,
1 serving, 20ml **1**
Concentrated Vegetable Liquid Stock,
1 serving, 20ml **1**
Cubes, All Types, 2 cubes, 6g **1**
Gravy Granules for Meat Dishes, 1 serving, 7g **1**
Gravy Granules for Roast Beef, 4 teaspoons, 18g **2**
Gravy Granules for Roast Chicken, 1 serving, 6g **0**

Gravy Granules for Vegetable Dishes,
1 serving, 7g **1**
Lamb Gravy with a Hint of Garden Mint,
1 serving, 7g **1**
Onion Gravy with a Hint of Sage & Thyme,
1 serving, 7g **1**
Pork Gravy with a Hint of Sage, 1 serving, 7g **1**
Real Stock Chicken, 1 serving, 125ml **0**
Turkey Gravy with a Hint of Parsley & Sage,
1 serving, 7g **1**

Schwartz

Classic Roast Chicken Gravy Mix, 1 sachet, 26g **1**
Classic Roast Turkey Gravy Mix, ¼ packet, 6g **1**
Mix for Classic Roast Onion Gravy,
1 sachet, 27g **2**
Rich Gravy, All Types, 1 serving, 20g **0**

Tesco

Finest Beef Gravy, 1 serving, 125g **2**
Free Range Chicken Stock, 1 serving, 125ml **0**
Onion Gravy, 1 serving, 125g **2**
Poultry Gravy, 1 serving, 125g **2**

The Co-operative

Gravy Browning, ½ teaspoons, 3g **0**
Gravy Granules for Chicken, 1 tablespoon, 20g **3**
Gravy Salt, 1 serving, 140ml **1**
Poultry Gravy, ¼ pot, 100g **1**
Ready to Serve Gravy for Poultry, 1 pot, 280g **3**
Ready to Serve Gravy for Red Meat, 1 pot, 280g **2**
Rich Brown Gravy Granules for Meat,
1 heaped teaspoon, 10g **1**

Waitrose

Beef Gravy, ⅙ pot, 83g **1**
Beef Stock, 1 quantity, 100ml **1**
Chicken Gravy, ⅙ pack, 83g **1**
Chicken Stock, 1 quantity, 100ml **1**
Cranberry & Mulled Wine Sauce, ⅙ pot, 50g **2**
Cranberry & Port Sauce, ⅙ pot, 50g **1**
Lamb Stock, 1 quantity, 100ml **2**
Onion Gravy, ⅙ pot, 83g **1**
Poultry Gravy, ⅙ pot, 83g **1**
Vegetable Stock, 1 quantity, 100ml **2**

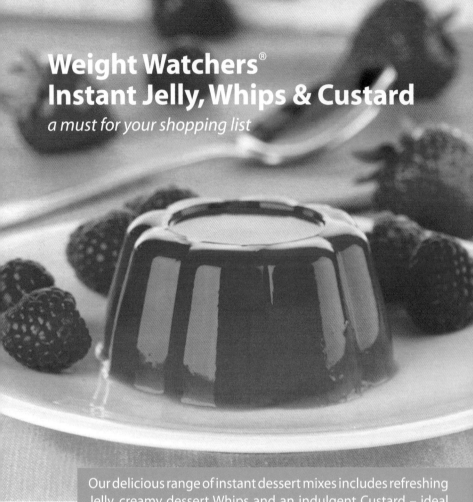

Weight Watchers®
Instant Jelly, Whips & Custard

a must for your shopping list

Our delicious range of instant dessert mixes includes refreshing Jelly, creamy dessert Whips and an indulgent Custard – ideal for a tasty treat!

0 ProPoints value *to* **3** ProPoints value

per serving

7 varieties including:
Orange Jelly, Chocolate Whip and Instant Custard

WeightWatchers Foods
Eat gorgeous. Feel gorgeous.

Jellies & Gelatines

Asda

Orange Jelly, 1 portion, 81g	1
Strawberry Jelly, 1 pack, 400g	5

Chivers

Blackcurrant Jelly, 1 pack, 135g	2
Frujies Mandarins in Orange Flavour Jelly, 1 serving, 125g	2
Frujies Peaches in Strawberry Flavour Jelly, 1 serving, 125g	2
Lemon Jelly, 1 pack, 135g	2
Orange Jelly, 1 pack, 135g	2
Pineapple in Jelly, 1 pot, 175g	3
Raspberries in Jelly, 1 pot, 175g	3
Raspberry Jelly, 1 pack, 135g	2

Dole

Fruit in Jelly Apples in Raspberry Flavour Jelly, 1 pot, 120g	3
Fruit in Jelly Mixed Fruit in Peach Flavour Jelly, 1 pot, 123g	3
Jelly Peaches in Strawberry Flavour Jelly, 1 pot, 123g	3
Mandarins in Orange Flavour Jelly, 1 pot, 123g	3
Pineapple in Lime Flavour Jelly, 1 pot, 123g	3

Hartley's

Blackcurrant Flavour Jelly, Ready to Eat, 1 pot, 125g	3
Frujies Mandarins in Orange Flavour Jelly, 1 pot, 125g	2
Frujies Peaches in Strawberry Flavour Jelly, 1 pot, 125g	2
Lemon & Lime Flavour Jelly, Ready to Eat, 1 pot, 125g	3
Lemon Flavour Jelly, ¼ pack, 34g	3
Lime Flavour Jelly, ¼ pack, 34g	3
Low Sugar Raspberry Flavour Jelly, 1 pot, 115g	0
Low Sugar Raspberry Flavour Jelly, 2 pots, 230g	1
Low Sugar Strawberry Flavour Jelly, 1 pot, 115g	0
Low Sugar Strawberry Flavour Jelly, 2 pots, 230g	1
Mango & Passionfruit Jelly, 1 pot, 175g	0
Mango & Passionfruit Jelly, 2 pots, 350g	1
Orange Flavour Jelly, ¼ pack, 34g	3

Orange Jelly, ¼ pack, 34g	3
Pineapple Flavour Jelly, ¼ pack, 34g	3
Raspberry Flavour Jelly, ¼ pack, 34g	3
Raspberry Jelly, Ready to Eat, 1 pot, 125g	3
Strawberry Flavoured Jelly, ¼ pack, 34g	3
Strawberry Jelly, Ready to Eat, 1 pot, 125g	3
Tangerine Flavour Jelly, ¼ pack, 34g	3

Tesco

Mandarin Jellies, 1 individual, 140g	7
Mixed Berry Jellies, 1 individual, 140g	4
Quince Jelly, 1 serving, 15g	1
Raspberry Jellies, 1 individual, 140g	4

The Co-operative

Lemon Flavour Jelly, ¼ pack, 34g	3
Orange Flavour Jelly, ¼ pack, 34g	3
Peach Flavour Jelly, ¼ pack, 34g	3
Pineapple Flavour Jelly, ¼ pack, 34g	3
Raspberry Flavour Jelly, ¼ pack, 34g	3
Strawberry Flavour Jelly, ¼ pack, 34g	3
Summer Fruits Flavour Jelly, ¼ pack, 34g	3

Waitrose

Cherry Jelly, 1 pot, 175g	4
Fruity Pineapple Jelly, 1 pot, 175g	3
Fruity Raspberry Jelly, 1 pot, 175g	4

Weight Watchers

Blackcurrant Flavour Sugar Free Jelly Crystals, 1 serving, 204g	0
Orange Flavour Sugar Free Jelly Crystals, 1 serving, 204g	0
Raspberry & Strawberry Flavour Sugar Free Jelly Crystals, 1 serving, 204g	0

Marzipan & Icing

Asda

Almond Marzipan, Smart Price, 1 quantity, 100g	12
Golden Marzipan, 1 quantity, 100g	12
Plain Chocolate Drops, 1 tablespoon, 10g	1
White Marzipan, 1 quantity, 100g	12

Dr Oetker

Golden Marzipan, 1 quantity, 100g	12
Ready Rolled Marzipan, ⅙ pack, 68g	8

Scotbloc Chocolate Flavour Cake Covering, Plain, 1 quantity, 100g	15
Scotbloc Chocolate Flavour Cake Covering, White, 1 quantity, 100g	16
Select 35% Cocoa Milk Chocolate, Organic, ⅓ pack, 40g	6
Select 85% Cocoa Dark Chocolate, Organic, ⅓ pack, 40g	6
Select Mediterranean Almond Marzipan, ¼ pack, 114g	14
Select Milk Chocolate Chips, Organic, ¼ pack, 25g	4
Select Milk Chocolate Chunks with Caramel Fudge, ¼ pack, 25g	3
Select White Chocolate Chunks with Cranberry, ¼ pack, 25g	3

Morrisons

Chocolate Flavour Frosting, 1 serving, 50g	6
Purple Cupcake Topper, 1 serving, 45g	6
Strawberry Flavour Frosting, 1 serving, 50g	7
Vanilla Flavour Frosting, 1 serving, 50g	7
White Cupcake Topper, 1 serving, 46g	6
Yellow Cupcake Topper, 1 serving, 45g	6

Silver Spoon – Cakecraft

Finest Quality Marzipan, 1 quantity, 100g	12
Ivory Ready to Roll Icing, 1 quantity, 100g	11
Ready Rolled Marzipan, 1 quantity, 100g	12
Ready Rolled White Icing, 1 quantity, 100g	11
White Ready to Roll Icing, 1 quantity, 100g	11

Meringues

Asda

Meringue Nests, 1 (13g)	1
Meringue Pavlova, 1 serving, 22g	2
Meringues, 1 portion, 25g	3

Asda – Extra Special

Belgian Chocolate Mini Meringues, 1 (6g)	1
Meringue Nests, 1 individual, 14g	1
Mini Meringues, 2 (9g)	1
Strawberry Mini Meringues, 2 (8g)	1

Morrisons

| Fresh Cream Meringues, 1 (81g) | 8 |
| Meringue Stack, 1 serving, 21g | 2 |

Oil & Vinegar

Asda – Extra Special

Balsamic Dipping Oil, 1 tablespoon, 15ml	3
Garlic-Infused Extra Virgin Olive Oil, 1 tablespoon, 15ml	4
Madras Spiced Blend, 1 tablespoon, 15ml	1
Roast Garlic Dipping Oil, 1 tablespoon, 15ml	3

FryLight

Better than Butter, 4 sprays, 1ml	0
Extra Virgin Olive Oil, 4 sprays, 1ml	0
Oriental Stir Fry, 4 sprays, 1ml	0
Sunflower Oil, 4 sprays, 1ml	0

The Co-operative

Chilli Dipping Oil, 1 tablespoon, 15ml	3
Corn Oil, 1 tablespoon, 15ml	4
Garlic Dipping Oil, 1 tablespoon, 15ml	3
Grapeseed Oil, 1 tablespoon, 15ml	4
Groundnut Oil, 1 tablespoon, 15ml	4
Light & Mild Olive Oil, 1 tablespoon, 15ml	4

Pastry, Ready Made – Fresh & Frozen

Asda

All-Butter Pastry Case, ½ pack, 92g	12
Ready to Roll Sweet Pastry, ¼ pack, 75g	11
Savoury Pastry Case, ¼ medium, 50g	7
Sweet Pastry Case, ¼ medium, 50g	7

Blue Dragon

| Spring Roll Wraps, 1 (11g) | 1 |

Jus-Rol

Jus-Rol Vol-Au-Vent, 1 (17g)	2
Puff Pastry Block, 1 serving, 50g	6
Puff Pastry Cases, 1 (38g)	5

ALL THE TASTE BUT ONLY HALF THE SUGAR

**GREAT IN TEA AND COFFEE,
OR SPRINKLED ON FRUIT OR CEREALS**

HALF A SPOON OF HALF SPOON IS THE EQUIVALENT OF A FULL SPOONFUL OF REGULAR SUGAR.

Shortcrust Pastry Block, 1 serving, 50g | 6

Sara Lee

Fresh Ready to Bake Dough for
Croissants, 1 (60g) | 6
Fresh Ready to Bake Dough for Pains au
Chocolat, 1 piece, 47g | 5

Syrups, Sweet Sauces, Sugars & Sweeteners

Asda

Passion Fruit & Mango Sauce, 1 serving, 15g | 1
Raspberry Sauce, 1 serving, 30g | 2
Strawberry Sauce, 1 serving, 15g | 1

Asda – Extra Special

Wild Cranberry & Orange Sauce, 1 teaspoon, 10g | 1
Old English Toffee Flavour Sauce,
1 serving, 30g | 3

Asda – Good For You

Belgian Chocolate Sauce, 1 serving, 30g | 3
Chocolate Sauce, 1 serving, 30g | 3
Toffee Sauce, 1 serving, 30g | 3

Aunty's

Sensational Butterscotch or Chocolate Dessert
Sauce, 1 serving, 30g | 3
Sensational Mixed Berry Dessert Sauce,
1 serving, 20g | 1

Billington's

Unrefined Demerara, 2 teaspoons, 8g | 1
Unrefined Dark Muscavado Sugar,
1 serving, 100g | 10
Unrefined Golden Caster Sugar, 1 serving, 100g | 11
Unrefined Golden Granulated Sugar,
1 teaspoon, 4g | 0
Unrefined Light Muscavado Sugar,
1 serving, 100g | 11
Unrefined Molasses, 1 serving, 100g | 10

Blue Dragon

Stem Ginger in Syrup, 1 serving, 30g | 2

Merchant Gourmet

Dulce de Leche Chocolate Toffee, 1 serving, 15g | 1

Nestlé

Carnation Caramel, 1 serving, 50g | 4

Sainsbury's

Stem Ginger in Sugar Syrup, ¼ jar, 52g | 4

Silver Spoon

White Granulated Sugar, 1 teaspoon, 4g | 0
White Granulated Sugar, 2 teaspoons, 8g | 1
Caster Sugar, 1 serving, 100g | 11
Icing Sugar, 1 serving, 100g | 11
Fondant Icing, 1 serving, 100g | 11
Royal Icing, 1 serving, 100g | 11
Half Spoon, Low Calorie Sugar, 2 teaspoons, 8g | 1
Silver Spoon, Sweetness & Light, Granulated
Sugar, 1 teaspoon, 0.5g | 0
Silver Spoon, Sweetness & Light, Sweetener
Cubes, 1 cube | 0
Silver Spoon, Sweetness & Light, Sweetener
Tablets, 1 tablet | 0

Splenda

Low Calorie Sugar Alternative,
Granulated, 1 (0g) | 0
Low Calorie Sugar Alternative, Sweet
Minis, 1 (0g) | 0

Tesco

Apple & Toffee Sauce, 1 serving, 100g | 5

The Co-operative

Fairtrade Chocolate Sauce, 1 serving, 20g | 2
Fairtrade Golden Granulated Sugar,
1 teaspoon, 5g | 1
Raspberry Coulis, 1 tablespoon, 20g | 1

The English Provender Co.

Belgian Chocolate Sauce, 1 serving, 15g | 2
Fairtrade Chocolate Sauce, 1 serving, 15g | 2
Fairtrade Coffee Sauce, 2 tablespoons, 60g | 7

Waitrose

Belgian Chocolate Sauce, 1 tablespoon, 15g | 1
Chinese Stem Ginger in Syrup, ¼ jar, 110g | 9
Maple Syrup No 1 Medium, 1 tablespoon, 15g | 1
Toffee Sauce, 1 tablespoon, 15g | 1

Kitchen
Cupboard

Basic Foods

Beans, Black Eyed, dried,
1 heaped tablespoon, 50g — **4**
Beans, Kidney, dried, 1 portion, 100g — **8**
Beans, Mung, dried, 1 tablespoon, 35g — **3**
Beans, Soya, dried, 1 portion, 100g — **10**
Bulgar Wheat, Cracked Wheat, dried,
1 small portion, 20g — **2**
Bulgar Wheat, Cracked Wheat, dried,
1 medium portion, 40g — **3**
Cannelloni Tube, dried, 1 tube, 10g — **1**
Chick Peas, dried, 1 portion, 100g — **9**
Couscous, cooked, 1 medium portion, 150g — **4**
Couscous, dried, 1 medium portion, 60g — **6**
Cous Cous, Wholewheat, dried,
1 medium portion, 60g — **6**
Gnocchi, fresh, 1 small portion, 125g — **5**
Lasagne Sheet, dried, 1 sheet, 20g — **2**
Lentils, Green & Brown, whole, dried,
1 portion, 100g — **8**
Lentils, Split Red, cooked,
1 heaped tablespoon, 35g — **1**
Lentils, Split Red, dried, 1 small portion, 20g — **2**
Millet, raw, 1 portion, 30g — **3**
Noodles, Egg, boiled, 1 portion, 150g — **3**
Noodles, Egg, dried, 1 medium portion, 40g — **4**
Noodles, Rice, cooked, 1 portion, 150g — **5**
Noodles, Rice, dried, 1 medium portion, 40g — **4**
Noodles, Spinach, cooked, 1 portion, 150g — **5**
Pasta, Corn, dried, 1 medium portion, 40g — **4**
Pasta, Plain, fresh, cooked, 1 portion, 100g — **4**
Pasta, Plain, fresh, uncooked, 1 portion, 100g — **8**
Pasta, White, cooked, 1 medium portion, 150g — **4**
Pasta, White, dried, 1 medium portion, 40g — **4**
Pasta, Wholemeal, cooked,
1 medium portion, 150g — **5**
Pasta, Wholemeal, dried, 1 medium portion, 40g — **4**
Pearl Barley, dried, 1 small portion, 30g — **3**
Peas, Yellow Split, dried, 1 quantity, 100g — **8**
Polenta, raw, 1 medium portion, 62g — **6**
Pudding Rice, dried (short grain),
1 medium portion, 60g — **6**
Quinoa, dried, 1 portion, 100g — **9**
Rice, Brown, boiled, 1 medium portion, 150g — **6**
Rice, Brown, dried, 1 medium portion, 60g — **6**
Rice, White, Basmati, raw, 1 medium portion, 60g — **6**

Rice, White, Arborio, dried,
1 medium portion, 60g — **6**
Rice, White, Easy Cook, boiled
1 medium portion, 150g — **6**
Rice, White, Easy Cook, dried,
1 medium portion, 60g — **7**
Rice, White, Long Grain, dried,
1 medium portion, 60g — **6**
Sago, dried, 1 heaped tablespoon, 30g — **3**
Semolina, dried, 1 quantity, 100g — **9**
Tapioca, dried mix, 1 heaped tablespoon, 30g — **3**
Wheat Bran, dried, 2 tablespoons, 14g — **1**
Wheatgerm, dried, 1 tablespoon, 5g — **1**

Pasta & Noodles

Amoy

Straight to Wok Medium Noodles, 1 pack, 150g — **7**
Straight to Wok Rice Noodles, 1 pack, 150g — **5**
Straight to Wok Singapore Noodles,
1 pack, 150g — **7**
Straight to Wok Thick Udon Noodles,
1 pack, 150g — **6**
Straight to Wok Thread Fine Noodles,
1 pack, 150g — **6**

Asda

Beef & Tomato Flavour Noodle Snack,
1 sachet, 93g — **4**
Cannelloni Italian Pasta, 1 serving, 80g — **7**
Cheese & Bacon Pasta in Sauce,
1 sachet, 115g — **13**
Chicken & Mushroom Pasta in Sauce,
½ pack (prepared), 200g — **6**
Chicken & Sweetcorn Savoury Rice,
1 pack, 120g — **5**
Chilli Penne Flavoured Italian Pasta,
1 pack, 500g — **20**
Garlic & Basil Linguine Flavoured Pasta,
¼ pack, 125g — **5**
Garlic & Herb Pasta in Sauce, 1 pack, 120g — **13**
Instant Beef Noodles, 1 serving, 167g — **6**
Instant Chicken Noodles, 1 serving, 172g — **6**
Instant Curry Noodles, 1 serving, 182g — **6**
Pad Thai Noodles, chilled, 1 pack, 350g — **12**
Paglia e Fieno Italian Egg Pasta, ¼ pack, 125g — **12**
Quick Cook Fusilli, 1 portion (medium), 185g — **17**
Ready to Wok Noodles, ½ pack, 125g — **6**

Rice Noodles with Spring Onions,
½ pack, 200g **7**
Tomato & Basil Pasta in Sauce, 1 sachet, 120g **12**

Batchelors

Low Fat Super Noodles, Chicken & Herb Flavour,
½ pack, cooked, 140g **4**
Low Fat Super Noodles, Chilli Chicken Flavour,
½ pack, cooked, 150g **4**
Low Fat Super Noodles, Smoky Bacon Flavour,
½ pack, cooked, 140g **4**
Low Fat Super Noodles, Sweet Thai Chilli
Flavour, ½ pack, cooked, 150g **4**
Pasta 'n' Sauce Cheese, Leek & Ham Flavour,
1 serving, 120g **12**
Pasta 'n' Sauce Chicken & Mushroom Flavour,
1 serving, 122g **12**
Pasta 'n' Sauce Creamy Chicken & Herbs,
1 pack, 116g **11**
Pasta 'n' Sauce Creamy Tikka Masala,
1 pack, 117g **11**
Pasta 'n' Sauce Macaroni Cheese,
1 serving, 108g **10**
Pasta 'n' Sauce Mild Cheese & Broccoli,
1 serving, 123g **12**
Savoury Rice Mild Mexican Flavour,
1 pack, 120g **12**
Savoury Rice Pilau Flavour, 1 pack, 120g **12**
Savoury Rice Thai Sweet Chilli Flavour,
1 pack, 120g **12**
Wholegrain Pasta 'n' Sauce Creamy Carbonara,
1 pack, 110g **11**
Wholegrain Pasta 'n' Sauce Creamy Tomato &
Basil, 1 pack, 110g **10**
Wholegrain Pasta 'n' Sauce Garlic & Herb,
1 pack, 110g **10**
Wholegrain Pasta 'n' Sauce Mediterranean
Tomato & Vegetable, 1 pack, 110g **10**

Batchelors – Super Noodles

Bacon Flavour, ½ pack, cooked, 150g **7**
BBQ Beef, ½ pack, cooked, 150g **7**
Cheese & Ham, ½ pack, cooked, 150g **7**
Chicken Flavour, ½ pack, cooked, 150g **7**
Mild Curry Flavour, ½ pack, cooked, 150g **7**
Spicy Curry Flavour, ½ pack, cooked, 150g **7**
Sweet & Sour Flavour, ½ pack, cooked, 150g **7**
Thai Green Curry Flavour,
½ pack, cooked, 150g **7**

Batchelors – Super Noodles To Go

Beef & Mushroom Flavour,
1 pot, 360g, as cooked **10**
Chicken Chow Mein Flavour,
1 pot, 360g, as cooked **10**
Chinese Spare Rib Flavour,
1 pot, 360g, as cooked **11**
Curry Flavour, 1 pot, 360g, as cooked **11**
Nice 'n' Spicy Flavour, 1 pot, 360g, as cooked **11**
Roast Chicken Flavour, 1 pot, 360g, as cooked **11**
Spicy Curry Flavour, 1 pot, 360g, as cooked **10**
Thai Green Curry Flavour,
1 pot, 360g, as cooked **10**

Blue Dragon

Chicken & Spring Onion Flavour Snack
Noodles, 1 serving, 85g **11**
Coriander Infused Quick Wok Noodles,
½ pack, 150g **7**
Crispy Noodles, 1 pack, 125g **12**
Fine Egg Noodle Nest, 1 portion, 50g **5**
Instant Noodles, 1 serving, 75g **9**
Japanese Ramen Noodles, ¼ pack, 63g **6**
Medium Egg Noodle Nest, 1 portion, 50g **5**
Medium Quick Noodles Infused with Chilli,
1 pouch, 150g **7**
Medium Rice Noodles, ½ pack, 125g **12**
Medium Wheat Quick Wok Noodles,
½ pack, 150g **7**
Medium Wholewheat Quick Wok Noodles,
½ pack, 150g **6**
Wholewheat Noodles, 1 serving, 50g **5**

Blue Dragon – Noodle Town

Beef & Black Pepper, 1 pack, 85g **11**
Chow Mein Instant Noodles, 1 pack, 85g **11**
Chicken & Chilli Flavour, 1 pack, 86g **7**
Crispy Duck Flavour, 1 pack, 85g **11**
Mushroom Flavour, 1 pack, 85g **11**
Oriental Chicken Flavour, 1 pack, 65g **7**
Won Ton Flavour, 1 pack, 85g **11**

Crosse & Blackwell

Pasta & Sauce Carbonara, 1 pack, 120g **12**
Pasta & Sauce Cheese & Broccoli,
1 pack, 120g **12**
Pasta & Sauce Cheese, Leek & Ham,
1 pack, 120g **12**

Pasta & Sauce Chicken & Mushroom,
1 pack, 120g **12**

Pasta & Sauce Tomato, Onion & Herb,
1 pack, 120g **12**

Golden Wonder
The Nation's Noodles

Beef & Tomato Flavour, 1 pot, 271g **11**
Chicken & Mushroom Flavour, 1 pot, 261g **10**
Chip Shop Curry Flavour, 1 pot, 269g **10**
Sweet & Sour Flavour, 1 pot, 280g **9**

Knorr – Micro Noodles

Barbecue Beef Flavour, 1 pack, 280g **14**
Chicken Flavour, 1 pack, 280g **13**
Mild Curry Flavour, 1 pack, 280g **14**

Morrisons

Beef and Tomato Flavour Noodle Tubs,
1 tub (made-up) 255g **13**

Chicken and Mushroom Flavour Noodle Tubs,
1 tub (made-up) 255g **13**

Chicken and Mushroom Flavour Noodle Tubs,
1 tub (made-up) 245g **14**

Curry Flavour Noodle Tubs,
1 tub (made-up) 255g **14**

Snack Pasta Cheese & Ham Flavour,
1 packet (made-up), 220g **7**

Snack Pasta Chicken & Mushroom Flavour,
1 packet (made-up), 234g **7**

Snack Pasta Tomato & Herb,
1 packet (made-up) 257g **7**

Southern Fried Chicken Flavour Noodle Tubs,
1 tub (made-up), 255g **11**

Morrisons – Eat Smart

Chicken & Sweetcorn Noodle Snack Pot,
1 pot (made-up) 247g **7**

Mug Shot

Noodle Snack Spicy Sweet 'n' Sour Flavour,
67g packet (made up) **7**

Noodle Snack Thai Style, 55g packet (made up) **6**

Pasta Snack Creamy Cheese,
68g packet (made up) **8**

Pasta Snack Roast Chicken Flavour,
55g packet (made up) **6**

Pasta Snack Tomato 'n' Herb,
64g packet (made up) **7**

Don't leave it to guesswork...

ProPoints® Kitchen Scales

- The ONLY kitchen scales that calculate *ProPoints* values
- Database with over 700 everyday items
- Recipe Builder feature works out the *ProPoints* values in any recipe

Please note that the actual product colour may vary from the item shown.

Available now... in your meetings or through at home

WeightWatchers®

Order today by calling: 08456 788 999
or visit: www.weightwatchers.co.uk

Weight Watchers and *ProPoints* are the registered trademarks of Weight Watchers International, Inc. The *ProPoints* Weight Loss System and formula are proprietary to Weight Watchers International, Inc. Patent pending. © (2011) Weight Watchers International, Inc. All rights reserved.

Pot Noodle

Beef & Tomato Flavour, 1 pot, 305g	**10**
Chicken & Mushroom, 1 pot, 305g	**10**
Chinese Chow Mein Flavour, 1 pot, 305g	**10**
Chinese Sweet & Sour Flavour, 1 pot, 305g	**11**
King Pot, Bombay Bad Boy, 1 pot, 420g	**15**
No 7 Sticky Rib Flavour, 1 pot, 305g	**11**
Original Curry Flavour, 1 pot, 305g	**11**

Sainsbury's

Asparagus Quadrotti, ½ pack, 125g	**4**
Basil & Pine Nut Margherite, ½ pack, 125g	**5**
Tomato & Basil Pasta, ¼ pot, 75g	**3**

Sharwood's

Lemongrass & Coriander Microwave Noodles, ½ pack, 125g	**5**
Plain Microwave Noodles, ½ pack, 125g	**6**
Ready to Wok Pad Thai Ribbon Noodles, 1 pack, 200g	**9**
Ready to Wok Soft Medium Noodles, 1 pack, 200g	**7**
Rich Soy & Sesame Microwave Noodles, 1 pack, 250g	**12**
Stir-Fry Soft Medium Noodles, 1 pack, 200g	**9**
Sweet & Sour Microwave Noodles, ½ pack, 125g	**6**
Sweet Chilli Microwave Noodles, ½ pack, 125g	**6**
Thai Rice Noodles, 1 serving, 68g	**7**

Tesco – Light Choices

Chicken & Mushroom Flavour Noodle Snack in a Pot, 1 pot, 247g	**6**
Chow Mein Noodles Snack in a Pot, 1 pot, 238g	**6**
Roasted Vegetable Couscous Snack in a Pot, 1 pot, 144g	**5**

The Co-operative

Cheese & Broccoli Flavour Pasta & Sauce, 1 pack, 110g	**4**
Cheese & Ham Flavour Pasta & Sauce, 1 pack, 110g	**4**
Chicken & Mushroom Flavour Pasta & Sauce, 1 pack, 110g	**4**
Mushroom & Garlic Flavour Pasta & Sauce, 1 pack, 110g	**4**
Spicy Chicken Pasta Pot, 1 pot, 300g	**12**

Rice, Pulses & Grains

Ainsley Harriott

Amazing Grains Lentil Dahl, 1 serving, 266g	**6**
Basmati Savoury Rice, Chicken Flavour, 1 serving, 181g	**5**
Basmati Savoury Rice, Golden Vegetable, 1 serving, 180g	**5**
Basmati Savoury Rice, Mixed Vegetable, 1 serving, 178g	**6**
Basmati Savoury Rice, Mushroom & Pepper, 1 serving, 173g	**5**
Citrus Kick Cous Cous, 1 serving, 130g, cooked	**5**
Moroccan Medley Cous Cous, 1 serving, 130g, cooked	**5**
Premium Risotto, Cheese, Onion & Wine Flavour, 1 serving, 360g	**18**
Premium Risotto, Wild Mushroom, 1 serving, 370g	**16**
Roasted Vegetable Style Cous Cous, 1 serving, 130g, cooked	**5**
Spice Sensation Cous Cous, 1 serving, 130g, cooked	**5**
Tomato Tango Cous Cous, 1 serving, 130g, cooked	**5**
Wickedly Wild Mushroom Cous Cous, 1 serving, 130g, cooked	**2**

Asda

Basmati Micro Rice, ½ pack, 200g	**8**
Boil in the Bag Basmati Rice, 1 bag, 125g	**12**
Boil in the Bag Long Grain Rice, 1 bag, 125g	**5**
Brown Long Grain Micro Rice, ½ pack, 200g	**9**
Carnaroli Risotto Rice, 1 serving, 125g, cooked	**5**
Cheese & Tomato Risotto, 1 serving, 250g	**9**
Long Grain Micro Rice, ½ pack, 200g	**9**
Mediterranean Style Tomato Cous Cous, 1 pot, 110g	**4**
Mediterranean Vegetable Risotto, 1 pack, 250g	**8**
Mushroom Risotto, 1 pack, 250g	**8**
Mushroom Savoury Rice, ½ pack, 60g	**2**
Paella Spanish Rice, 1 serving, 100g	**9**
Pilau Micro Rice, ½ pack, 200g	**8**
Pilau Rice, ½ pack, 170g	**7**
Quick Cook Lemon Pepper Savoury Rice, 1 serving, 105g	**4**

Quick Cook Paella Savoury Rice,
1 serving, 105g **5**

Quick Cook Thai Style Savoury Rice,
1 serving, 105g **4**

Spicy Vegetable Cous Cous, ½ pack, 55g **2**

Sweet & Sour Savoury Rice, 1 pack, 120g **4**

Batchelors

Beef Savoury Rice, ½ packet, 60g **6**

Chicken Savoury Rice, ½ packet, 60g **6**

Chinese Savoury Rice, ½ packet, 60g **6**

Egg Fried Savoury Rice, ½ packet, 60g **6**

Garlic Butter Savoury Rice, ½ packet, 60g **6**

Golden Savoury Rice, ½ packet, 60g **6**

Mild Curry Savoury Rice, ½ packet, 60g **6**

Mushroom Savoury Rice, ½ packet, 60g **6**

Blue Dragon

Wide Wheat Quick Wok Noodles, ½ pack, 150g **7**

Merchant Gourmet

Authentic French Puy Lentils, ¼ pack, 125g **4**

Black Beluga Lentils, ¼ pack, 125g **4**

Microwave Puy Lentils, ½ pouch, 125g **5**

Polenta, 1 serving, 62g **6**

Sainsbury's

Mixed Vegetable Savoury Rice, ½ pack, 186g **6**

Thai Sticky Rice, 1 pack, 200g **8**

Three Colour Pilau Rice, ½ pack, 250g **10**

Vegetable Biryani, 1 pack, 250g **12**

Sammy's

Moroccan Spices, Sultanas & Pine Nuts
Couscous, 1 serving, 50g **5**

Organic Couscous Aromatic Pesto & Herbs,
1 pack, 200g **7**

Snack Pack Couscous Chicken & Mushroom
Flavour, 1 pack, 70g **7**

Snack Pack Couscous Tomato & Roast
Vegetable, 1 pack, 70g **7**

Sundried Tomato & Italian Herb Couscous,
1 serving, 50g **5**

Tesco

Light Choices Moroccan Couscous Snack in
a Pot, (1), 144g **6**

Microwaveable Chinese Style Egg Rice,
1 serving (½ bag), 125g **5**

The Co-operative

Boil in the Bag Easy Cook Long Grain Rice,
1 bag, 125g **12**

Microwavable Basmati Rice, 1 pack, 250g **10**

Microwavable Long Grain Rice, 1 pack, 250g **11**

Microwaveable Chinese Rice, 1 pack, 250g **10**

Moroccan Cous Cous,
1 heaped tablespoon, 50g **5**

Tomato & Mediterranean Herb Cous Cous,
1 pack, 110g **10**

Tilda

American Easy Cook Rice, 1 pack, 100g **10**

Butternut Squash Steamed Brown Basmati
Rice, ¼ pack, 125g **4**

Chickpea, Yoghurt & Mint Steamed Basmati
Rice, ¼ pack, 125g **4**

Coconut & Lime Leaf Steamed Basmati Rice,
¼ pack, 125g **5**

Giant Wild Rice, 1 serving, 30g **3**

Golden Savoury Basmati Rice, 1 pack, 250g **8**

Italian Four Cheese Basmati Rice,
1 pack, 250g **8**

Mushroom & White Wine Steamed Brown
Basmati Rice, 1 pack, 250g **9**

Oriental Stir Fry Steamed Basmati Rice,
1 pack, 250g **9**

Pure Basmati Rice Cook in the Bag,
1 pack, 250g **24**

Rizazz Oriental Vegetable Rice, ½ pouch, 125g **5**

Rizazz & Brown Basmati Rice, 1 serving, 125g **4**

Steamed Basmati, Brown, ½ pouch, 125g **5**

Steamed Basmati, Coconut, Chilli &
Lemongrass, ½ pouch, 125g **5**

Steamed Basmati, Egg Fried, ½ pouch, 125g **4**

Steamed Basmati, Lime & Coriander,
½ pouch, 125g **4**

Steamed Basmati, Mushroom, ½ pouch, 125g **4**

Steamed Basmati, Pilau, ½ pouch, 125g **4**

Steamed Basmati, Pinto Bean & Chilli,
½ pouch, 125g **4**

Steamed Basmati, Pure, ½ pouch, 125g **5**

Steamed Basmati, Roasted Pepper &
Courgette, ½ pouch, 125g **5**

Steamed Basmati, Split Pea, Clove &
Cinnamon, ½ pouch, 125g **4**

Steamed Basmati, Sun-Dried Tomato,
½ pouch, 125g **4**

Steamed Basmati, Turtle Bean & Red Pepper,
½ pouch, 125g **4**

Steamed Basmati, Vegetable Biryani,	
½ pouch, 125g	**5**
Steamed Basmati, White & Brown,	
½ pouch, 125g	**5**
Tex Mex Basmati Rice, 1 pack, 250g	**11**
Thai Fragrant Rice, 1 pack, 100g	**9**
Thai Jasmine Rice, 1 medium portion, 60g	**6**

Uncle Ben's

Bacon & Mushroom Risotto, ½ pouch, 125g	**6**
Basmati & Thai Rice, Express, 1 serving, 125g	**6**
Basmati Rice, Express, ½ pouch, 125g	**5**
Chicken & Mushroom Risotto, ½ pouch, 125g	**6**
Chinese Style Rice, ½ pack, 125g	**5**
Egg Fried Rice, ½ pouch, 125g	**6**
Golden Vegetable Rice, ½ pack, 125g	**5**
Lemon & Rosemary Rice, ½ pack, 125g	**5**
Risotto Bacon & Mushroom, 1 portion, 125g	**6**
Risotto Chicken & Mushroom, 1 portion, 125g	**6**
Risotto Grilled Mediterranean Vegetables,	
1 portion, 125g	**6**
Risotto Grilled Mediterranean Vegetables,	
1 pack, 250g	**11**
Risotto Tomato & Italian Herbs,	
1 portion, 125g	**6**
Savoury Chicken Flavour Rice, ½ pack, 125g	**5**
Special Fried Rice, ½ pack, 125g	**6**
Spicy Mexican Rice, ½ pack, 125g	**6**
Thai Curry Rice, 1 serving, 125g	**5**
Thai Curry Rice, 1 pack, 250g	**10**
Vegetable Pilau Rice, ½ pouch, 125g	**5**
Wholegrain Rice with Mediterranean	
Vegetables, ½ pack, 125g	**6**
Wok Basmati Rice pre-steamed, 1 pack, 250g	**11**
Wok Rice Garlic & Herb, 1 pack, 250g	**12**
Wok Rice Oriental Pre-Steamed, 1 pack, 250g	**11**

Uncle Ben's – Express

Basmati & Thai Rice, 1 portion, 101g	**5**
Basmati Rice, 1 portion, 125g	**5**
Chinese Style Rice, 1 portion, 125g	**5**
Egg Fried Rice, 1 portion, 125g	**6**
Golden Vegetable Rice, 1 portion, 125g	**5**
Lemon & Rosemary Rice, 1 portion, 125g	**5**
Mexican Style Rice, ½ pouch, 125g	**5**
Mushroom Rice, 1 serving, 125g	**5**
Pilau Rice, ½ pouch, 125g	**6**
Savoury Chicken Flavour Rice, 1 portion, 125g	**5**
Special Fried Rice, 1 portion, 125g	**6**
Spicy Mexican Rice, 1 portion, 125g	**6**
Thai Curry Rice, 1 portion, 125g	**5**

Thai Sweet Chilli Rice, 1 serving, 125g	**5**
Tomato & Basil Rice, ½ pack, 125g	**6**
Vegetable Pilau Rice, 1 portion, 125g	**5**
Wholegrain Rice with Mediterranean	
Vegetables, 1 portion, 125g	**6**

Veetee – Dine In

Basmati & Wild Rice, 1 serving, 140g	**5**
Basmati Rice & Mushroom, 1 serving, 140g	**5**
Peri Peri Rice, 1 serving, 140g	**6**
Thai Lime & Herb Rice, 1 serving, 140g	**6**
Wholegrain Basmati Rice, 1 serving, 140g	**6**

Waitrose

Lemon & Garlic Couscous, ½ pack, 55g	**5**
Pilau Rice, 1 portion, 200g	**10**
Tomato & Onion Couscous, 1 pack, 110g	**10**

Tins, Packets & Jars

Basic Foods

Ackees, in brine, drained, 1 portion, 100g	0
Agar Flakes, canned , 1 portion, 100g	2
Anchovies, 1 small can, 45g	2
Apple Sauce, 2 tablespoons, 40g	1
Apricots, in juice, drained, 1 small can, 210g	0
Apricots, Ready-to-Eat, 1 small pack, 50g	2
Barbecue Sauce, 2 tablespoons, 30g	1
Beans, Aduki, cooked or canned, 1 heaped tablespoon, 35g	1
Beans, Baked, 3 tablespoons, 105g	2
Beans, Baked, 1 small can, 205g	5
Beans, Black Eyed, cooked or canned, 1 heaped tablespoon, 35g	1
Beans, Borlotti, cooked or canned, 1 heaped tablespoon, 35g	1
Beans, Butter, cooked or canned, 1 heaped tablespoon, 35g	1
Beans, Cannellini, cooked or canned, 1 heaped tablespoon, 35g	1
Beans, Flageolet, cooked or canned, 1 heaped tablespoon, 35g	1
Beans, Haricot, dried, 1 tablespoon, 15g	1
Beans, Kidney, cooked or canned, drained, 1 heaped tablespoon, 35g	1
Beans, Mung, cooked or canned, 1 heaped tablespoon, 35g	1
Beans, Pinto, cooked or canned, 1 heaped tablespoon, 35g	1
Beans, Soya, cooked or canned, 1 heaped tablespoon, 35g	1
Beef Extract, 1 teaspoon, 5g	0
Beef Extract, 1 tablespoon, 15g	1
Black Cherries, in Syrup, ½ can, 213g	4
Blackcurrants in juice, drained, 1 small can, 210g	0
Bread Sauce, made with Semi-Skimmed Milk, 1 serving, 35g	1
Bread Sauce, made with Whole Milk, 1 serving, 35g	1
Brown Sauce, 2 tablespoons, 30g	1
Caviar in Brine, drained, 2 tablespoons, 38g	1
Chick Peas, cooked or canned, 1 heaped tablespoon, 35g	1
Chilli Sauce, 2 tablespoons, 30g	0
Chilli Sauce, 1 serving, 50g	1
Chocolate Nut Spread, 1 heaped teaspoon, 15g	2
Chutney, Apple, 1 serving, 15g	1
Chutney, Mango, 1 serving, 15g	1
Chutney, Mango, 1 serving, 30g	2
Chutney, Tomato, 1 serving, 15g	1
Chutney, Tomato, 1 serving, 30g	1
Clams, in Brine, drained, ⅓ can, 47g	1
Crab, canned in Brine, 1 small can, 85g	2
Cranberry Sauce, 1 tablespoon, 30g	1
Fish, Mackerel in Brine, 1 can, 125g	8
Fish, Mackerel in Oil, 1 can, 125g	9
Fish, Mackerel in Tomato Sauce, 1 can, 125g	7
Fish, Pilchards in Brine, drained, 1 can, 108g	4
Fish, Pilchards in Tomato Sauce, 1 small can, 105g	4
Fish, Salmon, Pink, drained, ½ can, 106g	4
Fish, Salmon, Red, drained & cooked, ½ can, 106g	5
Fish, Sardines in Oil, drained, 1 can, 120g	7
Fish, Sardines in Tomato Sauce, 1 can, 120g	5
Fish, Tuna in Brine, drained, 1 small can, 56g	1
Fish, Tuna in Oil, drained, 1 small can, 56g	3
Fish, Tuna in Springwater, drained, 1 small can, 56g	1
Fruit Cocktail, in Juice, drained, 1 small can, 210g	0
Fruit Cocktail, in Syrup, 1 small can, 210g	4
Grapefruit Segments, in Juice, drained, 1 medium portion, 150g	0
Ham, canned, 1 medium slice, 35g	1
Hoisin Sauce, 1 tablespoon, 15g	1
Honey, 1 heaped teaspoon, 15g	1
Horseradish Sauce, 1 tablespoon, 20g	1
Hot Pepper Sauce (Tabasco), ½ teaspoon, 2ml	0
Jam, 2 heaped teaspoons, 36g	3
Jam, Low Calorie, 2 heaped teaspoons, 36g	1
Kombu, 1 quantity, 100g	3
Lemon Curd, 1 heaped teaspoon, 18g	1
Lentils, Green & Brown, Whole, cooked, 1 heaped tablespoon, 35g	1
Lychees in Syrup, 2 26g	1
Mandarin Segments, in Juice, drained, 1 small can, 210g	0
Mandarin Segments, in Syrup, 1 small can, 210g	3
Mango, in Syrup, ½ can, 212g	5
Mangosteen, in Syrup, 1 quantity, 100g	2
Maraschino Cherries, 5 (20g)	1
Marmalade, 2 heaped teaspoons, 36g	3
Marmalade, Reduced Sugar, 2 heaped teaspoons, 36g	2
Mayonnaise, 1 tablespoon, 15g	3
Mayonnaise, Reduced Fat, 1 tablespoon, 15g	1
Mint Jelly, 1 tablespoon, 20g	1

Mint Sauce, 3 teaspoons, 21g	1
Mixed Pulses, canned or cooked, 1 heaped tablespoon, 35g	1
Mushrooms, Creamed, 1 small can, 213g	5
Mustard, 1 level tablespoon, 15g	1
Mustard, Coarse Grain, 1 level tablespoon, 15g	1
Mustard, Dijon, 1 level tablespoon, 15g	1
Mustard, Wholegrain, 1 level tablespoon, 15g	1
Nori, 1 quantity, 100g	5
Olives, in brine, 10 (30g)	1
Onions, Pickled, drained, 1 large, 25g	0
Palm Hearts in Brine, ¼ can, 55g	1
Passata, ½ large jar, 280g	0
Peaches, in juice, drained, 1 small can, 210g	0
Peanut Butter, Crunchy, 1 serving, 15g	3
Peanut Butter, Reduced Fat, 1 serving, 15g	2
Peanut Butter, Smooth, 1 serving, 15g	3
Pears, in Juice, drained, 1 small can, 210g	0
Peppadew Peppers, ¼ jar, 94g	0
Pesto Sauce, 1 tablespoon, 15g	2
Piccalilli, 1 heaped tablespoon, 40g	1
Pickle, Sweet, 1 heaped tablespoon, 40g	2
Pickled Beetroot, 1 medium portion, 40g	0
Pickled Gherkin, 1 large, 60g	0
Pineapple, in juice, drained, 2 ring, 80g	0
Prunes, in juice, drained, 1 small can, 210g	5
Prunes, in syrup, 1 small can, 210g	6
Raspberries, in Juice, drained, 1 small can, 210g	0
Raspberries, in Syrup, 1 small can, 210g	5
Redcurrant Jelly, 1 teaspoon, 9g	1
Rhubarb, in Syrup, 1 medium portion, 150g	1
Rice Pudding, Low Fat, ½ large can, 215g	4
Salad Cream, 1 serving, 20g	2
Salad Cream, Light, 1 serving, 20g	1
Salad Dressing, Blue Cheese, 2 tablespoons, 30ml	4
Salad Dressing, Caesar, 2 tablespoons, 30ml	2
Salad Dressing, Caesar, Low Fat, 2 tablespoons, 30ml	1
Salad Dressing, Fat or Oil Free, 2 tablespoons, 30ml	1
Salad Dressing, French, 1 tablespoon, 15ml	2
Salad Dressing, Italian, 1 tablespoon, 15ml	1
Salad Dressing, Low Fat, 2 tablespoons, 30ml	1
Salad Dressing, Thousand Island, 1 tablespoon, 30g	3
Salad Dressing, Thousand Island, Reduced Calorie, 1 tablespoon, 30g	1
Sardines, in Brine, drained, 1 can, 120g	5
Sauerkraut, 1 tablespoon, 45g	0
Seafood Sauce (Marie Rose Sauce), 1 tablespoon, 15g	2

Shellfish, Cockles in Vinegar, 1 jar, 155g	2
Shellfish, Crab, Dressed, 1 serving, 100g	5
Soup Cream of Chicken, canned, 1 can, 400g	6
Soup Cream of Mushroom, canned, 1 can, 400g	5
Soup Cream of Tomato, 1 can, 400g	6
Soup Oxtail, 1 can, 400g	5
Soup Vegetable, 1 can, 400g	6
Soy Sauce, 1 tablespoon, 15g	0
Soy Sauce, 3 tablespoons, 45g	1
Spaghetti in tomato sauce, 1 small can, 200g	4
Strawberries, in Syrup, 1 small can, 200g	4
Sun-Dried Tomato Paste, 1 tablespoon, 15g	2
Sun-Dried Tomatoes in Oil, 1 quantity, 100g	7
Sun-Dried Tomatoes, ½ pack, 50g	2
Sweet Chilli Sauce, 2 tablespoons, 30g	2
Sweet Kombu, 1 quantity, 100g	0
Sweetcorn Relish, 1 heaped tablespoon, 40g	1
Tartare Sauce, 1 tablespoon, 15g	1
Teriyaki Sauce, 1 tablespoon, 15g	1
Tomato Ketchup, 1 tablespoon, 15g	0
Tomato Ketchup, 2 tablespoons, 30g	1
Tomato Purée, 2 tablespoons, 30g	1
Tomatoes, whole or chopped, canned, 1 small can, 200g	0
Water Chestnuts, 1 medium portion, 50g	0
Worcestershire Sauce, 1 tablespoon, 15g	0
Worcestershire Sauce, 2 tablespoons, 30g	1
Yeast Extract, 1 tablespoon, 15g	1

Condiments, Mayo, Sauces & Dressings

Asda

Barbecue Ketchup, 1 tablespoon, 15g	1
Blue Cheese Dressing, 1 tablespoon, 15ml	1
Bramley Apple Sauce, 2 tablespoons, 30g	1
Burger Ketchup or Sauce, 1 tablespoon, 15g	1
Caesar Dressing, 1 tablespoon, 15ml	1
Chilli Ketchup, 2 tablespoons, 30g	1
Curry Ketchup, 1 tablespoon, 15g	1
Garlic & Herb Dressing, 1 tablespoon, 15ml	1
Hot Chilli & Jalapeño Relish, 1 tablespoon, 17g	1
Juicy Burger Relish, 2 tablespoons, 30g	1
Light Mayonnaise, 1 tablespoon, 15ml	2
Real Mayonnaise, 1 tablespoon, 10g	2
Reduced Fat Salad Cream with Sugar & Sweetener, 2 tablespoons, 30g	1
Salad Cream, 1 tablespoon, 15g	2

Salad Cream, Reduced Fat, 2 tablespoons, 30g	1
Seafood Sauce, 1 tablespoon, 15g	2
Seafood Sauce, Reduced Fat, 1 tablespoon, 15g	2
Squeezy Tartare Sauce, 1 tablespoon, 15g	1
Sweet & Sour Dip, 1 pack, 70g	4
Thousand Island Dressing, 1 tablespoon, 15ml	1
Vinaigrette Dressing, 1 tablespoon, 15ml	2

Asda – Extra Special

Bramley Apple Sauce, 1 serving, 15g	1
Caramelised Onion Chutney, 1 tablespoon, 15g	1
French Dressing, 1 serving, 20g	2
Fresh Lemon Mayonnaise, 1 serving, 25g	4
Marie Rose Sauce, 1 serving, 25g	4
Mustard & Cider Vinaigrette, 1 tablespoon, 15g	2
Seafood Sauce with Brandy, 1 teaspoons, 10g	2

Asda – Good For You

Caesar Dressing, 2 tablespoons, 30g	1
Honey & Mustard Dressing, 2 tablespoons, 30g	1
Mayonnaise, Reduced Fat, 1 tablespoon, 10g	1
Salad Cream, squeezy, 2 tablespoons, 30g	1
Seafood Sauce, Reduced Fat, 1 tablespoon, 15g	2
Thai Style Dressing, 3 tablespoons, 45g	1
Yogurt & Mint Dressing, 2 tablespoons, 30g	1

Ashoka

Lime Pickle, 1 tablespoon, 15g	1
Mango Pickle, 1 tablespoon, 15g	1

Blue Dragon

Hoisin Sauce, ¼ jar, 50ml	4
Light Soy Sauce, 2 tablespoons, 30ml	1
Oyster Sauce, 1 teaspoon, 5ml	0
Plum Sauce, 1 serving, 15ml	1
Sweet Chilli Dipping Sauce, Squeezy, 1 serving, 30g	2
Thai Sweet Chilli Dipping Sauce Original, 1 tablespoon, 15ml	1

Branston

New Brown Sauce with Branston Bite, 1 serving, 15g	1
Red Onion & Cranberry Pickle, 1 serving, 30g	1

Chivers

Traditional Cranberry Sauce, 1 serving, 15g	1

Colman's

American Mild Squeezy Mustard, 1 teaspoon, 5g	0
Bramley Apple Sauce, 2 tablespoons, 30g	1
Classic Mint Sauce, 1 tablespoon, 15g	0

Double Superfine Mustard Powder, 1 teaspoon, 5g	1
Fruity Sauce, 2 tablespoons, 30g	1
Seafood Sauce, 1 tablespoon, 15g	1

Crosse & Blackwell

Bramley Apple Sauce, 1 serving, 20g	1
Cranberry Sauce, 1 serving, 30g	1
Waistline Salad Cream, 1 tablespoon, 15ml	1

Heinz

Deli Mayo Caramelised Onion, 1 tablespoon, 15g	2
Deli Mayo Moroccan Style, 1 tablespoon, 15g	2
Deli Mayo Roasted Garlic, 1 tablespoon, 15g	2
Deli Mayo Sun-Dried Tomatoes, 1 tablespoon, 15g	3
Extra Light Salad Cream, 1 serving, 15g	1
Garlic & Chive Sauce, 1 serving, 30g	3
Heinz BBQ Sauce, 1 serving, 15g	1
Hot 'N' Spicy BBQ Sauce, 1 tablespoon, 15g	1
Light Mayonnaise, 1 tablespoon, 15g	1
Mayonnaise, 1 tablespoon, 15g	3
Sweet Onion Relish, 1 serving, 25g	1
Sweet Tomato Relish, 1 serving, 25g	1
Tangy Tomato Pickle, 2 tablespoons, 30g	1
Tomato Frito with a Hint of Onion & Garlic, ½ jar, 150g	3

Hellmann's

Balsamic Vinaigrette Dressing, 2 tablespoons, 30ml	1
Burger Sauce, 1 tablespoon, 15g	1
Caesar Dressing, 2 tablespoons, 30ml	4
Chicken Thai Salad Dressing, 2 tablespoons, 30g	2
Chinese Light Warm Chicken Salad Dressing, 2 tablespoons, 30g	1
Classic Light Dressing, 2 tablespoons, 30g	1
Creamy Lemon Dressing, 2 tablespoons, 30ml	2
Dijon Mustard Mayonnaise, 1 tablespoon, 15ml	1
Extra Light Mayonnaise, 3 tablespoons, 45g	1
French Dressing, 1 tablespoon, 15ml	1
Garlic & Herb Dressing, 1 tablespoon, 15ml	1
Garlic Mayonnaise, 1 tablespoon, 15g	3
Honey & Mustard Dressing, 1 tablespoon, 15ml	1
Hot n Spicy Tomato Sauce, 2 tablespoons, 30g	1
Italian Dressing, 1 tablespoon, 15ml	1
Luxury Orange & Honey Dressing, 2 tablespoons, 30ml	1
Luxury Thousand Island Dressing, 1 tablespoon, 30ml	2
Olive Oil Mayonnaise, 1 tablespoon, 15g	3

Condiments, Mayo, Sauces & Dressings Tins, Packets & Jars

Real Mayonnaise, 1 tablespoon, 15g	**3**
Salad Cream, 2 tablespoons, 30ml	**2**
Saucy Chip Dip Sauce, 1 tablespoon, 15g	**1**

HP Foods

BBQ Sauce Classic Recipe, 2 tablespoons, 30g	**1**
Classic Woodsmoke Flavour BBQ Sauce, 1 tablespoon, 15g	**1**
Fruity Sauce, 2 tablespoons, 30g	**1**
Honey Woodsmoke Flavour BBQ Sauce, 1 serving, 15g	**1**
Hot BBQ Sauce Spicy Woodsmoke Flavour, 1 serving, 20g	**1**
Reduced Salt & Sugar Brown Sauce, 2 tablespoons, 30g	**1**
Steak Sauce, 1 serving, 15g	**1**
The Original Brown Sauce, 2 tablespoons, 30g	**1**

Kraft

Balsamic Dressing, Light, 2 tablespoons, 30ml	**1**
Classic Thousand Island Dressing, 1 serving, 15g	**1**
Garlic & Herb Dressing, Fat Free, 4 tablespoons, 60ml	**2**
Get Dressed Creamy Caesar Dressing, 2 tablespoons, 30ml	**1**
Get Dressed Honey & Mustard Dressing, 2 tablespoons, 30ml	**1**
Light Caesar Dressing, 2 tablespoons, 30ml	**1**
Light French Dressing, 2 tablespoons, 30ml	**0**
Original Italian Dressing, 1 tablespoon, 15ml	**0**

Levi Roots

Fiery Guava Dipping Sauce, 2 tablespoons, 30g	**1**
Reggae Reggae BBQ Sauce, 2 tablespoons, 30g	**1**
Reggae Reggae Love Apple Tomato Ketchup, 2 tablespoons, 30g	**1**

Maille

Dijonnaise, 1 serving, 20g	**2**
Salsa Bearnaise Sauce, 1 serving, 30g	**4**
Vinaigrette Balsamic Vinegar with a Hint of Orange, 1 serving, 15ml	**2**
Vinaigrette Cider Vinegar Apple Juice & Shallots, 1 serving, 15ml	**2**

Morrisons

Blue Cheese Dressing, 1 serving, 15ml	**1**
Caesar Dressing, 1 serving, 15ml	**2**
Extra Light Salad Cream, 1 serving, 15g	**1**
Fine Herb Dressing, 1 serving, 15ml	**0**
French Dressing, 1 serving, 15ml	**2**

Garlic & Herb Dressing, 1 serving, 15ml	**2**
Hamburger Relish, 1 serving, 15g	**1**
Honey & Mustard Dressing, 1 serving, 15ml	**2**
Light Salad Cream, 1 serving, 15g	**1**
Reduced Fat Seafood Sauce, 1 serving, 15g	**1**
Salad Cream, 1 serving, 15g	**1**
Seafood Sauce, 1 serving, 15g	**2**
Sweet Peri Peri Dressing, 1 serving, 1g	**1**
Tartare Sauce, 1 serving, 15g	**2**
Thousand Island Dressing, 1 serving, 15ml	**2**

Morrisons – Eat Smart

Thousand Island Dressing, 1 serving, 15ml	**1**
Honey & Mustard Dressing, 1 serving, 15ml	**0**
French Dressing, 1 serving, 15ml	**0**
Caesar Dressing, 1 serving, 15ml	**0**

Nando's

Extra Hot Peri-Peri Sauce, 2 tablespoons, 30ml	**1**
Extra Extra Hot! Peri-Peri Seasoning Rub, 1 serving, 5g	**0**
Medium Peri-Peri Sauce, 2 tablespoons, 30ml	**1**
Peri-Peri Ketchup, 2 tablespoons, 30ml	**1**
Peri-Peri Salsa, 1 serving, 50g	**1**
Sweet Chilli Peri-Peri Marinade, 1 serving, 40g	**1**

Newman's Own

Balsamic Vinaigrette, 1 tablespoon, 15ml	**2**
Creamy Caesar Dressing, 1 tablespoon, 15ml	**1**
Creamy Cajun Marinade, 2 tablespoons, 30ml	**2**
Italian Dressing, 1 tablespoon, 15ml	**2**
Light Caesar, 4 tablespoons, 60ml	**1**
Light Creamy Caesar Dressing, 2 tablespoons, 30ml	**1**
Light Raspberry & Orange Dressing, 2 tablespoons, 30ml	**1**
Ranch Dressing, 1 tablespoon, 15ml	**1**
Soy, Ginger & Chilli Dressing, 2 tablespoons, 30ml	**1**
Sticky BBQ Marinade, 2 tablespoons, 30ml	**1**
Two Thousand Island Dressing, 1 tablespoon, 15ml	**1**

Patak's

Mango Chutney, 1 tablespoon, 15g	**1**
Original Hot Mango Chutney, 1 serving, 30g	**2**

Pizza Express

Balsamic Dressing, 1 tablespoon, 15ml	**2**
Caesar Light Dressing, 1 serving, 30g	**3**
Honey & Lemon Dressing, 1 tablespoon, 15ml	**1**
Honey & Mustard Dressing, 1 tablespoon, 15ml	**2**

House Dressing, 1 tablespoon, 15ml	2
Light Dressing, 1 tablespoon, 15ml	1

Sainsbury's

Bramley Apple Sauce, 2 dessertspoons, 20g	1
Caesar Dressing, 2 tablespoons, 30ml	4
French Dressing, 1 dessertspoon, 15ml	2
French Dressing, Organic, 95% Fat Free, 2 tablespoons, 30ml	0
Marie Rose Sauce, ¼ pack, 38g	2
Mayonnaise, 1 serving, 15ml	3
Reduced Fat Caesar Dressing, 1 dessertspoon, 15ml	1
Roasted Garlic Mayonnaise, ⅓ pot, 50g	7
Spicy Tomato & Coriander Sauce, ½ pack, 75g	1
Tartare Sauce, ¼ pack, 38g	2

Sainsbury's– Be Good To Yourself

Balsamic & Garlic Dressing, 1 serving, 20g	0
Ceasar Dressing, 1 serving, 20g	0
Caesar Dressing, 2 servings, 40g	1
French Vinaigrette Dressing, 1 serving, 20g	0
Honey & Mustard, 1 serving, 60ml	1
Raspberry Dressing, 1 serving, 20g	0
Sweet Balsamic Dressing, 2 tablespoons, 40g	1
Vinaigrette Dressing, 2 tablespoons, 30ml	1

SaladLight

Balsamic Vinegar Dressing, 4 sprays, 1ml	0
Caesar Dressing, 4 sprays, 1ml	0

Sharwood's

Bengal Spice Mango Chutney, 1 tablespoon, 40g	3
Bengal Spiced Tomato & Red Pepper Dip, 1 tablespoon, 40g	1
Green Label Chutney Sauce, 1 tablespoon, 40g	2
Green Label Mango Chutney, 1 tablespoon, 40g	3
Green Label Mango Chutney & Chilli Dip, 1 tablespoon, 40g	3
Green Label Squeezy Mango Chutney, 1 tablespoon, 40g	3
Lime Pickle, 1 tablespoon, 40g	2
Mango Chutney Smooth, 1 tablespoon, 40g	3
Plum Sauce, 1 tablespoon, 15g	1
Spicy Tomato Szechuan Stir Fry Sauce, ½ jar, 98g	2

Sweet Chilli Sauce, 1 tablespoon, 15g	1
Sweet Major Grey Mango Chutney, 1 tablespoon, 40g	3
Tropical Lime Mango Chutney, 1 tablespoon, 40g	3

Tesco

BBQ Sauce, 1 serving, 15g	1
Blue Cheese Dressing, 1 serving, 15g	1
Burger Sauce, 1 serving, 15g	1
Caesar Dressing, 1 serving, 15g	2
Chinese Stir Fry Sauce, 1 serving, 44g	1
Classic Green Pesto, 1 serving, 48g	5
Classic Red Pesto, 1 serving, 48g	5
French Style Dressing, 1 serving, 15g	1
Garlic & Herb Dressing, 1 serving, 15g	1
Garlic Sauce, 1 serving, 15g	1
Honey & Mustard Dressing, 1 serving, 15g	1
Hot Chilli Sauce, 1 serving, 140g	2
Light Mayonnaise, 1 serving, 15ml	1
Lighter than Light Mayonnaise, 1 serving, 15ml	0
Red Chilli Purée, 1 serving, 5g	0
Thai Purée, 1 serving, 5g	0
Thousand Island Dressing, 1 serving, 15g	1

Tesco – Finest

Balsamic Dressing, 1 tablespoon, 15g	1
Caesar Dressing, 1 serving, 15g	1
Chilli & Sherry Vinegar Dressing, 1 serving, 15g	2
French Dressing, 1 serving, 15g	1
Honey & Three Mustard Dressing, 1 serving, 15g	1
Pesto Alla Genovese, 1 serving, 48g	6

The Co-operative

Barbecue Relish, 1 heaped teaspoon, 30g	1
Blackberry & Mint Salad Dressing, 1 tablespoon, 15ml	1
Blue Cheese Dressing, 1 tablespoon, 15ml	1
Caesar Dressing, 1 tablespoon, 15ml	2
Caramelised Red Onion Chutney, 1 heaped tablespoon, 30g	2
Exotic Salad with Mango & Chilli Dressing, ½ pack, 65g	1
French Dressing, 1 tablespoon, 15ml	2
Garlic & Herb Dressing, 1 level tablespoon, 15ml	1
Half Fat Salad Cream, 1 serving, 15g	1
Hamburger Relish, 1 heaped teaspoon, 30g	1
Honey & Mustard Dressing, 1 tablespoon, 15ml	2
Mango & Chilli Salad Dressing, 1 tablespoon, 15ml	1
Onion Relish, 1 heaped teaspoon, 30g	1

Condiments, Mayo, Sauces & Dressings Tins, Packets & Jars

Pesto & Parmesan Salad Dressing, 1 tablespoon, 15ml	**1**
Piccalilli, 2 heaped teaspoons, 60g	**1**
Reduced Fat French Dressing, 2 tablespoons, 30ml	**1**
Reduced Fat Honey & Mustard Dressing, 2 tablespoons, 30ml	**1**
Reduced Fat Mayonnaise, 1 level tablespoon, 15ml	**1**
Reduced Fat Thousand Island Dressing, 2 tablespoons, 30ml	**1**
Sweetcorn Relish, 1 heaped teaspoon, 30g	**1**
Tomato & Chilli Chutney, ¼ pack, 78g	**4**
Thousand Island Dressing, 1 level tablespoon, 15ml	**2**

The English Provender Co.

Apple Sauce with Scrumpy Cider, 2 servings, 30g	**1**
Apple Sauce with White Balsamic Vinegar, 1 serving, 15g	**1**
Caramelised Red Onions, 1 serving, 15g	**1**
Dill Mustard Sauce, 1 serving, 15g	**2**
English Mint Sauce with Balsamic Vinegar, 1 serving, 30g	**1**
Honey & Mustard Dressing, 2 tablespoons, 30ml	**3**
Hot Chilli Relish, 1 dessertspoon, 10g	**1**
Indulgent Balsamic Dressing, 2 tablespoons, 30ml	**2**
Indulgent Classic Vinaigrette, 2 tablespoons, 30ml	**4**
Lemongrass Paste, 1 pack, 110g	**1**
Lime & Coriander Dressing Singles, 1 (25g)	**1**
Ploughman's Plum Chutney, 1 tablespoon, 15g	**1**
Seafood Sauce, 1 serving, 15g	**2**
Tartare Sauce, 1 serving, 15g	**2**
Wild Cranberry Chutney, 1 tablespoon, 15g	**1**
Wild Cranberry Sauce, 1 serving, 15g	**1**

Waitrose

Apple Sauce with Cider, 1 tablespoon, 25g	**1**
Bramley Apple Sauce, 2 tablespoons, 40g	**1**
Cranberry Sauce with Burgundy, 1 tablespoon, 15g	**1**
Cranberry Sauce, 1 tablespoon, 30g	**1**
Creamed Horseradish Sauce, 1 tablespoon, 15g	**1**
Hot Horseradish Sauce, 1 tablespoon, 20g	**1**
Kalamata Olive & Anchovy Tapenade, 2 teaspoons, 10g	**1**
Kentish Cider & Mustard Sauce, ½ pot, 150g	**5**

Mango & Lime Coulis, 1 serving, 50g	**1**
Mint Jelly, 1 tablespoon, 20g	**1**
Mint Sauce with Wine Vinegar, 2 tablespoons, 30ml	**1**
Parsley Sauce, ½ pot, 150g	**5**
Peppercorn Sauce, ½ pot, 150g	**5**
Redcurrant Sauce with Port, 1 teaspoon, 9g	**1**
Red Wine & Shallot Sauce, ½ pot, 150g	**2**
Tartare Sauce, 1 tablespoon, 15g	**1**
Tomato & Chilli Marinade, 2 tablespoons, 30ml	**2**
Wholegrain Mustard with Sun-Dried Tomatoes, 1 tablespoon, 15g	**1**
Watercress Sauce, ½ pot, 150g	**3**

Desserts & Puddings

Asda

Creamed Rice Pudding, 1 pot, 212g	**5**
Custard, 1 serving, 197g	**4**
Rice Pudding, ½ can, 213g	**5**
Rice Pudding, Good for You, ¼ can, 156g	**3**
Strawberry Holey Poly Sponge Pudding, ¼ can, 75g	**6**
Syrup Sponge Pudding, 1 pot, 105g	**9**

Ambrosia

Creamed Rice with Sultanas & Nutmeg, ½ can, 212g	**6**
Creamed Rice Pudding, ½ can, 212g	**6**
Creamed Semolina, ½ can, 212g	**4**
Creamy Macaroni Pudding, ½ pack, 212g	**5**
Creamy Rice Pudding, 1 pot, 135g	**4**
Creamy Rice Pudding, ½ can, 212g	**6**
Custard with Strawberry Sauce, 1 pot, 160g	**5**
Devon Creamed Rice, 1 pot, 150g	**4**
Devon Creamed Rice, ½ can, 212g	**6**
Devon Custard, 1 pot, 150g	**4**
Devon Custard, ½ can, 212g	**6**
Layers Custard Dessert with Caramel Layer, 1 pot, 160g	**5**
Layers Custard Dessert with Chocolate Layer, 1 pot, 160g	**5**
Layers Custard Dessert with Peach Compote, 1 pot, 160g	**4**
Layers Custard Dessert with Rhubarb Compote, 1 pot, 160g	**4**
Layers Rice Dessert with Raspberry & Blackberry Compote, 1 pot, 160g	**5**

Layers Rice Dessert with Strawberry Compote,
1 pot, 160g **5**
Low Fat Devon Creamed Rice, 1 pack, 135g **3**
Low Fat Devon Creamed Rice, ½ can, 212g **5**

Asda

Custard, 1 serving, 197g **4**
Creamed Rice Pudding, 1 pot, 212g **5**
Rice Pudding, ½ can, 212g **5**
Strawberry Holey Poly Sponge Pudding,
⅓ can, 100g **8**
Syrup Sponge Pudding, 1 pot, 105g **9**

Asda – Good For You

Rice Pudding, ¼ can, 156g **3**

Bird's

Angel Delight No Added Sugar, ¼ sachet, 12g **2**
Angel Delight No Added Sugar, Butterscotch
Flavour, ¼ sachet, 12g **2**
Angel Delight No Added Sugar, Chocolate
Flavour, ¼ sachet, 12g **2**
Angel Delight No Added Sugar, Strawberry
Flavour, ¼ sachet, 12g **1**
Angel Delight, Banana, ¼ sachet, 15g **2**
Angel Delight, Butterscotch, ¼ sachet, 15g **2**
Angel Delight, Corking Chocolate, ¼ sachet, 12g **2**
Angel Delight, Rasping Raspberry,
¼ sachet, 15g **2**
Angel Delight, Stonking Strawberry,
¼ sachet, 15g **2**
Brandy Flavour Sauce, ¼ sachet, dried, 18g **2**
Cheesecake Mix Strawberry Flavour,
1 serving, 69g **8**
Custard Powder, 2 tablespoons, 36g **3**
Lemon Pie Filling Mix, 1 serving, 100g **10**
Mousse Chocolate Flavour, 1 serving, 100g **13**
Mousse Lemon Flavour, 1 serving, 100g **11**
Mousse Strawberry Flavour, 1 serving, 100g **11**

Heinz

Strawberry Jam Sponge Pudding, ¼ can, 82g **6**

Tesco

Chocolate Sponge Pudding, ½ can, 150g **12**
Creamed Rice Pudding, 1 can, 213g **5**
Healthy Living Creamed Rice Pudding,
1 can, 213g **4**
Value Ready to Serve Custard, ½ can, 198g **4**

Weight Watchers

Banoffee Flavour Dessert Whip, 1 serving, 69g **1**

Chocolate Flavour Dessert Whip, 1 serving, 69g **1**
Strawberry Flavour Dessert Whip,
1 serving, 69g **1**

Dried Vegetables

Asda

Instant Mashed Potato, 1 pack, 120g **12**
Mash Snackpot, Cheese & Broccoli,
1 pot (made-up), 240g **6**
Mash Snackpot, Roast Onion,
1 pot (made-up), 225g **7**
Mash Snackpot, Swede & Carrot,
1 pot (made-up), 223g **6**
Minute Mash Bubble & Squeak Instant Mash,
½ sachet, 50g **1**
Sun-Dried Tomatoes, ½ pack, 50g **3**

Batchelors

Bigga Marrowfat Processed Peas, 1 serving, 80g **2**
Mushy Chip Shop Processed Peas,
1 portion, 100g **2**

Blue Dragon

Crispy Seaweed, 1 serving, 55g **10**

Clearspring

Japanese Wakame Dried Sea Vegetable,
1 pack, 50g **2**
Japanese Sushi Nori Dried Sea Vegetable,
1 pack, 17g **1**

Crosse & Blackwell

Bigga Dried Peas, ¼ can, 63g **5**
Dried Peas, 1 pack, 100g **3**

Merchant Gourmet

Classic Mediterranean Sun-Dried Tomatoes,
½ pack, 100g **4**
Classic Mediterranean Sun-Dried Tomatoes in
Oil, ¼ pack, 68g **3**
Italian Sun-Dried Tomatoes, 1 serving, 25g **1**

Mr Mash

Instant Mash, made up, 1 serving, 142g **3**

Sainsbury's

Instant Mashed Potato Mix, ½ pack, 146g **2**

Smash

Smash Buttery, 1 serving, 30g	3
Smash Original, 1 serving, 30g	3

Jams, Honey & Preserves

Asda

Apricot Jam, 1 tablespoon, 15g	1
Beef Paste, ⅓ jar, 25g	1
Chicken & Ham Paste, ⅓ jar, 25g	2
Chicken & Stuffing Paste, ⅓ jar, 25g	1
Chicken Paste, ⅓ jar, 25g	1
Chicken Tikka Sandwich Spread, 1 tablespoon, 15g	1
Crab Paste, ⅓ jar, 25g	1
Ham & Beef Paste, ⅓ jar, 25g	2
Lemon Curd, 1 heaped teaspoon, 15g	1
Mincemeat, ¼ jar, 103g	8
Mixed Fruit Jam, 1 heaped teaspoon, 15g	1
Raspberry Jam, 1 tablespoon, 15g	1
Salmon Paste, ⅓ jar, 25g	1
Seedless Raspberry Jam, 1 tablespoon, 15g	1
Strawberry Jam, 1 tablespoon, 15g	1
Thick Cut Orange Marmalade, 1 tablespoon, 15g	1
Tuna & Mayonnaise Paste, ⅓ jar, 25g	2
Valencia Orange & Cranberry Mincemeat, ⅓ jar, 103g	8

Baxters

Country Berry Conserve, 1 serving, 15g	1
Orange, Lemon & Grapefruit Marmalade, 1 serving, 15g	1
Raspberry Conserve, 1 serving, 15g	1
Rhubarb & Ginger, 1 serving, 15g	1
Strawberry Jam, 1 serving, 15g	1
Thin Cut Lemon Marmalade, 1 serving, 15g	1
Thin Cut Seville Orange Marmalade, 1 serving, 15g	1

Bonne Maman

Apricot Conserve, 1 serving, 15g	1
Strawberry Conserve, 1 serving, 15g	1

Chivers

Apricot Jam, 1 serving, 20g	1
Blackcurrant Jam, 1 serving, 20g	1

Bramble Jelly, 1 serving, 23g	2
Citrus Conserve, 1 serving, 20g	1
Mango Jam, 1 serving, 20g	1
Mincemeat, 1 serving, 20g	2
Raspberry Conserve, 1 serving, 20g	1
Raspberry Jam, 1 serving, 20g	1
Redcurrant Jelly, 1 serving, 23g	0
Rhubarb Jam, 1 serving, 20g	1
Seedless Raspberry Jam, 1 serving, 20g	1
Smooth Squeezy Sweet Orange Jam, 1 serving, 20g	1
Strawberry & Apple Jam, 1 serving, 20g	1
Strawberry Conserve, 1 serving, 20g	1
Strawberry Jam, 1 serving, 20g	1

Frank Cooper's

Lemon & Lime Oxford Marmalade Fine Cut, 1 serving, 22g	2
Original Oxford Marmalade Coarse Cut, 1 tablespoon, 15g	1
Oxford Apple Sauce, 1 serving, 15g	1
Oxford Apricot Conserve, 1 serving, 22g	2
Oxford Blackcurrant Conserve, 1 serving, 22g	2
Oxford Fine Cut Oxford Marmalade, 1 serving, 15g	1
Oxford Marmalade with Ginger, 1 tablespoon, 15g	1
Oxford Original Oxford Marmalade, 1 serving, 15g	1
Oxford Raspberry Conserve, 1 serving, 22g	2
Oxford Strawberry Conserve, 1 serving, 22g	2
Oxford Three Fruit Oxford Marmalade, 1 serving, 15g	1
Oxford Vintage Oxford Marmalade, 1 serving, 15g	1
Redcurrant Jelly, 1 serving, 20g	2
Summer Berry Conserve, 1 serving, 20g	1
Superior Matured Mincemeat Steeped in Cognac, ¼ jar, 103g	8
Superior Mincemeat with Cranberries Ruby Port & Winter Spices, ¼ jar, 103g	8

Hartley's

Olde English Thick Cut Marmalade, 1 serving, 20g	1
Redcurrant Jelly, 1 serving, 15g	1
Reduced Sugar Apricot Jam, 1 serving, 20g	1
Reduced Sugar Blackcurrant Jam, 1 serving, 20g	1
Reduced Sugar Raspberry Jam, 1 serving, 20g	1
Reduced Sugar Strawberry Jam, 1 serving, 20g	1
Strawberry Jam, 1 serving, 20g	1

Heinz

Ham & Cheese Toast Toppers, 1 can, 128g	**3**
Light Sandwich Spread, 1 dessertspoon, 10g	**1**
Original Sandwich Spread, 1 tablespoon, 15g	**1**
Toast Toppers Chicken & Mushroom, 1 can, 128g	**2**
Toast Toppers Mushroom & Bacon, 1 can, 128g	**3**

Marmite

Marmite, 1 teaspoon, 5g	**0**
Marmite, 2 teaspoons, 10g	**1**

Morrisons

Beef Paste, ⅓ jar, 25g	**1**
Blend Clear Honey, 1 serving, 15g	**1**
Blend Set Honey, 1 serving, 15g	**1**
Chicken & Ham Paste, ⅓ jar, 25g	**2**
Chicken Paste, ⅓ jar, 25g	**2**
Crab Flavoured paste, ⅓ jar, 25g	**1**
Ham & Beef Paste, ⅓ jar, 25g	**2**
Salmon Paste, ⅓ jar, 25g	**1**
Sardine & Tomato Paste, ⅓ jar, 25g	**1**
Shredless Orange Marmalade, 1 serving, 15g	**1**
Thick Cut Orange Marmalade, 1 serving, 15g	**1**
Tuna & Mayonnaise Paste, ⅓ jar, 25g	**1**

Sainsbury's

Apricot Jam, 1 heaped teaspoon, 15g	**1**
Blackcurrant Jam, 1 heaped teaspoon, 15g	**1**
Bramble Jelly, 1 serving, 15g	**1**
Damson Jam, 1 heaped teaspoon, 15g	**1**
Lemon Curd, 1 serving, 15g	**1**
Medium Cut Orange Marmalade, 1 serving, 15g	**1**
Reduced Sugar Morello Cherry Jam, 1 heaped teaspoon, 15g	**1**
Seedless Raspberry Jam, 1 heaped teaspoon, 15g	**1**
Strawberry Jam, 1 serving, 15g	**1**

Sainsbury's – Taste the Difference

Apricot Preserve, Continental Soft Set, 1 serving, 15g	**1**
Bitter Seville Orange Marmalade, 1 serving, 15g	**1**
Blackcurrant Preserve, Continental Soft Set, 1 serving, 15g	**1**
Cherry Conserve, 1 serving, 15g	**1**
Lemon Curd, 1 serving, 15g	**2**
Raspberry Preserve, Continental Soft Set, 1 serving, 15g	**1**
Strawberry Preserve, Continental Soft Set, 1 serving, 15g	**1**
Sweet Valencia Orange Marmalade, 1 serving, 15g	**1**
Three Fruit Marmalade, 1 serving, 15g	**1**

Skippy

Smooth Peanut Butter, 1 serving, 20g	**4**
Super Crunch Peanut Butter, 1 serving, 20g	**4**

Stute

Diabetic Fine Cut Orange Extra Marmalade, 1 serving, 20g	**1**
Diabetic Strawberry Extra Jam, 1 serving, 20g	**1**

Sun-Pat

Creamy Smooth Peanut Butter, 1 heaped teaspoon, 15g	**3**
Extra Crunchy Peanut Butter, 1 heaped teaspoon, 15g	**3**
Original Crunchy Peanut Butter, 1 heaped teaspoon, 15g	**2**
Original Smooth Peanut Butter, 1 heaped teaspoon, 15g	**2**
Super Smooth Peanut Butter, 1 heaped teaspoon, 15g	**3**

Tesco

Beef Paste, 1 serving, 15g	**1**
Chicken & Ham Paste, 1 serving, 15g	**1**
Chicken Paste, 1 serving, 15g	**1**
Crab Paste, 1 serving, 15g	**1**
Ham & Beef Paste, 1 serving, 15g	**1**
Salmon & Shrimp Paste, 1 serving, 15g	**1**
Sardine & Tomato Paste, 1 serving, 15g	**1**
Tuna & Mayonnaise Paste, 1 serving, 15g	**1**

The Co-operative

Apricot Jam, 1 tablespoon, 15g	**1**
Blackcurrant Jam, 1 tablespoon, 15g	**1**
Bramble Jelly, 1 heaped teaspoon, 18g	**1**
Chocolate Spread, 1 serving, 10g	**2**
Coarse Cut Fresh Fruit Orange Marmalade, 1 heaped teaspoon, 18g	**1**
Damson Jam, 1 tablespoon, 15g	**1**
Fine Cut Orange Marmalade, 1 tablespoon, 15g	**1**
Orange & Ginger Jam, 1 heaped teaspoon, 18g	**1**
Plum Jam, 1 heaped teaspoon, 18g	**1**
Raspberry Jam, 1 heaped teaspoon, 18g	**1**
Raspberry Seedless Jam, 1 heaped teaspoon, 18g	**1**
Strawberry Jam, 1 heaped teaspoon, 18g	**1**

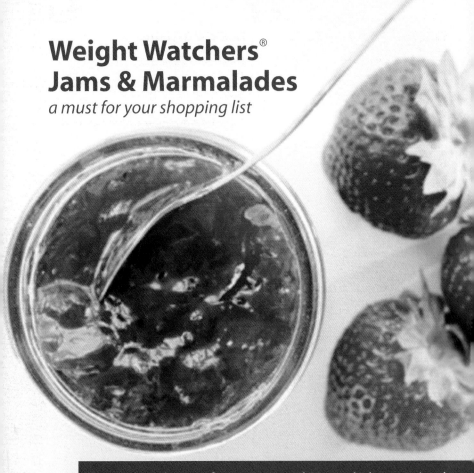

Weight Watchers®
Jams & Marmalades
a must for your shopping list

Our reduced sugar fruity Jams and Marmalades are simply delicious. Enjoy.

1 ProPoints value®

per 15g serving

Now available:
Apricot, Strawberry, Blackcurrant & Raspberry Jam, Orange Marmalade

FREE FROM ARTIFICIAL SWEETENERS, PRESERVATIVES, COLOURINGS AND FLAVOURINGS.

WeightWatchers Foods
Eat gorgeous. Feel gorgeous.

Thick Cut Fresh Fruit Three Fruits Marmalade,
1 heaped teaspoon, 18g | **1**
Thick Cut Orange Marmalade,
1 heaped teaspoon, 18g | **1**

Waitrose

Mincemeat, 1 serving, 50g | **4**
Redcurrant Jelly, 1 serving, 15g | **1**
Reduced Sugar High Fruit Strawberry Jam,
1 serving, 15g | **1**

Weight Watchers

Reduced Sugar Apricot Jam, 1 serving, 15g | **1**
Reduced Sugar Blackcurrant Jam,
1 serving, 15g | **1**
Reduced Sugar Orange Marmalade,
1 serving, 15g | **1**
Reduced Sugar Raspberry Jam, 1 serving, 15g | **1**
Reduced Sugar Strawberry Jam, 1 serving, 15g | **1**

Pickles, Olives & Peppers

Asda

Anchovy Stuffed Green Olives, 1 serving, 15g | **1**
Black or Green Olives, Pitted, 1 serving, 15g | **1**
Garlic Stuffed Olives Spanish Olives with
Garlic Paste, ¼ pack, 85g | **4**
Jalapeno Stuffed Olives Spanish Olives with
Jalapeño Paste, ⅛ jar, 42g | **2**
Marinated Mixed Olives, 1 serving, 25g | **1**
Pimento Stuffed Olives Spanish Olives with
Pimento Paste, ¼ tub, 85g | **4**
Pitted Black Olives Spanish Olives in brine,
¼ pack, 78g | **4**
Pitted Green Olives Spanish Olives in Brine,
¼ pack, 78g | **4**
Pitted Queen Olives Spanish Olives in Brine,
¼ pack, 78g | **3**
Sliced Black Olives Spanish Olives in Brine,
½ pack, 90g | **4**
Sunblush Tomatoes, 1 serving, 40g | **4**
Sweet Piccalilli, 2 tablespoons, 30g | **1**
Sweet Pickle, 2 tablespoons, 30g | **1**
Tasty Mixed Pickles, 1 pack, 440g | **1**

Branston

Beetroot Pickle, 1 tablespoon, 15g | **0**
Original, 1 tablespoon, 15g | **0**

Relish, Sweet Chilli with Ginger,
1 tablespoon, 15g | **1**
Wholegrain & Dijon Piccalilli,
1 tablespoon, 15g | **0**

Crosse & Blackwell

Piccalilli Traditional Quality, 1 tablespoon, 15g | **0**
Red Onion & Cranberry Pickle, 1 tablespoon, 15g | **0**

Cypressa

Mixed Olives with Lemon & Garlic, ¼ pack, 69g | **4**
Olives with Herbs de Provence, ¼ pack, 69g | **6**
Olives with Mixed Peppers, ¼ pack, 69g | **3**
Pitted Green Olives with Garlic & Chilli,
¼ tub, 69g | **3**
Pitted Green Olives with Garlic & Dill,
¼ tub, 69g | **2**

Discovery Foods

Latino Banana Chillies in Balsamic Vinegar,
1 jar, 200g | **4**
Mexican Green Jalapeños, 1 jar, 200g | **0**
Mexican Red Jalapeños, 1 jar, 200g | **0**
Mexican Vine Ripened Tomato Salsa,
1 pack, 200g | **3**
Sliced Cactus - Nopalitos, 1 jar, 17g | **0**

Heinz

Mild Mustard Pickle, 2 tablespoons, 30g | **1**
Piccalilli, 1 heaped tablespoon, 40g | **1**
Ploughman's Pickle, 2 tablespoons, 30g | **1**
Tangy Sandwich Pickle, 2 tablespoons, 30g | **1**

Morrisons

Country Sandwich Pickle, 1 serving, 15g | **1**
Sweet Pickle, 1 serving, 15g | **1**
Chilli Piccalilli, 1 serving, 15g | **0**
Sandwich Piccalilli, 1 serving, 15g | **0**
Green Halkidiki Olives stuffed with Sundried
Tomato, 1 serving, 50g | **3**
Mixed Pitted Olives, 1 serving, 50g | **3**
Pimento Stuffed Olives with Manchego Cheese,
1 serving, 50g | **3**
Marinated Italian Sundried Tomatoes with
Herbs in Sunflower Oil, 1 serving, 50g | **3**

Patak's

Brinjal Pickle (Aubergine), 1 serving, 30g | **3**
Chilli Pickle, 1 serving, 30g | **3**
Chilli Pickle Hot, 1 serving, 30g | **3**
Garlic Pickle, ¼ jar, 75g | **5**
Hot Mango Pickle, 1 serving, 30g | **2**

Lime Pickle, 1 tablespoon, 15g	**1**
Lime Pickle Medium/Hot, 1 tablespoon, 15g	**1**
Mango Pickle, ⅓ jar, 93g	**7**
Original Garlic Pickle Medium, 1 tablespoon, 15g	**1**
Original Mixed Pickle Hot, 1 tablespoon, 15g	**1**
Superior Sweet Lime Pickle Mild Medium, 1 tablespoon, 15g	**1**
Sweet Lime Pickle Mild Medium, 1 serving, 20g	**2**

Sacla

Italia Char-Grilled Borettane Onions Antipasto, ¼ jar, 70g	**2**
Italia Mixed Beans with Mushrooms Antipasto, ¼ jar, 72g	**3**
Italian Oven Roasted Tomatoes Marinated with Chilli Antipasto, ¼ jar, 48g	**2**
Italian Oven Roasted Tomatoes Marinated with Garlic & Capers Antipasto, ¼ jar, 48g	**2**

Sainsbury's

Black & Green Olives with Feta, ⅓ pack, 50g	**3**
Couchillo Olives with Pine Nuts, ⅓ pot, 53g	**1**
Gordal & Kalkidis Olive Mix, ⅓ pot, 59g	**4**
Mixed Olives, ⅓ pot, 59g	**3**
Pimento Stuffed Green Olives with Sweetflamed Peppers, ⅓ pack, 59g	**4**
Queen Green Olives, ⅓ pack, 59g	**2**

Tesco

Black & Green Pitted Olives with Feta Cheese, 1 serving, 50g	**3**
Marinated Greek Olives, 1 serving, 45g	**2**
Pimento Stuffed Olives, 1 serving, 45g	**2**
Spanish Pimento Stuffed Olives, 1 serving, 42g	**2**

The Co-operative

Green Olives Stuffed with Feta, ¼ jar, 82g	**4**
Green Olives stuffed with Sun-Dried Tomatoes, ¼ pack, 82g	**4**
Pimento Stuffed Manzanilla Olives, ¼ jar, 85g	**4**
Pimento Stuffed Olives, ¼ jar, 38g	**2**
Pitted Black Olives in Brine, ¼ jar, 85g	**3**
Pitted Green Olives in Brine, ¼ jar, 85g	**4**
Sandwich Pickle, 1 teaspoon, 15g	**1**
Sweet Piccalilli, 1 heaped teaspoon, 30g	**1**

Tinned & Packet Soup

Ainsley Harriott

Aromatic Thai Chicken & Lemongrass Cup Soup, 1 serving, 200ml	**3**
Asparagus Cup Soup, 1 serving, 200ml	**3**
Carrot & Coriander Cup Soup, 1 serving, 200ml	**2**
Chicken & Vegetable Cup Soup, 1 serving, 200ml	**2**
Classique French Onion Cup Soup with Crisp Crunchy Croutons, 1 serving, 200ml	**2**
Country Style Shropshire Pea Cup Soup, 1 serving, 200ml	**2**
East Indian Mulligatawny Cup Soup, 1 serving, 200ml	**3**
Italian Style Tomato & Herb Cup Soup, 1 serving, 200ml	**2**
Leek, Potato & Pea Cup Soup, 1 sachet, 200ml	**2**
Mediterranean Style Tomato Cup Soup, 1 serving, 200ml	**2**
Mexican Mixed Pepper & Chilli Cup Soup, 1 serving, 200ml	**2**
Moroccan Fusion with Cous Cous Cup Soup, 1 serving, 200ml	**2**
Mushroom Cup Soup, 1 serving, 200ml	**2**
New England Style Vegetable Chowder Cup Soup, 1 serving, 200ml	**2**
Oriental Style Hot & Sour Cup Soup, 1 serving, 200ml	**1**
Scottish Style Chicken & Leek Cup Soup, 1 serving, 200ml	**2**
Southern Cajun Gumbo Cup Soup, 1 serving, 200ml	**2**
Spicy Lentil Cup Soup, 1 serving, 200ml	**2**
Szechuan Hot & Sour Cup Soup, 1 serving, 200ml	**2**
Vegetable Cup Soup, 1 serving, 200ml	**2**
Wonderfully Wild Mushroom Cup Soup, 1 serving, 200ml	**2**

Asda

Beef & Vegetable, ½ can, 200g	**3**
Broccoli & Stilton, 1 serving, 200g	**3**
Chicken & Noodle, ½ can, 200g	**2**
Chicken & Vegetable in a Mug with Croutons, 1 sachet, 28g	**3**
Chicken Noodle Simmer, 1 packet, 30g	**3**

Country Vegetable, 1 serving, 200g	3
Cream of Chicken, ½ can, 200g	2
Cream of Mushroom, ½ can, 200g	2
Cream of Tomato, ½ can, 200g	3
Farmhouse Vegetable Simmer, 1 packet, 59g	6
Golden Vegetable in a Mug with Croutons, 1 sachet, 29g	3
Lentil, ½ can, 200g	3
Mighty Soup Chicken Noodle, 1 sachet, 30g	3
Mighty Soup Minestrone, 1 sachet, 38g	3
Mighty Soup Mushroom Noodle, 1 sachet, 42g	4
Mighty Soup Tomato & Vegetable, 1 sachet, 38g	4
Minestrone Simmer, 1 packet, 50g	5
Minestrone, ½ can, 200g	2
Minestrone Soup in a Mug with Croutons, 1 sachet, 23g	2
Oxtail Simmer, 1 packet, 50g	5
Oxtail, ½ can, 200g	3
Pea & Ham, ½ can, 200g	2
Potato & Leek, ½ can, 200g	3
Scotch Broth, ½ can, 200g	3
Spicy Tomato & Lentil, ½ can, 200g	3
Thick & Creamy Roast Chicken Cup, 1 packet, 26g	3
Thick & Creamy Tomato, Red Pepper & Basil Cup, 1 packet, 24g	2
Thick & Creamy Vegetable Chowder Cup, 1 packet, 26g	3
Thick & Creamy Mushroom Cup, 1 packet, 26g	3
Thick & Creamy Pea & Ham Cup, 1 packet, 25g	3
Tomato & Vegetable Soup in a Mug with Croutons, 1 sachet, 24g	3
Vegetable, ½ can, 200g	3

Asda – Good For You

Carrot & Coriander, ½ can, 200g	1
Farmhouse Vegetable Cup, 2 sachets, 132g	1
Golden Vegetable Cup, 2 sachets, 116g	1
Leek & Potato Cup, 2 sachets, 128g	1
Roast Chicken Flavour Cup, 2 sachets, 112g	1
Tomato & Basil, ½ can, 200g	2
Tomato & Basil Cup, 2 sachets, 132g	1

Batchelors

Chicken, 1 serving, 252ml	3
Chicken & Vegetable with Croutons, 1 sachet, 262ml	4
Classic Lentil, Condensed, 1 can, 295g	7
Classic Italian Tomato with Basil, ½ can, 148g	6
Classic Scotch Broth, ½ can, 148g	4
Cream of Asparagus, Condensed, ½ can, 148g	4
Cream of Celery, Condensed, ½ can, 148g	4

Cream of Chicken, ½ can, 148g	4
Cream of Chicken & Mushroom, Condensed, ½ can, 148g	5
Cream of Chicken & White Wine, Condensed, ½ can, 148g	4
Cream of Mushroom, Condensed, ½ can, 148g	5
Cream of Tomato & Red Pepper, ½ can, 148g	5
Cream of Tomato, Condensed, ½ can, 148g	6
Low Fat Chicken, Condensed, ½ can, 148g	2
Low Fat Mushroom, Condensed, ½ can, 148g	2
Low Fat Tomato, Condensed, ½ can, 148g	4
Minestrone with Croutons, 1 serving, 256ml	2
Original Golden Vegetable, 1 serving, 252ml	2
Oxtail, ½ can, 148g	3
Soupfulls Chicken & Country Vegetable, 1 pouch, 400g	5
Soupfulls Classic Beef & Vegetable, 1 pouch, 400g	5
Soupfulls Creamy Chicken Potato & Mushroom, 1 pouch, 400g	7
Soupfulls Harvest Vegetable, 1 pouch, 400g	4
Soupfulls Mediterranean Tomato & Vegetable, 1 pouch, 400g	5
Soupfulls Tuscan Tomato & Pasta, 1 pouch, 400g	6
Vegetable, ½ can, 148g	3

Batchelors – Cup a Soup

Cheese & Broccoli with Tagliatelle, 1 serving, 290g	4
Chicken & Leek, 1 serving, 248ml	3
Chicken & Vegetable with Croutons, 1 serving, 257g	4
Chicken, 1 serving, 250g	3
Chicken Noodle, 1 serving, 257ml	3
Cream of Asparagus with Croutons, 1 serving, 257ml	3
Cream of Vegetable with Croutons, 1 serving, 262ml	4
Creamy Broccoli & Cauliflower, 1 serving, 255ml	3
Creamy Carrot & Coriander, 1 serving, 258ml	3
Creamy Chicken & Tarragon, 1 serving, 258ml	3
Creamy Leek & Potato, 1 serving, 255ml	3
Creamy Thai, 1 serving, 254g	3
Creamy Winter Vegetable, 1 serving, 257g	2
Minestrone with Croutons, 1 serving, 258g	3
Original Beef & Tomato, 1 serving, 254g	2
Original Chicken, 1 serving, 250ml	3
Original Chicken & Leek, 1 serving, 254g	3
Original Golden Vegetable, 1 serving, 230ml	2
Original Oxtail, 1 serving, 252g	2

Original Tomato, 1 serving, 255g — 3
Rich Tomato & Basil, 1 serving, 250g — 2
Rich Woodland Mushroom, 1 serving, 257g — 3
Tomato & Vegetable with Croutons, 1 serving, 257g — 3

Batchelors –
Cup a Soup Extra

Cheese, Broccoli & Tagliatelle, 1 serving, 290ml — 4
Chicken & Mushroom with Pasta, 1 serving, 285ml — 4
Chinese Chicken Noodle, 1 serving, 279ml — 3
Leek & Potato, 1 serving, 283g — 3
Minestrone with Pasta, 1 serving, 286ml — 3
Potato & Leek, 1 serving, 285ml — 4
Soup n Crunch Creamy Chicken with Sage & Onion Croutons, 1 serving, 230ml — 5
Soup n Crunch Harvest Vegetable Soup with Herb Croutons, 1 serving, 264ml — 5
Soup n Crunch Rich Tomato & Herb with Black Pepper Croutons, 1 serving, 266ml — 4
Tangy Tomato with Pasta, 1 serving, 287ml — 4

Batchelors – Slim a Soup

Cajun Spicy Vegetable, 1 serving, 208ml — 1
Chicken & Mushroom, 1 serving, 207ml — 2
Chicken & Sweetcorn, 1 serving, 200ml — 2
Chicken Noodle & Vegetable, 1 serving, 205ml — 2
Leek & Potato, 1 serving, 204ml — 2
Mediterranean Tomato, 1 serving, 207ml — 2
Minestrone with Croutons, 1 serving, 208ml — 2
Spicy Lentil, 1 serving, 206ml — 2
Thick Broccoli & Cauliflower, 1 serving, 257ml — 2

Baxters

Chunky Carrot, Butterbean & Coriander, ½ can, 207g — 3
Chunky Chicken & Vegetable Casserole, ½ can, 208g — 3
Chunky Country Vegetable, ½ can, 208g — 3
Chunky Lamb Casserole, ½ can, 207g — 3
Chunky Smoked Bacon & Three Bean, ½ can, 208g — 3
Cream of Tomato, ½ can, 208g — 4
Italian Tomato with Basil, ½ can, 208g — 3
Traditional Haggis Broth, ½ can, 208g — 3

Baxters – Favourites

Beef & Winter Vegetable, ½ can, 208g — 3
Chicken Broth, ½ can, 208g — 2
Chicken Noodle with Sweetcorn, ½ can, 208g — 2
Cock-a-Leekie, ½ can, 208g — 1

Cream of Chicken, ½ can, 208g — 4
Cream of Leek, ½ can, 208g — 3
Cream of Mushroom, ½ can, 208g — 4
Cream of Tomato, ½ can, 206g — 4
Creamy Chicken & Mushroom, ½ can, 208g — 3
French Onion, ½ can, 208g — 2
Haggis Broth, ½ can, 206g — 3
Highlander's Broth, ½ can, 208g — 3
Lentil & Bacon, ½ can, 208g — 3
Minestrone, ½ can, 208g — 2
Mulligatawny, ½ can, 208g — 3
Oxtail, ½ can, 208g — 3
Pea & Ham, ½ can, 208g — 3
Potato & Leek, ½ can, 208g — 3
Red Lentil & Vegetable, ½ can, 208g — 2
Royal Game, ½ can, 208g — 2
Scotch Broth, ½ can, 208g — 3
Scotch Vegetable with Lamb, ½ can, 208g — 2
Turkey Broth, 1 serving, 207g — 2
Winter Vegetable with Yellow Split Peas, ½ can, 208g — 2

Baxters –
Healthy Choice

Autumn Vegetable, ½ can, 208g — 3
Broccoli & Cauliflower, 1 serving, 207ml — 2
Carrot, Onion & Chickpea, ½ can, 208g — 2
Chicken & Vegetable, ½ can, 208g — 2
Chunky Carrot, Bean & Quinoa, ½ can, 208g — 3
Chunky Chilli Beef & Bean, ½ can, 208g — 3
Chunky Spicy Lentil & Vegetable, ½ can, 208g — 3
Italian Bean & Pasta, ½ can, 208g — 3
Lentil & Vegetable, ½ can, 208g — 2
Minestrone with Wholemeal Pasta, ½ can, 208g — 2
Puy Lentil & Tomato, ½ can, 208g — 3
Spicy Tomato & Rice with Sweetcorn, ½ can, 208g — 3
Tomato & Brown Lentil, ½ can, 208g — 3

Baxters – Vegetarian

Butternut Squash & Red Pepper, ½ can, 208g — 2
Carrot & Butterbean, ½ can, 208g — 3
Carrot & Coriander, ½ can, 208g — 2
Country Garden, ½ can, 208g — 2
Cream of Red Pepper, ½ can, 208g — 3
Italian Tomato with Basil, ½ can, 207g — 3
Mediterranean Tomato, ½ can, 208g — 2
Spicy Parsnip, ½ can, 208g — 3
Tomato & Butterbean, ½ can, 208g — 3
Tomato & Orange, ½ can, 208g — 2

Blue Dragon

Chicken & Sweetcorn, ½ can, 205g	2
Thai Green Curry, ½ can, 205g	5
Thai Red Curry, ½ can, 205g	6
Wonton, ½ can, 205g	1

Campbell's

Carrot & Coriander Selection, ½ carton, 250ml	3
Hearty Vegetable, ½ can, 295g	5
Mediterranean Tomato, ½ can, 295g	4
Spring Vegetable, ½ can, 295g	3
Tomato & Basil Selection, ½ carton, 250ml	3

Campbell's – Condensed 99% Fat Free

Hearty Minestrone, ½ can, 295g	4

Heinz

Carrot & Lentil, 1 can, 100g	1
Chicken Noodle CupSoup, 1 pack, 200ml	1
Chicken, 1 can, 100g	1
Cream of Chicken, 1 serving, 200g	3
Heinz Vegetable, 1 serving, 200g	3
Mushroom & Croutons CupSoup, 1 cup, 80g	1
Oxtail, 1 serving, 290g	3
Special Edition Cream of Tomato with Red Pepper, ½ can, 200g	3
Tomato & Herb CupSoup, 2 cups, 136g	1
Tomato, 1 can, 100g	1
Vegetable CupSoup, 2 cups, 136g	1

Heinz – Big Soup

Beef & Vegetable, ½ can, 200g	3
Beef Broth, ½ can, 200g	3
Chicken & Leek, ½ can, 200g	3
Chicken & Vegetable, ½ can, 200g	3
Chicken, Potato & Bacon, ½ can, 258g	4
Chunky Minestrone, ½ can, 200g	2
Chunky Vegetable, ½ can, 200g	3
Cumberland Sausage & Vegetable, ½ can, 258g	3
Italian Meatball & Tomato, 1 serving, 260g	4
Lamb & Vegetable, ½ can, 200g	3
Mexican Chilli Beef & Bean, 1 serving, 258g	5
Minted Lamb Hotpot, ½ can, 200g	3
Smokey Bacon, Leek & Potato, ½ can, 258g	4
Spicy Mixed Bean, ½ can, 200g	2
Steak & Potato, ½ can, 258g	3

Heinz – Classic

Autumn Vegetable & Lentil, ½ can, 200g	2
Beef Broth, ½ can, 200g	2
Carrot & Lentil, ½ tin, 200g	2
Chicken & Vegetable, ½ can, 200g	2
Classic Chicken & Barley Broth, 1 serving, 197g	2
Classic Chicken Noodle, ½ can, 200g	2
Classic Pea & Ham, ½ can, 200g	3
Cream of Chicken, ½ can, 200g	3
Cream of Chicken & Mushroom, ½ can, 200g	3
Cream of Mushroom, ½ can, 200g	3
Cream of Tomato, ½ can, 200g	3
Cream of Tomato with a Hint of Basil, ½ can, 200g	3
Italian Chicken, Tomato & Red Pepper, ½ can, 200g	2
Lentil, ½ can, 200g	2
Minestrone, 1 can, 300g	3
Mulligatawny Beef Curry, ½ can, 200g	3
Oxtail, ½ can, 200g	2
Potato & Leek, ½ can, 200g	3
Scotch Broth, ½ can, 200g	2
Spring Vegetable, ½ can, 200g	2
Tomato, Sweet Chilli & Pasta, ½ can, 200g	2
Vegetable, ½ can, 200g	2
Vegetable, 1 small can, 300g	4
Winter Vegetable Broth, ½ can, 200g	2

Heinz – Farmers' Market

Autumn Three Bean & Tomato, ½ carton, 300g	4
Broccoli & Stilton, 1 serving, 255g	4
Chicken & Country Vegetable, ½ can, 258g	5
Chicken & Herb, ½ carton, 300g	5
Country Vegetable & Herb Fresh, ½ carton, 300g	3
Hearty Minestrone, ½ carton, 300g	3
Market Tomato & Red Pepper with Basil, ½ can, 258g	3
Pea & Smoked Ham, ½ can, 258g	3
Potato, Leek & Thyme, ½ can, 258g	4
Roast Parsnip & Caramelised Onion, ½ can, 258g	4
Root Vegetable & Sweet Potato, 1 portion, 260g	4
Three Bean & Smoked Bacon, ½ can, 258g	5
Wild Mushroom, ½ can, 258g	2
Woodland Mushroom, ½ can, 258g	3

Knorr

Broccoli & Stilton, 1 serving, 225ml	3
Cream of Mushroom, 1 serving, 225ml	3
Crofters Thick Vegetable, 1 serving, 225ml	2
Florida Spring Vegetable, 1 serving, 225ml	1
Leek & Chicken, 1 serving, 225ml	2
Minestrone, 1 serving, 225ml	1

| Super Chicken Noodle, 1 serving, 225ml | 1 |

Loyd Grossman

Bean Fusion, ½ can, 200g	4
Carrot & Coriander, ½ pouch, 210g	3
Chicken & Vegetable, ½ pouch, 210g	4
Minestrone, ½ can, 200g	4
Mushroom Pottage, ½ can, 200g	3
Tomato & Basil, ½ pouch, 210g	3

Morrisons

Asparagus with Croutons Cup Soup, 1 serving (made-up), 227g	3
Chicken & Sweetcorn Cup Soup with Croutons, 1 serving (made-up), 226g	3
Chicken & Vegetable Cup Soup with Croutons, 1 serving (made-up), 224g	3
Chicken & Vegetable, 1 can, 330g	4
Chunky Vegetable, 1 can, 330g	3
Golden Vegetable Cup Soup with Croutons, 1 serving (made-up, 228g	3
Minestrone with Pasta & Croutons Cup Soup, 1 serving (made-up), 221g	2
Mushroom Cup Soup with Croutons, 1 serving (made-up), 226g	3
Organic Carrot, Ginger & Parsnip, 1 can, 400g	6
Organic Four Bean, 1 can, 400g	5
Organic Tomato, 1 can, 400g	5
Organic Vegetable, 1 can, 400g	4
Oxtail Cup Soup with Croutons, 1 serving (made-up), 222g	2
Simmer Soup Chicken, 1 serving (made-up), 314g	4
Simmer Soup Mushroom, 1 serving (made-up), 315g	4
Spicy Lentil Soup, 1 can, 330g	5
Thick & Tasty Cup Soup Pea & Ham, 1 serving (made-up), 226g	3
Thick & Tasty Cup Soup Potato & Leek, 1 serving (made-up), 225g	3
Thick & Tasty Cup Soup Roast Chicken, 1 serving (made-up), 224g	3
Thick & Tasty Cup Soup Thai Style Chicken, 1 serving (made-up), 224g	3
Thick & Tasty Cup Soup Tomato, 1 serving (made-up), 226g	3
Thick & Tasty Cup Soup Vegetable, 1 serving (made-up), 226g	3
Tomato & Basil, 1 can, 330g	5
Tomato & Vegetable Cup Soup with Croutons, 1 serving (made-up), 224g	3

Morrisons – Eat Smart

Carrot & Coriander Cup Soup, 1 serving (made-up as per pack instructions), 221g	2
Carrot & Coriander, ½ can, 200g	2
Chicken & Mushroom Cup Soup, 1 serving (made-up), 214g	1
Chicken Noodle Cup Soup, 1 serving (made-up) 213g	1
Lentil & Vegetable, ½ can, 200g	3
Tomato & Basil Cup Soup, 1 serving (made-up), 217g	1
Tomato, ½ can, 200g	2
Vegetable Cup Soup, 1 serving (made-up), 215g	1

Sainsbury's

Chicken Noodle, ½ can, 200g	1
Chunky Beef & Vegetable, ½ can, 200g	3
Chunky Chicken & Vegetable, ½ can, 200g	2
Chunky Minestrone, ½ can, 200g	2
Cream of Tomato, 1 serving, 200g	3
Extra Thick Vegetable, ½ can, 200g	2
Minestrone, ½ can, 200g	2
Mulligatawny, ½ can, 200g	3
Vegetable Soup in a Cup, 1 serving, 220ml	2

Sainsbury's – Be Good To Yourself

Lentil, Carrot & Cumin, 1 serving, 200g	2
Parsnip, Butternut Squash & Ginger, 1 serving, 200g	2
Spicy Tomato & Lentil, 1 serving, 200g	3

Seeds of Change

Carrot & Coriander, ½ pouch, 175g	2
Creamy Tomato, ½ pouch, 175g	3
Curried Butternut Squash & Lentil, 1 can, 400g	4
Minestrone, ½ pouch, 175g	4
Spicy Lentil, ½ pouch, 175g	3
Three Bean, ½ pouch, 175g	3
Tomato, Basil & Crème Fraîche, ½ can, 200g	3

Spinnaker Seafood

| Bouillabaisse, ½ can, 200g | 5 |
| Clam Chowder, ½ can, 200g | 5 |

Tesco

Carrot & Coriander, ½ can, 200g	2
Chicken & Sweetcorn, ½ can, 200g	2
Lentil & Vegetable, ½ can, 200g	3
Soup in a Mug, Carrot & Coriander, 1 serving, 219ml	2

Soup in a Mug, Chinese Style Chicken Noodle, 1 sachet, 213ml	**1**
Soup in a Mug, Leek & Potato, 1 serving (made-up as per pack instructions), 216ml	**2**
Soup in a Mug, Mediterranean Style Tomato, 1 serving, 220ml	**2**
Soup in a Mug, Mediterranean Style Tomato, 1 serving, 220ml	**2**
Soup in a Mug, Vegetable, 1 serving, 218ml	**2**

The Co-operative

Carrot & Coriander, ½ can, 200g	**1**
Cream of Mushroom, ½ can, 200g	**2**
Cream of Tomato, ½ can, 200g	**3**
Creamy Golden Vegetable, ½ can, 200g	**2**
Lentil & Bacon, ½ can, 200g	**2**
Minestrone, ½ can, 200g	**3**
Oxtail, ½ can, 200g	**2**
Scotch Broth, ½ can, 200g	**3**
Simply Broccoli & Stilton, ½ pot, 300g	**5**
Simply Carrot & Coriander, ½ pot, 300g	**3**
Simply Chunky Vegetable, ½ pot, 300g	**3**
Simply Minestrone, ½ pot, 300g	**2**
Vegetable, ½ can, 200g	**2**

Waitrose

Beef Consommé, 1 can, 415g	**1**
Carrot & Coriander, 1 can, 415g	**2**
Celeriac, Leek & Bacon, 1 can, 350g	**4**
Chicken Consommé, 1 can, 415g	**1**
Chunky Beef & Vegetable, 1 can, 415g	**6**
Chunky Chicken & Vegetable, 1 can, 415g	**6**
Chunky Minestrone, 1 can, 415g	**5**
Chunky Tuscan Bean, 1 can, 415g	**4**
Cream of Chicken Quick Soup, 1 serving, 30g	**1**
Cream of Mushroom, ½ can, 212g	**3**
Cream of Petit Pois & Smoked Bacon, 1 can, 415g	**6**
Cream of Tomato, 1 can, 425g	**10**
French Onion & Cider, 1 can, 415g	**4**
Lentil & Smoked Bacon, 1 can, 415g	**6**
Moroccan Vegetable Tagine, 1 can, 350g	**5**
Oxtail Soup, ½ can, 212g	**2**
Parsnip & Ginger, 1 can, 350g	**3**
Scotch Broth, 1 can, 415g	**4**
Seafood Chowder, 1 can, 415g	**6**
Slow Roasted Tomato & Mascarpone, 1 can, 350g	**6**
Spicy Parsnip, 1 can, 415g	**4**
Sweet Potato, Parmesan & Sage, 1 can, 350g	**4**
Tomato & Basil, 1 can, 415g	**3**
Tomato & Red Pepper, 1 can, 415g	**4**

Weight Watchers from Heinz

Carrot & Lentil, 1 can, 295g	**1**
Chicken Noodle, 1 can, 295g	**1**
Chicken, 1 can, 295g	**2**
Chicken, Potato & Leek, 1 can, 295g	**2**
Country Vegetable, 1 can, 295g	**3**
Hearty Vegetable Broth, 1 can, 295g	**3**
Mediterranean Tomato & Vegetable, 1 can, 295g	**1**
Mexican Spicy Bean, 1 can, 295g	**3**
Mushroom, 1 can, 295g	**2**
Spiced Lentil & Potato, 1 can, 295g	**3**
Tangy Tomato & Rice, 1 can, 295g	**3**
Tomato & Basil, 1 can, 295g	**3**
Tomato & Red Pepper, 1 can, 295g	**1**
Tomato, 1 can, 295g	**2**
Tuscan Minestrone, 1 can, 295g	**3**

Tinned Beans & Pulses

Asda

Baked Beans & Sausages, 1 small can, 420g	**11**
Baked Beans & Vegetarian Sausages in Tomato Sauce, 1 can, 400g	**11**
Baked Beans with Jumbo Sausages, ½ can, 210g	**6**
Baked Beans, 1 can, 215g	**5**
Chick Pea Dahl, ½ can, 200g	**6**
Chilli Beans, ½ can, 145g	**3**
Mexican Style Bean Mix, ½ can, 200g	**5**
Mixed Beans Salad, ½ can, 145g	**3**
Mixed Beans, ½ can, 210g	**5**
Oriental Style Bean Mix, ½ can, 200g	**5**

Branston

Baked Beans, ½ can, 210g	**5**
Baked Beans with Sausages, ½ can, 210g	**6**
Baked Beans, 50% Reduced Sugar & Salt, ½ large can, 210g	**4**
Baked Beans, 50% Reduced Sugar & Salt, 1 small can, 220g	**4**
Bloomin' Big Baked Beans in a Rich & Tasty Tomato Sauce, ½ can, 210g	**5**
Chickpeas in a Masala Sauce, ½ can, 210g	**5**
Chickpeas in a Mediterranean Tomato Sauce, ½ can, 210g	**5**

Tinned Beans & Pulses — Tins, Packets & Jars

Reduced Salt & Sugar Baked Beans in a Rich & Tasty Tomato Sauce, 1 serving, 210g — **4**

Soya Beans in a Mediterranean Tomato Sauce, ½ can, 210g — **4**

Soya Beans in a Sweet Chilli Sauce, ½ can, 210g — **4**

Crosse & Blackwell

Baked Beans in a Rich Tasty Tomato Sauce, ¼ can, 105g — **2**

Baked Beans in Tomato Sauce, ½ can, 210g — **5**

Everyday Baked Beans in Tomato Sauce, 1 serving, 35g — **1**

Discovery Foods

Refried Beans, ¼ can, 104g — **3**

Spicy Refried Beans, ¼ can, 54g — **1**

Heinz

Baked Beans in Tomato Sauce, ½ can, 210g — **4**

Baked Beanz, 1 tin, 200g — **4**

Baked Beanz with Mini Pork Sausages in Tomato Sauce, 1 can, 200g — **5**

Beanz with Balls, ½ can, 208g — **6**

Beanz with Pork Sausages, ½ can, 208g — **6**

Beanz Reduced Sugar & Salt Snap Pots, 1 pot, 200g — **4**

Bumper Edition Spicy Meatballs with Beanz, 1 serving, 207g — **5**

Curry Beanz, 1 serving, 200g — **6**

Hidden Veg Beanz in Tomato Sauce, ½ can, 208g — **6**

Mean Beanz, Mexican, ½ can, 195g — **4**

Mean Beanz, Smokey BBQ, ½ can, 195g — **4**

Mean Beanz, Sweet Chilli, ½ can, 195g — **4**

Red Hot Balls, ½ can, 208g — **5**

Morrisons

Baked Beans in Tomato Sauce, ½ large can, 210g — **5**

Baked Beans & Sausages in Tomato Sauce, 1 small can, 220g — **6**

Chip Shop Style Mushy Peas with Mint Flavouring, 1 serving, 150g — **3**

Curried Beans with Sultanas in Curry Sauce, 1 small can, 220g — **5**

Mixed Beans in Tomato Sauce, ½ large can, 210g — **5**

Red Kidney Beans in Chilli Sauce, ½ large can, 210g — **5**

Morrisons – Eat Smart

Baked Beans in Tomato Sauce, 1 small can, 220g — **4**

Sainsbury's

Baked Beans & Pork Sausages in Tomato Sauce, ½ can, 210g — **7**

Baked Beans with Meatfree Sausages in Tomato Sauce, ½ can, 210g — **6**

Baked Beans in Tomato Sauce, Reduced Salt, Reduced Sugar, ½ can, 210g — **4**

Mixed Beans in a Mild Chilli Sauce, ½ large can, 210g — **4**

Reduced Sugar Reduced Salt Baked Beans in Tomato Sauce, 1 serving, 210g — **5**

Tarantella Organic

Tarantella®

Baked Beans, ½ can, 200g — **5**

Borlotti Beans, 1 can, drained, 240g — **5**

Butter Beans, 1 can, drained, 234g — **9**

Cannellini Beans, 1 can, drained, 240g — **5**

Chick Peas, 1 can, drained, 234g — **5**

Haricot Beans, 1 can, drained, 240g — **6**

Lentils, 1 can, drained, 240g — **5**

Mixed Bean & Chick Pea Salad, 1 can, drained, 230g — **8**

Pinto Beans, 1 can, drained, 240g — **8**

Red Kidney Beans, 1 can, drained, 240g — **5**

Tesco

Baked Beans & Vegetarian Sausages, ½ can, 203g — **5**

Baked Beans in Tomato Sauce, 1 can (large), 420g — **9**

Beans & Sausages, 1 can, 220g — **6**

Light Choices Baked Beans, 1 large can, 420g — **8**

Tuna & Mixed Bean Salad, ½ can, 140g — **6**

Value Baked Beans in Tomato Sauce, 1 can (large), 420g — **6**

Value Beans & Sausages in Tomato Sauce, 1 can, 405g — **13**

The Co-operative

Everyday Baked Beans, ½ can, 210g — **4**

Reduced Salt Baked Beans in Tomato Sauce, ½ can, 210g — **4**

Waitrose

Baked Beans, ½ can, 210g	**5**
Mixed Beans in a Spicy Tomato Sauce, 1 can, 410g	**8**

Weight Watchers from Heinz

Baked Beans in Tomato Sauce, 1 small can, 205g	**4**
Baked Beans in Tomato Sauce, 1 large can, 415g	**7**

Tinned Fish

Asda

Anchovy Fillets in Olive Oil, 1 can, 50g	**2**
Cantabrian Anchovy Fillets in Olive Oil, ½ can, 50g	**3**
Mackerel Fillets in Tomato Sauce, ½ can, 62g	**3**
Sardines in Brine, ½ can, 60g	**3**
Sardines in Sunflower Oil, ½ can, 60g	**3**
Sardines in Tomato Sauce, ½ can, 60g	**3**
Smoked Kipper Fillet, 1 fillet, 100g	**7**
Smoked Salmon Appetisers, 1 serving, 100g	**5**
Tuna Steaks in Sunflower Oil, ½ can, 100g	**5**
Yellowfin Tuna Mayonnaise with Sweetcorn & Peppers, ½ can, 46g	**3**

John West

Dressed Crab, 1 serving, 43g	**2**
Dressed Lobster, 1 serving, 43g	**1**
Herrings in Mustard & Dill Sauce, 1 serving, 95g	**7**
Herrings in Tomato Sauce, 1 serving, 95g	**5**
Kippers in Brine, drained, 1 serving, 140g	**7**
Kippers in Sunflower Oil, drained, 1 serving, 140g	**9**
Mackerel (Boneless) Fillets in Spicy Tomato Sauce, 1 serving, 190g	**11**
Mackerel Fillets in a Hot Chilli Dressing, 1 serving, 125g	**11**
Mackerel Fillets in Curry Sauce, 1 serving, 125g	**7**
Mackerel Fillets in Green Peppercorn Sauce, 1 serving, 125g	**8**
Mackerel Fillets in Mustard Sauce, 1 serving, 125g	**8**

Mackerel Fillets in Spicy Tomato Sauce, 1 serving, 125g	**6**
Mackerel Fillets in Tomato Sauce, 1 serving, 125g	**5**
Mackerel Fillets with Garlic & Herbs in Olive Oil, drained, 1 serving, 125g	**10**
Mild Oak Smoked Scottish Salmon, 1 serving, 50g	**2**
No drain No Mess Tuna Steak with a Little Brine, 1 serving, 130g	**3**
No drain No Mess Tuna Steak with a Little Sunflower Oil, 1 serving, 130g	**5**
Peppered Mackerel Fillets in Sunflower Oil, drained, 1 serving, 140g	**12**
Pressed Cod Roe, 1 serving, 100g	**3**
Salmon Light Lunch, Moroccan Style, 1 serving, 240g	**5**
Sardine Boneless Fillets in Sunflower Oil, drained, 1 serving, 67g	**4**
Sardine Boneless Fillets in Tomato Sauce, 1 serving, 95g	**4**
Sardines in BBQ Sauce, 1 serving, 120g	**5**
Sardines in Olive Oil, drained, 1 serving, 90g	**5**
Sardines in Spicy Tomato Sauce, 1 serving, 120g	**5**
Sardines in Tomato Sauce, 1 serving, 120g	**5**
Seared Tuna Fillets - Italian Herb, 1 serving, 142g	**4**
Seared Tuna Fillets - Lime & Cracked Black Pepper, 1 serving, 142g	**4**
Seared Tuna Fillets - Sweet Thai Red Chilli, 1 serving, 142g	**4**
Sild in Tomato Sauce, 1 serving, 110g	**6**
Skippers in Tomato Sauce, 1 serving, 106g	**5**
Smoked Mussels in Sunflower Oil, drained, 1 serving, 65g	**4**
Smoked Oysters in Sunflower Oil, drained, 1 serving, 65g	**4**
Tuna in Lime Mayonnaise with Peppers/Water Chestnuts, 1 serving, 92g	**6**
Tuna in Mayonnaise with Sweetcorn, 1 serving, 92g	**6**
Tuna Light Lunch in Tomato Salsa, 1 serving, 250g	**5**
Tuna Light Lunch Mediterranean with Chargrilled Onions, 1 serving, 240g	**6**
Tuna Light Lunch with a Lime & Cracked Black Pepper Dressing, 1 serving, 240g	**6**
Tuna Light Lunch, French Style, 1 serving, 240g	**6**
Tuna with a Twist, Dried Tomato & Herb, 1 serving, 85g	**3**

Tuna with a Twist, French Dressing, 1 serving, 85g	4
Tuna with a Twist, Lime & Black Pepper, 1 serving, 85g	3

Morrisons

Portuguese Sardines in Tomato Sauce, 1 can, 120g	5
Sardines in Tomato Sauce, 1 can, 120g	5
Sardines Skinned & Boned in Spicy Tomato Sauce, ½ can, 58g	3
Scottish Mackerel Fillets in Spicy Tomato Sauce, 1 can, 125g	6
Scottish Mackerel Fillets in Tomato Sauce, 1 can, 125g	6
Tuna Slices in Sweet Chilli Sauce, 1 can, 120g	4
Tuna Slices in Tomato, Garlic & Basil, 1 can, 120g	3
Tuna Slices in Sunflower Oil, 1 can (drained), 74g	3

Princes

Atlantic Pilchards in Lightly Salted Water, 1 tin, 155g	5
Brisling in a Rich Tomato Sauce, 1 tin, 110g	5
Brisling in Sunflower Oil, 1 tin, 110g	7
Herring Fillets in a Rich Tomato Sauce, 1 tin, 200g	13
Mackerel Fillets in a Spicy Tomato Sauce, ½ can, 125g	8
Pacific Pilchards in a Rich Tomato Sauce, 1 tin, 155g	5
Peppered Wood Smoked Mackerel Fillets in Sunflower Oil, 1 serving, 190g	13
Pilchard Fillets in a Spicy Tomato Sauce, 1 tin, 120g	5
Pilchards in Tomato Sauce, ½ can, 212g	9
Sild in a Rich Tomato Sauce, 1 tin, 110g	5
Sild in Sunflower Oil, 1 tin, 110g	7
Tuna Bites with Sun-Dried Tomato in Brine, ½ can, 188g	9
Tuna in an Authentic Thai Curry Sauce, ½ can, 92g	4
Tuna Mediterranean, 1 can, 80g	2
Tuna with Ginger & Lime, 1 can, 80g	2

Sainsbury's

Albacore Tuna in Extra Virgin Olive Oil, ½ pack, 80g	4
Fillets of Anchovies in Extra Virgin Olive Oil, 1 serving, 50g	2

Fillets of Anchovies in Olive Oil with Garlic & Herb, 1 serving, 50g	2
Fillets of Anchovies in Pure Olive Oil, 1 serving, 50g	2
Fillets of Mackerel in Spicy Tomato Sauce, 1 can, 125g	4
Mackerel Fillets in Spicy Tomato Sauce, 1 can, 125g	4
Portuguese Sardines in Olive Oil, 1 tin, 120g	7
Portuguese Sardines in Sunflower Oil, 1 can, 90g	4
Portuguese Sardines Skinless & Boneless in Tomato Sauce, 1 can, 120g	4
Skinless & Boneless Wild Pacific Red Salmon, 1 pack, 180g	6
Tuna Chunks in Sunflower Oil, ½ can, 69g	3

Weight Watchers

Salmon with Lemon Mayonnaise Style Dressing, 1 can, 80g	3
Tuna in Mango Chutney, 1 small can, 80g	2
Tuna in Mayonnaise Style Dressing with Sweetcorn, 1 small can, 80g	3
Tuna in Thousand Island Dressing, 1 small can, 80g	2
Tuna in Tomato & Herb Dressing, 1 small can, 80g	2

Weight Watchers from Heinz

Tuna & Noodles in a Chinese Sweet & Sour Dressing, 1 pot, 220g	5
Tuna & Noodles in a Thai Mild Chilli & Coriander Dressing, 1 pot, 220g	4
Tuna & Rice in an Indian Mild Curry Dressing, 1 pot, 220g	5

Tinned Fruit

Asda

Apple Slices, No Added Sugar, ½ can, 205g	2
Blackberries in Fruit Juice, ½ can, 145g	1
Blackberries in Juice, No Added Sugar, ½ can, 150g	1
Blackcurrants in Fruit Juice, No Added Sugar, ½ can, 145g	1
Blueberries in Light Syrup, ½ can, 150g	3
Fruit Cocktail in Grape Juice, ½ can, 200g	3

Fruit Cocktail in Syrup, ½ can, 206g	**4**
Fruit Medley in Grape Juice From Concentrate, 1 pack, 80g	**1**
Gooseberries in Fruit Juice, ½ can, 145g	**3**
Grapefruit & Mandarin Segments in Grape Juice, ½ can, 200g	**3**
Grapefruit Salad in Grapefruit Juice, 1 serving, 135g	**3**
Grapefruit Salad in Light Syrup, 1 serving, 96g	**2**
Guava Halves in Light Syrup, ½ can, 205g	**4**
Lychee in Light Syrup, 1 serving, 67g	**1**
Mandarin Segments in Orange Juice, No Added Sugar, ½ can, 149g	**1**
Mango Slices in Light Syrup, ½ can, 212g	**5**
Mixed Berries in Light Syrup, ½ can, 150g	**3**
No Added Sugar Raspberries in Fruit Juice, ½ can, 145g	**1**
Peach & Pear Pieces in Grape Juice, 1 can, 200g	**3**
Peach Chunks in Grape Juice, ½ can, 200g	**3**
Peach Halves in Light Syrup, 1 serving, 83g	**2**
Pear Quarters in Light Syrup, 1 pack, 213g	**3**
Pear Quarters in Pear Juice, 1 can, 213g	**2**
Prunes & Apricots in Grape Juice, ½ can, 100g	**2**
Prunes in Fruit Juice, 1 small can, 220g	**5**
Prunes in Grape Juice, 1 serving, 200g	**5**
Prunes in Light Syrup, ½ can, 210g	**4**
Raspberries in Fruit Juice, ½ can, 145g	**1**
Raspberries in Light Syrup, ½ can, 150g	**3**
Rhubarb in Light Syrup, ½ can, 270g	**4**
Strawberries in Fruit Juice, ½ can, 206g	**3**
Strawberries in Light Syrup, ½ can, 206g	**4**
Tropical Fruit Medley in Grape & Passion Fruit Juice, ½ can, 100g	**1**

Del Monte

Apricot Halves in Light Syrup, 1 can, 100g	**2**
Apricot Halves in Syrup, 1 can, 100g	**2**
Fruit Cocktail in Light Syrup, 1 can, 100g	**2**
Fruit Express Peach Pieces in Juice, 1 pot, 185g	**3**
Fruit Express Pineapple in Juice, 1 can, 100g	**1**
Fruit Express Tropical Fruit in Juice, 1 can, 100g	**1**
Fruitini Fruit Pieces in Juice Mixed Fruit, 1 small can, 140g	**2**
Fruitini Fruit Pieces in Juice Peach, 1 small can, 140g	**2**
Mandarin Oranges Whole Segments in Own Juice, 1 can, 175g	**2**
Sun Ripened Peaches in Juice, 1 can, 100g	**2**
Sun Ripened Pineapple in Juice, 1 serving, 205g	**3**

Sun Ripened Prunes in Juice, 1 serving, 205g	**5**
Sun Ripened Tropical Fruits in Juice, 1 serving, 205g	**3**

Dole

Mandarins in Grape Nectar, 1 can, 452g	**8**
Mandarins in Light Syrup, 1 can, 198g	**3**
Peaches in Grape Nectar, 1 can, 100g	**2**
Pears in Light Syrup, 1 serving, 100g	**2**
Pineapple Slices in Juice, 1 pack, 432g	**6**
Sunny Fruits in Grape Juice, 1 can, 452g	**8**
Sunny Fruits in Juice, 1 can, 198g	**3**
Tropical Fruit in Fruit Juices, 1 can, 452g	**8**

Hartley's

Gooseberries in Apple Juice, 1 serving, 100g	**1**
Gooseberries in Syrup, ½ can, 150g	**3**
Prunes, 1 can, 220g	**5**
Raspberries in Light Syrup, 1 serving, 100g	**2**
Rhubarb in Light Syrup, ½ can, 270g	**2**
Summer Fruits in Apple Juice, 1 serving, 100g	**1**
Summer Fruits in Light Syrup, 1 can, 300g	**6**

John West

Apricot Halves in Syrup, ½ can, 206g	**4**
Black Cherries in Syrup, ½ can, 212g	**4**
Fruit Cocktail in Fruit Juice, ½ can, 114g	**2**
Fruit Cocktail in Light Syrup, ½ can, 206g	**4**
Guava Halves in Syrup, ½ can, 205g	**4**
Lychees in Light Syrup, ½ can, 212g	**3**
Mandarin Orange Segments in Light Syrup, 1 serving, 100g	**1**
Mandarin Orange Segments in Light Syrup, ½ can, 156g	**2**
Mango Slices in Light Syrup, ½ can, 212g	**4**
Pear Halves in Fruit Juice, ½ can, 205g	**2**
Pear Halves in Syrup, ½ can, 110g	**2**
Raspberries in Fruit Juice, ½ can, 145g	**1**
Red Plums in Syrup, ½ can, 285g	**6**
Strawberries in Light Syrup, ½ can, 206g	**4**
Whole Green Figs in Syrup, ½ can, 208g	**4**

Sainsbury's

Blackberries in Fruit Juice, ½ can, 145g	**2**
Blackcurrants in Fruit Juice, ½ can, 145g	**1**
Breakfast Compote in Fruit Juice, 1 serving, 75g	**3**
Californian Prunes in Fruit Juice, ½ can, 205g	**6**
Fruit Cocktail in Fruit Juice, ½ can, 206g	**3**
Fruit Cocktail in Light Syrup, ½ can, 206g	**2**
Peach Slices in Syrup, ½ can, 206g	**3**

ProPoints value

Pitted Black Cherries in Fruit Juice, ½ can, 212g	3
Pitted Californian Breakfast Prunes in Fruit Juice, ½ can, 145g	4

The Co-operative

Apple & Blackberry Fruit Filling, 1 can, 395g	10
Apple Fruit Filling, 1 can, 395g	9
Blackcurrant Fruit Filling, ¼ can, 102g	3
Broken Mandarin Orange Segments in Light Syrup, ½ can, 156g	2
Prunes in Apple & Pear Juice from Concentrate, 1 can, 215g	5
Prunes in Syrup, 1 can, 215g	6
Raspberries in Apple & Blackcurrant Juice, ½ can, 145g	2
Raspberries in Light Syrup, ½ can, 150g	3
Red Cherry Fruit Filling, 1 can, 410g	11
Rhubarb in Light Syrup No Added Colour, ⅓ can, 178g	2
Strawberries in Light Syrup, ½ can, 210g	4
Two Fruits in Light Syrup, ½ can, 206g	3

Waitrose

Apple & Blackberry Fruit Filling, ½ can, 200g	4
Apricot Halves in Fruit Juice, 1 can, 220g	2
Apricot Halves, in Syrup, 1 can, 205g	4
Black Cherry Fruit Filling, ½ can, 195g	5
Blackcurrant Coulis, 1 serving, 50g	1
Fruit Salad in Syrup, ½ can, 205g	4
Grapefruit Segments, in Syrup, ¼ can, 135g	3
Mandarin Oranges in Light Syrup, 1 can, 310g	5
Mixed Fruit with Glacé Cherries, Apricots & Pineapple, 1 serving, 30g	2
Peach Halves in Light Syrup, 1 can, 410g	7
Peach Halves in Syrup, ½ can, 205g	4
Pear Quarters in Fruit Juice, 1 pack, 220g	3
Pink Grapefruit Segments in White Grapefruit Juice, ¼ can, 135g	1
Pitted Black Cherries in Syrup, 1 quantity, 100g	2
Pitted Black Cherries in Syrup, ½ can, 212g	4
Prunes in Juice, ¼ can, 54g	1
Prunes in Light Syrup, 1 can, 220g	5
Red Cherry Fruit Filling, ½ can, 200g	5
Rhubarb Chunks, in Light Syrup, 1 can, 560g	6
Tropical Fruit Salad in Light Syrup & Fruit Juice, ½ can, 212g	3

Tinned Meat & Poultry

Asda

Beef Bolognese, ½ can, 196g	4
Beef Ravioli, ½ can, 200g	5
Chicken Casserole, ½ can, 196g	4
Chicken Casserole, 1 pack, 400g	9
Chicken Korma, ½ can, 200g	8
Chicken Tikka Masala, ½ can, 200g	6
Chicken Vindaloo, ½ tin, 200g	6
Chilli con Carne, ½ can, 196g	4
Irish Stew, ½ can, 196g	4
Minced Beef & Onions, ½ tin, 200g	7
Stewed Steak, ½ can, 205g	6
Vegetable Balti, ½ can, 200g	5

Fray Bentos

Beef Stew, 1 pack, 400g	6
Chicken & Mushroom Pie, ½ can, 238g	11
Chicken Curry Hot, 1 pack, 400g	11
Chicken Curry Mild, 1 pack, 400g	11
Chicken Curry Pie, ½ can, 238g	10
Chicken in White Sauce, 1 pack, 400g	16
Chilli con Carne Hot, 1 pack, 400g	10
Chilli con Carne Medium, 1 pack, 400g	11
Classic' Steak & Kidney Pie, ½ pack, 238g	10
Fiery' Chicken Curry Pie, 1 portion, 237g	10
Meatballs in 'Gorgeous' Gravy, ½ can, 205g	4
Meatballs in Bolognese Sauce, 1 pack, 410g	10
Meatballs In 'Brilliant' Bolognese Sauce!, 1 pack, 100g	2
Meatballs in Gravy, 1 pack, 410g	9
Meatballs in Tomato Sauce, 1 pack, 410g	10
Minced Beef & Onion Pie, ½ can, 212g	10
Steak & Ale Pie, ½ can, 238g	10
Steak & Kidney Pie, 1 serving, 213g	10
Steak & Kidney Pudding, 1 can, 213g	12
Steak & Mushroom Pie, ½ can, 238g	10
Steak with Veg Pie, ½ pack, 213g	10
Tender' Just Steak, ½ pack, 238g	10

Heinz

Bumper Edition Big Saucy Bangers, 1 serving, 207g	6
Bumper Edition Saucy Steak, 1 serving, 206g	5
Chicken & Vegetable Curry Big Eat Pot, 1 serving, 350g	9

M&S – Eat Well

Chilli con Carne, ½ can, 200g	5
Chunky Steak in Rich Gravy, ½ can, 200g	5

Princes

American Big Hot Dog, 1 can, 50g	3
Chicken Roll with Sage & Onion, 1 can, 200g	10
Chopped Pork & Ham, 1 slice, 30g	2
Corned Beef, ¼ can, 75g	4
Cured Ham, 1 tin, 200g	9
Goulash, 1 pack, 410g	10
Hot Dogs in Brine, ⅛ tin, 50g	3
Jumbo Hot Dogs in Brine, ⅙ tin, 93g	5
Lean Corned Beef, ½ can, 100g	5
Mini Hot Dogs in Brine, 1 can, 20g	1
Premium Hot Dogs in Brine, 1 can, 50g	2
Steak & Kidney in a Rich Gravy, 1 tin, 410g	13
Stewed Steak, ½ can, 205g	7
Tasty & Tender Chicken Sweetcorn & Light Mayonnaise, 1 serving, 85g	3

Sainsbury's

Bolognese with Beef, 1 serving, 200g	4
Chicken Breast in Jelly, ¼ can, 50g	1
Chicken Curry, 1 portion, 195g	3
Chilli con Carne, 1 serving, 200g	4
Irish Stew, 1 portion, 196g	3
Meatballs in Tomato Sauce, 1 serving, 200g	7
Medium Chilli con Carne, ½ can, 200g	4
Minced Beef & Onions in Gravy, 1 portion, 195g	7
Turkey Breast in Jelly, ¼ can, 50g	1

Shippam's

Beef Stew, 1 can, 400g	10
Chicken Curry, 1 can, 400g	9
Chicken Supreme, 1 can, 400g	12

Stagg

Chili Chicken Grande, 1 can, 410g	9
Chili Classic Chili con Carne, 1 can, 410g	14
Chili Dynamite Hot Chili con Carne, 1 tin, 410g	14
Silverado Beef Chili con Carne, 1 tin, 410g	11

Tesco

Premium Hot Dogs, 1 individual, 23g	1
Beef Curry, 1 can, 400g	13
Chicken Curry, 1 can, 400g	12
Chilli con Carne, 1 can, 400g	12
Irish Stew, ½ can, 200g	4
Sweet & Sour Chicken, ½ can, 205g	6
Chicken & Vegetable Casserole, 1 can, 400g	8
Chicken in White Sauce, 1 can, 400g	12
Spaghetti Bolognese, ½ can, 205g	5
Chicken Tikka Masala, 1 can, 400g	15
Sausage Casserole, ½ can, 200g	5

The Co-operative

Beef Casserole, ½ can, 196g	3
Beef Madras Curry, ½ can, 196g	6
Chicken Casserole, ½ can, 196g	4
Chicken Curry, ½ can, 196g	5
Chicken in White Sauce, ½ small can, 103g	4
Chicken in White Sauce, ½ can, 196g	8
Chilli con Carne, ½ can, 196g	4
Chopped Ham & Pork, ½ can, 85g	7
Chopped Ham & Pork, ½ large can, 150g	12
Irish Stew, ½ can, 196g	4
Pork Luncheon Meat, ¼ can, 50g	3
Pork Luncheon Meat, ½ large can, 150g	8
Ravioli in Tomato Sauce, ½ can, 200g	4

Westler Foods

Burgers, 1 (54g)	4
Hamburgers, 1 (55g)	4
Hamburgers in a Rich Onion Gravy, ¼ can, 106g	3
Jumbo Pork Hot Dogs, 1 (136g)	7
King Size Reduced Fat & Salt Hot Dogs, 1 (55g)	2
Reduced Salt & Fat Hot Dogs, 1 (39g)	2
Reduced Salt Meatballs, 1 pack, 100g	3
Super Size Pork & Chicken Hot Dogs, 1 (100g)	5

Ye Olde Oak Foods

American Style Hot Dogs, 1 (33g)	1
Bockwurst, ¼ pack, 136g	10
Chicken Roll with Sage & Onion, ½ can, 100g	6
Giant Hot Dogs Sausages in Brine, ⅙ pack, 93g	4
Hot Dogs in Brine, ¼ pack, 100g	4
Mini Hot Dogs in Brine, ⅛ can, 50g	2
Pork Luncheon Meat, ¼ can, 50g	3
Premium Corned Beef, ¼ can, 85g	5
Turkey Roll, ¼ can, 50g	3

Tinned Pasta

Asda

Macaroni Cheese, Chosen by You, 1 pack, 400g	15
Macaroni Cheese, ½ can, 110g	3
Spaghetti in Tomato Sauce, 1 can, 410g	7

| Spaghetti in Tomato Sauce, 1 can (small), 215g | 4 |
| Spaghetti Loops & Sausages, ½ can, 205g | 5 |

Crosse & Blackwell

Beef Ravioli, 1 pack, 410g	9
Branston Spaghetti Loops, ½ can, 205g	3
Macaroni Cheese in a Rich Tasty Cheese Sauce, 1 pack, 410g	10
Spaghetti Bolognese in a Rich Tasty Bolognese Sauce, 1 pack, 410g	7
Spaghetti in a Rich Tomato Sauce, 1 pack, 410g	7
Spaghetti Loops in a Rich Tomato Sauce, 1 pack, 410g	7
Vegetable Ravioli, 1 pack, 410g	9

Heinz

Big Eat Spaghetti Bolognese, 1 can, 350g	7
Big Eat Sweet & Sour Chicken, 1 serving, 350g	9
Cheese & Tomato Ravioli in Tomato Sauce, ½ can, 205g	5
Creamy Cheese Pasta Big Eat Pot, 1 pot, 350g	12
Hoops 'n Hotdogs in a Smoky Bacon Sauce, ½ pot, 200g	5
Hoops in Tomato Sauce, 1 serving, 98g	1
Macaroni Cheese, 1 serving, 200g	5
Mini Pasta Spirals in Cheese Sauce, 1 can, 200g	4
Mini Vegetable Ravioli in Tomato Sauce, 1 serving, 202g	4
Ravioli in Tomato Sauce, 1 can, 410g	8
Spaghetti Bolognese, ½ can, 200g	4
Spaghetti in Tomato Sauce, ½ can, 200g	3
Spaghetti with Chicken Meatballs in Tomato Sauce, ½ can, 200g	5
Spaghetti with Sausages in Tomato Sauce, 1 small can, 200g	5

Morrisons

Macaroni Cheese, ½ large can, 205g	5
Ravioli in Bolognese Sauce, ½ large can, 200g	5
Ravioli in Tomato Sauce Low Fat, ½ large can, 200g	4
Rigatoni Carbonara, ½ large can, 205g	5
Spaghetti Bolognese, ½ large can, 205g	4
Spaghetti in Tomato Sauce, ½ large can, 205g	4
Spaghetti Rings & Sausages in Tomato Sauce, ½ large can, 205g	4
Spaghetti Rings in Tomato Sauce, 1 small can, 210g	3

Morrisons – Eat Smart Reduced

| Spaghetti in Tomato Sauce, 1 small can, 210g | 3 |

Sainsbury's

Cheese & Bacon Pasta, ½ can, 208g	4
Macaroni Cheese, ½ can, 205g	5
Spaghetti Rings & Pork Sausages in Tomato Sauce, ½ can, 205g	5
Spaghetti Rings in Tomato Sauce, ½ can, 205g	3
Spaghetti in Tomato Sauce, ½ can, 205g	3
Spicy Tomato Pasta, ½ can, 205g	5
Vegetarian Spaghetti Bolognese, ½ can, 208g	4

Sainsbury's – Be Good To Yourself

| Macaroni Cheese, ½ can, 200g | 7 |

The Co-operative

Everyday Spaghetti, ½ can, 205g	3
Spaghetti Rings in Tomato Sauce, ½ can, 106g	2
Spaghetti Rings in Tomato Sauce, ½ large can, 205g	3

Weight Watchers from Heinz

Cheese Tortellini, 1 can, 395g	7
Spaghetti in Tomato Sauce, 1 small can, 200g	3
Spaghetti in Tomato Sauce, 1 large can, 400g	5
Spaghetti in Tomato Sauce with Parsley, 1 serving, 200g	3

Tinned Tomatoes, Purée & Passata

Princes

| Pizza Topping, ¼ pack, 200g | 3 |

Sacla

| Sun-Dried Tomato Paste, 1 tablespoon, 15g | 2 |

Tarantella Organic

Cherry Tomatoes, 1 can, 240g	0
Chopped Tomatoes, 1 can, 240g	0
Passata, 1 jar, 690g	0
Plum Peeled Tomatoes, 1 can, 240g	0

Waitrose

Chopped Tomatoes with Mixed Sliced Olives,
1 can, 400g **5**

Chopped Tomatoes with Olive Oil & Chopped
Garlic, 1 can, 400g **4**

Tinned Vegetables

Asda

Bombay Potato, ½ can, 200g **5**
Chip Shop Style Mushy Peas, 1 serving, 150g **3**
Flame Roasted Red Pepper & Feta
Meze, 1 (100g) **4**
Haricot Beans, ½ can, 150g **3**
Kalamata Olive Tapenade, 1 serving, 100g **8**
Roasted Red Pepper Meze, 1 pack, 100g **2**
Water Chestnuts, ½ can, 112g **0**

Batchelors

Mushy Chip Shop Peas, 1 pack, 300g **6**
Mushy Original, 1 pack, 100g **2**
Mushy Original Processed Peas, 1 serving, 80g **2**
Small Processed Peas, 1 serving, 79g **2**

Blue Dragon

Baby Corn Cobs in Water, 1 can, 410g **0**
Bean Sprouts in Water, 1 can, 410g **0**
Chinese Stir Fry Vegetables in Water,
1 can, 410g **3**

Crosse & Blackwell

Garden Peas in Water, Sugar, Salt Added,
1 can, 300g **6**
Marrowfat Processed Peas, ¼ can, 75g **2**
Mushy Chip Shop Style Processed Peas,
1 can, 300g **6**
Mushy Peas Chip Shop Style, 1 pack, 300g **7**
Mushy Peas, Mint Sauce Flavour, ¼ can, 80g **2**
Mushy Processed Peas, ½ can, 150g **3**

Green Giant

Baby Cobs, 1 can, 410g **3**
Creamed Style Corn, ½ can, 209g **3**
Naturally Sweet Sweetcorn, 1 can, 198g **4**
Organic Sweetcorn, 1 can, 340g **9**
Original Sweet Niblets, ½ can, 99g **2**
Salad Crisp Sweet Corn, 1 can, 198g **4**
Sweet Corn with Peppers, 1 can, 198g **4**

Sainsbury's

Garden Peas in Water, 1 serving, 93g **2**
Jersey New Potatoes in Water, ½ can, 150g **2**
Marrowfat Peas in Water, ½ can, 90g **2**
Marrowfat Processed Peas, 1 serving, 90g **2**
Mushy Peas Chip Shop Style, 1 serving, 150g **3**
Mushy Processed Peas, ½ can, 150g **3**
Peeled New Potatoes in Water, 1 can, 191g **3**
Processed Peas in Water, ½ can, 95g **3**

The Co-operative

Everyday New Potatoes in Water, drained,
1 serving, 180g **3**
Everyday Processed Peas, 1 serving, 80g **2**
Jersey New Potatoes, ½ can, 150g **2**
Mixed Bean Salad, ½ can, 205g **4**
Mixed Vegetables in Water, ½ can, 150g **2**
Naturally Sweet Sweetcorn in Water, drained,
⅓ can, 92g **2**
New Potatoes, tinned, 1 can, 300g **5**
Petit Pois & Baby Carrots, drained, ⅓ can, 85g **1**
Petits Pois, 3 heaped tablespoon, 80g **1**
Processed Peas, ¼ can, 75g **2**
Ratatouille Provencale, ½ can, 195g **2**

Vegetarian Foods

Basic Foods

Nut Cutlet, 1 medium, 87g	8
Quorn Burger, 1 (50g)	2
Quorn Fillet, 1 (51g)	1
Quorn Mince, 1 medium portion, 100g	2
Quorn Pieces, 1 portion, 175g	4
Quorn Sausage, 1 (50g)	2
Sausages, Vegetarian, grilled, 1 medium, 30g	1
Soya Chunks, 1 quantity, 100g	9
Soya Mince, moist, 1 quantity, 100g	2
Tahini, Sesame Paste, 1 teaspoon, 5g	1
Textured Vegetable Protein, cooked, 1 medium portion, 50g	2
Tofu, Regular, 1 medium portion, 50g	1
Tofu, Smoked, 1 medium portion, 50g	1

Fresh Vegetarian Food

Alpro

Soya Tofu Mince, 1 pack, 180g	8
Soya Tofu Pieces Lightly Seasoned, 1 pack, 180g	9

Asda

Aubergine & Lentil Moussaka, 1 pack, 450g	10
Cherry Tomato & Pesto Spaghetti, 1 pack, 365g	7
Falafel, ½ pack, 100g	8
Lincolnshire Sausages, 1 (57g)	4
Meat Free Burger, 1 individual, 57g	2
Meat Free Butternut Squash & Pecan Roasts, 1 individual, 140g	8
Meat Free Nut Cutlets, 1 cutlet, 90g	9
Meat Free Spicy Vegetable Wraps, 1 individual, 150g	6
Mushroom, Leek & Stilton Bake, ½ pack, 200g	6
Potato & Spinach Saag, 1 pack, 370g	8
Sweet Potato & Red Pepper Korma, 1 pack, 400g	18
Three Cheese & Broccoli Pasta, 1 pack, 375g	17
Vegetable Enchiladas, ½ pack, 225g	8
Vegetarian Cannelloni, 1 pack, 450g	13
Vegetarian Chilli & Rice, 1 pack, 450g	12
Vegetarian Lasagne, 1 pack, 450g	13
Vegetarian Spaghetti Bolognese, 1 pack, 450g	11

Asda - Chosen by You

Vegetarian Roasted Vegetable Lasagne, 1 pack, 450g	14

Batchelors

Beanfeast Bolognese Style, 1 pack, 120g	2
Beanfeast Mexican Chilli, ½ pack, 278g	24

Cauldron Foods

Carrot & Onion Burgers, ½ pack, 88g	6
Chick Pea & Black Olive Pâtè, ½ tub, 56g	3
Cumberland Vegetarian Sausages, 1 (50g)	3
Falafel Bites, ¼ pack, 45g	2
Feta & Mint Falafel Bites, 1 serving, 15g	1
Goat's Cheese & Roasted Pepper Lasagne, 1 pack, 400g	14
Golden Marinated Tofu Pieces, ½ pack, 75g	5
Jalapeño & Jarlsberg Cheese Burgers, ½ pack, 88g	5
Leek, Cheddar & Rosemary Crispbakes, ½ pack, 114g	7
Lincolnshire Veggie Sausage, 1 (50g)	2
Marinated Tofu Pieces, ½ pack, 75g	5
Mediterranean Sun-Dried Tomato & Basil Pâtè, ½ tub, 58g	3
Moroccan Spiced Almond Tagine Roast, ½ pack, 142g	9
Moroccan Tagine with Couscous, Ready meal for one, 1 pack, 400g	15
Mushroom & Herb Sausages, 1 (50g)	2
Mushroom & Spinach Cannelloni, 1 pack, 400g	9
Mushroom Burger, 1 portion, 88g	3
Mushroom, Almond & Hazelnut Roast, ½ pack, 142g	6
Organic Black Bean Burgers, 1 portion, 88g	5
Organic Falafel, 1 (25g)	1
Organic Moroccan Chickpea Pâtè, ½ pot, 58g	3
Organic Moroccan Spiced Falafel Bites, ¼ pack, 45g	2
Organic Mushroom & Cheese Burgers, ½ pack, 88g	4
Organic Mushroom & Wensleydale Burgers, 1 (88g)	4
Organic Mushroom Pâtè, ½ pot, 56g	2
Organic Roasted Parsnip & Carrot Pâtè, ½ tub, 58g	2
Organic Rosemary & Cheese Crispbakes, ½ pack, 114g	7
Organic Spinach & Cheese Pâtè, 1 (115g)	6
Pesto & Mozzarella Risotto Bites, ¼ pack, 45g	3

Puy Lentil Casserole with Root Vegetables & Dumplings, 1 pack, 400g	10
Roast Veg & Basil Crispbakes, ½ pack, 115g	7
Roasted Vegetables & Feta Pâté, ½ tub, 58g	2
Smoked Paprika & Cheese Grills, 1 serving, 100g	5
Smoked Tofu, organic, ½ pack, 110g	3
Spicy Bean Chilli & Rice, 1 pack, 400g	6
Spinach & Sweetcorn Crisp Bakes, 1 portion, 115g	7
Thai Bites, 1 serving, 60g	3
Tuscan Four Bean Cannelloni, 1 pack, 400g	12

Dragonfly Organic

Mushroom Beany, 1 pack, 200g	13
Nut Beany, 1 pack, 200g	13
Original Soysage, 1 pack, 200g	13
Tomato Beany, 1 pack, 200g	15

Goodlife

Bistro Range Root Vegetable Roast, 1 serving, 180g	8
Nut Cutlets, 1 (90g)	8

Grassingtons Food Co.

Cauliflower Cheese Grills, 1 pack, 92g	4
Pepper & Courgette Sausages, 1 (44g)	2

Quorn

Barbecue Sliced Fillets, ½ pack, 70g	2
Beef Style & Onion Burgers, 1 pack, 100g	3
Beef Style & Sweet Red Onion Burgers, 1 pack, 160g	5
Beef Style & Tomato Burgers, 1 (80g)	3
Beef Style Pieces in Red Wine Sauce, 1 pack, 275g	4
Beef Style Pieces in Stroganoff Sauce, 1 pack, 275g	5
Bolognese Pasta Sauce, 1 serving, 150g	3
Bourguignon & Mash, 1 pack, 400g	8
Cheddar & Bacon Style Escalopes, 1 pack, 240g	14
Cheshire Cheese & Leek Sausages, 1 (50g)	2
Chicken Style & Mushroom Pies, 1 pie, 150g	7
Chicken Style & Mushroom Slice, 1 portion, 163g	11
Chicken Style Pieces in a Rich Jalfrezi Sauce, 1 pack, 275g	7
Chilli Beef Style Burgers, 1 (80g)	4
Classic Lasagne, 1 pack, 500g	11
Cocktail Sausages, 1 pack, 250g	10
Cornish Style Pasties, 1 (150g)	10
Cracked Black Pepper Fillets, 1 (80g)	3

Fajita Strips, ½ pack, 70g	2
Fresh Pasta Bolognese Ravioli, 1 pack, 250g	15
Goat's Cheese & Cranberry Escalopes, 1 (120g)	8
Golden Poppin Bites, ⅓ pack, 73g	4
Goujon, 1 (30g)	2
Hot Pot, 1 pack, 400g	7
Large Cornish Style Pasty, 1 (165g)	12
Lime & Chilli Dippers, 1 (23g)	1
Low Fat Chilli Pasta Bake, 1 pack, 400g	9
Loyd Grossman Marinated Dhania Masala Pieces, 1 pack, 220g	6
Loyd Grossman Marinated Sun-Dried Tomato & Basil Pieces, 1 serving, 220g	6
Mature Cheddar & Broccoli Escalopes, 1 pack, 120g	7
Mince & Onion Slice, 1 slice, 165g	10
Mini Ham Style & Cheese Quiches, ¼ pack, 50g	5
Mini Savoury Eggs, 1 (20g)	1
Mini Scotch Eggs, ¼ pack, 60g	4
Mozzarella & Pesto Escalopes, 1 pack, 240g	14
Picnic Eggs, 1 serving, 25g	2
Pork Style Pie, 1 (150g)	12
Quarter Pounders, 1 (112g)	4
Quorn Cottage Pie, 1 pack, 500g	8
Quorn Lasagne, 1 pack, 400g	9
Quorn Lasagne, 1 large pack, 500g	11
Quorn Lemon & Black Pepper Fillet, ½ pack, 100g	5
Quorn Mini Savoury Egg, 1 (20g)	1
Quorn Roast Style Sliced Fillets, 1 portion, 100g	3
Red Leicester & Onion Sausages, 1 (50g)	2
Red Pesto Pasta Snack, 1 pot, 200g	6
Roma Vine Tomato Fillets, 1 (80g)	3
Sage & Onion Turkey Style Escalopes, 1 (100g)	5
Sage & Onion Turkey Style Escalopes, ½ pack, 100g	5
Sausage, 1 (42g)	1
Smoky Bacon Style Slices, ¼ pack, 35g	2
Smoky Ham Style Slices, ½ pack, 50g	2
Soft Cheese & Ham Style Escalopes, 1 pack, 240g	14
Sticky Chilli Dippers, ½ pack, 130g	6
Sunblush Tomato & Italian Style Cheese Escalopes, 1 pack, 240g	13
Surprisingly Hearty Bangers, 1 (50g)	2
Surprisingly Hearty Bangers & Mash, 1 pack, 400g	9
Surprisingly Hearty Sausages, 1 (50g)	1
Surprisingly Juicy Sizzling Bangers, ⅓ pack, 50g	2
Surprisingly Juicy Smoky Red Pepper Sizzlers, 1 (50g)	2

Surprisingly Low Fat Chicken Style Pieces, 1 serving, 87g	**2**
Surprisingly Low Fat Cottage Pie, ½ pack, 250g	**4**
Surprisingly Low Fat Fajita Strips, 1 serving, 50g	**1**
Surprisingly Low Fat Family Roast, ⅕ pack, 91g	**2**
Surprisingly Low Fat Fillets, 2 fillets, 104g	**2**
Surprisingly Low Fat Sweet & Sour with Long Grain Rice, 1 pack, 400g	**10**
Surprisingly Satisfying Chicken Style Burgers, 1 (63g)	**3**
Surprisingly Satisfying Deep Filled Mince & Onion Pies, 1 (142g)	**10**
Surprisingly Satisfying Quarter Pounders, 1 (114g)	**4**
Surprisingly Satisfying Southern Style Burgers, 1 (63g)	**3**
Surprisingly Sizzling Bacon Style Rashers, ¼ pack, 38g	**2**
Surprisingly Succulent Bangers, 1 (50g)	**2**
Surprisingly Succulent Bramley Apple Bangers, 1 (50g)	**2**
Surprisingly Succulent Bramley Apple Quarter Pounders, ½ serving, 114g	**4**
Surprisingly Succulent Burgers, 1 (50g)	**2**
Surprisingly Succulent Cumberland Sausages, 1 (50g)	**2**
Surprisingly Succulent Lamb Style Grills, 1 (100g)	**4**
Surprisingly Succulent Pork Style & Leek Sausages, 1 (50g)	**2**
Surprisingly Succulent Sausages, 1 (42g)	**1**
Surprisingly Succulent Sizzling Burgers, 1 (50g)	**2**
Surprisingly Tasty Lasagne, 1 pack, 450g	**12**
Surprisingly Tempting Creamy Mushroom Pies, 1 (141g)	**10**
Surprisingly Tempting Garlic & Herb Fillets, 1 (100g)	**6**
Surprisingly Tempting Garlic & Mushroom Fillets, 1 (120g)	**7**
Surprisingly Tempting Lemon & Black Pepper Escalopes, 1 (110g)	**7**
Surprisingly Tempting Soft Cheese & Spinach Escalopes, 1 pack, 240g	**13**
Surprisingly Tempting Streaky Bacon Style Strips, 1 serving, 38g	**2**
Surprisingly Tempting Wensleydale & Blueberry Escalopes, 1 (120g)	**8**
Surprisingly Tempting Wild Mushroom & White Wine en Croutes, 1 (165g)	**11**
Surprisingly Tender Lamb Style Grills, ½ serving, 100g	**4**

Surprisingly Tender Peppered Steaks, 1 (98g)	**3**
Surprisingly Versatile Chicken Style Slices, ½ pack, 50g	**1**
Surprisingly Versatile Ham Flavour Slices, 1 serving, 51g	**1**
Surprisingly Versatile Peppered Beef Style Slices, ½ pack, 50g	**1**
Surprisingly Versatile Roast Chicken Style Slices, ½ pack, 50g	**1**
Surprisingly Versatile Tandoori Pieces, 1 serving, 140g	**5**
Surprisingly Versatile Turkey Style with Stuffing, ½ pack, 50g	**1**
Surprisingly Yummy Chicken Style Dippers, 1 (20g)	**1**
Tikka Fillet, 1 slice, 78g	**2**
Tomato & Sweet Pepper Pasta Snack, 1 pot, 200g	**4**
Wafer Thin Chicken Style Slices, ⅓ pack, 60g	**2**
Wafer Thin Ham Style Slices, ½ pack, 90g	**3**

Ross

Vegetable Hotpot, 1 pack, 300g	**5**
Vegetable Lasagne, 1 pack, 300g	**8**
Vegetarian Cauliflower Cheese, 1 pack, 300g	**5**
Vegetarian Macaroni Cheese, 1 pack, 300g	**10**
Vegetarian Vegetable Lasagne, 1 pack, 300g	**8**

Sainsbury's

Falafel, 1 piece, 17g	**1**
Meatfree Chicken Style Burgers, 1 portion, 50g	**3**
Meatfree Mince, ⅛ pack, 77g	**4**
Meatfree Thai Grill, 1 (100g)	**6**
Stuffed Vine Leaves, 1 piece, 50g	**2**
Vegetable Burger, 1 (56g)	**3**
Vegetable Kebab, 1 serving, 135g	**3**
Vegetable Masala, ½ pack, 200g	**4**
Vegetarian Glamorgan Leek & Cheese Sausages, 1 (49g)	**3**

Tesco

Bean Burger, 1 individual, 90g	**5**
Cheese & Leek Sausages, 1 individual, 55g	**4**
Lentil Moussaka, 1 pack, 300g	**14**
Light Choices Vegetable Masala Curry, 1 pack, 350g	**8**
Medium Veggie Sushi Pack, 1 pack, 147g	**6**
Mushroom Burger, 1 individual, 88g	**4**
Mushroom Lasagne, 1 pack, 400g	**18**
Three Bean Enchiladas, 1 pack, 450g	**18**
Vegelicious BBQ Chilli, 1 pack, 450g	**12**
Vegelicious Biryani, 1 pack, 450g	**14**

Vegelicious Bolognese, 1 pack, 400g	**11**
Vegelicious Hoisin Noodles, 1 pack, 400g	**11**
Vegelicious Hot Pot, 1 pack, 450g	**14**
Vegelicious Linguine, 1 pack, 380g	**11**
Vegetable Lasagne, 1 pack, 400g	**10**

Tivall

Breakfast Sausage, 1 (50g)	**4**
Chargrilled Burgers, 1 (75g)	**3**
Drumsticks, 1 serving, 80g	**4**
Frankfurters, 1 serving, 90g	**6**
Nuggets, ½ pack, 120g	**7**
Schnitzels, 1 (100g)	**5**

Frozen Vegetarian Food

Asda

Meat Free Apple & Rosemary Sausages, 2 individual, 112g	**5**
Meat Free Beef Style Pieces, 1 serving, 70g	**3**
Meat Free Broccoli & Leek Crsip Bakes, 1 serving, 132g	**7**
Meat Free Burgers, 1 individual, 57g	**2**
Meat Free Cauliflower Cheese Crispy Bakes, 1 individual, 99g	**6**
Meat Free Chicken Style Fillets, 1 fillet, 115g	**6**
Meat Free Creamy Leek & Gruyere Cheese Tarts, 1 individual, 120g	**10**
Meat Free Garlic Kievs, 1 serving, 125g	**7**
Meat Free Glamorgan Sausages, 1 individual, 50g	**3**
Meat Free Hotdogs, 3 serving, 81g	**5**
Meat Free Mediterranean Style Vegetable Parcels, ½ serving, 150g	**9**
Meat Free Potato & Spinach Curry Bakes, 1 individual, 140g	**5**
Meat Free Red Onion & Goats Cheese Parcels, 1 serving, 150g	**12**
Meat Free Southern Fried Chicken Style Pieces, 4 pieces, 120g	**10**
Meat Free Sun-dried Tomato & Mozzarella Quarter Pounders, 1 individual, 114g	**8**
Meat Free Vegetable & Cheese Crisp Bake, 1 serving, 132g	**7**
Meat Free Vegetable & Goats Cheese Crisp Bakes, 1 portion, 132g	**7**
Meatballs, 5 serving, 70g	**3**
Mega Meat Feast Pizza, ½ pack, 196g	**11**

Spicy Vegetable & Bean Quarter Pounder, 1 individual, 108g	**4**
Vegetable Fingers, 3 finger, 90g	**5**
Vegetarian Burgers, 1 individual, 57g	**2**
Vegetarian Toad in the Hole, 1 pack, 190g	**10**
Veggie Quarter Pounder, 1 individual, 114g	**7**
Vegetarian Spinach & Ricotta Cannelloni, 1 pack, 400g	**12**

Asda - Chosen by You

Meat Free Cauliflower Cheese Crispy Grills, 1 individual, 91g	**5**
Meat Free Lincolnshire Sausages, 1 (cooked), 47g	**2**
Meat Free Meat Balls, 1 serving (baked), 80g	**3**
Meat Free Mince, 1 serving (boiled), 75g	**2**
Meat Free Spicy Bean & Nacho Burgers, 1 burger (baked), 112g	**8**
Vegetarian Shepherd's Pie, 1 pack, 400g	**10**
Vegetarian Spinach & Ricotta Cannelloni, 1 pack, 400g	**12**

Aunt Bessie's

Oven Ready Toad in the Hole, 1 pack, 190g	**14**

Dalepak

Spicy Bean Quarter Pounders, 1 (114g)	**6**
Vegetable Fingers, 1 finger, 28g	**2**

Goodlife

Butternut Squash Roasts, 1 portion, 200g	**9**
Falafel, 4 (126g)	**7**

Grassingtons Food Co.

Chicken Style Fillets in a Tomato & Herb Marinade, 1 pack, 200g	**8**
Chicken Style Nugget, 1 serving, 73g	**4**
Multigrain Vegetable Bakes, 1 pack, 106g	**4**
Vegetable Burgers, 1 portion, 106g	**3**
Vegetable Quarter Pounders, 1 portion, 106g	**5**
Vegetable Sausages, 1 pack, 44g	**2**

Linda McCartney

Aubergine & Courgette Bake, 1 pack, 360g	**7**
Cheese, Leek & Red Onion Plaits, ½ pack, 170g	**13**
Chicken Style Burgers, 1 (65g)	**4**
Chilli Non Carne, 1 pack, 340g	**7**
Deep Country Pie, 1 (165g)	**11**
Falafel, 1 serving, 20g	**1**
Food to Come Home to Balti Curry, 1 pack, 340g	**10**
Lasagne, 1 pack, 320g	**11**

Macaroni Cheese, 1 pack, 360g	**17**
Vegetarian Cornish Pasties, ⅙ pack, 125g	**8**
Vegetarian Country Pies, ¼ pack, 166g	**11**
Vegetarian Lasagne, 1 pack, 360g	**12**
Vegetarian Mince, 1 serving, 300g	**8**
Quarter Pounder Burgers, 1 serving, 114g	**5**
Vegetarian Roast, 1 serving, 114g	**6**
Sausage Rolls, ¼ pack, 86g	**6**
Sausages, 1 serving, 50g	**3**

Morrisons

Meat Free Burger, Quarter Pounder, 1 individual, 114g	**4**
Meat Free Chicken Style Pieces, 1 serving, 75g	**3**
Meat Free Garlic & Cream Cheese Kievs, 1 individual, 125g	**6**
Meat Free Hot Dog Sausages, 1 (60g)	**4**
Meat Free Lincolnshire Sausages, 1 (93g)	**4**
Meat Free Ravioli in Tomato Sauce, ½ large can, 200g	**4**
Meat Free Southern Fried Chicken Fillet, 1 (100g)	**5**
Vegetable Lasagne, 1 pack, 450g	**13**

Quorn

Cheese & Broccoli Escalopes, 1 serving, 120g	**7**
Cheese & Leek Escalopes, 1 serving, 120g	**7**
Chicken Style Roast, 1 serving, 90g	**3**
Deep Filled Chicken Style & Mushroom Pie, 1 portion, 225g	**16**
Deli Bacon Style Rasher, 1 (19g)	**1**
Garlic Mushroom Escalope, 1 (120g)	**7**
Italian Style Balls, ¼ pack, 70g	**2**
Mince & Onion Pudding, 1 pack, 195g	**11**
Mini Kievs, ¼ pack, 55g	**3**
Quorn Burgers, 1 (70g)	**3**
Quorn Cocktail Sausage, 1 (10g)	**0**
Quorn Crispy Fillet, 1 fillet, 100g	**5**
Quorn Fillet, 1 (52g)	**1**
Quorn Goujon, 1 serving, 30g	**2**
Satay Skewers, 1 pack, 120g	**6**
Surprisingly Satisfying Sausage Rolls, 1 roll, 75g	**5**
Surprisingly Tempting Goujons, 1 (30g)	**2**
Surprisingly Versatile Turkey Style & Cranberry Slices, ½ pack, 50g	**1**
Taco Mince, 1 portion, 132g	**5**

Realeat

Chicken Style Pieces, 1 serving, 75g	**3**
Chicken Style Vege Roast, 1 portion, 113g	**5**

Vege Bacon Meat-Free Rashers, 1 portion, 37g	**3**
Vege Roast Chicken Style with Sage & Onion Stuffing, 1 portion, 114g	**6**

Ross

Spinach & Ricotta Cannelloni, 1 pack, 300g	**8**

Sainsbury's

Meatfree Chicken Style Kievs with a Cheesy Garlic Sauce, 1 portion, 125g	**8**
Meatfree Meatballs, 1 (18g)	**1**
Vegetable Quarter Pounders, 1 serving, 104g	**6**

Tesco

Quorn Tikka Masala & Rice, 1 pack, 400g	**10**
Vegetarian Chargrilled Quarter Pounders, 1 individual, 114g	**5**
Vegetarian Creamy Mushroom Escalope, 1 individual, 150g	**11**

Waitrose

Cheddar Cheese & Cauliflower Burgers, ¼ pack, 95g	**6**
Moroccan-Spiced Couscous Grills, 1 (88g)	**4**

Vegetarian Ingredients

Asda

Bolognese, ½ sachet, 60g	**1**
Chicken Style Pieces, ½ pack, 155g	**5**
Mexican Style Chilli, ½ sachet, 60g	**1**
Savoury Mince, ½ sachet, 60g	**1**

Batchelors

Beanfeast Mince & Onion, 1 pack, 120g	**10**

Crosse & Blackwell

Beanfeast Bolognese, ½ packet, 362g	**6**

Granose

Meat-Free Sausage Mix, 3 pieces, 75g	**5**
Soya Mince, 1 portion, 100g	**2**

Quorn

Surprisingly Low Fat Mince, 1 serving, 87g	**2**